Human Rights in Nigeria's External Relations in the Age of General Muhammadu Buhari and His Successors

Philip C. Aka
Dominican University
River Forest, IL, USA

ISBN 978-3-031-63230-3 ISBN 978-3-031-63231-0 (eBook)
https://doi.org/10.1007/978-3-031-63231-0

This Palgrave Macmillan imprint is published by the registered company Springer Nature Switzerland AG
The registered company address is: Gewerbestrasse 11, 6330 Cham, Switzerland

For Philip Jr., first son and first child, together with his siblings. And to the still mostly unsung and un-mourned victims of human-right abuses in Nigeria, atop the 3.5 million Igbo who died in the abominable civil war from 1967 to 1970.

Preface

This book critically assesses Nigeria's progress or lack thereof toward a human-right policy under the Fourth Republic since 1999, taking advantage of the inestimable opportunity afforded by General Muhammadu Buhari's departure from the political scene on May 29, 2023, after the double famine, domestically and externally, of his two terms of office as President. It is a broad-ranging argument, draped in the less arcane constitutional vocabulary of human rights, for thoroughgoing reforms at home and abroad as the only antidote to the state-building dilemmas Nigeria confronts in the first quarter of the Twenty-First Century. The 2023 presidential election in Nigeria was the first since the inception of the Fourth Republic in 1999 in which a retired army general did not run for office. Buhari's departure marks the end of military teleguidance of Nigerian politics under the Fourth Republic in the camouflage of democratic rule, a birthmark of remote control dating back to the first military coup d'etat in the country in January 1966.

In the globalized world steeped in complex interdependence that we live in, two presidential terms in office of the type Nigerians endured under General Buhari from 2015 until 2023 can spell existential threats for ordinary citizens, with ramifications for their relations with other countries. Under the Fourth Republic, the challenge Nigerian leaders face like never before is how to create a state that matches the expectations of their diverse peoples at home and abroad. The decline of military influence in Nigerian politics, symptomized by General Buhari's departure from the political scene, affords an opportunity for stocktaking, to the benefit of democracy, human rights, and the rule of law in Nigeria, that this book undertakes.

Taking the foregoing propositions as starting point, four interlinked questions frame this research. First, what factors at this moment in Nigeria's checkered history make embracement and internalization of international standards of governance, signified by increased application of human rights in external affairs, exigent for the country and its citizenry? Second, what quantifiable influence do human rights have in Nigeria's external relations? Put differently, how far does the country need to go to join the club of "global Good Samaritans," the hallowed list of countries in the world who consistently apply human rights in their external affairs for their own domestic good and to the glory of the international human rights regime. Third, what possible methods can Nigeria use to facilitate the application of more human rights in its external relations? Fourth, what are possible objections to the case for more human rights in Nigeria's external relations and conceivable rebuttals of those objections.

This book builds on a convergence of three genres of literature: garden-variety studies on Nigerian foreign policies; works which deal tangentially with application of human rights in Nigeria's external relations, including studies, such as those on peacekeeping, which touch human rights only incidentally or sporadically; and works on human rights in comparative foreign policy or the application of these values in national foreign policies in comparative perspective. In sum, simultaneously, the book responds to pressures for Nigeria to: use the implements of human rights to improve its still-fledgling democracy at home, while increasing its contribution to the international human rights regime, à la global Good Samaritan, within the boundaries spelled out in this work. The theoretical framework that informs this book is Constructivism, an exploratory and explanatory tool in-between Political Realism and Idealism, based on the extent to which each of these competing worldviews permits introduction of human rights into external affairs.

This book celebrates my abiding interest in human rights spanning over three decades back to Temple University School of Law in Philadelphia, subsequently named after the trial lawyer James E. Beasley, Sr., where I took my first courses in human rights. Like the Biblical seed sown on a fertile ground, over the years, the interest took deeper roots in the ground through subsequent programs that include an LL.M. in International

Human Rights Law and a Doctor of Juridical Science (SJD) in the same field, both from the Robert H. McKinney School of Law at Indianapolis, as well as a certificate in Conflict Resolution from Cornell University, and numerous publications over this time-frame that gave voice to that interest.

For persons familiar with America's bill-paying tradition, acknowledging a debt from completing a book is more pain-free because of the surpassing joy in gladness that it brings. Craving the indulgence of the reader to inebriate from that gladness, I acknowledge those I encountered in the long road to my human-right journey for various forms of support, *nwanne di namba* (siblings fortuitously found abroad), within the best tradition of generosity in Igbo worldview, among them: Opoku Agyeman, Firas Al-Douri, Yvette Alex-Assensoh, Curtbert Anidobu, Nonye Anidobu, A.B. Assensoh, Joseph Balogun, Chris Botanga, Agber Dimah, George Edwards, Virginia Ejindu, Frank Emmert, Michael Eskay, the late Rev. Fr. Celestine Ibe, Gabriel Ibe, Rev. Fr. John Ibe, Richard Ibe, Kenneth Ihenetu, Emmanuel Iheukwumere, Aliya Latif-Wahab, Nkuzi Nnam, Rev. Sister Francisca Nzeke, Kanayo Odeluga, Joel Ogbonna, Obasi Okafor-Obasi, Sampson Onwueyi, Felix Onyeise, Hassan Wahab, and Sencer Yeralan. I acknowledge these fine individuals within the best tradition of Igbo folklore—guided by the wisdom that a person who forgets the old (as in past deeds) does not deserve the beneficence of future favors.

Another set of individuals whose debt I acknowledge in this preface are the numerous authors whose works I have, like any other writer, relied upon to build my argument in this book. My appreciation goes well beyond the citation in the text and footnotes of the work. A third are the conscientious reviewers of the manuscript that metamorphosed into this book for their insights and suggestions, some of which helped shape the final form of this work, as well as for their contribution to the peer-review system.

Last but not least is the team of editors and publishers at Palgrave Macmillan, quite unlike any other, for the opportunity to publish with them, for their congeniality, and for competently shepherding the book through production: Angie Merila, Editor for International Studies in New York; and Divya Sakkaravathi, Production Editor in India, along with their coterie of assistants, such as Henry Rodgers in New York, and Leonie Sittner in Germany. If I may use the memorable language of one US product advertisement many years ago that still rings in my ears, together, you all bring good things to life. Consistent with the canons of academic writing, I alone take responsibility for any error of analysis and interpretation in this book.

Park Forest, IL, USA
April 2024

Philip C. Aka

List of Cases by the ECOWAS Community Court of Justice (CCJ) Cited in the Book

Community Court of Justice. 2022. *SERAP and 176 Other Concerned Nigerians v. Nigeria*. Suit No. ECW/CCJ/APP/23/21. Judgment No. ECW/CCJ/JUD/40/22. July 14.

Community Court of Justice. 2021. *Fodi Mohamed & Others v. Niger*. Suit No. ECW/CCJ/APP/27/19. Judgment No. ECW/CCJ/JUD/19/21. June 24. https://caselaw.ihrda.org/en/entity/pcaiwdusd5?page=1 (text in French).

Community Court of Justice. 2021. *Kadiaton Siby v. Mali*. Suit No. ECW/CCJ/APP/42/19. Judgment No. ECW/CCJ/JUD/15/21. June 22. *Reprinted* in African Human Rights Case Law Analyzer. https://caselaw.ihrda.org/en/entity/16tp7b9q7l7h (text in French).

Community Court of Justice. 2020. *Amnesty International and 7 Others v. the Togolese Republic*. Suit No. ECW/CCJ/APP/61/18. Judgment No. ECW/CCJ/JUD/09/20. June 25. https://www.eods.eu/elex/uploads/files/642e998c687ef-JUD-ECW-CCJ-JUD-09-20-Amnesty-Int.-TOGO-7-ORS-vs.-REP.-OF-TOGO-25_06_20-vA.pdf.

Community Court of Justice. 2019. *Rev. Fr. Solomon Mfa & 11 Others v. Nigeria and 5 Others*. Suit No. ECW/CCJ/APP/11/16. Judgment No. ECW/CCJ/JUD/06/19. February 26. https://caselaw.ihrda.org/en/entity/y1vuecy8gz.

Community Court of Justice. 2018. *Raymond Oguche & 4 Others v. Nigeria*. Suit No. ECW/CCJ/APP/11/15. Judgment No. ECW/CCJ/JUD/24/18. July 4. https://caselaw.ihrda.org/en/entity/v7dx0uzx5h36xsri94ojn61or?page=1.

Community Court of Justice. 2017. *Nosa Ehanire Osaghae & 3 Others (on Behalf of Niger Delta People) v. Nigeria*. Suit No. ECW/CCJ/APP/2015. Judgment No. ECW/CCJ/JUD/03/07. October 10. https://caselaw.ihrda.org/en/entity/5rot9qij7oijzfuyfghr1i3sor?page=1.

Community Court of Justice. 2015. *Rose M. Ako v. West African Monetary Agency and 4 Others*. Suit No. ECW/CCJ/APP/01/14/SUPP. Judgment No. ECW/CCJ/JUD/2815. December 2. https://caselaw.ihrda.org/en/entity/jcp55cz4kcrjbp0nc7bck57b9?page=2.

Community Court of Justice. 2012. *SERAP v. Nigeria*. Suit No. ECW/CCJ/APP/08/09. Judgment ECW/CCJ/JUD/18/12. December 14. https://caselaw.ihrda.org/en/entity/pftlz3gneo0wxsgq0kdszto6r?page=30.

Community Court of Justice. 2011. *Starcrest Investment Ltd. v. President of ECOWAS Commission*. Suit No. ECW/CCJ/APP/01/08. Judgment No. ECW/CCJ/JUD/06/11. July 8. https://www.worldcourts.com/ecowasccj/eng/decisions/2011.07.08_Starcrest_Investment_Ltd_v_President_of_ECOWAS_Comm.htm.

Community Court of Justice. 2010. *Musa Saidykhan v. The Gambia*. Suit No. ECW/CCJ/APP/11/07. Judgment No. ECW/CCJ/JUD/08/10. December 16. https://caselaw.ihrda.org/en/entity/froafttgl56tn7350qszzd7vi.

Community Court of Justice. 2010. *SERAP v. Nigeria and Anor*. Suit No. ECW/CCJ/APP/12/07. Judgment No. ECW/CCJ/JUD/07/10. November 30. https://www.worldcourts.com/ecowasccj/eng/decisions/2010.11.30_SERAP_v_Nigeria.htm.

Community Court of Justice. 2008. *Hadijatou Mani Koraou v. Niger*. Suit No. ECW/CCJ/APP/08/08. Judgment No. ECW/CCJ/JUD/06/08. October 27. http://www.courtecowas.org/wp-content/uploads/2023/12/JUD-ECW-CCJ-JUD-06-08-Dame-Hadijatou-Mani-Koraou-c.-La-R%C3%A9p-du-NIGER-27_10_08-vA-1.pdf.

Community Court of Justice. 2008. *Manneh v. The Gambia*. Suit No. ECW/CCJ/APP/04/07. Judgment No. ECW/CCJ/JUD/03/08. June 5. https://www.worldcourts.com/ecowasccj/eng/decisions/2008.06.05_Manneh_v_Gambia.htm.

Community Court of Justice. 2004. *Olajide Afolabi v. Nigeria*. ECW/CJ/JUD/01/04. April 27. *Reprinted* in African Human Rights Case Law Analyzer. https://caselaw.ihrda.org/en/entity/6dp0llnd6hr82kc18ylbjiqkt9?page=6.

Contents

Abbreviations

ACHPR	African Charter on Human and Peoples' Rights (Banjul Charter)
ACOSTA	African Contingency Operations Training and Assistance
ACP Countries	African, Caribbean, and Pacific Countries
ACRI	African Crisis Response Initiative
AEC	African Economic Community
AHSG	[ECOWAS's] Authority of Heads of State and Government
APC	All Progressives Congress
AU	African Union (from 1963 until 2000, Organization of African Unity, OAU)
CCJ	ECOWAS Community Court of Justice
CEAO	Communauté Economique de l'Afrique de l'Quest
CEN-SAD	Community of Sahel-Saharan States
CJEU	Court of Justice of the European Union
CLO	Civil Liberties Organization
CM	[ECOWAS's] Council of Ministers
COMESA	Common Market for Eastern and Southern Africa
DTAC	Directorate of Technical Aid Corps
EAC	East African Community
EBID	ECOWAS Bank for Investment and Development
ECA	UN Economic Commission for Africa
ECCAS	Economic Community of Central African States
ECOMOG	ECOWAS Monitoring Group
ECOWAS	The Economic Community of West African States
FCFA	Franc of the Financial Community of Africa
FDI	Foreign direct investment

GDP	Gross Domestic Product
HL	Humanitarian Law
HRVIC	The Human Rights Violations Investigation Commission (Oputa Panel)
ICCPR	The International Covenant on Civil and Political Rights
ICESCR	The International Covenant on Economic, Social, and Cultural Rights
ICPC	Independent Corrupt Practices Commission
IDEA	International Institute for Democracy and Electoral Assistance
IGAD	Intergovernmental Authority on Development
INEC	Independent National Electoral Commission
IPI	International Press Institute
ISIS	Islamic State of Iraq and Syria
MFWA	Media Foundation for West Africa
MOPOL	[Nigerian] Mobile Police
MPLA	Movement for the Popular Liberation of Angola
MRU	Mano River Union
MTAP	Military Training Assistance Program
NAPKC	Nigerian Army Peacekeeping Center
NEPAD	New Partnership for Africa's Development
NGOs	Non-Governmental Organizations
NIDCOM	Nigerians in Diaspora Commission
NIIA	Nigerian Institute of International Affairs
NIPSS	National Institute for Policy and Strategic Studies
OACPS	Organization of African, Caribbean, and Pacific States
OAU	Organization of African Unity (since 2000 renamed the African Union, AU)
OECD	Organization for Economic Cooperation and Development
ONUC	United Nations Organization in the Congo
OPEC	Organization of the Petroleum Exporting Countries
OSCE	Organization for Security and Cooperation in Europe
PDP	Peoples Democratic Party
PKW	Peacekeeper Wing
R2P	Responsibility to Protect
RECAMP	Reinforcement of African Capacity to Maintain Peace
SADC	Southern African Development Community
TAC	Technical Aid Corps
TI	Transparency International
UDHR	Universal Declaration of Human Rights
UK	The United Kingdom of Great Britain and Northern Island
UMA	Arab Maghreb Union
UN	The United Nations
UNAMSIL	The United Nations Mission in Sierra Leone

UNITAR	United Nations Institute for Training and Research
UNVS	United Nations Volunteer Service
US	The United States of America
VOA	Voice of America
WCC	Within-Case Comparison
WCHR	World Conference on Human Rights (1993)
WHO	World Health Organization

List of Tables

CHAPTER 1

Argument

This is the entrance of the book and a succinct embodiment of its argument, including a statement of the problem revolved around the reduced influence of the military in Nigerian politics, signified by the departure of General Muhammadu Buhari after two underwhelming terms in office as President; brief introduction of Nigeria; justifications for a human-right policy; and a statement on the book's organization.

Statement of the Problem

This book studies the application of human rights in Nigeria's external relations under the Fourth Republic, post-Buhari, since 2023. The Fourth Republic is the third instalment of civilian rule, shorn of military intervention, in Nigeria's body politic since independence. A projected Third Republic preceding this latest one died stillborn following the cancellation by the military regime then under General Ibrahim Babangida of the presidential election in 1993 that would have given birth to that Republic.[1]

[1] See, for example, Ian Campbell, "Nigeria's Failed Transition: The 1993 Presidential Election," *Journal of Contemporary African Studies*, 12(2) (1994), 179–199, 10.1080/02589009408729556; and Emeka Nwokedi, "Nigeria's Democratic Transition: Explaining the Annulled 1993 Presidential Election," *The Round Table*, 83(330) (April 1994), 189–204, 10.1080/00358539408454202.

P. C. Aka, *Human Rights in Nigeria's External Relations in the Age of General Muhammadu Buhari and His Successors*,
https://doi.org/10.1007/978-3-031-63231-0_1

Democracy scholars like Larry Diamond assessed General Babangida as "the first personal dictator in [Nigeria's] history."[2] Such was the extent of the military's direct intervention into the country's body politic before 1999, the start date of the Fourth Republic, within which period, as one Nigerian public affairs analyst pointed out, "the military appropriated responsibility for more and more facets of daily life."[3]

General Buhari was Nigeria's president from 2015 until 2023. Defying all hope and expectation for someone with an earlier stint in government as a military head of state,[4] Buhari's presidency marked a new low in governmental performance for a country already notorious for lackluster results matched against its vast human and material endowments.[5] "When Nigerians needed him to deliver, President Muhammadu Buhari fell short."[6] Instead, his eight years in office was a textbook example of "squandered goodwill," matched against modest delivery expectations of

[2] Larry Diamond, "Nigeria: The Uncivic Society and the Descent into Praetorianism," in *Politics in Developing Countries: Comparing Experiences with Democracy*, 2d Ed., eds. Larry Diamond et al. (Boulder, CO: Lynne Rienner, 1995), 417, 443. For one recent assessment of the Babangida regime, see James Falode Adewunmi, "The Military and Nation-Building in Nigeria: The General Ibrahim Babangida Regime, 1985–1993," *International Letters of Social and Humanistic Sciences*, 85 (2019), 37–48.

[3] Max Siollun, "Nigeria's Military Is Part of the Problem[;] It's Also the Solution," *Foreign Policy* (June 7, 2021), https://foreignpolicy.com/2021/06/07/nigerias-military-is-part-of-the-problem-its-also-the-solution/.

[4] David Smith, "Muhammadu Buhari: Reformed Dictator Returns to Power in Democratic Nigeria," *Guardian* (London) (March 31, 2015), https://www.theguardian.com/world/2015/mar/31/muhammadu-buhari-military-dictator-nigeria-new-democratic-president. From December 31, 1983 to August 27, 1985, when he was removed from office in a countercoup, Buhari held office as Nigeria's head of state. Ibid.

[5] See Eghosa E. Osaghae, *The Crippled Giant: Nigeria since Independence* (Bloomington, IN: Indiana University Press, 1998) (likening the suboptimal experiences of governance in the country through civilian and military regimes from 1960 until 1996 to that of a "crippled giant").

[6] Ebenezer Obadare, "Why Buhari Failed," Council on Foreign Relations (May 22, 2023), https://www.cfr.org/blog/why-buhari-failed. For an assessment of the former president's performance in office, see Kabir Yusuf, "Fact-Check: How True is Buhari's Claim that Nigeria is Better off Today Than in 2015?" *Premium Times* (Abuja) (July 4, 2022), https://www.premiumtimesng.com/news/headlines/540682-fact-check-how-true-is-buharis-claim-that-nigeria-is-better-off-today-than-in-2015.html (finding Buhari's claim to be untrue, based on assessment of his performance in managing the economy, on security, and on corruption or governmental transparency).

Nigeria's longsuffering citizens.[7] In the complexly interdependent world we live in, two presidential terms in office of the type Nigerians endured under Buhari from 2015 until 2023, can spell existential threats for ordinary citizens, with ramifications for external relations. The doubt about performance was one that reared its head from the get go within Buhari's first year in office that, however, he made no attempt to dispel over the ill-fated eight years of his period in office.[8]

In the light of this report card, many Nigerians view General Buhari as "inescapably the worst President Nigeria ever had."[9] The 2023 presidential election in Nigeria was the first since the inception of the Fourth Republic in 1999 that a retired army general did not run for office.[10] The decline of military influence in Nigerian politics, epitomized by General

[7] Oromo Egbejule et al., "'Squandered Goodwill': How Buhari Failed Nigeria a Second Time," *Alja Zeera* (May 29, 2023), https://www.aljazeera.com/features/2023/5/29/squandered-goodwill-how-buhari-failed-nigeria-a-second-time.

[8] In a report published in November 2015, nearly six months after Buhari took office, Bloomberg, the international business news outlet, assessed that Buhari lacked the economic "capacity to run Nigeria." Paul Wallace and Michael Cohen, "Buhari Bounce Becomes Bust as Nigeria Policies Irk Investors," *Bloomberg* (November 26, updated November 27, 2015), https://www.bloomberg.com/news/articles/2015-11-26/buhari-bounce-becomes-bust-as-nigeria-policies-annoy-investors#xj4y7vzkg.

[9] Kiikpoye K. Aaron, "Buhari's Eight Years of Governance Disaster," *Guardian* (Lagos) (May 24, 2023), https://guardian.ng/opinion/buharis-eight-years-of-governance-disaster/ ("Clearly, Mr. Buhari's Aso Rock odyssey would, for long, be remembered for what it is: eight years of governance disaster"). Aso Rock is the name of Nigeria's national government's seat of power in Abuja, the country's capital city. See also Kabir Yusuf, "Scorecard: Key Metrics Show Buhari Failed as Nigeria's President," *Premium Times* (Abuja) (May 28, 2023), https://www.premiumtimesng.com/features-and-interviews/600912-scorecard-key-metrics-show-buhari-failed-as-nigerias-president.html ("Buhari's eight-year reign as president has seen Nigeria struggle through numerous challenges, with inflation and unemployment at worse levels than he met them"); and Elfredah Kevin-Alerechi, "Nigerians Experiencing Worst Security Crisis since Civil War: Buhari," *People's Gazette* (Abuja) (October 1, 2021), https://gazettengr.com/nigerians-experiencing-worst-security-crisis-since-civil-war-buhari/. ("Nigeria's economy has plunged into recession three times since Mr. Buhari assumed power in May 2015, a record under a single administration").

[10] See Nasir Ayitogo, "2023: Military Influence 'Dwindles' in Nigerian Elections," *Premium Times* (Abuja) (July 9, 2022), https://www.premiumtimesng.com/news/headlines/541716-2023-military-influence-dwindles-in-nigerian-elections.html; and K'ọlá Túb`ọsún, "Nigeria's Last General Departs the Political Stage," *Foreign Policy* (May 30, 2023), https://foreignpolicy.com/2023/05/30/nigeria-democracy-elections-tinubu-bulhari/.

Buhari's departure from the political scene, affords an inestimable opportunity for critical assessment of Nigeria's progress in the journey toward a human-right policy, to the benefit of democracy and human rights at home.

To put the matter in closer analytical perspective, the Fourth Republic as it has evolved is military-rule lite.[11] First, General Olusegun Obasanjo, whose regime initiated this new dispensation, served two terms in office, and handpicked his successor—after failing to change the constitution to permit him to run for a third term.[12] Second, no need for a third-term gambit, Buhari did the same, serving two terms in office and making way for Bola A. Tinubu to take his own "turn" at the presidency.[13] To all intents and purposes, the Tinubu era since May 29, 2023, is an extension of the Buhari period; Tinubu, a member of Buhari's All Progressives Congress (APC), was handpicked to succeed Buhari as a payback for providing the organizational and monetary clout that saw Buhari through two terms in office.[14]

As the story goes, ahead of the presidential election in 2015, Buhari and Tinubu entered "a Faustian pact [...] under which Tinubu would help Buhari become president [...], and Buhari would help Tinubu become president after his [Buhari's] two terms [...]."[15] Although it does not justify it, this was the basis for Tinubu's reported claim to the effect that "[w]ithout [Tinubu], Buhari won't be president," adding to good effect in Yoruba, "*Emi lokan*!" translatable into English as

[11] See Philip C. Aka, *Navigating the Tension Between Sovereignty and Self-Determination in Postcolonial Africa: Blueprints for the Midcentury* (Cham, Switzerland, 2023), 371 (contending that "Nigeria under the Fourth Republic is little better than military rule," commenting on the necessity for more quality in civil-democratic rule). See also Philip C. Aka and Joseph Abiodun Balogun, *Improving Disability Laws under Nigeria's Fourth Republic: Ten Measured Steps into the Future* (Lanham, Boulder, New York, and London: Lexington Books, 2022), 147–151 (outlining the need for improved civilian rule as the foundation for improvement in the implementation of disability laws in the country).

[12] John Campbell, "Obasanjo's Costly Failed Third-Term Bid," Council on Foreign Relations (September 27, 2018), https://www.cfr.org/blog/obasanjos-costly-failed-third-term-bid.

[13] See note 16 below and accompanying text.

[14] Olu Fasan, "Buhari Wants Tinubu as Next President; He's Nigeria's Worst Enemy," *Business Day* (Lagos) (November 28, 2022), https://businessday.ng/columnist/article/buhari-wants-tinubu-as-next-president-hes-nigerias-worst-enemy/.

[15] Ibid.

"It's my turn!"[16] However, based on questionable issues in his background, political analysts like Olu Fasan are unsure that Tinubu possesses the character and integrity to be president.[17] Instead, they are worried that a Tinubu presidency would "divide and destabilize Nigeria internally," and "damage [it] externally, making it a big laughingstock, a butt of dark international jokes."[18] Given this assessment, they contend, Buhari's "campaign for Tinubu to succeed him" is anything but in the overall interest of the Nigeria people, such that "Buhari must really hate Nigeria."[19]

Buhari participated in the unlawful overthrow of the government of the Second Republic in 1983 on the theory that "a flawed democracy was worse than no democracy at all."[20] It is therefore ironic, even hypocritical, that he should bequeath Nigeria with a democracy more flawed

[16] Ibid. Another iteration of the claim goes that, in a speech broadcast on local television, Tinubu told party faithful in Ogun state: "It is my time, I'm educated, I'm experienced. I have been serving you (Buhari) for a long time, bring me (the) presidency, it is my turn." Macdonald Dzirutwe, "Tinubu Says It is His Turn to Rule Nigeria in Election Appeal to Buhari," *Reuters* (June 3, 2022), https://www.reuters.com/world/africa/tinubu-says-it-is-his-turn-rule-nigeria-election-appeal-buhari-2022-06-03/#:~:text=%22It%20is%20my%20time%2C%20I,t%20have%20become%20the%20president.%22.

He reportedly claimed, "If not for me that stood behind Buhari he wouldn't have become the president." Ibid.

[17] Fasan, note 14.

[18] Ibid.

[19] Ibid. Fasan's analysis calls to mind the contribution of Sanusi Lamido Sanusi, a traditional ruler and one-time governor of Nigeria's Central Bank in July 2002, years before Buhari became president in 2015. See Sanusi Lamido Sanusi, "Buharism: Economic Theory and Political Economy," *Gamji* (July 22, 2002), http://www.gamji.com/sanusi/sanusi26.htm. Sanusi opined that "the situation of Nigeria and its elite today is worse than it was in 1983," adding that "[c]ompared to the politicians who populate [Nigeria's political parties] today, [S]econd [R]epublic politicians were angels." Ibid. He accused Buhari of joining the very same group of politicians that in the past he waged a battle against, in the sense that many of those who hold key offices at the national and subnational levels in Nigeria today were creatures of the corrupt system he fought against. Ibid. In Sanusi's assessment, "Nigeria needs people like Buhari in politics but not to contest elections. Buhari should be in politics to develop Civil Society and strengthen the conscience of the nation. He should try to develop many Buharis who will continue to challenge the elements that have hijacked the nation." Ibid. Despite these serious reservations about a Buhari candidacy, strangely and nonsensically, Sanusi still indicated he would vote for him. See ibid.

[20] Clifford D. May, "Military Rule is Contagious in Africa," *New York Times* (May 6, 1984), § 4, p. 4.

than the one that impelled him and his colleagues to seize power in the military coup four decades ago that ended Nigeria's second experiment in civilian rule just four years after thirteen years of military dictatorship. All this feeds into the proposition of commentators like Olu Fasan who, in criticizing the former president's quid pro quo electoral agreement with Tinubu, labelled him "Nigeria's worst enemy."[21]

A third factor cementing these first two points is the failure to hold free, fair, and credible elections that meet international standards. Elections serve the consolidative role of legitimizing and routinizing democracies.[22] However, on account of their fraudulence, all the seven elections bar none over the 24 years of the Fourth Republic since 1999, as of this book, were controversial.[23] The one in February 2023 organized by General Buhari, which brought Mr. Tinubu into office, seems to top these elections in pervasive irregularity matched by electoral violence and low voter turnout.[24] This is against the enjoinment of the Economic Commission of West African States (ECOWAS), a regional political and economic organization Nigeria helped create in 1975, related to regional security.[25] A revised treaty of the organization adopted in 1993 obligated Nigeria and co-member-states "to safeguard and consolidate relations

[21] Fasan, note 14.

[22] See Winrich Kühne, "The Role of Elections in Emerging Democracies and Post-Conflict Countries," *Friedrich Ebert Stiftung* (August 2010), https://library.fes.de/pdf-files/iez/07416.pdf (electoral malpractices "in emerging democracies and post-conflict societies have a great potential to plunge a country back into violent conflict, to undermine processes of stabilization and to discredit democratization").

[23] See, for example, Aka and Balogun, note 11, p. 147 ("Despite the numerous elections Nigeria has held under the Fourth Republic, Nigeria's electoral system remains flawed with irregularities, election season after election season"). See also Emmanuel Remi Aiyede, "Nigeria's Electoral System is Still Broken," *Conversation* (May 9, 2021), https://theconversation.com/nigerias-electoral-system-is-still-broken-heres-a-list-of-whats-urgent-159693; and Michael M. Ogbeidi, "A Culture of Failed Elections: Revisiting Democratic Elections in Nigeria, 1959–2003," *Historia Actual Online,* 21 (2010), 43–56.

[24] A report by observers from the European Union assessed that the election fell below international standards in transparency and accountability. See "Nigeria's 2023 Election Eroded Voters' Trust: EU Observers," *Alja Zeera* (June 29, 2023), https://www.aljazeera.com/news/2023/6/29/nigerias-2023-election-eroded-voters-trust-eu-observers.

[25] See Economic Community of West African States (ECOWAS), Revised Treaty of the Economic Community of West African States (ECOWAS) (July 24, 1993), http://www.refworld.org/docid/492182d92.html [hereinafter ECOWAS Revised Treaty], art. 58 ("Regional Security").

conducive to the maintenance of peace, stability, and security within the [sub]region,"[26] including, where necessary, securement of assistance related to "democratic elections."[27]

Months after he took office, the election of Mr. Tinubu was challenged by two opponents who contended that he did not win the polls.[28] It was a vociferous challenge that spread beyond the borders of Nigeria with allegations in US courtrooms against Mr. Tinubu for criminal indictment related to drug dealing and certificate forgery.[29] Tinubu lived in the US from the 1970s until his return to Nigeria in 1998 at the dawn of the Fourth Republic.[30] The challenge came to an end on October 26, 2023, when the Nigerian Supreme Court refused to void the election on ground of the complained irregularities.[31] Since the inception of the Fourth Republic in 1999, the Court has not voided a presidential election, no matter how egregious the irregularities are.[32]

A fourth and final indicator, more anecdotal than substantive, is the number of US presidential visits to the country under the Fourth Republic. There was one such visit, by President William J. Clinton, in August of 2000,[33] sequel to an earlier one by President Jimmy Carter

[26] Ibid., art. 58(1).

[27] Ibid., art. 58(2)(g).

[28] Timothy Obiezu, "Opposition Parties Reject Nigeria's Presidential Election Court Verdict," *VOA News* (September 7, 2023), https://www.voanews.com/a/opposition-parties-reject-nigeria-s-presidential-election-court-verdict-/7258597.html.

[29] See, for example, Chinedu Asadu, "Nigeria's President Faces New Challenge to Election Victory as Opposition Claims He Forged Diploma," *AP News* (October 5, 2023), https://apnews.com/article/nigeria-tinubu-abubakar-election-challenge-ba0fd3483678b84747bd38aba53d5bf9.

[30] See Ebenezer Obadare, "Paper Truths and Counterfeit Lives," Council on Foreign Relations (October 10, 2023), https://www.cfr.org/blog/paper-truths-and-counterfeit-lives.

[31] See Camillus Eboh, "Nigerian Supreme Court Affirms President Tinubu's Election Win," *Reuters* (October 26, 2023), https://www.reuters.com/world/africa/nigerian-supreme-court-upholds-president-tinubus-election-win-2023-10-26/#:~:text=ABUJA%2C%20Oct%2026%20(Reuters),victory%20was%20marred%20by%20irregularities.

[32] See Chinedu Asadu, "Nigeria's Supreme Court Refuses to Void President's Election and Dismisses Opposition Challenges," *AP News* (October 26, 2023), https://apnews.com/article/nigeria-election-supreme-court-abubakar-tinubu-ad610050879e5a0178bcb52934c56054.

[33] Marc Lacey, "Clinton in Nigeria to Show Support for Civilian Rule," *New York Times* (August 27, 2000), § 1, p. 1.

in April 1978, twenty-two years before.[34] Nigerians maintain close ties with America whose political system they adopted in 1979, relatively on the eve of President Carter's visit to the country March ending 1978, in place of the Westminster model they inherited from the UK at independence.[35] Despite its known imperfections, the US is viewed by many as a prima donna in the orchestra of modern democracy.[36]

Introducing Nigeria

Nigeria is a country in West Africa overlooking the Gulf of Guinea with a landmass slightly more than twice the size of California.[37] It is bordered to the East by Cameroon, West by Benin, North by Niger, and South by the Atlantic Ocean.[38] A slight reshaping of the country's border took place soon after independence when, in a referendum on February 11 and 12, 1961, Northern Cameroon voted to join Nigeria,

[34] David B. Ottaway, "Carter Arrives in Nigeria on State Visit," *Washington Post* (April 1, 1978), https://www.washingtonpost.com/archive/politics/1978/04/01/carter-arrives-in-nigeria-on-state-visit/bd7821e0-271a-49c6-b16d-0252f1efeb74/.

[35] See Constitution of the Federal Republic of Nigeria, 1979, *Constitution Net*, www.constitutionnet.org/files/nig_const_79.pdf, art. 5, § 1(a) (stipulating that the executive powers of the Federation "shall be vested in the President, and may [...] be exercised by him directly or through the Vice-President and Ministers of the Government of the Federation or officers in the public service of the Federation"); and Constitution of the Federal Republic of Nigeria, 1999, *Constitute Project*, https://www.constituteproject.org/constitution/Nigeria_1999 [hereinafter Nigerian Const. 1999], art. 5, §1(a) (providing similarly).

[36] Richard Haass, "The World's Stake in American Democracy," *Project Syndicate* (January 24, 2023), https://www.project-syndicate.org/commentary/world-still-depends-on-us-leadership-by-richard-haass-2023-01 (pointing out that US resources and leadership are needed to promote stability and prosperity in the world). Haass quoted a dictum attributable to sometime British Prime Minister Winston Churchill to the effect that "You can always count on Americans to do the right thing—after they've tried everything else." Ibid. See also David Leonhardt, *Ours Was the Shining Future: The Story of the American Dream* (New York: Random House, 2023), xxxiii ("[W]hile America is a flawed embodiment of its founding ideals of equality, liberty, opportunity, and democracy, those ideals matter").

[37] CIA World Factbook, "Nigeria" (last updated September 5, 2023), https://www.cia.gov/the-world-factbook/countries/nigeria/.

[38] "Political Map of Nigeria," *Nations Online*, https://www.nationsonline.org/oneworld/map/nigeria-political-map.htm.

while Southern Cameroon chose to join French-speaking Cameroon.[39] Before the referendum, Northern Cameroon was administered separately within Nigeria, while Southern Cameroon was part of Eastern Nigeria.[40] More recently, the International Court of Justice (World Court) heard a land and maritime dispute between Nigeria and Cameroon in which it awarded ownership of the Bakassi Peninsula to Cameroon but a stretch of land in the area around Lake Chad to Nigeria.[41]

Nigeria is a wholesale creature of British colonialism. The country took its name from the Niger River which courses through its territory.[42] The name was coined in 1897 by Flora Shaw, a British journalist, later married to Frederick Lugard (1858–1945), first governor-general of the country.[43] Nigeria is not "an African creation that reflect[s] the affiliation and sentiments of the people living there"; instead, it is "the result of British colonial conquest."[44]

Nigeria came into being on January 1, 1914, when, in the wake of the scramble for Africa underscored by the Berlin Conference (1884–1885),[45] the British government by fiat amalgamated three territories it acquired in the area to form the country, with no regard for preexisting divisions, ethnic, cultural, and linguistic. These were areas hitherto

[39] Dieter Nohlen et al., eds., *Elections in Africa: A Data Handbook* (London: Oxford University Press, 1999), 177.

[40] "Brief Notes on Nigeria," *Online Nigeria*, http://www.onlinenigeria.com/history.asp.

[41] See International Court of Justice, Land and Maritime Boundary Between Cameroon and Nigeria (Cameroon v. Nigeria: Equatorial Guinea Intervening) (October 10, 2002), http://www.icj-cij.org/docket/index.php?p1=3&p2=3&k=74&case=94&code=cn&p3=4.

[42] See Toyin Falola and Matthew M. Heaton, *A History of Nigeria* (New York: Cambridge University Press, 2008), 85–104.

[43] International Crisis Group, *Nigeria: Want in the Midst of Plenty*, Africa Report No. 113 (July 19, 2006), 2, https://www.crisisgroup.org/africa/west-africa/nigeria/nigeria-want-midst-plenty.

[44] April A. Gordon, *Nigeria's Diverse Peoples: A Reference Sourcebook* (Santa Barbara, CA: ABC-CLIO, 2003), 3.

[45] This was a meeting at which the major European powers negotiated and formalized claims to territory in Africa. Elizabeth Heath, "Berlin Conference of 1884–1885," in *Encyclopedia of Africa*, eds. Henry Louis Gates, Jr. and Kwame Anthony Appiah (New York: Oxford University Press, 2010), https://www.oxfordreference.com/display/10.1093/acref/9780195337709.001.0001/acref-9780195337709-e-0467. The conference "marked the climax of the European competition for territory in Africa, a process commonly known as the Scramble for Africa." Ibid.

inhabited by "a heterogeneous population of strangers" who established "many economic, social, and political links among themselves," but "did not recognize themselves as one people or as one political community."[46] The architect of the amalgamation was Lugard.[47] The three territories involved were the Northern and Southern Protectorates, which Britain acquired in 1900, and the Colony of Lagos, which it acquired on March 5, 1862.[48] The colonization of Lagos followed its annexation on August 6, 1861, and its bombardment ten years before in 1851.[49]

Following forty-six years of British control, counting from the amalgamation in 1914, Nigeria became independent in October 1960,[50] and a republic three years later,[51] in a move designed to shake off residues of British control and consolidate its independence.[52] Republican status did away with two major relics of British control. First was the change in the job title of the Governor-General of the country who represented the British monarch to President.[53] Second, the Nigerian Supreme Court

[46] Ignatius Akaayar Ayua and Dakas C.J. Dakas, "Federal Republic of Nigeria," in *Constitutional Origins, Structure, and Change in Federal Countries*, eds. John Kincaid and George Alan Tarr (Montreal, Canada: McGill-Queen's University Press, 2005), 242.

[47] See Reuters, "Lord Lugard, 87, African Pioneer; Former Governor General of Nigeria Dies—Occupied Uganda, Fought Slavers," *New York Times* (April 12, 1945), 23, https://www.nytimes.com/1945/04/12/archives/lord-lugard-87-african-pioneer-former-governor-general-of-nigeria.html.

[48] See The Centenary Project, "Colonial Footprints: Lagos, Then and Now," *Google Arts and Culture*, https://artsandculture.google.com/story/colonial-footprints-lagos-then-and-now/LAUBxuvCARsA8A.

[49] Ibid.

[50] See Nigeria Independence Act, 1960, 8 & 9 Eliz., 2 CH. 55 (July 29, 1960), www.legislation.gov.uk/ukpga/1960/55/pdfs/ukpga_19600055_en.pdf (granting the country "fully responsible status" within the British Commonwealth of Nations, effective October 1, 1960).

[51] See Nigeria Republican Act 1963, 1963 CH. 57 (December 18, 1963), http://www.legislation.gov.uk/ukpga/1963/57 (making the country "a Republic within the Commonwealth," effective Oct. 1, 1963). See also Constitution of the Federal Republic of Nigeria 1963, http://www.unesco.org/fileadmin/MULTIMEDIA/HQ/CI/WPFD2009/pdf/Nigeria%20Constitution.pdf.

[52] See Nigeria (Republic) Bill, H.L., Deb. December 17, 1963, Vol. 254 cc208–14 *Hansard*, hansard.millbanksystems.com/lords/1963/dec/17/Nigeria-republic-bill.

[53] Ibid.

became the tribunal of final appeal, rather than the Judicial Committee of the Privy Council, which hitherto assumed that role.[54]

From a federation of one national government (headquartered in Lagos) and three regions at independence,[55] four in 1963,[56] Nigerian governments have ballooned into a bureaucratic Leviathan of one national government in Abuja, 36 states, and 774 local governments.[57] Testament to the strong military influence in Nigerian politics, commented upon in the preceding paragraphs, all of these but the 1963 reorganization were created through military fiat.[58] As indicated earlier, in constitutional and political practice, since 1979, Nigeria has adopted the US's presidential system of government which replaced the parliamentary system bequeathed to it by the UK.[59] However, unlike the US, where formerly unaffiliated territories joined the union, in the process expanding the landmass of the country,[60] state creations in Nigeria involve the breakup of a fixed and unchanging landmass into smaller entities.[61] In the apt observation of some legal scholars, "one prominent theme of Nigeria's federal history has been an urge to subdivide."[62] Also unlike the US's, the Nigerian Constitution contains no provision on the admission of new territories as states, should such a situation arise, nor does it include any provision permitting the merger of preexisting states.[63]

[54] Ibid.

[55] See Paul E. Lovejoy, "Historical Setting," in *Nigeria: A Country Study*, 5th Ed. Helen Chapin Metz, ed. (Washington, DC: Library of Congress, 1992), 1, 47, https://www.marines.mil/Portals/1/Publications/Nigeria%20Study_1.pdf.

[56] The state was created on August 9, 1963, following a referendum on July 13, 1963 in which 89% of the voters in the area approved the creation. See Rotimi T. Suberu, *Public Policies and National Unity in Nigeria* (Ibadan, Nigeria: Development Policy Center, 1999), 12.

[57] See Nigerian Const. 1999, note 35, 1st schedule Part I (listing the states, capital cities, and local governments).

[58] See Suberu, note 56, p. 11.

[59] See note 35 and accompanying text.

[60] See "States of the United States," *Statoids,* http://statoids.com/uus.html; "Statehood Dates," 50States.com, http://www.50states.com/statehood.htm#.VoL53xUrKls.

[61] See Ayua and Dakas, note 46, p. 253.

[62] Ibid.

[63] Ibid.

The Case for a Human-Right Policy

Some of the changes Nigeria has witnessed since independence, such as the humanitarian convulsions of the civil war from 1967 to 1970 and the repressive experience of military rule across seven juntas for nearly three decades until 1999,[64] are negative. But others, such as the experiments in democracy, are heart-warming. Albeit low quality, as indicated in the preceding paragraphs, Nigeria is currently living through the longest spurt of civilian rule since independence in 1960 Nigerians celebrate as the Fourth Republic. This bout of non-military rule provides the setting and context for this study.

Like many other countries in the world, Nigeria participates a bit in the international human rights regime. The country played an instrumental role in the establishment of the Organization of African Unity (OAU) and its successor, the African Union (AU);[65] participated robustly in

[64] The seven regimes in chronological order are: Johnson Aguiyi-Ironsi, January-July 1966; Yakubu Gowon, July 1966-July 1975; Murtala Muhammed and Olusegun Obasanjo (two regimes usually counted as one because Obasanjo continued the policies of Muhammed after the assassination of his principal in a failed military coup), July 1975–1979; Muhammadu Buhari, 1983–1985; Ibrahim Babangida, 1985–1993; Sani Abacha, 1993–1998; and Abdulsalami Abubakar, 1998–May 29, 1999. For studies of Nigerian foreign policy during these military eras, see Olayiwola Abegunrin, *Nigerian Foreign Policy under Military Rule, 1966–1999* (Westport, CT: Praeger, 2003) (covering the entire military period); Alade W. Fawole, *Nigeria's External Relations and Foreign Policy under Military Rule, 1966–1999* (Ile-Ife: Obafemi Awolowo University Press, 2003) (same); and Joe Garba, *Diplomatic Soldiering: The Conduct of Nigerian Foreign Policy, 1975–1979* (Ibadan, Nigeria: Spectrum Books, 1991) (limited to the Muhammed-Obasanjo regime). More discussion on this and their civilian counterparts is saved for Chapter 3 devoted to background history.

[65] See J. Peter Pham, "Nigeria's Foreign Policy: An Inquiry into Sources and Prospects," Presentation for International Conference, Lisbon, Portugal (November 8–9, 2007), www.ipri.pt/eventos/pdf/JPeterPham_paper.pdf. (opining that "[t]he creation of both the AU and NEPAD would have been exceedingly difficult [...] without the combined diplomatic and political efforts of" Nigeria and South Africa). The AU replaced the Organization of African Unity, the association of independent African states, set up in May 1963. The Constitutive Act of the organization, its enabling law, stressed the determination of the AU "to promote and protect human and peoples' rights, consolidate democratic institutions and culture, and to ensure good governance and the rule of law." Organization of African Unity, Constitutive Act of the African Union (2000), OAU Doc. CAB/LEG/23.15 (July 11, 2000), http://www.africa-union.org (preamble). NEPAD is a voluntary "peer review" tool of the organization, rooted in democratic principles and sound economic practice. "Profile: African Union," *BBC News* (February 1, 2012), http://news.bbc.co.uk/2/hi/africa/country_profiles/3870303.stm. See also

the decolonization and anti-racialist campaigns in Africa that culminated with the achievement of majority rule in South Africa in 1994;[66] and espouses "respect for international law and treaty obligations."[67] Nigeria also puts a premium on peace and international cooperation that it seeks

Philip C. Aka, "NEPAD and the Movement for Popular Participation in Development (MPPD) in Africa," *Human Rights & Globalization Law Review,* 3 (2009–2010), 79, 81 (indicating that NEPAD presages a new kind of cooperative arrangement between African countries and outside donors, embedded in good governance, democracy, and human rights, "that embodies the vision and aspirations of African Governments and their peoples for development").

[66] Bonn O. Nwanolue and Victor C. Iwuoha, "A Reflection on Nigeria's Past: Africa as the Centerpiece of Nigeria's Foreign Policy Revisited," *Developing Country Studies*, 2 (2012), 78–79, http://www.iiste.org/Journals/index.php/DCS/article/view/1756/1709.

[67] See Nigerian Const. 1999, note 35, § 19(d). Nigeria is a party to numerous global and regional human rights instruments. See University of Minnesota, Human Rights Library, Ratification of International Human Rights Treaties—Nigeria, http://www1.umn.edu/humanrts/research/ratification-nigeria.html (last visited February 26, 2015) (listing various categories of instruments Nigeria ratified from 1960 to 2012). These include the six core global human rights instruments: the International Convention on the Elimination of All Forms of Racial Discrimination in 1967; the International Covenant on Civil and Political Rights (1993); the International Covenant on Economic, Social, and Cultural Rights same year; the Convention on the Elimination of All forms of Discrimination against Women (1985); the Convention against Torture and Other Cruel, Inhuman or Degrading Treatment or Punishment (2001); and the Convention on the Rights of the Child (1991). See ibid. Other key global human rights instruments Nigeria has ratified are: the Convention Relating to the Status of Refugees in 1967; Convention on the Prevention and Punishment of the Crime of Genocide in 2009, only following its civil war from 1967 to 1970, interestingly given the allegation of genocide that shrouded the conflict; and the Rome Statute of the International Criminal Court in 2001. Ibid. African regional human rights instruments Nigeria is a state party to include the African [Banjul] Charter on Human and Peoples' Right in 1983; Convention Governing the Specific Aspects of Refugee Problems in Africa (1986); and the African Charter on the Rights and Welfare of the Child (2001). See ibid. Similarly, Nigeria has ratified all four main instruments and two protocols of the Geneva Convention, all four in 1961, excepting the Geneva Convention Relative to the Protection of Civilian Persons in Time of War, which it ratified in 1988, the same year as the protocol instruments. Ibid. However, the country's 1999 constitution forbids the enforcement of treaties that have not been enacted into law by the national legislature, a process fraught with long delay, and Nigeria ratifies treaties, such as the Geneva Conventions, that it makes little effort to comply with. See, for example, Babatunde Isaac Olutoyin, "Treaty Making and Its Application under Nigerian Law: The Journey So Far," *International Journal of Business and Management Invention*, 3 (2004), 7, http://www.ijbmi.org/papers/Vol%283%293/Version-3/B033307018.pdf.

to promote through peacekeeping;[68] and eschews the use of force in resolving conflicts with neighbors.

Regarding the use of force, Nigeria's 1999 constitution includes peaceful "settlement of international disputes by negotiation, mediation, conciliation, arbitration[,] and adjudication" among the foreign policy objectives of the country.[69] Constitutional provision aside or because of it, Nigeria has a reputation as a gentle giant that never uses force to settle a dispute with a neighbor, not even when pushed to the point of provocation. For example, for many years, the country had a boundary dispute with Cameroon over Bakassi, an oil-rich peninsula that both countries claimed. Skirmishes erupted occasionally from the Cameroonian side that at times involved the death of Nigerians, but the country never responded in kind. Ultimately the dispute was settled via a lawsuit at the International Court of Justice that in 2002 awarded the peninsula to Cameroon.[70]

Despite pressures from many Nigerians at home and abroad displeased with the judgment, Nigeria obeyed the judgment.[71] About 90% of the peninsula's population, estimated at about 300,000 people, is made up of Nigerian fishermen.[72] Ban Ki-Moon, then UN Secretary General, praised the peaceful transfer as "a model for negotiated settlements of border disputes."[73] In short, Nigeria tends to limit its use of violence within its borders, rather than extend it overseas. Finally, going back to the early days of its independence, Nigeria operates a technical assistance program that in 1987 it formalized into a Technical Aid Corps (TAC) scheme.[74]

[68] See Adekeye Adebajo, *Liberia's Civil War: Nigeria, ECOMOG, and Regional Security in West Africa* (Boulder, CO: Lynne Rienner Publishers, 2002); and 'Funmi Olonisakin, *Reinventing Peacekeeping in Africa: Conceptual and Legal Issues in ECOMOG Operations* (London: Kluwer Law International, 2000).

[69] Nigerian Const. 1999, note 35, § 19(d).

[70] See note 41 and accompanying text.

[71] See "Nigeria Cedes Bakassi to Cameroon," *BBC News* (August 14, 2008), http://news.bbc.co.uk/2/hi/africa/7559895.stm.

[72] Ani Akpan, "Nigeria Hands Over Oil-Rich Bakassi to Cameroon," *Reuters* (August 14, 2008), https://www.reuters.com/article/us-nigeria-cameroon-bakassi/nigeria-hands-over-oil-rich-bakassi-to-cameroon-idUSLE14871520080814.

[73] "Nigeria Cedes Bakassi to Cameroon," note 71.

[74] See, for example, Salami B. Olawale, "The Preclude to Babangida Regime's Foreign Policy Initiatives," *Mediterranean Journal of Social Sciences*, 5 (2014), 83, http://www.mcser.org/journal/index.php/mjss/article/view/2120. More discussion of this scheme is saved for Chapter 7 dedicated to the program.

However, for a country its size and potentials, this is barely enough. Building on auspicious foundations, such as the ones recounted in the preceding paragraph, Nigeria can do more to increase the role of human rights in its external affairs while contributing to the international human rights regime,[75] through various practical steps that include "build[ing] global governance," and "reshap[ing] the meaning of sovereignty" in a manner that helps to incorporate human rights as a norm of legitimacy.[76] In the post-Cold War period, "[m]any states have made substantial progress toward a more serious incorporation of human rights into their foreign policy [,]" but many too "could readily do more."[77] This study identifies Nigeria as one of those laggards needing to do more, outlines the justification for that assessment but more so the extent of the deficit, and marshals several practical measures the country could use to enhance its contribution to international human rights for its own domestic well-being and to the benefit of its known aspirations for a leadership role within the sphere of its influence in West Africa and beyond.

This book advances proposals for a human-right policy, referred to alternately in this book as principled foreign policy,[78] for Nigeria under the Fourth Republic, taking advantage of the inestimable opportunity afforded by General Buhari's departure from the political scene on May

[75] *International regimes* are "are sets of implicit or explicit principles, norms, rules, and decision-making procedures around which actors' expectations converge in a given area of international relations." Stephen D. Krasner, "Structural Causes and Regime Consequences: Regimes as Intervening Variable," *International Organization*, 36 (1982), 186. See also Alison Brysk, *Global Good Samaritans: Human Rights as Foreign Policy* (New York: Oxford University Press, 2009), 4 (defining international human rights regime as "the thin layer of international understandings, institutions, and exchanges that seek to protect individual human dignity from abuses of power").

[76] See Brysk, note 75, p. 4. As Professor Brysk explains, the influence of these states "can be critical for framing and ratifying treaties, creating and staffing multilateral institutions, monitoring and sanctioning offenders, assisting victims, directing resources, implementing peace processes, catalyzing transnational initiatives or emerging issues, and introducing new understandings of rights to the global agenda." Ibid., p. 3. One gets the sense why, for their uncommon altruism, Brysk variously praised these countries as global Good Samaritans, humanitarian internationalists, and principled states.

[77] Jack Donnelly, *International Human Rights*, 4th Ed. (Boulder, CO: Westview Press, 2013), 147.

[78] The appellation does not suggest or imply that countries whose foreign policies do not follow this approach are not necessarily principled, for they may still be, only that they are sub-optimally different.

29, 2023, after the double famine,[79] domestically and externally, of two terms of office as President. It is a broad-ranging argument, draped in the less arcane constitutional material of human rights, for thoroughgoing reforms at home and abroad as the only antidote to the national-building dilemmas Nigeria confronts in the first quarter of the twenty-first century. Buhari's departure marks the end of military teleguidance of Nigerian politics under the Fourth Republic in the camouflage of democratic rule, a birthmark of remote control dating back to the first military intervention in the country in January 1966.[80]

These momentous events within Nigeria coincide with equally momentous developments in the UK, Nigeria's former colonial overlord, with ripple effects in Nigeria, signified by the death of Queen Elizabeth II, after seven decades on the throne, and the emergence of Prince Charles as King of England.[81] Queen Elizabeth's reign and headship of the Commonwealth of Nations coincided with human right atrocities in Nigeria signified by the Nigerian civil war from 1967 until 1970 which many legal scholars assess as a genocide perpetrated against the Igbo.[82] It was under her rule that then Prime Minister Harold Wilson indicated that he would "accept a half million dead Biafrans if that was what it

[79] *Holy Bible*, New International Version 41:29–32 ("Seven years of great abundance are coming throughout the land of Egypt, but seven years of famine will follow. Then all the abundance in Egypt will be forgotten, and the famine will ravage the land. The abundance in the land will not be remembered, because the famine that follows it will be so severe").

[80] See generally Toyin Falola et al., *Military Factor in Nigeria, 1966–1985* (Lewiston, NY: E. Mellen Press, 1994).

[81] See "Queen Elizabeth II Has Died," BBC (September 8, 2022), https://www.bbc.com/news/uk-61585886. Queen Elizabeth became the head of the Commonwealth following the death of King George VI in 1952. She became queen on February 2, 1952, during a visit to Kenya when her father died. Her first overseas tour as monarch was also in Africa, specifically South Africa. Mohammed Yusuf, "Africans Say Goodbye to Queen Who Led Britain into Post-Colonial Era," *Voice of America* (September 9, 2022), https://www.voanews.com/a/africans-say-goodbye-to-queen-who-led-britain-into-post-colonial-era/6738394.html. British rule in Africa is associated with conflicts, forceful extraction of natural resources, and expropriation of private lands. Ibid. With respect to conflicts, Kenya gained independence from the UK in 1963 after an 8-year war, minimized-ly denominated rebellion, that left an estimated 10,000 people dead. This was just few years apart from the civil war over Biafra (1967–1970), text next after this footnote.

[82] See Philip C. Aka, "Prospects for Igbo Human Rights in Nigeria in the New Century," *Howard Law Journal*, 48(1) (Fall 2004), 165–266.

took" to keep Nigeria one.[83] The British government got more than its wish: an estimated 3.5 million Igbo perished in Biafra, the name of the new nation under whose umbrella the Igbo and other Easterners-turned-Biafrans fought for self-determination.[84] A new monarch in Britain adds to the opportunity that falls open for the recreation of Nigeria's external relations with ramifications for Nigerian domestic events of the type this book proposes.

Under the Fourth Republic, the challenge Nigerian leaders face like never before is how to create a state that matches the expectations of their diverse people*s* at home and abroad—markedly for a country since its independence from Britain sixty-three years ago as of this book notorious for dashing those expectations.[85] Building upon this proposition, four interlinked and internally-consistent questions frame this research. First, what factors at this moment in Nigeria's checkered history make embracement and internalization of international standards in governance, signified by increased application of human rights in external affairs, exigent for the country and its citizenry? Second, what quantifiable influence do human rights have in Nigeria's external relations? Put differently, how far does the country have or need to go to join the club of "global Good Samaritans"[86] the hallowed list of countries in the world who consistently apply human rights in their external affairs for

[83] Herbert Ekwe-Ekwe, "Africans Had No Business Fighting in Either the 1914–1918 War or the 1939–1945 War," *Journal of Asian and African Studies*, 57(1) (2022), 11, 13, citing R. Morris, *Uncertain Greatness: Henry Kissinger and American Foreign Policy* (London and New York: Quartet Books, 1977), 122.

[84] See Aka, *Navigating the Tension Between Sovereignty and Self-Determination in Postcolonial Africa*, note 11, pp. 211–231.

[85] In his memoir on the Nigerian civil war, the renowned writer Chinua Achebe (1930–2013) made uncomplimentary remarks concerning Nigerian leaders whom he, alternately, described as "bum in suit," "poorly-educated," "half-baked," and "politicians with plenty of money and very low IQs," among other expressions. See Chinua Achebe, *There Was a Country: A Personal History of Biafra* (New York: Penguin Press, 2012) (part IV). Most to the point, in the perceptive summary of one reviewer of the book, "Achebe's memoir is not just an epitaph for Biafra. It is also a warning to Nigeria. *If Nigeria fails to find its purpose and achieve it for all its people, a new generation of writers may have the misfortune of writing a similar epitaph for Nigeria*—There Was a Country Called Nigeria." Rudolf Ogoo Okonkwo, "Achebe Administers a Sacrament for Biafra," *Nairaland Forum* (October 9, 2012), https://www.nairaland.com/1069497/rudolph-okonkwo-reviews-chinua-achebes. Emphasis added.

[86] Brysk, note 75, *passim*.

their own domestic good and to the glory of the international human rights regime. Third, what possible methods can Nigeria use to facilitate the application of more human rights in its external relations? Fourth, what are possible objections to the case for more human rights in Nigeria's external relations and conceivable rebuttals of those objections.

This book draws on a convergence of three genres of literature. The first consists of garden-variety studies on Nigerian foreign policies.[87] A second category are works which deal tangentially with application of human rights in Nigeria's external relations, including studies, such as those on peacekeeping, which touch human rights only incidentally or

[87] A rough sample includes: Osita C. Eze and Peter A. Egom, eds., *Foreign Policy and Nigeria's Economic Development* (Lagos: Nigerian Institute of International Affairs, 2009); Adekeye Adebajo and Abdul R. Mustapha, eds., *Gulliver's Troubles: Nigeria's Foreign Policy after the Cold War* (Scottsville, South Africa: University of KwaZulu Press, 2008); Akintola Bukola, "Nigeria and the World: A Review of Nigeria's Foreign Policy (1960–2007)," *Nigerian Army Quarterly Journal*, 3 (2007), 438–471; Emeka A. Obi, *Fundamentals of Nigerian Foreign Policy: A Study on the Role of National Interest in Foreign Policy Making* (Abingdon, U.K.: Bookpoint Ltd., 2006); L.E. Okogwu and A. Akpuru-Aja, *Nigerian Diplomacy and the Conflict of Laws: An Insight into the Practice of Nigeria's Foreign Policy* (Abakaliki, Nigeria: WillyRose and Appleseed Publishing Co., 2004); Steve Egbo, *Nigeria and the World: A Treatise on Foreign Policy* (Enugu, Nigeria: John Jacobs Classic Publishers, 2003); Ufot Bassey Inamete, *Foreign Policy Decision-Making in Nigeria* (Selinsgrove, PA: Susquehanna University Press, 2001); Richard A. Akindele and Bassey Ate, eds., *Selected Readings on Nigeria's Foreign Policy and International Relations* (Lagos: Nigerian Institute of International Affairs and Vantage Publishers, 2000); Mae C. King, *Basic Currents of Nigerian Foreign Policy* (Washington, DC: Howard University Press, 1996); G. O. Olusanya and R. A. Akindele, eds., *The Structure and Processes of Foreign Policy Making and Implementation in Nigeria, 1960–1990* (Lagos: Nigerian Institute of International Affairs, 1990); Ibrahim A. Gambari, *Theory and Reality in Foreign Policy Making: Nigeria after the Second Republic* (Humanities Press, Inc., 1989); G.O. Olusanya and R.A. Akindele, *Nigeria's External Relations: The First Twenty-Five Years* (Ibadan, Nigeria: Ibadan University Press, 1986); and Ibrahim A. Gambari, *Party Politics and Foreign Policy: Nigeria under the First Republic* (Zaria, Nigeria: Ahmadu Bello University Press, 1980).

sporadically.[88] A third comprises works on human rights in comparative foreign policy or the application of these values in national foreign policies in comparative perspective.[89] In sum, simultaneously, the book responds to pressures for Nigeria to: use the implements of human rights to improve its still-fledgling democracy at home, while increasing its contribution to the international human rights regime, à la global Good Samaritan,[90] within the meaning of this book, by so doing unearthing the package of thoroughgoing reforms at home and abroad that it needs to more confidently confront the state-building challenges it faces in the first quarter of the twenty-first century and beyond.

Theory is part of the foundation of social science research that makes the world of analysis go round. The theoretical framework that informs this book is Constructivism, an exploratory-cum-explanatory tool in-between Realism and Idealism, based on the extent to which each of these competing worldviews permits introduction of human rights into external affairs.[91] More than its two rivals, Constructivism also has utility for the discussion in Chapter 4 of the book on the reconstruction of Nigeria's national interest to improve its readiness for international human-right

[88] Includable in this category is Sylvester S. Shikyil, Human Rights in Foreign Policy: Nigeria's Experience since 1979. Ph.D. Dissertation, Department of Law, University of Jos (2000), http://datad.aau.org/handle/123456789/42302?show=full. This book departs from Shikyil's dissertation in several respects. First, it spans a longer period (over 63 years from 1960 as of this book, compared to the 21 years from 1979 until 2000 of Shikyil's research). Second, the goals of the two studies are also different. Although, like this book, Shikyil's dissertation focused on human rights policies that matched the profiles of Nigeria as a rising power, his goal was "to provide the background to the discussion of human rights in contemporary international politics," specifically "the analysis of the reasons for and consequences of the internationalization of human rights, its determinants, objectives, and future perspectives." Ibid. Not to minimize his contribution, this was a diffuse goal matched against the more comprehensive project in this book revolved around the design of a human rights policy for Nigeria under the Fourth Republic in the aftermath of General Buhari.

[89] See, for example, David P. Forsythe, ed., *Human Rights and Comparative Foreign Policy* (New York: United Nations University Press, 2000), 17 (stating that "[w]ith an unlimited budget and a multi-volume project, we could have added numerous states that merit study: France, Norway, Germany, Nigeria, Kenya, Mexico, Brazil, Pakistan, Israel, the Philippines, etc."). This study fills this needed gap with respect to Nigeria.

[90] See generally Brysk, note 75.

[91] Chapter 2 focused on the exigency of a human-right policy for Nigeria under the Fourth Republic in the age of Buhari and his progenies, elaborates these competing worldviews.

work, to the lasting benefit of democracy and human rights at home. The stocktaking of sort this book conducts coincides with a season of democratic decline in Africa, no different from Nigeria's, signified by the spate of recent military coups in West Africa, with ramifications for Nigeria's leadership role in the subregion, including within the Economic Community of West African States (ECOWAS).[92]

Plan of This Book

This book consists of ten chapters, divided into three parts, including this introduction as Chapter 1. Part I, Exigency, comprises two chapters; Part II, Methods, five chapters, and Part III, Rebuttable Objections, two chapters, including the conclusions (see Table 1.1). This chapter is the entrance of the book and embodiment of its argument, revolved around the pursuit of a principled foreign policy for Nigeria, taking advantage of the inestimable opportunities afforded by an intersection of fortuitous events, emblematized in Nigeria by the declining influence of the military in Nigerian politics, signified in turn by General Buhari's departure from office after two underwhelming terms as President, and abroad by the coronation of a new monarch in Britain.

Chapters 2–3 answers the *why* question the book addresses. They comprise the two discussions in the work under Part II on the exigency of a human-right policy for Nigeria. Chapter 2 builds on the statement of the problem in this chapter. Severally, it explains the relationship between human rights and foreign policy, key to any enlightened appreciation of a human rights policy; marshals several reasons why Nigeria needs to continue its journey toward a human-right policy abroad to the benefit of democracy and human rights at home that General Buhari's

[92] See Paul Melly, "Niger Coup Underlines Challenge to Democracy across West Africa," Chatham House (August 18, 2023), https://www.chathamhouse.org/2023/08/niger-coup-underlines-challenge-democracy-across-west-africa; and Soonest Nathaniel, "Increasing Coups in West Africa: Falana Explores Key Issues Ahead of ECOWAS Summit," *Channels TV* (Lagos) (Updated August 10, 2023), https://www.channelstv.com/2023/08/10/increasing-coups-in-west-africa-falana-explores-key-issues-ahead-ecowas-summit/. See also Mohammed Yusuf, "ECOWAS Unity Put to Test as West African Coup Crisis Deepens," *VOA News* (September 11, 2023), https://www.voanews.com/a/ecowas-unity-put-to-test-as-west-african-coup-crisis-deepens-/7263280.html (stating that the coups question the legitimacy of the constitutionally-elected governments in these countries, no different from Nigeria).

Table 1.1 Recap on the organization of the book

Chapter	*Topic*	*Analytical thrust*	*Part*
1.	Argument	Introduction	
2.	Creating a state worthy of its peoples' dreams at home and abroad	Exigency	I
3.	Historical background	Exigency	I
4.	Reconstructing Nigeria's national interest in readiness for human-right duties	Method	II
5.	Increased respect for human rights at home	Method	II
6.	Peacekeeping	Method	II
7.	The Technical Aid Corps (TAC)	Method	II
8.	Community Court of Justice (CCJ)	Method	II
9.	Enacting serious reforms at home and abroad	Rebuttable objection	III
10.	Conclusions and prospects for the future	Rebuttable objection	III

two terms in office impeded; and introduces the theoretical framework anchored in Constructivism, in-between Realism and Idealism, based on the allowance each theory makes regarding the interjection of human rights in external relations, that informs the book. Chapter 3 unearths five discernible periods in Nigeria's foreign policy since independence with an eye on their human-right contents. To provide more depth in time duration necessary for thorough understanding and to start the story from its proverbial beginning, the discussion includes the precolonial and colonial eras.

Chapters 4–8 respond to the *how* question of this book. They comprise the five chapters grouped under methods, the assortment of tools open to Nigeria for the formulation and implementation of principled human-right policy. The five tools are a sample that do not exhaust all the possibilities. Chapter 4 is dedicated to reconstructing Nigeria's national interest within the worldview of Constructivism, to improve its readiness for international human-right work, including the definition of national interest, the evolution of the doctrine since independence, and conceivable means for reconstructing Nigeria's national interest to render it human-right-compliant. The discussion includes strategies for reshaping Nigeria's foreign policy machine in a human right-sensitive direction.

For its part, Chapter 5 comments on the necessity for increased respect for human rights within the Nigerian homeland. Charity begins at home; Nigeria cannot seriously export abroad values that it neither produces nor practices at home. Takeaways from the presentation are the various steps it lays down for achieving increased human rights at home, including decentralization of political powers, achieved through political restructuring, stemming the influence of religion in politics, electing governments able and willing to handle the steps prescribed, and well-targeted external support. Foreign policy is a continuation of domestic policy by facilitative non-domestic means. Inclusion of increased respects for human rights within the Nigerian homeland among the methods speaks to that complementarity, the teachable lesson to scholars and policymakers being to refrain from erecting sharp distinctions between the two domains of policy.

Chapter 6 analyzes the possibilities and limits of peacekeeping. As a foreign-policy implementation tool, peacekeeping reached its apogee with Nigeria's interventions in Liberia and Sierra Leone, the first to stop a civil war, and the second to restore an overthrown civilian government. This was the context in which President Bill Clinton, during a highly-publicized state visit to the country in August 2000, at the inception of the Fourth Republic, commended Nigerian leaders for their creativity in "building the record of a moral superpower."[93]

In the aftermath of Nigeria's civil war from 1967–1970 and some teachable lessons learned from that war, ECOWAS, a regional customs union,[94] Nigeria played an instrumental role in creating after that conflict, emerged as a key tool for the implementation of Nigerian foreign policy. Many of the peace operations ECOWAS conducts took place through ECOMOG, its military arm. Given the intertwinement with peacekeeping, Chapter 6 includes an extended discussion on the role of ECOWAS as a tool for a Nigerian human-right policy, one sensitive

[93] William J. Clinton, "Remarks to a Joint Session of the Nigerian National Assembly in Abuja, Aug. 26, 2000," in *Public Papers of the Presidents of the United States: William J. Clinton, 2000–2001* (Washington, DC: 2000), 1705. Text of the same document is available in *American Presidency Project* (August 26, 2000), https://www.presidency.ucsb.edu/documents/remarks-joint-session-the-nigerian-national-assembly-abuja.

[94] "Customs Union," *Britannica Money*, https://www.britannica.com/money/customs-union (a trade agreement and a form of economic integration "by which a group of countries charges a common set of tariffs to the rest of the world while granting free trade among themselves").

to the abuses from ECOMOG but that also addresses the issue of its proper boundary as a multilateral tool of choice for Nigeria, in an era of democratic fermentation in West Africa with ramifications for its composition, signified by the embracement of military rule in three member-states of ECOWAS, Burkina Faso, Niger, and Mali, all three of whom have threatened to leave the economic union.[95]

Chapter 7 focuses on the possibilities and limits of the Technical Aid Corps (TAC), a foreign aid program Nigeria established in 1978 to facilitate its external relations with states in Africa, Caribbean, and Pacific, known for short as ACP countries. To punch within its weight, rather than below it, Nigeria needs a mixture of multilateral and bilateral activities in its human-right foreign policy toolbox fit for a would-be global Good Samaritan which infuses and enriches its external relations with human-right deeds in the sense we use this term in this book. More than for peacekeeping, the question for this tool is whether, in addition to being human-right-compliant, it is also bilateral enough to get the job of international human-right job properly done.

Chapter 8 focuses on the ECOWAS Court of Justice, hereinafter for short referred to as the Community Court of Justice (CCJ), a key

[95] See note 92 and accompanying text. In January 2024, Burkina Faso, Mali, and Niger, three countries hit by military coups, announced their intention to withdraw from ECOWAS. Leaders of the three countries accused the organization of a lack of support, based on coup-related sanctions they jointly assessed as "inhumane." See Chinedu Asadu, "What is ECOWAS and Why Have [Three] Coup-Hit Nations Quit the West Africa Bloc?" *Associated Press* (January 29, 2024), https://apnews.com/article/mali-burkina-faso-niger-ecowas-africa-d2e8b1e5448d9a7823e6b9d3d8ec774b. See also David Rich, "With ECOWAS Exit, Mali, Burkina Faso and Niger Leave Democratic Transition in Limbo," *France 24* (February 2, 2024), https://www.france24.com/en/africa/20240202-with-ecowas-exit-mali-burkina-faso-and-niger-leave-democratic-transition-in-limbo. Parenthetically speaking, it is doubtful whether the intention to withdraw here serves enough notice under ECOWAS rules. The statute creating the organization stipulates that a member-state wishing to withdraw from the Community must serve a one-year "written notice at the end of which, if not withdrawn, the member shall cease to be a member." Economic Community of West African States (ECOWAS), Treaty of the Economic Community of West African States (ECOWAS) (May 28, 1975), https://www.refworld.org/legal/constinstr/ecowas/1975/en/63881, art. 64(1). Meanwhile, "the member-state shall nevertheless observe the provisions of this Treaty and shall remain liable for the discharge of its obligations under the Treaty." Ibid., art. 64(2). See also ECOWAS Revised Treaty, note 25, art. 91(1)-(2) (providing similarly). Moreover, the announcement to leave negated other provisions of the Revised Treaty of July 1993, specifically the commitment to promote and consolidate "a democratic system of governance in each Member State," pursuant to the Declaration of Political Principles of July 1991. Ibid., art. 4(j).

institution of ECOWAS, created under the revised treaty of the subregional economic organization adopted in 1993. Located in Nigeria's capital city at Abuja, the Court hears cases from member-states and adjudicates human-right violations, either by individuals or corporate bodies, although its jurisdiction on human-right abuses does not extend to complaints pertaining to violations of regional economic rules. And while still a multilateral tool, vis-à-vis its obvious co-methods (i.e., peacekeeping, and the TAC), fortuitously, the CCJ holds tremendous promise with respect to application of human rights in Nigeria's external relations. Fortunately, the achievements embodied in the CCJ's human-right jurisprudence contract the portraiture of multilateralism as necessarily and automatically an impediment in the application of human rights in external relations.

Chapters 9–10, grouped under Part III of the book, address the *so what?* question of this book, specifically conceivable objections to the argument of this book and possible rebuttals to those objections. Legitimate objections to this manner of foreign policy for Nigeria revolve around the concern about whether the country possesses the wherewithal for the formulation and implementation of an effective human-right policy, given the many existential problems it faces at home. The answer to these objections, as Chapter 9 fields them, lies in a calibrated yes answer embedded in reforms: serious changes at home and abroad, including increased harmonization of domestic and foreign policies, designed to help the country punch within its weight, rather than below it, and by so doing, enhancing its contribution to international human rights to the dual benefit of its own domestic well-being and in foreign policy related to its known aspirations for a leadership role in Africa and beyond.

Giving the dismaying failure of Nigeria to realize its potential in the crush of rising expectations from an ever-growing population in the age of Instagram, orthodoxy and conventionalism are not enough. Instead, in this third decade of the 21st century, Nigerian leaders will need to enact reforms in multiple areas of the country's national life, all the way to external relations in a spirit of bold and persistent experimentation. Along with the masses of the citizenry, they must do so guided by the thrust and analogy of Nigeria as "a work in progress, an unfinished enterprise that would constantly be in need of change, adjustment, and repair."[96]

Chapter 10 recapitulates the achievements of the book with an introspective look into the future, including the theme of loving the foreigner as oneself central to the message of this book, and Constructivism, the exploratory-cum-explanatory framework that drives the work. With his disinterest in external relations bordering on insularity, economic famine at home, with negative impact on foreign relations, and slow motion in ethnic relations (measured by centrifugal markers signified by unceasing campaigns by ethnic groups, notably the Igbo, for self-determination),[97] Buhari complicated Nigeria's journey to a human-right policy on several fronts, including even the signature tool of peacekeeping. Thus, in the wake of the eight years of his administration under the Fourth Republic, the exigency for a human-right policy for the betterment of domestic policy has increased while the means for attaining that policy in several areas, including peacekeeping, have measurably diminished.

Social science research views the world as it *is*, but also as it *should* be in instances when agreed-upon criteria exist among social scientists for the ideals of what should be.[98] This research combines the best of what is and what should be, describing the application of human rights in Nigeria's foreign policy where it meets it while prescriptively incorporating suggestions on the way forward. Among its other merits spelled out above, this work contributes significantly to the literature on human rights and governance in a manner that hopefully minimizes the "endless teardrops" associated with the study of human rights in postcolonial Africa.[99] Similarly, as indicated before, it is a progress report on Nigeria's

[96] See Fareed Zakaria, "Are America's Best Days Behind Us?" *Time* (March 3, 2011), http://content.time.com/time/magazine/article/0,9171,2056723,00.html (referring to the US).

[97] See Aka, *Navigating the Tension Between Sovereignty and Self-Determination in Postcolonial Africa,* note 11.

[98] See Gary Gutting, "How Reliable Are the Social Sciences?" *New York Times* (May 17, 2012), https://archive.nytimes.com/opinionator.blogs.nytimes.com/2012/05/17/how-reliable-are-the-social-sciences/ (Although the social sciences lack the capacity for detailed and precise predictions of the physical sciences, social science conclusions "can supplement the general knowledge, practical experience, good sense, and critical intelligence" that policy makers need to make decisions).

[99] See generally Ronald Cohen et al., eds., *Human Rights and Governance in Africa* (Gainesville, FL: University Press of Florida, 1993).

journey toward a human-right policy in an era of democratic fermentation in West Africa,[100] and of reduced military influence in Nigeria's body politic, signified by General Buhari's departure from the Nigerian political scene after two deleterious terms in office with negative ramifications for Nigeria's domestic and foreign policies.

100 See notes 92 and 95 and accompanying texts.

PART I

Exigency

CHAPTER 2

A State Worthy of Its Peoples' Dreams at Home and Abroad

Introduction

To make Nigeria "the world's next great opportunity to advance the cause of peace, justice, and prosperity," as then US President William J. Clinton predicted for the country during a state visit there in August 2000, its leaders must work to make their country a state worthy of its peoples' dreams at home and abroad.[1] One conceivable way to approach the achievement of this high-minded goal is for Nigeria to apply human rights in its external relations.[2] This chapter is the first of two complementary accounts on the exigency of a human-right policy for Nigeria

[1] William J. Clinton, "Remarks Following Discussions with President Olusegun Obasanjo of Nigeria and an Exchange with Reporters in Abuja, Nigeria, August 26, 2000," in *Public Papers of the President of the United States: William J. Clinton, 2000–2001* (Washington DC: Best Books, 2000), 1701. The Scripture enjoined, "Let each of you look not only to his own interests, but also to the interests of others." *Holy Bible*, English Standard Version, Philippians 2:4. Testament to the theme of love-the-foreigner-as-thyself that drives this whole book is that this admonition came from a foreign leader.

[2] This would be the closest to a guiding philosophy that, "to survive as one political entity" under the Fourth Republic, its various peoples must voluntarily commit themselves to. See Emeka Odumegwu Ojukwu, "Nigeria: The Truths Which are Self-Evident," *Sunday Magazine* (Lagos) (March 6, 1994), 15–18, https://nigeriaworld.com/feature/speech/ojukwu_archives.html.

P. C. Aka, *Human Rights in Nigeria's External Relations in the Age of General Muhammadu Buhari and His Successors*,
https://doi.org/10.1007/978-3-031-63231-0_2

under its Fourth Republic after Buhari; the other is a chronicle of the book's background history.

This discussion spells out the contours of a human-right policy for Nigeria, including the factors that make such a policy exigent under the Fourth Republic. Specifically, it performs three interlinked tasks: explains the relationship between human rights and foreign policy key to understanding of a human-right policy; marshals several reasons why Nigeria needs to continue its journey toward a human-right policy abroad to the benefit of democracy and human rights at home that General Buhari's two terms in office truncated; and introduces a theoretical framework anchored in Constructivism that frames and informs the book.

Nature of the Relationship Between Human Rights and Foreign Policy

Human Rights

Human rights are freedom guarantees of various descriptions, that "ideally, individuals and groups everywhere have equally free of invidious discrimination, by virtue of the fact that they are human beings who need these rights to live a life of dignity."[3] The human rights instrument which, more than any other, popularized these rights is the Universal Declaration of Human Rights (UDHR).[4] The UDHR was adopted by the UN General Assembly in December 1948, "in the aftermath of a bloody global war hallmarked by denial of every measure of basic rights, including the right to life, and of access to food."[5] As the human rights scholar and administrator Kenneth Roth aptly put it, persons "who live in countries that respect the Universal Declaration in all its dimensions enjoy the freedom and means to live life to its fullest[,]" given that "[t]hey are able to speak their minds, practice the religions of their cho[ice], meet with their compatriots, be treated fairly by their government[s], and

[3] Philip C. Aka, "Fidel Castro and Socioeconomic Human Rights in Africa: A Multi-Level Analysis," *Fordham International Law Journal*, 43(1) (2019), 41, 47.

[4] Universal Declaration of Human Rights, UN General Assembly, 217 A (III) (December 10, 1948), https://www.refworld.org/docid/3ae6b3712c.html.

[5] Aka, "Fidel Castro and Socioeconomic Human Rights in Africa," note 3, p. 48.

enjoy access to the necessities of life."[6] Traceable to President Franklin D. Roosevelt's doctrine of four freedoms,[7] the document established the idea of human rights "as the ideology of our times" by, among other means, providing that idea "with a universally acceptable foundation."[8]

To accomplish the job of analysis mapped out for them, terms should be defined robustly. Based on this wisdom, the term *human rights* is defined broadly here to include collective rights. In fact, the definition of human rights set forth in the previous paragraph includes group or collective rights. In our time, safeguarding minority rights and affording all citizens the opportunity "to participate in the national life in a climate of justice and peace" have become the mark of "a morally adult society."[9] Because abusive state policies in Nigeria and other African countries put groups at risk, "[n]o strategy for human rights promotion in Nigeria will succeed that does not pay strong attention to group rights."[10] Fear of majority domination by minority groups was the major factor that led to the enshrinement of "fundamental rights" in the country's 1960 Constitution and subsequent ones.[11]

In the 1950s, as Nigeria moved inexorably toward independence, minority groups in each of the country's three regions voiced the concern that the dominant ethnic group in each region, the Igbo in the East, the Yoruba in the West, and the Hausa-Fulani in the North, would dominate them once the country became independent from Britain. These groups demanded their own separate states to prevent that occurrence or minimize its effect. In response, in 1957, the British colonial authority set up

[6] See Kenneth Roth, "Human Rights Organizations: A New Force for Social Change," in *Realizing Human Rights: Moving from Inspiration to Impact*, eds. Samantha Power and Graham Alison (New York: St. Martin's Press, 2000), 230–231.

[7] The four are freedom of speech and expression, freedom of religion, freedom from want, and freedom from fear. See Louis Henkin, "Human Rights: Ideology and Aspiration, Reality and Prospect," in *Realizing Human Rights*, note 6, p. 4.

[8] Ibid., p. 11.

[9] Emilio J. Cárdenas and Maria Fernanda Cañás, "The Limits of Self-Determination," in *The Self-Determination of Peoples: Community, Nation, and State in an Interdependent World*, ed. Wolfgang Danspeckgruber (Boulder, CO: Lynne Rienner, 2001), 101 (quoting Pope John Paul II).

[10] Philip C. Aka, "Nigeria Since May 1999: Understanding the Paradox of Civil Rule and Human Rights Violations under President Olusegun Obasanjo," *San Diego International Law Journal*, 4 (2003), 273–274.

[11] Ibid., p. 274.

a commission of inquiry to examine their claim. With independence just three years away, the commission left the regional structure unchanged the way it was, but recommended the equivalent of a bill of basic rights that it adapted from the European Convention on Human Rights of 1950, to be inserted in the country's independence constitution. The colonial government accepted the recommendations.[12]

In the light of the foregoing, "[p]romoting increased access to state power for all groups is a human rights issue in Nigeria," with a good chance of minimizing "opportunities for conflict that could result in human rights violations."[13] In a word, human rights are individual guarantees, "a rule in the interest of individuals,"[14] that are complemented by the rights of groups, the entity from which, in many societies, individuals draw their identity—and anchor. Recall the advice of President Clinton during his state visit to Nigeria in 2000 for Nigerian leaders to create a country "worthy of its *people's* dreams."[15] Given the multiethnic character of Nigeria and its still-loose integration as one nation, the advice can equally pass as a challenge for these leaders to create a country worthy of its *peoples'* dreams.[16]

Foreign Policy

Colloquially, *foreign policy* signifies the "interplay between the outside and the inside"[17]; it is an "extension of domestic policy" that defines our relations with persons outside our borders, the putative strangers or

[12] See *Report of the Commission Appointed to Inquire into the Fears of Minorities and the Means of Allaying Them* (London: Her Majesty's Stationery Office, 1958), *passim*. For more on this commission, see Chapter 3, note 115, and accompanying text (laying out the historical background of this book).

[13] Aka, "Nigeria Since May 1999," note 10, p. 274.

[14] David P. Forsythe, "Human Rights Fifty Years after the Universal Declaration," *PS: Political Science and Politics*, 31(September 1998), 507, 508.

[15] Clinton, note 1. Emphasis added.

[16] See Ojukwu, note 2, p. 18 (stating that "the *peoples* of Nigeria have not [...] had the same or similar benefits and privileges from the Nigerian polity[,]" but that, instead, "while some have experienced joy, others experienced pain"). Emphasis added.

[17] F.S. Northedge, "The Nature of Foreign Policy," in *The Foreign Policies of the Powers,* ed. F.S. Northedge (Westport, CT: Praeger, 1969), 15.

foreigners.[18] It is "a dynamic process involving the interaction between a country's internal and external environments."[19] In more practical terms, *foreign policy* is "the formulation, implementation, and evaluation of external choices within one country, viewed from the perspective of that country."[20] Three key elements to the foreign policy of any state are the national *objectives* the state in question seeks to achieve by that policy, the *means* to reach those objectives, and "the *interaction* between objectives and means."[21] In sum, foreign relations are a continuation of domestic policy by other means, or, alternatively, engagements abroad to support the work of security and economic development at home, the point being that enlightened leaders cannot weaken at home the very same thing they are trying to strengthen abroad.[22]

Intersection of Human Rights and Foreign Policy

Different scholars have commented on the essentially "national character of human rights."[23] Given this occurrence, how does a country apply human rights in its external relations? Stated differently, what features make the application of human rights in external relations different from its application domestically and why should the distinction matter? Proper answers to these questions demand that we understand the key influence

[18] Mae C. King, *Basic Currents of Nigerian Foreign Policy* (Washington, DC: Howard University Press, 1996), 237.

[19] J. Peter Pham, "Nigeria's Foreign Policy: An Inquiry into Sources and Prospects," Presentation for an International Conference, Lisbon, Portugal (November 8–9, 2007), www.ipri.pt/eventos/pdf/JPeterPham_paper.pdf.

[20] James E. Dougherty and Robert L. Pfaltzgraff, *Contending Theories of International Relations: A Comprehensive Survey,* 3rd Ed. (New York: Harper & Row, 1990), 15.

[21] Cecil V. Crabb Jr., *American Foreign Policy in the Nuclear Age*, 3rd Ed. (New York: Harper & Row, 1972), 1.

[22] For elaboration of this strand of argument, see Chapter 5 on the need for increased respect for human rights in Nigeria.

[23] See, for example, Jack Donnelly, *International Human Rights,* 4th Ed. (Boulder, CO: Westview Press, 2013), 14–16 (commenting on the system of national implementation that marks the global human rights regime); Henkin, note 7, p. 8 (defining international human rights as "an international movement to promote and protect and assume and assert international responsibility for national human rights, that is, rights within national societies"); and Louis Henkin, "The Universal Declaration and the U.S. Constitution," *PS: Political Science and Politics*, 31 (September 1998), 512–513 (characterizing "international human rights as national rights").

of politics on human rights. Human rights are "a matter of law," codified in international instruments and interpreted by international lawyers as well as officials in global and regional treaty supervision bodies, that have also, in our time, equally evolved into "a matter of diplomacy and politics."[24] To hit the nail on the head, human right-based policies "are promoted, selected, disseminated, contested, and reconstructed through political processes."[25]

Applying human rights in foreign relations means adoption of a human-right policy, referred to alternately, as indicated in Chapter 1, the introduction of this book, as principled foreign policy. No universal definition of such a policy exists. Instead, different analysts posit different requirements with more or less connection to human rights for such policy. For Kathryn Sikkink, a state has a human rights policy when the state in question "has explicit mechanisms for integrating human rights concerns into foreign policy and when those mechanisms have modified foreign policy decisions in some cases."[26] For Jack Donnelly, for states that chose to apply human rights in their external relations, "we can reasonably demand that human rights actually enter into calculations balancing competing interests, with a weight that roughly matches their stated place in the hierarchy of national interests."[27] For David Gilles,

[24] Peter R. Baehr, "Foreign Policy," in *Encyclopedia of Human Rights*, Vol. 5 (New York: Oxford University Press, 2009), 237. See also J. Oloka-Onyango, *Battling Over Human Rights: Twenty Essays on Law, Politics, and Governance* (Bamenda, Cameroon: Langaa Research & Publishing, 2015), *passim* (set of essays depicting human rights as the intersection of laws, politics, and governance).

[25] Alison Brysk, *Global Good Samaritans: Human Rights as Foreign Policy* (New York: Oxford University Press, 2009), 37. See also Abdullahi An-Naim, "The National Question, Secession, and Constitutionalism: The Mediation of Competing Claims to Self-Determination," in *Constitutionalism and Democracy: Transition in the Contemporary World*, eds. Douglas Greenberg et al. (New York: Oxford University Press, 1993), 111, 112–113 (depicting human rights as "legal rights enforceable in a court of law" that have also immense "utility in political discourse").

[26] Kathryn Sikkink, "The Power of Principled Ideas: Human Rights Policies in the United States and Western Europe," in *Ideas and Foreign Policy: Beliefs, Institutions, and Political Change*, eds. Judith Goldstein and Robert O. Keohane (Ithaca, New York: Cornell University Press, 1993), 143.

[27] Donnelly, note 23, p. 146. This configuration is not as stringent as it looks on the surface. This is because, as Professor Donnelly pointed out elsewhere, commenting on US foreign policy, the key point is to assess "the impact of the full range of [...] foreign policy behavior on international human rights practices, not just those initiatives that explicitly address human rights." Jack Donnelly and Debra Liang-Fenton, "Introduction,"

pursuit of a human-right-based foreign policy involves some measure of opportunity cost defined to mean "any action which, to a significant extent, will be likely to disrupt normal diplomatic relations, limit commercial opportunities, inflict domestic economic hardship, strain alliance structures, or provoke retaliation by a target state."[28]

For Alison Brysk, an external activity rises to a human-right policy when such activity "seek[s] to protect and empower citizens of other countries in order to secure the" key rights embodied in the international bill of human rights—the Universal Declaration of Human Rights, the International Covenant on Civil and Political Rights, and the International Covenant on Economic, Cultural, and Social Rights.[29] Specifically, an international activity qualifies as a human-right policy when, keeping aside the ultimate impact and effectiveness of that activity, "(1) its primary announced goal is humanitarian protection or empowerment, and (2) the resources and strategies used correspond to a reasonable outside observer's standard of humanitarian orientation."[30] Professor Brysk calls states who apply human rights in their foreign affairs "global good Samaritans."[31] In their foreign relations, these states project a "kindness of

in *Implementing U.S. Human Rights Policy*, ed. Debra Liang-Fenton (Washington, DC: United States Institute of Peace Press, 2004), 6. In Donnelly's view, "a moral add-on after the 'real' foreign policy decisions have been made" isn't enough. Donnelly, note 23, p. 146.

[28] David Gilles, *Between Principles and Practice: Human Rights in North-South Relations* (Montreal, Canada: McGill-Queen's University Press, 1996), 50.

[29] Brysk, note 25, p. 5.

[30] Ibid.

[31] Seven Good Samaritans Brysk's book surveyed, six of them states, and each of which applied human rights in external affairs in varying degrees, were Sweden, Canada, Costa Rica, The Netherlands, Japan, South Africa, and a set of transnational human rights organizations, "coalitions of the caring," such as the Organization for Security and Cooperation in Europe (OSCE), the Human Security Network, the Community of Democracies (Club Dem, comprising 10 states), the International Institute for Democracy and Electoral Assistance (IDEA), the Organization for Economic Cooperation and Development (OECD) Donor Assistance Committee (comprising 30 developed northern states), and the Network of National Human Rights institutions (Team Gov). Brysk, note 25, pp. 28–30, 42, 197–219.

strangers,"[32] no different from the biblical injunction to "love your neighbor as yourself."[33]

Last World on the Relationship Between Human Rights and Foreign Policy

First, although important in that it can lay the foundation for principled foreign policy, application of human rights in external affairs in the sense we define it in this work is a more deep-seated concept that rises beyond sheer emergence of human rights in world politics.[34] Nor of occasional interjections of ethical values into external affairs. Instead, the requisite application "is a pattern of persistent principled politics" that rises beyond "episodic altruism."[35] What is more, interjecting moral principles embedded in human rights in external affairs does *not* violate the principle of non-interference in the domestic affairs of another state, the principle in the UN Charter that forbids member-states from intervening into "matters which are essentially within the domestic jurisdiction of any state."[36] Because "breaches of human rights, especially gross breaches, are taken out of domestic jurisdiction[,]" concern for human rights does not negate the principle of non-interference.[37]

[32] Brysk, note 25, book's frontispiece (poem on "The Kindness of Strangers").

[33] Brysk built the theme of her work on the biblical parable of the Good Samaritan, Luke 10: 25–37 (*Holy Bible,* New International Version).

[34] See, for example, Donnelly, note 23, pp. 3–16 (sketching the emergence of human rights as an issue in world politics); David P. Forsythe, *Human Rights in International Relations*, 3rd Ed. (New York: Cambridge University Press, 2012), especially 3–33 (commenting on "human rights in international relations"); and R.J. Vincent, *Human Rights and International Relations* (New York: Cambridge University Press, 1986), 7 ("The idea that human beings have rights as humans is a staple of contemporary world politics").

[35] Brysk, note 25, p. 3.

[36] United Nations, Charter of the United Nations (1945), 59 Stat. 1031, T.S. 993, 3 Bevans 1153 [hereinafter UN Charter], art. 2, ¶ 7 ("Nothing contained in the present Charter shall authorize the United Nations to intervene in matters which are essentially within the domestic jurisdiction of any state [...]").

[37] U. Oji Umozurike, *The African Charter on Human and Peoples' Rights* (Leiden, Netherlands and Boston, MA: Brill, 1997), 7.

Human rights emerged in world politics, distinguished from its distinct application in external affairs by way of a human rights policy,[38] as a counterweight against the unrestrained *exercise* of sovereignty fingered as a factor in the atrocities of World War II. The atrocities Adolf Hitler and his National Socialist German Workers' Party (known for short as the Nazi Party) perpetrated against Jews, Slavs, Gypsies, and other supposedly "inferior" peoples during World War II, leading to the death of about 6 million people, "gave sovereignty a bad name."[39] The felt need to moderate the raw exercise of sovereignty in the interest of human rights became evident even while World War II was still raging. The Allied Powers built their opposition against the Nazis on human rights grounds, citing the Declaration of the United Nations, precursor to the UN Charter of 1945, that they, these winning countries, adopted in January of 1942.[40] In the document the allied nations claimed that "complete victory over their enemies is essential to defend life, liberty, independence and religious freedom, and to preserve human rights and justice in their own lands as well as in other lands."[41]

In sum, "[t]he shock of the Second World War led very quickly to the realization that it was no longer appropriate or possible to leave the business of protecting human rights to the sovereign state alone."[42] Underscoring the role of the atrocities of World War II as key factor in the emergence of human rights as a counterweight to abuses in the unrestrained exercise of sovereign powers, the Convention on the Prevention and Punishment of the Crime of Genocide (the Genocide Convention) was adopted one day before the adoption of the Universal Declaration of Human Rights on December 10, 1948.[43] Before the Second World War,

[38] See note 34 and accompanying text.

[39] Forsythe, note 34, p. 31.

[40] Donnelly, note 23, p. 4. Matched against the Axis Powers (comprising Germany, Italy, and Japan), the Allied Powers included China, Soviet Russia, the UK, and the US, along with France before its occupation. See Adam Volle, "Allied Powers," *Encyclopedia Britannica* (May 17, 2023), https://www.britannica.com/topic/Allied-powers-World-War-II.

[41] Donnelly, note 23, p. 4.

[42] J. Oloka-Onyango, note 24, p. 12.

[43] Donnelly, note 23, p. 191 (noting that the occurrence both marked "the central role of the Holocaust in crystallizing international concern with human rights, as well

explicit interjection of moral values into international affairs was "historically unusual."[44] Following the War, such application came into vogue, reaching a highpoint with the Carter administration in the United States from 1977 until 1981.[45] Pursuit of a human rights policy requires a state conducting that policy to "transgress the norm of non-interference and sacrifice short-term gains to safeguard long-range values."[46]

There is no intention here to minimize the secular commandment of non-interference in international law meant to protect all states, powerful and non-powerful alike. This is because, as even human-right scholars like David F. Forsythe and Jack Donnelly uniformly acknowledge, a state's national self-image is not "exhausted by a commitment to human rights."[47] Instead, "human rights exist within a set of hegemonic ideas constituting the reigning mantra of world politics,"[48] if only in the sense that, "in addition to human rights, sovereignty and non-intervention are vital norms of international society."[49]

High on the set of hegemonic ideas which frames world politics and animates international society is sovereignty, which doctrine still exerts a lingering influence on the behavior of even major states like the US and China.[50] The point, as Professor Donnelly advised, is for enlightened

as "the creation of a separate legal regime[,] genocide, largely divorced from the global human rights regime" until the 1990s).

[44] See Donnelly, note 23, p. 16 (under 1 in the list of "discussion questions.").

[45] Jimmy Carter, "The American Road to a Human Rights Policy," in *Realizing Human Rights,* note 6, pp. 49–61 (commenting on the sources of increased human rights awareness in the US and abroad along with the road to a human rights policy that the US treaded under his leadership from 1977 to 1981).

[46] Gilles, note 28, p. 50.

[47] Jack Donnelly, "An Overview," in *Human Rights and Comparative Foreign Policy,* ed. David P. Forsythe (New York: United Nations University Press, 2000), 315.

[48] Forsythe, "Human Rights Fifty Years after the Universal Declaration," note 14, p. 508.

[49] Donnelly, "An Overview," note 47, p. 318.

[50] See Forsythe, "Human Rights Fifty Years after the Universal Declaration," note 14, p. 510. See also Donnelly, "An Overview," note 47, p. 318 (stating that "[a]ll states, in fact, have a deeper and more enthusiastic commitment to sovereignty than to human rights"). China is one country that appears to support this proposition. In its human-right action plan for 2000–2010, the country confessed its fidelity to human rights. Yet, that did not prevent the Chinese leadership from linking human rights with the country's identity as a socialist state, claiming that "the task of our party is to establish the rule of law and construct a socialist country with the rule of law." See Philip C. Aka, "Introductory Note

policymakers not to "overestimate either human rights or sovereignty" when it comes to the external behavior of states.[51] While keeping this cautionary well in mind, for Nigeria under the Fourth Republic after Buhari, an inescapable point going to the relationship between human rights and foreign policy lies in the application of human rights in external relations, indicated by the adoption of a principled human rights policy, with keen eyes for the multiple benefits of that application for democracy and human rights at home.

Necessity for Infusing More Human Rights in Nigeria's External Relations to Engender a Culture of the Rule of Law at Home

Several reasons make increased infusion of more human rights into Nigeria's external relations exigent. Two of those reasons, both interrelated, that this section highlights are Nigeria's status as the largest society in Africa, and its possession of the infrastructure for human-right work, despite its known disabilities.

Largest Society in Africa

In the light of its vast size and endowments, Nigeria has a reputation in the academic literature of comparative politics as "the largest society in Africa."[52] Injecting more human rights into Nigeria's external relations could harmonize Nigeria's domestic and foreign policies, to the benefit of democracy at home, as it has done for countries with human rights-based foreign policies, such as Costa Rica.[53] As the partition of the Sudan in 2013 makes clear,[54] unabated abuses of human rights can have

to the Human Rights Action Plan for China (2009–2010)," *International Legal Material*, 48 (2009), 842.

[51] Donnelly, "An Overview," note 47, p. 318.

[52] J. Tyler Dickovick and Jonathan Eastwood, *Comparative Politics: Integrating Theories, Methods, and Cases* (New York: Oxford University Press, 2013), 578.

[53] Brysk, note 25, pp. 95–118.

[54] See, for example, Jeffrey Gettleman, "After Years of Struggle, South Sudan Becomes a New Nation," *New York Times* (July 9, 2011), www.nytimes.com/2011/07/10/world/africa/10sudan.html?pagewanted=1&r=2&hp&adxnn1x=1310234502-5nvX4GUBg0fK28Wp4F.

dire consequences for the integrity of a country. And should Nigeria, like Sudan, disintegrate, due to its piling human rights abuses, successor states from the ashes of the parent state will grapple with the same human rights challenges without the benefit of "a large republic" that Nigeria now, for its seeming incoherence,[55] affords.

Building on the first factor and reinforcing it, infusion of more human rights into Nigeria's foreign relations will also help to build a culture of the rule of law, critical for the consolidation of democracy within the country itself.[56] The rule of law is a concept encapsulated in the description of the US's political system as "a government of laws, not of men."[57] The concept signifies two mandates: first, that all who hold the reins of power, no matter how highly placed in rank, are under the law, rather than above it; and, second, that the powers of the government to make and enforce laws are subject to legal restraints.[58] In a political system that operates under this rule, "the legal authority of the state and its officials is limited by the law, and [...] no one is above the law."[59]

The connection between human rights and the rule of law is indicated by the fact, for example, that the strictures of the rule of law forbid the government from engaging in arbitrary practices that signify abuse of its powers, such as unlawful arrest, torture, kangaroo or fraud trials, corruption, and the like.[60] Under such a system, "[t]he Law rests upon known, general principles applicable on equal terms to all persons," and it is "superior to, and thus binds, the government and all of its officials."[61]

[55] The expression "large republic" comes from US founding father James Madison (1751–1836), President from 1809–1817. See James Madison, "Federalist No. 10," Bill of Rights Institute (1787), https://billofrightsinstitute.org/primary-sources/federalist-no-10.

[56] See Michael J. Sodaro, *Comparative Politics: A Global Introduction*, 3rd Ed. (Boston, MA: McGraw-Hill, 2008), 171, fig. 7.1 (positioning the rule of law as a foundation step in the textbook's diagram of democracy as a temple).

[57] Ibid., p. 177.

[58] Ibid.

[59] Ibid.

[60] Ibid., p. 104.

[61] Anthony M. Kennedy, Associate Justice, US Supreme Court, Keynote Address at the Meeting of the American Bar Association, Honolulu, HI, CSPAN (August 5, 2006), www.c-span.org/video/?193757-1/justice-kennedy-address.

An independent judiciary is a critical monitor in a system based on the rule of law.[62]

Third, given their legendary passion for international relations,[63] increased application of human rights in external affairs will give Nigerians and their leaders the opportunity to fashion their bilateral relations with foreign countries and conduct business in multilateral settings in a more principled format than is currently the case. Human-right policies may be "the most rapid way to improve the lives of" beleaguered citizens of foreign lands.[64] As Professors Hannum and his colleagues elaborate, using the US as example, the attitude of a foreign government toward a regime that is perpetrating human-right abuses "might have far more impact on the lives of people living under that regime than, for example, petitions filed with the United Nations or regional human rights bodies."[65] Such a disapproving attitude bilaterally can also reinforce initiatives at the multilateral level. For Nigeria, as for many other countries, application of these values in external affairs may be a low-hanging-fruit opportunity to contribute to the international human rights regime.[66]

A fourth factor relates to Nigeria's origins arguably laced in human rights. The territory known today as Nigeria was once colloquially called the *Slave Coast*, in testament to the immense slave activities that took

[62] Philip C. Aka, "Judicial Independence under Nigeria's Fourth Republic: Problems and Prospects," *California Western International Law Journal*, 45(1) (2014), 1, 4.

[63] "Foreign Relations," in *Nigeria: A Country Study*, 5th Ed. Helen Chapin Metz, ed. (Washington, DC: Library of Congress, 1992), https://www.marines.mil/Portals/1/Publications/Nigeria%20Study_1.pdf (discussing Nigeria's active participation in international organizations); and Toyin Falola and Matthew M. Heaton, *A History of Nigeria* (New York: Cambridge University Press, 2008), 243–270 (extended discussion on "Nigeria and Nigerians in world history," including foreign policy in the period since independence in 1960).

[64] Hurst Hannum et al., *International Human Rights: Problems of Law, Policy, and Practice,* 5th Ed. (Alphen aan den Rijn, Netherlands: Wolters Kluwer, 2011), 1118.

[65] Ibid.

[66] Otherwise, for these countries, the standard operating procedure is to pay lip service to human rights. See Forsythe, *Human Rights in International Relations*, note 34, p. vii (pointing out that "states continue to profess their commitment to at least some of [these human rights] standards, even as their record of compliance is often far short of what it should be").

place there for hundreds of years.[67] The piecemeal occupation and subsequent colonization of Nigeria was an attempt to stop these activities and to set in motion legitimate commercial and economic activities that would replace the obnoxious trade in humans.[68] Certain dignitaries affiliated with regions that became subsumed into present-day Nigeria, such as the former Igbo slave, Olaudah Equiano, participated in this anti-slavery campaign.[69] To whom much is given, much is expected. As former US President Jimmy Carter once observed regarding the US, in important respects, Nigeria is a state *invented* by human rights.[70]

Bearing on this fourth factor, although colonial rule severely impeded human rights,[71] events in the later leg of British rule in Nigeria, especially after World War II and the formation of the UN system, helped give rise to Nigeria's non-violent independence in 1960.[72] The "protracted negotiations with British colonial power[,]"[73] short of the violent

[67] See "Slave Coast," *Encyclopedia Britannica*, http://www.britannica.com/EBchecked/topic/548212/Slave-Coast; "Slavery Fact Sheets," *Digital History*, www.digitalhistory.uh.edu/disp_textbook.cfm?smtID=11&psid=3807; and Robin Law, *The Slave Coast of West Africa 1550–1750: The Impact of the Atlantic Slave Trade on an African Society* (Oxford, UK: Clarendon Press, 1991).

[68] See Jenny S. Martinez, *The Slave Trade and the Origins of International Human Rights Law* (New York: Oxford University Press, 2011) (tracing modern-day international human rights law to the anti-slavery movement of the nineteenth century).

[69] Olaudah Equiano, *The Interesting Narrative of the Life of Olaudah Equiano: Written by Himself*, ed. with an introduction by Robert J. Allison (New York: Bedford/St. Martin's Press, 1995 [1789]).

[70] Carter, note 45, p. 49 ("In 1981, as I left the U.S. presidency, I said, 'America did not invent human rights. In a very real sense [...] human rights invented America'"). The matter of the human rights content or lack thereof of slavery and colonialism is a complex topic, subject to careful qualification, that is revisited in the historical background portion of this study, Chapter 3, under Section II dealing with the colonial era.

[71] For more on this issue, see Chapter 3 of this book, dedicated to historical background.

[72] See Henkin, "Human Rights: Ideology and Aspiration, Reality and Prospect," note 7, p. 12 (stating that "[o]ne might trace a path from the [Universal Declaration of Human Rights] to historic developments in the second half of the century," including the "end of colonialism and the proliferation of new states," and the "eradication of apartheid" and the birth of black majority rule in South Africa).

[73] King, note 18, p. 16.

blow-out elsewhere,[74] became arguably possible due to the mellowing influence of human rights. Thus, by 1954, several years before independence, British authorities transferred authority for foreign affairs to Nigerians.[75] A country birthed by human rights like Nigeria can do more for human rights in external affairs than its leaders so far have done. Nigeria can punch more within its weight, not below it, by contributing more through its word and action to international human rights.

Potential Infrastructure for Human-Right Work

Despite its known disabilities, Nigeria has the infrastructure to conduct a human-right policy, if it rationalizes its resources more properly. One of these resources is a sizable population. With a population of approximately 225 million people in 2023,[76] Nigeria is the most populous country in Africa and the sixth most-populous state in the world, after India, China, the US, Indonesia, and Pakistan, in this order.[77] This population factor lends it "a demographic weight equal to second-ranked Egypt and third-ranked Democratic Republic of Congo combined."[78] This does not include Nigerians in the Diaspora estimated to be anywhere from 5 to 17 million people.[79]

The Nigerian Diaspora "covers practically every part of the world, but the largest populations of Nigerians can be found in the UK, USA, and

[74] Kenya serves as an example of a violent decolonization during this period. See Martin Meredith, *The Fate of Africa: A History of the Continent since Independence*, revised and updated edition (Public Affairs, 2011), 79–87 (commenting on the Mau Mau insurgency).

[75] See Joseph Effiong, "Reflections on Nigeria's Foreign Policy," *Journal of Social and Psychological Sciences*, 5 (2012), www.questia.com/read/1G1-314443206/reflections-on-nigeria-s-foreign-policy.

[76] "Nigeria Population (Live)," *Worldometer*, https://www.worldometers.info/world-population/nigeria-population/.

[77] "Countries in the World by Population (2023)," *Worldometer*, https://www.worldometers.info/world-population/population-by-country/.

[78] Pham, note 19, p. 90.

[79] See "The Nigerian Diaspora," *Nigerian Diaspora*, http://www.nigeriandiaspora.com/nigerian-diaspora.php; and "Nigerians Abroad: Secret Weapon," *Economist* (London), http://www.economist.com/news/special-report/21654360-nigerias-diaspora-source-money-markets-skills-and-ideas-secret-weapon.

South Africa."[80] Based on World Bank data, in 2013, Nigerians in the Diaspora remitted an estimated US $21 billion into Nigeria, an amount said to represent about one-quarter of the country's earnings that year from oil exports.[81] It was probably in recognition of this contribution, including the "abiding love of [this community] for their native land and their greater unity abroad," that, in 2017, the Nigerian government established the Nigerians in Diaspora Commission (NIDCOM).[82] One perceptive analyst praised NIDCOM as "an important institution," one of few positive legacies from the Buhari period.[83] Moreover, Nigeria's "population includes, in both relative and absolute terms, a large number of well-educated citizens who represent a wealth of human capital."[84] However, concededly, there are also downsides to this resource, including a relatively low literacy rate,[85] a massive brain drain to foreign countries of a cream of its educated labor force.[86]

[80] "Nigerian Diaspora," note 79.

[81] Ibid.

[82] Chris Adetayo, "A Foreign Policy Guide for President Tinubu," *Cable* (June 13, 2023), https://www.thecable.ng/a-foreign-policy-guide-for-president-tinubu.

[83] Ibid.

[84] Pham, note 19, p. 90. See also William J. Clinton, "Remarks at a State Dinner Hosted by President Olusegun Obasanjo of Nigeria in Abuja, August 26, 2000," in *Public Papers of the Presidents of the United States: William J. Clinton, 2000–2001*, note 1, p. 1711 (pointing out that additional to its reputation as "an important supplier of energy[,]" Nigeria deserves to be also known and honored "for its greatest energy resource," namely, its people). During the same state visit, in his address to the Nigerian National Assembly, President Clinton commented on another type of economy, a "new" one, tied to education: "Building a stronger economy also means helping all children learn. In the old economy, a country's economic prospects were limited by its place on the map and its natural resources. Location was everything. In the new economy, information, education, and motivation are everything." William J. Clinton, "Remarks to a Joint Session of the Nigerian National Assembly in Abuja," *American Presidency Project* (August 26, 2000), https://www.presidency.ucsb.edu/documents/remarks-joint-session-the-nigerian-national-assembly-abuja.

[85] In 2023, Nigeria ranked 185 out of 204 countries in literacy, with an educational attainment of 59.57 percent (measured as persons 15 and above who can read and write). "Literacy Rate by Country" (2023), *Wisevoter*, https://wisevoter.com/country-rankings/literacy-rate-by-country/.

[86] See David H. Shinn, "Reversing the Brain Drain in Ethiopia," Address to the Ethiopian North American Health Professionals Association (November 23, 2002), http://chora.virtualave.net/brain-drain8.htm (disclosing that "[m]ore than 2,000 Nigerian doctors work in the United States even though there continues to be a critical

Another element of infrastructure is natural resources. Nigeria is home to large quantities of hydrocarbon,[87] and other mineral resources.[88] As of 2016, for which year information is available, Nigeria produced nearly 2 million barrels of crude oil per day, ranking it Number 15 in the world, much of it for export to global markets,[89] and a good part to US markets, until America's achievement of "energy independence," began under Barack Obama (2009–2017),[90] which reached its highest level

need for health professionals in Nigeria[,]" and that "[a]bout 10,000 Nigerian academics are employed in the United States alone"); and Anya O. Anya, "Nigeria: The Human Capital Challenge," *African Journal of Physics*, 30 (2010), 5, http://sirius-b.ncat.edu.ncat.edu/asn/afps/ajp/ajp-ISOTPAND10/Proc%20ISPD%20book5-30.pdf (lamenting Nigeria's "failure to develop her human resources," effects of which include the drain of medical professionals in its educated labor force who migrate to foreign countries).

[87] As of 2023, Nigeria has an estimated 37.1 billion barrels of proved crude oil reserves. The country produces mostly light, sweet (meaning low sulfur) crude oil, most of which it exports to global markets. See Energy Information Administration, "Petroleum and Other Liquids" (April 26, 2023), table 2 (selected crude oil grades produced in Nigeria), https://www.eia.gov/international/content/analysis/countries_long/Nigeria/#:~:text=Nigeria%20held%20an%20estimated%2037.1,at%20the%20beginning%20of%202023.&text=Nigeria%20produces%20mostly%20light%2C%20sweet,global%20markets%20(Table%202.

[88] Other mineral resources found in commercial quantities on Nigerian soils include natural gas, coal and numerous others like iron ore, uranium, copper, gold, and diamond. See Center for Energy Economics, "Gas Monetization in Nigeria," http://www.beg.utexas.edu/energyecon/new–era/case_studies/Gas_Monetization_in_Nigeria.pdf; and Nuhu George Obaje, *Geology and Mineral Resources of Nigeria* (Berlin, Germany: Springer-Verlag, 2009), 117–119.

[89] See "Nigeria Oil," *Worldometer*, https://www.worldometers.info/oil/nigeria-oil/ (summary table). For an overview of the country's oil industry, including the evolution of petroleum production as a mainstay of Nigeria's economy, see Jedrzej G. Frynas, *Oil in Nigeria: Conflict and Litigation Between Oil Companies and Village Communities* (Hamburg and London: Lit Verlag, 2000), 8–58.

[90] The pursuit of "energy independence" was designed to insulate the US and its citizenry from untoward dependency on oil exports by potentially unstable political regimes abroad. See The White House, "Advancing American Energy," https://www.whitehouse.gov/energy/securing-american-energy (particularly the section on "[r]educing [American] [d]ependence on [f]oreign [o]il."). A factor that facilitated that pursuit was the "shale revolution," arising from advances in oil and natural gas production technology, notably a new combination of horizontal drilling and hydraulic fracturing (or fracking), that has stimulated tremendous production of oil and natural gas in the US. See Edward L. Morse, "Welcome to the Revolution," *Foreign Affairs* (May/June 2014), https://www.foreignaffairs.com/articles/2014-04-17/welcome-revolution. An underlying point is that US oil drillers are able to access oil and gas reserves previously too expensive to tap. The negative impact on Nigeria is signified by the fact that "[a]t its peak in February 2006,

under Joseph R. Biden Jr., president since 2021.[91] Due to its natural resource endowment, spruced up in recent years with services from the entertainment industry anchored on Nollywood, Nigeria is home to the biggest economy in Africa.[92] Nollywood results in the export of Nigerian music and related entertainment products to many parts of the world.[93] It is, in prolific-ness, reputed to be the second-largest film industry in the world after Hollywood in the US, and Bollywood in India.[94] Nollywood

the US imported 1.3 m b/d from Nigeria—equal to roughly one super-tanker the size of the Exxon Valdez every day[,]" but "[b]y 2012, Nigeria was already selling just 0.5 b/d." Javier Blas, "Victim of Shale Revolution, Nigeria Stops Exporting Oil to U.S.," Blogger (October 2, 2014), http://blogs.ft.com/beyond-brics/2014/10/02/victim-of-shale-revolution-nigeria-stops-exporting-oil-to-us/. And by early 2014 "sales dropped to a trickle of about 100,000 b/d[,]" stopping completely in July of that year. Ibid.

[91] See Evans Halper and Toluse Olurunnipa, "U.S. Oil Production Hit[s] a Record under Biden: He Seldom Mentions It," *Washington Post* (December 31, 2023), https://www.washingtonpost.com/politics/2023/12/31/us-oil-production-has-hit-record-under-biden-he-hardly-mentions-it/. See also Seth Borenstein, "US Oil Production Hits All-Time High, Conflicting with Efforts to Cut Heat-Trapping Pollution," *AP* (Updated October 20, 2023), https://apnews.com/article/oil-fossil-fuels-climate-change-biden-df27160fc81f28d21fbf1fc5575b77bc (citing a report by the US Department of Energy to the effect that American oil production in the first week of October 2023 hit 13.2 million barrels per day, surpassing the previous record set in 2020 by 100,000 barrels).

[92] Based on the figures provided by Nigeria's office of statistics at the end of 2013, Nigeria had a gross domestic product (GDP) of US $510 billion, compared to South Africa's little over US $370 billion. See "Nigeria Becomes Africa's Biggest Economy," *BBC News* (April 6, 2014), http://www.bbc.com/news/business-26913497 (commenting on the rebasing of the country's GDP). The rebasing means that Nigeria included in its GDP calculations, industries like telecom, information technology, music, online sales, airlines, and film production that previously were uncounted. Ibid. Rebasing is carried out to give a nation's GDP statistics the most up-to-date picture of an economy as possible. It is an updating that many countries conduct about once every three years that Nigeria last did in 1990. Ibid. Although with the updating, Nigeria surpasses South Africa as Africa's largest economy, Nigerian citizens do not enjoy a higher standard of living than their counterparts in South Africa. This is because at the time Nigeria's population was more than three times larger than South Africa's, even though on a per-capita basis, South Africa's GDP numbers were three times larger than Nigeria's. Ibid.

[93] See Philip C. Aka and Joseph Abiodun Balogun, *Healthcare and Economic Restructuring: Nigeria in Comparative Perspective* (Gateway East, Singapore: Palgrave Macmillan, 2022), 86–87. Coined in 2002 by Norimitsu Onisha, then reporter for the *New York Times*, the term *Nollywood* is an adaptation of Hollywood in the US and Bollywood in India. Ibid. p. 87, n.38.

[94] Ibid.

produces about 2,500 films a year under more exacting circumstances than in India, talk less the US.[95]

But the Nigerian economy is excessively based on the export of crude oil.[96] This is despite reckonable strides in service areas like telecommunication and entertainment recounted before.[97] The overdependence breeds troubles, conceivable "paradoxes of plenty," both those that Nigeria shares with other oil-producing countries,[98] and those unique to the country. One of the shared troubles relates to the incompetence of these states in collecting taxes from their nationals, with the result that their citizens tend to "feel disconnected from the state, regarding it as an alien organization force or seeing it simply as a distributor of resources."[99] A "resource curse" unique to Nigeria is the conflict in the Niger Delta, source of the country's oil wealth,[100] with its trio narratives of "environmental disaster, economic destitution, and political repression" steeped in the intricacies of oil production.[101]

On environmental disaster, studies by the UN indicate that drinking water in some parts of the Delta region contains some 900 times the amount of benzene, a cancer-causing ingredient, deemed safe by the

[95] Ibid. See also Dickovick and Eastwood, note 52, p. 585 (observing that Nigeria's film industry Nollywood "distributes movies across Africa at a rate faster than Hollywood itself").

[96] Aka and Balogun, note 93 (arguing for restructure of Nigeria's oil-based economy to generate more money for healthcare services).

[97] See note 92 and accompanying text. On telecommunication, one source assessed that "[t]he Nigerian telecommunications sector is among the best performing sectors of the Nigerian economy and one of the fastest growing employers of labor in the country." Lanre Adedeji, "Telecommunications and the Nigerian Economy," *Lawyers Chronicle*, http://thelawyerschronicle.com/telecommunications-and-the-nigerian-economy/ (last visited March 23, 2015). With respect to entertainment, Dickovich and Eastman observe that the Nigerian film industry, Nollywood, "distributes movies across Africa at a rate faster than Hollywood itself." Dickovick and Eastwood, note 52, p. 585.

[98] See Terry Lynn Karl, *The Paradox of Plenty: Oil Booms and Petro-States* (Berkeley, CA: University of California Press, 1997), 189–220.

[99] Dickovick and Eastwood, note 52, pp. 54–55.

[100] See Frynas, note 89, *passim*; and International Crisis Group, *Nigeria: Want in the Midst of Plenty*, Africa Report No. 113 (July 19, 2006).

[101] Larry Diamond, "Foreword," in Rotimi T. Suberu, *Federalism and Ethnic Conflict in Nigeria* (Washington, DC: United States Institute of Peace, 2001), xv.

World Health Organization (WHO).[102] The same studies predict that cleaning the crude oil residue in the affected areas will take decades and billions in US dollars.[103] Next to economic destitution, the narrative pertains to the revenue allocation formula the Nigerian government has applied since the discovery of oil in commercial quantity which the oil-producing communities complain is unfair. From a high of 50% at independence, the size of allocation based on "derivation" (i.e., revenue allocation for oil found on one's land) has gyrated from 45 to 20% to 0% to 1.5% to 3% to its current 13%, reaching their lowest percentage levels during periods of military rule.[104] Finally on political repression, the narrative is signified by the actions of Nigeria's government at both the national and subnational levels who use their coercive authority, including military and police forces, to muffle protests by oil-producing communities, many of those protests peaceful, out of apprehension for the negative impact of the protests on oil production.[105] In sum, the trouble in the Niger Delta is an assault on political-civil and socioeconomic rights; it is a deprivation of the right to economic self-determination, contrary to the injunction of the international bill of human rights that "[i]n no case may a people be deprived of its own means of subsistence."[106]

Nigeria's paradoxes of plenty arising from overdependence on oil production are compounded by persistent poor economic management.[107] These human and natural resource impediments were probably among the reasons that Nigeria ranked low on the list of states "most

[102] See Patrick H. O'Neil et al., *Cases in Comparative Politics*, 4th Ed. (New York: W. W. Norton & Co., 2012), 724.

[103] Ibid.

[104] See Ayakeme Whisky, "The South-South Position: A Stitch in Time Saves Nine," *Vanguard* (Lagos) (June 5, 2014), http://www.vanguardngr.com/2014/06/south-south-position-stitch-time-saves-nine/.

[105] See Frynas, note 89, *passim*.

[106] See International Covenant on Civil and Political Rights, December 16, 1966, S. Treaty Doc. No. 95–20, 6 I.L.M. 368 (1967), 999 U.N.T.S. 171, art. 1, §§ 1–2; and International Covenant on Economic, Social, and Cultural Rights, December 16, 1966, S. Treaty Doc. No. 95–19, I.L.M. 360 (1967), 993 U.N.T.S. 3, art. 1, §§ 1–2.

[107] See, for example, Reuben Abati, "Cardoso, CBN, and the Nigerian Economy," *Premium Times* (Abuja) (February 6, 2024), https://www.premiumtimesng.com/opinion/665839-cardoso-cbn-and-the-nigerian-economy-by-reuben-abati.html ("The [Nigerian] economy is too narrow it has to be expanded to generate better activities and opportunities beyond oil," given a noticeable lag in productivity in many sectors in an

likely to succeed" as "multilateral internationals" in Professor Brysk's seminal work on the small ranks of "global good Samaritans" needed to beef up the US's slackening leadership of the international human rights movement.[108] There is no question that the country's disabilities in potential infrastructure when it comes to the conduct of a human right foreign policy are real. Foreshadowed by colonial rule, some of the problems were evident in the early years of independence, deepened during the nearly thirty years of sustained military rule, and have witnessed little alleviation during the twenty-five years of the Fourth Republic since 1999.

However, these problems are *not* destiny. Nigeria is living through the longest stretch of civilian rule since independence. For all its unevenness, democratic rule affords a better canvas than authoritarian military rule for resolution of these and other issues.[109] Nigeria's infrastructure for the pursuit of a human-right-based foreign policy is not limited to resources within its borders. Instead, it includes resources outside its borders, including the Economic Community of West African States (ECOWAS), an economic integration organization that Nigeria helped to found in 1975,[110] covered in Chapter 6 of this book under peacekeeping.

environment of plentiful oil theft and unceasing vandalism of oil pipelines in the Niger Delta).

[108] Brysk, note 25, pp. 8–17 (Table 1.1, with countries that meet the threshold for potential global good citizenship highlighted in light gray). Regarding that slackening leadership, Brysk lambasted the US as the "deadbeat dad of global governance." Ibid., pp. 232–234. See also Michael Ignatieff, "Is the Human Rights Era Ending?" in *Perspectives on Terrorism: How 9/11 Changed U.S. Politics*, ed. Allan J. Cigler (Boston, MA: Houghton Mifflin Co., 2002), 103–106 (positing that in the wake of the war against terror that attended the terrorist attacks against the US in September 2001, "[t]he new element in determining American foreign policy is what assets—bases, intelligence[,] and diplomatic leverage—it can bring to bear against Al Qaeda"). With the rise of illiberal democracy (i.e., nominal democracy lacking in constitutionalism), the International Relations analyst Fareed Zakaria advised that it is about time the US national government worked to make democracy safe for the world, rather than making the world safe for the democracy. Fareed Zakaria, "The Rise of Illiberal Democracy," *Foreign Affairs*, 76(6) (November-December 1997), https://doi.org/10.2307/20048274.

[109] One still festering issue is insecurity arising from terrorist activities with its arrowhead in the northeastern portion of the country. See Farouk Chothia, "Who are Nigeria's Boko Haram Islamists," *BBC News Africa* (May 4, 2015), http://www.bbc.com/news/world-africa-13809501.

[110] Olufemi A. Babarinde, "Regionalism and African Foreign Policies," in *African Foreign Policies*, ed. Stephen Wright (Boulder, CO: Westview Press, 1999), 215–236.

Over six decades since its independence, "Nigeria has not forged the vibrant and effective foreign policy" that matches its human and material endowments and the basis for its self-perception as the giant of Africa and the black world.[111] Nigeria should rank among the regional "tiger" from the global South that Brysk indicated are aspiring to take their place in the conduct of human-rights-based foreign policies.[112] Countries like Costa Rica, which distinctively punch above their weight in international human rights, "did not require wealth or power to afford the luxury of pursuing a principled foreign policy."[113] Global good Samaritans notable for their human-right-based foreign policies, are made, not born.[114] Instead, as Brysk elaborated, "although some national values and experiences harmonize readily with human rights, foreign policy projection of those norms must be learned and mobilized."[115]

For Nigeria, the requisite national values harmonizing with human rights that can form the basis for learning would include its experience in peacekeeping, habit of general obedience to international law, and its commitment to peaceful settlement of international disputes.[116] There is no requirement that the country punch above its weight in applying human rights in external affairs the way "global Good Samaritans" like Costa Rica have impressively done. But it needs to punch within its weight, something it has yet to do, hence this book.

[111] Pham, note 19, p. 91.

[112] Brysk, note 25, p. 230. These tigers, none of them from Africa, are Argentina, Brazil, Chile, and South Korea. Ibid.

[113] Ibid., p. 118. Judging by population size alone, Costa Rica has 3 million people, compared to Nigeria's 135 million denizens as of 2009 when the Brysk study was published. Ibid., pp. 8–17.

[114] Ibid., p. 221.

[115] Ibid.

[116] See Chapter 1, notes 65–74, and accompanying texts.

Theoretical Framework Grounding This Book

Constructivism

Theory embeds the "foundations of social science" research.[117] Because, among other salient functions, it helps the researcher make sense of and order the phenomenon under observation, explain it, and, where appropriate, make predictions, distinctively, theory is the ingredient in social science research that makes the world of analysis go round.[118] Although the appellation theory suggests a unity, such impression can be misleading, given that, as we will see shortly, some theories have variants.

The theoretical framework that undergirds and informs this book is Constructivism, the school of international relations which holds that states and other actors "interpret the structural conditions in which they find themselves, based on their own experiences, norms, and values."[119] The following discussion expounds Constructivism. Specifically, it juxtaposes the theoretical framework with its two rivals, Political Realism, and Idealism, to draw it out; and formally justifies the choice of Constructivism over the two rival theories.

Juxtaposing Constructivism with its Two Rivals

To better understand a phenomenon under examination, one possible way is to match that phenomenon with its opposite(s). This wisdom justifies the juxtaposition of Constructivism with two rival theories in-between it: Idealism on the left of the political spectrum and Political Realism on the *right* (see Table 2.1).[120] Several salient and interrelated features and concepts of international relations conveniently used to draw out

[117] Michael G. Maxfield and Earl R. Babbie, *Research Methods for Criminal Justice and Criminology*, 7th Ed. (Stamford, CT: Cengage Learning, 2015), 31–32.

[118] Ibid., p. 14.

[119] James N. Danziger, *Understanding the Political World: A Comparative Introduction to Political Science*, 11th Ed. (New York: Pearson, 2013), 287.

[120] *Left* and *right* on the political spectrum is a manner of classifying political positions, ideologies, and parties, with *left* signifying radicalism and *right* conservatism. The terms take their origins from the seating order in the first National Assembly following the French Revolution of 1789. Supporters of the revolution sat on the left, while lawmakers supporting the king (or the status quo) sat on the right. See Marcel Gauchet, "Right and Left," *in Realms of Memory: Conflicts and Divisions,* eds. Pierre Nora and Lawrence D. Kritzman (New York: Columbia University Press, 1997), 242–245.

the three theories here at issue are teachings related to human nature, the nature of the state, anarchy, national interest, war, and the role of diplomacy (Table 2.1).

Table 2.1 Narratives of constructivism vis-à-vis idealism and political realism on selected key concepts of international relations

Item no	*Concepts*	*Theories* *Idealism*	*Constructivism*	*Political Realism*
1	View of human nature	Inherently positive	Could be positive or negative, depending on a state's construction of a situation	Inherently negative
2	Nature of the state	Emphasis on individuals and private groups alongside the state	Emphasis on norms, identities, and interests	State sovereignty and national interest (two rows below), defined in terms of power and security
3	Anarchy	International cooperation is still possible, resulting in "positive sum"[121]	Anarchy is what a state makes of it, meaning it does not have to unrelievedly lead to conflict	Heavy emphasis on the "condition" and its negative consequence for state behavior
4	National interest	Recognizes concept, but does *not* limit it to survival and security	National interest is what the state makes it to be	Ties concept unrelievedly to survival and security
5	War	Recognizes concept, but stresses that cooperation is still possible regardless	War is not imminent or even inevitable, unless states choose to make it so	Points to international conflicts as one of the unavoidable consequences of anarchy
6	Role of diplomacy	Assigns diplomacy an enhanced role not limited to the imperatives of anarchy	Puts the most stress on concept, compared to Idealism and Realism	Diplomacy is important, but subject to the imperatives of anarchy

[121] "Positive-sum" outcome are occurrences where all parties gain and no one loses. They are contrasted with "zero-sum" scenarios where, in the case of power for realists, "an

Political Realism dates back to the Fifth Century BCE,[122] and since the other two responses evolved in response to its explanatory inadequacies, it makes sense to begin with this worldview. The theory is also referred to alternately as *realpolitik* or *power politics*. *Realism* is a school of thought in international relations that stresses the primacy of power, security, and survival in political life.[123] Its basic premise is that individuals, along with the states that represent them, are self-centered.[124] Given this attribute, made no less urgent by the situation of anarchy in the international system, meaning the lack of a world government that mimics the set up domestically, rather than chaos, realists advise that states neither base their domestic or foreign policies on universal moral principles nor use those principles in evaluating the actions of other states.[125] Prisoners' dilemmas and game theories are all spinoff of classic realist theory.[126] Additionally, variants exist within the theory. For example, while classic

increase in power for one another results in an equivalent decrease for others." Danziger, note 119, p. 286.

[122] See "Political Realism in International Relations," *Stanford Encyclopedia of Philosophy* (July 26, 2010, revised April 2, 2013), http://plato.stanford.edu/entries/realism-intl-relations/ (sketching the roots of the realist tradition to include Thucydides' thesis on the importance of power, Machiavelli's critique of the moral tradition, and Hobbes's concept of the state of nature).

[123] Donnelly, note 23, p. 29; see also Dickovick and Eastwood, note 52, p. 400.

[124] Danziger, note 119, p. 286. A *state* is the tool for control over a specific territory that comes in a range of sizes with some, such as China, big (pop. over 1.3 billion people) and others, such as Andorra (pop. over 79,000 people), small. "What is a 'State,'" *Global Policy Forum*, https://www.globalpolicy.org/nations-a-states/what-is-a-state.html. Altogether, there are 196 states in the world, all of which, but Kosovo, Taiwan, and the Vatican, are members of the United Nations. United Nations, "Member States," http://www.un.org/depts/dhl/unms/cms.shtml; Matt Rosenberg, "Non-Members of the United Nations," *About*, http://geography.about.com/od/politicalgeography/a/nun.htm.

[125] Donnelly, note 23, p. 29. "To pursue a moral foreign policy," realists contend, "would not only be foolishly unsuccessful, but also leave one's country vulnerable to the power of self-interested states." Ibid.

[126] See Dickovick and Eastwood, note 52, pp. 400–402. *Prisoner's dilemma* is a game model wherein two actors would benefit from cooperation, but where both parties have individual incentives that lead them to ultimately defect from cooperation. *Game theory* consists of strategic interactions between actors, rooted in mathematical modeling, wherein the "players" respond rationally to incentives and to the expected actions of other players. Ibid., p. 400.

realists insist on absolute gain in power, neo-realists contend that states pursue relative gains.[127]

Political Realism takes a negative view of human nature. For realists, human beings are self-centered species whose behaviors are essentially driven by self-interest.[128] On the nature of the state, realists regard states as the primary and most important actors in international relations,[129] an orientation that puts a heavy stress on sovereignty.[130] They also view the world as *anarchic*, meaning absence of centralized authority at the world level necessary to enforce compliance among states.[131] The "condition" of anarchy results in a "security dilemma" leading sometimes to war,[132] which states seek to overcome through various self-help measures meant to promote security and survival, including maximizing their power, and promoting national interests defined in terms of power resources.[133]

[127] David Weissbrodt et al., *International Human Rights: Law, Policy, and Process,* 4th Ed. (San Francisco, CA: LexisNexis, 2009), 26. Incidentally, neo-realism appears to be little different from institutionalism which framework Professors Weissbrodt and his colleagues include among their theories of why states ratify and enforce human rights treaties and accept other human rights norms.

[128] See Danziger, note 119, p. 286; Donnelly, note 23, p. 29; and Hans J. Morgenthau, *Politics Among Nations: The Struggle for Power and Peace,* Revised 5th Ed. (New York: Alfred A. Knopf, 1978), 6 (warning that "[w]e cannot conclude from the good intentions of a statesman that his foreign policies will be either morally praiseworthy or politically successful").

[129] Weissbrodt et al., note 127, p. 26; and Danziger, note 119, p. 286.

[130] Sovereignty "requires independence from any outside power and final authority over men who live within certain boundaries." Joseph R. Strayer, *On the Medieval Origins of the Modern State* (Princeton, NJ: Princeton University Press, 2005), 58. It also forbids intervention into "matters which are essentially within the domestic jurisdiction of any state [...]." UN Charter, note 36, art. 2 (7). In addition to control over a territory, the doctrine also implies a source of legitimate authority.

[131] See Brian C. Schmidt, *The Political Discourse of Anarchy: A Disciplinary History of International Relations* (Albany, NY: State University of New York Press, 1998), *passim.*

[132] This does not necessarily mean that realists like war. To the contrary, many realists study the causes of war to reduce the chances of future conflicts. See Robert Jervis, "Realism in the Study of World Politics," *in Explorations and Contestation in the Study of World Politics,* eds. Peter J. Katzenstein et al. (Cambridge, MA: MIT Press, 1999), 334.

[133] See Morgenthau, note 128, p. 5 (positing that "[t]he main signpost that helps political realism to find its way through the landscape of international politics is the concept of interest defined in terms of *power*"—in the same manner that economics, for example, defines interest in terms of *wealth*).

Diplomacy is critical under this model, but only as a secondary issue subject to the imperatives of anarchy.[134]

Idealism is a school of thought in international relations that insists that, along with self-interest, cooperation and altruistic behavior are possible between states and in the international community in general.[135] Idealism takes a decidedly positive view of human nature; for idealists, human beings can be intrinsically selfless entities capable of altruistic and cooperative behaviors.[136] Overall, idealists take a more complicated view of human beings and international relations. On the nature of the state, idealists finger individuals and private groups, rather than the state all by itself, as primary actors in international relations.[137] Idealism posits that states "have different preferences and internal structures that lead them to behave in different ways."[138]

Accordingly, the theory "pays greater attention to the role of domestic institutions in international relations, and it makes efforts to explain cooperation and peace between some states while also accounting for conflict in other circumstances."[139] Because states have many goals they pursue at home and abroad, "aggressive, power-maximizing behavior is not inevitable."[140] For idealists, vis-à-vis realists, it is possible to create an international system wherein well-designed institutions facilitate cooperative behavior among all actors, whether state and non-state, wherein no one loses and actually some win (positive sum), rather than zero-sum

[134] See Paul Sharp, *Diplomatic Theory of International Relations* (New York: Cambridge University Press, 2009), 53–73 (discussing diplomacy and diplomats in realist theory).

[135] A term used interchangeably with Idealism is Liberalism. See Danziger, note 119, p. 286; and Donnelly, note 23, p. 29. This researcher chose Idealism to keep things simple, given the several variants within this worldview that can confuse all but the most initiated reader. See Terence Ball et al., *Political Ideologies and the Democratic Ideal*, 9th Ed. (Boston, MA: Pearson, 2014), 44–93 (highlighting three divisions—classical liberalism, neoclassical liberalism, and reformist (or welfare)—within this one school of thought).

[136] See Danziger, note 119, p. 286. For example, idealists see no reason why the nonviolent principles and cooperative techniques, key to nonviolent resolution of disputes at the domestic level, should not be extended to the international level. See Jonathan Schell, *The Unconquerable World: Power, Nonviolence, and the Will of the People* (New York: Henry Holt & Co., 2003), 265–279.

[137] Weissbrodt et al., note 127, p. 29.

[138] Dickovick and Eastwood, note 52, p. 402.

[139] Ibid.

[140] Danziger, note 119, p. 286.

scenario where "an increase in power for one actor results in an equivalent decrease for others."[141]

Idealists concede anarchy and the other concepts associated with it, such as war, national interest, and balance of power, to the point that some within this school accept war as a legitimate means of settling international disputes.[142] However, consistent with the theory's positive view of human nature, their narrative related to anarchy and its consequences for international relations is much less gloomy, compared to that of realists. Finally, idealists perceive a much broader role for diplomacy in international relations than the limited role dictated by the imperatives of anarchy that realists bestow this tool. Perceiving the dominant international role of states to be weakening, the result of various international forces that include globalization, idealists posit that, alongside states, other forces, such as international law and institutions, today contribute importantly to an evolving international community that, together with the state, deserve analytical attention.[143]

Constructivism takes a middle ground between Realism and Idealism that straddles the views of these two contending and competing theories regarding human nature,[144] as opposed to depicting it categorically as

[141] Ibid. For idealists, "[i]f a state's actions reduce the welfare of people in any country or increase interstate conflict and war, it is usually because of poorly designed institutions (e.g., governments, economic systems, and legal systems), not because people and states are evil or selfish." Ibid.

[142] Surely, the position of idealists on the consequences for international relations arising from the "condition" of anarchy is more complex than is sketched here. On the one hand, there are the so-called liberal hawks who accept war as a legitimate means for settling international disputes. See Joseph S. Nye, Jr., *Understanding International Conflicts: An Introduction to Theory and History,* 7th Ed. (New York: Longman, 2008), 4. On the other hand, consistent with the vision of Woodrow Wilson, many idealists espouse a collective security arrangement in place of balance of power. See Margaret MacMillan, *Paris 1919: Six Months That Changed the World* (New York: Random House, 2003), 3–16 (focusing on Woodrow Wilson).

[143] For example, for idealists, state power matters, but it is a power exercised within a framework of international rules and institutions capable of facilitating cooperation—or stimulating conflict. See Karen A. Mingst and Margaret P. Karns, *The United Nations in the 21st Century,* 4th Ed. (Westview Press, 2012), 10. Similarly, for idealists, states are pluralistic (not unitary actors as realists see them) who, because their goals vary and their interests change, do not apply one single definition of national interests. Ibid.

[144] Emanuel Adler, "Seizing the Middle Ground: Constructivism in World Politics," *European Journal of International Relations,* 3(1997), 319–363 (situating Constructivism as a "middle ground" between realism and idealism).

positive or negative. On the nature of the state, Constructivism stresses the impact of norms, interests, and identities on state behavior.[145] Specifically, constructivists argue "that states come to accept norms and ideas through a process of socialization and internationalization."[146] Where realists "seem to take the goal of power as a given" and idealists imagine broader possibilities within the security dilemma of anarchy permitting international cooperation among states, constructivists "question[] the underlying goal of seeking power or, minimally strive[] to explain why states pursue certain goals to obtain social acceptance within the community of nations."[147] Finally, compared to the two rival theories, constructivism spots the least extreme narrative on anarchy and the consequences of this "condition" for international relations. For example, constructivists posit that the absence of a world government with authority to enforce compliance among states need not automatically lead to conflict, given that "anarchy is what states make of it."[148] Similarly, "foreign policy is what states make of it."[149]

In sum, on international affairs and foreign policy, Constructivism is a theory in the middle that consciously seeks to overcome some of the embedded weaknesses of realism and idealism. The theory's location within these two rival theories calls to mind the answer of former Secretary of State Madeleine Albright responding to the question, "[h]ow often in the world of politics do reality and pragmatic considerations step on moral ideals?"[150]

> I think that I am somebody who has a good moral basis, foundation — an idealist, but also at various times pragmatic and realistic. That's why I've never liked the division between idealist and realist ... because the two

[145] See Weissbrodt et al., note 127, p. 30; Brysk, note 25, pp. 33–34.

[146] Weissbrodt et al., note 127, p. 29.

[147] Ibid.

[148] Alexander Wendt, "Anarchy Is What States Make of It: The Social Construction of Power Politics," *International Organization*, 46 (1992), 391–425.

[149] Steve Smith, "Foreign Policy Is What States Make of It: Social Construction and International Relations Theory," in *Foreign Policy in a Constructed World*, ed. Vendulka Kubálková (Armonk, NY: M.E. Sharpe, 2001), 38–55.

[150] "Madeleine Albright Extended Interview," *PBS* (May 19, 2006), http://www.pbs.org/wnet/religionandethics/2006/05/19/may-19-2006-madeleine-albright-extended-interview/2838/.

> have to combine. So I sometimes call myself an idealistic realist or a realistic idealist. I believe that you have to have an overall set of goals and principles. But ultimately politics and foreign policy have to have compromise in it, because you're dealing with more than just what you want. Foreign policy is trying to get some other country to do what you want. But you do have to figure out what is acceptable, what is doable.[151]

More than its competitors, Constructivism holds the key to the compromise former Secretary Albright talked about.

Three Justifications for the Choice of Constructivism Over Political Realism and Idealism as Theoretical Framework

Three justifications for the choice of Constructivism over Political Realism and Idealism as appropriate framework for the study of human rights in Nigeria's external relations are that, vis-à-vis its two famous rivals, Constructivism affords the most scope for interjecting human rights in external affairs; more than liberalism, the theory stands a better chance of correcting the moralistic excesses of realism; and there are a growing number of studies this book joins that have successfully used Constructivism in their works.

Most-Scope Argument

The first justification supporting the preference of Constructivism over its two famous rivals is that Constructivism affords the most scope for interjecting human rights in external affairs. Political Realism sees little utility in bringing moral principles into international relations[152]; accordingly, realists counsel states to forswear such integration.[153] And with its

[151] Ibid.

[152] See Donnelly, note 23, p. 28 (observing that for realists, "there is no significant independent international community, let alone an international body with the right to act on behalf of human rights"). In realists' view, the only permissible guide to foreign policy should be considerations of the national interest, defined in terms of power and security. Ibid., p. 29.

[153] George Kennan, a contemporary realist thinker and an architect of US post-World War II foreign policy, argued that "[t]he process of government [...] is a practical exercise and not a moral one." Opining that misgovernment has been and will always remain "the

stress on opportunities for cooperative behavior and by multiple actors on the international stage besides just states, idealism represents a welcome improvement on realism. However, the theory still takes as given some of the supposed consequences arising from the "condition" of anarchy, such as war and the necessity for balance of power, whether in its classic form or as collective security.

These inadequacies of Political Realism and Idealism leave Constructivism as the only plausible explanatory alternative. Constructivists perceive the contexts in which states interact to range from competitive to cooperative, in a manner that permits states to respond in many different ways.[154] It treats national identity, whether essentialist or aspirational, as a primary site of political contestation and "constant process" that is "continuously shaped by various actors and communities, both domestically and internationally."[155] Under the framework, states display their inclinations to human rights norms, including the application of those norms in external relations, based on identities and mutually constitutive interests that are continuously shaped through social interaction. Constructivism regards foreign policy as a means through which a state all at once achieves several goals, including expressing its national identity and interest, projecting a self-image that differentiates it from other states or political communities, providing a forum for political contestation, and interacting with other international actors, both state and non-state actors alike, in the process of socialization.[156]

In sum, quite unlike any other, the framework adopts "a wider remit of how interests are defined."[157] If national interests are viewed as "intersubjective understanding of what it takes to advance power, influence, and wealth," then Constructivism "is equipped to show how national interests are born, how they acquire their status of general political understandings,

common condition of most of mankind," Kennan likened the U.S. government's attempt to correct "the political habits of large parts of the world's population" to "tilting against the windmills." Donnelly, note 23, pp. 29–30 (citing three works Kennan published from 1954 to 1986).

[154] See Alexander Wendt, *Social Theory of International Politics* (New York: Cambridge University Press, 1999), *passim*.

[155] Andrew Lui, *Why Canada Cares: Human Rights and Foreign Policy in Theory and Practice* (Montreal, Canada: McGill-Queen's University Press, 2012), 117.

[156] See ibid.

[157] Ibid., p. 116.

and how such understandings are politically selected in through political processes."[158] Under the theory, foreign policy is what a state makes of it and the "condition" of anarchy in international relations poses no barriers to pursuit of a human-right policy unless a state so chooses. This is in contradistinction to realism which equates these interests narrowly with power and security and assumes them a priori.[159]

Given the foregoing reasons, Constructivism "offers a valuable way of studying how shared beliefs, rules, organizations, and cultural practices shape the behavior of states and other actors as well as their identities and interests."[160] As an explanatory tool, these factors add up to lend Constructivism a realistic quality that its two competitors lack.[161] Constructivism embodies elements beyond the limited confines of its rivals, especially Political Realism, that takes international relations and foreign policy, including the influence of human rights in these fields, "into new areas of inquiry."[162] By exploring the ever-evolving identities and interests that drive state behavior, Constructivism "provide[s] unique insight into the underlying motivations of states international human rights policies."[163]

Moderating the Moralistic Excesses of Political Realism

Professor Donnelly presents one of the most broad-ranging criticisms of realist teaching related to human rights,[164] one revolved around the concern that realists may have "wildly exaggerated" "[a] valuable caution against moralistic excesses" "into a general principle of politics."[165] First, he concedes "a kernel of truth" to realists regarding the possibility that

[158] Adler, note 144, p. 337.

[159] Lui, note 155, p. 116.

[160] Mingst and Karns, note 143, p. 11.

[161] See Daniel C. Thomas, *The Helsinki Effect: International Norms, Human Rights, and the Demise of Communism* (Princeton, NJ: Princeton University Press, 2001), 15 (reasoning that the more salient the identity specified by an international norm, the more the actor will seek to fulfill its obligations under that norm").

[162] Lui, note 155, p. 112.

[163] Ibid.

[164] See Donnelly, note 23, pp. 29–30.V.

[165] Ibid., p. 30.

the demands of morality may conflict with the national interest defined in terms of power.[166] The problem, however, he noted is that "all objectives of foreign policy, not just moral ones, may compete with the national interest thus defined."[167] Second, "most moral objectives," including human rights goals, "can be pursued at a cost far less than national survival[]" critical to realism.[168] Third, nothing prevents a country, if it wishes, from including moral concerns, such as human rights, in its configuration of the national interest.[169]

True, "[s]ecurity, independence, and prosperity may be unavoidable necessities of national political life."[170] However, governments need not limit themselves to just these concerns. "Even if the primary obligation of governments must be to the national interest defined in terms of power, this need not be their sole, or even ultimate, obligation."[171] Fourth, Donnelly takes issue with realist suggestion that moral behavior in foreign policy is not possible without the existence first of "an effective government that can deter and punish illegal actions."[172] He argues that "[j]ust as individuals may behave morally without government to enforce moral rules, so moral behavior is possible in international relations."[173]

Finally, Donnelly concedes the point regarding the possible costs of moral behavior. Notwithstanding those costs, he said, "states often can act on moral concerns without harm, and sometimes with success. There may be good policy reasons to pursue amoral, or even immoral, policies in particular instances. There are, however, no good theoretical reasons for requiring amoral policies, or even accepting them as the norm."[174]

Given the plasticity embedded in its notion that foreign policy is what states make of it, more than Idealism, Constructivism holds a better explanatory chance of correcting the moralistic excesses of realism. Political Realism provided the dominant explanation for international politics

[166] Ibid., p. 30.

[167] Ibid.

[168] Ibid.

[169] Ibid.

[170] Donnelly, note 23, p. 30.

[171] Ibid.

[172] Ibid.

[173] Ibid.

[174] Ibid.

for much of the period during the era of the Cold War, the ideological competition between East and West that ended in 1991 with the breakup of the Soviet Union.[175] But because of sea changes in world politics since then, including the expanded multilateralism globally within the UN and regionally as well as the increased advocacy for human rights by non-governmental organizations (NGOs)—events unanticipated by realism—the consensus is that the theory has become an inadequate framework for analyzing world politics, including the influence of human rights in external affairs.[176] The inadequacy leaves an explanatory hole that, because of its plasticity and robustness vis-à-vis idealism, Constructivism has stepped up to fill.[177]

The Growing Number of Studies Using Constructivism This Book Joins

The third and final justification for the choice of Constructivism over its two rival theories revolves around the growing number of studies that have successfully applied the framework in their own works—that this book joins. These studies include Andrew Lui, *Why Canada Cares: Human Rights and Foreign Policy in Theory and Practice*[178]; Alison Brysk, *Global Samaritans: Human Rights as Foreign Policy*[179]; David P. Forsythe, editor, *Human Rights and Comparative Foreign Policy*[180] (notwithstanding that the volume did not explicitly use the term Constructivism); and Philip C. Aka, *Human Rights in Nigeria's External Relations: Building the Record of a Moral Superpower*.[181] As we see shortly, among these works, the most elaborate for our purpose here is Alison Brysk's.

[175] For more on this ideological competition, see, for example, Edward H. Judge and John W. Langdon, *The Cold War: A Global History with Documents*, 2d Ed. (Upper Saddle River, NJ: Prentice Hall, 2010).

[176] Mingst and Karns, note 143, p. 10.

[177] Lui, note 155, p. 112.

[178] Lui, note 155, *passim*.

[179] Brysk, note 25.

[180] David P. Forsythe, ed., *Human Rights and Comparative Foreign Policy* (New York: United Nations University Press, 2000).

[181] Philip C. Aka, *Human Rights in Nigeria's External Relations: Building the Record of a Moral Superpower* (Lanham, Boulder, New York, and London: Lexington Books, 2017).

In *Why Canada Cares*, Lui argued that while, on the one hand, Canada has rarely shown a willingness to sacrifice material advantages for international human rights causes, on the other hand, the country has pursued human rights in a broader attempt to cement individual rights as the cornerstone of Canadian federalism as well as to mitigate friction between the country's diverse social groups.[182] The book includes a postscript on the conservative administration of Stephen Harper, prime minister from 2006 to 2015, under whose government Canada managed to maintain its human rights foreign policy, even though initial indications, including failure to adopt a government White Paper on Canadian foreign policy released by the previous government, suggested otherwise.[183] In tracing and testing the influence of Constructivism on Canadian policy, Liu began with realism as a baseline in Part 1, "interests all the way down," encompassing two chapters,[184] before delving into Part II, "ideas all the way down," in an analysis, in three chapters, devoted specifically to Constructivism.[185]

Overall, Lui takes the position that in examining Canadian policies, "realist and constructivist accounts should be regarded as complementary rather than as competing and mutually exclusive."[186] Because both Realism and Constructivism offer useful, albeit "immoderate and incomplete," insights on Canadian foreign policies,[187] Lui advised adoption of a "theoretical eclecticism" that "bridge both perspectives," instead of each in its pure form,[188] assuming that pure form exists for Constructivism.

In *Global Samaritans*, Brysk enquires into factors that impel political communities to pay prices, including the risk of lives, treasure, and diplomatic repercussions, to promote human rights in their external relations.[189] Using six states—Canada, Costa Rica, Japan, The Netherlands, South Africa, and Sweden,[190] plus a coalition of equally six groups, some

[182] See generally Lui, note 155; ibid., p. 7.

[183] Ibid., pp. 177–181.

[184] Ibid., pp. 21–95.

[185] Ibid., pp. 99–176.

[186] Ibid., p. 164.

[187] Ibid., p. 168.

[188] Ibid., p. 169.

[189] *See* Brysk, note 25, *passim*.

[190] Ibid., pp. 42–196.

of them states,[191] as case study, Professor Brysk illustrated how, even in a world of realist security dilemmas, some political communities reconstruct their national interests as a long-term common good to embed human rights in their foreign relations.[192] The book closed with a set of recommendations, instructively titled, "The World Needs More Canada,"[193] including nine learned lessons.[194]

Eight of these lessons relevant here are: the reward in goodness; identity politics can be constructive; good citizens are made, rather than born; and good Samaritans need only to be good enough, not perfect. Other lessons are: different strokes for different folks, meaning that countries can and should specialize in projecting areas of domestic strength; it takes a global village; size is not everything as even small countries can punch above their weight when that weight is well-developed and well-distributed; and eternal vigilance is the price of global citizenship, given that the adoption of human rights foreign policies is progressive, rather than permanent.[195] The theoretical framework of the Brysk book anchored in Constructivism revolved around the reconstruction of national interest necessary for a human right-based foreign policy.[196]

Compared to Lui's work, as suggested already in the previous statement, the application of Constructivism in Professor Brysk's book was an indirect one that synonymized or integrated Constructivism and reconstructing the national interest. Principled foreign policy evident in Constructivism "is possible," she said, "but it requires the continuous reconstruction of national interest through the constitution and projection of norms of cosmopolitan interdependence."[197] Brysk posited that, compared to states which do not consistently apply human rights in external relations, global Good Samaritans "have a broader, long-term vision of national interest. Global good citizens have reconstructed their national identity in accordance with universalist norms, roles, and

[191] These transnational human rights organizations, which Brysk praised as "Coalitions of the Caring," are enumerated in note 31.

[192] See Brysk, note 25, *passim*.

[193] Brysk, note 25, pp. 220–234.

[194] Ibid., pp. 220–224.

[195] Ibid.

[196] Ibid., pp. 31–40.

[197] Ibid., p. 40.

expectations."[198] For these states, "the principled pursuit of human rights is a consciously constructed alternative pathway of enlightened self-interest."[199]

More than rival theories, Constructivism "draws our attention to the active and political work of putting ideas into practice"[200]; for Brysk "[a] constructivist theory of foreign policy can help us to understand how cosmopolitan political cultures like human rights values make sense—and how such cultures are learned."[201] Moreover, a human right-based foreign policy need not preclude realism.[202] "Ideas matter, but constructivism tells us that human rights norms are always competing with alternative discourses of security threat, parochial nationalism, and narrowly material, short-term calculation."[203] In fact, "the interplay of moral and material interests can help to explain the selectivity and targeting of principled foreign policy."[204]

Brysk's theoretical framework embedded in Constructivism includes a showing of "identities as interests."[205] Because "[s]tates are political communities that seek values and identity[,]"[206] in contradistinction to realist teaching, under Constructivism "what interests a nation is not always state security."[207] Instead, "[n]ations also expend scarce resources in pursuit of identity, which is often formed in international relationships."[208]

In *Human Rights and Comparative Foreign Policy*, Professors Forsythe and his colleagues examined the influence or lack thereof of human rights in the foreign policies of a wide range of contemporary states,

[198] Ibid., p. 31.

[199] Ibid., p. 32.

[200] Ibid.

[201] Ibid., p. 31.

[202] See ibid., p. 32 (pointing out that "[a]n emphasis on normative change can be combined with a recognition of rationalist parameters or structural dialectics of foreign policy").

[203] Ibid., p. 40.

[204] Ibid., p. 33.

[205] Ibid., pp. 33–37.

[206] Ibid., p. 33.

[207] Ibid.

[208] Ibid.

using a common framework of analysis consisting of an intersection of domestic and foreign factors for the ten political communities covered in their work.[209] The authors made several important points relating to the subject matter. First is an increased salience to human rights in the foreign policies of many contemporary states. However, secondly, many states who interject human rights in their external affairs, including even liberal-democratic ones, such as the UK and the US, much of the time fail to accord human rights issues the same level they assign traditional security and economic concerns. Related to this second factor, due to factors, such as national political culture and perceived national interests, different states bring different emphases to their human rights diplomacy. A fourth and final issue is the matter of inconsistency that arises when human rights are balanced against competing foreign policy when, for example, states treat comparable human rights violations in different countries differently.[210]

Although the introduction unveils some useful conceptual ideas that frame the work, the theoretical chapter of the volume by Jack Donnelly, modestly titled "An Overview," is Chapter 12.[211] Professor Donnelly's discussion covers four separate issues, two of which—the influence of national identity on human rights, and self-image[212]—are germane to this discussion justifying the choice of the theory as an appropriate framework for this study on human rights in Nigeria's external relations. In statements that smack of Constructivism, Donnelly posited that a state's national interest "is a matter of what [that] state values," based partly on "how that state sees itself, both nationally and internationally[,]"[213] and that many states' human rights policies are largely "identity based," in

[209] Forsythe, ed., *Human Rights and Comparative Foreign Policy*, note 180, *passim*. The ten political communities covered in the book are the US, the Netherlands, the UK, and Japan, classified under "liberal democracies," along with Russia, India, Iran, Central Europe (consisting of Hungary, the Czech Republic, and Poland), South Africa since 1994, and Latin America. Ibid., pp. 21–309.

[210] Forsythe, ed., *Human Rights and Comparative Foreign Policy*, note 181, *passim*. See also Donnelly, note 23, p. 145 (discussing the charge of inconsistency in international human rights policies).

[211] Donnelly, "An Overview," note 47, pp. 310–334.

[212] Ibid. The two not relevant here are his comments relating to the intensity of human rights commitments, ibid., pp. 321–324, and evaluation of international human rights policies, ibid., pp. 324–331.

[213] Ibid., p. 311.

that "they reflect the extent to which (national and international) human rights values have shaped or re-shaped understandings of who they are and what they value."[214]

Next on self-images, Donnelly indicated that a state's national self-image is not "exhausted by a commitment to human rights."[215] Instead, "in addition to human rights, sovereignty and non-intervention are vital norms of international society."[216] And because "[a]ll states, in fact, have a deeper and more enthusiastic commitment to sovereignty than to human rights," he indicated, it is foolhardy to "overestimate either human rights or sovereignty" in the external behavior of states.[217] He depicted on a quadrant based on "orientation toward international society" from "nationalist" on the left to "internationalist" on the right, the range of national attitudes toward international human rights of ten states covered in the volume.[218]

In *Human Rights in Nigeria's External Relations*, Professor Aka applied Alison Brysk's concept of global Good Samaritan to Nigeria in an attempt to boost its contributions to the international human rights movements, just as Aka did subsequently with respect to Cuba's often-neglected humanitarian missions in Africa under Fidel Castro,[219] Cuba being the only socialist country in the lineup.[220] The book built its contributions on a secular temple of Nigerian Human Rights Foreign Policy, in two steps and four pillars, powered by thoroughgoing reforms at home and abroad, comprising: reconstructed national interest, increased respect

[214] Ibid.

[215] Ibid., p. 315.

[216] Ibid., p. 318.

[217] Ibid.

[218] Ibid., p. 320 (fig. 12.1). Six of the countries—South Africa, Hungary, Japan, Netherlands, Costa Rica, and the UK clustered on the "international" end of the quadrant with the last three close to the right-hand margin. Three of the countries, Russia, India, and the US placed around the center of the quadrant with Russia and India much closer to the "nationalist" end, compared to the US. Iran stood alone under the "nationalist" end of the diagram. Ibid.

[219] See Aka, "Fidel Castro and Socioeconomic Human Rights in Africa," note 3, pp. 41–78.

[220] Ibid. See also Philip C. Aka, *Bosnia as Civic State and Global Citizen: Alternative Futures Outside the EU* (Lanham, Boulder, New York, and London: Rowman & Littlefield, 2022), 162–185 (featuring Cuba on a list of seven countries that includes Canada, Costa Rica, Japan, the Netherlands (or Holland), South Africa, and Sweden).

for human rights at home, redesigned peacekeeping, reshaped foreign policy machine, increased bilateralism in foreign relations, as well as the resourceful use of ECOWAS as a human-right tool.[221]

Last Word on the Choice of Constructivism as Theoretical Framework

The foregoing discussion entailed juxtaposition of Constructivism to two other leading theories to better understand it; justification of its choice over those two rival theories; and a review of previous works that successfully applied Constructivism the study here now joins. Weissbrodt and his colleagues observe that Constructivism may "suffer from a lack of sincerity on the part of the state actors."[222] But rather than a flaw as such, this may be a compliment that speaks to the theory's plasticity. And assuming, for the sake of argument, that the theory is not a strong connection, it may be the best under the circumstances where no other theory comes close. The fact of the matter is that, vis-à-vis its two rival theories, Constructivism is more "adequately sensitive to the socially constructed nature of the identities and norms that shape beliefs and guide actions taken by" states and other actors in international relations.[223] For their seminal volume, Professor Forsythe and his team could not include numerous states like Nigeria that deserve examination because of budgetary constraints.[224] This study fills that gap with a study on the country that tests the theory of Constructivism using the country.

Conclusion

Three issues this chapter addressed, all converged around the theme of Nigeria as a state worthy of the dreams of its diverse peoples at home and abroad, were:

[221] See Aka, *Human Rights in Nigeria's External Relations*, note 181, p. 5 (Fig. 1.1), and pp. 247–254 (reforms at home and abroad).

[222] Weissbrodt et al., note 127, p. 29.

[223] Danziger, note 119, p. 287.

[224] See David P. Forsythe, "Introduction," *in Human Rights and Comparative Foreign Policy*, note 181, p. 17 (indicating, "[w]ith an unlimited budget and a multi-volume project, we could have added numerous states that merit study: France, Norway, Germany, Nigeria, Kenya, Mexico, Brazil, Pakistan, Israel, the Philippines, etc.").

- the nature of the relationship between human rights and foreign policy,
- the necessity for Nigeria to infuse more human rights in its external relations to the glory and benefit of democracy and human rights at home, and
- the theoretical framework that grounds this book.

For Nigeria, the nature of the relationship between human rights and foreign policy boils down to the application of human rights in external relations, signified by the adoption of a principled foreign policy under its still ongoing Fourth Republic, after Buhari, with keen eyes for the numerous benefits of that application for democracy and human rights at home. On the necessity for Nigeria to adopt a human-right policy, taking advantage of a new era opened up by the departure of the military from Nigeria's body politic, we canvassed various factors revolved around the existence of an incipient infrastructure for human-right work, including Nigeria's celebrated status in the literature of comparative politics as the largest society in Africa.

Finally on the theoretical framework that informs this book, Constructivism is singled out as the applicable worldview because of the middle ground that it affords over and above the inadequacies of Political Realism and Idealism. Spelling out a theoretical framework upfront precludes hidden or implicit assumptions within the best tradition in the conduct of social science research,[225] with the additional value here that it is tied to the reconstruction of Nigeria's national interest to improve its readiness for human rights work, spelled out in Chapter 4. To provide a hint, as perceptive analysts have recommended, leveraging the growing popularity of Nigeria's Afro-beats music on the global stage as soft power[226] mandates attention to a worldview different from the prevailing paradigm anchored on Political Realism. This over, the next topic up for examination as Chapter 3 is a historical background account, that complements and completes this presentation.

[225] See *Scientific Research in Education* (Washington, DC: National Academies Press, 2002), 68 ("Assumptions underlying the inferences made should be clearly stated and justified").

[226] Adetayo, note 82.

CHAPTER 3

Historical Background

Introduction

This chapter complements and completes the discussion in Chapter 2 on the imperatives of a human-right policy for Nigeria under the Fourth Republic, in the wake of the reduced influence of the military in the country's body politic, symptomized by General Buhari's departure on May 29, 2023, after two unimpressive terms in office as President. Within the best tradition of comparative analysis, this chapter chronicles activities from the past that shape the current patterns of politics.[1] Arguably, those patterns include the need and modalities for applying human rights in Nigeria's external relations to strengthen democracy and human rights at home while contributing to the international human rights regime abroad.

Nigerian foreign policy since independence is classifiable into five distinctive periods: the First Republic from 1960 to 1966, the first round of military rule from 1966 to 1979, the Second Republic from 1979 to 1983, the second round of military rule from 1983 to 1999, and the Fourth Republic since 1999 (see Table 3.1). The five periods form the focus in this chapter. However, the picture is incomplete without a

[1] Frank L. Wilson, *Concepts and Issues in Comparative Politics: An Introduction to Comparative Analysis* (Upper Saddle River, NJ: Prentice Hall, 1996), 17.

P. C. Aka, *Human Rights in Nigeria's External Relations in the Age of General Muhammadu Buhari and His Successors*,
https://doi.org/10.1007/978-3-031-63231-0_3

statement on the precolonial and colonial eras. Including the eras before independence starts the story of human rights in Nigeria's external relations from its proverbial beginning and shines useful insights pertaining to the topic. Comprehension of "the nature and issues of contemporary politics" of a country under examination is predicated on an awareness of the past history of the country in question.[2] Including the pre-independence eras sits well with this wisdom and is consistent with the tenets of comparative analysis, specifically Within-Case Comparison (WCC), involving the study of one country at different points in time and space.[3] Under this technique, a researcher scrutinizes his or her case material with a sharp eye for variations at different points in time to better understand the evidence.[4] In a word, this chapter is prefaced with a sketch of the precolonial and colonial eras.

In addition to this introduction, this chapter has four sections, organized mostly around the various eras. The first is a brief statement on ethics as moral consideration in foreign affairs, short of full-blown human rights, as a trade that connects all three periods in the areas today known as Nigeria. The discussion is next followed by a chronicle of each era, much of it devoted to the postcolonial era with the five periods and the sixteen governments from Abubakar Tafawa Balewa to Bola A. Tinubu that this era encompasses. The chronicle is preceded by sketches of three concentric circles that power Nigerian foreign relations and the abiding influence of the civil war on those circles.

[2] Ibid.

[3] J. Tyler Dickovick and Jonathan Eastwood, *Comparative Politics: Integrating Theories, Methods, and Cases* (New York: Oxford University Press, 2013), 19.

[4] Ibid. WCC is often associated with "process-tracing" by which "the researcher examines histories, archival documents, interview transcripts and other sources to see whether the causal process a theory hypothesizes or implies in a case is in fact evident in the sequence and values of the intervening variable in that case." Alexander L. George and Andrew Bennett, *Case Studies and Theory Development in the Social Sciences* (Cambridge, MA: MIT Press, 2005), 6.

Table 3.1 Recap of five distinctive periods in Nigerian foreign policy since independence

Item no	*Period*	*Leader*	*How rule ended*
1	First Republic (1960–1966)	Abubakar T. Balewa	Assassination; military coup
2	First round of military rule (1966–1975)	Johnson Aguiyi-Ironsi (January-July 1966)	Assassination; countercoup
		Yakubu D. Gowon (July 1966-July 1975)	Countercoup
		Murtala Muhammed (July 1975-February 1976)	Death by assassination during a failed coup
		Olusegun Obasanjo (February 1976-October 1979)	Transfer of power to a civilian government
3	Second Republic (Oct. 1979–Dec. 1983)	Shehu U. Shagari	Military coup
4	Second round of military rule (Dec. 1983–May 1999)	Muhammadu Buhari (December 1983–August 1985)	Countercoup
		Ibrahim Babangida (August 1985–August 1993)	Forced resignation following controversies in the wake of an annulled presidential election in June 1993
		Ernest Shonekan (August–November 1993)	Interim government; forced resignation; military coup
		Sani Abacha (November 1993–June 1998)	Died in office
		Abdulsalami Abubakar (June 1998–May 1999)	Transfer of power to a civilian government
5	Fourth Republic (May 1999 to Present Time)	Olusegun Obasanjo (May 1999–May 2007)	Term limited
		Umaru Musa Yar'Adua (May 2007–May 2010)	Died in office
		Goodluck E. Jonathan (May 2010–May 2015)	Failed reelection attempt
		Muhammadu Buhari (May 2015–May 2023)	Term limited
		Bola A. Tinubu (since May 2023)	2023-

Ethics in Foreign Relations

Ethics is an element of normative analysis involving the "examination, justification, and critical analysis of morality."[5] Ethical considerations, presaging what today we might call human rights, play and continue to play a role in the foreign policy of many nations.[6] Different ways through which moral norms influence international relations include the conscience of decision makers, and the influence of domestic public opinion, as well as a country's international reputation.[7] As the experience of the US exemplifies, ethical considerations in the foreign policy of a nation can go on for a long time, all the while lacking in systematization as far as meets the eyes, before congealing into "a pattern of persistent principled politics" going beyond "episodic altruism" that defines the adoption of a human rights policy.[8] Accordingly, a common streak that runs through the three timeframes analyzed below—the precolonial, colonial, and postcolonial eras—is the influence of ethical considerations, short and shorn so far of a full-blown human rights policy, in Nigeria's external relations.[9]

[5] Mark R. Amstutz, *International Ethics: Concepts, Theories, and Cases in Global Politics* (Lanham, MD: Rowland & Littlefield Publishers, 1999), 2.

[6] See ibid., p. xv (identifying the role of moral values in foreign policy, and the ethical foundation of the rules and structures of global society as two dimensions of international political morality); ibid., pp. 1–25 (commenting on the influence on morality in foreign policy); and ibid., pp. 47–69 (analyzing "the role of ethical traditions").

[7] Robert W. McElroy, *Morality and American Foreign Policy* (Princeton, NJ: Princeton University Press, 1992), 30.

[8] Alison Brysk, *Global Good Samaritans: Human Rights as Foreign Policy* (New York: Oxford University Press, 2009), 3. It was not until 1976, under the presidency of Jimmy Carter, backed by a Congress controlled by the Democratic Party and public support from a country, chastened by the turbulence of US's involvement in the long war in Vietnam, and the Watergate scandal, that these ethical concerns crystallized into full-scale human rights policy. Philip C. Aka, "The *Country Reports on Human Rights Practices* and U.S. Human Rights Policy in a Changing World," *Perspectives on Global Development and Technology*, 14 (2015), 240.

[9] The reference to ethics is consistent with the definition of human rights as ethical precepts. See Philip C. Aka, "Analyzing U.S. Commitment to Socioeconomic Human Rights," *Akron Law Review*, 39 (2006), 417, 423 (defining human rights as "international ethical standards that uphold, as a birthright, the minimum thresholds individuals and communities everywhere require to live in dignity and to realize their potentials").

Precolonial Era

Modern-day Nigeria came into existence in 1914 when three territories previously maintained separately by Britain—the Northern Protectorate, Southern Protectorate, and the Colony of Lagos—were consolidated into one entity in a process the consolidators and many Nigerian historians till today call "the amalgamation."[10] Nigeria is a "new state" superimposed on numerous "old societies"[11]; the period before then, dating back more than 5,000 years, constitute the country's precolonial era.[12] Specifically, present-day Nigeria is a multinational state with over 250 ethnic

[10] See Dapo Fafowora, "Lord Lugard and the 1914 Amalgamation of Nigeria," *Nation* (February 28, 2013), http://thenationonlineng.net/lord-lugard-and-the-1914-amalgamation-of-nigeria-2/; and F.D. Lugard and A.H.M. Kirk-Greene, *Lugard and the Amalgamation of Nigeria: A Documentary Record* (London: Cass, 1968). See also Chapter 1, notes 37–63, and accompanying texts ("Introducing Nigeria").

[11] Clifford Geertz, ed., *Old Societies and New States: The Quest for Modernity in Asia and Africa* (New York: Free Press of Glencoe, 1963). Prior to European engagement, societies in Nigeria and other parts of Africa witnessed the emergence of states as well as attained a certain level of technological development and capacity. See Osita C. Eze, *Human Rights in Africa: Some Selected Problems* (Lagos: Nigerian Institute of International Affairs and Macmillan Nigeria, 1984), 10; Ignatius Akaayar Ayua and Dakas C.J. Dakas, "Federal Republic of Nigeria," in *Constitutional Origins, Structure, and Change in Federal Countries*, eds. John Kincaid and George Alan Tarr (Montreal, Canada: McGill-Queen's University Press, 2005), 240 (observing that "[p]recolonial Nigeria consisted of a bewildering variety of communities and entities of varying sizes, levels of political and social development, and degrees of independence and autonomy [...]; at no time before the British arrived was Nigeria even loosely ruled by one government."); International Crisis Group, *Nigeria: Want in the Midst of Plenty*, Africa Report No. 113 (July 19, 2006), 5 (pointing out that "[t]he boundaries of present-day Nigeria contain a prodigious variety of historical political units, social orders, economies, and cultures"). Little wonder that some scholars consider the independence of African countries in the second half of the twentieth century as "reestablishment" of an original independence lost following European "conquest" of these societies. See Herbert Ekwe-Ekwe, *Biafra Revisited* (Dakar, Senegal: African Renaissance, 2006), 18 (viewing Nigeria's independence in 1960 as "the reestablishment of independence for its various peoples, after 60 years of British conquest and occupation"); and Ibrahim A. Gambari, *Party Politics and Foreign Policy: Nigeria under the First Republic* (Zaria, Nigeria: Ahmadu Bello University Press, Ltd., 1980), 7 (depicting a cluster of indigenous independent states at the point of contact which "experienced the advent of the Europeans first as traders, then as explorers and missionaries, and finally as rulers").

[12] See Elizabeth Isichei, *A History of the Igbo People* (New York: Palgrave Macmillan, 1976), 3 ("[M]en have been living in Igboland for at least [5,000] years. One of the most notable factors of Igbo history is its length and continuity.").

groups, and language groups double that number.[13] Therefore, discussion on human rights in precolonial Nigeria boils down ultimately to ethical practices prevalent among ethnic groups, conveniently the major ones, within the areas that formed modern-day Nigeria. Three of the most populous groups are the Igbo in the East, the Yoruba in the West, and the Hausa-Fulani in the North.[14] This "ethnic triumvirate" makes up about two-thirds of the country's population.[15] The Hausa-Fulani had a highly-centralized system centered on Emirs who combined political and religious powers in a system marked by few checks and balances.[16] In contrast, Igbo societies were kingless communities, who organized themselves into about 2,000 villages, marked by decentralized political powers.[17] "[M]onarchical and hierarchically structured and centralized

[13] See "Nigeria," in *Ethnologue: Languages of the World,* 17th Ed., ed. M. Paul Lewis (SIL International, 2010), http://www.ethnologue.com/country/NG (listing the number of individual languages in the country as 527, of which 514 are living and 11 extinct).

[14] See A. Carl LeVan and Oladimeji Aborisade, "Politics in Nigeria," in *Comparative Politics Today: A World View*, 11th Ed., eds. G. Bingham Powell, Jr. et al. (New York: Pearson 2014), 633–634; and Donald Terfa Gaadi, "Ethnic Groups and Geo-Political Regions in Nigeria," *Eagle Reporters* (Abuja) (December 28, 2013), http://eaglereporters.com/2013/12/28/ethnic-group-and-geo-political-region-in-nigeria-by-donald-terfa/.

[15] Larry Diamond, "Nigeria: The Uncivic Society and the Descent into Praetorianism," in *Politics in Developing Countries: Comparing Experiences with Democracy*, 2d Ed., eds. Larry Diamond et al. (Boulder, CO: Lynne Rienner, 1995), 419. Each of these groups has a population that runs into tens of millions. See Larry Diamond, "Nigeria: Pluralism, Statism, and the Struggle for Democracy," in *Democracy in Developing Countries: Africa*, Vol. 2, eds. Larry Diamond et al. (Boulder, CO: Lynne Rienner Publishers, 1988), 35, Table 2.1 (listing the populations of ten major ethnic groups alphabetically: Edo, Fulani, Hausa, Ibibio-Efik, Igbo, Ijaw, Kanuri, Nupe, Tiv, and Yoruba). Many of the remaining more than 200 groups are small, some of them numbering only in the tens of thousands. Philip C. Aka, "Prospects for Igbo Human Rights in Nigeria in the New Century," *Howard Law Journal*, 48(1) (2004), 165, 180, n.87.

[16] Oyediji O. Babatunde, "Hausa/Fulani Pre-Colonial Political System in Nigeria," *Word Press* (March 30, 2014), http://www.profseunoyediji.wordpress.com/2014/03/30/hausafulani-pre-colonial-political-system-in-nigeria (characterizing the Emir as an "absolute ruler" who exercised his authority unrestrained by any "principle of checks and balance").

[17] See Elizabeth Isichei, *The Ibo People and the Europeans: The Genesis of a Relationship—To 1906* (New York: St. Martin's Press, 1973), 47; and Elizabeth Isichei, *A History of Christianity in Africa: From Antiquity to the Present* (Grand Rapids, MI: Wm. B. Eerdmans Publishing, 1995), 155.

with some measure of republicanism," the Yoruba represented a midpoint between the Hausa-Fulani and the Igbo.[18]

Complexity surrounds the search for human rights in precolonial Nigeria, mostly because of the paucity of available data related to this era.[19] A temptation is to regard this period as an era of pre-rights when humans lived "in small tribes" isolated from outsiders whom they perceive as possible threat to survival.[20] After all, as the human rights scholar Chidi Odinkalu points out, some African languages lack the term *human rights*.[21] Add to these the fact that understanding of human rights in the sense we know it today as "the rights of all people, and of all people equally,"[22] is an occurrence of recent vintage that goes back to the end of World War II with the inauguration of the UN.[23] As Pope Francis averred in a different context, "it is difficult to judge the past by the criteria of the present."[24]

[18] Mojeed Olujinmi A. Alabi, "Law Making in Pre-Colonial Yorubaland," in *The Yoruba in Transition: History, Values, and Modernity*, eds. Toyin Falola and Ann Genova (Durham, NC: Carolina Academic Press, 2006), 122.

[19] Part of the reason for the occurrence, as Professor Eze points out, is that, except for portions that came under Islamic influence, African customary law is oral, rather than written. Eze, note 11, p. 9. Related to this factor, much of what available information that exists is derived from colonial laws and practices that either confirm or abrogate precolonial practices. Ibid.

[20] Chip Pitts, "'Mobilizing Shame' Can Bring Abuses Up Short," *Topeka Capital-Journal* (March 11, 2005), http://cjonline.com/stories/031105/opi_pitts.shtml (tribute to Peter Benenson, founder of Amnesty International, upon his death that year).

[21] Chidi A. Odinkalu, "Why More Africans Don't Use Human Rights Language," *Human Rights Dialog*, 2 (December 1999), www.carnegiecouncil.org/publications/archive/dialogue/2_01/articles/602.html (pointing out that "in some African languages there is no direct equivalent to the phrase 'human rights'").

[22] R. J. Vincent, *Human Rights and International Relations* (New York: Cambridge University Press, 1986), 136.

[23] See Karen A. Mingst and Margaret P. Karns, *The United Nations in the 21st Century*, 4th Ed. (Boulder, CO: Westview Press, 2012), 197–246 (commenting on the role of the United Nations in human rights); and Louis Henkin, "Human Rights: Ideology and Aspiration, Reality and Prospect," in *Realizing Human Rights: Moving from Inspiration to Impact*, eds. Samantha Power and Graham Allison (New York: St. Martin's Press, 2000), 17–18 (including the UN as one of six forces responsible for the emergence, survival, and flourishing of international human rights "as a shared ideology in the latter half of the twentieth century").

[24] Pope Francis, Text of Address to a Joint Session of the US Congress (September 24, 2015), http://www.politico.com/story/2015/09/pope-francis-speech-to-congress-transcript-text-video-214016 (commenting on the (mis)treatment of Native Americans, of

However, the matter is more complicated than it seems at first sight. "Although in some African languages there is no direct equivalent to the phrase 'human rights,'" both the notion of justice that underlies human rights and the experience of struggle to realize these rights are well known to Africa.[25] This is because with or without the formal language of human rights, individuals and communities "will struggle for their rights."[26] Accordingly, some societies in the areas subsequently brought together as Nigeria promoted as well as violated approximations or simulacrums of these rights.[27]

Take the Igbo as example.[28] On the one hand, precolonial Igbo communities "organized themselves into village democracies, over 2,000 in all, where they practiced a direct democracy characterized by a system of checks and balances, the pursuit of consensus through protracted discussion, the use of religious sanctions, and political institutions designed to combine popular participation with weighting for experience, among other features."[29] As the historian Elizabeth Isichei recounted in her work on Igbo history, "[o]ne of the things that struck the first Western visitors to Igboland, was the extent to which democracy was truly practiced."[30] And although in precolonial Igbo societies, elderly males ran affairs, "there was also much scope for individual mobility, and political participation was open to many, including women."[31] On the other hand, these societies also perpetrated practices that today would militate against human rights. These derogations include human sacrifice, trial by

whom His Holiness observed that "[t]ragically, the rights of those who were here [in the US] long before us were not always respected[;]" instead, "[t]hose first contacts were often turbulent and violent").

[25] Odinkalu, note 21.

[26] Ibid.

[27] See Eze, note 11, *passim*.

[28] For more on this group, see Aka, "Prospects for Igbo Human Rights in Nigeria in the New Century," note 15, pp. 177–184 ("[t]he Igbo People and Nation").

[29] Ibid., p. 177 (internal quotes omitted).

[30] Isichei, *The Ibo People and the Europeans*, note 17, p. 21.

[31] Aka, "Prospects for Igbo Human Rights in Nigeria in the New Century," note 15, pp. 177–178 (internal quotes omitted).

ordeal, rampant kidnapping, twin killings, and maintenance of the *osu* caste system.[32]

Of the last, one commentator elaborated that the practice "involves inequality in freedom of movement and choice of residence, inequality in the right of peaceful association, inequality of residence, in[e]quality in the right of peaceful association, inequality in the enjoyment of the right to marry and establish a family, [and] inequality in access to public office."[33] The practice was abolished in Eastern Nigeria in 1956, though the law did not change attitude in some communities where the discrimination lingered.[34] However, Nigeria's 1999 Constitution forbids discrimination against individuals based on circumstances of birth, by interpretation including any caste system.[35]

Not all Igbo communities perpetrated these derogations.[36] Moreover, some of these practices, such as human sacrifice, trial by order, and rampant kidnapping, were occurrences associated with the slave trade.[37] In sum, using the Igbo as example, it is fair to conclude on the note of Professor Eze's calibrated assessment to the effect that, while societies in precolonial Nigeria, like elsewhere in Africa, "witness[ed] some measure of *concern* for human rights," they "did not go far enough" in *protecting* these rights.[38]

[32] Eze, note 10, pp. 9–14 (covering the pre-colonial period); and Isichei, *The Ibo People and the Europeans,* note 17, pp. 59–60.

[33] Tony Uchenna, "Osu Caste in Igboland," *Vanguard* (Lagos) (October 9, 2010), http://www.vanguardngr.com/2010/10/osu-caste-in-igboland/. See also Andrew Walker, "The Story of Nigeria's 'Untouchables,'" *BBC News* (April 7, 2009), http://news.bbc.co.uk/2/hi/africa/7977734.stm.

[34] E.I. Nwogugu, *Family Law in Nigeria* (Ibadan, Nigeria: HEBN Publishers, 2014), 65.

[35] Ibid., citing art. 42(2) which stipulates that "no citizen of Nigeria shall be subjected to any disability or deprivation merely by reason of the circumstances of his birth."

[36] Eze, note 11, p. 13. Some Igbo communities killed twins in the superstitious belief that their existence brings evil or back luck. Ibid. But there were also Igbo communities who did not. Such was the case in Enugu-Ezike, a town near Nsukka in northern Igbo, whose indigenes regarded twin and multiple births "as symbol of good luck and fortune." Gloria Chuku, "Olaudah Equiano and the Foundation of Igbo Intellectual Tradition," in *The Igbo Intellectual Tradition: Creative Conflict in African and African Diasporic Thought*, ed. Gloria Chuku (New York: Palgrave Macmillan, 2013), 62, n.64.

[37] Isichei, *The Ibo People and the Europeans*, note 17, pp. 59–60.

[38] Eze, note 11, p. 228.

Colonial Era

British control of Nigeria took place from the late nineteenth century until the country's independence in 1960. Although European colonial authorities justified some of their imperialist activities in Africa on human rights grounds,[39] colonial control marked a frontal assault on every category of human rights—political and civil (or political-civil) rights; economic, social, and cultural (or socioeconomic) rights; and collective (or group) rights.[40] Repressive practices like forced labor, forced taxation, and the use of sedition laws as a weapon designed to stamp out opposition to foreign rule and impede the evolution of a free press marked its negation of political-civil rights.[41] Colonial governance was also an attack on socioeconomic rights because foreign rule is inconsistent with any meaningful notion of economic development.[42] Instead, in Nigeria and other dependent territories, European colonialism sowed the seed for distortion of economic life that till date many of these societies have yet to overcome.[43] As Professor Isichei observed concerning the paucity of British socioeconomic human rights benefits in Eastern Nigeria, "the important thing to the historian of Igboland is the sobering reflection that after half

[39] One such ironic occurrence was the Berlin Conference in 1885 where European countries formalized the partition of African territories among themselves, with the US there as witness to ensure its interests were protected. What made the conference and the partitioned that it occasioned ironic were that they were premised on human rights embedded in the abolition of the slave trade. See Matthew Craven, "Between Law and History: The Berlin Conference of 1884–1885 and the Logic of Free Trade," *London Review of International Law*, 3(2015), 31–59; U. Oji Umozurike, *The African Charter on Human and Peoples' Rights* (Leiden, Netherlands: Brill, 1997), 20; and Frederick J.D. Lugard, *The Dual Mandate in British Tropical Africa* (London: Frank Cass & Co., 1922) (self-serving narrative by Nigeria's former governor-general and major brain behind the creation of the country that recounts the supposed benefits of British rule in Nigeria).

[40] For an explanation of the various categories of human rights, see Philip C. Aka, "Fidel Castro and Socioeconomic Human Rights in Africa," *Fordham International Law Journal*, 43(1) (2019), 41, 47–50.

[41] Philip C. Aka, "The Military, Globalization, and Human Rights in Africa," *Journal of Human Rights*, 18 (2002), 380, 382.

[42] Ibid., p. 381.

[43] See Eze, note 11, p. 228 (observing that European colonialism in Africa left in place "[i]nstitutional structures [designed] to serve the predatory interests of the colonial powers" which till today "continue to impose major obstacles" to economic development of many African states).

a century of colonial rule and mission, over 80 [percent] of the population was illiterate."[44]

Lastly, colonial rule contradicted collective rights because foreign rule violated the right of people to determine their destiny for themselves rather than have foreigners do so for them.[45] During World War II, British Prime Minister Winston S. Churchill opposed extending to Nigeria and other British colonies the self-determination concept embedded in the Atlantic Charter of 1941,[46] on the ground that these colonies were not "sovereign," compared to countries like Poland occupied by Nazi-ruled Germany, which were accorded the right.[47] In contrast, President Franklin D. Roosevelt, with whom Churchill signed the Atlantic Charter, seemed committed to the dismantling of all colonial empires, including those held by the UK because of the conditions that lead to war the colonial system represented.[48] Therefore, the "wind of change" in nationalism

[44] Isichei, *The Ibo People and the Europeans*, note 17, p. 199.

[45] Aka, "The Military, Globalization, and Human Rights in Africa," note 41, p. 381. See also Eze, note 11, p. 228 (observing that "[t]he civilizing mission of colonialism was [...] antithetical to human rights" and "[i]ts racist overtone compounded other forms of discrimination that existed in Africa").

[46] The Atlantic Charter is an eight-point agreement between Churchill and US President Franklin D. Roosevelt regarding the goals of their two countries (and the Allied Group) for World War II and their collective vision of the world after that conflict. See "Atlantic Charter" (August 14, 1941), http://avalon.law.yale.edu/wwii/atlantic.asp. The third of these "common principles" was "respect[ing] the right of all peoples to choose the form of government under which they will live" and restoring "sovereign rights and self-government" "to those who have been forcibly deprived of" these guarantees. Ibid.

[47] Henkin, "Human Rights: Ideology and Aspiration, Reality and Prospect," note 23, p. 7 (noting that "[t]he ideology of rights was not encouraged in, and did not spread to, to the colonies of the British and French empires"); J.A.A. Ayoade, "Nigeria: Positive Pessimism and Negative Optimism: A Valedictory Lecture," *Nigerian Voice* (September 17, 2010), 5, http://www.thenigerianvoice.com/print/34992/1/nigeria-positive-pessimism-and-negative-optimism-a.html. Lord Moyne, British Colonial Secretary, took the position that self-determination applied only to territories occupied by the Germans because these territories were "not in need of political tutelage." Ibid.

[48] For Franklin D. Roosevelt, the colonial system took wealth from dependent territories without putting anything back into those territories by way of education, healthcare, or jobs, among other guarantees people need for a life of dignity, a deprivation that creates the conditions that lead inevitably to war. Ayoade, note 47, p. 5.

that ultimately reached the shores of these British colonies in Africa[49] occurred *in spite* of British opposition. Instead, "[f]or most of the colonial period the British rulers hardly saw their role as one of producing a cohesive independent state and even when this task was accepted, late in the day, it was indifferently performed."[50]

In sum, against the grain of dignity that underlines the concept of human rights, "[t]he entire architecture of colonial rule, like that of military rule down the road in [Africa], was built and maintained solely and completely on naked force designed to *crush* any and every 'native' resistance to external domination."[51] Europe had little in the way of a human rights plan for its colonies in Africa beyond their use as sources of raw materials for European industrialization and as markets for excess outputs. As opposed to being vehicles for promoting human rights, European colonial institutions were primarily "structures of exploitation, despotism, and degradation"[52]; colonialism, wherever it existed in Africa, was something "imposed by violence, and maintained by its potential capacity for violence."[53]

There is no suggestion that every aspect of British rule in Nigeria was unrelievedly evil, given the existence of certain positive features with ramifications for human rights from the experience. First, British rule injected

[49] This refers to a speech at the South African Parliament in Cape Town on February 3, 1960, wherein Harold Macmillan, British Prime Minister from 1957 to 1963, indicated that his government recognized the "growth of national consciousness" sweeping through Africa as "a political fact." Harold Macmillan, Speech at the South African Parliament, Cape Town, http://www.bbc.co.uk/archive/apartheid/7203.shtml (video). Macmillan declared, "The wind of change is blowing through this continent. Whether we like it or not, this growth of national consciousness, is a political fact." Ibid. A highlight of his tour of British colonies in Africa starting January 6 of that year, including stopovers in Ghana, and Nigeria, the speech, acknowledged, *inter alia*, that the campaigns for self-rule by still-dependent Africans were legitimate and that the British government had a responsibility to promote the creation of societies that uphold the rights of citizens. "'Wind of Change' Speech," *About*, http://africanhistory.about.com/od/eraindependence/a/wind_of_change1.htm.

[50] John A. Wiseman, *Democracy in Black Africa: Survival and Revival* (Salt Lake City, UT: Paragon, 1990), 93.

[51] Aka, "The Military, Globalization, and Human Rights in Africa," note 41, p. 379. Emphasis added.

[52] Robert Fatton, Jr., "Liberal Democracy in Africa," *Political Science Quarterly*, 105 (1990), 457.

[53] Isichei, Isichei, *The Ibo People and the Europeans*, note 17, p. 119.

a "capitalist mode of production and the principles of liberal democracy" that inspired subsequent economic and political developments in Nigeria and other British colonies.[54] Secondly, British rule eliminated precolonial practices, with negative ramifications for human rights, such as human sacrifices, trial by ordeal, rampant kidnapping, twin-killings, and the operation of a caste system,[55] some of which, like the first three, are traceable to the slave trade,[56] which the colonial system replaced. Thirdly, uniquely for Nigeria, the benefits of colonial rule included the creation of a big state with the potential to play a major role in international relations, including international human rights.

Due to these serendipities, at independence in 1960, Nigeria had all the features and trappings of a democratic state that, for many commentators, made it "a beacon of hope for democracy" in Africa.[57] These features included a federal constitution, one of few in Africa, that guaranteed a measure of autonomy to three regions, increased to four in 1963; a parliamentary democracy on the British Westminster model, based on majority rule; bill of rights embedded in a constitutional document that calls to mind the American constitution; and a regional, multiparty system, that set the country apart from many African countries that adopted a one-party system soon after independence.[58] Finally, under British tutelage, Nigeria made important strides in constitutionalism,[59] including the

[54] Eze, note 11, p. 229.

[55] Isichei, *The Ibo People and the Europeans*, note 17, pp. 59–60; Eze, note 11, p. 229.

[56] Isichei, *The Ibo People and the Europeans*, note 17, pp. 59–60.

[57] "The First Republic," in *Nigeria: A Country Study*, ed. Helen Chapin Metz (Washington, DC: GPO for the Library of Congress, 1991), https://countrystudies.us/nigeria/68.htm.

[58] See ibid.

[59] Under British rule, Nigeria witnessed the production and unveiling of five quasi-constitutions, each named after the British administrator who introduced it: the Lugard Constitution of 1914 amalgamating the country, Clifford's Constitution of 1922, the Richard's Constitution of 1946, the McPherson Constitution of 1951, and the Littleton Constitution of 1954 setting up the country's federal system of government. Anthony Kirk-Greene, "The Remedial Imperatives of the Nigerian Constitution, 1922–1992," in *Transition Without End: Nigerian Politics and Civil Society under Babangida*, eds. Larry Diamond et al. (Boulder, CO: Lynne Rienner, 1997), 31.

growth of political parties,[60] some of which, revealingly, had their origins in opposition to British foreign rule.

But there were also several downsides to colonial rule that over time has defied easy resolution. First, following the forced amalgamated of incompatible ethnic groups with no prior history of living together, British colonial authorities made little attempt to create a coherent country out of these disparate groups.[61] Professor Ayoade described Nigeria's birth in 1914 variously as an "amalgamation without integration" aimed mainly at "freeing the British treasury of the financial responsibility for Northern Nigeria" in a manner that invokes the analogy of a "prisoner pa[ying] "for his own handcuffs."[62] He likened British indirect rule experiment in the country to a "LEGO, a line of construction toys consisting of colorful interlocking plastic blocks[,]" so un-tightly "assembled to require more than a child's effort to separate and re-assemble to make other objects."[63]

Second, related to this first factor, British rule engendered domination by the north. Implementation of British "indirect rule" in Nigeria created a system that insulated the Islamic North from the "corruption" of the South.[64] The insulation included restriction of missionary activities with the accompanying educational benefits those activities brought along, an occurrence which stunted educational growth in the North vis-à-vis the South.[65] Moreover, British rule engendered preferences for Fulanis, reeked of racism, that some analysts called "British-supervised indigenous or internal colonialism."[66] British writers and administrators repeatedly referred to the Fulani as ruler race in glowing terms that included "capable race," "European in form," "races higher than the negroid type," and "races born to conquer."[67] With British support, rather than dissuasion, in the lead up to independence, northern leaders in

[60] See Richard L. Sklar, *Nigerian Political Parties: Power in an Emergent African Nation* (Princeton, NJ: Princeton University Press, 1963), *passim*.

[61] See Ayoade, note 47, pp. 2–3.

[62] Ibid., p. 2.

[63] Ibid., p. 3.

[64] Ibid.

[65] Ibid.

[66] Ayoade, note 47, p. 12.

[67] Ibid.

two conferences (one at Ibadan in 1950 and another in London in 1953), made demands for autonomy,[68] which reinforced northern domination in the period after independence.

These concessions, inconsistent with the theory of federalism, included assignment of 50% of the seats in the national legislature and a separate public service.[69] The advantages were codified in the Lyttleton Constitution of 1954 which created a federal arrangement for the country where the Northern Region had more seats in the national legislature than the Eastern and Western Regions combined.[70] Since independence, northern leaders have striven hard to maintain these advantages, to the detriment of nation-building and national integration.[71]

Even the positive contributions of colonial rule over time turned up to be dubious. For example, some commentators, including surviving British public servants who saw colonial service in Nigeria, have wondered whether the experiment of forcibly transmuting disagreeable ethnic groups into one mega-state as the UK did in Nigeria was a good idea.[72] Similarly, the model of constitutional development bequeathed to Nigeria from British colonial rule has come under question because of its slowness in generating the habit of constitutionalism and the culture of the rule of law among the citizenry of the country.[73] For these various reasons, while there is no question regarding "the influence of human rights ideas" at

[68] See Adisa Adeleye, "The Old and the New: Which Way Forward?" *Vanguard* (Lagos) (November 15, 2013), http://www.vanguardngr.com/2013/11/old-new-way-forward/ (enumerating the eight-point demand of northern leaders in 1953).

[69] Ibid.

[70] See Eghosa E. Osaghae, *The Crippled Giant: Nigeria since Independence* (Bloomington, IN: Indiana University Press, 1998), 6.

[71] Ibid.

[72] See Idowu Ajanaku, "Ex-Colonial Officer Faults Amalgamation of Nigeria," *Guardian* (Lagos) (April 28, 2005), cited in Ekwe-Ekwe, note 11, p. 18, n.1 (reporting the confession of Peter Smithers, a former colonial official to the effect that, in retrospect, the amalgamation "was a grave mistake which has cost many lives and will probably continue to do so," including the conviction of this official that "[i]t should have been better to establish several smaller states in a free trade area").

[73] See Kirk-Greene, note 59 (contrasting the "remedial" system consisting of the unveiling of numerous constitutions that are created and quickly discarded utilized in the country vis-à-vis the US system of one document with piecemeal amendments as the need arises for change); Ayoade, note 47, p. 3 (noting that Nigerian constitutionalism "did not match the growth of the Nigerian territory" and that "most of the colonial constitutional reforms de-emphasized the essence of corporate existence of Nigerians").

home and abroad in dismantling the British colonial system,[74] ultimately making way for Nigeria's independence, in the final analysis, given its abstruse and diffuse nature, that influence seems more apparent than real.

Postcolonial Era: Survey of Five Distinctive Periods Encompassing Sixteen Governments

Dependency status is inconsistent with conduct of foreign policy. Nigeria shed that status when it gained independence on October 1, 1960, sealing the achievement with admission into the UN on October 7, 1960, as the 99th member of the organization.[75] Accordingly, compared to the colonial era, the postcolonial era—ushered in by independence in 1960, and capped by severance of the ligament of ties to the British monarchy through the achievement of republican status three years later—afforded Nigerian leaders the opportunity, hitherto lacking, to design and implement an indigenous foreign policy.[76] To restate, five periods mark this era: the First Republic spanning over five years from 1960 to 1966, the first round of military rule spanning thirteen years from 1966 to 1979, the Second Republic lasting little more than four years from 1979 to 1983, the second round of military rule spanning over fifteen years from 1983 to 1999, and the Fourth Republic since 1999 going on now for more than twenty-four years as of this book (Table 3.1).

[74] Jack Donnelly, "An Overview," in *Human Rights and Comparative Foreign Policy*, ed. David P. Forsythe (New York: United Nations University Press, 2000), 313 (attributing the dismantling of the British colonial empire partly to "the influence of human rights ideas" in both the home country and the colony); and Neta C. Crawford, *Argument and Change in World Politics: Ethics, Decolonization, and Humanitarian Intervention* (New York: Cambridge University Press, 2002), 2, 388 (pinpointing human rights as a factor in the demise of slavery and colonialism which prompted "the biggest change in the structure and practice of international relations in the last 500 years").

[75] S. O. Akinboye, "Beautiful Abroad but Ugly at Home: Issues and Contra[di]ctions in Nigeria's Foreign Policy," University of Lagos Inaugural Lecture Series (2013), www.unilag.edu.ng/opendocnew.php?.

[76] The opportunity to design an indigenous policy calls to mind Kwame Nkrumah's notion of "African Personality." Nkrumah declared, "For too long in our history, Africa has spoken through the voices of others. Now, what I have called an African Personality in international affairs will have a chance of making its proper impact and will let the world know it through the voices of Africa's own sons." Quoted in Olayiwola Abegunrin, *Africa in Global Politics in the Twenty-First Century: A Pan-African Perspective* (New York: Palgrave Macmillan, 2009), 1.

Within these five periods, sixteen administrations have piloted Nigeria's foreign policy ("leader" column, Table 3.1). Four of the periods comprised multiple political chief executives, while two, the brief First Republic and the even shorter Second Republic, featured only one leader each. Testament to the spate of instability that marks Nigeria's politics since independence, nine out of the sixteen governments from the womb of these periods, amounting to 56% of the lot or nearly 6 out of 10 cases, ended inauspiciously: assassination of the leader in question during a military coup (Balewa, Aguiyi-Ironsi, and Muhammed), death in office (Abacha, and Yar'Adua), forced resignation (Babangida, and Shonekan), and the interim or transitional nature of the regime in question (Obasanjo as military head of state, Shonekan, and Abubakar). The discussion that follows is a survey of the sixteen governments ensconced in five distinctive periods. Before then, a commentary on the three concentric circles of Nigerian foreign policy, followed by a statement on the influence of the civil war on those circles.

Three Concentric Circles of Nigerian Foreign Policy

Concentric circles are two or more circles, from inside to outside, with the same center point. Three concentric circles and their intersection, powered by events at home, which drive Nigerian foreign policy endeavors are: West Africa, Africa, and the larger world (or international community) (see Table 3.2). The brainchild for this concept is credited to Oko Arikpo, Nigeria's external affairs minister from 1967 to 1975.[77] Focus on West Africa reflects an awareness that Nigeria's security is tied

[77] The notion of "concentric circles" in Nigeria's foreign policy was developed under Okoi Arikpo, external affairs minister from 1967 to 1975. Keith Campbell, Nigerian Foreign Policy and the Economic Community of West African States (ECOWAS), Occasional Paper, South African Institute of International Affairs (September 1978), 1. Different authors sketch these circles differently. See, for example, Ibrahim Gambari, "From Balewa to Obasanjo: The Theory and Practice of Nigeria's Foreign Policy," in *Gulliver's Troubles: Nigeria's Foreign Policy after the Cold War*, eds. Adekeye Adebajo and Abdul Raufu Mustapha (Scottsville, South Africa: University of Kwazulu-Natal Press, 2008), 58–80 (sketching four concentric circles comprising: a first circle of four immediate neighbors; a second circle revolved around relations with the Economic Community of West African States (ECOWAS); a third circle focused on Africa; and a fourth with states and organizations outside Africa); and "Foreign Relations," in *Nigeria: A Country Study*, note 57 (sketching four, without explicitly using the term concentric circles, comprising relations with neighboring states, relations with the rest of Africa, relations with major

Table 3.2 Recap on three concentric circles that power Nigeria's external relations

Item no	*Circle*	*Moving forces*
1	West Africa	Belief that Nigeria's security is inescapably tied to that of its neighbor, a recognition that undergirded Nigeria's leadership role in the formation of ECOWAS
2	Africa	The focus is dictated by the notion of Nigeria as "giant of Africa" and embodied in the portraiture of Africa as "centerpiece" of Nigerian foreign policy that, in the post-decolonization period, Nigerian leaders have struggled to invest with new meaning
3	International community	Covers everything else not in the first two circles in pursuit of true nonalignment beyond the capitalist world, drawing from the lessons of the civil war

to that of its neighbors,[78] beginning with its five immediate neighbors, Cameroon, Chad, Niger, Benin, and Togo,[79] and encompassing other ECOWAS countries.[80] The logic behind deepening relations with immediate neighbors, as one Nigerian ambassador put it, is that "while we can choose our friends, we cannot choose our neighbors."[81] To the extent that it featured at all in Nigerian foreign policy, before 1975, the West African sub-region was subsumed within the Africa circle.

The next concentric circle is Africa. The common expression used to convey this notion is the portraiture of Africa as "centerpiece" of Nigerian

powers, and relations with international organizations). To keep things simple, this book stays with three concentric circles.

[78] Campbell, note 77.

[79] Nigeria shares 1,500 km of land border in the North with Niger and Chad, about 1,000 km in the West with Benin, 1,700 km in the East with Cameroon, and 700 km of Atlantic coastlines in the South. Victor A.O. Adetula, "Between National Security Considerations and the Challenge of Cross-Border Crime in West Africa," in *Governance and Border Security in Africa*, eds. Celestine Oyom Bassey and Oshita D. Oshita (Lagos: Malthouse Press Ltd., 2010), 300.

[80] Only the last three states are members of ECOWAS; the first two, Cameroon and Chad, are not. The community is covered in Chapter 6 within the context of peacekeeping.

[81] Ambassador Olugbenga Ashiru, Seminar to Review Nigeria's Foreign Policy (July 28, 2011), http://www.mfa.gov.ng/news_one.php?article=41.

foreign policy.[82] Put differently, the country's "engagement in the international system will be looked at through the binoculars of Africa."[83] It is a concept borne out of the related notion of Nigeria as the "giant" of Africa, meaning that as the most populous country in Africa and the entire black world, Nigeria perceives itself as the potential leader of the black world.[84] It is a position the early shapers of Nigerian foreign policy, civilian and military alike, agreed on. These shapers include Prime Minister Abubakar T. Balewa, and Jaja Wachuku, first Speaker of the House of Representatives and first Foreign Minister.

Balewa declared that "[o]n the question of colonialism and racial discrimination, I am afraid that we in Nigeria will never compromise."[85] Wachuku posited that "the whole black continent is looking up to this country to liberate it from thralldom. The whole negroid race is looking up to Nigeria to be free from slavery."[86] But the "expectation" witnessed

[82] See Adebayo Adedeji, *Report of the Committee on the Review of Nigerian Foreign Policy, Including Economic and Technical Cooperation* (Lagos: Government Printer, 1976), *passim*.

[83] Atah Pine, "Nigerian Foreign Policy, 1960–2011: Fifty Years of Conceptual Confusion," *Modern Ghana* (October 4, 2011), http://www.modernghana.com/print/354264/1/nigeria-foreign-policy-1960-2011-fifty-one-years-o.html.

[84] "Foreign Relations," in *Nigeria: A Country Study*, note 57.

[85] Quoted in Abegunrin, note 76, p.5. In retrospect, the focus on Africa was an outlook that predated Nigeria's independence and an accent that many other African leaders shared. For example, in his "midnight" address to mark the achievement of Ghana's independence on March 5, 1957, Dr. Kwame Nkrumah stated that "our [Ghana's] independence is meaningless unless it is linked up with the total liberation of the African continent." "Kwame Nkrumah's Vision," BBC World Service (September 14, 2000), www.bbc.co.uk/worldservice/people/highlights/000914_nkrumah.shtml. Subsequently, this principle found its way into the Charter of the Organization of African Unity (OAU). One of the principles of the organization is "absolute dedication to the total emancipation" of still dependent African territories. OAU, Charter of the Organization of African Unity, 479 U.N.T.S. 39 (entered into force September 13, 1963), http://www1.umn.edu/humanrts/africa/OAU_Charter_1993.html, art. III.6. The idea goes even further back to pan-Africanism, an ideology which stresses the solidarity and common destiny of black people, irrespective of where they make their home. See Pine, note 83 (opining that "the ideals of pan-Africanism […] lubricated the wheels of this foreign policy conceptualization."); and P. Olisanwuche Esedebe, *Pan-Africanism: The Idea and Movement 1776–1991,* 2d Ed. (Washington, DC: Howard University Press, 1994) (tracing the roots of Pan-Africanism from the period of the American revolution in 1776 to the early 1990s).

[86] Federal Parliamentary Debate Reports, Independence Motion (January 4, 1960), 89, quoted in Gambari, *Party Politics and Foreign Policy*, note 11, p. 68.

its most robust expression by General Johnson T. Aguiyi-Ironsi, then Head of State who linked the expectation to a "destiny" built on a role in Africa:

> In the whole sphere of Nigeria's external relations, the Government attaches the greatest importance to our African policy. We are aware that because of our population and potentials, the majority of opinion in the civilized world looks up to us to provide responsible leadership in Africa; and we realize that we shall be judged, to a very great extent, by the degree of success or failure with which we face up to this challenge which this expectation throws on us. We are convinced that whether in the political, economic or cultural sphere, our destiny lies in our role in the continent of Africa.[87]

Several issues which give practical expression to this world view include "the remnants of colonialism [in Africa], apartheid in South Africa, liberation war, [as well as] ideological and proxy conflicts."[88] The decolonization of formerly-dependent portions of Africa, initially the Lusophone territories of Angola and Mozambique, Zimbabwe and subsequently Namibia followed by the attainment of Black-majority rule in South Africa in 1994, raises question regarding what is still left of this field of concentration of Nigerian foreign relations.[89] At the risk of over-simplification, emphasis in recent policies on "economic diplomacy," "citizen diplomacy," and related slogans may properly be seen as attempts by different administrations to answer this question.[90]

[87] Johnson T. Aguiyi-Ironsi, Remarks by the Head of State to the Regional Conference of Heads of Missions in Africa, Lagos (June 9, 1966, Cn 1/21/I, 114), cited in John J. Stremlau, *The International Politics of the Nigerian Civil War, 1967–1970* (Princeton, NJ: Princeton University Press, 2015), 3.

[88] Pine, note 83.

[89] See, for example, John Danfulani, "The End of Apartheid: A Redefinition of Nigerian Foreign Policy," *IQSRJ Journal of Humanities & Social Science*, 19(2014), 53–57, http://iosrjournals.org/iosr-jhss/papers/Vol19-issue11/Version-3/I0191135357.pdf. (arguing for the "imperatives of [a] paradigm shift" in Nigeria's Africa-centered foreign policy, given the end of apartheid and the emergence of Black majority rule in South Africa).

[90] Developed in 1987 by General Ike Nwachukwu, foreign minister (1987–1989 and 1990–1993), *economic diplomacy* emerged as a foreign policy theme during the period of General Ibrahim Babangida, Head of State (1985–1993). Under this formula, Nigeria

Last but not least, the larger international community. This circle covers everything else that is not encompassed in the first two categories. In addition to the UN and its affiliated agencies, this category includes the Eastern Europe, Middle East, North America, and Western Europe. On this category, Nigerian foreign policy makers initially focused narrowly on relations with West European countries but subsequently broadened the focus of this category to encompass countries in the former Soviet orbit as Nigeria, after the First Republic, but particularly following the civil war from 1967 to 1970, became more non-aligned in its foreign relations. With the fall of the Soviet Union and demise of what used to be the Eastern bloc, there is pressure for attention in this field of concentration to extend to a much broader spectrum that includes influential players in the global economy, such as Argentina, Brazil, China, India, Mexico, Singapore, and South Korea.[91]

Influence of Nigeria's Civil War on the Three Circles

Although some of the ideas behind these concentric circles predated the catastrophe, the circles mirrored or internalized lessons about foreign policy from the civil war (1967–1970) that successive Nigerian regimes took to heart. The first is that the maintenance of the country as one entity should be the primary purpose of foreign policy, not something to

foreign policy is said to serve the purpose of economic development at home, in a calculated attempt to tackle the parlous state of Nigeria's oil-based economy. See C.N. Ajaebili, "The Option of Economic Diplomacy in Nigeria's Foreign Policy," *International Journal of Humanities & Social Science*, 1 (2011), 277–280, http://www.ijhssnet.com/journals/Vol_1_No_17_Special_Issue_November_2011/30.pdf. Several practical issues the concept embeds include a focus "on export promotion, encouragement of direct foreign investment, debt rescheduling, [and] embracing of neo-liberal economic measures[,]" among others. Pine, note 83. Developed by Ojo Maduekwe, foreign minister (2007–2010) under the administration of Umaru Musa Yar'Adua (2007–2010), *citizen diplomacy* stands for the proposition that "Nigeria's foreign policy will henceforth be focused on [...] Nigerian citizens at home and in [the] [D]iaspora." Monday Dickson, "Citizen Diplomacy in President Umaru Musa Yar'Adua's Nigeria, 2007–2009: An Assessment," *International Journal of Politics & Good Governance*, 1(2010), 1, http://onlineresearchjournals.com/ijopagg/art/59.pdf. Under this worldview, "[t]he country will strive for a synergy between foreign policy and domestic affairs in such a way that the citizen is taken as the focus of foreign policy." Ibid.

[91] See Dapo Fafowora, "Review of Nigeria's Foreign Policy," *Nation* (June 14, 2015), http://thenationonlineng.net/review-of-nigerias-foreign-policy/.

be taken for granted.[92] Second is the need to secure its backyard in West Africa to limit the influence of extra-African powers like France whose close ally Côte d'Ivoire (formerly Ivory Coast) there, at France's instigation, backed Biafrans during the war.[93] Third is the need for strong pan-African institutions necessary to support the country's national security.[94] Last but not least is the need to cultivate extensive ties with major power blocs that extend to Eastern countries (such as the then Soviet Union) rather than limited exclusively to the West.[95]

Over the years, various policy tools Nigerian foreign policy makers have used in implementing these concentric circles include peacekeeping and technical assistance. Beginning with the 1979 Constitution, some of the tools of Nigerian foreign policy have been codified in the Nigerian charter document.[96] The following discussion recounts key events, some pertaining to human rights, that drove Nigerian foreign policies during each of the five periods delineated in Table 3.1.

First Republic, 1960–1966

This period featured only one chief executive, Abubakar T. Balewa, who combined his role as Prime Minister with foreign minister until July

[92] J. Peter Pham, "Nigeria's Foreign Policy: An Inquiry into Sources and Prospects," Paper Prepared for Presentation at an International Conference in Lisbon, Portugal (November 8–9), 95, www.ipri.pt/eventos/pdf/JPeterPham_paper.pdf.

[93] Ibid.

[94] Ibid.

[95] Ibid.

[96] See Constitution of the Fed. Republic of Nigeria 1979, *Constitution Net*, https://constitutionnet.org/vl/item/constitution-federal-republic-nigeria-1979, art. 19 (spelling out the "foreign policy objectives" of the country); and Constitution of the Fed. Republic of Nigeria 1999, *Constitute Project*, https://www.constituteproject.org/constitution/Nigeria_1999, art. 19 (a)-(3).The latter is more elaborate and spells out the objectives to include: promoting and protecting the national interest; promoting African integration and support for African unity; promoting international cooperation for consolidating universal peace and mutual respect among nations; eliminating all forms of discrimination; respect for international law and treaty obligations as well as seeking pacific settlement of international disputes; and promoting a just world economic order.

1961,[97] when he ceded the latter position to Jaja Wachuku,[98] who held the position until 1965.[99] As first political chief executive, Balewa helped shape the early foreign policy of the country.[100] Under him, Nigeria operated a low-quality democracy at home[101] that drove a diplomacy of "uncertainty and timidity" abroad,[102] including a "low-keyed, hesitant, and often apologetic approach to African affairs."[103] On the major issues of the day, Nigeria "did not speak with one voice and when she spoke she leaned toward the West."[104] These issues included a secret defense agreement between the Nigerian government which the Nigerian masses opposed when it came to their notice, the crisis in the Congo, and the

[97] Under the parliamentary system of government modelled after Britain's that Nigeria practiced during the First Republic, a fusion of legislative and executive powers existed wherein the Prime Minister, as leader of the party that won the most or majority seats in the legislature, participated in legislative business in a manner not possible in a presidential system of government (such as the US's), marked by strict separation of the powers of the legislative and executive branches. See, for example, Michael J. Sodaro, *Comparative Politics: A Global Introduction*, 3rd Ed. (Boston, MA: McGraw-Hill Higher Education, 2008), 194–205 (juxtaposing features of the parliamentary and presidential systems).

[98] Courtney Faal, "Balewa, Sir Abubakar Tafawa (1912–1966)," *Black Past*, http://www.blackpast.org/gah/balewa-sir-abubakar-tafawa-1912-1966.

[99] "Wachuku, Jaja Anucha," *S9.com Biographical Dictionary*, http://www.s9.com/Biography/Wachuku-Jaja-Anucha.

[100] Faal, note 98. Following the first military coup in January of 1966, Nigeria abandoned the parliamentary system of government, blamed for some of the instability of the First Republic years, in place of the presidential system of government which it has used in the Second Republic (1979–1983) and in the still ongoing Fourth Republic. See Embassy of the Federal Republic of Nigeria, Washington, DC, "Nigeria: Past, Present[,] and Future," http://www.nigeriaembassyusa.org/index.php?page=nigeria-past-present-and-future.

[101] See Diamond, "Nigeria: Pluralism, Statism, and the Struggle for Democracy," note 15, p. 40 (assessing Nigeria under the First Republic as a "quasi-democracy struggling to establish fully democratic government[,]" given "the shallow commitment of political elites to democratic norms of tolerance and fair play" which made "it difficult to classify Nigeria at independence as a democracy").

[102] Ibrahim A. Gambari, *Theory and Reality in Foreign Policy Making: Nigeria after the Second Republic* (Atlantic Highlands, NJ: Humanities Press International Inc., 1989), 6.

[103] Ibid., p. 7.

[104] Ibid., p. 6.

Arab-Israel conflict, among others.[105] During this period, because what passed for the national government was "a weak coalition of regional and ethnic-based political parties" where the prime minister did not have the power to override divergent groups' encroachments upon Nigeria's foreign policy, the country lacked a "national ideology or even nation-wide political consciousness" to guide the formation and implementation of foreign policy.[106]

Given these policymaking disabilities, Nigeria operated "a nonaligned policy that was in reality pro-West."[107] As Ibrahim Gambari illustrated with some key issues of Nigerian foreign policy, Nigerian ratified, then abrogated, but later retained the basic elements of a contentious defense agreement with Britain; "sent troops to the Congo under the United Nations umbrella without fully supporting Patrice Lumumba, who requested the troops; opted for a weak OAU; negotiated and signed but did not ratify an agreement with the European Economic Community; and professed a 'neutral' federal policy toward the Arabs and Israelis in the Middle East that was actually inoperative in northern Nigeria."[108] Additionally, strange for a supposedly independent state, Prime Minister Balewa reportedly had a practice of asking the British High Commissioner in Nigeria to brief him on foreign policy questions, to the chagrin of oppositions groups in the country.[109] Few of the many signals of the country's pro-Western orientation included Prime Minister Balewa's pledge of the country's eternal friendship with Britain in his inaugural address,[110] and the fact that the official title of the head of

[105] Professor Gambari examined these and other issues in some detail in his *Party Politics and Foreign Policy*, note 11, pp. 33–131 (covering the Anglo-Nigerian Defense Pact, the Congo crisis and relations with Ghana, relations with South Africa and then Rhodesia, the Arab-Israeli conflict, and Nigeria's relations with the then European Economic Community).

[106] Gambari, *Theory and Reality in Foreign Policy Making*, note 102, pp. 6–7.

[107] Ibid., p. 7.

[108] Ibid.

[109] Gambari, *Party Politics and Foreign Policy*, note 11, pp. 50–51.

[110] See Speech of Sir Abubakar Tafawa Balewa (October 1, 1960), *reprinted* in *Black Past* (August 20, 2009), https://www.blackpast.org/global-african-history/1960-sir-abubakar-tawafa-balewa-independence-day/ ("We are grateful to the British officers whom we have known, first as masters, and then as leaders, and finally as partners, but always as friends").

the foreign ministry was Minister of Foreign Affairs and Commonwealth Relations.[111]

Operating under the then-available two concentric circles of Africa and the global community, the Balewa government conducted peacekeeping operation in the Congo (later Zaïre),[112] participated in the anti-apartheid campaign in South Africa,[113] and help found the OAU.[114] During Balewa's period, Nigeria was the first African country to enshrine elaborate fundamental human rights guarantees in its constitution.[115] The occurrence followed the work of the Willink's Commission.[116] However, more accurately, this was an accomplishment predating Balewa that was part of the negotiations in the lead up to independence.

The First Republic ended cataclysmically on January 15, 1966, the result of a bloody coup which claimed the life of Balewa as well as those of a number of the country's other leaders, including ministers and regional leaders.[117] The overthrow of the Balewa government culminated

[111] "Wachuku, Jaja Anucha," note 99.

[112] "The Gowon Regime," in *Nigeria: A Country Study*, note 57 ("By 1964 Nigerian army units, under General Johnson Aguiyi-Ironsi's command, formed the backbone of the UN force").

[113] His government lodged a vocal protest of the massacre in Sharpeville, South Africa, and, working with other countries in the British Commonwealth, attempted to expel South African from the Commonwealth because of its apartheid policies. Faal, note 98.

[114] Ibid.

[115] See "The First Republic," in *Nigeria: A Country Study*, note 57.

[116] Minority ethnic groups in the country expressed the fear that majority groups in their regions would dominate them once the country became independent from the United Kingdom. To look into this fear, in 1957, the British government appointed a commission head by Sir Henry Willink. Rather than recommend the separate regions these minority groups requested as antidote, the Commission took the seemingly middle ground of fundamental guarantees in a constitutional document, which the British authorities, desirous of avoiding any delay in the road to independence, readily accepted. See *Report of the Commission Appointed to Inquire into the Fears of the Minorities and the Means of Allaying Them* (London: Her Majesty's Stationery Office, 1958). In sum, the inclusion of fundamental guarantees, a bill of rights, in the 1960 and subsequent constitutions of Nigeria, including the 1963, 1979, and 1999 constitutions, was because of the Willink Commission which recommended guarantees of human rights, adapted from the European Convention on Human Rights of 1950, in lieu of the separate regions the minority ethnic groups requested.

[117] Works on the first coup, some by participants in the act, include: Adewale Ademoyega, *Why We Struck: The Story of the First Nigerian Coup* (Ibadan, Nigeria: Evans Brothers Ltd., 1981) (participant); and Ben Gbulie, *Nigeria's Five Majors: Coup d'état of*

a succession of crisis that buffeted the country, almost from the moment of independence, that included the persistent troubles and violence in the Western Region, controversies over the accuracy of census figures, a devastating workers' general strike in June 1964, and a dispute over the rigging and other electoral irregularities that marred the conduct of the general elections in 1964, among other troubles.[118] An overarching factor in the demise of the First Republic "was the disproportionate power of the north" in what should have been to be a federal system of more balanced federating units.[119] "The departing colonial authority had hoped that the development of national politics would forestall any sectional domination of power, but it underestimated the effects of a regionalized party system in a country where political power depended on population."[120]

First Round of Military Regimes, 1966–1979

Vis-à-vis the First Republic, this period featured multiple leaders—Johnson A. Aguiyi-Ironsi, Yakubu Gowon, Murtala Muhammed, and Olusegun Obasanjo (see Table 3.1)—testimony to a longer timeframe double that earlier period, even though it does not justify it. Two interrelated developments marked this period. First was a reassessment of Nigeria's diplomacy of uncertainty shrouded in lack of self-assurance under the First Republic. The second, building on the reassessment, was the implementation of an assertive foreign policy that commentators praise as the golden era of Nigerian foreign policy.[121] Despite its brevity, Aguiyi-Ironsi's regime set the tone for the important changes in Nigeria's foreign policy. In June of 1966, under Aguiyi-Ironsi's watch, the country hosted a six-day Ambassadors' Conference in Lagos, the first

15th January 1966, First Inside Account (Lagos: Africana Educational Publishers, 1981) (participant); Olusegun Obasanjo, *Nzeogwu: An Intimate Portrait of Major Chukwuma Kaduna Nzeogwu* (Ibadan, Nigeria: Spectrum Books, 1987); and Robin Luckham, *The Nigerian Military: A Sociological Analysis of Authority and Revolt, 1960–1967* (New York: Cambridge University Press, 1971).

118 Aka, "Prospects for Igbo Human Rights in Nigeria in the New Century," note 15, p. 206.

119 "The First Republic," in *Nigeria: A Country Study*, note 57.

120 Ibid.

121 Ufot Bassey Inamete, *Foreign Policy Decision-Making in Nigeria* (Selinsgrove, PA: Susquehanna University Press, 2001), 103.

of its kind since the country's independence in 1960, to re-examine the premises and directions of Nigeria's foreign policy.[122] Evidently informed by General Aguiyi-Ironsi's expressed position that "in the whole sphere of external relations, the Government attached greatest import to our African policy," the conference underscored Nigeria's commitment to the total emancipation of all African territories still under colonial control.[123]

Under Gowon, Nigeria fought a ghastly civil war, from 1967 to 1970, conducted *outside* the strictures of the Geneva Conventions on treatment of noncombatants during a war.[124] The occurrence led to unsurpassed abuses of the individual and collective human rights of Easterners (who declared independence from Nigeria as Biafrans) about which till date a fierce debate still rages within and beyond Nigeria.[125] Throughout the period of the war, Nigerian foreign policy "was defensive, aimed at limiting Biafra's penetration of the international system" by, among other means, prevailing on African governments "to maintain a solid front of diplomatic support as a means of discouraging intervention that would foster Biafran independence."[126]

Abroad, the Nigerian government under Gowon became more truly non-aligned,[127] drawing from the lessons during the war of undependable

[122] Stremlau, note 87, p. 3.

[123] Ibid.

[124] See Aka, "Prospects for Igbo Human Rights in Nigeria in the New Century," note 15, pp. 196–209 (commenting on the "Conduct of the Biafran War," including assessment of allegations of genocide against the Igbo, the major ethnic group in Biafra). The Geneva Conventions comprise international treaties dating back to 1864 and amplified by numerous updates, some as recent as 1978, dealing with a multiplicity of topics, including the treatment of civilians during wars, humane treatment of prisoners of war, and treatment rules relating to care of the wounded and sick. See, for example, Emily Crawford and Alison Pert, *International Humanitarian Law* (New York: Cambridge University Press, 2015), 1–27.

[125] See Chinua Achebe, *There Was a Country: A Personal History of Biafra* (New York: Penguin Press, 2012), 209–211, 228–239 (memoir on the war by a distinguished Igbo writer who supported the secession); and Chimamanda N. Adichie, *Half of a Yellow Sun* (New York: Alfred A. Knopf, 2006) (work of fiction based on the war by an Igbo born after the war).

[126] Stremlau, note 87, pp. 3–4.

[127] Indicators of this posture include "warmer attitude toward the Soviet Union," recognition of the People's Republic of China, stepped up condemnation of the activities and policies of Western powers toward Southern Africa, and increased financial and other support for the liberation movements in Southern Africa. Gambari, *Theory and Reality in*

support from Western countries vis-à-vis the military support of the Soviet Union and other East European countries. The war taught the Nigerian leadership a lesson regarding the necessity to spread the range of its bilateral and multilateral relations beyond the traditional West European countries. But with the war over, Nigerian foreign policy experienced a loss of momentum that tracked the deteriorating domestic political situation which reached an all-time high in October of 1974 when Gowon assessed as unrealistic his promise to return the country to civilian rule.[128] In sum, despites the shortcomings recounted above, the Gowon regime made notable contributions to Nigerian foreign policy embedded in two concentric circles: West Africa via its efforts in founding ECOWAS, and Africa manifested in support for liberation movements in Africa.[129] These foreign policy achievements were facilitated by increased earnings from hydro-carbon products, which, in the aftermath of the civil war, replaced exports of agricultural products as the mainstay of Nigeria's economy.[130]

Injecting more assertiveness into Nigerian foreign policy, through nonalignment in the rivalry between East or West, reached its highest point under Murtala Muhammed, Head of State from August 1975 until his assassination during a failed military coup in February 1976. Domestically, Muhammed formulated a robust transition-to-civilian rule program[131] that his successor, General Olusegun Obasanjo, successfully completed, finally keeping the promise Aguiyi-Ironsi made in 1966 to return power to civilians that, in the final analysis, took thirteen years to accomplish.[132] Abroad, Muhammed's most notable act was the recognition of the Movement for the Popular Liberation of Angola (MPLA)

Foreign Policy Making, note 102, p. 7. See also "The Gowon Regime," in *Nigeria: A Country Study*, note 57 (stating that the regime committed itself to eliminating the policy of apartheid in South Africa, and, under the auspices of the OAU, channeled financial and military assistance to liberation movements in Africa).

[128] Ifeoma Azikiwe, *Nigeria: Echoes of a Century: 1914–1999*, Vol. 1 (Bloomington, IN: AuthorHouse, 2013), 217.

[129] For example, at the time of his overthrow in July of 1975, General Gowon was attending an OAU meeting in Kampala, Uganda, over the Angolan civil war. Terry M. Mays and Mark W. Delancey, *Historical Dictionary of International Organizations in Sub-Saharan Africa* (Lanham, MD: Scarecrow Press, 2002), 161.

[130] Gambari, *Theory and Reality in Foreign Policy Making*, note 102, p. 7.

[131] See Diamond, "Nigeria: Pluralism, Statism, and the Struggle for Democracy," note 15, pp. 45–49 (commenting on "[t]he [t]ransition to the Second Republic").

[132] See ibid.

"as the sole legitimate representative of the people and government of Angola," a recognition that ultimately garnered OAU support for the MPLA.[133] His regime backed this up with increased "diplomatic, financial, and material support to the liberation movements in Southern Africa."[134]

Based on a speech at an OAU summit meeting in Addis Ababa, Ethiopia, in January 1976, General Muhammed was not afraid to call out Western powers when the occasion warranted it.[135] In the speech, instructively titled, "Africa Has Come of Age," Mohammed declared that African countries "are capable of resolving African problems without presumptuous lessons in ideological dangers":

> Africa has come of age. It's no longer under the orbit of any extra continental power. It should no longer take orders from any country, however powerful. The fortunes of Africa are in our hands to make or to mar. For too long have we been kicked around: for too long have we been treated like adolescents who cannot discern their interests and act accordingly. For too long has it been presumed that the African needs outside "experts" to tell him who are his friends and who are his enemies. ... The time has come when we should make it clear that we can decide for ourselves; that we know our own interests and how to protect those interests; that we are capable of resolving African problems without presumptuous lessons in ideological dangers which, more often than not, have no relevance for us, nor for the problem at hand.[136]

[133] Gambari, *Theory and Reality in Foreign Policy Making*, note 102 p. 8.

[134] Ibid. Under Mohammed and subsequently Obasanjo, Nigeria earned the honor of unofficial or informal membership in the Frontline States (FLS). Abba Mahmood, "Nigeria's Africa Policy in Perspective," *Leadership* (December 26, 2013), leadership.ng/columns/Thursday-column/343/nigerias-africa-policy-in-perspective. The FLS was an organization of independent African states formed in 1975 designed to achieve majority rule in South Africa. Its members included Angola, Botswana, Lesotho, Malawi, Mozambique, Swaziland, Tanzania, Zambia, and Zimbabwe. These countries, all led by black majority governments, formed a ring around South Africa. Nigeria was the only such member of the group that was not geographically located in Southern Africa. See *Building Security in Southern Africa: An Update on the Evolving Architecture*, Monograph No. 43 (Pretoria, South Africa: Institute for Security, November 1999).

[135] Gambari, *Theory and Reality in Foreign Policy Making*, note 102, p. 8.

[136] Murtala Muhammed, "Africa Has Come of Age," Speech to the OAU Extraordinary Summit Conference, Addis Ababa (January 11, 1976), Africa Youth Union (December 3, 2013), https://www.facebook.com/Africanyouthunion/posts/726490580710778.

In sum, Africa would no longer be a pawn in the cold war struggle between East and West. The speech was triggered by a private letter from then US President Gerald Ford to many African leaders, warning them against Soviet-Cuban role in Angola and calling for support of the United States position in Southern Africa.[137] Not only did the Nigerian government reject the request, it also as well published the private letter to the approval of informed public opinion in the country.[138]

Building on the foundations laid by Muhammed, Obasanjo contributed to the liberation struggle in Southern Africa, reaching a high point with the nationalization of the assets of British Petroleum, the British oil and gas mega-company, over the British government's position in Rhodesia, later Zimbabwe.[139] However, a discernable soft-pedalling in the pursuit of an activist foreign policy occurred under General Obasanjo, due partly to a slowdown in Nigeria's oil-based economy.[140] Reflecting on the leverage of cartel power to some developing countries arising from export of a precious mineral resource, the London *Economist* observed in August of 1979 that "a world outside the old Euro-American heartland has developed its own centers of power: its Arabias, Brazils, and Nigerias."[141] The credit is due much more to Muhammed than to Obasanjo.

[137] Gambari, *Theory and Reality in Foreign Policy Making*, note 102, p. 8.

[138] The speech is a perfect example of an outcome that would not have occurred but for the stroke of serendipity. Mohammed initially planned to send his second-in-command, General Obasanjo, to attend this meeting, but changed his mind after he received a letter from US President Gerald Ford, hand-delivered on January 3, 1976, through Donald Easum, US Ambassador to Nigeria regarding the conflict in Angola where the US government supported UNITA, the Portuguese acronym of the National Union for the Total Independence of Angola (UNITA), in opposition to the Marxist-oriented Movement for the People's Liberation of Angola (MPLA). The Muhammed regime considered the letter a "gross insult." Africa Youth Union, note 136. This was among the setting wherein General Muhammed chose to attend the OAU conference himself rather than send an emissary. Ibid.

[139] See Gambari, *Theory and Reality in Foreign Policy Making*, note 102, pp. 8–9.

[140] Ibid.

[141] Ibid., quoting the *Economist* (London) (August 4, 1979), 11.

Second Republic, 1979–1983

Like with the First Republic, President Shagari was the only leader during this period. His tenure was even shorter than the First Republic lasting only until December 1983 when it was cut short by a military coup. The logical assumption was that a civilian administration would build on the momentum in foreign policy activism established during the first round of military rule from 1966 to 1979. Unfortunately, things did not pan out that way. Instead, Shagari turned out to be an ineffective leader whose administration drew comparison with the First Republic,[142] under which coincidentally he served.[143] During his watch, the wheels figuratively came off the train of Nigerian foreign policy in that "[t]he innovativeness and assertiveness" of the Mohammed-Obasanjo era evaporated, "replaced with a lack of forthrightness and excessive caution in approaching issues."[144] This was ironic given the enormous executive power of the president under the presidential system of government patterned on the US that Shagari's regime inaugurated, compared to the parliamentary system under the First Republic where the prime minister,

[142] See Gambari, *Theory and Reality in Foreign Policy Making*, note 102, p. 11 (stating that under Shagari, "it was as if Nigeria had rapidly slipped back into the policies of subservience to the West and hesitancy in African affairs, closer to the situation in the 1960s"); and Diamond, "Nigeria: Pluralism, Statism, and the Struggle for Democracy," note 15, p. 65 (positing that this time around, though ethnic polarization failed to metamorphose into conflict, "politics were not significantly less violent, vituperative, and chaotic in the Second Republic than they had been in the First Republic").

[143] Appointed parliamentary secretary to future Prime Minister Abubakar T. Balewa in 1959, Shagari went on to hold several positions in the Cabinet, including minister of economic development in 1959, minister of internal affairs in 1962, and minister of labor in 1965. "Biography of Alhaji Shehu Usman Aliyu Shagari," *The Biography*, http://thebiography.us/en/shagari-alhaji-shehu-usman-aliyu.

[144] Steve Egbo, *Nigeria and the World: A Treatise on Foreign Policy* (Enugu, Nigeria: John Jacobs Classic Publishers, 2003), 78. See also A.I. Pogoson, "Leadership Roles and Foreign Policy: A Study of President Shehu Shagari's Foreign Policy Posture," *Africa Bib.*, http://www.africabib.org/rec.php?RID=170748693 (stating that, despite the promise of "a vigorous and active foreign policy," Shagari is generally acknowledged to have been "weak and indecisive," judging by the positions of his government on a range of major foreign policy issues, including "decolonization, Namibian independence, [and] racism in South Africa").

by definition, wielded less power,[145] with important ramifications for foreign policies.

At home, massive corruption and bad management of the economy at a time of declining oil prices[146] destroyed the domestic base for creative foreign policymaking. Abroad, under Shagari, Nigeria witnessed little progress in both the West Africa and Africa concentric circles of its foreign policy. On West Africa, faced with economic difficulties at home, the Shagari government expelled undocumented foreign workers from West Africa,[147] whom his administration made the hapless scapegoats of Nigeria's economic troubles. With respect to Africa, Nigeria failed to translate its resources and power position in Africa into reality by bringing its weight to bear creatively and constructively in solving African problems.[148]

Second Round of Military Regimes, 1983–1999

Like Round One, Round Two of military rule in Nigeria encompassed multiple leaders—Muhammadu Buhari, Ibrahim Babangida, Ernest Shonekan, Sani Abacha, and Abdulsalami Abubakar—and lasted more years, six longer, to boot. Buhari's regime failed to contribute to the tradition for assertive foreign policy laid down during the first installment of military rule in the country.[149] Instead, save for a campaign against corruption domestically, his rule intriguingly appeared to clone the discredited NPN

[145] See Sodaro, note 97, pp. 194–205 (juxtaposing features of the parliamentary and presidential systems).

[146] See Diamond, "Nigeria: Pluralism, Statism, and the Struggle for Democracy," note 15, pp. 65–63 (commenting on "Why the Second Republic Failed").

[147] See Associated Press, "Expelled Foreigners Pouring Out of Nigeria," *New York Times* (May 4, 1985), http://www.nytimes.com/1985/05/05/world/expelled-foreigners-pouringout-of-nigeriaby-the-associated-press.html?pagewanted=print. See also Micah Bump, "Ghana: Searching for Opportunities at Home and Abroad," *Migration Info Source* (March 1, 2006), http://www.migrationpolicy.org/article/ghana-searching-opportunities-home-and-abroad (section commenting on "expulsion from Nigeria").

[148] Gambari, *Theory and Reality in Foreign Policy Making*, note 102, p. 13.

[149] Diamond, "Nigeria: Pluralism, Statism, and the Struggle for Democracy," note 15, pp. 55–57.

government that he overthrew.[150] His regime was also, even by military standards, a repressive one,[151] that did not commit itself to return the country to civilian rule.[152] In sum, Buhari was a leader of insular dispositions who expressed distinct aversion for matters of external affairs that would take away from his focus on the Nigerian economy battered by corruption that he inherited,[153] and whose regime continued the anti-ECOWAS initiatives of the Shagari administration that detracted from the energized Africa-centered policy of the Mohammed-Obasanjo regimes.[154]

Babangida equally operated a repressive regime, albeit less blatantly,[155] that also dubiously reached new heights in political corruption.[156] He set the record for a convoluted return to civil rule program that some

[150] "Return to Military Rule," in *Nigeria: A Country Study*, note 57.

[151] See Diamond, "Nigeria: Pluralism, Statism, and the Struggle for Democracy," note 15, pp. 56–57 (commenting on several controversial decrees unleashed by the regime permitting trials by military tribunals, curtailing expression, and detentions without trial).

[152] "Political Transition," in *Nigeria: A Country Study*, note 57 (pointing out that "political transition has been on the agenda of every military government since Ironsi's, with the [...] exception of that of Buhari").

[153] Seyi Gesinde, "Nigeria's Foreign Policy in the Eye of Global Challenge," *Tribune Online* (Lagos) (May 28, 2015), http://tribuneonlineng.com/content/nigeria%E2%80%99s-foreign-policy-eye-global-challenge. Under him, in December 1984, Nigeria signed a tripartite security agreement with Benin, Togo, and Niger, to deal with the challenges of national security arising from drugs and psychotropic substances, smuggling in small arms, human trafficking, and currency trafficking. See Hugo Odiogor and Abiodun Alade, "I Cannot Rest When the World Is Being Terrorized—Prof. Ibrahim Gambari," *Vanguard* (Lagos) (June 21, 2015), http://www.vanguardngr.com/2015/06/i-cannot-rest-when-the-world-is-being-terrorised-prof-ibrahim-gambari/ (interview with Professor Gambari). While this agreement could go as foreign policy achievement for Buhari, it also reinforces the need for a stronger action, lacking under his regime, in the West Africa circle of Nigerian foreign policy.

[154] See "Return to Military Rule," *in Nigeria: A Country Study*, note 57.

[155] One incident that easily comes to mind is the death by letter bomb of the investigative journalist Dele Giwa in October 1986. See Diamond, "Nigeria: The Uncivic Society and the Descent into Praetorianism," note 15, p. 486, n.100 (enumerating evidence tying the Babanginda regime to the murder).

[156] See Diamond, "Nigeria: The Uncivic Society and the Descent into Praetorianism," note 15, p. 449 (recounting reasons why "[i]ncreasingly, Babangida was seen as the most massively corrupt ruler in Nigerian history").

commentators legitimately likened to a permanent transition.[157] This was inconsistent with popular expectation, dating back to Aguiyi-Ironsi, that counseled return of power to civilians after the army has fixed the problem that brought them into office. In the view of some analysts, for the most part, "rhetorics, emptiness, inaction, policy somersault, and indecision," marked his regime.[158]

No government is totally evil and there are some good deeds credited to his regime. One of these relates to ECOWAS covered in greater details in Chapter 6 under peacekeeping. His regime chalked in some memorable accomplishments in two concentric circles—West Africa and Africa—that resonate with the assertive foreign policy program associated with the latter leg of the first round of military rule. For West Africa, Babangida gave the integration impetus of ECOWAS, stalled under Shagari and Buhari, a proverbial shot in the arm. Under him, Nigeria donated land in Abuja for the building of the ECOWAS Secretariat and contributed money toward its construction.[159] It was also during his period that the community's Protocol on Free Movement of Citizens took effect in July 1986; the Protocol was adopted seven years before in 1979.[160] Another achievement to his credit was the formalization of technical assistance under the Technical Aid Corps (TAC) scheme,[161] covered in more details in Chapter 7. With the troops of professional volunteers that it exported to many corners of the developing world, including West Africa, Africa, and the Caribbean, the scheme encompassed all three concentric circles of Nigerian foreign policy.[162]

With a lifespan of under three months, the interim government under Shonekan, a Yoruba, had hardly settled down before it was sacked. From every indication, his government was little more than a ploy by the

[157] See *Transition Without End*, note 59, *passim* (providing a critical analysis of Babangida's non-transparent transition-to-democracy program).

[158] Egbo, note 144, p. 95.

[159] John N. Shagaya, *Governance in Nigeria: The IBB Era: An Insider's View* (Lagos: Viewpoint Communications Ltd., 2003), 86.

[160] See Comfort Asaa Mantey, Ensuring Free Border Movements in ECOWAS Integration: Challenges to National Security, M.A. Thesis, University of Ghana (July 2013). The multiparty agreement eliminated travel restrictions, such as visa, among members of the community. Ibid.

[161] Egbo, note 144, p. 95. Chapter 7 of this book is devoted to the TAC program.

[162] Egbo, note 144, p. 95.

Babangida regime to douse the earth-rending protests which accompanied his invalidation of the June 12 1993 presidential election believed by many to have been won by another Yoruba, businessman Moshood Abiola.[163] Abacha held the all-time record for human-right atrocities. Under him, dissidents were routinely tortured, political prisoners were tried in camera before military tribunals that hardly set them free, and execution for offenses, such as armed robbery, were commonplace. His massive abuses of human rights drew widespread condemnation, including suspension of Nigeria's membership in the Commonwealth of Nation following the hanging death in October 1995 of Keni Saro-Wiwa, along with 9 other Ogoni activists.[164] Under him, the pariah status of the country in the international community, instigated by Babangida's annulment of the 1993 presidential election, reached new proportions. His regime implemented peacekeeping in Liberia to end a raging civil war and another in Sierra Leone to restore an elected leader forced out of office in a military coup.[165]

However, these peacekeeping initiatives in no way mitigated Abacha's failures in domestic and foreign policies. For example, it is hard to miss the solecism embodied in a Nigerian military regime's leading an interventionist force to restore democracy in Sierra Leone. Also, part of the Abacha legacy was the monstrous scale of corruption that

[163] Babangida's Decree No. 61 establishing the Interim National Government stated that Sani Abacha, Chief of Defense Staff under Babangida and a member of the Armed Forces Ruling Council, the country's highest policymaking body, shall be "Vice President, Defense Secretary, and Senior Minister." Ibid., quoted in "Ernest Shonekan, Nigeria's Most Fugacious Leader," *Nairaland Forum*, http://www.nairaland.com/1336063/ernest-shonekan-nigerias-most-fugacious. Taking advantage of this decree, on November 17, 1993, Abacha ousted Shonekan, and replaced him as head of state. "Nigerian Military Leader Ousts Interim President," *New York Times* (November 18, 1993), http://www.nytimes.com/1993/11/18/world/nigeria-military-leader-ousts-interim-president.html.

[164] See Howard W. French, "Nigeria Executes Critic of Regime; Nations Protest," *New York Times* (November 11, 1995), http://www.nytimes.com/1995/11/11/world/nigeria-executes-critic-of-regime-nations-protest.html?pagewanted=all; and "Nigeria Suspended from Commonwealth," *CNN* (November 11, 1995), http://www.cnn.com/WORLD/9511/nigeria/11-11/.

[165] See Adekeye Adebajo, *Building Peace in West Africa: Liberia, Sierra Leone, and Guinea-Bissau* (Boulder, CO: Lynne Rienner Publishers, 2002), 43–78, 79–110 (Sierra Leone).

occurred under his regime.[166] Under his kleptocratic watch, corruption moved from being part of Nigeria's government to being "the object of government."[167]

By the time of Abacha's death on June 8 1993, after three decades in office, only interrupted by four years of civilian rule under the Second Republic, it was obvious that a Nigerian army "[c]onsumed with fear, factionalism, and greed" "could hardly any longer be viewed as a potential source of rescue for democracy."[168] Moreover, it is foolhardy "to weaken at home what one is trying to strengthen abroad."[169] This was the setting in which Abubakar emerged to start the process of repairing Nigeria's sick image abroad needing to be preceded by a genuine transition to civil rule program.[170]

Abubakar was Chief of Defense under Abacha before the ruling junta selected him as Head of State.[171] He was chosen because "he was seen a professional soldier without political ambitions of his own," but also equally because, although an Abacha loyalist, Abubakar believed that

[166] See James Rupert, "Corruption Flourished in Abacha's Regime," *Washington Post* (June 9, 1998), A01. See also "U.S. Freezes $458 m Stolen by Sani Abacha," *Vanguard* (Lagos) (March 6, 2014), http://www.vanguardngr.com/2014/03/us-freezes-458-mn-stolen-nigeria-dictator-abacha/ (story includes a quote attributed to a US Department of Justice official who called the freeze "the biggest civil forfeiture action to recover the proceeds of foreign official corruption ever brought by" the department). In addition to the usual kickbacks, under General Abacha, avenues for corruption included subsidies of refined petroleum products imported from abroad (leaving the country's refineries under-utilized), creating artificial scarcity of fuel that negatively impacted Nigeria's economy. Ibid.

[167] Rupert, note 166 (quoting one Nigerian political scientist).

[168] Diamond, "Nigeria: The Uncivic Society and the Descent into Praetorianism," note 15, note 1, p. 464.

[169] Thomas E. Patterson, *The American Democracy,* 8th Ed. (New York: McGraw-Hill, 2008), 513–514 (citing the warning of former US President Dwight D. Eisenhower against "the unwarranted influence" and "misplaced power" of the military-industrial complex, made up of the coalition of military establishment, industries that manufacture weapons, and members of Congress from constituencies that depend heavily on the arms industry that mutually benefit from a high level of defense spending).

[170] Gerald E. Ezirim, "Fifty Years of Nigeria's Foreign Policy: A Critical Review," *Sacha International Academic Journal* (2011), http://www.academia.edu/345652/Fifty_Years_of_Nigeria_s_Foreign_Policy_A_Critical_Review.

[171] "Abdulsalam Abubakar," *Online Nigeria,* http://www.onlinenigeria.com/abubakar.asp.

"the survival of the country depends on a rapid and peaceful transition to a lasting democracy."[172] He dismantled Abacha's transition program together, embedded in five political parties, "five fingers of a leprous hand," as one Nigerian politician derisively called them,[173] finally completing the return-to-civil-rule agenda that the Nigerian army initiated in 1986 under Babangida—and with it the long-overdue retreat of Nigerian soldiers to the barracks.[174]

Fourth Republic, 1999 to the Present

Five heads of state, Olusegun Obasanjo, Umaru Yar'Adua, Goodluck Jonathan, Muhammadu Buhari, and Bola A. Tinubu, feature(d) in Nigeria's long-running period of civilian rule since independence. The fact that two of these individuals, Obasanjo and Buhari, are former military leaders, speak to the continuing influence of the army in the political system twenty-four years after the Nigerian army retreated to the barracks. Testimony further to that lingering influence, which ended with Buhari's departure from the Nigerian political scene on May 29, 2023, after two terms in office, is that the two leaders handpicked their successors: Obasanjo, Umaru Yar'Adua, as president and Goodluck Jonathan as vice-president,[175] and Buhari, Tinubu.

[172] Ibid.

[173] This was a reference to Abacha's spurious transition program aimed at self-succession before the dictator's death on June 8, 1998. Each of the five political parties supposedly unanimously adopted Abacha as its sole presidential candidate. See 'Kunle Amuwo, "Introduction: Transition as Democratic Regression," in *Nigeria during the Abacha Years (1993–1998)*, eds. 'Kunle Amuwo et al. (Lagos: IFRA-Nigeria, 2001), 1–56.

[174] The occurrence calls to mind the ignominious humiliation in 1982 arising from the defeat of the Argentine army by British forces over control of the Falkland Islands, which both countries claimed, that eased it out of partisan politics. See Jack Donnelly, *International Human Rights*, 4th Ed. (Boulder, CO: Westview Press, 2013), 65 ("Having attacked its own people, brought the economy to the brink of ruin, and then embarrassed itself and the country before the entire world, the Argentine military had little choice but to permit a return to civilian government").

[175] See Christine Purefoy, "Goodluck Jonathan: By Name and Nature?" *CNN* (April 17, 2011), http://www.cnn.com/2010/WORLD/africa/05/06/nigeria.jonathan/; and Robyn Dixon, "Umaru Yar'Adua Dies at 58; Nigerian President," *L. A. Times* (May 7, 2010), http://articles.latimes.com/2010/may/07/local/la-me-umaru-yaradua-20100507.

Obasanjo continued the rehabilitation of Nigeria's international image that Abubakar initiated.[176] He equally made important strides in domestic politics that included reduction of Nigeria's external debt and laid the groundwork for expansion of telecommunication services that caught fire in the country after he left office.[177] However, after two terms in office which he sought unsuccessfully to extend into a third term,[178] there was little evidence of "democratic dividend" for the citizenry,[179] a large segment of whom remained mired in poverty.[180] Next to external relations, while certain gains were made in all concentric circles of Nigerian foreign policy, those achievements lacked the sharpness the country witnessed during his first time around for a variety of reasons that includes inability to reshape the country's Africa-centered prong in the architecture of the country's foreign policy to reflect a changed world. In a speech in 2005, Obasanjo indicated why he "believe[d] that Africa should remain the centerpiece of our foreign policy."[181] His justification was a defensive one that evinced poverty of imagination on how to reshape Nigeria's Africa-centered policy in the wake of the decolonization in Africa capped

[176] Ezirim, note 170.

[177] See, for example, "The Obasanjo Years: His Legacy," *Lawyers Chronicle*, http://thelawyerschronicle.com/the-obasanjo-years-his-legacy/ (including his period as military Head of State from 1976 to 1979); and Emmanuel Ojameruaye, "A Tentative Analytical Evaluation of President Obasanjo's Performance (May 1999–May 2007)," *Gamji*, http://www.gamji.com/article6000/NEWS7024.htm (finding his overall performance "barely satisfactory," yet "better than most other past Nigerian presidents" based on promises and result on a range of domestic issues, including human development, corruption, healthcare, and education as well as foreign policy).

[178] See Darren Kew and Peter Lewis, "Nigeria," in *Introduction to Politics of the Developing World: Political Challenges and Changing Agendas*, ed. Mark Kesselman (Boston, MA: Cengage Learning, 2013), 214; Ofeibea Quist-Arcton, "Nigeria Rejects Term-Limit Change in Constitution," *NPR* (May 17, 2006), http://www.npr.org/templates/story/story.php?storyID=5410582; and Craig Timberg, "Bid to Allow Nigerian a Third Term Hits Snag," *Washington Post* (May 13, 2006), http://www.gpo.gov/fdsys/pkg/CHRG-105shrg48230/html/CHRG-105shrg48230.htm.

[179] See, for example, Philip C. Aka, "The 'Dividend of Democracy': Analyzing U.S. Support for Nigerian Democratization," *Boston College Third World Law Journal*, 22 (2) (2002), 225–279.

[180] Ojameruaye, note 177 (finding that on human development, "about 60% to 70%" of Nigerians still live below the poverty line, defined as less than US $1 per day).

[181] Obasanjo, quoted in Ezirim, note 170.

by the achievement of majority rule in South Africa in 1994, several years before he took office.[182]

To compound matters, in the aftermath of Obasanjo's second coming, Nigerian foreign policy, "has been rudderless, [...] ineffectual for the most part," and direly in need of "strategy, focus, and leadership."[183] As indicated before, both Yar'Adua and Jonathan were handpicked by Obasanjo. Both had no military background. Both administrations were imbued with a truly civilian atmosphere and mien that represented a marked departure from the military approach to non-military issues that marked Obasanjo's civilian years in office,[184] and the Buhari regime after them.

Given a chronic health condition that kept him hospitalized for long periods, Yar'Adua remained a transitional leader for much of the less than three years he served in office before his death on May 5, 2010, three months of which period from February 9, 2010, vice-president Jonathan filled in acting capacity while his principal received treatment in Saudi Arabia.[185] Jonathan won his own separate term in 2011 and left office in 2015 after he lost his bid for reelection.[186] With an earned doctorate degree in science when he took office, Jonathan is the best-educated of

[182] Obasanjo declared that "[t]he renewed determination of African leaders, our strengthening of regional economic communities, the restructuring of the OAU into the AU, and a better global disposition toward Africa, the AU and the AU's program, NEPAD, are indicators that we are indeed in a new Africa." Ibid.

[183] Chris Adetayo, "A Foreign Policy Guide for President Tinubu," *Cable* (June 13, 2023), https://www.thecable.ng/a-foreign-policy-guide-for-president-tinubu.

[184] See Philip C. Aka, "Nigeria since May 1999: Understanding the Paradox of Civil Rule and Human Rights Violations under President Olusegun Obasanjo," *San Diego International Law Journal*, 4 (2003), 209, 237–255 (commenting on Obasanjo's handling of four crises, including the military reprisals at Odi and Benue State).

[185] See "Obituary: President Yar'Adua," *BBC News* (May 6, 2010), http://news.bbc.co.uk/2/hi/africa/6187249.stm.; and Ademola Bello, "Umaru Yar'Adua: A Mediocre Administrator, the Least Prepared Nigerian President since Shehu Shagari," *Huffington Post* (May 13, 2010, updated May 25, 2011), http://www.huffingtonpost.com/ademola-bellow/umaru-musa-yaradua-a-medi_b_575125.html (noting that under Yar'Adua, "Nigeria's celebrated peace-keeping roles, leadership of ECOWAS, and the country's Giant of Africa status all took a back seat").

[186] Will Ross, "Nigeria Elections: Buhari Scores Historic Win," *BBC News* (April 1, 2015), http://www.bbc.com/news/world-africa-32141703; and Damian Zane, "Nigeria's Goodluck Jonathan: Five Reasons Why He Lost," *BBC News* (March 31, 2015), http://www.bbc.com/news/world-africa-32136295.

Nigerian chief executives since independence.[187] This is a notable first for a country whose achievements in the educational field internationally include a Nobel Laureate in literature. However, although he maintained momentum on the three concentric circles in the architecture of Nigerian foreign policy, Jonathan was an effete leader.[188] One singular issue more any other which manifested this want of strong leadership skill—and a major factor in his failure to win a second term in office—was his ineffective response to the crisis of terrorism by the insurgency group, Boko Haram, that rocked the northeast of the country under his watch.[189]

Boko Harm stands for the notion that "Western education is evil" which evilness these terrorists are convinced can be resolved by turning Nigeria into an Islamic state in the mold of Iran or Saudi Arabia.[190] Populated by retired and serving soldiers, policemen, and immigration personnel from Nigeria and foreign nationals from Niger, Chad, and Sudan, the group has conducted relentlessly bombings and gun attacks on ordinary citizens and more well-known ones, such as politicians, and religious leaders.[191] It has also targeted government infrastructure of all types within and outside the epicenter of its operation in northeastern Nigeria, including police stations, army barracks, the UN office in Abuja, churches, and recreation centers, among other seeming symbols of Western education.[192]

[187] Jonathan earned a doctor of philosophy (Ph.D.) degree in Zoology from the University of Port Harcourt. Amy McKenna, "Goodluck Jonathan, President of Nigeria," *Encyclopedia Britannica*, http://www.britannica.com/biography/Goodluck-Jonathan.

[188] See Fisayo Soyombo, "Why is Nigeria's Jonathan Worried?" *Al Jazeera* (November 27, 2014), http://www.aljazeera.com/indepth/opinion/2014/11/why-nigeria-jonathan-worried-20141123104313818965.html (opining that "[a] Jonathan win in 2015 will not invalidate the fact that his first-term performance was underwhelming").

[189] Ibid.

[190] For a sample of the numerous commentaries in academic and popular media on this terrorist group, see John Ford, "The Origins of Boko Haram," *National Interest* (June 6, 2014), http://nationalinterest.org/print/feature/the-origins-boko-haram-10609; and Farouk Chothia, "Who are Nigeria's Boko Haram Islamists?" *BBC News* (May 4, 2015), http://www.bbc.com/news/world-africa-13809501.

[191] See Chothia, note 190.

[192] Ibid.

The group is linked to al-Qaeda, the global terrorist group founded by Osama bin Ladin, and professes allegiance to another terrorist organization, the Islamic State of Iraq and Syria (ISIS).[193] Since inaugurating its violent phase in 2009, the group has killed or maimed over 20,000 people, displaced millions of others from their homes, kidnapped hundreds, including school girls, and blew off public and private property running into millions in US dollars.[194] Because the group aims to make Nigeria an Islamic theocracy in the model of Iran, the conflict appears to cap the continued salience of religion in Nigerian politics under the Fourth Republic that began with the institution of sharia as legal code in twelve northern states between 2000 and 2001.[195]

Some individuals are creatures of habit. Thus, as civilian president, General Buhari brought to his new role much of the same mindset from his period as military head of state from 1983 to 1985.[196] In practical terms, this translated into a focus first on Nigeria, then on its immediate neighbors, followed by other West African countries, Africa, and the rest of the world.[197] Except for Niger Republic on the country's northern borders, that policy translated effectively to insularity. With respect to Niger, under Buhari, Nigeria implemented controversial projects with little benefit to Nigeria like a rail line from Nigeria to Niger that the Nigerian government funded, among other largess.[198]

[193] Ibid.

[194] See Michelle Gavin, "Nigeria Security Tracker," Council on Foreign Relations (Last updated July 1, 2023), https://www.cfr.org/nigeria/nigeria-security-tracker/p29483.

[195] See Philip C. Aka, "Judicial Independence under Nigeria's Fourth Republic: Problems and Prospects," *California Western International Law Journal*, 45 (1) (2014), 1, 42, n.170 (indicating that "the bloody campaign since 2009 by Boko Haram" "amplifies the upgrading of sharia into legal code in Northern Nigeria[.]").

[196] Chiamaka Okafor, "Gambari Explains Buhari's Foreign Policy Mindset," *Premium Times* (Abuja) (August 15, 2022), https://www.premiumtimesng.com/news/headlines/548864-gambari-explains-buharis-foreign-policy-mindset.html#:~:text=According%20to%20Mr%20Gambari%2C%20Mr,the%20rest%20of%20the%20world.

[197] Ibid. Instructively, the official performing this explanation was the President's Chief of Staff, not the country's Foreign Minister, Geoffrey Onyeama, said to have been a "painfully low key and diffident" public servant who "sleep-walk[ed]" through his eight long years in office. Adetayo, note 183. In fairness to him, Ibrahim Gambari, who served as Nigeria's permanent representative to the UN from 1990 to 1999, and before then under Buhari as external affairs minister from 1984 to 1985, some of whose insights we have referenced in this book, is a scholar-diplomat.

[198] Okafor, note 196.

In foreign policy, Buhari focused his energies on combating the Boko Harmam insurgency in the country's northeast and promoting food production to minimize food imports.[199] To achieve these goals, he paid state visits to Niger and Chad, Nigeria's two northern neighbors, and created a multinational joint task force made up of troops from Nigeria, Niger, Chad, and Cameroon to bring peace in the Lake Chad area.[200] To stop the smuggling of small arms and ammunitions as well as of foreign rice into Nigeria, for months his regime closed the borders between Nigeria and neighboring ECOWAS countries.[201] In the sphere of domestic and foreign affairs alike, Buhari accumulated an achievement far below the general expectation when he took office in 2015.[202] Overall, between his two periods in office, military and civilian alike totaling nearly 10 years, dispassionate analysts assessed that Buhari left a legacy of "squandered goodwill," one starkly different than the one Nigerian voters hoped for when he took office, especially in the civilian setting.[203]

Conclusion

This chapter completes Part II of the book on the exigency of a human-right foreign policy for Nigeria under the Fourth Republic. The reduced influence of the military in Nigerian politics, signified by Buhari's departure from the Nigerian political scene after two underwhelming terms of office on May 29, 2023, provides an inestimable opportunity for this exploration. Although focused on the period since Nigeria's independence from the UK in 1960 at the heartbeat of this research, the discussion also included a pre-independence timeline consisting of the precolonial and colonial eras, necessary to present a complete story,

[199] See Adoba Echono, "Nigeria's Foreign Policy Giant Strides under President Buhari Administration." *Voice of Nigeria* (Last updated May 23, 2023), https://von.gov.ng/nigerias-foreign-policy-giant-strides-under-president-buhari-administration/.

[200] Adetayo, note 183.

[201] Ibid.

[202] Fiayo Soyombo, "How Will Nigeria Fare Under Buhari?" *Alja Zeera* (June 9, 2015), https://www.aljazeera.com/opinions/2015/6/9/how-will-nigeria-fare-under-buhari (predicting that by the end of his first term in office, "Nigerians will have a government that will be genuinely trying to meet their needs").

[203] Oromo Egbejule et al., "'Squandered Goodwill': How Buhari Failed Nigeria a Second Time," *Alja Zeera* (May 29, 2023), https://www.aljazeera.com/features/2023/5/29/squandered-goodwill-how-buhari-failed-nigeria-a-second-time.

consistent with the methodology of Within-Case Comparison (WCC), involving the study of one country at different points in time and space. The jury is still out with respect to the Tinubu administration, which has been in office for little over one year as this book goes to press.

Several lessons emerge from this presentation, particularly the material on the postcolonial era. First is the interrelatedness of domestic and foreign policies. To "build [its] national prestige on the global scale," Nigeria needs leaders versed in the "intricacies of the international system, [and who] underst[an]d what it mean[s] to set foreign policy to drive domestic goals."[204] Second is the instability in the Nigerian political system with ramifications for the conduct of domestic and foreign policies. Tied to the instability of the Nigerian political system referenced in the introduction, as Table 3.1 makes clear, sixteen administrations have governed Nigeria in the sixty-three years since its independence—from a high of 8 years under General Obasanjo and General Buhari, respectively, to only 84 days for Ernest Shonekan. Speaking to the domination of the Nigerian political system by military leaders that extended into the Fourth Republic, both Obasanjo and Buhari were also former military heads of state. Excluding the Tinubu regime, which took office only in May 2023, in lifespan, this comes to an average of 4.2 years for each administration. Third is the influence of military rule in Nigerian politics. Only eight of the sixteen administrations surveyed, amounting to 47%, including the transitional government under Shonekan, are civilian.

Even if for no other reason, background histories are important because of the starting point they provide to every story in the light of the tendency for past events to shape contemporary politics, whether for one country or for a set of countries.[205] With Part I now completed, the train of this book moves to its next stop, Part II on the methods Nigeria can use to continue its pursuit of a principled foreign policy in the aftermath of the setback from the Buhari years. The conversation begins with Chapter 4 on the redesign of the country's national interest to increase its readiness for and amenability to international human-right functions.

[204] Adetayo, note 183.

[205] Wilson, note 1, p. 17.

PART II

Methods: Sample of Five Distinctive Tools

CHAPTER 4

Reconstructing Nigeria's National Interest in Readiness for Human-Right Duties

Introduction

Reconstructing the national interest is a requisite first step for any country, Nigeria no different, which seeks to adopt a human-right policy.[1] Applying human rights in external relations is no mean endeavor; it "reflects a fundamental redefinition of the national interest."[2] Using these propositions as starting point, this chapter unearths modalities for the reconstruction of Nigeria's national interest to increase its amenability for human-right work, consistent with Constructivism's worldview of foreign policy as what a state makes of it. The worldview contrasts with the teaching of Political Realism which defines national interest, more soon below, in terms of power and security.[3] Building on Part I relating to exigency, Part II of this book is devoted to *methods* for designing and implementing a human-right policy for Nigeria under the Fourth Republic in the wake of the reduced praetorian influence in Nigeria's body

[1] See, for example, Alison Brysk, *Global Good Samaritans: Human Rights as Foreign Policy* (New York: Oxford University Press, 2009), 31–41.

[2] Jack Donnelly, *International Human Rights*, 4th Ed. (Boulder, CO: Westview Press, 2013), 139.

[3] Never mind the tenets of idealistic Realism or realistic Idealism of former US Secretary of State Madeline Albright laid out elsewhere. See Chapter 2, notes 150–151, and accompanying texts.

P. C. Aka, *Human Rights in Nigeria's External Relations in the Age of General Muhammadu Buhari and His Successors*,
https://doi.org/10.1007/978-3-031-63231-0_4

politic, signified by the departure of General Buhari from the Nigerian political scene.

This chapter is the first in a sample of five discussions on methods; the four complementary others are Chapter 5 on the necessity for increased respect for human rights at home, Chapter 6 on peacekeeping, Chapter 7 on the Technical Aid Corps (TAC), and Chapter 8 on the Community Court of Justice (CCJ). Three interrelated issues this chapter covers are: the intricacies of national interest, the evolution of Nigeria's national interest since independence in 1960, and strategies for reconstructing Nigeria's national interest to make it human right-compliant, including reshaping the country's foreign policy machinery.

The Intricacies of National Interest

There is no universally agreed-upon definition of national interest; instead, different writers define the term differently. Three examples make this point clear. These include the realist scholar Hans J. Morgenthau who defined the concept in terms of survival,[4] the political scientist Vernon Von Dyke who summed it up colloquially as "desires on the part of sovereign states,"[5] and Brookings Institution, a think tank, which likened it to "the general and continuing ends for which a nation acts."[6] More elaborately, national interests are "the claims, objectives, goals, demands[,] and interests which a nation always tried to preserve, protect, defend and secure in relations with other nations."[7] Other points of common or emerged agreement include that: a state has the *right* to promote its national interest; that the national interest is *the* principle by

[4] See Morgenthau, quoted in "National Interest: Meaning, Components[,] and Methods," *Your Article Library*, http://www.yourarticlelibrary.com/international-politics/national-interest-meaning-components-and-methods/48487/ [hereinafter Your Article Library Essay] ("[t]he meaning of national interest is survival—the protection of physical, political[,] and cultural identity against encroachments by other nation-states").

[5] See Vernon Von Dyke, quoted in Your Article Library Essay, note 4 ("[n]ational interest is that which states seek to protect or achieve in relation to each other[,]" or "desires on the part of sovereign states").

[6] See Brookings Institution, quoted in Your Article Library Essay, note 4 ("[w]hat a nation feels to be necessary to its security and wellbeing" that "reflects the general and continuing ends for which a nation acts").

[7] Morgenthau, in Your Article Library Essay, note 4.

which every state justifies its actions in international relations and conditions its behavior;[8] and that a litmus test, so to speak, of every foreign policy decision is whether it serves the national interest.[9]

National interests may be vital or non-vital, based on whether a state is willing to go to war to protect those interests.[10] Vital interests include values like territorial identity, political-economic benefits, and historical achievements or endowments that a nation upholds as part of its cultural heritage and over which it will to go to war, if necessary, to protect.[11] Non-vital interests are values outside the vital category, such as peace, justice, and prestige, sometimes dictated by the necessity of securing the vital interests, that a state would like to see realized but over which it will not go to war.[12]

Popular means through which states seek to secure their national interests in the international system include: diplomacy, propaganda, economic investments or activities, alliances and treaties, and coercive means only as a last resort.[13] *Diplomacy,* the tool through which "the foreign policy of a nation travels to other nations," "involves the presentation of the goals and objectives of national interest in such a way as can persuade others to accept these as just and rightful demands of the nation."[14]

[8] Ibid.

[9] Lee H. Hamilton, "Defining National Interest," *Christian Science Monitor* (March 30, 1998), http://www.csmonitor.com/1998/0330/033098.opin.opin.2.html (commenting on US's national interest).

[10] Ibid.; Morgenthau, in Your Article Library Essay, note 4.

[11] Hamilton, note 9; Morgenthau, in Your Article Library Essay, note 4. The idea that comes to mind here is the US journalist Walter Lippman's definition of *security* to mean the extent to which a country "is not in danger of having to sacrifice core values if it wishes to avoid war, and is able, if challenged, to maintain them in such a war." Walter Lippman, *U.S. Foreign Policy: Shield of the Republic* (Boston, MA: Little Brown, 1943), 5.

[12] Morgenthau, in Your Article Library Essay, note 4. Other systems for classifying these interests exist. For the US, former Congressman Hamilton identified the following components: preserving the territorial integrity of the US and the safety and security of its people; sustaining US's economic prosperity, e.g., through free markets and reacting to financial crises abroad to minimize their domestic impact; promoting democratic values; promoting basic human rights, including economic rights (freedom from starvation), political-civil rights (religious freedom and freedom of expression), and group rights (freedom from genocide); and protecting the health and welfare of Americans. Hamilton, note 9.

[13] Morgenthau, in Your Article Library Essay, note 4.

[14] Ibid.

Propaganda is the art of salesmanship by which the nation using this tool seeks to convince the target nation(s) "about the justness of the goals and objectives or ends" that the nation using this tool seeks to accomplish.[15] *Economic means* consist of material tools, such as aid and loans as a means for promoting interests in another country or countries by the nation using that tool.[16] *Alliances and treaties,* military or economic, are agreement concluded by two or more states for achieving common interests.[17]

National interest has two usages revolved around what is *best* for an affected state in foreign affairs: as an instrument of *political action* in justifying, denouncing, or proposing policies; and as *political analysis* (or *analytic tool*) in describing, explaining, or evaluating the sources or adequacy of a nation's foreign policy.[18] The term's function as an instrument of *political action* goes back a long time to the sixteenth century in Italy and the seventeenth century in England.[19] In this first sense, the evolution of the term coincided with the emergence of the nation-state as a new form of political organization and allegiance, in replacement of the then existing feudal order.[20] The use of the term in *political analysis* evolved much later in the twentieth century, particularly to evaluate the policies of certain European states—the UK, France, and the US on the one hand and Germany on the other hand—in the lead up to World War II. In this latter sense, the term is distinguished from the *public interest* at the domestic level.[21]

[15] Ibid.

[16] Ibid.

[17] Ibid. Though discouraged in modern international relations, states can use force (such as war) to secure their national interests, but more advisedly coercive means short of war, such as intervention, embargoes, boycotts, reprisals, etc. See ibid. An exception that makes the rule here is international terrorism against which threat today world public opinion permits the use of military power. Ibid.

[18] James N. Rosenau, "National Interest," *International Encyclopedia of the Social Sciences* (1968), http://www.encyclopedia.com/doc/1G2-3045000855.html.

[19] Charles A. Beard and G. H. E. Smith, *The Idea of National Interest: An Analytical Study in American Foreign Policy* (New York: Macmillan, 1934), 22–24.

[20] Ibid.

[21] Rosenau, note 18. In his essay, Professor Rosenau identified two schools regarding the use of national interest as political analysis. The first are the "objectivists" because of their interest in analyzing the contents of foreign policy, including their underlying assumption that the national interest can be objectively determined. Hans J. Morgenthau,

Whether in political action or political inquiry, national interest is a concept fraught with inherent limitations that also lends itself to opportunistic use.[22] In a nutshell, the national interest calls to mind the teachings of the realist school, dwelt upon extensively in Chapter 2, which suggests that the pursuit of human right concerns in external relations does not promote the national interest of a state and goes as far as to advise against such interjection of ethical values on the ground that it may impede protection of a country's vital interests.[23] Instead, Political Realists advocate a concept of national interest defined in terms of power

Politics Among Nations: The Struggle for Power and Peace, Revised 5th Ed. (New York: Alfred A. Knopf, 1978 [1948]), exemplifies this first school. The second school consists of "subjectivists" so called because of their interest in explaining why nations do what they do when they engage in international action—or the decision-making approach to international politics. Rosenau, note 18. There are weaknesses with each school, which speak to the inherent limitations of national interest as political analysis. For the objectivists, it is the premise that the national interest can be objectified. For the subjectivists, it is the notion that the national interest is a reflection—and aggregation—of the individual and sometimes conflicting preferences of many groups within a nation. Ibid.

[22] One infamous abuse of the term that comes quickly to mind is Adolf Hitler's invocation of "German national interests" to justify his expansionist policies before and during World War II. Morgenthau, in Your Article Library Essay, note 4. On a much less extreme note, one analyst lists national interest among several most-abused clichés in foreign policy. Paul J. Saunders, "The Five Most Abuses Foreign-Policy Clichés," *National Interest* (January 20, 2016), http://nationalinterest.org/commentary/the-five-most-abused-foreign-policy-cliches-9978. The four others are isolationism, someone "must" do something, the international community, and on the right/wrong side of history. Ibid. For this reason, the scholar Rosenau painted a mixed picture regarding the future of the term in political inquiry. See Rosenau, note 18 (commenting on the limitations of the term as well as on its future). Professor Rosenau predicted that "[a]s political inquiry becomes more systematic and explicit, the concept is [...] likely to be used less and less[,]" a process that he expected to accelerate with "[t]he ever greater interdependence of nations and the emergence of increasing number of supranational actors." Ibid. At the same time, he said, the term "cannot be entirely abandoned" because "[p]olitical actors will no doubt continue to make extensive use of the national interest in their thinking about foreign-policy goals and in their efforts to mobilize support for them. And, to the extent that they do, political observers must take cognizance of the national interest." Ibid. In short, "while the national interest has little future as an analytic concept, its use in politics will long continue to be a datum requiring analysis." Ibid.

[23] Realists make a sharp distinction between *high politics*, denoting issues supposedly vital to the survival of a state, such as sovereignty, and national security, and *low politics*, matters supposedly secondary to core security interests, such as trade, finance, migration, and social welfare. Russell Bova, *How the World Works: A Brief Survey of International Relations* (New York: Longman, 2010), 211.

which relegates human right to "a (merely) moral concern."[24] For them, ethical concerns like human right may be appropriate at the domestic level but *not* at the international level.[25]

Next to Idealism, although this school emphasizes cooperation in international relations among a larger group of actors other than states, no different from Political Realism, it embraces the anarchic view of international politics, centered around the absence of centralized authority at the world level necessary to enforce good behavior and compliance among errant states.[26] In contrast to these two contending and competing theories, Constructivism, the theoretical framework of choice in this study, views foreign policies as what states make of them,[27] an accommodation which permits the pursuit of human rights in external relations as national interest, should a state so choose.

Evolution of Nigeria's National Interest Since Independence

Nigeria is a land rife with frequent changes in government. As the human-right scholar, Chidi Odinkalu, put it in 1996,

> in its 36 years as an independent state, Nigeria has had seven military rulers, six military inspired changes of government (five of which have been successful military coups), four constitutions (including one that was never

[24] Donnelly, note 2, p. 139. While under this formula, "states may choose to pursue international human rights objectives, out of a sense of compassion or justice," such objectives "must be rigorously subordinated to vital material national interests." Ibid.

[25] See Morgenthau, *Politics Among Nations*, note 21, p. 11 (positing that "[p]olitical realism refuses to identify the moral aspirations of a particular nation with the moral laws that govern the universe[,]" because "[t]o know that nations are subject to the moral law is one thing, while to pretend to know with certainty what is good and evil in the relations among nations is quite another."); Hans J. Morgenthau, "The Pathology of American Power," *International Security*, 1 (Winter 1977), 20 (warning, as President Jimmy Carter poised to take office in 1977, that "[t]o establish and maintain stability in an existentially unstable world requires of necessity an anti-reformist and anti-revolutionary foreign policy").

[26] See Brian C. Schmidt, *The Political Discourse of Anarchy: A Disciplinary History of International Relations* (Albany, NY: State University of New York Press, 1998), *passim*.

[27] Steve Smith, "Foreign Policy Is What States Make of It: Social Construction and International Relations Theory," *in Foreign Policy in a Constructed World*, ed. Vendulka Kubálková (Armonk, NY: M.E. Sharpe, 2001), 38–55.

> used!), four constitution drafting processes, at least four programs of transition from military to civilian government, at least three unsuccessful coup attempts, three national censuses, two civilian regimes, two constituent assemblies, one civil war[,] and one successful transition program.[28]

In the twenty-eight years since these words were written, Nigeria has undergone five other changes in government: one successful transition to civil rule in 1999 and five administrations under the Fourth Republic since then.

As Table 3.1, recap of five distinctive periods in Nigerian foreign policy in Chapter 3 makes clear, altogether sixteen administrations have run Nigeria and managed its foreign policies since its independence in 1960. This comes down to a lifespan of 4 years for each administration. The number drops to little over 2 years when the years since independence are divided by the twenty-eight foreign ministers as of 2024 that have superintended the foreign policies of the country (Table 4.1).[29] This translates into about one minister every two years. The focus on foreign ministers is justified because, vis-à-vis administrations, in gauging national interest or lack thereof, foreign ministers are a more reliable tool of measurement. In Nigeria, foreign ministers, as head of the Ministry of Foreign Affairs, have "direct[] responsib[ility] for foreign policy formulation and implementation."[30] Moreover, "[b]ecause matters were usually left in the hands of the minister and his officials, foreign policy positions could change radically from one minister to another, depending on the minister's orientation."[31]

[28] Chidi A. Odinkalu, "The Management of Transition to Civil Rule by the Military in Nigeria (1966–1999)," *in Nigeria during the Abacha Years*, eds. 'Kunle Amuwo et al. (Lagos: IFRA Nigeria, 2001), 57.

[29] These ministers and the ministry they head had gone through several nomenclatures since the country's independence. Pre-independence, the ministry was christened Department of External Affairs. At independence in 1960, it was renamed Ministry of Foreign and Commonwealth Affairs, then Ministry of External Affairs in 1963, which name it bore until 1989 when it assumed its current name as Ministry of Foreign Affairs. See Ministry of Foreign Affairs, Headquarters Abuja, "Our History," https://foreignaffairs.gov.ng/about-us/our-history/#:~:text=On%20attainment%20of%20a%20Republican,the%20Ministry%20of%20Foreign%20Affairs.

[30] "Foreign Relations," *in Nigeria: A Country Study*, ed. Helen Chapin Metz (Washington, DC: GPO for the Library of Congress, 1991), http://countrystudies.us/nigeria/80.htm.

[31] Ibid.

Table 4.1 Roster of Nigeria's foreign ministers since 1960

Item no.	*Name of minister*	*Period*	*Administration*	*Years in office*
1	Abubakar T. Balewa	First Republic, 1960–1966	Abubakar T. Balewa	1960–1961
2	Jaja Wachuku	First Republic, 1960–1966	Abubakar T. Balewa	1961–1965
3	Nuhu Bamali	First Republic, 1960–1966	Abubakar T. Balewa	1965–1966
4	Okoi Arikpo	First round of military rule, 1966–1979	Yakubu Gowon	1967–1975
5	Joseph Garba	First round of military rule, 1966–1979	Murtala Muhammed-Olusegun Obasanjo	1975–1978
6	Henry Adefope	First round of military rule, 1966–1979	Olusegun Obasanjo	1978–1979
7	Ishaya Audu	Second Republic, 1979–1983	Shehu Shagari	1979–1983
8	Emeka Anyaoku	Second round of military rule, 1983–1999	Muhammadu Buhari	1983–1984
9	Ibrahim Gambari	Second round of military rule, 1983–1999	Muhammadu Buhari	1984–1985
10	Bolaji Akinyemi	Second round of military rule, 1983–1999	Ibrahim Babangida	1985–1987
11	Ike Nwachukwu	Second round of military rule, 1983–1999	Ibrahim Babangida	1987–1989
12	Rilwanu Lukman	Second round of military rule, 1983–1999	Ibrahim Babangida	1989–1990
13	Ike Nwachukwu	Second round of military rule, 1983–1999	Ibrahim Babangida	1990–1993
14	Matthew Mbu	Second round of military rule, 1983–1999	Ibrahim Babangida-Ernest Shonekan	1993
15	Babagana Kingibe	Second round of military rule, 1983–1999	Sani Abacha	1993–1995

(continued)

Table 4.1 (continued)

Item no.	*Name of minister*	*Period*	*Administration*	*Years in office*
16	Tom Ikimi	Second round of military rule, 1983–1999	Sani Abacha	1995–1998
17	Ignatius Olisemeka	Second round of military rule, 1983–1999	Abdulsalami Abubakar	1998–1999
18	Sule Lamido	Fourth Republic since 1999	Olusegun Obasanjo	1999–2003
19	Oluyemi Adeniju	Fourth Republic since 1999	Olusegun Obasanjo	2003–2006
20	Ngozi Okonjo-Iweala	Fourth Republic since 1999	Olusegun Obasanjo	2006
21	U. Joy Ogwu	Fourth Republic since 1999	Olusegun Obasanjo	2006–2007
22	Ojo Maduekwe	Fourth Republic since 1999	Umaru Musa Yar'Adua	2007–2010
23	Henry Ajumogobia	Fourth Republic since 1999	Goodluck Jonathan	2010–2011
24	Olugbenga Ashiru	Fourth Republic since 1999	Goodluck Jonathan	2011–2013
25	Viola Onwuliri	Fourth Republic since 1999	Goodluck Jonathan	2013–2014
26	Aminu B. Wali	Fourth Republic since 1999	Goodluck Jonathan	2014–2015
27	Geoffrey Onyeama	Fourth Republic since 1999	Muhammadu Buhari	2015–2023
28	Yusuf Tuggar	Fourth Republic since 1999	Bola A. Tinubu	2023–

In the light of this history of political instability with consequences for foreign relations or in spite of it, in academic and popular forums, many Nigerian analysts take the position that the country lacks the compass of national interests, especially given the fact that, contrary to the requirements of national interest, Nigeria as a country has ceded territory. We will take these two issues in turn, rather than conflate them, beginning with the first. A sample of analysts who posit that Nigerian foreign policies lack the canvas of any national interest include: Jonathan Ajere who likened Nigerian foreign policy since independence as "regional voluntarism" and "Afrocentrism"[32]; Atah Pine who lambasts the composite of that policy from independence until 2011 (when this piece appeared) as "fifty-one years of conceptual confusion"[33]; Stevens Okoro who observed that "in most countries, Nigeria is represented by diplomats who have no idea of their functional responsibilities[,] hence they cannot protect Nigeria's national interest feverishly even in the face [of] violations;"[34] and Hadi Y. Al-Hassa who opined that the "omnibus nature" of the country's Africa-centered foreign policy "does not appear to be well aligned to the country's national interests or has not served the national interest in a commensurate measure."[35]

Ajere posited, inter alia, that "Nigeria's self-assumption of African interest promotion responsibility is indicative of the role of a volunteer[,]" a posture he said is inconsistent with realist theory.[36] However, he concedes that Nigeria's "commitment[] to African security and development" and the "achievement of its national interests are not incompatible[,]" if the country improves its "local politics and economic

[32] Jonathan Ajere, "Regional Voluntarism: The Sustainability of Nigerian Afrocentrism," *E-International Relations* (July 19, 2012), *passim*, http://www.e-ir.info/2012/07/19/regional-voluntarism-the-sustainability-of-nigerian-afrocentrism/.

[33] Atah Pine, "Nigerian Foreign Policy, 1960–2011: Fifty One Years of Conceptual Confusion," *Modern Ghana* (October 4, 2011), *passim*, http://www.modernghana.com/print/354264/1/nigeria-foreign-policy-1960-2011-fifty-one-years-o.html.

[34] Stevens Okoro, "Nigeria and the Concept of National Interest," *Daily Independent* (Lagos) (July 2012), http://dailyindependentnig.com/2012/07/nigeria-and-concept-of-national-interest/. Emphasis added.

[35] Hadi Y. Al-Hassa, "Evaluating Nigerian Foreign Policy at 50," *Gamji* (Circa 2010), http://www.gamji.com/article9000/news9139.htm.

[36] Ajere, note 32, p. 4.

management."[37] Four slogans in Nigeria's foreign policy that Pine singled out for criticism were dynamic foreign policy, Africa as the centerpiece of Nigeria's foreign policy, economic diplomacy, and citizen diplomacy.[38]

Pine opined that what Nigeria needs but currently lacks "is a foreign policy that will contain the crisis of underdevelopment, the challenges of poverty, leadership, political development, and a host of other maladies and launch her as a modern state in the twenty[-]first century in order to realize her full potentials and cravings for continental and global leadership."[39] Instead, what currently passes for policies are regime-specific pronouncements "not grounded in deep philosophical thought, visionary imagination[,] and broad[-]based considerations of long-lasting benefits to the national interests."[40] According to Pine, Nigeria's foreign policies since independence may be summed up as "change and continuity, motion without movement, dynamism without surge."[41]

For Okoro, the solution to Nigerian diplomats unable to protect Nigeria's national interest because they are not versed in their "functional responsibilities" is for Nigerians to "experiment with a new and different tactics in the fervent pursuits of [their] national interest."[42] After extensive reviews of the country's numerous engagements and commitments in Africa since independence, Al-Hassa posited, "[i]t seems that there is apparent disconnect between national interest and Nigeria-African relations. It is apparent that the nation is doing too much in the African continent without corresponding positive outcome."[43] He advised that the country's "attention should be more focused toward achieving our vital national interests[,] such as the socio-economic growth and development so as to improve the standard of living of the populace."[44] Al-Hassa called for the convention of a foreign policy summit on a range of issues, including "redefining our national interest, refocusing our foreign policy in such a way that we will minimize loss and increase gains as well as

[37] Ibid., p. 9.

[38] Pine, note 33.

[39] Ibid.

[40] Ibid.

[41] Ibid.

[42] Okoro, note 34.

[43] Al-Hassa, note 35.

[44] Ibid.

tying it to the socio-economic growth and development of our great country."[45]

Next to cession of territory, a key element in the definition of national interest is whether a country has encountered an issue over which it will go to war. In its national history, Nigeria has ceded territory, something which works against territorial wholeness and a value which many definitions of the national interest will classify as vital interest, in defense of which a country would be willing to go to war, if necessary.[46] As indicated in Chapter 1, the Nigerian government obeyed an unfavorable 2002 judgment against it by the International Court of Justice that awarded the Bakassi peninsula, a territory rich in oil located in the boundary between Nigeria and Cameroon, to Cameroon in a long-standing dispute between the two countries over ownership of the territory.[47] Nigeria complied with the ruling despite the fact that 9 out of 10 of the peninsula's estimated 300,000 residents are Nigerians.[48]

Despite these tabled concerns going to the formulation and implementation of Nigeria's foreign policy, Nigeria has national interests that guide its external relations. First, every state which conducts external relations has a national interest that animates those relations. Nigeria is no different. The country is a non-autarkic state born in international relations through British colonialism.[49] If nothing else, as a leading oil producer, Nigeria possesses national interest sufficient enough to facilitate export of its crude oil and related raw materials to the capitalist-dominated global economy.

Secondly, several times in the post-independence life of the country, Nigerian leaders have convened conferences or empaneled committees to review the country's foreign policies and map the way forward. These initiatives include: the Ambassadors' Conference in 1966 under General Aguiyi-Ironsi, the Adedeji Panel in 1976 under the Mohammed-Obasanjo regime, and a conference in 1986 under General Babangida to "review

[45] Ibid.

[46] See notes 10–12.

[47] See Chapter 1, note 70, and accompanying text.

[48] Chapter 1, note 71, and accompanying text.

[49] Inspiration for this idea comes from Hanes Walton Jr. and Robert C. Smith, *American Politics and the African American Quest for Universal Freedom,* 5th Ed. (Longman, 2010), 283 (depicting African Americans as a people "born in foreign affairs through African slavery and the slave trade").

the country's foreign policy and recommend broad policy frameworks for the 1990s and beyond."[50] In each of these instances, covered in Chapter 3, dealing with the historical background of the study, the conferees recommitted the country to the principle of Africa as centerpiece of Nigeria's foreign relations laid down in the early days of the country's independence.

In addition to these reviews, various Nigerian governments have created think tanks to help them formulate foreign policies. The most notable of these institutions are: the Nigerian Institute of International Affairs (NIIA), formed in 1961,[51] and the National Institute for Policy and Strategic Studies (NIPSS) established in 1979.[52] The NIIA avowedly "seeks to promote a deeper understanding of Nigeria's foreign policy, international relations, and global cultures and peoples," through "painstaking research, national and international conferences and seminars, workshops[,] and public lectures on crucial issues in world affairs."[53] The Institute is modelled after Chattam House of the Royal Institute of International Affairs in London.[54] For its part, the NIPSS touts itself "as a high[-]level center for reflection, research[,] and dialog" where "academics of excellence, seasoned policy initiators and executors and other citizens of mature experience and wisdom, drawn from all walks of life, meet to reflect and exchange ideas on the great and critical issues of society, particularly as they relate to Nigeria and Africa, within the context of a constantly changing world."[55] To add to these deliberate energies, beginning from 1979, Nigerians codified the country's foreign policy objectives by including them in its constitution.[56]

[50] "Foreign Relations," note 30.

[51] Nigerian Institute of International Affairs, "Director-General's Message," http://niianet.org/dgmessage.htm; Nigerian Institute of International Affairs, "About Us," http://niianet.org/aboutus.htm.

[52] National Institute for Policy and Strategic Studies, "Objectives," http://nipsskuru.gov.ng/index.php/similar-tags.html.

[53] "Director-General's Message," note 51.

[54] Ibrahim A. Gambari, *Theory and Reality in Foreign Policy Making: Nigeria after the Second Republic* (Atlantic Highlands, NJ: Humanities Press International, Inc., 1989), 11.

[55] National Institute for Policy and Strategic Studies, "Objectives," note 52.

[56] See Constitution of the Federal Republic of Nigeria, 1999, *Constitute Project*, https://www.constituteproject.org/constitution/Nigeria_1999, art. 19 (enumerating the

Rather than assailments directed at the national interest as such, critics who complain that Nigerian foreign policy lacks the compass of a national interest direct their anger at what they consider the excessive emphasis on Africa in Nigerian foreign policy—not sufficiently rooted in "enlightened self-interest or deliberate search for sustainable advantages."[57] This is the reason Ajere saw no conflict between Nigeria's commitment to Africa and its national interest, *if* the country implements the necessary reforms in domestic politics that should form the basis for an African-centered foreign policy.[58] Atah argued similarly with his view that, for all its benefits and Nigeria's laudable energies in this respect, the focus on Africa in Nigerian foreign policy soon took a life all its own, "reproduc[ing] itself, like the ever[-]recurring mathematical decimal," without regard to any merit rooted in economic or other tangible benefits.[59] Atah cited Nigeria's interventions in Liberia and Sierra Leone on humanitarian missions whose interventions in the aftermath of the conflicts earned the country no reckonable economic rewards.[60] To overcome this problem, he said, the country needs a coherent foreign policy, *not* regime specific, that will stem its hosts of "maladies," including "the crisis of underdevelopment" and poverty at home that it must overcome to realize its potentials for leadership in Africa and the world.[61]

And to create the strong economic base that it needs to use its economy as an "instrument of diplomatic engagement," Nigeria must build its still "grossly underdeveloped" economy.[62] For Okoro, the main concern is a lack of sync between domestic and foreign policies, contradictions evident in a "false generosity" abroad and "penury at home," as well as in the country's "stupidly overstretching [itself] to maintain peace in other countries" that it lacks at home.[63] Last but not least is Al-Hassa the

five objectives of the country in foreign policy, instructively including as the very first, "promotion and protection of the national interest.").

[57] Reuben Abati, "The President as Chief Diplomat," *YNaija* (April 17, 2016), http://ynaija.com/president-travel-reuben-abati/.

[58] Ajere, note 32.

[59] See Atah, note 33.

[60] Ibid.

[61] Atah, note 33.

[62] Ibid.

[63] Okoro, note 34.

gravamen of whose argument is that the Africa-centered orientation takes an "omnibus nature" that puts it out of alignment with the country's national interests.[64]

A resolution by the Nigerian Senate in December of 2015 mirrored these popular sentiments.[65] The resolution pled with the Nigerian government to review the objectives of the country's foreign policy to ensure that its relationship with other countries produces tangible benefits for Nigeria.[66] More specifically, it advised the national government to "imbibe Nigeria's economic interest as vital component of our foreign policy objectives in countries where the nation invested her enormous human and material resources to restore security, peace, stability[,] and democracy[.]".[67]

In addition, activities that critics view as altruism may actually be undergirded by considerations of national interest. An example would be the decision in 1974 by the Gowon regime (1966–1975) to extend subsidy on oil to some African countries by selling crude oil to them at concessionary rates, provided they had their own refineries and would not re-export the oil to third countries.[68] The decision came in spite of Nigeria's role as a member of the Organization of the Petroleum Exporting Countries (OPEC), which role impels it to favor higher oil prices.[69] However, there was a substantial dose of national interest embedded in this seemly altruistic policy. As one perceptive source explained, "[p]roviding subsidies for African countries was a safe move for Nigeria" for a number of good reasons, including that "it enhanced [the country's]

64 Al-Hassa, note 35.

65 See "Senate Asks Buhari to Review Nigeria's Foreign Policy," *Premium Times* (Abuja) (December 8, 2015), http://www.premiumtimesng.com/news/top-news/194812-%E2%80%8Bs%E2%80%8Benate-asks-buhari-to-review-nigerias-foreign-policy.html; and Johnbosco Agbakwuru and Joseph Erunke, "Senate Urges Buhari to Review Nigeria's Foreign Policy," *Vanguard* (Lagos) (June 3, 2015), https://www.vanguardngr.com/2015/06/senate-urges-buhari-to-review-nigerias-foreign-policy/.

66 Ibid.

67 Ibid.

68 "Foreign Relations," note 30.

69 Ibid.

position and influence in Africa while building African solidarity," "protected security interests by preventing economic decline[,]" and "aided Nigeria in its efforts to create ECOWAS."[70]

Another example not focused directly on Africa would be the importance that Nigeria placed on international organizations anchored on its commitment to peace and international cooperation. On the surface this does not sound like promotion of national interest. But more critically examined, it *is*, given that "in the cases of the OAU and ECOWAS, these organizations also served to increase African unity," a key goal in Nigeria's foreign relations.[71] Besides the right, states also have the *duty* to protect their national interests. Based on the foregoing, including the continuity across leaderships in the emphasis on Africa in Nigerian foreign policy, there is no *prima facie* evidence that Nigerian decision makers failed in their duty to protect the national interest.

Strategies for Reconstructing Nigeria's National Interest to Make It Human-Right-Compliant

A reconstructed national interest is a critical starting point in the adoption of a human-right foreign policy. Such reconstruction takes place when a state remakes its "national identity in accordance with universalist norms, roles, and expectations[,]" and views itself "as [an] interconnected member[] of a global community that works best for everyone when human rights are respected."[72] States who apply human rights in their external relations do *not* and need not do so at the expense of their national interests.[73] To the contrary, they are following their national interests, the only difference being that, unlike states who define their national interest based on power, consistent with the commandment of realist theory, states with a human-right-based policy spot "a broader, longer-term vision of national interest."[74]

What is more, pursuit of a human-right policy need not spell abandonment of complementary material interests. Instead, "the interplay

[70] Ibid.

[71] Ibid.

[72] Brysk, note 1, p. 31.

[73] See ibid.

[74] Ibid.

of moral and material interests can help to explain the selectivity and targeting of principled foreign policy" by states who apply human rights in their external affairs.[75] As the discussion in the preceding section bears out, in its amorphousness, Nigeria's foreign policy since independence has not conformed strictly to realist teaching. Given this reality, Nigeria should experience little difficulty making the transition to a human-right or principled foreign policy. Next to strategies, Nigeria needs a doctrinal (re)orientation of its national interest and a reshaping of its foreign policy machinery embedded in a range of practical techniques. We take these two issues in turn.

Doctrinal (Re)Orientation

(Re)orienting its national interest doctrine requires Nigeria to make that interest whatever the country and its citizens are interested in.[76] Under the Constructivist worldview that informs this work, "what interests a nation is not always state security."[77] Accordingly, if Nigeria "feel[s] that it is in [its] interest to expend some of [its] foreign policy resources and attention on the rights of foreigners, there is no reason [it] should not[,]"[78] and for intrinsically human-right reason, rather than on instrumental ground(s). For example, living in a more just world, rather than justifications, such as "rights-protective regimes are more peaceful or better trading partners."[79] Staying with the bifurcation of national interest into vital and non-vital values, human-right concerns should sometimes make it into the vital category, rather than be forever relegated to the non-vital category as would normally be the case, based on realist commandment.

But this does not mean that the national interest and the objectives of foreign policy are "reducible to human rights"; instead, they can sometimes include other components.[80] More elaborately,

[75] Ibid., p. 33.

[76] See Donnelly, note 2, p. 139.

[77] Brysk, note 1, p. 33.

[78] Donnelly, note 2, p. 140.

[79] Ibid.

[80] Ibid.

> Setting priorities among various national interests is an essential part of the process of defining the national interest. International human rights law leaves states considerable latitude with respect to the weight they attach to human rights objectives in their foreign policy. There is no requirement that they include international human rights goals. …
>
> For those states that have included international human rights in their foreign policies, however, we can reasonably demand that human rights actually enter into their stated place in the hierarchy of national interests.[81]

This counsels the use of a decision-making formula that assigns human rights a weight that matches its stated place in the hierarchy of national interest.

This standard is not as onerous as it seems on the surface; as Professor Donnelly clarified elsewhere, the main point is to assess "the impact of the full range of […] foreign policy behavior on international human rights practices, not just those initiatives that explicitly address human rights."[82] Still on this matter of the national interest of the country being whatever the country and its citizens are interested, using a decision making formula that assigns human rights a weight that roughly matches its stated place in the hierarchy of national interest,[83] it helps if the country puts things in writing. Apart from the promotional materials of the Ministry of Foreign Affairs, one good place to start would be in a national security strategy document of the type that, under the force of law, US Presidents write up and adopt.[84]

[81] Ibid., p. 146.

[82] Jack Donnelly and Debra Liang-Fenton, *Introduction, in Implementing U.S. Human Rights Policy,* ed. Debra Liang-Fenton (Washington, DC: United States Institute of Peace Press, 2004), 6.

[83] Donnelly, note 2, p. 146.

[84] As its name suggests, US National Security Strategy is a coherent document, not a promotional brochure on the policy of an affected US administration that sets the priorities of a particular U.S. administration and communicates those priorities to Congress, the American people, and the world. Karen DeYoung, "Obama Redefines National Security Strategy, Looks Beyond Military Might," *Washington Post* (May 27, 2010), http://www.washingtonpost.com/wp-dyn/content/article/2010/05/27/AR2010052701044.html. The document is prepared annually, pursuant to the Goldwater-Nichols Act of 1986, Pub. L.99-433, which mandates the President to submit to Congress an annual strategic statement. National security is something that presidents do whether or not they report to Congress, but by requiring the White House to make its policy explicit, Congress asserts greater control over the military while affording itself

Reshaping Nigeria's Foreign Policy Machinery

Another strategy in the road to the adoption of a human-right policy is to reshape Nigeria's foreign policy machine in a more human-right-sensitive direction. Every state which conducts relations with other countries has institutions involved in the formulation and implementation of its foreign policies. Nigeria is no different. Given their classified nature, the intricacies of foreign policy decision making are a topic where relatively little information exists.[85] This is especially so for a developing country like Nigeria.[86] A way around this problem is to sketch a template of the US foreign policy machine (like the US, Nigeria is a federation with a presidential system of government), next applied to Nigeria.[87]

That heavy-lifting is not necessary here. Instead, the more limited task is to highlight the techniques necessary for reshaping Nigeria's foreign policy machine in a human-right specific direction. Doing so mandates that we first articulate the problems that confront that apparatus. There are two such interlocked problems: lack of public input,

an opportunity to exert greater influence on the President's national security strategy. "National Security Strategy, United States," *Encyclopedia of Espionage, Intelligence & Security* (2004), http://www.encyclopedia.com/doc/1G2-3403300516.html.

[85] For a pioneering work dissecting the nature of these decisions and the models that can be applied to understand them, see Graham Allison, *Essence of Decision: Explaining the Cuban Missile Crisis* (Boston, MA: Little Brown, 1971) (study on the decision making relating to the dispute between the United States and the Soviet Union regarding the unimplemented attempt of the Soviet Union to place nuclear weapons in Cuba supposedly to insulate it from possible United States invasion).

[86] One of the few studies on decision making in Nigerian foreign policy that turned up during my research is Ufot Bassey Inamete, *Foreign Policy Decision-Making in Nigeria* (Selinsgrove, PA: Susquehanna University Press, 2001). The study is dated and, except for the first 2 years up to its appearance in 2001, does not cover the period of the Fourth Republic since 1999.

[87] See Philip C. Aka, *Human Rights in Nigeria's External Relations: Building the Record of a Moral Superpower* (Lanham, Boulder, New York, and London: Lexington Books, 2017), 193–200. US foreign policy machinery comprises five separate yet interconnected components: the Constitution; Congress; the president; an executive branch made up of foreign affairs, defense, the intelligence community, and the economic agencies; and public opinion. Ibid., pp. 193–196. Of these five elements, the one Nigeria lacks is public opinion. See ibid., p. 201 (Table 8.1, recapping Nigeria's foreign policy machine). The table indicated no input from the public to foreign policy formulation during the first and second rounds of military rule (little surprise), none during the Second Republic (a bit surprising), and little to no input during the First Republic from 1960 until 1966 and Fourth Republic since 1999. Ibid.

and lack of cohesiveness. Understanding the distinction between foreign policy *formulation* and *implementation* is necessary for the discussion that follows. Under the US system that Nigeria copies, foreign policy *formulation* requires the participation of the President, Congress, the executive branch, and the public. Conversely, implementation of foreign policy is the exclusive responsibility of the President and his subordinates in the executive branch.

Lack of Public or Popular Input

Societal forces, including the mass media, interest groups, and public opinion, play an important role in US foreign relations.[88] Moreover, along with the media, public opinion ranks among key "democratic checks on" US foreign policy.[89] The public has a duty to assess US's interests in world affairs, among other obligations.[90] Issues for public consideration relating to foreign policy include the proper relationship between the US and the United Nations, the proper role of peacekeeping operations and foreign aid programs, and the balance of economic and political interests against humanitarian and environmental concerns.[91] Decision makers respond to these questions within the context the American people's never-ending "experiment in self-government and the democratic limits established in the Constitution."[92] In the US, "[t]he voice of public opinion occasionally penetrates the carefully encrypted speech and muffled secrecy of foreign policy making to have an impact."[93] While there is no clarity regarding the impact of public opinion in US foreign policy, at the very least, that opinion "plac[es] new items on the political agenda."[94]

[88] See Eugene R. Wittkopf et al., *American Foreign Policy: Patterns and Process,* 7th Ed. (Belmont, CA: Thomson Wadsworth, 2008), 239–323.

[89] See Larry Berman and Bruce Allen Murphy, *Approaching Democracy*, 8th Ed. (New York: Pearson Education, Inc., 2013), 534–545.

[90] Ibid., p. 535.

[91] Ibid.

[92] Ibid.

[93] Ibid. An example that Professors Berman and Murphy cited here was the Vietnam War (1955–1975) wherein popular discontent impelled the US government to retrace its steps and reverse a longstanding policy. Ibid.

[94] Glenn P. Hastedt, *American Foreign Policy: Past, Present, Future*, 6th Ed. (Upper Saddle River, NJ: Pearson Prentice Hall, 2006), 138–139.

In Nigeria, in contrast, the picture is a lack of popular input in foreign policy. Instead, the country's external relations "reflect the needs and aspirations of a national super elite of business, bureaucratic, military, and traditional ruling groups."[95] As a corollary, at any point in time, only "a tiny segment" of the Nigerian population is involved in foreign policy[96]; that does *not* include the masses of the people whose well-being should form the basis for the conduct of any foreign policy. To the contrary, oftentimes, foreign policy in Nigeria is "personality-influenced"[97] and steeped in formation and implementation "in highly elitist circles"[98] without the benefit of any input from the masses nor imbued with measurable regard for their needs.

To use as example the Ministry of Foreign Affairs, an agency closely associated with the formulation and implementation of Nigerian foreign policy, the foreign policy making team consists of the minister and his or her immediate staff, plus "a small foreign policy elite comprising other top government officials, interest group leaders, academicians, top military officers, religious leaders, and journalists."[99] This leads to the scenario where, as indicated before, radical changes take place in foreign policy depending on the idiosyncratic orientation of the foreign minister.[100] The same lack of popular input is observable in peacekeeping, one of the most visible faces of Nigerian foreign policy, covered in Chapter 6. This is not to suggest that public opinion should perfectly reflect majority preferences for it does not, not even in the US,[101] from which Nigeria draws its model.

In sum, in the US, there is a better appreciation and sensitivity by officialdom, roundly lacking in Nigeria, that public input should be a natural part of the foreign policy making machinery. Under the administration of President Umaru Musa Yar'Adua from 2007 to 2010, Nigeria espoused

[95] Gambari, note 54, p. 5.

[96] Ibid.

[97] J. Peter Pham, "Nigeria's Foreign Policy: An Inquiry into Sources and Prospects," Presentation for International Conference, Lisbon, Portugal (November 8–9, 2007), 95–96, www.ipri.pt/eventos/pdf/JPeterPham_paper.pdf.

[98] Gambari, note 54, p. 5.

[99] "Foreign Relations," note 30.

[100] See note 31 and accompanying text.

[101] See Berman and Murphy, note 89, pp. 266–267 (reflecting on the extent to which public policy in the US mirrors public opinion).

the notion of a citizen diplomacy revolved around foreign policy focused on Nigerian citizens at home and abroad.[102] However, this concept did not take root in Nigerian diplomacy until the death of Yar'Adua in May 2010, not even during the period of his successor.[103]

Lack of Cohesiveness

Adding to the lack of popular input in the design and implementation of Nigerian foreign policy and compounding it is a lack of cohesiveness. According to Professor Ibrahim Gambari, former foreign minister of Nigeria,[104] Nigerian foreign policy is controlled by a super-elite, not known for its selflessness,[105] that is "deeply divided along ethnic, regional, religious, and ideological lines[.]"[106] This is an assessment other scholars share. These include the Africanist Peter Pham who posits that under the Fourth Republic, as in the past, foreign policy making and implementation in the land lacked systematization[107]; as well as Professors Ayua and Dakas, writing jointly, who pointed out that Nigeria's Constitution lacked provision for intergovernmental consultation in foreign affairs and defense.[108]

Conceivable Solutions

From a human-right standpoint, the solutions track the problems. First, foreign policy decision making in Nigeria somehow needs to integrate public opinion than is presently the case now. The opportunity for the

[102] See Chapter 3, note 90, and accompanying text.

[103] Adekeye Adebajo, "Sad Deterioration of Nigeria's Foreign Policy," *B[usiness] D[ay] L[ive]* (Johannesburg) (May 6, 2013), http://za.news.yahoo.com/sad-deterioration-nigeria-foreign-policy-051439591.html (contending that Nigeria's foreign policy under Goodluck Jonathan, President from 2010–2015, "lack[ed] strategic vision").

[104] See item 9 on Table 4.1, listing Nigerian ministers since 1960.

[105] Gambari, note 54, p. x.

[106] Ibid., p. 5.

[107] Pham, note 97, pp. 95–96.

[108] Ignatius Akaayar Ayua and Dakas C.J. Dakas, "Federal Republic of Nigeria," in *Constitutional Origins, Structure, and Change in Federal Countries*, eds. John Kincaid and George Alan Tarr (Montreal, Canada: McGill-Queen's University Press, 2005), 266. See also Adebajo, "Sad Deterioration of Nigeria's Foreign Policy," note 103, who observed that under Jonathan, Nigeria's foreign policy "lack[ed] strategic vision."

public to have a say in their own government is both an issue of democracy as well as a human rights concern.[109] Second, Nigeria should create more sense of nationhood necessary for effective conduct of human rights by implementing the various strategies for increased human rights at home discussed in Chapter 5. Third, it may be necessary for Nigeria to integrate intergovernmental consultation in the Nigerian Constitution (along with any national security strategy document) additional to the informal channels that now exist.

Nigeria may also consider the possibility of assigning its embassies some human rights role the way the US has done since the presidency of Jimmy Carter from 1976 to 1980. US embassies today play a critical role in the preparation and production of the *Country Reports on Human Rights Practices* published by the US State Department in spring every year.[110] On his narrative regarding the US's road to a human rights policy, Carter asserted that soon after he took office, he declared his "intention to regard every American ambassador as my personal human rights rapporteur: I asked them to take person responsibility for writing and submitting their Country Reports on human rights."[111]

Similarly, Nigerian Fourth Republic leaders should use the language of human rights in formulating and implementing domestic and foreign policy[112]; they need their own "personal human rights rapporteurs." Although there is no suggestion for anything the scale of the *Country Reports*, Nigerian foreign desks could develop a niche in human rights, additional to their present roles. Because foreign policy should not be run

[109] For example, the Universal Declaration of Human Rights provides that "[t]he will of the people" "expressed in periodic and genuine elections" "shall be the basis of the authority of government." See Universal Declaration of Human Rights, art. 21(3), G.A. Res. 217 A (III), U.N. GAOR, 3d Sess., U.N. Doc. A/810 (1948).

[110] For more on this important human rights tool, see Philip C. Aka, "The *Country Reports on Human Rights Practices* and U.S. Human Rights Policy in a Changing World," *Perspectives on Global Development & Technology*, 14 (2015), 238.

[111] Jimmy Carter, "The American Road to a Human Rights Policy," *in Realizing Human Rights: Moving from Inspiration to Impact,* eds. Samantha Power and Graham Allison (New York: St. Martin's Press, 2000), 54.

[112] This insight comes from South Africa where, under Nelson Mandela (President from 1994–1999), an exchange ensued regarding application of human rights in the country's foreign policy. See Tiyanjana Maluwa, "Human Rights and Foreign Policy in Post-Apartheid South Africa," in *Human Rights and Comparative Foreign Policy*, ed. David P. Forsythe (New York: United Nations University Press, 2000), 250.

on a shoe-string budget, part of the reforms needing to be implemented should include proper funding of its foreign missions.[113] And it does not hurt if Nigeria prunes down the number of its diplomatic missions abroad to a more manageable number, paying attention to factors, such as the "economic or strategic interests" of each mission and eschewing the turning of diplomatic postings into the sinecure of political patronage and expedience.[114] As of 2024, Nigeria has about 103 diplomatic missions, including embassies, high commissions, consulates, and the like, in 94 countries,[115] some of which it cannot afford to maintain.

To facilitate these changes, Nigeria must rationalize its resources better, top of which would be diversification of its economy for too long based on oil and gas, as well as the maintenance of a proper balance between fertility rate and economic growth to tease out the means for principled foreign policy work. This may necessitate forging new relations outside Africa over and above its policy thrust for too long centered on Africa. To borrow the wisdom of one commentator, its "search for a new role [...] in world affairs should involve a region-by-region review of its foreign policy with a view to redefining its national interests and foreign policy objectives,"[116] and it should specifically focus on "bilateral relations with certain regional economic and military powers that have emerged" recently: China and India in Asia, the US and the European Union, specifically Germany and France; Argentina, Brazil, and Mexico in Latin America; and mutually-beneficial relationships with the World Bank and the International Monetary Fund while expanding ties with the African Development Bank.[117] Chapter 9 on the imperativeness of serious reforms at home builds on and complements these insights.

[113] Dapo Fafowora, "Review of Nigeria's Foreign Policy," *Nation* (June 4, 2015), http://thenationonlineng.net/review_of_nigerias-foreign-policy.

[114] Fafowora, note 113. Fafowora advised that the number be cut down "immediately to 100, and thereafter to not more than 80." Ibid.

[115] "Nigerian Embassies and Consulates," *Embassies*, https://embassies.net/nigeria-embassy#:~:text=Nigeria%20currently%20maintains%20about%20102%20diplomatic%20representations%20worldwide. Fafowora advised that the number be cut down "immediately to 100, and thereafter to not more than 80." Fafowora, note 113.

[116] Fafowora, note 113.

[117] Ibid.

Conclusion

This chapter expounded reconstruction of the national interest as the first port of call in the transition to a human-right policy for Nigeria, including the modalities for that transition in readiness for human-right duties in the new era post-Buhari that Nigeria finds itself. Three issues covered in the discussion were the definition of national interest as a starting point; the evolution of that interest in Nigeria since independence; and strategies, doctrine as well as practical techniques, for reconstructing the country's national interest to render it human-right-compliant. Beginning with definition, on account of its plasticity, more than Realism and Idealism, Constructivism accommodates the interjection of human rights in external affairs, the main reason why, as well indicated in Chapter 2 (which sketched the exigency for principled foreign policy for Nigeria) this theoretical framework was chosen over its two rivals. Next to evolution, the overconcentration on Africa as centerpiece of Nigeria's foreign policy long after the decolonization of the continent raised legitimate questions regarding the extent to which the country's foreign policies is undergirded by the compass of national interest. Despite the perceived amorphousness in the articulation and implementation of the country's foreign policy the overconcentration unearths, Nigeria still has a national interest sufficient to facilitate the export of crude oil, which it produces in large quantity, to the capitalist-dominated world economy.

Next on strategies, a logical starting point was a (re)orientation of the national interest doctrine embedded, as indicated already, on Constructivism. Because the contours of Nigeria's foreign policy since independence does not strictly follow realist strictures and commandments, there is a small gap between where the country is now and where it needs to be that makes a transition to principled foreign policy relatively pain-free. Moreover, transition to principled foreign policy does not require that the country abandon pursuit of complementary material interests. Applying human rights in external affairs is predicated on a set of national interests in dealing with other countries that includes human-right concerns, but is also not limited to just these concerns. In the apt observation of Professor Donnelly, "in addition to human rights, sovereignty and non-intervention are vital norms of international society."[118] As Donnelly cautioned, it is

[118] Jack Donnelly, "An Overview," in *Human Rights and Comparative Foreign Policy*, ed. David P. Forsythe (New York: United Nations University Press, 2000), 318.

foolhardy to "overestimate either human rights or sovereignty" in the external behavior of states.[119] And it does not hurt if Nigerian leaders codify these ideas in a national security strategy document, drawing from the example of the US from which it draws its model.

Lastly on strategy for shaping Nigeria's foreign policy and activities to render them human-right-compliant, possible practical steps to this goal include increased popular participation in the design and implementation of foreign policy, as the US exemplifies. There is also the need to strengthen the cohesiveness of foreign policy formulation and implementation through interjection of more strategic vision, the growth of human rights at home (object of Chapter 5 next after this chapter), and the need for Nigerian leaders to couch policies in human-right language, down to the assignment of human-right duties, as the US State Department does, to Nigerian diplomatic missions around the world.

119 Ibid.

CHAPTER 5

Increased Respect for Human Rights at Home

Introduction

Increased respect for human rights within Nigeria is a desideratum for successful design and implementation of a human-right policy for the country in the wake of General Buhari's departure from the Nigerian political scene in May 2023, in an age of equally momentous changes in British politics, signified by the coronation of a new monarch. This chapter unearths and presents techniques for achieving that goal. It is the second, after Chapter 4 on reconstructing Nigeria's national interest for human-right work, in a sample of five distinctive methods marked out for analysis in this book. The remaining three methods are peacekeeping, analyzed in Chapter 6, the TAC in Chapter 7, and the ECOWAS Community Court of Justice, referred for short in this book as the Community Court of Justice (CCJ), in Chapter 8.

A threshold question revolves around the meaning of "increased respect for human rights at home." The phrase raises a question regarding what *depth* of respect for human rights is appropriate.[1] The appropriate depth is not an inchoate desire to treat citizens "fairly and seek to realize

[1] This is an issue that sometimes comes up in the literature. For example, should the appropriate minimal commitment to rights be respect or toleration or more. See Amy Gutmann, "Introduction," in *Human Rights as Politics and Idolatry*, ed. Michael Ignatieff (Princeton, NJ: Princeton University Press, 2001), xxvi–xxvii (disagreeing that toleration

P. C. Aka, *Human Rights in Nigeria's External Relations in the Age of General Muhammadu Buhari and His Successors*,
https://doi.org/10.1007/978-3-031-63231-0_5

their interests."[2] Instead, it is solicitude of a more general or universal nature embedded in "recognized rights of [...] citizens that can be exercised against their rulers."[3] Put differently, the focus here, as in co-chapters under Part II of the book devoted to methods, is not a verbal commitment to human rights ideals. Instead, it is a conversation animated by an essentialist instinct for a transition from inspiration to impact in realizing human rights.[4]

But there are also distinguishing markers. First, except perhaps for reconstruction of Nigeria's national interest for human right work, this chapter looks less than a method, though a method it *is*. Secondly, probably more than its co-chapters under Part II on methods, this discussion underscores the futility of a sharp distinction between domestic and foreign policies, conceptually as well as policy-wise. There are two main segments to the ensuing discussion: justification for increased human rights at home, and a layout of seven steps designed to facilitate the achievement of that target.

Justifying Increased Human Rights at Home

Charity begins at home. The do-gooder should help himself and his family before helping others. Charity beginning at home is the pointed flip-side to the proposition of "beautiful abroad but ugly at home"[5]; persons uncharitable to themselves are not in a position to extend charity, which property they lack, toward others. In a word, foreign policy begins at

is enough but, instead, arguing for a moral commitment anchored on toleration plus respect).

[2] Jack Donnelly, "An Overview," in *Human Rights and Comparative Foreign Policy*, ed. David P. Forsythe (New York: United Nations University Press, 2000), 312.

[3] Ibid.

[4] See Samantha Power and Graham Allison, eds., *Realizing Human Rights: Moving from Inspiration to Impact* (New York: St. Martin's Press, 2000), xiv (observing that "if a key challenge of the second half of the twentieth century was gaining universal acceptance of the idea that human rights existed or mattered, the key challenge for the decades ahead is to identify the policies and actions that most effectively realize human rights").

[5] S.O. Akinboye, Beautiful Abroad but Ugly at Home: Issues and Contra[di]ctions in Nigerian Foreign Policy. University of Lagos Inaugural Lecture Series (2013), www.unilag.edu.ng/opendocnew.php?.

home.[6] Foreign policy initiatives, including demonstrations of national sovereignty in international relations, are nominal if a state is unable to protect the basic rights of its citizens, beginning with the right to life.[7] "It is folly to weaken at home what one is trying to strengthen abroad."[8] Instead, a country's human-right record is the basis for projection of human rights abroad[9]; projecting human rights abroad must be rooted in and reflect respect of human rights at home.[10]

Accordingly, Nigeria's foreign policy should be the tool for externalizing the "domestic priorities and the aspirations of [Nigerian] citizens, including the values of democracy within the country."[11] For Nigeria, increased human rights at home comes with certain domestic and external benefits. First, more human rights at home is the answer to the apology of "beautiful abroad but ugly at home,"[12] emblematized by "the solecism of abuses at home, and a nominal commitment to international law

[6] Richard N. Haass, *Foreign Policy Begins at Home: The Case for Putting America's House in Order* (New York: Basic Books, 2014) (focusing on the US). Haass was then President of US Council of Foreign Relations and since June 2023 President Emeritus of the organization.

[7] A.J. Vincent, *Human Rights and International Relations* (New York: Cambridge University Press, 1986), 130.

[8] Thomas E. Patterson, *The American Democracy*, 8th Ed. (New York: McGraw-Hill, 2008), 513–514 (discussing the economic dimension of national security policy, citing the warning of former US President Dwight D. Eisenhower against "the unwarranted influence" and "misplaced power" of the military-industrial complex, the coalition of military establishment, industries that manufacture weapons, and members of Congress from constituencies that depend heavily on the arms industry). Between them, these three mutually benefit from a high level of defense spending. The source of Eisenhower's concern was that sustained high levels of military and secrecy would only weaken America in the long run. Eisenhower warned that excessive government secrecy, justified in the name of national security, threatened liberty. Ibid., pp. 514 (box), and 522.

[9] Alison Brysk, *Global Good Samaritans: Human Rights as Foreign Policy* (New York: Oxford University Press, 2009), 19.

[10] See Andrew Lui, *Why Canada Cares: Human Rights and Foreign Policy in Theory and Practice* (Montreal, Canada: McGill-Queen's University Press, 2012), 75 (commenting on the statement of Lloyd Axworthy, then Canadian Foreign Affairs Minister).

[11] Goodluck Jonathan, Address at the Retreat on the Review of Nigeria's Foreign Policy (August 1, 2011), http://www.nigeriavillagesquare.com/index.php?option=com_content&allposts=1&catid=590&id=19313&view=arti cle&Itemid=1719, ¶¶ 16 and 18.

[12] Akinboye, note 5.

abroad."[13] As indicated in Chapter 1, Nigeria is a party to numerous global and regional human rights instruments, consistent with a proclamation of "respect for international law and treaty obligations" in its domestic Constitution.[14] Despite this pledge, the country remains a hotbed of human-right abuses of every category, individual and group, both during military and civilian regimes alike.[15] Therefore, secondly, building on the first benefit, increased human rights at home will lend a sliver of credibility to Nigeria's known aspiration for a leadership role in international affairs.

Third, Nigeria can perform important service for international law just by getting its human-right house in order. Given its status as the largest black society in the world, human-right peace in Nigeria is a boon for the international human rights regime. The reverse is true when violations are rife. For example, the tragic humanitarian fallouts of the Nigerian civil war from 1967 to 1970 immensely occupied the attention of the international community and generated debate about excessive use of force by the Nigerian central government, in its attempt to suppress the secession of Eastern Nigeria, that till today still rages within the country.[16] A similar human-right crisis today, in a country that has more than tripled its population in the over 50 years since the war and within the context of a post-Cold War world marked by increased globalization, would divide the world and occupy its attention more.

[13] Philip C. Aka, "Human Rights in Nigeria's External Relations: Exigency, Methods, and Rebuttable Objections," *Buffalo Human Rights Law Review*, 21 (2014–2015), 1, 25.

[14] See Constitution of the Federal Republic of Nigeria, 1999, *Constitute Project*, https://www.constituteproject.org/constitution/Nigeria_1999 [hereinafter Nigerian Const. 1999], § 19(d).

[15] See, for example, Jacob Abiodun Dada, "Impediments to Human Rights Protection in Nigeria," *Annual Survey of International & Comparative Law*, 18 (2012), 67 (enumerating various factors, including absence of judicial independence, that constrain realization of human rights in the land as well as possible solutions, including steps like maintaining civilian rule covered in this chapter).

[16] See Chinua Achebe, *There Was a Country: Personal History of Biafra* (New York: Penguin Press, 2012), 209–211, 228–239; and Chimamanda N. Adichie, *Half of a Yellow Sun* (New York: Alfred A. Knopf, 2006), *passim* (work of fiction based on the Nigerian civil war from 1967 to 1970).

Seven Steps to Increased Human Rights at Home

In the light of the justification set forth above, how does Nigeria generate the human rights at home necessary for the pursuit of principled foreign policy? A conceivable answer is the seven interrelated steps set forth in this section, namely: maintaining civilian rule; extending the dividend of democracy under the Fourth Republic since 1999 to socioeconomic rights; taking collective rights seriously; taking power devolution, à la political restructuring, seriously; stemming the influence of religion in politics; electing competent governments able and willing to handle the foregoing tasks; and external support or assistance. Table 5.1 pulls together the seven steps.

Several prefatory observations are in order before delving into the steps. First, the list is illustrative, rather than exhaustive. For example, it does not include the critical contributions of individuals and other non-state actors in protecting and promoting human rights.[17] Second, the list mirrors the recommendations of other scholars, with more or less connection to this topic.[18] Third, as the ensuing discussion makes clear, these steps are not mutually exclusive but instead overlap at various points. Fourth, for the best result, many of these steps must be synchronized, rather than implemented sequentially.

[17] See, for example, Icelandic Human Rights Center, "The Role of Non-State Entities," http://www.humanrights.is/en/human-rights-education-project/human-rights-concepts-ideas-and-fora/human-rights-actors/the-role-of-non-state-entities; and Office of the UN High Commissioner for Human Rights, Declaration on the Right and Responsibility of Individuals, Groups[,] and Organs of Society to Promote and Protect Universally Recognized Human Rights and Fundamental Freedoms, Res. 53/144 (adopted by the UN General Assembly December 9, 1998), http://www.ohchr.org/EN/ProfessionalInterest/Pages/RightAndResponsibility.aspx.

[18] See, for example, Dada, note 15, *passim*; and Toure Kazah-Toure, "Nigeria: Challenge to the State and Ways of Breaking through the Quagmire," *in Beyond State Failure and Collapse: Making the State Relevant in Africa*, ed. George Klay Kieh Jr., 170–194 (Lanham, MD: Lexington Books, 2007) (citing a range of problems that includes lack of real democracy, no negotiated guarantees of collective rights, no adequate mechanism for tackling ethnic and religious conflicts, no true multiparty system, no genuinely democratic institutions, no agreement on ownership, control, and distribution of resources, and no agreement on citizenship rights, among others).

Table 5.1 Recap of seven steps to increased respect for human rights in Nigeria

Item no	*Step or technique*	*Justification or means*
1	Maintaining civilian rule	In the light of the arbitrariness and known abuses of military rule before 1999, staying with democracy, despite its imperfections, provides the minimum default (predicate) condition for possible improvement that military rule forecloses for a country the size of Nigeria
2	Extending the dividend of democracy to socioeconomic rights	This step adds value to the predicate of civilian rule. The Fourth Republic risks the fate of the failed Second Republic (1979–1983) if it continues with its dance of slow or no motion on socioeconomic rights
3	Taking collective rights seriously	Historically, group rights has been important in Nigeria because of the structure and nature of the country as a conglomerated patchwork of numerous, many times disagreeable, ethnic groups
4	Taking power devolution, à la political restructuring, seriously	Same as Item No. 3. Going further, devolution of political powers was the basis for the introduction of federalism in Nigeria in 1954. Given the political overtone associated with political restructuring, the vocabulary of choice is decentralization or devolution of political powers
5	Stemming the influence of religion in Nigerian politics	A conceivable way to achieve the moderation in the interest of a human-right policy is for Nigeria to stay within the secular boundaries of the Settlement of 1960
6	Electing competent governments	Arguably, this step falls within the legal-rational basis of authority formulated by Max Weber. Moreover, since the Weberian formulation, performance has emerged as a distinctive source of legitimacy
7	External support or assistance	This step is justified by the character of Nigeria as an artificial state, brainchild of British imperialism. Going further, like maintenance of civilian rule, it is a predicate, auxiliary precaution, matched against Items 2–6, the five steps in-between

Because, arguably, steps Nos. 1, staying the course on civilian rule, and 7, external support, are predicates, the applicable steps needing synchronization are the five in-between these factors, namely: more economic rights to make democracy more meaningful for longsuffering citizens, taking collective rights seriously, decentralizing political powers, stemming the influence of religion in politics, and electing more capable governments able to accomplish the enumerated tasks. Consistent with its importance in the scheme of analysis, mostly because of the emotive debate that swirls the topic, vis-à-vis the other steps, decentralization of political powers received extended discussion.

Maintaining Civilian Rule

For an elongated period since independence, Nigeria was a land paved with military rule. Until 1999, the only government many Nigerians grew up in, back to 1966 when the military seized power for the first time, was a military dictatorship. Accordingly, civilian rule, practiced only three times in the entire history of Nigeria with the period since 1999 as the longest of the three periods, is the flipside of military rule. Another name for civilian rule would be *democracy*, "government of the people, by the people, for the people," as Abraham Lincoln famously defined the term.[19]

But people-centered governance, in the sense Lincoln used the term, is yet to take root in Nigeria, hence the preference for the term *civilian rule*. Although important, procedures, such as elections, are not the only constituent features of a democracy; instead, *quality* is also a key ingredient in the definition of any democracy.[20] In both theory and practice, democracy is a dynamic notion that entails progressive and widespread application of democratic principles that proceed apace until democracy becomes the "only game in town,"[21] through routinization and internalization "in social, institutional, and even psychological life, as well

[19] "A Short Definition of Democracy," *Democracy Building*, http://www.democracy-building.info/definition-democracy.html.

[20] Assuming, for the sake of argument that we call Nigeria a democracy, it would be "illiberal democracy," rather than liberal democracy. *Illiberal democracies* are political systems that satisfy the procedural but not the substantive requirements of democracy. In these systems, leaders "routinely ignor[e] constitutional limits on their power," "depriv[e] their citizens of basic rights and freedoms[,]" and elections are held that "do not reflect the reality of popular participation in politics and support for those elected." Fareed Zakaria, "The Rise of Illiberal Democracy," *Foreign Affairs* (November/December 1997), http://www.foreignaffairs.com/articles/53577/fareed-zakaria/the-rise-of-illiberal-democracy. These regimes are contrasted from liberal democracies, such as in the US and Europe, that are "marked not only by free and fair elections, but also by the rule of law, a separation of powers, and the protection of basic liberties," such as freedom of speech, assembly, religion, and property. Ibid.

[21] Juan J. Linz and Alfred Stepan, *Problems of Democratic Transition and Consolidation: Southern Europe, South America, and Post-Communist Europe* (Baltimore, MD: Johns Hopkins University Press, 1996), 5.

as in political calculations for achieving success."[22] There is something else. Civilian control of the military and the police is a key element of democracy.[23] Such control is present when there is supremacy of elected officials of state over appointed officers at all levels but is lacking where, instead, security forces control the civilian population.[24] Domination of the political system by former military general negates civilian control.

We commented earlier in Chapter 1 that democracy in Nigeria under the Fourth Republic is nominal to the point of being analogized to military rule because of its domination by former military generals who brought military command ethos into their rules indicated by non-compliance with judicial orders among other attributes. Related to domination and mirroring it, is the issue of leadership style. Both Obasanjo and Buhari in their respective times adopted military solutions to nonmilitary issues, more so Buhari.[25]

[22] Juan J. Linz and Alfred Stepan, "Toward Consolidated Democracies," *in Consolidating the Third Wave Democracies: Themes and Perspectives*, eds. Larry Diamond et al. (Baltimore, MD: Johns Hopkins University Press, 1997), 16. See also Adam Przeworski, *Democracy and the Market* (New York: Cambridge University Press, 1991), 30, 31 (stating that democracy works "when all the relevant political forces have some specific minimum probability of doing well," such that those who lose elections or fail to have their demands met "may stay with the democratic game if they believe that even losing repeatedly under democracy is better for them than a future under an alternative system").

[23] Larry Berman and Bruce Allen Murphy, *Approaching Democracy*, 8th Ed. (New York: Pearson, 2013), 15.

[24] See ibid., p.15.

[25] For Obasanjo, see Philip C. Aka, "Nigeria Since May 1999: Understanding the Paradox of Civil Rule and Human Rights Violations under President Olusegun Obasanjo," *San Diego International Law Journal*, 4 (2003), 209, 237–255 (analyzing General Obasanjo's record relating to a set of four crises: the trouble over resource control and environmental degradation in the Niger Delta, the trouble relating to the adoption of sharia law as legal code by 12 northern states, the agitation for self-determination in the Southeast, and military reprisals at Odi and Benue State for security forces killed by warring groups in these communities). For Buhari, see Reuters, "A Year on From Nigerian Election Victory, Buhari's Reforms Founder," *New York Times* (February 25, 2016), http://www.nytimes.com/reuters/2016/02/25/world/africa/25reuters-nigeria-politics.html?_r=0. See also Alabi Williams, "It's Time to Review Nigeria," *Guardian* (Lagos) (June 12, 2016), http://guardian.ng/opinion/its-time-to-review-nigeria/ (portraying Buhari as a leader who "would rather deploy arms to deal with certain issues [...]").

Maintaining civilian rule is the foundation for any sustained progress in human rights in Nigeria. True, many of the country's political institutions, such as the 36-state structure,[26] transfer of the country's national capital from Lagos to Abuja,[27] and adoption of the presidential system of government in place of the parliamentary system, occurred during the years of military rule.[28] Similarly, some of the gains in Nigerian foreign policy, including the evolution of peacekeeping as a niche in the implementation of the country's external affairs, covered in Chapter 7, took place during military rule. However, these changes are little more than a testament to military domination of the political system. First, abuses of human rights in the country reached their apogee during periods of military rule.[29] Secondly, prolonged military rule has a severely negative effect on many political values necessary for the growth of the rule of law, including judicial independence.[30] Third, political corruption, the use of public offices and trusts for private ends,[31] reached dubiously new heights during the two long stretches of military rule for nearly thirty

[26] See Toyin Falola and Matthew M. Heaton, *A History of Nigeria* (New York: Cambridge University Press, 2008), 192–193 (snapshot of the country's 36 states).

[27] "Federal Capital Abuja," *Online Nigeria* (December 2, 2003), http://www.onlinenigeria.com/links/abujaadv.asp?blurb=387 (providing background information on the logic behind the relocation to Abuja as well as the personalities that planned the movement).

[28] See Larry Diamond, "Nigeria: Pluralism, Statism, and the Struggle for Democracy," *in Democracy in Developing Countries: Africa*, Vol. 2, eds. Larry Diamond et al. [hereinafter Diamond, "Struggle for Democracy in Nigeria"] (Boulder, CO: Lynne Rienner, 1988), 45–49 (discussing the transition to the Second Republic from 1975 to 1979).

[29] See Chinonye Obiagwu and Chidi Anselm Odinkalu, "Nigeria: Combating Legacies of Colonialism and Militarism," *in Human Rights under African Constitutions: Realizing the Promise for Ourselves*, ed. Abdullahi Ahmed An-Na'im (Philadelphia, PA: University of Pennsylvania Press, 2003), 211–250 (including military rule among the factors responsible for human right abuses in the country).

[30] *Executive lawlessness*, marked by contempt for judicial rulings, and utter disrespect of judicial institutions, took root during the period of military rule in Nigeria. See, for example, Mike A. A. Ozekhome, "The Nigerian Judiciary–15 Years of Democracy," *Point Blank News*, http://pointblanknews.com/pbn/articles-opinions/the-nigerian-judiciary-15-years-of-democracy/ (last visited November 24, 2014).

[31] See also Richard A. Joseph, *Democracy and Prebendal Politics in Nigeria: The Rise and Fall of the Second Republic* (New York: Cambridge University Press, 1987), *passim* (documenting and lamenting the massive corruption that led to the demise of Nigeria's Second Republic from 1979 to 1983). Derived somewhat impertinently from the Roman Catholic prebend doctrine, *prebendalism* is the term Joseph coined for the Nigerian variety of patronage.

years.[32] In his chronicles of the troubles with Nigeria, Chinua Achebe commented on how "[f]rom fairly timid manifestations in the 1960s," corruption grew "bold[ly] and ravenous[ly]" in Nigeria.[33] Much of this ravenousness took place during periods of military rule.[34]

As indicated in Chapter 1, which unearthed the argument of this book, concededly, the quality of civilian rule under the Fourth Republic has been distinctively low. The first point relates to the incidence of political corruption in Nigeria. Plato taught in his allegory of the Cave that "the well-governed city is impossible" where "beggars hungry for private goods go into public life, thinking that the good is there for the seizing[.]"[35] This feature appears to characterize Nigerian governments under the Fourth Republic since 1999. Nigeria ranks dubiously high on many perceptions-of-corruption indicators. For two straight years

[32] See James Rupert, "Corruption Flourished in Abacha's Regime," *Washington Post* (June 9, 1998), A01, http://www.washingtonpost.com/wp-srv/inatl/longterm/nigeria/stories/corrupt060998.htm (reporting on the unmatched scale of corruption that marked the military government under General Sani Abacha from 1993 to 1998); and David Imhonopi and Moses Urim Ugochukwu, "Leadership Crisis and Corruption in the Nigerian Public Sector: An Albatross of National Development," *African Symposium: An Online Journal of the African Educational Research Network*, 13(1) (June 2013), 78, 82. http://www.ncsu.edu/aern/TAS13.1/TAS13.1_Imhonopi.pdf (commenting on the Babaginda regime (1985–1993)).

[33] Chinua Achebe, *The Trouble with Nigeria* (Ibadan, Nigeria: Heinemann, 1983), 42.

[34] Unlike their counterparts in East Asia (China, Hong Kong, Singapore, South Korea, and Taiwan), said to have used authoritarianism to build the economy, Nigerian military dictators produced slow or negative economic progress. Philip C. Aka, "The Military, Globalization, and Human Rights in Africa," *Journal of Human Rights*, 18 (2002), 361, 387. Scholars like the late Claude Ake questioned the hypothesis postulating positive relationship between authoritarianism and development. See Claude Ake, *Democracy and Development in Africa* (Washington, D.C.: Brookings Institution, 1996), 158 (maintaining essentially that "development is part of what democracy is about"; therefore, that "[a] case for authoritarianism's being positively correlated to development does not really arise, because democracy is part of the very meaning of political development"). Ake contended that "[p]olitical authoritarianism has its own specificity, which markedly affects its consequences." Ibid., p. 128. Part of this specificity is that in East Asia, unlike in Africa, the political class "was able to realize some of the economically functional values of democracy, such as accountability, transparency, the rule of law, and negotiated consensus." Ibid., p. 158.

[35] Plato, "The Myth of the Cave," in *Philosophical Inquiry: Classic and Contemporary Readings*, eds. Jonathan E. Adler and Catherine Z. Elgin (Indianapolis, IN: Hackett Publishing Company, Inc., 2007), 26. Based on this premise, Plato advised that "it is those who are not lovers of ruling who must rule." Ibid.

(2002 and 2003), under General Obasanjo, Transparency International (TI) ranked Nigeria the second most corrupt country in the world—despite the fact that Obasanjo was a co-founder of the organization.[36] Because, by its laws and examples, the government sets the tone for behavior in society, corruption stimulates a culture of graft in the larger community.[37] For Nigeria, political corruption creates collateral problems coalesced around the negative effects that the ill casts on the country's image abroad with negative ramifications for the inflow of foreign direct investment (FDI),[38] all of which have the potential to complicate the conduct of foreign relations. Second, although various legal measures have been unveiled designed to deal with this problem,[39] these laws lack vigorous enforcement for various reasons, including a lack of political will.[40]

Despite the low quality of civilian rule recounted above, civilian governments are preferable because of the opportunity they afford, vis-à-vis repressive military regimes, for experimentation in self-governance necessary for the growth of the rule of law.[41] Democracy is "freedom

[36] "Nigeria Angry at Being Rated Second Most Corrupt," *IRIN* (October 9, 2003), http://www.irinnews.org/report/46630/nigeria-nigeria-angry-at-being-rated-second-most-corrupt. Obasanjo was president of TI from 1999 to 2007.

[37] See Daniel Jordan Smith, *A Culture of Corruption: Everyday Deception and Popular Discontent in Nigeria* (Princeton, NJ: Princeton University Press, 2008), *passim* (portraying the widespread nature of corruption in the daily lives of many Nigerians).

[38] J. Peter Pham, "Nigeria's Foreign Policy: An Inquiry into Sources and Prospects," Paper Prepared for Presentation at an Int'l Conference in Lisbon, Portugal (November 8–9, 2007), 99, www.ipri.pt/eventos/pdf/JPeterPham_paper.pdf.

[39] See Ben Nwabueze, "Corrupt Practices: Igbo Leaders' Position on Probe of Past Governments," *Vanguard* (August 13, 2015), http://www.vanguardngr.com/2015/08/corrupt-practices-igbo-leaders-position-on-probe-of-past-govts/ (detailing various sources of law dealing with corruption in Nigeria—common law, statutory law, and the Constitution—the last two of which include §172 of the 1999 Constitution (§ 209 in the case of States), the Code of Conduct Bureau and Tribunal Act, Cap. 56 of the Laws of the Federation, 1990 ed., the Corrupt Practices and Related Offenses Act, 2000, and the Economic and Financial Crimes Commission Act); and Patrick H. O'Neill et al., *Cases in Comparative Politics,* 4th Ed. (New York: W. W. Norton & Co., 2012), 719 (recounting other reform initiatives, including a bill to reform the oil industry that stalled in the National Assembly).

[40] See Nwabueze, note 39.

[41] See Amartya Sen, "Democracy as a Universal Value," in *Readings in Comparative Politics: Political Challenges and Changing Agendas*, eds. Mark Kesselman and Joel Krieger (Boston, MA: Cengage Learning, 2006), 175–176 (commenting on three ways,

institutionalized."[42] In contrast, military regimes and safeguard of human rights are oxymoron. Military rule was among the key factors that impeded progress in human rights after independence. "All eight military regimes that ruled Nigeria since independence have put the constitution on hold."[43]

Agitation for human rights in the country coincided with the harshness of military rule during the second instalment of military rule from 1984 to 1999, with the birth of the Civil Liberties Organization (CLO), a key human rights organization in the country, in 1987.[44] "[A]s the military effectively silenced, co-opted, or intimidated all other pressure groups in the polity, including the trade union, professional associations, and religious organizations," non-governmental organizations (NGOs) formed the only entity that the population looked up to as alternative voice.[45] Conscious of the repression of military regimes and convinced that civilian rule provides a more conducive environment for human rights, many of these NGOs fought for a return to democracy, mobilizing local and international support for this purpose.[46]

Compared to military regimes, civilian rule affords an atmosphere conducive for the safeguard of all categories of human rights in Nigeria. This includes the group right to self-determination. As one analyst observed, "[f]or three decades after the war, military dictatorships suppressed all secessionist" agitations that under the Fourth Republic are now coming to the fore.[47] Therefore, vis-à-vis military regime,

direct, instrumental, and constructive, through which democracy "enriches the lives of the citizens").

[42] Adam Michnik, "After the Revolution," *New Republic* (April 17, 1993), https://newrepublic.com/article/89495/revolution-poland-communism-christianity.

[43] Obiagwu and Odinkalu, note 29, p. 232.

[44] Immigration and Refugee Board of Canada, Nigeria: Information on the Civil Liberty Organization (CLO), Its Leadership, Its Activities, the Arrest of Its Members and Its Members and Its Involvement in Demonstrations that Followed the Annulment of the 12 June 1993 Elections (March 1, 1994), http://www.refworld.org/docid/3ae6ab3a24.html; and Abdul Raufu Mustapha, "Civil Rights and Pro-Democracy Groups in and Outside Nigeria," in *Nigeria during the Abacha Years (1993–1998)*, eds. 'Kunle Amuwo et al. (Lagos: IFRA Nigeria, 2001), 148–183.

[45] Obiagwu and Odinkalu, note 29, p. 243.

[46] Ibid.

[47] Max Siollun, "Nigeria is Coming Apart at the Seams," *Foreign Policy* (February 8, 2016), https://foreignpolicy.com/2016/02/08/nigeria-is-coming-apart-at-the-seamsbiafra/.

civilian rule provides ampler room for ventilating and rectifying "historically unjust relationships."[48] A key feature of the post-Cold War landscape in Africa is that, to be effective, any system of governance in the region must be *more* democratic than in the past. This is because in the age of globalization, the Internet, Worldwide Web, social media, and Artificial Intelligence, political techniques used in the past to maintain non-democratic governments, such as adherence to artificial boundaries, have eroded to the point of no return.[49]

To play on Winston Churchill's famous dictum about democracy as the worst form of government,[50] for human rights and the rule of law, the worst civilian government in Nigeria is better than the most benevolent military rule.[51] Moreover, the immense diversity of Nigeria makes the country hard to manage by military means.[52] This is one reason military rule in Nigeria is considered an aberrational episode justified on the grounds that soldiers are cleaning up the mess in the political system to clear the ground for a timely return to civilian rule.[53]

[48] Constitution of the Federal Republic of Ethiopia, *reprinted* in *Ref World* (August 21, 1995) [hereinafter Ethiopian Const. 1995], http://www.refworld.org/docid/3ae6b5a84.html.

[49] See Christopher Clapham, "Democratization in Africa: Obstacles and Prospects," *Third World Quarterly*, 14 (1993), 437–438 (advising African governments to wrap themselves with popular legitimacy, given that if "the mighty Soviet Union breaks up into fifteen different fragments, there is no way in which an artificial African state can hold together unless most of its people want it to").

[50] *Winston Churchill, Churchill by Himself: The Definitive Collection of Quotations*, ed. Richard M. Langworth (New York: Public Affairs, 2008), 574 (observing that "[n]o one pretends that democracy is perfect or all-wise[,]" but, to the contrary, "democracy is the worst form of Government except for all those other forms that have been tried from time to time").

[51] See, for example, Frank L. Wilson, *Concepts and Issues in Comparative Politics: An Introduction to Comparative Analysis* (Upper Saddle River, NJ: Prentice Hall, 1996), 142–143 (positing that "[m]ilitary regimes are, after all, authoritarian regimes[,] [i]nherently illegitimate, [...] [and] abusive of basic human rights"); and Paul Brooker, *Non-Democratic Regimes: Theory, Government, and Politics*, 2d Ed. (New York: Palgrave Macmillan, 2009), 2 (observing that "there are major behavioral differences between dictatorship by military and by a political party").

[52] Diamond, "Struggle for Democracy in Nigeria" note 28, p. 33 (observing that "the ethnic complexity of the country [...] represents an irrepressible social pluralism that cannot be effectively managed by authoritarian means").

[53] Philip C. Aka, "Nigeria: The Need for an Effective Policy of Ethnic Reconciliation in the New Century," *Temple International & Comparative Law Journal*, 14(2) (2000),

A human-right policy is *not* a value anchored on authoritarianism.[54] Because foreign policy is the product of a self-governing people that also mirrors their values and interests at home, by definition, military rule is inconsistent with people-based foreign policy. The stability of civilian rule over military dictatorship as a political system is indicated by the fact that under the presidential system of government that Nigeria practices, General Buhari is guaranteed four years in office, a protection that a military regime lacks—considering that in his first outing, Buhari was schemed out of office by his colleagues in a "palace coup" after only 20 months in office. Little wonder regarding the growing consensus for democracy as a political and human right way of life in the country. Then President Goodluck E. Jonathan described democracy as the tool Nigerians need to "build a just, fair, and inclusive nation," adding that "there is no greater indignity, no greater disrespect for the values that bind us together as a nation than to deprive citizens of a say in who would govern them."[55] Not to be outdone, Buhari advocated for Nigerians to adopt democracy as "a lifestyle" for development and that to achieve their goals, they "must consciously work to improve the democratic system."[56]

Yet the impediments to democracy are real in Nigeria and should not be minimized. These deficiencies are the reason why, although a necessary condition, maintaining civilian rule in and of itself is insufficient.

327, 352. All military regimes in the country, from Ironsi to Gowon to Muhammad/ Obasanjo to Babangida to even Abacha, including those like Gowon and Babangida that ultimately failed to keep their promise, embraced this formula. The exception was the Buhari regime from 1983 to 1985. "Political Transitions," in *Nigeria: A Country Study*, ed. Helen Chapin Metz (Washington, DC: GPO for the Library of Congress, 1991), http://countrystudies.us/nigeria/74.htm.

[54] Garth le Pere, review of Adekeye Adebajo and Abdul Raufu Mustapha, eds., *Gulliver's Troubles: Nigeria's Foreign Policy after the Cold War* (Scottsville, South Africa: University of KwaZulu-Natal Press, 2008), *African Journal of Conflict Resolution*, 8 (2008), http://www.accord.org.za/publications/book-reviews/638-gullivers-troubles-nigerias-foreign-policy-after-the-cold-war.

[55] See Jonathan, Address at a Retreat on the Review of Nigeria's Foreign Policy, note 11.

[56] "Accept Democracy as Lifestyle, Not Government[al] System, Buhari Urges Nigerians," *The Will* (Online) (June 19, 2015), http://thewillnigeria.com/news/accept-democracy-as-lifestyle-not-government-system-buhari-urges-nigerians/; and Olalekan Adetayo, "Nigerians Won't Regret Electing Me, Says Buhari," *Punch* (Lagos) (June 4, 2015), http://www.punchng.com/news/nigerians-wont-regret-electing-me-says-buhari-2/ (quoting Buhari).

Instead, those deficiencies counsel the "auxiliary precautions" embedded in a backup of the other six factors,[57] considering that no political system in the world, not even the US with its long history of constitutional democracy, perfectly respects human-rights.[58]

Extending the Dividend of Democracy to Socioeconomic Rights

Maintaining civilian rule is nominal if it does not come with improved wellbeing for ordinary Nigerians—something which, to begin with, makes this predicate unsustainable. This is where this second step to a principled foreign policy for Nigeria kicks in. Under the Fourth Republic since 1999, Nigerians arguably enjoy more freedom than they did during the repressive eras of military rule. But there should be more to it than that. A free society must "help the many who are poor."[59] More elaborately, as then US president Bill Clinton intoned in his address to the Nigerian National Assembly in August 2000, "in the end, successful political change must begin to improve people's daily lives. That is the democracy dividend Nigerians have waited for."[60]

[57] In Federalist Paper No. 51, James Madison stressed the "necessity of auxiliary precautions," "[i]n framing a government which is to be administered by men over men," as an antidote against the imperfectness of human beings. James Madison, Federalist No. 10, Bill of Rights Institute (November 22, 1787), https://billofrightsinstitute.org/primary-sources/federalist-no-10. Madison observed that "It may be a reflection on human nature" that the elaborate separationist devices he recommended "should be necessary to control the abuses of government," adding rhetorically: "But what is government itself but the greatest of all reflections on human nature?" Ibid. The same need for auxiliary precautions is advised here.

[58] See, for example, Peter R. Baehr, "Mobilization of the Conscience of Mankind: Conditions of Effectiveness of Human Rights NGOs," in *Reflections on International Law from the Low Countries*, ed. Peter R. Baehr (Leiden, Netherlands: Brill Publishers, 1998), 135–155 (commenting on the discrepancy between norm and practice, embedded in the fact that "most governments in the world at some time or other violate" human rights, a discrepancy that "creates the space in which human rights [N]on-[G]overnmental [O]rganizations can operate").

[59] John F. Kennedy, Inaugural Address of President John F. Kennedy (January 20, 1961), John F. Kennedy Presidential Library and Museum, http://www.jfklibrary.org/Research/Research-Aids/Ready-Reference/JFK-Quotations/Inaugural-Address.aspx.

[60] William J. Clinton, "Remarks to a Joint Session of the Nigerian National Assembly in Abuja (August 26, 2000), in Public Papers of the Presidents of the United States: William J. Clinton, 2000–2001 (Washington, DC: Best Books, 2000), 1706. The YouTube video

Despite the advice, civilian rule is shorn of the "dividend of democracy" for the masses of Nigerian citizens[61]; instead, Nigeria is a land of "abundant human and natural resources [that] still struggles with mass impoverishment."[62] And although continuously under civilian rule now for nearly two and a half decades as of this book, Nigeria remains a rich country of many poor people.[63] Nigeria is a stalwart of NEPAD that has yet to live up to the poverty-alleviation mission of the organization.[64] Instead, about two-thirds of Nigerians still live below the poverty line.[65] The result is that under its Fourth Republic, Nigeria has "produce[d]

of the address published April 19, 2012, is available at https://www.youtube.com/watch?v=Z0uzicpbIIs.

[61] Philip C. Aka, "The 'Dividend of Democracy': Analyzing U.S. Support for Nigerian Democratization," *Boston College Third World Law Journal*, 22 (2002), 225–279 (commenting on the external factor embedded in US support for Nigeria's democracy).

[62] International Crisis Group, *Nigeria: Want in the Midst of Plenty*, Africa Report No. 113 (July 19, 2006), 1, https://icg-prod.s3.amazonaws.com/113-nigeria-want-in-the-midst-of-plenty.pdf. See also World Bank, *Nigeria—Poverty in the Midst of Plenty: The Challenge of Growth with Inclusion: A World Bank Poverty Assessment* (Washington, DC: World Bank Group, 1996), http://documents.worldbank.org/curated/en/582991468759320261/Nigeria-Poverty-in-the-midst-of-plenty-the-challenge-of-growth-with-inclusion-a-World-Bank-poverty-assessment.

[63] See Sam Nda-Isaiah, "Is Nigeria a Poor Country of Rich Men or a Rich Country of Poor Men?" *Leadership* (Abuja) (April 7, 2014), http://leadership.ng/columns/363727/nigeria-poor-country-rich-men-rich-country-poor-men; "Poverty in Nigeria: Rich Country, Poor People," *Poverties* (March 2012, updated April 2013), http://www.poverties.org/poverty-in-nigeria.html. See also "Protests in Biafra: Go Your Own Way," *Economist* (London) (November 28, 2015), http://www.economist.com/news/middle-east-and-africa/21679210-half-century-after-war-angry-biafrans-are-agitating-again-go-your-own-way (pointing out that "[d]espite oil wealth, Nigerians were twice as likely to be poor in 2010 as they were in 1980").

[64] Adopted in 2001 by African leaders, NEPAD is a program designed to promote sustainable economic development and reduce poverty, among other goals. See Philip C. Aka, "NEPAD and the Movement for Popular Participation in Development (MPPD) in Africa," *Human Rights & Globalization Law Review*, 3 (2009–2010), 79–148.

[65] "Reforming Nigeria: A Conversation with Ngozi Okonjo-Iweala," *Foreign Affairs* (March/April 2014), http://www.foreignaffairs.com/discussions/interviews/-nigeria. See also Abba Mahmood, "Nigeria's Africa Policy in Perspective," *Leadership* (December 26, 2013), leadership.ng/columns/Thursday-column/343/nigerias-africa-policy-in-perspective (observing instructively that, "[w]ith over 100 million people living below poverty line, Nigeria's population is not an asset but a burden").

millions of migrants, essentially economic refugees, who live throughout Africa, Europe, and the U.S."[66]

Nigerian leaders should keep in mind the injunction of the World Conference on Human Rights that "[t]he existence of widespread extreme poverty inhibits the full and effective enjoyment of human rights," an occurrence that makes the "immediate alleviation and eventual elimination" of such poverty "high priority."[67] How can Nigeria be so rich while its citizens are so poor?[68] Appeals by leaders to the masses for patience and continued sacrifice are unwarranted and less likely to be heeded if citizens believe that their contributions to democracy are not leading to any improvement in their economic circumstances.[69]

Life for ordinary Nigerians under the Fourth Republic is one marked by economic misery and marginality. Due to its sparse economic achievements, many observers mocked the People's Democratic Party (PDP), the ruling party in the country from 1999 until 2015 as the "Poverty Development Party."[70] And under Buhari's two terms in office from 2015 until 2023, Nigeria displaced India as the country with the highest number of poor people in the world.[71] Democracy is meaningless to many Nigerians who, after nearly 25 years under the Fourth Republic are yet to taste the economic dividends of democratic rule. Although it does not justify it,

[66] International Crisis Group, *Nigeria: Want in the Midst of Plenty*, note 62, p. 1.

[67] Office of the UN High Commissioner for Human Rights, Vienna Declaration and Program of Action (June 25, 1993), ¶14, http://www.ohchr.org/EN/ProfessionalInterest/Pages/Vienna.aspx.

[68] See John Campbell, *Nigeria: Dancing on the Brink* (Lanham, MD: Rowman & Littlefield Publishers, 2013), 11–24.

[69] Philip C. Aka, "Human Rights as Conflict Resolution in Africa in the New Century," *Tulsa Journal of Comparative & International Law*, 11 (Fall 2003), 201.

[70] Patrick H. O'Neil et al., note 39, p. 710.

[71] See Peter Beaumont and Isaac Abrak, "Oil-Rich Nigeria Outstrips India as Country with Most People in Poverty," *Guardian* (London) (July 16, 2018), https://www.theguardian.com/global-development/2018/jul/16/oil-rich-nigeria-outstrips-india-most-people-in-poverty#:~:text=According%20to%20the%20authors%2C%20energy,with%20India's%2073%20million%20peopleand Bukola Adebayo, "Nigeria Overtakes India in Extreme Poverty Ranking," *CNN* (June 26, 2018), https://www.cnn.com/2018/06/26/africa/nigeria-overtakes-india-extreme-poverty-intl/index.html.

this occurrence helps explain the decreasing number of Nigerians who bother to vote in presidential and legislative elections.[72]

To put the matter of economic dividend necessary to maintain democracy differently, under its Fourth Republic, Nigeria is a land sorely lacking in social justice. The term refers to gestures rooted in the idea that every human being deserves dignity and is therefore entitled to equal opportunity, equal treatment, and equal rights.[73] Moreover, it is mechanism for perfecting the humanness of individuals signified by a fair and equitable division of resources, opportunities, and privileges in society,[74] whose imperatives "impose[] on [every individual] a personal responsibility to work with others to design and continually perfect [societal] institutions as tools for personal and social development."[75] In short, social justice is an equalitarian doctrine with strong economic roots,[76] indicated by a

[72] Kabir Yusuf, "Analysis: Trend of Low Voter Turnout Continues in Nigerian Elections," *Premium Times* (Abuja) (March 5, 2023), https://www.premiumtimesng.com/news/top-news/586193-analysis-trend-of-low-voter-turnout-continues-in-nigerian-elections.html.

[73] San Diego Foundation, "What Is Social Justice?" (September 24, 2022), https://www.sdfoundation.org/news-events/sdf-news/what-is-social-justice/.

[74] Daniel Thomas Mollenkamp, "Social Justice Meaning and Main Principles Explained," *Investopedia* (Updated July 8, 2022), https://www.investopedia.com/terms/s/social-justice.asp.

[75] Cited in "What is Social Justice?" note 73. This is a phenomenon where, like in many things, ordinary citizens play a critically supporting role. Colloquially, the act of social justice is whatever individuals, in partnership with their fellow human beings, do to restructure existing laws and related societal institutions to promote the perfection of every person or group (such as the family). We measure social justice with respect to each institution, based on its success in elevating the well-being and overall dignity of every individual or group. On our own, many a time, even the best efforts can be inadequate. Individuals have a personal responsibility to engage in acts of social justice that reduce the gap between those at the top of the economic ladder and those at the bottom. They close the gap by restructuring the institutions in which we work and live, as well as by reforming the laws which shape their social interactions. In this endeavor, nothing is impossible, the reason being that what has been made possible by people can be remade by people. See William J. Ferree, *Introduction to Social Justice* (Arlington, VA: Center for Economic and Social Justice, 1997 [1948]), 43–54, https://www.cesj.org/wp-content/uploads/2012/08/introtosocialjustice.pdf (commenting on the characteristics of social justice). For Father Ferree, relegating social justice to the state in helplessness is unnecessary and wrong to the point of sinfulness. Ibid.

[76] This calls to mind the prayer in the Bible for a "daily bread" in-between poverty and wealth. *Holy Bible*, English Standard Version, Proverbs 30:8 ("Give me neither poverty nor riches, but give me only my daily bread").

"fair and compassionate distribution of the fruits of economic growth."[77] In addition to poverty-reduction referenced above, social justice may be achieved in Nigeria through the means of social protection programs, equally lacking in the country. These are benefits like cash transfers, food subsidies, housing allowance, as well as job training and skill development opportunities for the poor designed to minimize the worst effects of poverty and marginality.[78]

To boost popular attachment to democracy in Nigeria, civilian rule must, in addition to a government less tainted by political corruption, produce improved living standards, including more jobs, and better public service.[79] Like many Africans, Nigerians are outcome-oriented in their support of democracy. The attraction of democracy for many Nigerians stems from "its association with prosperity"[80]; agitation in Nigeria for democratic rule in the lead up to the Fourth Republic "has something to do with the belief most Nigerians held that the only government [that is] [...] able to improve their lot is a democratically-elected one."[81] A factor responsible for the fall of the Second Republic from 1979 to 1983 was the lack of any "serious effort to fight poverty[,]" creating a situation where "many losers in th[e] corrupt system welcomed military intervention."[82]

[77] Quoted in "What is Social Justice?" note 73.

[78] See, for example, "Social Protection," UNICEF, https://www.unicef.org/social-policy/social-protection; and *Leaving No One Behind: A Social Protection* (New York: UN Development Program, October 6, 2016).

[79] Regarding public service, one galling topic that immediately comes to mind is the inability of the various governments under the Fourth Republic since 1999 to generate enough electricity to serve the needs of the Nigerian public. With a population of about 170 million people circa 2014, Nigerian leaders generated only about 4,000 megawatts (MW) of electricity, compared, for example, to South Africa with 53 million (less than one-third Nigeria's population) of 44,175 MW. See Adewale Maja-Pearce, "Nigeria Does Generate More Electricity Now than It Did [Fifteen] Years Ago," *Africa Check* (November 2014), https://africacheck.org/reports/nigeria-does-generate-more-electricity-now-than-it-did-15-years-ago/.

[80] Robert J. Mundt and Oladimeji Aborisade, "Politics in Nigeria," in *Comparative Politics Today: A World View*, 7th Ed., eds. Gabriel A. Almond et al. (New York: Longman, 2000), 727.

[81] Philip C. Aka, "Education, Economic Development, and Return to Democratic Politics in Nigeria," *Journal of Third World Studies*, 18(1) (2001), 22.

[82] Ignatius Akaayar Ayua and Dakas C.J. Dakas, "Federal Republic of Nigeria," in *Constitutional Origins, Structure, and Change in Federal Countries*, eds. John Kincaid

The Fourth Republic risks a similar fate if it continues to make no progress on socioeconomic rights.

Nigeria's constitution enumerates both political and civil (political-civil) and socioeconomic rights.[83] Political-civil rights are guarantees of freedom with which governments must not interfere. These guarantees include the right to life, personal liberty, fair hearing, privacy and family life, the right to freedom of thought, conscience, and religion; freedom of expression and the press, peaceful assembly and association; and freedom of movement. Socioeconomic rights are material-based guarantees of freedom that require governmental preparation for the enjoyment of these rights. Without such preparation, the realization of these rights is made difficult or impossible. These guarantees include access to education, healthcare, food, shelter, and clean water; the right to work, including protection against unemployment; right to form and join trade unions; and the right to social security, among others. Global and regional human rights instruments that the Nigerian government ratified, pledging as a matter of international law to protect these rights for its citizens, include the International Covenant on Civil and Political Rights (ICCPR)[84]; the International Covenant on Economic, Social, and Cultural Rights (ICESCR)[85]; and the African [Banjul] Charter on Human and Peoples' Rights (ACHPR).[86]

However, while it protects political-civil rights, Nigeria's constitutions make socioeconomic rights non-justiciable, meaning that these rights are merely aspirations that individuals, as a matter of law, cannot sue on

and George Alan Tarr (Montreal, Canada: McGill-Queen's University Press, 2005), 239, 246.

[83] Nigerian Const. 1999, note 14, Chap. II, arts. 13–24 (setting forth the "Fundamental Objectives and Directive Principles of State Policy"), and Chap. IV, arts. 33–44 (dealing with "Fundamental Rights").

[84] UN General Assembly, International Covenant on Civil and Political Rights, UNTS, vol. 999 (December 16, 1966) [hereinafter ICCPR], 171, https://www.refworld.org/docid/3ae6b3aa0.htm.

[85] UN General Assembly, International Covenant on Economic, Social and Cultural Rights, UNTS, vol. 993 (December 16, 1966) [hereinafter ICESCR], 3, https://www.refworld.org/docid/3ae6b36c0.html.

[86] Organization of African Unity (OAU), African Charter on Human and Peoples' Rights ("Banjul Charter") (June 27, 1981), CAB/LEG/67/3 rev. 5, 21 I.L.M. 58 (1982), https://www.refworld.org/docid/3ae6b3630.html.

when these "guarantees" are violated.[87] Small wonder that one non-governmental organization in Nigeria laments that the socioeconomic profile of Nigeria's 1999 constitution reduces it to little more than "a treatise on abdication of responsibilities."[88] One way to stir Nigerian governments from their slumber on economic rights would be to make these rights—access to education, healthcare, food, shelter, clean water, and so forth—justiciable under the Nigerian constitution.[89] This would give citizens a legal reference point, currently non-existent, to bring lawsuits for breaches of these rights when they are violated, as has repeatedly been the case since the country's independence in 1960. To stem the high level of unemployment that riles its economy, especially among the youth, Nigerian governments at all three levels must work harder to create jobs,[90] while keeping close tabs on rapid population growth.[91]

[87] See, for example, Aka, "Nigeria Since May 1999," note 25, p. 216.

[88] Ibid., quoting Committee for the Defense of Human Rights, *Annual Report on the Human Rights Situation in Nigeria 1999* (July 2000), 100.

[89] See, for example, National Human Rights Commission, "Ojukwu Urges Lawmakers to Make Socio-Economic Rights Justiciable" (March 28, 2022), https://www.nigeriarights.gov.ng/nhrc-media/news-and-events/320-ojukwu-urges-lawmakers-to-make-socio-economic-rights-justiciable.html; and Silver Nwokoro, "Falana, Others Call for Enforcement of Socio-Economic Rights of Nigerians," *Guardian* (Lagos) (March 8, 2022), https://guardian.ng/features/falana-others-call-for-enforcement-of-socio-economic-rights-of-nigerians/. See also Femi Falana, "Making Chapter II of the Constitutional Justiciable," *This Day* (Lagos) March 2, 2022), https://www.thisdaylive.com/index.php/2022/03/02/making-chapter-ii-of-the-constitution-justiciable.

[90] Susan Lund and Arend van Wamelen, "Lions on the Move: 10 Things You Don't Know about Africa's Booming Economy," in *Current Debates in Comparative Politics*, eds. J. Tyler Dickovick and Jonathan Eastwood (New York: Oxford University Press, 2015), 44 (advising Nigerian and other African governments to invest on "a job strategy").

[91] See "Nigeria: Fears Over Population Growth as World Hits [Eight] Billion," *Africa News* (Last updated November 15, 2022), billion, https://www.africanews.com/2022/11/15/nigeria-fears-over-population-growth-as-world-hits-8-billion//; and Uche Charlie Isiugo-Abanihe, "Why Nigeria Can't Fix Its Development Agenda: And Where the Solutions Lie," *Conversation* (October 25, 2020), https://theconversation.com/why-nigeria-cant-fix-its-development-agenda-and-where-the-solutions-lie-123638 (contending that "[t]he combination of high fertility and declining mortality, resulting in a period of high population growth rate, puts Nigeria in a 'demographic trap'").

Taking Collective Rights Seriously

This step builds on extension of the dividend of democracy to socioeconomic rights and it facilitates the challenge of maintaining civilian rule in Nigeria, all aimed at promoting increased respect for human rights at home. Collective rights are guarantees which an individual may enjoy as a member of a particular society. Referred to sometimes as "solidarity rights,"[92] these guarantees complement individual rights (both political-civil and socioeconomic rights). Although "[t]he subject of a right, the right-holder, might be most obviously an individual[,]" "[b]ut it might also be a group—a family, a tribe, a company, a nation, a state, a region, a culture, even the globe itself."[93] These collective rights include the equality of peoples, the right to existence and self-determination, the right to free disposal of natural wealth and resources, the right to development, the right to international peace and security, and the right to a clean environment. Like individualized or nongroup political-civil rights and socioeconomic rights, these guarantees are consecrated in global and regional human rights multilateral treaties, which, as indicated above, Nigeria is a state party to and therefore obligated under international law to comply with.[94]

The enjoinment for states to "promote and protect *all* human rights and fundamental freedoms" for all citizens[95] encompasses collective

[92] See U. Oji Umozurike, *The African Charter on Human and Peoples' Rights* (Leiden, Netherlands: Brill Publishers, 1997), 51 (stating that these rights require "the solidarity of all peoples," including "the cooperation of the other members of the international community to carry into effect").

[93] See Vincent, note 7, p. 3. Collective rights are credited to the new states which became members of the United Nations following decolonization in Africa and Asia in the post-World World II period. See Louis Henkin, "Human Rights: Ideology and Aspiration, Reality and Prospect," in Power and Allison, eds., note 4, p. 8; Peter R. Baehr and Monique Castermans-Hollerman, *The Role of Human Rights in Foreign Policy*, 3rd Ed. (New York: Palgrave Macmillan, 2004), 14. Arguably, even the Universal Declaration of Human Rights anticipated these group rights. After observing in its opening article that human beings are persons "endowed with reason and conscience" who "should act toward one another in a spirit of brotherhood[,]" the document stipulated that "[e]veryone has duties to the *community* in which alone the free and full development of his personality is possible." Universal Declaration of Human Rights, G.A. Res. 217 A (III), U.N. GAOR, 3d Sess., U.N. Doc. A/810 (1948), art. 29. Emphasis added.

[94] See notes 82–84 and accompanying texts.

[95] Vienna Declaration and Program of Action, note 67, ¶ 5.

rights. The reason is the interconnectedness of human rights: "[p]olitical-civil rights and socioeconomic rights are individual rights that may also be enjoyed by groups; and solidarity rights, like the rights to peace, development, a clean environment, and the right to self-determination, are group rights that individuals may also enjoy."[96] Given this occurrence, along with the indivisibility of all categories of human rights,[97] privileging individual rights over group rights makes little sense.

Group rights have always been critical in Nigeria. As we see in the next section related to decentralization, concern about these rights led to the introduction of federalism as a political system in 1954.[98] Going further, in the period before independence in 1960, fear of possible domination of minority groups by the major ethnic groups as Nigeria moved progressively toward independence led to the entrenchment of "fundamental rights" in the country's constitutions, beginning with the 1960 charter.[99] Yet, Nigeria has a poor record of respect for these collective rights. Using the right to self-determination as case in point, under the Fourth Republic since 1999, Nigeria has responded inadequately to campaigns for this right,[100] vis-à-vis similarly-situated countries.[101] For

[96] Aka, "Human Rights as Conflict Resolution in Africa," note 69, p. 186.

[97] Vienna Declaration and Program of Action, note 67, ¶ 5.

[98] See note 154 below and accompanying text.

[99] Aka, "Nigeria Since May 1999," note 25, pp. 215–216, 274; Chapter 2, notes 11–12 and accompanying texts; and Chapter 3, notes 114–115 and accompanying texts, all three referencing the Willink Minority Commission Report (1957).

[100] See Aka, "Nigeria Since May 1999," note 25, pp. 237–255 (commenting on the handling of a set of four crises under General Obasanjo, including: the trouble over resource control and environmental degradation in the Niger Delta, the trouble relating to the adoption of sharia law as legal code by 12 northern states, and the agitation for self-determination in the Southeast).

[101] One country that comes to mind here is Ethiopia. Like Nigeria, Ethiopia is densely populated with numerous ethnic groups (over 93 million people in 2015 with over 80 ethnic groups vs. over 182 million people same period with over 250 ethnic groups for Nigeria). Like Nigeria too, Ethiopia is a federal state. And like Nigeria, Ethiopia fought a civil war where many people died (from 1974 to 1991, over 16 years in which 1.4 million people died vs. a three-year period where 3.5 million people died in the case of Nigeria). For Ethiopia, from 1961, the country battled an insurgency from Eritrea following the (forcible) incorporation of the Eritrea-land into Ethiopia in 1952. Yet the two countries drew different lessons from their experiences with violence and human rights abuses. For Nigeria, the lesson was to centralize power out of an "apprehension that a weak federal center [w]ould enable secession" and lead to disintegration. Ayua

ethnic peace in the Niger Delta (the developmentally neglected source of Nigeria's oil wealth) and other trouble spots in the country, the Nigerian national government must heed the injunction in the international bill of human rights, regarding economic self-determination, that "[i]n no case may a people be deprived of its own means of subsistence."[102]

Although human rights "are usually taken to have a special reference to the ways in which states treat their own citizens," it is not only governments (standing for states) that violate these rights.[103] Instead, life, liberty, security, property and other freedoms to which people have human rights may also as well be denied by an array of non-state actors, including individuals and organizations.[104] What this means for the issue here at hand is that, in addition to respecting individual and collective human rights, the government has an obligation to ensure that individuals and groups (including corporate entities) in society also respect these rights and that they are held accountable for abuses of human rights that they perpetrate. Unfortunately, this is not the case in Nigeria where, instead, the government time and again tolerates the violations by individuals and groups of the human rights of politically powerless or disfavored

and Dakas, note 82, p. 251. For Ethiopia, on the other hand, the experience led to power devolution, including a constitutional provision permitting secession following the successful breakaway of Eritrea in 1991. Ethiopia's 1995 Constitution guarantees "an unconditional right to self-determination, including the right to secession," to eligible ethnic groups. Ethiopian Const. 1995, note 48, art. 39(1). Ethiopia is especially instructive because it is the site of the headquarters of the Organization of African Unity, since 2000 the African Union, noted for its insistence on maintenance of colonial boundaries in Africa to avoid "balkanization," which reason Ethiopia under Emperor Haile Selassie (1930–1974), opposed Biafra. See James Podesta, "Haile Selassie 1892–1975," *Contemporary Black Biography* (1994), http://www.encyclopedia.com/topic/Haile_Selassie.aspx.

[102] See ICCPR, note 84, art. 1 § 2; and ICESCR, note 85, art. 1, § 2. See also Aka, "Nigeria Since May 1999," note 25, p. 274 (observing that "[p]romoting increased access to state power for all groups is a human rights issue in Nigeria," and advising that "[a]ccomplishing this purpose can also minimize opportunities for conflict that could result in human rights violations").

[103] Jack Donnelly, *International Human Rights*, 4th Ed. (Boulder, CO: Westview Press, 2013), xvii.

[104] Ibid. See also Andrew Clapham, *Human Rights in the Private Sphere* (New York: Oxford University Press, 1993); and Mary Robinson, "The Business Case for Human Rights," http://www.unhchr.ch/hurricane/huricane.nsf/0/e47d352dedc39697802566de0043b28e?OpenDocument.

groups. One such group, going back to the early history of the country, but especially since the end of the Biafra war in 1970, is the Igbo.[105]

"Nigeria violates the human rights of all its inhabitants, but much more so the human rights of Igbos."[106] Or as one Igbo sociocultural group put it, the Igbo "enjoy *less* protection of the law than any other ethnic group in Nigeria."[107] The reason for this occurrence is because Nigerian governments have a history and practice of *not* holding abusers of Igbo human rights—whether private citizens, government officials or organizations—accountable.[108] Better attention to collective attention in Nigeria must include eschewal of impunity by taking more seriously punishment for human rights violations by individuals and public officials who, under color of law,[109] violate the rights of individuals or groups, especially politically powerless or disfavored entities.

Taking punishment for human rights violations seriously includes reparations for past human rights abuses. Reparation means to repair a victim or put that victim back, as much as possible, to his or her pre-damage condition. The principle also mandates restitution or the return to a victim of something wrongfully taken from that victim. However, like with punishment for human rights violations, and again as the Igbo experience evinces, Nigeria has a poor history of reparations for past human rights abuses.[110] Reparations "for past violations will compel individuals

[105] See Achebe, note 33, p. 45 (stating that Nigeria has an "Igbo problem" rooted in the fact that one singular issue on which non-Igbo groups agree is "their common resentment of the Igbo").

[106] Philip C. Aka, "Prospects for Igbo Human Rights in Nigeria in the New Century," *Howard Law Journal*, 48 (Fall 2004), 168.

[107] Ibid., p. 223, quoting *Oha-na-Eze Ndi-Igbo, The Violations of Human and Civil Rights of Ndi Igbo in the Federation of Nigeria (1966–1999): A Call for Reparation and Appropriate Restitution* (1999), 39, http://www.westafricareview.com/war/vol2.2/ohaneze.pdf.

[108] Aka, "Prospects for Igbo Human Rights in Nigeria," note 106, pp. 221–224 ("rebutting the claim that Igbos are no more victims of human rights atrocities than other Nigerians").

[109] This term is a legal jargon signifying "the appearance of legal authority or an apparently legal right that may not exist." Legal Information Institute (Cornell University), "Color of Law," https://www.law.cornell.edu/wex/color_of_law. It is "abuse of power under the guise of state authority," an occurrence which therefore makes such misuse of authority illegal. Ibid.

[110] Aka, "Prospects for Igbo Human Rights in Nigeria," note 106, pp. 224–228. See also Philip C. Aka, "Bridging the Gap Between Theory and Practice in

or groups to think twice before they violate other people's individual and collective human rights. Conversely, the lack of reparation for past human rights abuses in Nigeria is probably among the reasons these abuses recur."[111]

In 1999, the Obasanjo administration (1999–2007), established a commission, the Human Rights Violations Investigation Commission (HRVIC) (Oputa Panel), after former Supreme Court Justice Chukwudifu Oputa, who headed the Commission, to investigate past human rights abuses in the country and make recommendations on how to redress those abuses and deter future abuses.[112] However, the Commission submitted a report that the government never released, much less enforce.[113] To prevent impunity, human rights abuses, whether by state or non-state entities must be punished, regardless of which entity perpetrated the violations. Given the point made earlier that life, liberty, security, property, and other freedoms to which people have human rights may also as well be denied by non-state actors, the state fails in its obligation verged on human rights when it leaves abuses by non-state entities unpunished.

Taking Devolution of Political Powers, à la Political Restructuring, Seriously

This step is an outgrowth of the prior one on collective rights. As indicated in that section, fear of majority domination by minority groups

Humanitarian Action: Seven Practical Steps to Humanitarian Integrity in Nigeria," *Critical Investigations into Humanitarianism in Africa (CIHA) Blog* (February 25, 2016), http://www.cihablog.com/bridging-the-gap-between-theory-and-practice-in-humanitarian-action-seven-practical-steps-to-humanitarian-integrity-in-nigeria/ (pointing out that "Nigeria has a poor history of reparations for past human rights abuses, with possible negative ramifications for humanitarian integrity").

[111] Aka, "Prospects for Igbo Human Rights in Nigeria," note 106, p. 226.

[112] See Hakeem O. Yusuf, "Human Rights Violations Investigations Commission, the Oputa Panel (Nigeria)," *in Encyclopedia of Transitional Justice*, eds. Lavinia Stan and Nadia Nedelsky (New York: Cambridge University Press, 2013), 161–165.

[113] See Charles Manga Fombad, "Transitional Justice in Africa: The Experience with Truth Commissions," Hauser Global Law School Program (May/June 2008), http://www.nyulawglobal.org/globalex/Africa_Truth_Commissions.html (discussion focused on Nigeria).

across the country in the period before independence led to the introduction of fundamental rights and the incorporation of those guarantees in Nigerian constitutionalism, beginning with the 1960 charter.[114] Going further, as we see in this section, concerns about group rights were, for starters, the factor that led to introduction of federalism the country under the 1954 constitution.[115] The devolution of political powers debate in Nigeria can be an emotive argument loaded with political overtones. Those overtones reach their highest decibel when the debate is cast in the vocabulary of political restructuring, instead of power devolution embedded in decentralization. Consistent with the thrust of this book anchored on universal human rights, the focus is on decentralization, free of political suggestions.

Prelude to the Power Devolution Debate

Back to the early days of the country's independence, reaching new heights under military rules, Nigeria's leadership, for the most part dominated by northern Muslims, has operated the country's federal system in a unitary format—much to the chagrin of many non-northern critics.[116] Under the Fourth Republic since 1999, "[a] recurring theme in Nigerian federalism is the federal government's dominance vis-à-vis the state and local governments," evidenced by various provisions in the 1999 Constitution, including exclusive control of the police and the armed forces, a sizable listing of subject areas over which only the national government can legislate and judicial powers for the national government that extends to state courts.[117] To put the matter in proper perspective, Nigeria is a country of 36 states, one federal capital territory at Abuja, and 774 local governments[118] underlain by six geo-political zones, the Southeast,

[114] See note 97 and accompanying text.

[115] See notes 153–154 below and accompanying texts.

[116] One such critic was Chukwuemeka Odumegwu Ojukwu, former Biafran leader, who in a 1994 lecture analogized the country's unity to Jonah in the belly of the Whale—the Whale being Hausa-Fulani and Jonah the rest of the country, notably the Igbo, who have craved fruitlessly for inclusion into the mainstream of Nigerian politics since their forced re-annexation into the country in 1970. Emeka Odumegwu Ojukwu, "Nigeria: The Truths Which Are Self-Evident," *Sunday Magazine* (March 6, 1994), 17, https://nigeriaworld.com/feature/speech/ojukwu_archives.html.

[117] Ayua and Dakas, note 82, p. 250.

[118] Nigerian Const. 1999, note 14, art. 1(3).

Southwest, South-South, Northeast, Northwest, and North Central, not reflected in the constitution.[119] However, the 1999 Constitution allocates 68 items of power to the national government[120]; twelve others which it shares with the states,[121] some smattering of residual powers, nothing spelled out like the reserved powers of the states under the Tenth Amendment of the US Constitution[122]; and two for the numerous local governments.[123] One measure of the size of a government is the proportion of money it controls.[124] Under Nigeria's revenue allocation formula since 1999, the national government based in Abuja keeps 56% of all revenues, leaving only 44% for the sub-national governments made up of 36 states, and 774 local governments.[125]

The Power Devolution Debate Before Buhari: Appeals for Return to "True Federalism"

Before the onset of the Buhari regime in 2015, advocacy for political restructure took the form of appeals for a return to "true federalism." One such call came from Emeka Anyaoku, Nigerian-born Secretary-General of the Commonwealth of Nations from 1990–2000. In 2016,

[119] See Philip C. Aka, "Why Nigeria Needs Restructuring Now and How It Can Peacefully Do It," *Denver Journal of International Law and Policy*, 46(2) (Winter 2018), 123–157; and Calista Ezeaku, "Should the Six Geopolitical Zones Become Federating Units in Nigeria?" *Tide* (Lagos) (February 11, 2013), http://www.thetidenewsonline.com/2013/02/11/should-the-six-geopolitical-zones-become-federating-units-in-nigeria/.

[120] Nigerian Const. 1999, note 14, 2d schedule, Part I (enumerating the "exclusive legislative list").

[121] Ibid., 2d schedule, Part II (enumerating the "concurrent legislative list").

[122] See Nigerian Const. 1999, note 14, art. 4(7)(a) (leaving to the States "any matter not included in the Exclusive Legislative List"). Compare with The Constitution of the United States (1789), https://www.usconstitution.net/const.html., 10th Amend. (providing that "[t]he powers not delegated to the United States by the Constitution, nor prohibited by it to the States, are reserved to the States respectively, or to the people").

[123] Nigerian Const. 1999, note 14, 4th schedule (specifying the "functions of a local council").

[124] As Everett McKinley Dirksen, US Senator from Illinois from 1951–1969, once famously stated, commenting on the U.S. federal budget, "A billion here, a billion there, and pretty soon you're talking about real money!" Cited in Michael E. Milakovich and George J. Gordon, *Public Administration in America,* 11th Ed. (Boston, MA: Wadsworth Cengage Learning, 2013), 327.

[125] Ayua and Dakas, note 82, p. 265.

Anyaoku proposed a reduction of Nigeria's 36 states into six units,[126] after initially lamenting the Nigerian state structure as "drift[ing] toward chaos."[127] General Olusegun Obasanjo (1999–2007) and Goodluck Jonathan (2010–2015) made feeble moves toward power devolution, signified by more or less self-serving national conferences, each of which produced laborious reports that were never implemented.[128]

This was despite findings by a presidential committee the Obasanjo administration set up in 1999, which reviewed the Fourth Republic Constitution. The committee observed that "[o]ne of the dominant issues which featured in a large number of submissions and representations is the preferred political structure for Nigeria."[129] It found that "so strong is the concern and agitation for the desired restructuring that Nigerians cannot seem to wait longer for them to witness the emergence of a True Federation with more powers, responsibilities[,] and resources [...] decentralized and devolved in favor of the lower tiers of Government."[130]

General Obasanjo set up the committee because of recurring questions regarding the legitimacy of the charter imposed on Nigerians by the departing military regime. In its preamble, the Constitution proclaimed, "We the People" of Nigeria "having firmly and solemnly resolved [on various issues, including living "in unity and harmony as one indivisible and indissoluble sovereign nation under God"], do hereby make,

[126] See "Anyaoku Proposes Reduction of Nigeria's 36 States into 6 Units," *Sun* (Lagos) (February 3, 2016), http://sunnewsonline.com/new/anyaoku-proposes-reduction-of-nigerias-36-states-into-6-units/ (quoting Anyaoku's remarks during a conference at the University of Ibadan on February 1, 2016, attributing Radio Nigeria as source for the news story).

[127] Emeka Anyaoku, "Nigeria's Current Drift Towards Chaos," *Vanguard* (Lagos) (November 12, 2013), http://www.vanguardngr.com/2013/11/nigerias-current-drift-towards-chaos-emeka-anyaoku/#sthas.3H7LjLA6.dpuf.

[128] See Festus Owete, "Between Jonathan's National Conference and Obasanjo's National Political Reform Conference: What You Need to Know," *Premium Times* (Abuja) (February 16, 2014), http://www.premiumtimesng.com/news/155237-between-jonathans-national-conference-and-obasanjos-national-political-reform-conference.html. Obasanjo convened his conference in 2005, while Jonathan inaugurated his own in 2014. To restate, each of these conferences produced reports that were never implemented.

[129] Ayua and Dakas, note 82, p. 250, citing Report of the Presidential Committee on the Review of the 1999 Constitution: Vol.1: Main Report (February 2001), 3.

[130] Ibid., p. 250, citing Report of the Presidential Committee on the Review of the 1999 Constitution: Vol.1: Main Report (February 2001), 37.

enact, and give to ourselves the following Constitution."[131] This was despite the fact that the document was adopted by military decree with no input from the public, and no opportunity to approve it in a national referendum. The template for this Constitution was the one of 1979, which was amended in several key respects that separated it from its 1979 predecessor.[132]

The Power Devolution Debate under Buhari: Decentralization as Political Restructuring

Under Buhari since May of 2015, calls for power devolution reached a din that his regime resisted until he left office on May 29, 2023, because the debate took the form of the politically-loaded vocabulary of political restructuring. A sample of three opinions by three Nigerians illustrates this point. These are the views of Atiku Abubakar,[133] Vice President from 1999 until 2007, the political analyst Reuben Abati,[134] and the journalist Alabi Williams.[135]

Abubakar opines that an excessively powerful center militates against (rather than facilitates), national unity, and that the country must renegotiate its union to make it stronger.[136] He contended that "no federal system is set for all time[,]" and that "the rising tide of agitations" in the country, some of them "militant and violent," mandate "a reset in our

[131] Nigerian Const. 1999, note 14 (preamble).

[132] See Ayua and Dakas, note 82, pp. 246–247. The military chose this document over a 1989 constitution under Babangida (1985–1993) that was never fully implemented and a 1995 draft constitution by Abacha (1993–1998) that was abandoned in 1998 after his sudden death. Ibid.

[133] Atiku Abubakar, Restructuring Nigeria for Greater National Integration and Democratic Stability, Paper Presented at the Umaru Musa Yar'Adua Memorial Hall, Kaduna (July 30, 2016) [hereinafter Abubakar, Second Restructure Speech], http://www.elombah.com/index.php/special-reports/9123-how-to-restructure-nigeria-written-by-atiku-abubakar; and Atiku Abubakar, Restructuring for Nigeria's National Unity, Remarks during a Book Launching at the Yar'Adua Center, Abuja (May 31, 2016) [hereinafter Abubakar, First Restructure Speech], http://opinion.premiumtimesng.com/2016/05/31/173089/.

[134] Reuben Abati, "Why We Need to Restructure Nigeria to Save It," *Info Square* (Online) (June 3, 2016), http://infosquare.com.ng/tag/why-we-need-to-restructure-nigeria-to-save-it-by-reuben-abati/.

[135] Williams, note 25.

[136] Abubakar, First Restructure Speech, note 133.

relations as a united nation."[137] Agitations for restructuring in the land have become so wide-spread ranging beyond the traditional "regional, ethnic[,] and religious groupings[,]" to encompass "labor and professional groups[,]" and many, such as unemployed youths, who increasingly feel that "their voices are not being heard or that they are unable to hold those in power to account."[138] While the government has in the past responded to these agitations through certain techniques, such as creation of new states, these measures have proven inadequate or in some cases, such as concentrating power at the federal level, even contradictory.[139]

Abubakar believes that there is no point in the government waiting to resolve the governance and economic challenges the country faces before it implements restructuring.[140] He opines that restructuring is good for *every* section of the country, including the North which has held political powers for much of the period since independence, and advised Nigerians to refrain from the habit of assuming that anyone calling for restructuring the country means to break it up.[141] Abubakar proposed several measures to achieve the goal of political restructuring in the land, including: a smaller, leaner federal government with reduced responsibilities; a tax-centered revenue base; common citizenship for all, based on residency, rather than ethnic group at birth; and state police forces to augment federal law enforcement.[142]

For his part, Abati maintained that Nigeria "is in urgent need of a [...] redesign" away from the nominal federalism it has operated since the first military coup in the country in 1966.[143] This is the only antidote against the present situation where Nigerians "feel excluded from the current power-sharing arrangement; [...] marginalized, treated unfairly

[137] Ibid.

[138] Abubakar, Second Restructure Speech, note 133.

[139] Ibid.

[140] Abubakar, First Restructure Speech, note 133.

[141] Ibid. This statement calls to mind the observation of Professor Achebe regarding the price Nigeria pays contending with "the legitimate grievance of a wrong citizen" each time it perpetrates "social injustice and the cult of mediocrity" against a section of its own population. Achebe, note 33, p. 19.

[142] Abubakar, First Restructure Speech, note 133.

[143] Abati, note 134.

and alienated by a compromised state that is in need of reinvention."[144] His proposal for change includes the following. First, organization of the current 36 states "on a zonal basis, to reflect the existing six geopolitical zones, with each zone having its own government, and responsible for its own development."[145] Second, each of the six autonomous zones will make financial contributions to the coffers of "a central government whose functions will be limited to defense, foreign affairs, national security" and other mutually-agreed-upon functions that must be spelled out in a new constitution.[146] Third, institution of a unicameral legislature at the center with equal number of members from each of the six zones, and presidential power at the center rotated "from one geo-political zone to the other, for a single term each of about six years."[147] Abati asserted that details of the new order "can be negotiated once there is a commitment to change and a broad consensus on what exactly will work for Nigeria."[148]

Williams shares the same sense of urgency as Abati with his proposition that, given the magnitude of the national security challenges Nigeria faces, including deadly conflicts over access to grazing lands, agitation for Biafra, and bombing of oil installations in the Niger Delta by militants advocating for resource control, "this is the best time to review Nigeria."[149] Plus, as he stated, the centripetal rumblings in the land "are direct responses of aggrieved nationalities to the attitude of [the] government in conceptualizing issues of restructuring the polity."[150] But because the national government then under Buhari, and, as of this book, Tinubu, lacks the motivation or incentive to deal with these problems, there is small chance that the political capital in consensus needed to address them will be mustered.

Power Devolution as Decentralization

Bereft of the political overtones that in Nigeria makes it controversial, in simpliciter, this step revolves around decentralization or devolution

[144] Ibid.

[145] Ibid.

[146] Ibid.

[147] Ibid.

[148] Ibid.

[149] Williams, note 25.

[150] Ibid.

of political powers. It follows logically from the historical importance of collective rights, given the status of Nigeria as a patchwork of numerous ethnic groups,[151] some of which, like the Igbo, Hausa-Fulani, and Yoruba, with populations running into tens of millions, are sizable enough to form their own separate countries. This line of thinking, even in those early days in the evolution of the country, led to the introduction of a federal system by colonial authorities more versed with a unitary system from their home state.[152]

Nigerian federalism goes back, pre-independence, to the 1946 constitution, but reached full blooming in the Lyttleton Constitution of 1954, named after Oliver Lyttleton, then British colonial secretary. Orchestrated killings of Igbo in Kano, a metropolitan city in northern Nigeria, along with large-scale destruction of Igbo businesses, convinced British colonial authorities that Nigeria, "if it was to be a nation, must be a federation, with as few subjects reserved for the Central Government as would preserve national unity."[153] The constitution created a federation of three autonomous regions in the country that was, however, lopsided, setting the ground for future instability in the political system, given that under the document, the northern region had more representation in the House of Representative than the Eastern and Western Regions joined together. For how much longer can the country continue to buck the global trend toward power-sharing and devolution? Why would a country like Nigeria, included in the comparative politics literature among examples of a federal system,[154] continue to *operate*, as it has done since the end of the civil war

[151] See "Nigeria," *in Ethnologue: Languages of the World*, 17th Ed., ed. M. Paul Lewis (Dallas, TX: SIL International, 2010).

[152] At the risk of over-simplification, the occurrence calls to mind the US's imposition of a parliamentary democracy on Japan after World War II, a political system polarly different from the presidential system of government in the US homeland. See "Why Did the Americans Choose the British System of Government for the Japanese, Instead of the American System?" *Reddit*, https://www.reddit.com/r/AskHistorians/comments/1b6gys/why_did_the_americans_choose_the_british_system/?rdt=61002.

[153] A.H.M. Kirk-Greene, *Crisis and Conflict in Nigeria: A Documentary Sourcebook*, Vol. 1 (London: Oxford University Press, 1971), 10 (quoting the diary of the British Colonial Secretary).

[154] See, for example, J. Tyler Dickovick and Jonathan Eastwood, *Comparative Politics: Integrating Theories, Methods, and Cases* (New York: Oxford University Press, 2013), 179 (map of federal systems around the world). Based on the map, Nigeria is one of only four federal countries in Africa, the others being Comoros, Ethiopia, and South Africa. Ibid.

in 1970, like a unitary system, at a time unitary systems like China and the UK, through extensive devolution of power to constituent units, are "seek[ing] the benefits of decentralized government without necessarily establishing federalism[?]".[155]

Shape of a Properly-Decentralized Nigeria

Based on insights from the multiple sources discussed above, a properly decentralized Nigeria will be a cross between a federal and con-federal systems,[156] with ingredients designed to promote the economic viability of each "federating" unit within the political system. It should have six units, whether named regions, provinces, or zones, based on the six geopolitical zones, either each by itself in place of the current thirty-six states or as "a cluster of states put together on the basis of ethnic homogeneity."[157] Second, similar to the practice during the First Republic from 1960 until 1966, each geopolitical zone should have its own constitution. Third, each zone should be responsible for its own census. Fourth, each should have control of its own resources, specifically revenue allocation based on a principle of ownership rooted on the proposition that "everybody owns all that is [on] one's land or under it."[158]

Fifth, each zone should recruit and control its police force and, to minimize the known propensity of the Nigerian army to stage coups,

[155] Dickovick and Eastwood, note 154, p. 179.

[156] Both a federal and con-federal systems are marked by division of powers between a central government and its constituent units. For a graphic explanation of the main elements of distinction between these two systems, vis-à-vis the unitary format, see Steffen W. Schmidt et al., *American Government and Politics Today 2005–2006 Edition* (Belmont, CA: Thomson Wadsworth, 2005), 83, Fig. 3-1 (in a confederal system, the non-center units are strong while the center is weak; in contrast, in a federal system, both the center and non-centers are strong in the issue areas assigned to them by the constitution. Additionally, in a federal system, both the center and the non-centers can act directly on the people, for example, through taxation, whereas in a confederal system, the central government can only act on the people only through the non-centers).

[157] Ojukwu, note 116, p. 22.

[158] Ibid. Elsewhere in the lecture, Ojukwu asserted that "[t]he oil, the gas, the mineral found under a man's property belongs to the man. This is a principle we must establish in this country." Ibid., p. 23. Ojukwu's proposition that "everybody owns all that is one's land or under it" appears to rhyme with the injunction in the international bill of human rights, regarding economic self-determination, that "[i]n no case may a people be deprived of its own means of subsistence." See note 116 and accompanying text (referring to the ICCPR and ICESCR, notes 84-85 above).

the armed forces should be decentralized along the lines of the Aburi Accord.[159] Sixthly, taking a cue from the Ethiopian constitution adopted one year after Ojukwu's speech, the Constitution should integrate a secession clause to give any zone that wants to leave the union the opportunity to do so.[160] Finally the Constitution of the national government should be mandatorily reviewed about every twenty years.[161] Now as in 1954, the goal should be to assign to the central government as few subjects as it needs to preserve unity[162]—foreign affairs, defense, and coordination of economic activities among the states. This would translate into an exclusive legislative list of no more than ten items, compared to the current 68.[163] As a corollary, "[t]he funds for running the Federal account shall be allocated to reflect the duties of the Federal Government."[164]

Given its known history of political instability, wouldn't implementation of the foregoing proposal set the stage for the dissolution of Nigeria as we know it? The response to this concern is that the Nigerian state is not sustainable in its current shape; accordingly, the argument for human

[159] The Aburi Accord is an agreement hammered out at a summit meeting on Jan. 4–5, 1967, between representatives of Nigerian federal government and the Eastern Nigerian government at the initiation of the Ghanaian government in a last-ditch attempt, ultimately unsuccessful, to prevent a civil war. The agreement included a decision on the regionalization (decentralization) of the Nigerian army. The Aburi Accord envisaged a confederal system of government, explained in note 156. See Dapo Akinrefon, "Let's Return to Aburi Accord—Adeniyi," *Vanguard* (Lagos) (January 30, 2012), http://stephendieseruvwe.com/2012/03/14/lets-return-to-aburi-accord-adeniyi/.

[160] For the provision of the Ethiopian Constitution relating to right to self-determination up to and including secession, see note 101.

[161] See Ojukwu, note 116, p. 22 (recommending every 15 years).

[162] See note 153 and accompanying text.

[163] See note 118–119 and accompanying texts.

[164] Ojukwu, note 116, p. 22. The restructure proposal laid out here may be analogized to the Swiss model. Switzerland (population 8.3 million as of 2016) has a long tradition of republicanism. Its constitution adopted initially in 1848 following a civil war (but amended several times since then) provides for a (con)federation of one central government and 26 cantons with far-reaching autonomy. See "Switzerland's Political System and Government," *All About Switzerland*, http://swiss-government-politics.all-about-switzerland.info/. Under the constitution, the central government is charged with responsibility for foreign relations, national defense, customs examinations and tariffs, value added taxes, railways, communications, and the like. Responsibility for all other matters, including police forces, education, health, and other social services belongs to the cantons. Ibid. The un-adopted Aburi Accord, referenced above, note 159, is the closest Nigeria has come to adopting a confederal system.

rights in external affairs made in this study is dependent on throughgoing reforms in domestic and foreign policies draped in the accessible vocabulary of universal human rights. Left as it is, concentration of political powers at Abuja is an albatross that undermines the unity, safety, and stability of the country.[165]

Stemming the Influence of Religion in Nigerian Politics

A disquieting issue in Nigerian politics under the Fourth Republic since 1999 is the increased salience of religion in politics and public life. Therefore, additional to the four above, there is need for Nigeria to stem the influence of religion in politics. While fundamentalism is a problem for all religions in Nigeria,[166] Islamic extremism is particularly troubling because of the intertwining of Islam and ethnicity in northern Nigeria.[167] Before Nigeria's independence in 1960, Islamic (or sharia) law formed the legal system in northern Nigeria.[168] On the eve of independence, under an agreement some commentators refer to as "the Settlement of 1960," application of sharia law was confined to family and personal issues, such as marriage, divorce, child custody, and inheritance.[169] Supported by the

[165] Abubakar, First Restructure Speech, note 133 (stating that excessive centralization of political powers at the center makes Nigeria's "unity more fragile, [its] government more unstable[,] and [the] country more unsafe."

[166] See Ryan Lenora Brown, "A Top Nigerian Export: Fervent Christianity," *Christian Science Monitor* (September 28, 2015), http://news.yahoo.com/top-nigerian-export-fervent-christianity-135101567.html; and Toyin Falola, *Violence in Nigeria: The Crisis of Religious Politics and Secular Ideologies* (Rochester, NY: University of Rochester Press, 1998), *passim.*

[167] See Aka, "Nigeria: The Need for an Effective Policy of Ethnic Reconciliation," note 53, p. 335.

[168] See J. N. D. Anderson, *Law Reform in the Muslim World* (London: Athlone Press, 1976), 27–28 (depicting northern Nigeria as "the only place outside the Arabian Peninsula in which the Islamic law, both substantive and procedural, was applied in criminal litigation—sometimes even in regard to capital offenses"). At the same time, during the colonial period, British authorities limited the forms of punishment that could take place under sharia law, abolishing mutilation and torture and subjecting other harsh penalties to a repugnancy test, which test precluded application of a punishment form determined to be contrary to "natural law, equity, and good conscience"). Ayua and Dakas, note 82, p. 248, n. 31.

[169] Philip Ostien and Albert Dekker, "Sharia and National Law in Nigeria," in *Sharia Incorporated: A Comparative Overview of the Legal Systems of Twelve Muslim Countries*

departing British colonial authorities, the agreement was necessary to protect basic rights for all citizens and to promote economic relations in the new nation.[170]

Contrary to the letter and spirit of the Settlement of 1960, some northern Nigerian leaders worked diligently in the post-independence period to expand the role of sharia law in the Nigerian public square. The campaign for more sharia began somewhat modestly in 1979 when northern Muslims staged a walk-out during the drafting of the Constitution for the Second Republic, following the defeat of their proposal to include a Federal Sharia Court of Appeal in the constitution. The impasse was resolved by then Head of State General Olusegun Obasanjo, a Christian from the Yoruba ethnic group, only following agreement by the Constituent Assembly, which wrote into the new constitution provisions for Sharia Court of Appeal "for any state that requires it," and, in the same manner, Customary Court of Appeal, "for any state that requires it."[171] Successive military rulers, all of whom were Muslims, did not approach the sharia issue with the same even-handedness. For example, in 1986, General Ibrahim Babangida, Head of State from 1985 to 1993, clandestinely enrolled the country into the Organization of the Islamic Conference, backing off only following a deafening public outcry from Christians in all parts of the country.[172]

Two events that have unfolded under the Fourth Republic since 1999 speak to the increased salience of religion into Nigerian politics. The first is the upgrading of sharia law into criminal code by twelve northern states in northern Nigeria in 2000–2001, beginning with Zamfara.[173] Going further, Nigeria's sharia states created *hisbah* organization (sharia police), charged with responsibility for prosecuting a range of offenses, including "social vices" like prostitution, mixing of the sexes, and drinking in public

in Past and Present, ed. Jan Michiel Otto (Leiden, Netherlands: Leiden University Press, 2010), 567.

170 Ibid., pp. 566–567.

171 See Philip C. Aka, "Judicial Independence under Nigeria's Fourth Republic: Problems and Prospects," *California Western International Law Journal*, 45 (Fall 2014), 38–39.

172 Ibid., p. 39.

173 The twelve sharia states are Bauchi, Borno, Gombe, Jigawa, Kaduna, Kano, Katsina, Kebbi, Niger, Sokoto, Yobe, and Zamfara. See "Analysis: Nigeria's Sharia Split," *BBC News* (January 7, 2003), news.bbc.co.uk/2/hi/Africa/2632939.stm.

places. Taken together, these actions had the effect of restoring sharia law in northern Nigeria "to a state of completeness and a degree of autonomy" never seen before in the country "for over a century."[174]

Another event under the Fourth Republic, coming from northern Nigeria, that lend testimony to the growing salience of religion in politics is the insurgency group known as Boko Haram, which colloquially means "Western education is a sin."[175] The group works feverishly to turn Nigeria into an Islamic state.[176] In pursuit of its bigoted goal, Boko Haram members have waged war on any target—police stations, rival Muslim clerics, politicians, public institutions, ordinary citizens, name it—which they consider insignia of Western education, using every terroristic tool of violence within their reach, including arson, fire-bombing, suicide bombing, kidnapping, raping, and maiming.[177] The group has killed about 50,000 people, maimed an untold number, engaged in incalculable destruction of private and public property, and rendered over two and a half million people homeless both within their area of operation in northeastern Nigeria and beyond.[178] Dubious highlights of the group's terroristic campaign include the kidnapping of over 200 schoolgirls in

[174] Ostien and Dekker, note 169, p. 576.

[175] The group calls itself *Jama'atul Alhul Sunnah Lidda'wati wal jihad* in Arabic, meaning "people committed to the propagation of the prophet's teachings and jihad." Jeff Haynes, "Religion," *in Politics in the Developing World,* 4th Ed., eds. Peter Burnell et al. (New York: Oxford University Press, 2014), 123.

[176] See Farouk Chothia, "Who Are Boko Harm Islamists?" *BBC News* (May 4, 2015), http://www.bbc.com/news/world-africa-13809501.

[177] See "Boko Haram Fast Facts," *CNN Library* (Updated February 19, 2016), http://www.cnn.com/2014/06/09/world/boko-haram-fast-facts/.

[178] See National Counterterrorism Center, "Boko Haram" (October 2022), https://www.dni.gov/nctc/ftos/boko_haram_fto.html#:~:text=OVERVIEW&text=Boko%20Haram%2C%20which%20aims%20to,it%20was%20established%20in%202002; Conor Gaffey, "Biafra Protests Prompt Separation Anxiety in Nigeria," *Newsweek* (March 1, 2016), http://www.newsweek.com/2016/03/11/nigeria-biafra-nnamdi-kanu-protests-432002.html (estimating the number of people killed as 20,000); and Charlotte Alfred, "Boko Haram Actually Kills More People in Terror Attacks than ISIS," *Huffington Post* (November 18, 2015), http://www.huffingtonpost.com/entry/boko-haram-isis_us_564cd890e4b00b7997f8c15d. (commenting on reports that found Boko Haram to have overtaken the Islamic State of Iraq and Syria (ISIS), as the "most deadly terror group in the world").

April 2014, and the bombing in August of 2011 of a United Nations building in Abuja.[179]

Electing Competent Governments Able and Willing to Handle the Preceding Four Tasks

Although political restructuring, covered in the penultimate section, is important, a political system is only as good as the men and women who run it.[180] This is where competent governments able to discharge the four tasks highlighted above—protecting socioeconomic human rights alongside political-civil rights, protecting collective rights, implementing political restructuring, and reducing the influence of religion in politics, all four conducted within the canvas of civilian rule—comes in as step six in generating the human rights at home that Nigeria needs for a human right-based foreign policy. Back to the Treaty of Westphalia (1648) setting up the nation-state system, governments have played a critical role in the life of every society.[181] The emphasis is on competent governments able and willing to serve the needs of their society.[182]

The social scientist Max Weber (1864–1920) hypothesized traditional, charismatic, and legal-rational authorities as sources of legitimacy or three reasons why citizens obey their leaders.[183] Overtime, performance emerged as a distinctive source of legitimacy.[184] For one thing, performance within the context of a selection process, not rooted in arbitrary

[179] See "Boko Haram Fast Facts," note 177. See also Adam Nossiter, "In Town of Missing Girls, Sorrow, but Little Progress," *New York Times* (May 12, 2015), http://www.nytimes.com/2014/05/12/world/africa/in-town-of-missing-girls-sorrow-but-little-progress.html.

[180] Leaders are distinguished from mere power holders. Instead, they are office holders capable of producing social change that will satisfy the authentic yearnings of their followers. See James MacGregor Burns, *Leadership* (New York: Harper Torchbooks, 1978), 4–5.

[181] See Office of the UN High Commissioner for Human Rights, "Good Governance and Human Rights," http://www.ohchr.org/EN/Issues/Development/GoodGovernance/Pages/GoodGovernanceIndex.aspx (tying governance to human rights).

[182] Ibid.; see also Burns, note 180.

[183] See generally Max Weber, *Economy and Society: An Outline of Interpretive Sociology* (New York: Bedminster Press, 1968).

[184] See Ben Cross, "Performance Legitimacy for Realists," *Philosophy East and West*, Project MUSE (2022), https://doi.org/10.1353/pew.0.0241.

military rule, belongs in the Weberian category of legal-rational authority. This line of thinking forms the basis for the inclusion of this step among the factors in the road to increased respect for human rights at home necessary for the design of a human right foreign policy for Nigeria in the age of Buhari and his progenies in an era of momentous changes in British politics.

One issue which points to the poverty of creative leadership under the Fourth Republic is the increased salience of religion highlighted in the preceding section. Although the Nigerian constitution forbids the adoption of a state religion, none of the four presidents who ruled Nigeria since 1999 saw it fit to get a clarification from the Nigerian Supreme Court regarding the constitutionality of the twelve northern states' upgrading of sharia law into criminal code, contrary to the Settlement of 1960, referred to in the previous section.[185] Three of these presidents, Olusegun Obasanjo, Shehu Musa Yar'Adua, and Goodluck Jonathan, were members of the People's Democratic Party (PDP),[186] which dominated the political system until it lost the presidential election in March 2015 to General Muhammadu Buhari of the All Progressives Congress (APC).[187] Buhari remained in office until May 2023 when he handed power to Bola A. Tinubu, his fellow APC chieftain.

During his two terms in office as civilian president, Obasanjo took the position that the issue was the use of religion for political ends that will fizzle out on its own with time.[188] It did not. Yar'Adua, a Muslim, was too sick during the brief period he served as President to even broach the issue. Neither did Jonathan, a Christian who spent five whole years in office before he left office in May 2015. Nor did Buhari, a Muslim who expressed support for sharia law prior to his assumption of office in 2015.[189] No one expects Tinubu, a Muslim who chose a fellow Muslim as

[185] See notes 169–170 and accompanying texts.

[186] "People's Democratic Party (PDP)," *Encyclopedia Britannica*, http://www.britannica.com/topic/Peoples-Democratic-Party-political-party-Nigeria.

[187] All Progressives Congress, "About APC," http://apc.com.ng/index.php/about-apc.

[188] Benson Ohihon Igboin, "'The President of Nigeria Has No Final Say': Sharia Law Controversies and Implications for Nigeria," *Central & East European Online Library* (2014), 265–290, http://www.ceeol.com/search/article-detail?id=180187.

[189] Buhari expressed support for strong implementation of sharia law, but walked back that position and defended freedom of religion for all when he ran for president in 2015.

running mate, contrary to past convention,[190] to be the leader who tests the constitutionality of sharia law. Failures like this validate the observation of the political analyst and former US diplomat John Campbell to the effect that "Nigeria's top political personalities have largely remained the same since the end of the civil war—they have merely aged in place."[191]

There is a more urgent issue tied to elections, the tool for instituting, maintaining, and legitimizing governments. It has nothing to do with the concern about popular passion, the strange presumption that ordinary people can be predisposed to work against their own common interests by electing unwise leaders, a propensity that the framers of the US Constitution sought to curb by instituting the Electoral College.[192] A more

See Brenda Daldorph, "Muhammadu Buhari: 'The Converted Democrat?'" *France 24* (Latest update April 13, 2015), http://www.france24.com/en/20150401–nigeria-buhari-president-elections-coup-africa.

[190] See Editorial Board, *Guardian*, "The Muslim-Muslim Ticket Challenge," *Guardian* (Lagos) (June 17, 2022), https://guardian.ng/opinion/the-muslim-muslim-ticket-challenge/ ("… [G]oing by convention, [Tinubu] [was] […] expected to choose a running mate from the Northern Christians to balance the geopolitical permutations and to create a feeling of belonging to most ethnic and religious groups in the country"). The editorial noted that, under the Fourth Republic since 1999, "politicians and the major political parties have avoided fielding Christian-Christian or Muslim-Muslim presidential and vice-presidential candidates to balance religious sentiments prevalent in the country." Ibid. It voiced the concern that "a joint Muslim-Muslim ticket by any party has the potential of raising apprehension in [a] country already divided along religious and ethnic cleavages." Ibid. This is especially given the "Islamization agenda" of the outgoing Buhari regime. Ibid. Despite this warning, the Independent National Electoral Commission, Nigeria's election czar, not only approved the ticket but also went ahead to call the presidential election in March 2023, which many observers adjudged to be marred by irregularities that direly question its credibility, for this same ticket. In its prescience, this editorial wondered what it will profit Nigeria if its leaders pursued devious "brinkmanship" that win them elections now, but in the end lose their country. Ibid. Herein lies the significance of this book.

[191] See Campbell, note 68, p. 141.

[192] Under the US's political system, the Electoral College refers to the body of electors that chooses the president. Thomas E. Patterson, *The American Democracy*, 11th Ed. (New York: McGraw-Hill, 2013), 46. During the Constitutional Convention in Philadelphia in 1787, "[d]irect election of the president was twice proposed and twice rejected because it would link executive power directly to popular majorities." Ibid. The compromise became the Electoral College, under which "[e]ach state would have the same number of electoral votes as it had members in Congress and could select it electors by a method of its choosing." Ibid. See also Eric Black, "Why the Constitution's Framers Didn't Want Us to Direct Elect the President," *Minn Post* (October

immediate problem the Nigerian masses face, ab initio, is the scarcity of free and fair elections under the Fourth Republic. All the elections since 1999, including the one conducted by the departing military that brought General Obasanjo into office lacked the free and fair quality.[193] An exception, arguably, is the 2015 presidential election where Goodluck Jonathan conceded defeat to General Buhari.[194] Given this occurrence, it is fair to conclude that, under the Fourth Republic, Nigeria's illiberal democracy holds elections barely free and fair that neither "reflect the reality of popular participation in politics" nor of "support for those elected."[195] Accordingly, Nigerian masses need free, fair, and credible elections, now missing in action, to elect competent governments able to get the job of governance accomplished within the best tradition of legal-rational legitimacy propounded by Max Weber.[196]

17, 2012), https://www.minnpost.com/eric-black-ink/2012/why-constitution-s-framers-didn-t-want-us-directly-elect-president. Over time, however, the US Constitution was altered in a manner that gave more power to the people. Andrew Jackson, president from 1828 to 1837, is the chief executive credited with linking the people and the presidency. Patterson, p. 48 (explaining how Jackson created that linkage with the positive result that, today, except for few instances where a candidate wins the presidency after losing the popular vote, "[t]he candidate who gets the most popular votes nationally is also likely to finish first in enough states to win a majority of the electoral votes").

193 See, for example, Salahu Mohammed Lawal, "An Appraisal of Corruption in the Nigerian Electoral System," *European Scientific Journal*, 11 (2015), 256–273 (analysis ranging up to the 2011 elections wherein the author reached the verdict that "conduct of credible, free and fair election has been eluding [the] Nigerian nation"); J. Oshola Omotola, "Elections and Democratic Transition in Nigeria under the Fourth Republic," *African Affairs*, 109 (2010), 535–553 (covering the 1999, 2003, and 2007 general elections); and Victor Oguejiofor Okafor, ed., *Nigeria's Stumbling Democracy and Its Implications for Africa's Democratic Movement* (Westport, CT: Praeger, 2008 (commenting on the 2007 general elections).

194 See, for example, Babatunde Oyekanmi, 2015 General Elections and the Role of INEC, Paper Presented at a Conference Organized by INEC (July 2015), http://www.inecnigeria.org/wp-content/uploads/2015/07/Conference-Paper-by-Tunde-Oyekanmi.pdf (observing that, vis-à-vis prior votes, the "2015 general elections were a huge success, but there is the need to continue to reform"). INEC is the acronym for Independent National Electoral Commission, the agency charged with responsibility for the conduct of elections in Nigeria.

195 Zakaria, note 20.

196 Weber, note 183.

External Support or Assistance

National action has priority in human rights protection and promotion, and external support is never a substitute for national action.[197] "[T]he long-term fate of human rights depends largely on the citizens whose rights are in question."[198] Professor Donnelly recounts various practical reasons why this is the case. First, external actors lack the capacity for the intensive monitoring ultimately necessary to make human rights secure. Second, they lack the immediate incentives that, as a practical matter, are necessary to engage in the sustained efforts to force states to respect human rights. Third, ultimately external actors lack the power that ordinary citizens have to pressure their governments to respect and enforce their international human rights obligations.[199] In a word, people develop themselves "or they do not develop at all."[200] Ultimately "it is up to a free people to defend their own rights[,]" because "if they don't do that, international action almost certainly will come to nothing."[201] Individually and collectively, citizens must "demand that their governments respect" their human rights.[202] They must work to create "for themselves a society and a legal and political system where their human rights are respected, implemented, enforced, and enjoyed."[203]

Yet, no discounting or gainsaying the primacy of national action, that primacy does not preclude the necessity for external support or assistance in building the human rights at home necessary for the conduct of a human right-based foreign policy. The entire UN system is built on "international cooperation"[204]; in a non-autarkic international system,

[197] See Donnelly, note 103, pp. 162–163 (commenting on "[t]he priority of national action" in human rights struggles).

[198] Ibid., p. 163.

[199] Ibid.

[200] Basil Davidson, *Modern Africa: A Social and Political History*, 3rd Ed. (New York: Longman, 1994), 265–268 (commenting on the imperatives of self-development).

[201] Donnelly, note 103, p. 163.

[202] Ibid.

[203] Ibid.

[204] United Nations, Charter of the United Nations (1945), 59 Stat. 1031, T.S. 993, 3 Bevans 1153, United Nations. Charter of the United Nations. 1945. 59 Stat. 1031, T.S. 993, 3 Bevans 1153, https://www.un.org/en/about-us/un-charter, art. 56 (stating that "[a]ll Members pledge themselves to take joint and separate action in cooperation with the Organization for the achievement of the purposes set forth in Article 55").

few countries can assist its people without help from abroad. For Nigeria as for any other United Nations member-state, international support is critical in the growth of human rights, as it can be for democracy.[205] International support is necessary, even decisive, both when violations are occurring[206] and when seemly they are not occurring.[207] "[M]ajor states and international organizations" can be "active partners of governments in making basic human rights part of the working foundations of contemporary states."[208] Infusing human rights in domestic and external relations are "a matter of joint, global responsibility" "too important to be left [exclusively] to national governments."[209]

Conclusion

Nigeria is a state born in foreign affairs via British colonialism in Africa[210]; over 63 years since independence as of this book, the country still anchors the bulk of its legitimacy on "juridical statehood," embedded in legal recognition as a sovereign state under international law, rather than the

[205] See Michael J. Sodaro, *Comparative Politics: A Global Introduction* (Boston, MA: McGraw-Hill Higher Education, 2008), 233–234 (spotlighting a "favorable international environment" among ten conditions for democracy). Professor Sodaro defines these "external" or "outside influences" that can support democracy at home to include "[t]ransnational networks of nongovernmental organizations[,]" but instructively noted that "while external influences may be important," they do not preclude national action—given that, among other things, "[u]ltimately, the sources and nutrients of democracy must be homegrown if democracy is to germinate and blossom to its full potential." Ibid., p. 234. As is with democracy, so it is too with human rights.

[206] See Donnelly, note 103, p. 163 (stating that where the environment is most repressive "external actors may have a decisive role in keeping the idea of human rights alive in national political discussions," but where the environment is "less repressive," they "may be able to provide vital support to isolated or fledgling local human rights advocates").

[207] Ibid. (stating that "[i]n countries where the overall human rights situation ranges from not too bad to excellent, external actors can often achieve incremental changes in policies and may provide a useful, occasionally even vital, supplement to national actors").

[208] John W. Harbeson and Donald Rothchild, "The African State and State System in Flux," *in Africa in World Politics: The African State System in Flux*, 3rd Ed., eds. John W. Harbeson and Donald Rothchild (Boulder, CO: Westview Press, 2000), 11.

[209] Paul Redmond, "Transnational Enterprise and Human Rights: Options for Standard Setting and Compliance," *International Law*, 37 (2003), 70.

[210] See Chapter 1, notes 37–63 and accompanying texts ("Introducing Nigeria").

empirical ability to perform the functions of a state.[211] Nigeria espouses and promotes ethical values abroad that it does not practice at home. For example, it keeps peace abroad that its longsuffering citizenry lacks at home. The jury is out as to whether the departure of General Buhari from the Nigerian scene after two terms in office changed this. Implementing human rights at home is a necessary step in the transition to principled foreign policy. Nigeria needs to "remove the solecism of abuses at home, and a nominal commitment to international law abroad that currently" passes for human-right policy.[212]

This chapter expounds the need for increased respect for human rights, next only to reconstructing Nigeria national interest in readiness for human-right work, on the road to principled foreign policy that Buhari eight years in office as president until 2023 impeded. In addition to a statement of justification, the discussion encompasses a layout of seven conceivable steps to that haven that, for best results, must be synchronized, rather than implemented sequentially: extending the dividends of democracy to economic rights; protecting collective rights; devolution of powers packaged as decentralization instead of the more politically-sensitive restructure vernacular; stemming the influence of religion in politics. These tasks are to be implemented by a competent government, within the predicate of civilian rule and the auxiliary precaution of external support. Of these steps, decentralization received extended discussion in the light of its importance, given the ethnic complexity of Nigeria, an importance evident in the premium historically placed on group rights in the country's politics.

At first appearance, international assistance seems out of place among these factors. However, such support necessary to consolidate human

[211] See Robert Jackson and Carl Rosberg, "Why Africa's Weak States Persist: The Empirical and the Juridical in Statehood," *World Politics* (1982), 1–24. Strong states control their boundaries and perform effectively the functions of security and provision of competent public services for their citizenry. In contrast, weak states base their statehood on non-empirical variables, including the legal notions and trappings of sovereignty and non-interference in the internal affairs of a country.

[212] Aka, "Human Rights in Nigeria's External Relations," note 13, p. 25. See also See also Douglas C. Lovelace, Jr., "Foreword," in Clarence J. Bouchat, *The Causes of Instability in Nigeria and Implications for the United States* (Carlisle, PA: Strategic Studies Institute & U.S. Army War College Press, August 2013), iii (dubbing the country "a swirling paradox of riches and poverty, growth and stagnation, *international influence and domestic paralysis*, cultural diversity, and ethnic and religious clashes"). Emphasis added.

rights at home does not in any way preclude national action. Implementing the seven steps will eliminate or ameliorate the problems of political corruption, with negative ramifications for the country's international image and for foreign direct investment, while generating the national cohesion that the country needs to formulate and execute foreign policy.[213] Otherwise, Nigerian leaders will be unable to consummate the "active role in world affairs commensurate with their country's aspirations,"[214] that going back since independence, especially under the Fourth Republic since 1999, they have pined for. With this chapter over, the book turns its searchlight to Chapter 6 on peacekeeping, the next station on methods in Nigeria's journey post-Buhari on the road to a principled foreign policy.

[213] Pham, note 38, pp. 91–100 (discussion the historical and conceptual background related to the country).

[214] Ibid., p. 100.

CHAPTER 6

Peacekeeping

Introduction

This chapter analyzes the possibilities and limits of peacekeeping in the toolbox of a projected human-right policy for Nigeria in an era of decreased influence of the military in the country's body politic, emblematized by the departure of General Buhari after two unimpressive terms in office as President. Put differently, the chapter explores peacekeeping, a key implement in the arsenal of methods set forth in this book for the pursuit and realization of a principled foreign policy for Nigeria post-Buhari. It is the third of five materials on methods, after Chapter 4 focused on reconstructing Nigeria's national interest in readiness for human-right work, and Chapter 5 on increased respect for human rights in the Nigerian homeland. This discussion is complemented and completed by Chapter 7 on the TAC (next after this conversation), and Chapter 8 on the CCJ.

Peacekeeping is *the* lifeblood of Nigerian foreign policy. It is the tool with which, even pre-independence in 1960, Nigeria cut its teeth in foreign affairs.[1] Since its formation in 1975 in the aftermath of the

[1] See Festus Ugboaja Ohaegbulam, *Nigeria and the United Nations' Mission to the Democratic Republic of the Congo: A Case Study of the Formative Stages of Nigeria's Foreign Policy* (Gainesville, FL: University Press of Florida, 1982), *passim*. Because the United

P. C. Aka, *Human Rights in Nigeria's External Relations in the Age of General Muhammadu Buhari and His Successors*,
https://doi.org/10.1007/978-3-031-63231-0_6

bloody civil war in Nigeria, ECOWAS has been the foreign policy tool of choice that Nigerian leaders use to conduct—and showcase their putative prowess in—peacekeeping. Given its embedment in peacekeeping, logically, this chapter includes a statement on the possibilities and limits of ECOWAS as a tool in the application of Nigeria's external relations. The extended discussion accorded the economic union reflects its preeminence in the formulation and implementation of Nigerian foreign policy. Such is the importance that the CCJ, explored in the next chapter of this book, ranks among the key institutions of the organization. Four issues that, in sum, this chapter covers are: the intricacies of peacekeeping; evolution of Nigerian peacekeeping since independence; strategies designed to make Nigerian peacekeeping human-right-compliant; and the possibilities and limits of ECOWAS, human-right speaking, as an embedded tool of Nigeria's foreign policy.

Intricacies of Peacekeeping

Peacekeeping is "a technique designed to preserve the peace [...] where fighting has been halted, and to assist in implementing agreements achieved by the peacemakers."[2] It is a third-party intervention designed to maintain peace with a set of guiding principles that includes the consent of the parties to the conflict, impartiality (or neutrality), and the non-use of force, save in self-defense.[3] Peacekeepers are charged with several functions that, in addition to maintaining peace and security, include protecting civilians; assisting in the disarmament, demobilization,

Nations Operation in the Congo (ONUC) spans the period July 1960–June 1964, see UN, "Republic of the Congo: United Nations Operation in the Congo" (ONUC) (July 1960–June 1964), http://www.un.org/en/peacekeeping/missions/past/onuc.htm, Nigeria's participation in peace operations predated the country's independence on October 1, 1960, by more than two months. ONUC is the acronym in French of *Organisation des Nations Unies au Congo*, translatable into English as the United Nations Organization in the Congo. The Congo, today the Democratic Republic of the Congo, is a French-speaking country. From 1971 until 1997, the country went by the name Zaire.

[2] United Nations, *United Nations Peacekeeping Operations: Principles and Guidelines* (New York: Department of Peacekeeping Operations, 2008) [hereinafter UN Peacekeeping Operations], 18.

[3] United Nations, "What Is Peacekeeping," http://www.un.org/en/peacekeeping/operations/peacekeeping.shtml; *United Nations Peacekeeping*, "Principles of Peacekeeping," https://peacekeeping.un.org/en/principles-of-peacekeeping.

and integration of former combatants; supporting organization of elections, as well as protecting and promoting human rights and assisting in restoring the rule of law.[4] In a word, as UN literature indicates, "[o]ver the years, peacekeeping has evolved from a primarily military model of observing ceasefires and the separation of forces after inter-state wars, to incorporate a complex model of many elements—military, police[,] and civilian—working together to help lay the foundations for sustainable peace."[5]

Peacekeeping is related to but also distinguished from three other concepts: peacemaking, peacebuilding, and peace enforcement, defined based on their location in the peace process. *Peacemaking* consists of measures designed to address ongoing conflicts, such as diplomatic action, designed to help hostile parties understand their differences with a view to bringing them to a negotiated agreement.[6] This is irrespective of whether the initiative in question was undertaken by officials within or outside the UN system, by unofficial and nongovernmental groups, or by private individuals working independently.[7]

Newly-won peace is a fragile commodity that could relapse into conflict, if not preserved. This is where *peacebuilding* kicks in. This peace technique is designed to reduce the risk of such relapse by strengthening national capacities for conflict management, thereby laying the foundation for sustainable peace and development.[8] In contrast to peacemaking, which involves ongoing conflicts, peacebuilding is post-conflict.

Last but not least is *peace enforcement*. The term involves the application of a range of coercive measures, including the use of military force, requiring the explicit authorization of the Security Council,[9] consistent with the collective security imperatives of the UN.[10] Although the word

[4] "What Is Peacekeeping," note 3; and Claire Klobucista and Mariel Ferragamo, "Backgrounder: The Role of Peacekeeping in Africa," Council on Foreign Relations (last updated December 12, 2023), https://www.cfr.org/backgrounder/role-peacekeeping-africa.

[5] *UN Peacekeeping Operations*, note 2, p. 18.

[6] United Nations, "Peace and Security," http://www.un.org/en/peacekeeping/.

[7] Ibid.

[8] Ibid.

[9] Ibid.

[10] *Collective security* is a collective defense arrangement guaranteeing "security for individual nations by collective means" to maintain international peace. Roland N. Stromberg,

"enforcement" in the concept suggests a post-conflict process, it is hard to figure out precisely where, between an ongoing conflict (associated with peacemaking) and post-conflict (linked with peacebuilding), peace enforcement comes in.

In sum, the connection of the three terms (peacemaking, peacebuilding, and peace enforcement) to peacekeeping is borne out by the fact that today, "[p]eace operations are rarely limited to one type of activity."[11] Instead, the boundaries of the concepts blur. For example, "[w]hile U.N. *peacekeeping* operations are, in principle, deployed to support the implementation of a ceasefire or peace agreement, they are often required to play an active role in *peacemaking* efforts and may also be involved in early *peacebuilding* activities."[12] It should be obvious by now that peacekeeping, as we know it today, is a UN invention.[13] Yet, although the UN Charter arguably anticipated the practice, it is a thing of serendipity not explicitly expressed in the document. Instead, peacekeeping evolved as an innovative attempt to deal with emergent regional conflicts needing to be dealt with in the interest of international security, but where, due to the ideological competition and rivalry between the US and the Soviet Union that marked the Cold War (1945–1991), great-power agreement was difficult or impossible. In short, in the perceptive observation of Inis L. Claude Jr., peacekeeping dramatically changed the role of the great powers vis-à-vis the UN: from "the proposition that the [UN] should [...] promote order by bringing the great powers into troubled situations[,]" to the notion that the UN should "keep[] the great powers out of such situations."[14]

"Collective Security," *Encyclopedia of the New American Nation,* http://www.americanforeignrelations.com/A-D/Collective-Security.html. Under this arrangement, which predated the UN's formation, "an aggressor against any one state is considered an aggressor against all other states, which act together to repel the aggressor." "Collective Security," *Encyclopedia Britannica*, http://www.britannica.com/topic/collective-security.

[11] "Peace and Security," note 6.

[12] Ibid. See also Ronald Hatto, "From Peacekeeping to Peacebuilding: The Evolution of the Role of the United Nations in Peace Operations," *International Review of the Red Cross*, 95 (2013), 495–515 (tracing the evolution of the UN's role in peace operations).

[13] See Hatto, note 12 (depicting the UN as the main player in setting up peace operations).

[14] Inis L. Claude Jr., *The Changing United Nations* (New York: Random House, 1965), 32.

Evolution of Nigerian Peacekeeping Since Independence in 1960

The following section has four interrelated portions: a sketch of Nigeria's record in peacekeeping before the negative watershed of General Buhari's two terms in office which ended May 29, 2023; gaps in years that give pause to the robustness of this activity, material rewards that question the altruism of the operations, and contradictions of the Nigerian state that these operations unearth. We take these issues in turn.

Sketch of Nigeria's Record in Peacekeeping Before General Buhari

Since its independence in 1960, Nigeria has participated actively in peace missions and in multiple settings: under the auspices of ECOWAS, and its military arm, ECOMOG, the OAU, the AU, the UN, and under "bilateral agreements" outside these conventional settings (see Appendix to this chapter). From 2000 to 2010, under the Fourth Republic since 1999, Nigeria ranked among the top seven contributors to UN peacekeeping.[15] By 2010, for about 50 years, Nigeria contributed over 150,000 troops to peace operations.[16] These troops include soldiers, police officers, and civilian experts.[17] Nigeria commanded six of these peace operations, namely: the missions in Angola, Congo, Liberia (twice), Sierra Leone, and South Sudan.[18] Six soldiers who have served as UN force commanders are:

[15] See table of contents of contents, pp. vii–viii, in *Providing Peacekeepers: The Politics, Challenges, and Future of United Nations Peacekeeping Contributions*, eds. Alex J. Bellamy and Paul D. Williams (New York: Oxford University Press, 2010). As of February 2012, Nigeria deployed 5,726 peacekeepers in UN missions in Sudan's Darfur region, Liberia, Côte d'Ivoire, the Democratic Republic of Congo, South Sudan, Western Sahara, Haiti, Lebanon, and East Timor. This placed the country fifth largest contributor after Bangladesh, Pakistan, India, and Ethiopia. Adekeye Adebajo, "Nigeria," in *Providing Peacekeepers*, p. 245.

[16] Adebajo, note 15, p. 245.

[17] Ibid.

[18] Adesoji Adeniji, "Peacekeeping Contributor Profile: Nigeria," *Providing for Peacekeeping* (April 24, 2015), http://www.providingforpeacekeeping.org/2015/04/24/peacekeeping-contributor-profile-nigeria.

- Major-General Johnson Aguiyi-Ironsi, who rose to become the country's first military Head of State (Congo)
- Major-General Chris Garuba (Angola)
- Lt. General Isaac Obiakor (Liberia)
- Major-General Joseph Owonibi (Liberia)
- Gen. Martin Luther Agwai (Darfur), and
- Major-General Moses Obi (South Sudan).[19]

Obiakor and Agwai also served as Chief Military Adviser and Deputy Military Adviser, respectively, at UN Headquarters.[20] Some Nigerian civilians have similarly occupied important positions in UN peacekeeping as Special Representative of the UN Secretary General. These include: Ibrahim Gambari, Joint AU-UN Special Representative and Head of the UN Mission in Darfur; Olu Adeniji, Central African Republic, and Sierra Leone; and Margaret Vogt, Central African Republic.[21]

Nigeria has lost over 2,000 of its nationals, who died in active duty while participating in peace operations and expended over US$10 billion of its own money on peacekeeping missions.[22] Key highlights of the country's peacekeeping undertakings include the OAU mission in Chad which cost it an estimated US$82 million,[23] as well as its participation in the conflicts in Liberia and Sierra Leone which claimed the lives of about 1,500 peacekeepers and cost the country about US$8 billion.[24] "Although Nigeria's positions on various issues have changed over the

[19] Ibid.

[20] Ibid.

[21] Ibid.

[22] See Henry Umoru, "Nigeria Lost 2,000 Soldiers, $10 [Billion] in Peacekeeping Operations," *Vanguard* (Lagos) (October 25, 2010). Different analysts quote different figures and over what time-period that Nigeria has spent on peacekeeping. See, for example, "The Perils of Liberian Peacekeeping," *BBC News* (August 4, 2003), http://news.bbc.co.uk/2/hi/africa/3113009.stm (putting the amount as about 12 billion US dollars, "without any help from the [W]est," quoting General Olusegun Obasanjo, then president of the country).

[23] Umoru, note 22.

[24] Adebajo, note 15, p. 245.

years, its level of activity in international organizations has increased."[25] The sustained activism is creditable in no small part to peacekeeping.

Nigeria's engagements in peace operations span many regions of the world, including the Caribbean, Europe, and Asia. However, consistent with the country's longstanding focus on Africa in its foreign relations, justified perhaps by the rifeness of conflicts in Africa which reached new heights during the Cold War (1945–1991),[26] Nigeria devotes much of its peacekeeping energies to African countries. requiring regional and international attention. In the light of the high level of conflicts in the region that continues even in the post-Cold War period, in choosing peacekeeping as an anchor of its foreign policy, Nigeria presciently selected an area of particular need for Africa. Although Nigerian peacekeepers come from three sectors of the Nigerian society, namely, the military, the police, and civilian experts,[27] most peacekeepers are soldiers. This could be why many of Nigerian peacekeeping missions are military observations (see Appendix to this chapter). And given their dominance in peacekeeping dating back to the early days of the country's independence, arguably the Nigerian military[28] plays an oversized role in the implementation (if not only formation) of Nigerian foreign policy, second only to diplomats.

In 2004, after many years of participation in peacekeeping operations, Nigeria established a training center, Peacekeeper Wing (PKW), to facilitate its peacekeeping activities. Initially part of the Nigerian Army Infantry Corps Center, the institution was upgraded to a freestanding center in 2009, on which date it also took its current name Nigeria Army Peacekeeping Center (NAPKC).[29] Based in Kaduna, a metropolitan city in

[25] "Foreign Relations," in Helen Chapin Metz, ed., *Nigeria: A Country Study* (Washington, DC: GPO for the Library of Congress, 1991), http://countrystudies.us/nigeria/80.htm.

[26] See Philip C. Aka, "Human Rights as Conflict Resolution in Africa in the New Century," *Tulsa Journal of Comparative & International Law*, 11 (Fall 2003), 179–180 (pointing out that "[o]f forty-two peacekeeping missions in the world organized by the United Nations as of 2000, thirteen, or little less than one-third of the overall number, took place in Africa").

[27] See note 17 and accompanying text.

[28] The Nigerian military consists of three branches: the army and navy, established in 1958, and the air force, founded in 1964. "Nigeria—Ministry of Defense," *Global Security*, http://www.globalsecurity.org/military/world/nigeria/mod.htm.

[29] Adeniyi, note 18.

northern Nigeria (population: over 1.2 residents in 2024),[30] the Center is headed by a commandant.

The Nigerian government announced that it upgraded the Center because of "the overriding need to ensure that [Nigerian] peacekeepers are placed on the same pedestal of professional competence" supposedly with their counterparts elsewhere, "in accordance with U.N. requirements."[31] The Center provides training to Nigerian troops before they are shipped for peacekeeping duties abroad. According to information taken from its website, as of 2014, the Center has delivered "over 230 courses and trained over 53,000 peacekeepers."[32] Training activities at the Center include courses in: pre-deployment training; command-and-staff operations skill; train-the-trainers; driver's training; combat life savers; junior leadership; military observation; peace operations planning; disarmament, demobilization, and reintegration; civil-military cooperation; negotiation skills; effective methods of instruction; basic peace support operations for defense correspondents; and protecting civilians.[33]

To increase the training exposure of its peacekeepers, the Center collaborates with external agencies, including the UN Institute for Training and Research (UNITAR), the US's Africa Contingency Operations Training and Assistance (ACOSTA), France's Reinforcement of African Capacity to Maintain Peace (RECAMP in its French acronym), and Canada's Military Training Assistance Program (MTAP). Established in 1963 by UN Generally Assembly Resolution 1934 (XVIII) of December 11, 1963, UNITAR is the training arm of the UN system.[34] The mission of the organization "is to develop capacities of individuals, organizations, and institutions to enhance global decision-making and to support country-level action for shaping a better future."[35] It is an autonomous body within the UN system, governed by a Board of Trustees and headed by an executive director. UNITAR is supported

[30] "Kaduna, Nigeria," *Encyclopedia Britannica* (December 10, 2023), https://www.britannica.com/place/Kaduna-Nigeria.

[31] Nigeria Army Peacekeeping Center, "About Us," http://www.napkc.org/training.php.

[32] Ibid.

[33] Nigeria Army Peacekeeping Center, "Highlight," http://www.napkc.org/training.php.

[34] UNITAR, "About Us: The Institute," http://www.unitar.org/the-institute.

[35] Ibid.

solely by voluntary contributions from governments, intergovernmental organizations, foundations, and other non-government sources.[36]

Funded by the US Department of State, which also manages it, ACOTA is an American initiative designed to improve the ability of African countries to respond quickly to crises by providing militaries who are beneficiaries of the program with the training and equipment they need to implement peace support or humanitarian operations. The organization replaced the African Crisis Response Initiative (ACRI) in 2004.[37] Operating under the aegis of the UN and in unison with the AU, France's RECAMP aims to help African states to acquire military capabilities that will enable them to conduct peace operations in Africa.[38] Last but not least is MTAP. The Canadian organization supports and reinforces the international mission of the Canadian military by training the military forces of other countries, particularly states in the developing world, in peace operations, including developing the capability of these militaries to operate effectively in joint forces with the Canadian military. The program originated in agreements Canada made in the early 1960s to provide military training assistance to certain newly independent Commonwealth countries.[39]

During his visit to Nigeria in August 2000, referred to repeatedly in this book, then US President Bill Clinton praised Nigeria for the "extraordinary extent of [its] leadership for peace in West Africa and around the world," crystallized in "its commitment to peacekeeping."[40] Clinton likened Nigeria's commitment to this activity as "building the record of

[36] Ibid.

[37] Council on Foreign Relations, "Fact Sheet on Africa Contingency Operations Training and Assistance (ACOTA)" (June 15, 2008), http://www.cfr.org/africa-sub-saharan/fact-sheet-africa-contingency-operations-training-assistance-acota/p22318.

[38] See Ruth Nabakwe, "France Continues Peacekeeping Initiatives for Africa," Pan African News Agency (January 23, 2002), https://www.globalpolicy.org/component/content/article/199/41018.html.

[39] Andrew P. Rasiulis, "The Military Training Assistance Program (MTAP): An Instrument of Diplomacy," *Canadian Military Journal* (Autumn 2001), 63–64, http://www.journal.forces.gc.ca/vo2/no3/doc/63-64-eng.pdf.

[40] William J. Clinton, "Remarks to a Joint Session of the Nigerian National Assembly in Abuja, August 26, 2000," in *Public Papers of the Presidents of the United States: William J. Clinton, 2000–2001* (Washington, DC: Best Books, 2000), 1710; and President Clinton's Address to the Nigerian Joint Assembly (August 26, 2000), https://www.youtube.com/watch?v=Z0uzicpb1Is (YouTube video of the speech published April 19, 2012).

a moral superpower."[41] However, under the insular regime of General Buhari from 2015 until 2023, this activity and other tools in the quiver of Nigeria's external relations took a hit, to the detriment of the country's already negligible contributions to international human rights and nominal application of human rights in external affairs.[42]

Gaps That Question the Robustness of Nigeria's Peacekeeping Operations

As robust as it seems at first sight, there are two gaps, totaling seventeen years in Nigeria's otherwise consistent engagement since independence in peace operations, that require some explanation. Those gaps—the first for twelve years from 1966 to 1978, and the second for five years from 1983 to 1988, considerably overlap the regimes of General Gowon (1966–1975), and General Buhari (1983–1985). One possible explanation for the relative inactivity is national security challenges at home of a kind that foreclosed mobilizing troops abroad. For Gowon that domestic issue was the civil war from 1967 to 1970. Additionally, the lack of activity might also have spelled antipathy for peacekeeping operations as a tool of foreign policy given that Gowon remained in office for five long years after the civil war during which time-period he helped form ECOWAS. This point bears noting, given that, with two other leaders who served as military Head of State (General Johnson Aguiyi-Ironsi in 1966 before him and General Olusegun Obasanjo after him), Gowon was part of the UN peacekeeping mission in the Congo.[43]

Secondly, even here too, the civil war appears to be a factor. ECOWAS was an attempt to secure the West African subregion, beginning with close-door neighbors, to avoid the type of interference in Nigeria's

[41] Clinton, "Remarks to a Joint Session of the Nigerian National Assembly," note 40, p. 1705. See also "Clinton Praises 'New Nigeria,'" *BBC News* (August 26, 2000), http://news.bbc.co.uk/2/hi/africa/897423.stm.

[42] Some scholars take the position that the retrogression started under Goodluck E. Jonathan, President from 2010 to 2015. See Adekeye Adebajo, "Sad Deterioration of Nigeria's Foreign Policy," *B[usiness] D[ay] L[ive]* (Johannesburg) (May 6, 2013), http://za.news.yahoo.com/sad-deterioration-nigeria-foreign-policy-051439591.html (commenting on the "deterioration of Nigeria's foreign policy" in the Fourth Republic, during the presidency of Goodluck Jonathan [2010–2015], including the performance of Nigerian peacekeepers which Adebajo assessed as below UN standards).

[43] Adebajo, note 15, p. 247.

internal affairs by foreign actors, including Western powers, that led to the recognition of Biafra, by two states in the subregion, Gabon and then Ivory Coast, which were, and still are, allies of France. Biafra was the former Eastern Region of the country that attempted unsuccessfully to break away from Nigeria. Next to Buhari, as military Head of State, he was an insular leader who focused exclusively on the economic troubles that his junta presented as the basis for the overthrow of the Shagari administration (1979–1983) that he unconstitutionally replaced.[44] He was succeeded by General Babangida (1985–1993) whose rulership was marked by unprecedented repression at home, including fallouts from the annulment of a presidential election in 1993 that forced him out of office.

Nigeria's Peacekeeping Operations Are Less Altruistic Than They Appear at First Sight

Nigeria's engagement in peacekeeping is not 100% altruistic as it appears at first sight[45]; instead, various material reasons, both economic and non-pecuniary, animate the country's peacekeeping undertakings.[46] Starting with economic reason, Nigeria received generous reimbursements (in some cases running into hundreds of thousands in US dollars) for its participation in UN peacekeeping, to the financial benefits of the country and the peacekeepers.[47] For instance, for its participation in the UN Mission in Sierra Leone (UNAMSIL), Nigeria received a reimbursement of over US$798,000 for use of major equipment and provision for "self-sustainment" for the initial two battalions deployed in the mission from December 27, 1999, to January 26, 2000.[48] However, the country

[44] See "Nigeria's Muhammadu Buhari in Profile," *BBC News* (March 31, 2015), http://www.bbc.com/news/world-africa-12890807 (observing that in addition to a "war against indiscipline," as military leader, Buhari opened another war front involving about 500 politicians, officials, and businessmen, whom he sent to jail as part of his campaign against corruption).

[45] On the role of self-interest motivations in International Law and Relations, see, for example, Jason Rudall, *Altruism in International Law* (London and New York: Cambridge University Press, 2021) (commenting on the emergence and denouement of self-interest rules and behaviors in international law).

[46] See Adeniyi, note 18 (dividing those reasons into political, normative, security, economic, and international).

[47] See ibid.

[48] Ibid.

spends its own money rather than gets reimbursed when it participates in peace operations mandated by ECOWAS or the AU. For instance, as indicated before, Nigeria spent over $10 billion without reimbursement on ECOMOG missions in Liberia and Sierra Leone during the conflicts in those two countries.[49]

In sum, because Nigeria is reimbursed for costs incurred in UN peacekeeping missions, the financial challenge for the country in peacekeeping occurs with respect to regional and subregional peace operations.[50] "[D]espite the importance and centrality of Africa to Nigeria's foreign policy[,]" vis-à-vis ECOWAS and AU engagements, the economic attraction of UN operations makes these missions more appealing for the country.[51] For the soldiers as a group that form the face of Nigerian peace operations, participation in these activities has become "part of the military's internal rewards system."[52] This and the opportunity for training in modern peace techniques that these rounds of duty afford explain the Nigerian Armed Force's strong support for UN peacekeeping.[53] Next to the non-pecuniary reasons, Nigeria embraced peacekeeping initially out of a desire to play a leadership role in Africa—a goal that expanded over time to include others, such as exposure of soldiers and police personnel to the techniques of modern peace operations that UN peacekeeping affords;

[49] See note 22–24 and accompanying texts. The civil war in Sierra Leone took place from 1991 to 2002. See "Sierra Leone," *Global Security*, http://www.globalsecurity.org/military/world/war/sierra_leone.htm; and Se Young Jang, "The Causes of the Sierra Leone Civil War," *E-International Relations Students* (October 25, 2012), http://www.e-ir.info/2012/10/25/the-causes-of-the-sierra-leone-civil-war-underlying-grievances-and-the-role-of-the-revolutionary-united-front/. The conflict in Liberia took place in two stages, the first from 1989 to 1996, and the second from 1999 to 2003. Part of the reason the amount was hefty was that Nigeria had to provide support to keep participating countries in West Africa aboard who threatened to pull out due to lack of funds. Adeniji, note 18.

[50] Adeniji, note 18.

[51] Ibid.

[52] Ibid. By 1993, the UN paid its peacekeeping soldiers almost US$1,000 per month, compared to about $150–$300 per month (US$5–$10 per day), that ECOMOG paid its soldiers. Human Rights Watch, *Waging War to Keep the Peace: The ECOMOG Intervention and Human Rights*, 5 (June 1993), 17, https://www.hrw.org/legacy/reports/1993/liberia/.

[53] See Adeniji, note 18. With respect to the opportunity it affords for practical training, there are some within the armed forces who view peacekeeping missions as "police work" that erodes rather than build their battle-readiness. Adebajo, note 15, p. 247.

and a desire to build up credentials for a seat in a modified UN Security Council.[54]

Contradictions of the Nigerian State That Its Peacekeeping Operations Expose

Peacekeeping demonstrates one of the contradictions of the Nigerian state, speaking to the paradox of "beautiful abroad and ugly" at home[55] that the adoption of a human-right policy can resolve for the country. "Physician, heal thyself!" is a wisdom that Nigerian leaders need to heed, given that their country is burdened by the very same troubles that Nigeria uses its peacekeeping energies to resolve abroad. Reading from the Appendix to this chapter, in 1964–1966, Nigeria was involved in peacekeeping activities in the India-Pakistan conflict the latter of which period (1966) overlapped the pogrom of about 100,000 Igbo and other Easterners in non-Eastern portions of the country, particularly northern Nigeria.[56] Under Babangida, in another era, Nigeria performed peacekeeping in various parts of the world—Bosnia and Herzegovina, Croatia, and Rwanda, where in one instance (Rwanda), it deployed one military battalion, the same year in 1993 that the regime annulled a presidential election that created so much uproar, especially in Lagos and surrounding areas in the Southwest, that are home of Moshood Abiola, the presumed winner of the cancelled election.[57] Finally, in 1998, a crisis-ridden military regime under the Abacha dictatorship undertook peacekeeping initiatives

[54] Ibid.

[55] S.O. Akinboye, Beautiful Abroad But Ugly at Home: Issues and Contra[di]ctions in Nigerian Foreign Policy. University of Lagos Inaugural Lecture Series (2013), www.unilag.edu.ng/opendocnew.php?

[56] See Herbert Ekwe-Ekwe, *Biafra Revisited* (Dakar, Senegal: African Renaissance, 2006), 77.

[57] See, for example, Aderemi Suleiman Ajala, Yoruba Nationalism: Culture, Politics[,] and Violence in South-Western Nigeria (1900–2009), Institut für Ethnologie und Afrikastudien, Johannes Gutenberg-Universität, Mainz, Germany, Working Paper No. 107 (2009), http://www.ifeas.uni-mainz.de/Dateien/AP107.pdf (commenting on agitations within and outside the country, including the establishment of a radio station in the US in the wake of the annulment); "Rioting in Nigeria Kills at Least 11," *New York Times* (July 7, 1993), http://www.nytimes.com/1993/07/07/world/rioting-in-nigeria-kills-at-least-11.html.

to restore a civilian regime in Sierra Leone.[58] In sum, it is fair to say that, save for a war or the idiosyncratic disposition of an insular leader who chooses to focus his attention on domestic issues, Nigeria engaged in peacekeeping abroad even when it lacks peace at home.

To put the issue of crisis at home and peacekeeping abroad into closer perspective, since 2009, Nigeria has battled terrorist violence by the Boko Haram group that has fought to turn the country into an Islamic state in a bloody campaign that has killed over 20,000 citizens, displaced millions from their homes, and inflicted untold damage to government and private property.[59] This is in addition to the longstanding militancy in the Niger Delta over environmental degradation from oil exploration and demands for more revenue allocation by impoverished communities in that region.[60] Due to these security issues, the Nigerian government has, as the security analyst Adesoji Adeniji pointed out, reprioritized its troop deployments such that "[a]n increasing number of troops are being recalled from peace operations, [...], and redeployed to restive regions within the country."[61]

[58] See Suleiman Hamman et al., "The Role of Nigeria in Peacekeeping Operations from 1960 to 2013," *International Affairs & Global Strategy*, 21 (2014), 43; Norimitsu Onishi, "What War Has Wrought: Sierra Leone's Sad State," *New York Times* (January 31, 1999), http://www.nytimes.com/1999/01/31/world/what-war-has-wrought-sierra-leone-s-sad-state.html?pagewanted=all.

[59] For two among the numerous commentaries in academic and popular media on the group, see John Ford, "The Origins of Boko Haram," *National Interest* (June 6, 2014), http://nationalinterest.org/print/feature/the-origins-boko-haram-10609; and Farouk Chothia, "Who Are Nigeria's Boko Haram Islamists?" *BBC News* (May 4, 2015), http://www.bbc.com/news/world-africa-13809501.

[60] See, for example, International Crisis Group, *Nigeria: Want in the Midst of Plenty*, Africa Report No. 113 (July 19, 2006); Larry Diamond, "Foreword," in Rotimi T. Suberu, *Federalism and Ethnic Conflict in Nigeria* (Washington, DC: United States Institute of Peace, 2001), x; Jedrzej F. Frynas, *Oil in Nigeria: Conflict and Litigation Between Oil Companies and Village Communities* (Hamburg and London: Lit Verlag, 2000); and Ken Saro-Wiwa, *A Month and a Day: A Detention Diary* (London: Penguin Books, 1996). See also Chapter 2, notes 100–106, and accompanying texts.

[61] Adeniji, note 18.

Strategies Designed to Make Nigerian Peacekeeping Operations Human-Right-Compliant

In and of itself, peacekeeping is *not* a human rights tool, if it is not human-right-compliant. Thus, as one study observed, pointing to UNAMSIL, the peacekeeping mission in Sierra Leone as example, "[t]he initial success of the peacekeepers helped obscure some of the troubling aspects of the intervention[,]" some inconsistent with human rights, that included "the lack of an international mandate, the use of mercenary in peacekeeping operations[,] and the very undemocratic nature of the Nigerian regime."[62] In the light of this proposition, one conceivable way for Nigeria to make its peacekeeping enterprise human-right-compliant is to embrace international standards embedded in human rights and humanitarian law, appreciation of the intersection between the two, and investment in human-right education. First, explication of the relationship between human rights and humanitarian law, followed by an elucidation of the imperativeness of human-right education for Nigerian peacekeepers in the journey toward principled foreign policy.

Nature of the Relationship Between Human Rights and Humanitarian Law and Its Connection to Nigeria

The two concepts are complementary in that: "[b]oth strive to protect the lives, health[,] and dignity of individuals, albeit from a different angle," and "[t]he duty to implement [humanitarian law] and human rights lies first and foremost with States."[63] Next to distinction, humanitarian law (HL) applies in situations of armed conflict and aims to protect people who are not fighters (noncombatants) or are no longer taking part in hostilities (because they are wounded or have surrendered or are taken as prisoners of war).[64] Building on this distinction, the rules embodied in HL impose duties on all parties to a conflict, whereas human rights applies to everyone; whether during peace or war, precepts of human right protect the individual.[65]

[62] Hamman et al., note 58, p. 43.

[63] International Committee of the Red Cross, "What Is the Difference Between Humanitarian Law and Human Rights Law?" https://www.icrc.org/eng/resources/documents/misc/5kzmuy.htm.

[64] Ibid.

[65] Ibid.

To put the matter more precisely, some human-right treaties permit governments to derogate from certain rights in situations of public emergency, whereas HL permits no such derogations—given that HL was inherently conceived for emergency situations, including armed conflicts.[66] The legal anchor of human rights comprises the UN Charter, and other core global human rights instruments, including the UDHR (1948), the ICCPR, and the ICESCR (1966), both of which came into force in 1976.[67] On the other hand, the legal anchor of HL consists of the Geneva Conventions, a set of international treaties dating back to 1864 and amplified by numerous revisions, some as recent as 1978, dealing with a multiplicity of topics, including the treatment of civilians during wars, humane treatment of prisoners of wars, and treatment rules regarding care of the wounded and sick.[68] That foundation necessarily includes the Convention on the Prevention and Punishment of the Crime of Genocide (1948), known for short as the Genocide Convention.

In a Nigerian society riven with regional, ethnic, religious, and class divisions,[69] the military and police perceive themselves to be among the only "national institutions."[70] It is probably this feature that pushed these two groups to the forefront as the face of the country in peacekeeping missions abroad.[71] But, historically, none of the two has a reputation

[66] Ibid.

[67] Ibid.

[68] See, for example, Emily Crawford and Alison Pert, *International Humanitarian Law* (New York: Cambridge University Press, 2015), 1–27 (discussing the historical development of international humanitarian law).

[69] See Gerald McLoughlin and Clarence J. Bouchat, *Nigerian Unity: In the Balance* (Carlisle, PA: Strategic Studies Institute & U.S. Army War College Press, June 2013), http://www.strategicstudiesinstitute.army.mil/pdffiles/PUB1159.pdf.

[70] See "Nigeria—Ministry of Defense," note 28 (stating that Nigerian military leaders "revel in and brag about" their role "as the bulwark against Nigerian anarchy[,]" and the country's "one indispensable institution, committed to Nigerian unity and sovereign survival"); and Max Siollun, *Oil, Politics[,] and Violence: Nigeria's Military Coup Culture (1966–1976)* (New York: Algora Publishing, 2009), 172 (commenting on how, before the Second Republic in 1979–1983, some within the army justified continued military rule on the ground that the military was "the only truly national institution" that could, ironically, guarantee political stability).

[71] During the period of military rule in Nigeria that spanned nearly three decades, some military regimes ruled in partnership with the police. The two that particularly come to mind are the Gowon Administration (1966–1975) and Muhammadu Buhari (1983–1985). Both governments included senior police officers as governors and members of the highest policymaking bodies. See Tekena N. Tamuno, "The Nigeria Police Force and Public

for respecting human rights and humanitarian laws at home.[72] The Nigerian army participated in the pogrom against the Igbo in northern Nigeria in 1966.[73] Similarly, during the Nigerian civil war from 1967 to 1970, Nigerian federal troops perpetrated human rights abuses against the Igbo and other Easterners for breaking away from Nigeria for which until today they have not been held accountable. Dispensing with provisions of the Geneva Conventions for the "humane" conduct of war, these "troops incessantly and wantonly bombed unarmed civilian targets, including open busy markets, and deliberately used economic blockades and starvation as a weapon of war," all atrocities suggestive of genocide.[74]

Most recently, in responding to the wave of terrorist activities in northeastern Nigeria since 2009 that has spread out into some other parts of the country, Nigerian security forces have abused the human rights of suspects to the extent that the US government and some human rights groups have voiced concerns on human-right grounds.[75] The Nigeria police have a similar dubious reputation for cruelty in its dealings with

Security and Safety: Major Challenges and Opportunities Since 1930," in *Security, Crime and Segregation in West African Cities Since the 19th Century*, eds. Laurent Fourchard and Isaac Olawale Albert (Paris, France: Karthala Editions, 2003), 127.

[72] For works on the history of the Nigerian Army, see Nigerian Army Education Corps and School, *History of the Nigerian Army 1863–1992* (Abuja: Nigerian Army Headquarters, 1992); and Norman J. Miners, *The Nigerian Army, 1956–1966* (London: Methuen, 1971) (covering the period 1956–1966). On the police, see Cheta Nwanze, "A Short History of the Nigerian Police Force," *The Trent Online*, http://www.thetrentonline.com/cheta-nwanze-short-history-nigeria-police-force/.

[73] See Mark Curtis, "Nigeria's War Over Biafra, 1967–70," edited extract from Mark Curtis, *Unpeople: Britain's Secret Human Rights Abuses* (New York: Vintage Books, 2004), 2, https://markcurtis.wordpress.com/2007/02/13/nigeriabiafra-1967-70/ (stating that "[r]eports circulated that troops from the northern region had participated in the massacres" of Igbo in September 1966).

[74] Aka, "Human Rights as Conflict Resolution," note 26, p. 180, n.7; Toyin Falola and Adebayo Oyebade, *Hot Spot: Sub-Saharan Africa* (Santa Barbara, CA: ABC-CLIO, 2010), 74–76 (wondering whether the untold killings, infliction of human suffering, and destruction of property that took place in the four years from 1966 until 1970 were in the legitimate pursuit of a "war of unity" or amounted to genocide as Biafrans alleged).

[75] See, for example, Michael Martinez, "Kerry: Nigeria Acknowledged Human Rights Abuses in Terror Fight," *CNN* (May 25, 2013), www.cnn/com/2013/05/25/world/africa/nigeria-kerry-human-rights (US Secretary of State John Kerry conceded that the Nigerian government had a right to defend itself against terror groups, but simultaneously criticized its human rights abuses in responding to terrorist attacks); Amnesty International, *Stars on Their Shoulders[,] Blood on Their Hands: War Crimes Committed by the Nigerian Military* (June 3, 2015), http://www.amnestyusa.org/research/reports/stars-on-their-shoulders-blood-on-their-hands-war-crimes-committed-by-the-nigerian-military (finding that

citizens at home.[76] This is particularly true with the Nigerian Mobile Police (MOPOL) nick-named "kill and go" by the masses of the Nigerian people because of its tendency to perpetrate extrajudicial murder with impunity.[77] Between them, Nigerian soldiers and the police share a history of corruption, the (ab)use of public office—and trust—for private ends. One shameful monument of the symbiosis are police so-called roadside checkpoints which Daniel J. Smith pinpointed as "the most notorious and popularly recognized symbol of everyday corruption" in Nigeria.[78] This is a practice of illegal extortion wherein the police and soldiers set up makeshift roadblocks, enabling them to stop and besiege the drivers of countless private and public vehicles who ply on Nigerian roads as well as hassle the passengers of these vehicles.[79] Smith averred that during the period he lived in Nigeria from 1989 to 1997, "hardly a month passed without media reports or oral testimony from my friends and acquaintances about people who had been harassed, beaten, or shot in confrontations at checkpoints with the police or military."[80]

Regrettably, the attitude of general disrespect of human rights at home by Nigerian security forces extended abroad into peacekeeping missions. In 1989, a civil war erupted in Liberia, generating mass killings, homelessness and dislocations and related loads of humanitarian disasters that spilled over into neighboring Sierra Leone.[81] To quell the violence and

since March 2011, more than 7,000 persons died in military detention and more than 1,200 were unlawfully killed since February 2012).

[76] See Human Rights Watch, *"Rest in Pieces": Police Torture and Deaths in Custody in Nigeria* (July 2005), https://www.hrw.org/reports/2005/nigeria0705/ (report documenting the frequent use of torture by the Nigerian police); and Adewale Maja-Pearce, "Changing Nigeria's Cruel Police Culture," *New York Times* (October 7, 2014), http://www.nytimes.com/2014/10/08/opinion/adewale-maja-pearce-changing-nigerias-cruel-police-culture.html (commenting on sensitivity to the need to respect human rights, against the background of a culture of lawlessness and cruelty, marked aplenty by extrajudicial executions of suspected armed robbers, detentions without trial, use of torture to extract confessions, and unrelieved assault and battery of suspects).

[77] Sam Olukoya, "Nigeria's Trigger-Happy Police," *BBC News* (May 11, 2001), http://news.bbc.co.uk/2/hi/africa/1322017.stm.

[78] Daniel Jordan Smith, *A Culture of Corruption: Everyday Deception and Popular Discontent in Nigeria* (Princeton, NJ: Princeton University Press, 2008), 61.

[79] Ibid.

[80] Ibid.

[81] See, for example, Caitriona Dowd and Clionadh Raleigh, "Mapping Conflict Across Liberia and Sierra Leone," *Accord*, 23, 13–18, https://rc-services-assets.s3.eu-west-1.amazonaws.com/s3fs-public/CON1222_Accord_23_2.pdf; and Human Rights Watch, *Waging War to Keep the Peace*, note 52.

minimize the spread of instability, ECOWAS sent troops, led by Nigeria, invoking dormant security protocols adopted since the formation of the economic union in 1975, but until the conflicts dormant, to justify the interventions.[82]

Several reports on human-right abuses perpetrated by ECOMOG peacekeeper, such as looting, theft and expropriation, and sexual exploitation of women and children spoke to the lack of discipline and impunity by the troops involved, most of them from Nigeria, alongside the failure of ECOWAS to infuse human rights in its conflict resolution initiatives.[83] Regarding the last point, a report by Human Rights Watch published in 1993 found that the ECOMOG forces in Liberia, led by Nigeria, failed to integrate human rights into its peace campaigns largely because, for the Nigerian commanders, observing human rights during the operation was a mission left for "[o]ther organizations" that soldiers should not be bothered with.[84] Ten years later, the problem remained not only in Liberia but also as well in Sierra Leone where, like in Liberia, Nigeria troops formed the bulk of ECOWAS peacekeepers.

In July 2003, Human Rights Watch wrote an open letter to President John Kufuor of Ghana in his capacity as ECOWAS President, as the organization braced itself to send soldiers into Liberia to end the conflict in the country.[85] The letter urged Kufuor to ensure that the peacekeepers deployed in Liberia "act[] in full accordance with international human rights and humanitarian law, and with a clear mandate to protect

[82] Alter et al., "A New International Human Rights Court for West Africa: The ECOWAS Community Court of Justice," *American Journal of International Law*, 107(4) (October 2013), 737, 771.

[83] Ibid., p. 772.

[84] Human Rights Watch, *Waging War to Keep the Peace*, note 52, p. 3, n. 8, quoting an interview in Monrovia, Liberia, on March 9, 1993, with ECOMOG Chief of Staff, Brigadier S.V.L. Malu.

[85] Janet Fleischman, Human Rights Watch, ECOWAS: Troops to Liberia Must Respect Human Rights, Letter to President John Kufuor, then Chairman of ECOWAS (July 18, 2003), https://www.hrw.org/news/2003/07/18/ecowas-troops-liberia-must-respect-human-rights. At the time she issued this letter, Fleischman was Human Rights Watch's Washington Director for Africa. The letter was copied to several world leaders, including President Joaquim Chissano, Chair of the African Union; Mohammad Ibn Chambas, Executive Secretary of ECOWAS; Olusegun Obasanjo, then President of Nigeria; Jacques Paul Klein, Special Representative of the Secretary-General and Coordinator of UN Operations in Liberia; Walter H. Kansteiner III, US Assistant Secretary of State for African Affairs; and Dr. Jendayi Frazier, Senior Director for Africa, US National Security Council.

civilians."[86] On the one hand, Human Rights Watch gave ECOMOG credit for helping to "restore security, which resulted in an improvement in the human rights situation."[87] On the other hand, the organization called the troops out for a litany of abuses, with impunity, that included responsibility "for extensive looting, harassment and arbitrary detention of civilians," as well as violation of "international humanitarian law by conducting indiscriminate air strikes against civilians and civilian objects, including violations of medical neutrality."[88]

In Sierra Leone, the violations no less egregiously included "summary executions of suspected rebels or collaborators," in some of which atrocities senior officers were present or took part; "use of child soldiers, and indiscriminate bombings against civilians;" violation of medical neutrality during a January 11, 1999, operation wherein ECOMOG troops "stormed a hospital, proceeded to drag wounded rebels from their beds, and executed them on hospital grounds;" and sexual exploitation of women and solicitation of child prostitutes.[89] In the light of the violations that it recounted, Human Rights Watch made a number of recommendations aimed at minimizing abuses of human rights, including providing the peacekeepers about to be sent to Liberia with appropriate training in international human rights and humanitarian law before they ship.[90]

It was not until 2004 that Nigeria set up separate training programs for its peacekeepers. This is an unduly long period for a country with a long history of participation in these missions as a pathway to a leadership role in Africa and the world. Yet when a center was created, old habits die

[86] Fleischman, note 85. Leading up to this appeal, Human Rights Watch made several important observations. These include the point that it "has documented human rights abuses by all sides to the conflicts in Liberia and Sierra Leone, including abuses by [...] ECOMOG," and that the "important successes" made in ECOMOG operations "have been offset by serious human rights abuses and a lack of accountability." Ibid. Among other things, it advised ECOWAS to "commit itself to ensuring its troops are adequately trained and able to meet their obligations under human rights and humanitarian law and to investigate and prosecute any officers or soldiers implicated in abuses." Ibid.

[87] Fleischman, note 85.

[88] Ibid.

[89] Ibid.

[90] Fleischman, note 85. Other pertinent recommendations include: integrating advisors with expertise in humanitarian law, establishing a disciplinary unit within the various ECOWAS contingent to secure accountability for human rights abuses by troops, and demobilizing and disarming all child soldiers. Ibid.

hard, none of the various courses it offered for peacekeepers on its face included human-right law and humanitarian law. Assuming the Center offered courses which integrated these laws, there is no evidence that Nigerian peacekeepers internalized these values, judging by the accounts of their stewardship in Liberia and Sierra Leone from the preceding paragraphs that Human Rights Watch presented. Armed forces which violate the rights of their citizens at home will have difficulty respecting these values for proverbial strangers abroad. The good news in all this, a silver lining, if you may, is that the humanitarian abuses in Liberia and Sierra Leone helped trigger "a re-examination of the role of human rights in" regional security,[91] leading to the unvarnished option for human rights by the CCJ two chapters away from this material—making the move from authorizing collective military intervention in a member state to granting the CCJ the power to adjudicate human-right abuses "a relatively modest step."[92]

Chapter 4 on reconfiguring Nigeria's national interest doctrine to improve its readiness for human-right duties commented on the lack of popular input that afflicts the Nigerian foreign policy machinery.[93] The same lack of popular input bedeviled peacekeeping. Domestic public opinion plays little to no role in the decision to recruit and deploy peacekeepers.[94] As proverbial voice of the people, Nigerian lawmakers should play a checkmating role that, regrettably, they do not. Instead, "[o]n this matter, there seem[s] to be very good understanding between the executive and legislative arms of government[,]" with virtually no need for popular input.[95]

Human-Right Education for Nigerian Peacekeepers

Along with appreciation of the connection between human rights and humanitarian law, Nigerian peacekeepers need to pay due attention to human-right education. As the US diplomat David Scheffer once observed in a lecture in February 1998 on war crimes, combatants

[91] Alter et al., note 82, p. 772.

[92] Ibid.

[93] See Chapter 4, notes 88–103, and accompanying texts.

[94] See Adeniji, note 18.

[95] Ibid.

know little to nothing about the laws of war.[96] Peacekeepers, including those from Nigeria, are no different. This is where human-right education comes in. Beginning with the UDHR in 1948, *education*, broadly defined, has been an important tool for promoting the "strengthening of respect for human rights and fundamental freedoms."[97] Among other benefits of enlightenment, human-right education open the eyes of citizens regarding their rights; "lead to an understanding of, and sympathy for, the concepts of democracy, justice, equality, freedom, solidarity, peace, dignity, and rights and responsibilities; and build their awareness that oppressive laws and inappropriate traditions may be reformed."[98]

While there is no one-size-fits-all related to the content of that education, the common core should include "familiarity with the main international documents on human rights; people, movements, and key events in the historical struggle for human rights, the main categories of human rights, along with duties or obligations, and incidents of discrimination, including racism and sexism."[99] The key, as the UN Commission on Human Rights advised, is that "knowledge of human rights, both in its theoretical dimension and in its practical application [...] be established as a priority in educational policies."[100] The Commission oversaw the drafting of the UDHR and other core human rights instruments. Eleanor Roosevelt, its first chairperson taught in 1958 that "the destiny of human

[96] David Scheffer, The Clear and Present Danger of War Crimes, Address, University of Oklahoma College of Law (February 24, 1998), in David P. Forsythe, *Human Rights in International Relations*, 3rd Ed. (New York: Cambridge University Press, 2012), 317 ("Combatants are as likely to know as much about the laws of war as they do about quantum mechanics").

[97] Universal Declaration of Human Rights, G.A. Res.217 A (III), U.N. GAOR, 3d Sess., at art. 26, U.N. Doc. A/810 (1948).

[98] Philip C. Aka, "The Military, Globalization, and Human Rights in Africa," *Journal of Human Rights*, 18 (2002), 435.

[99] Ibid.

[100] Ibid.

rights is in the hands of all our citizens in all our communities."[101] Education on human rights is the "small places close to home," "the world of the individual person," where human rights begin.[102]

Adopting international standard embedded in human rights, humanitarian law, as well as the intersection between the two, and human-right education, facilitates the peacekeeping role of Nigerian peacekeepers. It fits the needs of the victims of conflicts that Nigerian peacekeepers serve, while facilitating better cooperation with external agencies, such as UNITAR, ACOTA, RECAMP, and MTAP, with whom NAPKC, the Nigerian training agency, collaborates.[103] Because these external agencies follow international standards, they offer themselves as the role model Nigerian peacekeepers need.

The Possibilities and Limits of ECOWAS as an Embedded Tool of Nigeria's Peacekeeping Operations

Consistent with the study plan of this book, this section uncovers the connection or lack thereof between ECOWAS and the application of human rights in Nigeria's external relations. Getting there requires that we deal with four threshold issues, all of them interrelated, and each within the context of the international standard embedded in the application of human rights in external affairs that grounds this book: a primer on ECOWAS premised around the narrative and theme of an economic union of West Africa; key institutions of ECOWAS, of which the CCJ,

[101] Eleanor Roosevelt, "In Your Hands: A Guide for Community Action for the Tenth Anniversary of the Universal Declaration of Human Rights" (March 27, 1958), quoted in Jo Anne Wilson-Keenan, *From Small Places: Toward the Realization of Literacy as a Human Right* (Rotterdam, Zuid-Holland, The Netherlands: Sense Publishers, 2015), 28.

[102] Ibid. For studies on Mrs. Roosevelt's contributions to human rights, particularly her role in the drafting and adoption of the UDHR, see Mary Ann Glendon, *A World Made New: Eleanor Roosevelt and the Universal Declaration of Human Rights* (New York: Random House, 2001); and Carol Anderson, *Eyes on the Prize: The United Nations and the African American Struggle for Human Rights, 1944–1955* (New York: Cambridge University Press, 2003) (a less hagiographic chronicle which documented how Eleanor Roosevelt worked against any enforcement powers for UN human rights bodies, thereby assuring Southern Democrats that racial segregation had nothing to fear from human rights).

[103] See notes 29–39 and accompanying texts.

two chapters removed, is one; commentary on the distinctive characteristics of ECOWAS member-states; and forces within and outside Nigeria which lent impetus to the formation of ECOWAS in May 1975.

The Rugged Journey to an Economic Union of West Africa

As its name gives out, ECOWAS is a West African economic-integration organization headquartered in Abuja, Nigeria's capital city.[104] It is an entity imbued with international legal personality, the legal attribute-cum-capacity necessary for the performance of its functions under the treaty setting up the union, including the "power to acquire, hold or dispose" property, movable or immovable.[105] The official and working languages of the organization are English, French, and Portuguese.[106]

ECOWAS came into being on May 28, 1975, when the Heads of State and Government of fifteen countries met in Lagos where they executed the Treaty of Lagos which established the economic union.[107] Strictly

[104] See Economic Community of West African States (ECOWAS), Revised Treaty of the Economic Community of West African States (ECOWAS) (July 24, 1993) [hereinafter ECOWAS Revised Treaty], http://www.refworld.org/docid/492182d92.html, art. 86 ("The Headquarters of the Community shall be situated in the capital of the Federal Republic of Nigeria").

[105] Economic Community of West African States (ECOWAS), Treaty of the Economic Community of West African States (ECOWAS) (May 28, 1975) [hereinafter ECOWAS 1975 Treaty], https://www.refworld.org/legal/constinstr/ecowas/1975/en/63881, art. 60(1)–(2)(a)–(b); ECOWAS Revised Treaty, note 104, art. 88(1)–(2)(a)–(b). See also ECOWAS 1975 Treaty, note 105, art. 60(3) and ECOWAS Revised Treaty, note 104, art. 88(3) (stipulating that "[i]n the exercise of its legal personality under this Article, the Community shall be represented by the Executive Secretary"). For an enunciation of the doctrine of international legal personality, see Tushar Kanti Saha, *Textbook on Legal Methods, Legal Systems and Research* (New Delhi: Universal Law Publishing, 2010), 81 (articulating five legal rights embodied in this doctrine: the power to make and sign contract, to sue and be sued, to own property, the right to hire agents (employees), and self-governance embedded in the right to make regulations).

[106] ECOWAS 1975 Treaty, note 105, art. 87(1)–(2).

[107] See ECOWAS 1975 Treaty, note 105. The treaty contains 65 articles broken up into 14 chapters, plus preambles, eight of them altogether. By our own count, the treaty has eleven parts: **Part 1**, Chapter I, "Principles," including establishment of the organization and its membership, aims, and general undertaking, three articles; **Part 2**, Chapter II, "Institutions of the Community," eight articles; **Part 3**, Chapter III, "Customs and Trade Matters," fifteen articles; **Part 4**, Chapter IV, "Freedom of Movement and Residence," one article; and **Part 5**, Chapter V, "Industrial Development and Harmonization," five articles. Other coverages are: **Part 6**, relating to cooperation in four fields: Chapter VI

speaking, the organization became operational in November 1976, on which date the five protocols annexed to the treaty received the minimum number of ratifications to bring them into force.[108] These founder-heads

on agriculture and natural resources, three articles; Chapter VII on monetary and financial matters, four articles; Chapter IX on energy and mineral resources, one article; and Chapter X on social and cultural matters, one article; **Part 7**, Chapter VIII, "Infrastructural Links in the Fields of Transport and Communication," eight articles; **Part 8**, Chapter XI, "Fund for Cooperation, Compensation, and Development," three articles; **Part 9**, Chapter XII, "Financial Provisions," three articles; **Part 10**, Chapter XIII, "Settlement of Disputes," one article; and **Part 11**, Chapter XIV, "General and Final Provisions" (miscellaneous matters, such as headquarters of the organization, international legal personality, withdrawal of membership, entry into force, and depository location), nine articles.

The treaty specified that the goal of the Community is "to promote co-operation and development" in various fields of economic activity, in the cooperation categories enumerated above, aimed at "raising the standard of living of its peoples, of increasing and maintaining economic stability, of fostering closer relations among its members and of contributing to the progress and development of the African continent." ECOWAS 1975 Treaty, note 105, art. 2(1). The goal ultimately is "accelerated and sustained economic development [...] and the creation of a homogeneous society," achieved through "the elimination of all [...] obstacles to the free movement of goods, capital, and persons." Ibid., preamble. The treaty laid out various methods for achieving this goal, including harmonizing policies in various field, such as agriculture, industry, and monetary matters, and adopting a common policy in these fields, as well as removing "obstacles to the free movement of persons, services, and capital." See ibid., art. 2(2)(a)–(j). The document also created a set of six institutions designed to facilitate achievement of the goal, including an Authority of Heads of State and Government (AHSG), a Council of Ministers, an Executive Secretariat, a legal Tribunal of the Community, and technical and specialized Commissions in four issue-areas. Ibid., art. 4(1)(a)–(e). The commissions are for trade, customs, immigration, monetary and payments; industry, agriculture, and natural resources; transport, telecommunications, and energy; and social and cultural affairs. Ibid., art. 4(1)(e). Art. 4(1) left open room for the AHSG to create new institutions as needed in the future. Of the sixty-five articles embodied in the Treaty, one for us stands out: Art. 54 on contributions by member states. It mandates member-states "to pay regularly their annual contributions to the budget of the Commission," ECOWAS 1975 Treaty, note 105, art. 54(2), failing which, the member risks suspension from participating in the activities of the economic union. Ibid., art. 54(3) ("Where a Member State is in arrears at the end the financial year in the payment of its contributions for reasons other than those caused by public or natural calamity or exceptional circumstances that gravely affect its economy, such Member States may, by a resolution of the Authority, be suspended from taking part in the activities of the institutions of the Community").

108 Charles D. Jebuni et al., "A Case-Study of the Economic Community of West African States (ECOWAS)," in Ademola Oyejide et al., eds., *Regional Integration and Trade Liberalization in Sub-Saharan Africa: Regional Case-Studies*, Vol. 3 (London: Macmillan Press Ltd., 1999), 24. The protocols are enumerated along with 24 others, in an appendix to the Jebuni et al. article. See ibid., pp. 56–59 (Table 2A.1, Summary of the Protocols Annexed to the ECOWAS Treaty). In other words, rather than "a record

(or their representatives) were those of Dahomey (later Benin), Ghana, The Gambia, Guinea, Guinea-Bissau, Ivory Coast (later Côte d'Ivoire), Liberia, Mali, Mauritania, Niger, Nigeria, Senegal, Sierra Leone, Togo, and Upper Volta (later Burkina Faso).[109] See also Table 6.1 (enumerating these fifteen states).[110] The fifteen countries are out of the nineteen countries that comprise the subregion, meaning that ECOWAS is not coterminous with West Africa.[111] Treaties, supported by a roster of protocols, supplementary protocols, decisions, resolutions, and related legal instruments, form the constitutional framework for the establishment of ECOWAS and the source of authority for its operation.[112]

The Revised Treaty of ECOWAS, adopted July 24, 1993, at Cotonou in Togo, by the Heads of State and Government of sixteen West

of negotiated agreement," the 1975 treaty was little more than "a detailed declaration of interest" that provided the basis for more work. Ibrahim A. Gambari, *Theory and Reality in Foreign Policy Making: Nigeria After the Second Republic* (Atlantic Highlands, NJ: Humanities Press International, Inc., 1989), 30.

[109] See ECOWAS 1975 Treaty, note 105 (fifteen signatories appended on the last page of the document).

[110] See also Economic Community of West African States (ECOWAS), http://www.ecowas.int/. Cape Verde (Cabo Verde) on this list joined in 1977, swelling the number of member-states to sixteen. See José Luís Rocha, "Cape Verde and ECOWAS: The Challenge of Regional Integration," *Portuguese Journal of International Affairs* (Autumn/Winter, 2010), 1. However, the number fell back to fifteen, its current number, when Mauritania left the organization in 2000 over issues that include a disagreement relating to ECOWAS's decision to establish a common currency by 2004, which would have displaced Mauritania's currency, the Quguiya, that Nouakchott did not want displaced. See David Oladipupo Kuranga, *The Power of Interdependence: Lessons from Africa* (New York: Palgrave Macmillan, 2012), 112. Upon leaving ECOWAS, Mauritania concentrated its economic-cooperation-and-integration energies on the Arab Maghreb Union (UMA), note 141 below, of which it was a founding member.

[111] Four West African countries not members of economic union are: Cameroon, Chad, Equatorial Guinea, and Mauritania (which joined initially but left in 2000, as indicated in footnote 110).

[112] See ECOWAS Revised Treaty, note 104, art. 92(3). See also Adedamola Adeosun, "Measuring the Quality of the International Judiciary: The ECOWAS Community Court of Justice," Ph.D. Dissertation, School of Law, Open University, UK (May 2023), 92–93, https://oro.open.ac.uk/86967/1/Measuring%20the%20Quality%20of%20the%20International%20Judiciary%20PDF.pdf; and generally Jerry Ukaigwe, *ECOWAS Laws* (New York: Springer, 2016).

Table 6.1 ECOWAS member-states with distinctive characteristics as of 2024

Item No.	*Country*	*Population (in millions)*	*Land area (in sq. km)*	*GDP estimates (billions in US$)*	*Former colonizer*
English-speaking					
1.	Liberia	5.5	111,370	13.60	None, but has close ties to the US
2.	The Gambia	2.8	11,300	10	UK
3.	Ghana	34.7	238,540	75.65	UK
4.	Nigeria	229	923,540	2,175.40	UK
5.	Sierra Leone	Over 8.9	71,740	27.12	UK
French-speaking					
6.	Benin	Approx. 14	112,620	76.83	France
7.	Burkina Faso (formerly Upper Volta)	Approx. 24	274,200	82.92	France
8.	Côte d'Ivoire	Over 29	322,463	86.89	France
9.	Guinea	14.5	245,860	22.20	France
10.	Mali	24	1,240,000	101.48	France
11.	Niger	28	1,267,000	19.54	France
12.	Senegal	Over 18	196,190	30.56	France
13.	Togo	Over 9	56,785	9.86	Germany and France
Portuguese-speaking					
14.	Cape Verde (Cabo Verde)	0.6	4,033	2.37	Portugal
15.	Guinea-Bissau	2.1	36,120	1.71	Portugal

African countries, including Mauritania,[113] which left the organization

[113] See ECOWAS Revised Treaty, note 104 (sixteen signatories appended on the last two pages of the document). The treaty contains 93 articles broken up into 22 chapters, plus preambles, fifteen of them altogether. By our own count, the treaty has eleven parts: **Part 1**, Chapter I, "Definitions," one article; **Part 2**, Chapter II, "Establishment, Composition, Aims and Objectives and Fundamental Principles of the Community," four articles; **Part 3**, Chapter III, "Institutions of the Community: Establishment, Composition, and Functions," nineteen articles; **Part 4** relating to cooperation in seven-plus fields: Chapter IV on "Cooperation in Food and Agriculture," one article; Chapter V on "Cooperation in Industry, Science and Technology, and Energy," three articles; Chapter VI on "Cooperation in Environment and Natural Resources," three articles; Chapter VII on "Cooperation in Transport, Communications, and Tourism," three articles; Chapter

in 2000,[114] revised and replaced the 1975 treaty,[115] taking into due account developments in the eighteen years since 1975.[116] Therefore, except where necessary and appropriate, the following discussion focuses

VIII on "Cooperation in Trade, Customs, Taxation, Statistics, Money, and Payments," nineteen articles; Chapter X on "Cooperation in Political [i.e., nonaggression, mutual assistance in defense, as well as democracy and human rights], Judicial and Legal Affairs, Regional Security and Immigration," four articles; Chapter XI on "Cooperation in Human Resources, Information, Social, and Cultural Affairs," seven articles; and Chapter XII on "Cooperation in Other Areas," one article, the "plus" field by our definition. Other coverages are: **Part 5** in five areas of relations within and outside ECOWAS: Chapter XVIII on "Relations Between the Community and Other Regional Economic Communities," one article; Chapter XIX on "Relations Between the Executive, Secretariat, and the Specialized Institutions of the Community," three articles; Chapter XX on "Relations Between the Community, Third Countries, and International Organizations," one article; Chapter XXI on "Relations Between Member States, Non-Member States, Regional Organizations, and International Organizations," two articles; and Chapter IXVII on "Relations Between the Community and the African Economic Community," one article. **Part 6**, Chapter IX on "Establishment and Completion of an Economic and Monetary Union," two articles; **Part 7**, Chapter XIII on "Land-Locked and Island Member States," one article; **Part 8**, Chapter XIV on "Financial Provisions," seven articles; **Part 9**, Chapter XV on "Disputes," one article; **Part 10**, Chapter XVI on "Sanctions," one article; and **Part 11**, Chapter XXII on "General and Final Provisions," eight articles.

114 See notes 110–112 and accompanying texts.

115 See ECOWAS Revised Treaty, note 104, art. 92(2) ("The ECOWAS Treaty of 1975 shall be deemed terminated when the Executive Secretariat has received instruments of ratification of this revised Treaty from all Member States").

116 The revisions were preceded a Committee of Eminent Persons, convened in 1991, to assess the progress of ECOWAS toward economic cooperation and integration and make recommendations for change, as appropriate. Alter et al., note 82, p. 771. Recent developments reflected in the preamble include: the African Charter on Human and People's Rights, adopted June 27, 1981 and effective October 21, 1986, and the ECOWAS Declaration of Political Principles, adopted July 6, 1991; the Lagos Plan of Action and the Final Act of Lagos of April 1980, stipulating the establishment by 2000 of an African Economic Community based on existing and future regional economic communities; the African Economic Community, established June, 3, 1991; the need to adapt to the changes on the international scene to derive greater benefits from those changes; and the need to modify the Community's strategies to accelerate the economic integration process in the subregion. Ibid., preamble. Others are "the need to establish Community institutions vested with relevant and adequate powers," coupled with a conviction that integrating member states "into a viable regional Community may demand the partial and gradual pooling of national sovereignties to the Community within the context of a collective political will." Ibid.

on the 1993 treaty. The revised framework is more elaborate.[117] It also updates documents of the economic union before 1993.[118]

The goal of the Community remained very much what it was in 1975, still revolved around promoting cooperation and integration in the road to an economic union in West Africa to raise the living standards of its peoples and to enhance economic stability, thereby contributing to African development.[119] Put differently, the revised treaty "reaffirmed the establishment of" ECOWAS and the vision of its founders that "it shall ultimately be the sole economic community in the [sub]region for the purpose of economic integration and the realization of the objectives of the African Economic Community."[120] The organization is a lodestar for

[117] Compared to the 65 articles in 14 Chapters of its predecessor-document, the revised treaty has 93 articles, twenty-eight provisions more, broken up into 22 Chapters, eight chapters more than in 1975, plus preambles. The preambles are also more numerous: fifteen in 1993, compared to eight in 1975.

[118] See ECOWAS Revised Treaty, note 104, art. 92(3) ("Notwithstanding the provisions of paragraph 2 of this Article [terminating the 1975 treaty], all Community Conventions, Protocols, Decisions, and Resolutions made since 1975 shall remain valid and in force, except where they are incompatible with the present Treaty"). These include the Protocol Relating to Non-Aggression (1978), the Protocol Relating to Mutual Assistance on Defense (1981), and the Declaration of Political Principles (1991). Institute for Security Studies, "Profile: Economic Community of West African States (ECOWAS) [hereinafter Institute for Security Studies, "Profile: ECOWAS"], https://www.issafrica.org/AF/RegOrg/unity_to_union/ecowasprof.htm. The 1978 protocol enjoined member-states to "refrain from the threat and use of force or aggression" against one another; the protocol of 1986 committed them to a collective defense agreement, while the declaration of 1991 embodied commitments related to human rights, democracy, and the rule of law. Ibid. Crowning off these documents was the Protocol on Democracy and Good Governance, adopted in 2001, at the dawn of a new century. See The Economic Community of West African States (ECOWAS), Protocol on Democracy and Good Governance: Supplementary to the Protocol Relating to the Mechanism for Conflict Prevention, Management, Resolution, Peacekeeping, and Security, A/SPI/12/01 (December 2001), https://www.eisa.org/pdf/ecowas2001protocol.pdf. Issued as supplement to an earlier protocol on mechanisms for managing conflicts in Africa, this document sought to address the root causes embedded in abuses of political powers capable of leading to conflicts in the continent, such as political corruption, which ECOWAS member-states pledged to fight, ibid., art. 38(1)–(2), and unlawful exercises of powers, regarding which the document enumerated a list of constitutional principles shared by these members, see ibid., art. 1(a)-(l), among them, "zero tolerance for power obtained or maintained by unconstitutional means." Ibid., art. 1(c).

[119] ECOWAS Revised Treaty, note 104, art. (3)(1).

[120] Ibid., art.2.

"accelerated and sustained economic development [...], culminating in [an] economic union of West Africa."[121]

Rather than static, with the passage of time, the statement of that mission took on an expansive tone, broadening, by June 2007, to encompass the creation of "a borderless, peaceful, prosperous[,] and cohesive [sub]region, built on good governance," within an environment laden with "opportunities for sustainable development and environmental preservation."[122] Yet, from the get go, these founders understood this was no easy task; they were under no illusion that integrating their fifteen countries and economies "into a viable regional Community may demand the partial and gradual pooling of national sovereignties to the Community within the context of a collective political will."[123] This is especially given the existence of competing economic integration organizations in West Africa which, in addition to the Arab Maghreb Union (UMA), described below,[124] include Communauté Economique de l'Afrique de l'Quest (CEAO),[125] and the Mano River Union (MRU).[126]

[121] Ibid., preamble.

[122] See ECOWAS, "Vision 2020," www.ecowas.int/about_ecowas/vision-2020/; and The Economic Community of West African States (ECOWAS), *ECOWAS Vision 2020: Toward a Democratic and Prosperous Community* (June 2010), www.ecowas.int/wp-content/uploads/2015/01/ECOWAS-VISION-2020.

[123] ECOWAS Revised Treaty, note 104, preamble. The notion is revealing given the tendency of many African states to guard their sovereignties jealously. During the period of the Cold War (1945–1991), the Organization of African Unity (OAU) tolerated human rights atrocities under the guise of doctrines like respect for the territorial integrity of African states and non-interference in the domestic affairs of other countries. Aka, "Human Rights as Conflict Resolution in Africa," note 26, pp. 187–190 (commenting on human rights in Africa up to the end of the Cold War); and Rhoda E. Howard, *Human Rights in Commonwealth Africa* (Lanham, MD: Rowman & Littlefield, 1986), 5 (observing that during this period, "[t]he rights of black Africans inside the borders of independent African states appear[ed] to be of little real concern to the OAU").

[124] See note 141 below and accompanying text.

[125] See Allechi M'Bet, The CEAO and UEMOA within ECOWAS: The Road Ahead Toward West African Economic Integration, in Ademola Oyejide et al. eds., *Regional Integration and Trade Liberalization in Sub-Saharan Africa: Synthesis and Review*, Vol. 4 (London: Macmillan Press Ltd., 1999), 66–85.

[126] CEAO was founded in 1973 to replace a predecessor, the Union Douaniere de l'Afrique de l'Quest (UDEAO) or West African Customs Union, established in June 1966. Like its predecessor, CEAO comprised six countries: Burkina Faso, Côte d'Ivoire, Mali, Mauritania, Niger, and Senegal, plus Benin and Togo as observer-members. Ibid., pp. 66–67. Founded in 1973, the MRU comprises four countries: Côte d'Ivoire, Guinea,

Compared to the treaty of 1975, the revised treaty enumerated the means for achieving the goal of economic cooperation and integration in greater details.[127] Among others, they include: harmonizing and coordinating national policies and promoting integration in multiple areas of human activity, such as agriculture, trade and industry, information and technology, law, education, health, and environmental protection;[128] establishing a common market[129]; establishing an enabling legal environment[130]; harmonizing standards and measures[131]; and adopting a Community population policy which takes into account the need for a balance between demographic factors and socio-economic development.[132] In pursuing this goal of cooperation for integration, member-states "solemnly affirm and declare their adherence" to certain guiding principles, including "equitable and just distribution of the costs and benefits of economic co-operation and integration"; promoting and consolidating a democratic system of governance in each member[-]state, pursuant to the Declaration of Political Principles (1991); and accountability, economic and social justice, and popular participation in development.[133] Other principles are: recognizing, protecting, and promoting human and peoples' rights, consistent with the African Charter on Human and Peoples' Rights; peaceful settlement of disputes among Member States, including a peaceful environment as a prerequisite for economic development; promoting and strengthening good neighborliness; nonaggression; and collective self-reliance.[134] On an overarching note, among other things, member-states also undertook "to create favorable conditions for the attainment of" the goal they set for themselves,

Liberia, and Sierra Leone. Mano River Union, "About Us," http://manoriverunion.int/About_Us.html.

[127] Compare ECOWAS 1975 Treaty, note 105, art. 2(2)(a)–(j) with ECOWAS Revised Treaty, note 104, art. 3(2)(a)–(o). This translates into a difference of five means, (a)–(o), compared to (a)–(j) in the 1975 treaty.

[128] ECOWAS Revised Treaty, note 104, art. 3(2)(a)–(b).

[129] Ibid., art. 3(2)(d)(i)–(iii).

[130] Ibid., art. 3(2)(h).

[131] Ibid., art. 3(2)(j).

[132] Ibid., art. 3(2)(m).

[133] See ibid., art. 4(a)–(k).

[134] Ibid.

including taking "all necessary measures to harmonize their strategies and policies," and "refrain[ing] from any action that may hinder the attainment of" of the goal.[135]

Certain provisions of the revised treaty for us stand out. These are Art. 73 on membership contributions, Art. 77 on sanctions for non-fulfilment of membership obligations, Art. 78 on relations between the Community and the African Economic Community, and Art. 64 on population and development. The last is addressed later below in this Chapter. Art. 73 stipulated that member-states "undertake to promptly transfer their assessed contributions to the Community."[136] Art. 77 specifies multiple sanctions that, based on the particular circumstance, the Authority of Heads of State and Government (AHSG), discussed below, could, in its sound judgment, apply against a member state that fails to fulfil its obligation to the economic union.[137] Art. 78 embodies a more nuanced (and less hardline) provision on membership contribution, compared to Art. 54 of the 1975 treaty.[138] Art. 78 made the integration of the subregion "an essential component of the integration of the African Continent," and requires member-states "to facilitate the co-ordination and harmonization of the policies and program of the Community with those of the African Economic Community."[139]

ECOWAS is one of eight regional economic communities in Africa recognized by the African Union (AU).[140] The other seven communities recognized by the AU are the Arab Maghreb Union (UMA),

[135] See ibid., art. 5(1)–(3) ("General Undertakings").

[136] ECOWAS Revised Treaty, note 104, art. 73(2).

[137] See ibid., art. 77(1)–(4). The treaty empowers the Authority to decide the modalities for applying this article. Ibid., art. 77(4). The sanctions the Authority may decide to impose can include: suspending new loans or assistance to the member-state, suspending disbursement on ongoing Community project, assistance, or program, suspending voting rights, or precluding the defaulting member from participating in the activities of the Community. Ibid., art. 77(2)(i)–(v). It may also refrain from imposing any sanction where it is satisfied that the non-fulfilment of its obligations is due to forces beyond the control of the member-state in question. Ibid., art. 77(3).

[138] See notes 107.

[139] ECOWAS Revised Treaty, note 104, art. 78.

[140] The AU is the association of independent states in Africa that, in 2000, replaced the Organization of African Unity (OAU) established in May of 1963. See Organization of African Unity (OAU), Constitutive Act of the African Union, OAU Doc. CAB/LEG/23.15 (July 11, 2000), http://www.africa-union.org; and Rachael L. Swarns, "African

Common Market for Eastern and Southern Africa (COMESA), Community of Sahel-Saharan States (CEN-SAD), East African Community (EAC), Economic Community of Central African States (ECCAS), the Intergovernmental Authority on Development (IGAD), and the Southern African Development Community (SADC).[141] Five of the eight regional economic communities have been designated as "pillars," or building blocks, of the African Economic Community (AEC), an Africa-wide economic union of 54 member-states,[142] created during a meeting in

Leaders Drop Old Group for One That Has Power," *New York Times* (July 9, 2002), http://www.nytimes.com/2002/07/09/international/africa/09AFR.html.

[141] UMA is French for L'Union du Maghreb arabe. Formed in February 1989, the organization comprises five member-states: Algeria, Libya, Mauritania, Morocco, and Tunisia. See UMA, http://www.maghrebarabe.org/en/. COMESA was formed in December 1994 and comprises 20 member-states: Burundi, Comoros, Democratic Republic of the Congo, Djibouti, Egypt, Eritrea, Ethiopia, Kenya, Libya, Madagascar, Malawi, Mauritius, Rwanda, Seychelles, South Sudan, Sudan, Swaziland, Uganda, Zambia, and Zimbabwe. See Common Market for Eastern and South Africa, http://www.comesa.int/. CEN-SAD is French for Communauté des Etats Sáhélo-Sahariens. The organization was formed in February 1993 and has 28 member-states: Benin, Burkina Faso, Central African Republic, Chad, Comoros, Côte d'Ivoire, Djibouti, Egypt, Equatorial Guinea, Eritrea, Gambia, Ghana, Guinea, Guinea-Bissau, Kenya, Libya, Liberia, Mali, Morocco, Niger, Nigeria, Sao Tomé & Principe, Senegal, Sierra Leone, Somalia, Sudan, Togo, and Tunisia. See "CEN-SAD Celebrates 13th Anniversary," *Pana Press*, http://www.panapress.com/CEN-SAD-celebrates-13th-anniversary---12-756752-29-lang2-index.html. The EAC was originally founded in 1967, collapsed in 1977, and was revived in July of 2000. The organization comprises five states: Burundi, Kenya, Rwanda, Tanzania, and Uganda. See East African Community: One People, One Destiny, http://www.eac.int/. The ECCAS was founded in October 1983 and comprises 10 member-states: Angola, Burundi, Cameroon, Central African Republic, Chad, Democratic Republic of the Congo, Equatorial Guinea, Gabon, Republic of the Congo, and Sao Tomé & Principe. See Economic Community of Central African States, http://www.ceeac-eccas.org/index.php/fr/. The IGAD was founded in January 1986 and comprises eight member-states: Djibouti, Eritrea, Ethiopia, Kenya, Somali, South Sudan, Sudan, and Uganda. See IGAD, http://www.igad.org/. The SADC was founded in April 1980 (as South African Development Coordinating Conference, SADCC) and comprises 15 member-states: Angola, Botswana, Democratic Republic of the Congo, Lesotho, Madagascar, Malawi, Mauritius, Mozambique, Namibia, Seychelles, South Africa, Swaziland, Tanzania, Zambia, and Zimbabwe. See Southern African Development Community: Toward a Common Future, http://www.sadc.int/.

[142] ECOWAS, "Basic Information," www.ecowas.int/about-ecowas/basic-information/.

June 1991 in Abuja.[143] Along with ECOWAS, these four are COMESA, ECCAS, the IGAD, and SADC.[144]

Key Institutions of ECOWAS

To facilitate its work of economic integration, ECOWAS founders created a set of several institutions.[145] The Treaty of 1975 established six of these institutions, leaving open the possibility of new ones in the future,[146] should the need arise, which opened door the revised treaty seized in 1993. In addition to the AHSG, the Council of Ministers (CM), the Executive Secretariat, the Community Parliament, and the Specialized Technical Commissions, the revised treaty created (or upgraded) three new institutions, namely: the Economic and Social Council, the Fund for Cooperation, Compensation and Development, and the Community Court of Justice (CCJ), presumably in place of the Tribunal of

[143] "African Economic Community (AEC)," *AU Watch News*, https://www.au-watch.org/african-economic-community-aec/#:~:text=The%20commitments%20in%20this%20Plan,Ordinary%20Session%20of%20the%20Assembly.

[144] See Institute for Security Studies, "Profile: ECOWAS," note 118; and UN Economic Commission for Africa, "African Union (AU) and Regional Economic Communities (RECs) in Africa," http://www.uneca.org/oria/pages/african-union-au-regional-economic-communities-recs-africa. In February 1998, these five "pillars" signed the Protocol on Relations Between the AEC and Regional Economic Communities (RECs). Institute for Security Studies, "Profile: ECOWAS," note 118.

[145] Alter and her coauthors observed that although the names ECOWAS founders gave to the institutions they created mimicked those of the European Community, in reality, the ECOWAS Treaty of 1975, "created a system of policymaking bodies that [the] governments [of these ECOWAS member state countries] tightly controlled." Alter et al., note 82, p. 741. Put differently, unlike those of the European Community, the institutions created by the 1975 Treaty "left national sovereignty intact" in that the decisions of the AHSG and the Council of Ministers, two of these institutions discussed below, were binding only on ECOWAS institutions, with little legal binding force for member-states, who, under art. 3 of the Treaty, only committed themselves to "make every effort to plan and direct their policies with a view to creating favorable conditions for the achievement of" the Community's aims. Ibid. Absent delegated supranational decision-making powers of the type found in the European Community, ECOWAS resorted to the use of Protocols in policymaking, a cumbersome tool of decision-making and mechanism for Community lawmaking, prone to politicization, which accorded governments capacious discretion with respect to ratification and implementation, and which entered into force only after a majority of countries had ratified. See ibid.

[146] See note 107.

the Community.[147] Like with the 1975 treaty, it also left open "[a]ny other institutions that may be established by the Authority."[148] In the light of its importance in the scheme of things in this book, the CCJ receives a separate treatment in Chapter 8. Alongside these institutions, ECOWAS has a financial house, the ECOWAS Bank for Investment and Development (EBID).[149]

As its very name implies, the AHSG comprises Heads of State and Government of member-states.[150] Headed by a Chairperson, elected by the authority from its own ranks,[151] the Authority meets at least once a year in ordinary session.[152] The AHSG is the foremost decision-making body of ECOWAS,[153] and the institution charged with responsibility for the general direction and control of the Community.[154] To anticipate the material on the CCJ covered in Chapter 8, in this role, the Authority initiates the legal framework, such as Protocols, Supplementary Protocols, regulations, decisions and related documents, which facilitates the work of the CCJ, as well as approves its budget and remuneration of the judges.[155] And in going about its business of directing and controlling the Community, the AHSG may "request the Community Court of Justice, as and when necessary, to give advisory opinion on any legal questions."[156]

[147] See ECOWAS Revised Treaty, note 104, art. 6(1)(a)–(h).

[148] Ibid., art. 6(1) (i).

[149] See "Economic Community of West African States (ECOWAS)," *ECOWAS in Brief*, http://www.comm.ecowas.int/sec/index.php?id=about_a&; and Terry M. Mays, *Historical Dictionary of International Organizations and the Middle East* (Lanham, MD: Rowman & Littlefield, 2015), 165.

[150] ECOWAS Revised Treaty, note 104, art. 7(2).

[151] Ibid., art. 8(2).

[152] Ibid., art. 8(1). The Authority could meet in extraordinary session if the Chairperson convenes that session or a member-state requests it, provided the request is supported by a simple majority of the member-states. Ibid.

[153] ECOWAS Revised Treaty, note 104, art. 7(1) (creating the AHSG as "the supreme institution of the Community").

[154] Ibid., art. 7(2).

[155] Adeosun, note 112, pp. 85–86.

[156] ECOWAS Revised Treaty, note 104, art. 7(3)(h).

Next in importance to the AHGS is the CM,[157] which reports to the AHSG on an advisory basis.[158] The Council is tasked with a range of responsibilities that includes reviewing the functionality of the economic union, consistent with the treaty, making recommendations to the AHSG, giving directions to all subordinate institutions of ECOWAS, and overseeing the operations of the organization.[159] It comprises the minister in charge of ECOWAS affairs of every member-state or any other minister an affected member-state may choose to represent it in the Council,[160] Headed by a Chairperson of Council elected from its own ranks,[161] the Council meets at least twice a year in ordinary session.[162]

After the AHGS and the CM comes the Executive Secretariat in importance.[163] The Secretariat is headed by an Executive Secretary,[164] chief executive officer of the Community and all its institutions.[165] He or she is tasked with day-to-day administration of the affairs of the economic union, is accountable to the AHGS and the CM,[166] and serves as "the legal representative of the Institutions of the Community in their totality."[167] These key tasks include drafting protocol that elaborate and complement the treaties.[168] The Executive Secretary is elected for a four-year term,[169] and assisted by four deputies,[170] each in four areas critical

[157] Ibid., art. 10(1) (establishing the Council).

[158] Alter et al., note 82, p. 741.

[159] ECOWAS Revised Treaty, note 104, art. 10(3) (a)–(i).

[160] Ibid, art. 10(2).

[161] Ibid., art. 11(2).

[162] Ibid., art. 11(1). The Council is also authorized to meet in extraordinary session convened by the Chairperson of the Council at the request of a member-state, supported by a simple majority of the council. Ibid.

[163] Ibid., art. 17(1) (establishing the Secretariat).

[164] Ibid., art. 17(1)–(2).

[165] Ibid., art. 19(1).

[166] See ibid., art. 19(1)(2)(3)(a)–(i).

[167] Ibid., art. 19(2).

[168] See Alter et al., note 82, p. 757.

[169] ECOWAS Revised Treaty, note 104, art. 18(1).

[170] Ibid., art. 17(2) (providing that the Executive Secretary shall be "assisted by Deputy Executive Secretaries and such other staff as may be required for the smooth functioning of the Community").

to the work of the community.[171] In 2006, the Secretariat was converted into an Commission, comprised of a President, a Vice President, and fifteen Commissioners.[172]

Yet another institution from 1975 is the Community Parliament.[173] The Parliament comprises 115 persons; each member-state has at least five seats, while the remaining forty seats are distributed based on population.[174] It is headed by a speaker who is elected for the life of the legislature.[175] Rather than directly elected, its membership is constituted from the membership of the legislatures of each member-state.[176] The Parliament is empowered to "consider any matter concerning the community, […] particular[ly] issues relating to human rights and fundamental freedoms, and make recommendations to the institutions and organs of the Community."[177] And although currently a consultative and advisory body, the game plan is to progressively enhance its power "from advisory to co-decision making and subsequently to a lawmaking role in areas to be defined by the" AHSG.[178]

The revised treaty established specialized technical commissions on eight issue-areas, members of which will be drawn from member states,

[171] Institute for Security Studies, "Profile: ECOWAS," note 118. The four such areas now are political affairs, defense, and security; integration (involving agriculture and environment, trade and industry, human development, and the Community Computer Center); policies harmonization (involving economic policy and trade as well as customs policy); and administration and finance. Ibid.

[172] See ECOWAS, Supplementary Protocol A/SP.1/06/06 Amending the Revised Treaty (Abuja) (June 14, 2006), https://journal.cfcomlaw.com/wp-content/uploads/2021/10/scan0004.pdf. The idea behind the change was to transform the Secretariat to improve its chances of adapting to the international environment as it "fulfil[s] its role in the subregional integration process." Ibid. preamble. See also ECOWAS, "Basic Information," note 142.

[173] ECOWAS Revised Treaty, note 104, art. 13(1) (creating the Parliament).

[174] ECOWAS Parliament, "Parliament at a Glance," https://www.parl.ecowas.int/ecowas-parliament-at-a-glance/#:~:text=COMPOSITION%20OF%20PARLIAMENT,on%20the%20basis%20of%20population.

[175] ECOWAS, Supplementary Protocol A/SP.3/06/06 Amending Protocol AP.2.8/94 Relating to the Community Parliament (June 14, 2006) [hereinafter Supplementary Protocol on the Community Parliament], https://journal.cfcomlaw.com/wp-content/uploads/2021/10/scan0005.pdf.

[176] See "Parliament at a Glance," note 174.

[177] Supplementary Protocol on the Community Parliament, note 175.

[178] Ibid.

including: food and agriculture; industry, energy, science, and technology; environment and natural resources; transport, communications, and tourism; political, judicial, and legal affairs; regional security and immigration; and finance and administration, among others.[179] The AHSG may, as it deems appropriate, restructure the existing commissions or establish new ones.[180] The Treaty also created an advisory Economic and Social Council, composed of "representatives of the various categories of economic and social activity," whose specific functions and related matters will be defined in a protocol.[181] Ditto with respect to the Fund for Cooperation, Compensation and Development of the Community.[182]

Although not recognized as such by the revised treaty of 1993, over time, the Economic Community of West African States Monitoring Group (ECOMOG) emerged, never mind the deceptively modest appellation of monitor, in its own right as a key institution of the economic union. It is a non-standing army tasked with responsibility for monitoring ceasefires, even though in practical terms its peacekeeping role is more expansive.[183] Formed in 1990 on the eve of Liberia's first civil war (1989–1997), ECOMOG has since then featured in several peacekeeping missions: Liberia in 1990 until 1997 when the troops left following the elections that year in that country; Sierra Leone in 1997 until 1998 when ECOMOG troops helped reinstate a president dislodged from power by rebels; Guinea-Bissau in 1999 to keep peace after an armed conflict between the president and a rebel military chief; Sierra Leone in

[179] ECOWAS Revised Treaty, note 104, art. 22(1)–(4). See also ibid., art. 3(a)–(d) (specifying the functions of each Commission), and ibid., art. 24 (regarding its meetings).

[180] Ibid., art. 22(2).

[181] ECOWAS Revised Treaty, note 104, art. 14(1)–(2).

[182] Ibid., art. 21(1)–(2).

[183] To use an example from US politics, an analogy would be the rebranding of the Department of War in 1949 as the Department of Defense. See Chris Edwards et al., "Department of Defense Timeline," *Downsizing the Federal Government*, https://www.downsizinggovernment.org/defense/timeline#:~:text=1946%3A%20The%20War%20Department%20establishes,Department%20of%20Defense%20in%201949. From the standpoint of sheer nomenclature, which sane country wants to keep a department of war in an international system like the UN that outlaws aggression, which is what a department of war, as opposed to defense, connotes.

1999, whose capital Freetown ECOMOG troops recaptured after a guerrilla offensive; and Guinea-Liberia borders where ECOMOG troops were stationed to stop guerrilla infiltration.[184]

As Karen J. Alter and her colleagues insightfully pointed out, although the revised treaty of 1993 "reads primarily as a recommitment to economic integration, in practice th[is] second phase of ECOWAS came to be dominated by security, good governance, and human rights concerns[,]" built on "a role in promoting regional security" that the Community developed earlier.[185] For them, the Protocol on Non-Aggression (1978) and the Protocol Relating to Mutual Assistance on Defense (1981), referred to before,[186] both deflected foreign interventions and provided the legal basis for these tasks. ECOMOG played an indispensable role in the implementation of this regional security agenda.[187]

Distinctive Characteristics of ECOWAS Member-States

An expression in the law of evidence is that the thing speaks for itself. But nothing really speaks for itself. Therefore, Table 6.1 needs a bit of explanation. The first observation relates to three languages from the colonial past, each of which is now entrenched in the Revised

Treaty of 1993 as official and working languages.[188]

A second observation relates to the composition of the economic union. As presently constituted, ECOWAS has fifteen member-states, which will decrease to twelve if three, Burkina Faso, Mali, and Niger, all of them from the French-speaking section of the economic union, leave. As indicated in Chapter 1, the military rulers who seized power in these

[184] See "Profile: ECOMOG," *BBC News* (June 17, 2004), http://news.bbc.co.uk/2/hi/africa/country_profiles/2364029.stm; and "ECOMOG: Peacekeeping or Participant?" *BBC News* (February 11, 1998), http://news.bbc.co.uk/2/hi/Africa/55719.stm. The question in the last news story, revolved around "participant," goes to the abuses by Nigerian peacekeepers recounted in notes 88–90 and accompanying texts.

[185] Alter et al., note 82, p. 744.

[186] See note 118.

[187] Alter et al., note 82, p. 744.

[188] See note 106 and accompanying text.

three countries have expressed a collective intention to pull their countries out of ECOWAS.[189] However, as also indicated therein, none of the trio meets the requirement for withdrawal laid out in the Community's treaties.[190]

A third observation relates to Nigeria. ECOWAS covers a landmass of about 5.1 million square kilometers with a population estimated at over 441 million people in 2024. Reading and extrapolating from the diagram, Nigeria makes up approximately 52% of the community's population and about 79% of its total GDP estimated at over US$2,736 billion (over $2.7 trillion) in 2024. The treaty of 1975 sent a message to many ECOWAS countries, especially poorer neighbors, that Nigeria, their putative "big brother," at the time accounting for nearly 70% of the subregion's total GDP, had braced itself ready for subregional economic cooperation.[191]

From 2004 to 2020, for sixteen years, Nigeria contributed the sum of 1.17 billion in US dollars, representing about 40% of the total levies paid by all member-states, to the coffers of ECOWAS as levies.[192] The contribution is higher than those of twelve member-states combined.[193] In short, "ECOWAS institutions have always depended on the largesse of Nigerian oil revenues[.]"[194] He who pays the piper calls the tune; the bulk of the money for running ECOWAS coming from Nigeria makes Abuja a linchpin of the Community.[195]

A fourth and final point revolves around rapid growth of population in non-expanding land spaces for all countries, some more than others, vis-à-vis the rate of economic development with negative ramification for provision of social services like education and healthcare. To use Nigeria, the biggest member of the Community, as example, its population grew

[189] See Chapter 1, note 96.

[190] Ibid.

[191] Alter et al., note 82, p. 742.

[192] Adeosun, note 112, pp. 113–114 (citing Agency Report, "Nigeria Contributed $1.17 [Billion] to ECOWAS in [Sixteen] Years," *Premium Times* (Abuja) (July 29, 2020), https://www.premiumtimesng.com/news/top-news/405792-nigeria-contributed-1-17bn-to-ecowas-in-16-years.html.

[193] Ibid.

[194] Alter et al., note 82, pp. 745–746.

[195] See Femi Aribisala, "ECOWAS Imperative for Nigeria," *Nigeria Development and Finance Forum*, http://www.nigeriadevelopmentandfinanceforum.org/PolicyDialogue/Dialogue.aspx?Edition=63 (February 28, 2015).

from about 63 million in 1975 to 103 million in 1999, representing a 63% increase in less than 20 years.[196] The occurrence creates a scenario where infrastructural development mercilessly lags behind economic growth.[197]

As of 2020, the population of ECOWAS stood at approximately 402 million, with young people making up 60% of the population.[198] The situation made West Africa "one of the youngest [sub]regions in the world, with high urban growth."[199] Based on calculation from the table, four years after, the population of the subregion grew to over 441 million.

ECOWAS revised treaty of 1993 provides for the adoption of a population policy within the Community which takes into account the need for a balance between demographic factors and socioeconomic development.[200] Article 64 of the document elaborates this relationship between population and development.[201] It mandates member-states "to adopt, individually and collectively, national population policies and mechanism," including measures designed "to ensure a balance between demographic factors and socioeconomic development."[202] Means they could use to achieve this goal include: integrating population issues as components in the formulating and implementing national policies, establishing national population institutions, sensitizing target groups on population matters, as well as collecting, analyzing, and exchanging data on population issues.[203]

"[E]ffective economic cooperation and integration" achieved through "a determined and concerted policy of [collective] self-reliance" ranked among the principles underlying the formation of ECOWAS.[204]

[196] Calculated based on Google search, drawing on data from multiple sources that include Worldometer and Statista.

[197] See Philip C. Aka, *Healthcare and Economic Restructuring: Nigeria in Comparative Perspective* (Gateway East, Singapore: Palgrave Macmillan, 2022), 110–111 (commenting on healthcare services in Nigeria).

[198] Economic Commission of West African States (ECOWAS), *ECOWAS Vision 2050: ECOWAS of the Peoples: Peace and Prosperity for All* (Abuja, 2022), 18, https://ecowas.int/wp-content/uploads/2022/09/Vision2050_EN_Web.pdf.

[199] Ibid.

[200] See ECOWAS Revised Treaty, note 104, art. 3(m).

[201] Ibid., art. 64 ("Population and Development").

[202] Ibid., art. 64(1).

[203] Ibid., art. 64(2)(a)–(d).

[204] Ibid., preamble.

However, the imbalance between demographic factors and socioeconomic development works against such self-reliance. In the wisdom of one Nigerian demographer which applies broadly here, "[p]opulation is key[,]" and there is little any country can do to promote economic development if it does not bring population under control.[205] "If [it does not] take care of population, schools can't cope, hospitals can't cope, there's not enough housing."[206]

Forces Within and Outside Nigeria Which Lent Impetus to the Formation of ECOWAS in May 1975

An intersection of multiple individual and collective events gave impetus to the formation of ECOWAS in 1975. They may conveniently be divided into Nigerian and non-Nigerian forces. Nigeria's "big brother" role recounted in discussion above related to the characteristics of ECOWAS member-states justify this classification, along with the additional comment on the country. Also, the two categories are not watertight, given that in an international system like ours steeped in "complex interdependence,"[207] Nigerian is *not* insulated from the effect of the non-Nigerian forces. On the one hand, ECOWAS institutions depends on "the largesse of Nigerian oil revenues"; on the other hand, Abuja is reluctant to embrace "an organ that could circumscribe its role as [...] hegemon" in West Africa.[208]

Nigerian Factors

The Nigerian factors at play with respect to the formation of ECOWAS in 1975 revolved around a crystallization or internalization of several lessons learned from the civil war of 1967–1970 enumerated in Chapter 3 on the historical background of this book, specifically the comments on the three concentric circles of Nigeria's foreign policy, together with the influence of the civil war on the three circles. The analysis here builds on that prior

[205] Quoted in Elisabeth Rosenthal, "Nigeria Tested by Rapid Rise in Population," *New York Times* (April 14, 2012), https://www.nytimes.com/2012/04/15/world/africa/in-nigeria-a-preview-of-an-overcrowded-planet.html.

[206] Ibid.

[207] See generally Joseph S. Keohane and Robert O. Nye, *Power and Interdependence: World Politics in Transition* (Boston, MA: Little, Brown, and Company, 1977).

[208] Alter et al., note 82, pp. 745–746.

discussion. The first of those factors was to pay more attention to its West African neighbors to minimize the possibility of these neighbors providing "staging grounds for extra-regional powers" who may want to "destabilize or dismember Nigeria."[209] Gabon and Côte d'Ivoire, two of the four African countries that recognized Biafra as an independent state, free and separate from Nigeria, are in West Africa.[210]

Moreover, following the war, the Biafran leader, Chukwuemeka Odumegwu Ojukwu (1933–2011) lived in Côte d'Ivoire until his pardon and return to Nigeria in 1982.[211] In place of France (or any other extra-regional power), ECOWAS offered itself "as an alternative source of funds, ideas, and economic and trade relations" for West African countries, thereby minimizing the potential influence of these extra-regional powers on these neighboring countries.[212] Lastly, in the apt observation of one scholar, "except for contributions to the African Development Bank, what passed for Nigeria's foreign aid in the region tended to be haphazard and dependent on the whims of the [then] head of state, General Yakubu Gowon."[213] Therefore, on a happier note, and no different from the TAC, covered in Chapter 7, ECOWAS also afforded a more structured tool, formerly non-existent, for channeling assistance to countries in the developing world, African as well as non-African states.

Non-Nigerian Factors

These factors external to Nigeria include the creation in 1945 of the CFA franc that brought the French-speaking portion of West Africa into a single currency union; a proposal in 1964 by Liberian president William Tubman for an economic union for West Africa; signature of an agreement for an economic union in 1965 by Côte d'Ivoire, Guinea,

[209] Ibrahim A. Gambari, *Political and Comparative Dimensions of Regional Integration: The Case of ECOWAS* (Atlantic Highlands, NJ: Humanities Press International, 1991), 19.

[210] Ibid.

[211] Robert D. McFadden, "Odumegwu Ojukwu, Breakaway Biafra Leader, Dies at 78," *New York Times* (November 26, 2011), http://www.nytimes.com/2011/11/27/world/africa/odumegwu-ojukwu-leader-of-breakaway-republic-of-biafra-dies-at-78.html?_r=0.

[212] See Gambari, note 209, p. 19.

[213] Ibid., pp. 18–19.

Liberia, and Sierra Leone;[214] and the tour of twelve West African countries from July to August of 1972 by the leaders of Nigeria and Togo, General Yakubu Gowon and General Gnassingbe Eyadema, drumming up support for economic integration.[215] Others include Pan-Africanism,[216] and lobby energies by non-government organizations, crowned by the intergovernmental encouragement of the UN Economic Commission for Africa (ECA),[217] a UN agency different from the AEC referenced before.[218]

ECOWAS and the Application of Human Rights in Nigeria's External Relations

As it has evolved since its formation in the 1970s, ECOWAS has served a consolidated role as tool and context in the implementation of Nigerian foreign policy. Properly utilized, ECOWAS could be a vehicle for burden sharing that lifts some of the financial weight in peacekeeping operations

[214] In an address commemorating the 40th anniversary of ECOWAS, the political scientist and former Nigerian foreign minister Bolaji Akinyemi lent an artful interpretational spin on the failed attempt by these four countries to promote economic cooperation. His conclusion was that an existentialist security threat "drove that initiative but that threat was not sufficiently grave to bring the initiative to fruition." Akinyemi, address on May 25, 2015, in "ECOWAS at 40: The Driving Philosophy of Multinationalism," *Guardian* (Lagos) (June 3, 2015), http://www.ngrguardiannews.com/2015/06/ecowas-40-the-driving-philosophy-of-multinationalism/. The premise leading to that conclusion was: "The fact that the first West African coup d'état happened in Togo, a coup allegedly promoted by Ghana, which also was having a difficult relationship with Côte d'Ivoire, might have spurred Liberia to reach out to Sierra Leone, Côte d'Ivoire, Guinea for a security alliance. Liberia and Sierra Leone were and still are small states which were never nervous of a supposedly expansionist Ghana. Guinea was having a nervous relationship with France." Ibid.

[215] Institute for Security Studies, "Profile: ECOWAS," note 118; and ECOWAS, "History," www.ecowas.int/about-ecowas/history/.

[216] Jebuni, note 108, p. 24. See also Akinyemi's statement in his address referred to in note 214 where, among other things, he depicted ECOWAS as "a product of those institutions that started as far back as 1900 when the first pan-African congress was held, through the West African Students Union founded in 1925, through the West African National Congress formed in 1946 and through the Organization of African Unity established in 1963"; as a "consciousness that grew in a putative form on those trans-Atlantic slave ships, through its pan-African stage, now to a West African stage."

[217] Jebuni, note 108, p. 24.

[218] See notes 142–143 and accompanying texts.

off Nigeria at a time of declining government revenue from oil for its still undiversified economy. This was the point that President Clinton made in his address in August of 2000 to a joint session of the Nigerian National Assembly. After praising Nigeria and its leaders for "building the record of a moral superpower" through peacekeeping in Liberia and Sierra Leone, through the agency of ECOWAS,[219]

Clinton told Nigerian lawmakers "I know that many of you have often felt the burden of your peacekeeping was heavier than the benefit. I know you have felt that."[220] However, "there's no one else in West Africa with the size, the standing, the strength of military forces to do it. If you don't do it, who will do it?"[221] Yet, he said, not that Nigeria should go it alone. [D]espite your size, you cannot lead alone, and you shouldn't have to pay the enormous price."[222] Within the standpoint of human rights in external relations that form the motif in this book, the same point has been made elsewhere:

> ECOWAS holds great potential as an efficient tool for human rights-based foreign policy—not just for Nigeria, but also for the other members of the organization. In the pursuit of its foreign policy, Nigeria has shown a decided preference for multilateral forms (as opposed to bilateral dealings), consistent with its status as a developing nation. A revamped ECOWAS helps the country maintain that preference with the added benefit as an organization within its zone of influence that Nigeria leads—compared to broader forums, such as African regional and UN global institutions.[223]

The challenge for Nigerian leaders is how to achieve the proper utilization that will make ECOWAS efficient and effective burden-sharing tool of Nigerian foreign policy. Given the scale of Nigeria's problem with corruption, some of the estimated US$10 billion in peacekeeping that

[219] Clinton, "Remarks to a Joint Session of the Nigerian National Assembly in Abuja," note 40, p. 1710.

[220] Ibid.

[221] Ibid.

[222] Ibid.

[223] Philip C. Aka, "Human Rights in Nigeria's External Relations: Exigency, Methods, and Rebuttable Objections," *Buffalo Human Rights Law Review*, 21 (2014–2015), 22.

Clinton cited during his address[224] may have gone into the private pockets of corrupt Nigerian officials rather than invested in peacekeeping. Therefore, such streamlining must deal with the corruption in peacekeeping while eliminating the human-right abuses associated with Nigerian peacekeeping missions, both with respect to operations conducted under ECOWAS as well as those undertaken outside it. As in many things, the opportunity for cost-sharing and other multilateral benefits ECOWAS affords for Nigeria come with a bilateral downside that Chapter 7 on the TAC elaborated: the excessive weight of multilateral activities vis-à-vis bilateralism in Nigeria's external relations. The conceivable way around this problem is for Nigerian leaders to keep this factor in mind with a view to incorporating more bilateral arrows in their foreign policy quiver.

The reassessment should include the future of ECOWAS as a multilateral entity—and measurable changes in the fortunes garner-able from this instrument—in the face of popular disenchantment with the quality of democratic rule in West Africa indicated by military takeovers in Burkina Faso, Mali, and Niger, whose three countries, in January 2024, announced their intention to withdraw from ECOWAS.[225] In addition to its ramifications for ECOWAS as a political and economic union, the rumblings of military coups and regimes complicate democratic governance, not inconsistent with the broader objectives of ECOWAS, in the three countries.[226]

[224] Clinton, "Remarks to a Joint Session of the Nigerian National Assembly in Abuja," note 40, p. 1705 (observing that "[o]ver the past decade, with all its problems, Nigeria has spent $10 billion and sacrificed hundreds of its soldiers' lives for peace in West Africa").

[225] See Chinedu Asadu, "What is ECOWAS and Why Have [Three] Coup-Hit Nations Quit the West Africa Bloc?" *Associated Press* (January 29, 2024), https://apnews.com/article/mali-burkina-faso-niger-ecowas-africa-d2e8b1e5448d9a7823e6b9d3d8ec774b. Leaders of the three countries accused the organization of a lack of support, based on coup-related sanctions they jointly assessed as "inhumane." Ibid. But as indicated in Chapter 1, note 95, this justification does not meet the requirement for withdrawal from ECOWAS.

[226] David Rich, "With ECOWAS Exit, Mali, Burkina Faso and Niger Leave Democratic Transition in Limbo," *France 24* (February 2, 2024), https://www.france24.com/en/africa/20240202-with-ecowas-exit-mali-burkina-faso-and-niger-leave-democratic-transition-in-limbo.

Conclusion

This chapter integrates the perspective of peacekeeping in the toolbox of methods in a projected human-right policy for Nigeria in an era of momentous changes at home and abroad, signified by a decline in praetorian influence in Nigerian politics that the departure of General Buhari after two unimpactful terms in office bears out, and the coronation of a new king in the UK (creator and colonizer of the Nigerian state), following the death of Queen Elizabeth II in September 2022. The intent was to sketch the boundaries and limits of peacekeeping in the journey to a human-right policy for Nigeria post-Buhari through the proxy of four sample issues from intricacies of peacekeeping to the role of ECOWAS as an embedded tool of Nigeria's peacekeeping operations.

On intricacies of peacekeeping, the observation was that the lines in the UN literature dividing peacekeeping on the one hand and doctrines of peacemaking, peacebuilding, and peace enforcement on the other intersect and blur at several points. Regarding evolution, Nigerian activity in peacekeeping hit a new low during the insular administration of General Buhari from 2015 until 2023. The section also explained noticeable gaps in Nigeria's otherwise robust peacekeeping record that it attributes to the civil war and the idiosyncratic dispositions of certain Nigerian military rulers.

Other observations bearing on evolution relate to understandable economic and non-pecuniary benefits at play which minimize the altruism in Nigerian peacekeeping operations, as well as the contradictions of the Nigerian state embodied in Nigeria's making peace abroad that it lacks at home. Testament to the contradictions of the Nigerian state, inconsistent with human rights, recounted in the discussion on the evolution of Nigerian peacekeeping, the adoption and ratification of the revised treaty on July 24, 1993, took place after the controversial annulment by Babangida on June 23, 1993, less than one month of the June 12 elections that would have ushered in the Third Republic that year after nine and half years of dictatorial military rule at that point, initiated by General Buhari in December 1983 and complemented by General Babangida after Buhari's removal in August 1985.

Next to strategies for peacekeeping missions that are human-right-compliant, the key is embracement of international standards embedded in human rights and humanitarian law strewn in enhanced appreciation of the intersection between the two concepts along with investment in human-right education. Finally on the possibilities and limits of ECOWAS as an embedded tool of Nigeria's peace operations, the key is to build its utility as an invaluable multilateral, cost-sharing, tool, and to minimize human-right and humanitarian abuses coming from ECOMOG (its military arm), duly conscious of the downside that excessive reliance on this multilateral tool poses for independent bilateral activities. Compared to their military counterparts, Nigerian civilian leaders appear to be more wary about peace missions. For example, under the Second Republic from 1979 to 1983, President Shehu Shagari recalled Nigerian peacekeepers from Lebanon, following Israeli invasion of that country.[227] The issue raises a question regarding popular input into decisions on peacekeeping, broached in Chapter 4 on reconstructing Nigeria's national interest to improve its readiness for human-right work and touched upon in this chapter.[228] Whatever the challenges, on a practical note, peacekeeping will continue to occupy a cardinal position in the implementation of Nigeria's external relations simply because, currently, there are few arrows in the quiver of Nigeria's foreign policy ready to replace this signature tool. Consider this observation from Professor Alter and her coauthors, related to how retooling Nigeria's leadership contributed to improving the country's international profile, especially after a season of irrelevance, imposed by pariah-ship arising from human-right abuses during the second stretch of military dictatorship from 1983 to 1999. When General Obasanjo became President in 1999 and indicated a desire to revamp the country's leadership of the economic union, ECOWAS's institutions, including the CCJ, two chapters away, became a priority simply because the subregional powerhouse once again is serious about integration.[229]

In anticipation of the discussion in Chapter 8 on the CCJ, an organ of ECOWAS and a key institution created by the revised treaty of 1993, this chapter includes an extended conversation, well beyond a primership, on the subregional economic union. For while still a multilateral tool, for Nigeria more than for any other member-state, even if indirectly, ECOWAS has proven itself to be a key foreign policy instrument, largely due to the linchpin role of the country that includes the location of the country as the headquarters of the economic union. No institution speaks

[227] Adebajo, note 15, p. 247.

[228] See notes 94–95 and accompanying texts.

[229] Alter et al., note 82, pp. 747–748.

to that role better than the CCJ in Chapter 8, a judicial tribunal meant to promote economic cooperation and integration in West Africa that, fortuitously, metamorphosed into a human-right court.[230] As the chapter shows, multilateralism does not have to be an albatross in the dedicated pursuit of a human-right policy, unless an applicator makes it so.

Appendix: Nigerian Peacekeeping Operations Since 1960 (Most Recent to Least Recent)

Item No.	*Peacekeeping site*	*Date(s)*	*Mission description*	*Under whose auspice?*
1.	Central African Republic	2014–	Multidimensional integrated stabilization mission	UN
2.	Mali	2013–2023	Multidimensional integrated stabilization mission	AU and UN
3.	Guinea Bissau	2012	Ceasefire monitoring mission	ECOWAS (ECOMOG)
4.	South Sudan	2011–	Interim security mission	UN
5.	South Sudan (Abyei, border between the two Sudans)	2011–	To providing security and ensure the safety of civilians in the Abyei area	UN
6.	Democratic Republic of the Congo	2010–	Stabilization mission	UN
7.	Somalia	2007–	Nigeria sent 200 police officers	AU
8.	Darfur, Sudan	2007–	Hybrid operation	AU and UN
9.	Haiti	2004	Stabilization mission	UN
10.	Sudan	2004	Nigeria deployed 1,500 troops	AU

(continued)

[230] Nneoma Nwogu, "Regional Integration as an Instrument of Human Rights: Reconceptualizing ECOWAS, *Journal of Human Rights*, 6(3) (2007), 345–360, https://doi.org/10.1080/14754830701531112; and Alter et al., note 82, p. 740. See also Adeosun, note 112, p. 12 (commenting on the evolution of the CCJ "from adjudicating solely matters of regional integration to hearing matters relating to the protection of human rights in the [sub]region [...]; from being open to state parties and ECOWAS institutions only to giving access to private litigants").

(continued)

Item No.	*Peacekeeping site*	*Date(s)*	*Mission description*	*Under whose auspice?*
11.	Côte d'Ivoire	2004–	To facilitate peace agreement to end the Ivorian civil war (2002–2007)	UN
12.	Côte d'Ivoire	2003	Nigeria sent a medical and signals team	ECOWAS
13.	Liberia	2003	Nigeria deployed 1,500 troops plus 120 police officers	ECOWAS
14.	East Timor	2000	Transition authority mission	UN
15.	Democratic Republic of the Congo	2000–	Mission to enforce a ceasefire agreement	UN
16.	Sierra Leone	1995–2005	Mission to implement a peace agreement, to disarm, demobilize, and reintegrate armed factions	UN
17.	Dambe region, Croatia	1998	Civilian police support mission	UN
18.	Sierra Leone	1997–2000	Ceasefire monitoring mission (Operation Sandstorm)	ECOWAS (ECOMOG)
19.	Liberia	1990–1997	Ceasefire monitoring mission (Operation Harmony)	ECOWAS (ECOMOG)
20.	Angola	1997	Military observation mission	UN
21.	Prevlaka (Croatia)	1996–2000	Military observation mission	UN
22.	Eastern Slovenia	1996–1998	Transition administration mission	UN
23.	Macedonia	1995–2000	Prevention deployment mission	UN
24.	Tajikistan	1994–2000	Military observation mission	UN
25.	Aouzo Strip (northern Chad)	1994	Military observation mission	UN
26.	Croatia	1993–1995	Confidence restoration mission	UN
27.	Rwanda	1993–1995	Assistance mission	UN

(continued)

(continued)

Item No.	*Peacekeeping site*	*Date(s)*	*Mission description*	*Under whose auspice?*
28.	Bosnia and Herzegovina	1993	Nation-building mission, including law enforcement and police reform	UN
29.	Rwanda	1992–1993	Peace monitoring mission	OAU
30.	Sierra Leone	1992–	Peace observation mission	UN
31.	Mozambique	1992–1995	Mission to monitor and verify ceasefire	UN
32.	Former Yugoslavia	1992–1993	Protection force	UN
33.	Somalia	1992–1995	Nation-building mission	UN
34.	Somalia	1992–1995	Mission to monitor and observe ceasefire	UN
35.	Cambodia	1992–1993	Transitional authority mission	UN
36.	Kosovo	1991	Interim mission	UN
37.	Iraq–Kuwait	1991	Military observation mission	UN
38.	Western Sahara	1991–	Military observation mission	UN
39.	Namibia	1989–1990	Transition assistance mission	UN
40.	Angola	1992–1995	Verification mission (III)	UN
41.	Angola	1991–1992	Verification mission (II)	UN
42.	Angola	1989–1991	Verification mission (I)	UN
43.	Iran–Iraq conflict	1988–1991	Military observation mission	UN
44.	Chad	1982–1983	Mission codenamed "Operation Harmony II"	OAU
45.	Chad	1981–1982	Mission codenamed "Operation Harmony I"	Bilateral agreement
46.	Lebanon	1978–1983	Interim force	UN
47.	India–Pakistan conflict	1965–1966	Military observation mission	UN

(continued)

(continued)

Item No.	*Peacekeeping site*	*Date(s)*	*Mission description*	*Under whose auspice?*
48.	Tanzania	1964	Conflict January 12–September 26, 1964, triggered by an army mutiny wherein, on March 31, 1964, Nigeria deployed 500 troops to replace withdrawn British forces. The troops kept peace in Tanzania for six months before they left on September 26, 1964	Bilateral agreement
49.	New Guinea	1962–1963	Security force to which Nigeria sent military observers	UN
50.	Congo	1960–1964	In response to the Congo crisis	UN

CHAPTER 7

Technical Aid Corps (TAC)

Introduction

This chapter is a critical assessment of the possibilities and limits of the Technical Aid Corps (TAC), a volunteer program, related to the application of human rights in Nigeria's external relations in the age of General Buhari and his successors. It integrates the perspective of the program as the fourth of five methods in the proposal for a human-right policy for Nigeria, taking advantage of the inestimable opportunity presented by the reduced influence of the military in Nigerian politics, signified by the departure of General Buhari after two unimpressive terms in office as President until May 2023. Several salient issues bearing on the topic that the ensuing discussion explores are: the nuts and bolts of the TAC, as well as the history and evolution of this signature tool of Nigerian foreign policy, crowned by analysis of the possibilities and limits of the tool with respect to application of human rights in Nigeria's external relations.

Nuts and Bolts of the TAC

Nuts and bolts designates the basic practical details related to a program, here the TAC, whose basic features we sketch here. The following discussion covers four issues: overview of the TAC, its location as an agency under the Ministry of Foreign Affairs (MFA), volunteers under the

P. C. Aka, *Human Rights in Nigeria's External Relations in the Age of General Muhammadu Buhari and His Successors*, https://doi.org/10.1007/978-3-031-63231-0_7

scheme juxtaposed with the responsibilities of beneficiary countries, and funding the program.

Overview of the TAC

The law which created the TAC designed it as a tool meant to "share Nigeria's know-how and expertise with [...] African, Caribbean[,] and Pacific [ACP] countries."[1] In and of itself, the label APC countries harks back to the Organization of African, Caribbean, and Pacific States (OACPS).[2] Formed in 1975 and headquartered in Brussels, Belgium,the forum is made up of 79 member-states[3]: 48 from Africa (much of the

[1] "Nigerian Technical Aid Corps Act" (October 1, 1987), *Laws of Nigeria* [hereinafter NTAC Act, 1987], https://lawsofnigeria.placng.org/laws/N135.pdf. § 2(a). Decree No. 27, which established the scheme, was not signed into law by General Ibrahim Babangida until January 1993, six years after the inception of the program. Wale Adebanwi, *Globally-Oriented Citizenship and International Voluntary Service: Interrogating Nigeria's Technical Aid Corps Scheme*, Discussion Paper No. 71 (Uppsala, Sweden: Nordiska Afrikaininstitutet, 2011), 23.

[2] See The Organization of African, Caribbean, and Pacific States, Homepage, https://www.oacps.org/.

[3] Formerly known as African, Caribbean and Pacific Group of States, the OACPS works to promote sustainable development within its member-states and their increased integration into the world's economy. Ibid.

55 countries in the continent, including Nigeria itself),[4] 16 from the Caribbean,[5] and 15 from the Pacific.[6]

Channeling knowledge and expertise to ACP countries is one of four objectives of the TAC; the complementing three others are: extending assistance based on "the assessed and perceived needs of the recipient countries," promoting cooperation and understanding between Nigeria and these recipient countries, and facilitating "meaningful contacts between the youths of Nigeria and those of the recipient countries."[7] A recent iteration of these objectives by the Directorate of Technical Aid Corps (DTAC), the agency charged with responsibility for administering the program, enumerated them to include: ensuring a streamlined program of assistance that complements other forms of assistance to ACP countries; providing a channel for enhancing cooperation in the developing world; and establishing presence in countries with which, for some reason, such as economic factors, Nigeria lacks resident diplomatic missions.[8]

In sum, the TAC systematized and formalized sporadic technical assistance initiatives going back to the 1960s wherein Nigeria seconds (i.e.

[4] The 48 African countries are: Angola, Benin, Botswana, Burkina Faso, Burundi, Cameroon, Cape Verde, Central African Republic, Chad, Comoros, Democratic Republic of the Congo (formerly Zaire), Republic of the Congo (Congo Brazzaville), Côte d'Ivoire, Djibouti, Eritrea, Ethiopia, Gabon, Gambia, Ghana, Guinea, Guinea-Bissau, Equatorial Guinea, Eswatini (formerly Swaziland), Kenya, Lesotho, Madagascar, Liberia, Malawi, Mali, Mauritius, Mauritania, Mozambique, Namibia, Niger, Nigeria, Rwanda, Sao Tome and Principe, Senegal, Seychelles, Sierra Leone, Somalia, South Africa, Sudan, Tanzania, Togo, Uganda, Zambia, Zimbabwe. "[Seventy-Nine] Countries," *Business ACP* (December 2019), https://businessacp.com/wp-content/uploads/2019/12/79-countries-OACPS.pdf; and South-South Galaxy, "African, Caribbean and Pacific Group of States (ACP)," https://my.southsouth-galaxy.org/en/data/african-caribbean-and-pacific-group-of-states-acp.

[5] The 16 Caribbean countries are: Antigua and Barbuda, Bahamas, Barbados, Belize, Cuba, Dominica, Dominican Republic, Grenada, Guyana, Haiti, Jamaica, Saint Kitts and Nevis, St. Lucia, St. Vincent and the Grenadines, Suriname, and Trinidad and Tobago. Ibid.

[6] The 15 Pacific countries are: Cook Islands, Fiji, Kiribati, Marshall Islands, (Federated States of) Micronesia, Nauru, Niue, Palau, Papua New Guinea, Samoa, Solomon Islands, Timor-Leste, Tonga, Tuvalu, Vanuatu. Ibid.

[7] NTAC Act, 1987, note 1, § 2(b)–(d).

[8] Directorate of Technical Aid Corps, "About DTAC," https://www.dtac.gov.ng/DTAC/dtac/aboutDTAC#first. Note 17 below and accompanying text explains South-South cooperation.

temporarily posts) technical experts to various African counties.[9] Vis-à-vis these past initiatives, the TAC "place[s] less financial burden on the recipient countries."[10] In gestures that demonstrate Nigeria's commitment to cooperation with the developing world, the program provides "an alternative to direct financial (cash) assistance to [ACP] Countries;" forms "a practical transfer of knowledge and expertise from Nigerian professionals" to beneficiary countries "in a well-structured and more coordinated manner"; helps "cement[] existing relations between Nigeria and the recipient countries," and expands Nigeria's diplomatic presence in the world to countries where, again, for some reason, such as economic consideration, Nigeria lacks embassies.[11]

The TAC touts itself simultaneously as "a people-oriented and people-centered assistance [initiative] geared toward the development of recipient countries,"[12] as well as "a practical demonstration of South-South cooperation,"[13] matched against a "commonly-held perception that Africa is only a recipient of aid."[14] Variously, its admirers praise the scheme as the "only volunteer service of its kind currently operated by an African country,"[15] as well as a "pearl of South-South cooperation,"[16] in marked

[9] Salami B. Olawale, "The Prelude to Babangida Regime's Foreign Policy Initiatives," *Mediterranean Journal of Social Sciences*, 5 (2014), 83, www.mcser.org/journal/index.php/mjss/article/view/2120.

[10] Ibid.

[11] Directorate of Technical Aid Corps, "Welcome to the Directorate of Technical Aid Corps," http://www.dtac.gov.ng/DTAC/dtac/aboutDTAC#.

[12] "About DTAC," note 8.

[13] Wale Adebanwi, "International Service and Civic Nationalism in Nigeria and The Gambia," in *Youth Service in Comparative Perspective*, ed. Amanda Moore McBride (St. Louis, MO: Center for Social Development, Washington University in St. Louis, 2009), 65–72 (quoting the Directorate of Technical Aid Corps).

[14] "About DTAC," note 8. The quote is attributed to Meles Zenawi, Prime Minister of Ethiopia (1995–2012). See "Welcome to the Directorate of Technical Aid Corps," note 11.

[15] Meles Zenawi, quoted in "Welcome to the Director of Technical Aid Corps," note 11. See also Bethel Olujobi, "Nigeria Opens Door for Medical, Other Volunteer Missions Abroad," *Business Day* (January 3, 2024), https://businessday.ng/news/article/nigeria-opens-door-for-medical-other-volunteer-missions-abroad/#:~:text=The%20Federal%20Government%20of%20Nigeria,TAC)%20recruitment%20exercise%20for%202024.

[16] Samiu Babalola, "Nigeria's Technical Aid Corps: Pearl of South-South Cooperation," *Africa Platform for Development Effectiveness* (December 21, 2011), http://www.africa-platform.org/resources/nigerias-technical-aid-corps-pearl-south-south-cooperation.

departure from the conventional North–South pattern of aid.[17] Consistent with these showers of accolade, the program "is hugely popular with Nigerian professionals."[18] However, it is a popularity due as much to its inherent merits as to the high youth unemployment in Nigeria,[19] a crisis of joblessness that extends even to university graduates.[20]

[17] The literature on development makes a distinction between a Global North and a Global South. It is a distinction based on level of economic development, rather than strictly on geography as the name would suggest. The Global North includes the economically developed societies of Europe, North America, Australia, Israel, and others. In contrast, the Global South includes the developing societies of Africa, India, China, Brazil, Mexico, and others. Lemuel Ekedegwa Odeh, "A Comparative Analysis of Global North and Global South Economies," *Journal of Sustainable Development in Africa*, 12 (2010), 338, http://www.jsd-africa.com/Jsda/V12No3_Summer2010_A/PDF/A%20Comparative%20Analysis%20of%20Global%20North%20and%20Global%20South%20Economies%20(Odeh).pdf. Based on this distinction, "South-South cooperation" is another way of saying cooperation among developing countries that have yet to attain the high level of economic development found in the Global North.

[18] Adebanwi, "International Service and Civic Nationalism in Nigeria and The Gambia," note 13 (abstract).

[19] Ibid. (pointing out that the program aimed to "support [Nigeria's] young professionals during an economically-troubled time"). On youth unemployment in the country, see Tunji Akande, "Youth Unemployment in Nigeria: A Situation Analysis," Brookings (September 23, 2014), https://www.brookings.edu/articles/youth-unemployment-in-nigeria-a-situation-analysis/ (among other things, assessing the problem as a "largely structural" one in need of "structural solutions" that it has not received under the Fourth Republic since 1999). The Akande commentary described an "incredibly high and rising unemployment rate," signified by various dismal statistics, including youth unemployment in 2012 estimated at over 11 million (as the youth population grows steadily, so does the unemployment rate), and that, as of 2014, about "1.8 million youth [...] enter[] the labor market every year." Ibid. The commentary defines *youth* as persons between 15 and 34 years of age. Ibid.

[20] See Joshua Segun et al., "University-Industry Collaboration: A Panacea to Graduate Unemployment in Nigeria," BVIMSR's *Journal of Management Review*, 7(1) (2015), 17–25 (stating that Nigeria has "well over [one] hundred universities," public and private, which "churn[] out graduates every year without prospect[s] for employment"). Segun and his colleagues proposed collaboration between universities and industries designed to reduce some of the "mismatch between" preparation and "the world of work" as possible solution to the joblessness. A contributory and compounding factor is the retrograded status of higher education in Nigeria. See Dipo Awojide, "Solutions to Challenges Plaguing Tertiary Education in Nigeria," *LinkedIn* (November 20, 2023), https://www.linkedin.com/pulse/solutions-challenges-plaguing-tertiary-education-nigeria-awojide-r4hfe/ (listing inadequate funding, poor infrastructure, poorly renumerated academics, dated curriculum, bureaucracy, and insecurity among these challenges).

Location of the TAC as an Agency Under the Ministry of Foreign Affairs

Under its enabling law, the TAC is "an integral part of the Ministry of Foreign Affairs."[21] The law established the DTAC as a governing body for the scheme under the MFA, made up of a Director as chair, one person representing the MFA, and five other persons appointed by the President.[22] Members of the Directorate hold office for a four-year term, subject to reappointment for another four-year term.[23] The Minister of Foreign Affairs approves the "allowances and expenses" of these members.[24] Unlike the other members, the Director, who heads the Directorate, holds office for five years, subject to reappointment for another five years.[25] In the performance of his or her duties, the Director may be assisted by staff hired as employees of the Directorate.[26]

Functions of the Directorate include: overall management and general administration of the program; recruiting volunteers for the scheme and assigning them to recipient countries; organizing orientation courses for selected volunteers; receiving and debriefing volunteers upon their return at the end of their tours of duty; maintaining regular contacts with recipient countries to determine their technical aid needs, including the extent that those needs are being met; assessing and reviewing periodically the progress of the scheme; and carrying out any other functions or activities consistent with the objectives of the scheme.[27] Subject to the directive of the Foreign Affairs minister, the Directorate has the power to engage in any activity, in its assessment, calculated to facilitate the performance of its responsibilities under this law.[28] It may accept gifts of property, such as land and money, consistent with the objectives of the program or its functions,[29] and, in consultation with the Foreign Affairs minister,

[21] NTAC Act, 1987, note 1, § 3(1).

[22] Ibid., § 3(2)(a)–(c).

[23] Ibid., § 3(3)(a).

[24] Ibid., § 3(3)(b).

[25] Ibid., § 9(2)(b).

[26] Ibid., § 9(3).

[27] See NTAC Act, 1987, note 1, § 4 (a)–(h).

[28] Ibid., § 5.

[29] Ibid., § 14(1)–(2).

it may make regulations related to its work, including prescription of requirements volunteers must meet to participate in the program, and remuneration for their services.[30]

Volunteers Under the TAC and Responsibilities of Beneficiary Countries

Volunteers are a lifeblood of the TAC. Consistent with the enabling law, the program "consist[s] of such number of volunteers as shall, from time to time, be recruited by the Directorate to meet the technical aid needs of the recipient countries."[31] Put differently, the TAC is a volunteer program, something in the mold of the US Peace Corps program,[32] that draws from the wellspring of Nigeria's well-trained humanpower, made up of professionals from numerous disciplines, such as accounting, architecture, artisanry (such as textile design, and skill in the creation and production of musical instruments like drums), engineering, higher education administration, journalism and mass communication, law, and medicine (among them doctors, pharmacists, and nurses).[33] These professionals generally work in the education, health, legal, and public sector of the countries of their posting.[34]

To qualify as a volunteer, an individual must possess "at least a University degree or its equivalent," or "such other professional qualification as the Directorate may [periodically] specify," *and* "a minimum of three years post-qualification working experience."[35] In recruiting volunteers,

[30] Ibid., § 15(a)–(c).

[31] Ibid., § 6(1); see also ibid., § 1(2).

[32] See B.O. Salami, "Evaluating the Nigerian Technical Aids Corp Scheme, 1987–1993," *Journal of History and Diplomatic Studies*, 9 (2012), https://www.ajol.info/index.php/jhds/article/view/96974 (indicating that the creators of the program modelled it after the US Peace Corps); and Adebanwi, *Globally-Oriented Citizenship and International Voluntary Service*, note 1, pp. 22–23 ("Technical Aid Corps: From the US Peace Corps to TAC").

[33] See Olawale, note 9; Adebanwi, "International Service and Civic Nationalism in Nigeria and The Gambia," note 13; and "The Transformation of Technical Aid Corps Scheme," *Sun* (Lagos) (August 20, 2014), http://sunnewsonline.com/new/the-transformation-of-technical-aid-corps-scheme/.

[34] Adebanwi, "International Service and Civic Nationalism in Nigeria and The Gambia," note 13.

[35] NTAC Act, 1987, note 1, § 6(2)(a)–(c).

the Directorate may utilize guidelines like the nature of the requests received from a recipient country; willingness of the recipient country to receive the volunteers; and the availability of funds to defray the expenditure incurred in assigning volunteers to the recipient country.[36] Subject to the approval of the foreign minister, the Directorate determines the terms and duration of service of volunteers.[37] The same applies with respect to allowances for the volunteers, including the currency in which those allowances will be made.[38]

Volunteers are *not* national civil servant.[39] Thus, flowing from the power granted it under the enabling law,[40] the Directorate fashions and implements a regulation barring volunteers for applying after completing two years under the program. It is a biennial arrangement by which volunteers mandatorily serve for 24 months in their respective countries of deployment. In other words, they may not participate twice in the program, unless a beneficiary country chooses to retain a volunteer after his or her tour of duty is over.[41] Once the Corps concludes a Memorandum of Understanding (MoU) with the recipient country after assessing its needs,[42] the recipient country assumes responsibility for certain non-emolument benefits for volunteers, such as healthcare services, exemption from income tax, and housing.[43] A recipient country

[36] Ibid., § 6(3)(a)–(c).

[37] Ibid., § 6(4).

[38] Ibid., § 7(2).

[39] Ibid., § 6(5) ("A person shall not, by reason only of being a volunteer of the Corps, be treated as holding an office of emolument in the civil service of the Federation").

[40] See ibid., § 15(c) (granting the Directorate, in consultation with the foreign minister, the power to make regulations "generally for the purposes of carrying out or giving full effect to the provisions of this Act").

[41] Ibid., § 8(2) ("A recipient country may offer employment to a volunteer on completion of his assignment, on such terms and conditions as may be agreed upon by them").

[42] See ibid., § 2(b).

[43] Ibid., § 8(1)–(2). See also Godwin Onuh Odeh, "Nigeria's Technical Aid Corps Engagement in The Gambia, 1987–2012: A Neglected Aspect of Nigerian Foreign Relations," in *Culture and Nigeria's Foreign Relations in a Globalizing World* (Abuja: National Institute for Cultural Orientation Agency [NICO], 2021), chap. 14, https://www.researchgate.net/publication/353946774_Nigeria's_Technical_Aid_Corps_Engagement_in_The_Gambia_1987-2012_A_Neglected_Aspect_of_Nigerian_Foreign_Relations;

may also choose to retain a volunteer upon the expiration of his or her current assignment, on mutually-agreed terms and conditions.[44]

Funding the TAC

Adequate funding is a proverbial mother's milk in the effective administration of any program. The TAC is no different. Thus, to facilitate the running of the program, its enabling law established a Fund, to be sourced from: subventions and extra-budgetary allocations from the national government; monies accruing to the Directorate by way of gifts, endowments, bequests and other voluntary contributions by persons and organizations; and such other monies, consistent with the objectives of the Directorate or its functions, from any other source.[45] And to ensure proper records and probity, the enabling law mandates that the accounts of the Directorate must be "audited not later than six months after the end of the year to which it relates."[46]

History and Evolution of the TAC as a Tool of Nigerian Foreign Policy

This discussion builds on and amplifies the coverage in the preceding section. The program was born in 1987 during the regime of General Ibrahim Babangida, Head of State from 1985 to 1993.[47] It began modestly with 102 volunteers posted to 12 countries.[48] The country's external minister then and originator of the program was Bolaji Akinyemi.[49] Countries which have benefited from the TAC program include: Belize, Benin Republic, Brazil, Burkina Faso, Burundi,

and Adebanwi, *Globally-Oriented Citizenship and International Voluntary Service*, note 1, p. 26.

[44] See note 41 and accompanying text.

[45] NTAC Act, 1987, note 1, § 11(1)–(2).

[46] Ibid., § 13(1)–(3).

[47] See generally Olawale, note 9; and Salami, note 32.

[48] "About DTAC," note 8; and Adebanwi, Adebanwi, "International Service and Civic Nationalism in Nigeria and The Gambia," note 13, p. 66.

[49] Adebanwi, *Globally-Oriented Citizenship and International Voluntary Service*, note 1, pp. 22–23 ("Technical Aid Corps: From the US Peace Corps to TAC"). See also Dolapo Aina, "Technical Aid Corps: Nigeria's Soft Diplomacy Since 1987," *Guardian* (Lagos)

Cape Verde, Central African Republic, Democratic Republic of the Congo (formerly Zaire), Djibouti, Dominica, Equatorial Guinea, Eswatini (formerly Swaziland), Ethiopia, Fiji, The Gambia, Guinea-Bissau, Guyana, Jamaica, Kenya, Lesotho, Liberia, Mozambique, Namibia, Niger Republic, Rwanda, Sao Tome and Principe, Senegal, Seychelles, Sierra Leone, Uganda, Venezuela, Vietnam, and Zambia.[50] These are countries wherein volunteers under the scheme have completed their two-year assignments.

The number comes to 33 states, thirty of which are ACP countries. The other three—Brazil, Venezuela, and Vietnam—are states traditionally outside the ACP community, which expressed interest in the scheme and became beneficiaries in September 2014.[51] Some of these countries, such as The Gambia, have used the international volunteer service more than others. Based on need, from its inception until 2009, "The Gambia has received more volunteers than any other recipient country[.]"[52] Besides recipient states, the TAC has also attracted the attention or interest of international organization and development agencies like the UN Volunteer Service (UNVS).[53]

Beginning with 12 countries and 102 volunteers in 1987, by 2011, the TAC deployed over 4,000 volunteers to 38 countries.[54] The budget for the scheme, which has risen over the years, runs into tens of billions

(August 27, 2020), https://guardian.ng/opinion/technical-aid-corps-nigerias-soft-diplomacy-since-1987 (providing a hagiographic chronicle of the program).

50 "Welcome to the Directorate of Technical Aid Corps," note 11.

51 See "Nigeria's Technical Aid Corps for ACP Countries to Expand to Brazil, Venezuela, Vietnam," *ACP* (September 10, 2014), http://www.acp.int/content/news-nigerias-technical-aid-corps-acp-countries-expand-brazil-venezuela-vietnam.

52 Adebanwi, *Globally-Oriented Citizenship and International Voluntary Service*, note 1, p. 68; and Odeh, "Nigeria's Technical Aid Corps Engagement in The Gambia," note 43, p. 11 (Back to the inception of the program, The Gambia "receiv[es] the highest number of volunteers biennially, more than any other recipient country"). Nigeria's technical assistance to the country predates the TAC, goes back to the early days of Nigerian independence, and is driven by composite factors, that, besides sheer big-brother altruism, include similarities between the two countries embedded in culture and religion. See Odeh, "Nigeria's Technical Aid Corps Engagement in The Gambia," p. 9.

53 See, for example, Tom Bannister, "Volunteering, a Participatory Approach to South-South Cooperation," *UN Volunteers* (April 11, 2017), https://www.unv.org/news/volunteering-participatory-approach-south-south-cooperation.

54 Babalola, note 16.

in Nigeria's national currency.[55] Due partly to high youth unemployment in Nigeria,[56] the competition by volunteers for spaces in the program is stiff. By 2009, the number of applicants to the program hovered around 150,000.[57] This is despite the low odds of acceptance: in a typical biennial competition, less than 50% of the applicants invited for interview earn the opportunity to serve.

For the 2024–2026 application season, there were only 105 volunteer positions[58] that more than 100,000 applicants competed to fill. For a country like Nigeria with a huge population of young people, this is a proverbial drop in the ocean. The country has the largest population of youth in the world; about 70% of the population is under-30, with 42% under 15 years of age.[59] Millions of these youths are unemployed.[60] This is how one scholar described the arduous selection process volunteers endure:

> The process of recruiting TAC volunteers takes several months, sometimes more than a year. First, qualified volunteers apply to the federal ministry of foreign affairs, which then draws up a shortlist of applicants. The shortlisted candidates are invited for interviews, after which the final list is drawn. Specialized screening and selection committees coordinate the recruitment of volunteers. Those on the final list undergo security checks and medical check-ups. This is followed by the orientation course. [...] [N]ot all those who attend the orientation are subsequently deployed.[61]

[55] Ibid.

[56] See notes 19–20 and accompanying texts.

[57] Adebanwi, *Globally-Oriented Citizenship and International Voluntary Service*, note 1, p. 26.

[58] See Adam Ganiyu, "Ministry of Foreign Affairs Job Recruitment (2024–2026)—105 Positions," *Intel Region* (December 29, 2023), https://www.intelregion.com/jobs/ministry-of-foreign-affairs-job-recruitment/

[59] Akanmi I. Akinyemi, "Nigeria's Growing Population Can Be an Advantage, with Better Data and a Policy Focus on Young People," *Conversation* (July 11, 2023), https://theconversation.com/nigerias-growing-population-can-be-an-advantage-with-better-data-and-a-policy-focus-on-young-people-209530#:~:text=The%20country%20has%20the%20largest,under%20the%20age%20of%2015.

[60] See notes 19–20 and accompanying texts.

[61] Adebanwi, *Globally-Oriented Citizenship and International Voluntary Service*, note 1, p. 26.

Wale Adebanwi described a selection process in Kano between June and July 2005 where, out of a pool of 150,000 applicants, 10,000 persons were shortlisted and invited for interview, with only 2,000 volunteers ending up being selected.[62]

The number of volunteers has fluctuated over the years. Starting with 102 volunteers in 1987, that number reached a high of over 200 in August 2013.[63] Testament to the diminished contribution to the international human rights regime that took place under General Buhari (and the marked slow-down in Nigeria's journey toward a principled foreign policy), for nearly eight years from May 2015, when he took office, to January 2023, Nigeria deployed 2,500 TAC volunteers—and to a small(er) list of just sixteen countries: Belize, Benin, Ethiopia, The Gambia, Ghana, Guinea-Bissau, Jamaica, Liberia, Namibia, Niger, Rwanda, Seychelles, Sierra Leone, St. Kitts and Nevis, Tanzania, and Uganda.[64]

The TAC and Application of Human Rights in Nigeria's External Relations: Possibilities and Limits

Just like peacekeeping covered in the previous chapter, in and of itself, the TAC cannot be a human-right tool, if it is not human-right compliant—in word as well as in deed. In assessing the possibilities and limits of the program for its human-right content, two interrelated options out of many lend themselves for exploration. These are inadequacies related to funding and bilateralism, each of which we take in turn.

Inadequately Funded

Because the TAC is integrally tied to the Ministry of Finance, it also ipso facto shares some of the problems with the ministry related to funding. One unmistakable indicator of the intertwinement is the fact that the

62 Ibid., p. 27.

63 "About DTAC," note 8.

64 Wale Odunsi, "Nigeria Deploys 2,500 Technical Aid Volunteers to ACP Countries," *Daily Post* (Lagos) (February 2, 2023), https://dailypost.ng/2023/02/02/nigeria-deploys-2500-technical-aid-volunteers-to-acp-countries/.

agency fills in for those countries where, due to economic reasons, Nigeria does not field a resident mission.[65] Foreign policy is not something run on a shoestring budget[66]; instead, in Nigerian pidgin, *better soup na money kill am*, meaning that "good things in life don't come cheap."[67]

Contrary to these admonitions, one of the banes of Nigeria's government under the Fourth Republic is the underfunding of key public services, including diplomatic initiatives and activities.[68] Thus, for many years, coming to a head under General Buhari from 2015 to 2023, Nigeria has been underfunding its Ministry of Foreign Affairs, to the detriment abroad of its diplomatic obligations, and general economic development within the Nigerian homeland.[69] In 2020, Geoffrey Onyeama, then foreign minister, lamented that "Nigerian foreign missions are now a terrible embarrassment to the country abroad."[70] Testament to this observation, available record showed that, for the period 2015–2020, "Nigeria budgeted less than N200 billion for its foreign missions, representing a paltry 0.5% of all its budgetary proposals of ₦43.98 trillion."[71] Onyeama worried that the inadequate funding

[65] See notes 8 and 11, along with accompanying text.

[66] See Dapo Fafowora, "Review of Nigeria's Foreign Policy," *Nation* (June 4, 2015), http://thenationonlineng.net/review-of-nigerias-foreign-policy/.

[67] Nkem Ikeke, "[Seventeen] Hilarious Nigerian Pidgin Proverbs and Their Meanings," *Legit* (September 29, 2016) (Proverb No. 7), https://www.legit.ng/987866-17-nigerian-pidgin-proverbs-will-leave-rolling-floor-laughter-photos.html.

[68] Chiamaka Okafor, "Naira Depreciation Ridicules Increased Budgetary Allocation for Nigeria's Foreign Missions," *Premium Times* (Abuja) (January 11, 2024), https://www.premiumtimesng.com/news/657697-naira-depreciation-ridicules-increased-budgetary-allocation-for-nigerias-foreign-missions.html (citing the proposition of Ayoola Olukanni, former Nigerian ambassador to Australia, to the effect that the issue of underfunding Nigeria's foreign missions is an age-long challenge). On healthcare, see Philip C. Aka and Joseph Abiodun Balogun, *Healthcare and Economic Restructuring: Nigeria in Comparative Perspective* (Gateway East, Singapore: Palgrave Macmillan, 2022) (proffering suggestions on how to repair Nigeria's dysfunctional healthcare system through the medium of a healthier economy that provides sufficient revenue to meet the healthcare needs of citizens).

[69] See Aishat Babatunde and Yusuf Akinpelu, "Nigeria Underfunding Diplomatic Missions, Weakening Foreign Policy—Experts," *Premium Times* (Abuja) (December 11, 2020), https://www.premiumtimesng.com/news/headlines/430537-nigeria-underfunding-diplomatic-missions-weakening-foreign-policy-experts.html.

[70] Ibid.

[71] Ibid.

impedes the ability of Nigeria "to defend the interest of Africa and the black race around the world," and, most to the TAC scheme at the heart of this chapter, to maintain the "vast network of technical assistance" obligations to ACP countries.[72]

Due to the inadequate funding, Nigeria was unable to meet even basic diplomatic obligations like paying the rent for some of its embassies (such as the one in Hungary).[73] Nor adequately cater for the welfare of Nigerian citizens abroad.[74] For example, because of lack of money, in 2019, Nigeria's foreign ministry announced a plan to closing down its embassies in Sri Lanka, Czech Republic, and the Republic of Serbia, and downsizing another one,[75] all to the annoyance of Nigerians and their friends abroad who needed consular and related services. So much for the contrivance of giant of Africa.

Tying the matter to the disinterest in foreign affairs that marked the Buhari government, poor funding of diplomatic missions betrays the idiosyncrasy of a sitting president, the reason being because "[f]oreign policy is within the domain of the president," and because "[t]he vibrancy of foreign policy implementation depends on the nature of the president."[76] With respect to general economic development, competent handling of a country's foreign policy "can result in a creative economy"; therefore, underfunding diplomatic services is part of "the cavalier handing of the country's political economy" that took place under the watch of General Buhari.[77] Post-Buhari, the 2024 budget contained the highest allocation for Nigeria's foreign missions since 2020.[78] However, the decline of Nigeria's economy, emblematized by the depreciation of the Naira, Nigeria's national currency, which has taken a new turn since Tinubu's assumption of office in May 2023, has complicated the budgetary situation to the extent that "Nigerian missions will receive less

[72] Ibid.

[73] Ibid.

[74] Ibid.

[75] Ibid.

[76] Ibid. (citing Azeez Olaniyan, deputy director, Institute of Peace and Governance, Ekiti State University).

[77] Ibid. (citing Olutayo Adeshina, head of History department at the University of Ibadan).

[78] Okafor, note 68.

funding [in 2024] than they did in three of the last four years."[79] The reason is because "[w]hile the budgetary allocation for Nigeria's foreign missions is in [N]aira," for the more than 100 foreign missions Nigeria has around the world, "expenses are in US dollars."[80]

With respect to funding, some critics point to the expensiveness of the TAC in the face of myriad socioeconomic difficulties in Nigeria that supposedly makes it non-affordable.[81] But the positive features of the program outweigh the negatives.[82] In any case, this point was addressed in Chapter 2 related to the potential infrastructure for human-right duties that Nigeria possesses and explored at more length in Chapters 9–10 focusing on the rebuttable objections to the proposal in this book for a human-right policy for Nigeria, post-Buhari, to engender the growth of human rights and the rule of law in the country, while increasing its contributions to the international human rights regime.

[79] Ibid. On the decline of the Naira under Tinubu's presidency, see, for example, Ahmed Oluwasanjo, "Naira Falls to ₦1,600 Per $1 as Tinubu's Economic Collapse Continues," *Peoples Gazette* (Abuja) (February 15, 2024), https://gazettengr.com/just-in-naira-falls-to-n1600-per-1-as-tinubus-economic-collapse-continues/; Michael Cohen, "Why Nigeria Currency Exchange Mess Is So Hard to Fix," *Bloomberg* (January 29, 2024, Updated January 30, 2024), https://www.bloomberg.com/news/articles/2024-01-29/why-nigeria-s-naira-currency-exchange-regime-mess-is-so-hard-to-fix; and Chijioke Ohuocha, "Explainer: What Is Pushing the Nigerian Naira to Record Lows?" *Reuter* (October 27, 2023), https://www.reuters.com/markets/currencies/what-is-pushing-nigerian-naira-record-lows-2023-10-27/.

[80] Okafor, note 68.

[81] See Emmanuel C. Ojukwu and Chuka Enuka, "Nigeria and African Development Agenda: The Technical Aid Corps (TAC) Initiative," *Journal of African Studies and Sustainable Development*, 3(6) (2020), 107–119, 10.13140/RG.2.2.29758.72006 (lambasting the program as "an economically unprofitable Africa-centered foreign policy [...] not worth Nigeria's commitment").

[82] See Wale Adebanwi, "Government-Led Service: The Example of the Nigerian Technical Aid Corps," *Voluntary Action: The Journal of the Institute for Volunteering Research*, 7(2) (2005), https://www.bl.uk/collection-items/government-led-service. To the criticism of expensiveness and brain drawn, Adebanwi recounts that supporters of the program point to international goodwill credited to the program and the personal benefits to volunteers within an economy still marked by high unemployment, especially among the youth. Ibid. His weigh-in was that the positive results attributable to the program outweigh any negatives enough to justify the maintenance of the scheme. Ibid.

Insufficiently Bilateral

Successful application of human rights in external affairs requires a proper mixture between multilateral and bilateral activities in external relations. Stated differently, to engage in principled foreign policy of the type associated with global Good Samarians, the hallowed rank of political communities, marked out for recognition on grounds of their robust application of human rights in their external relations,[83] Nigeria must include more bilateral activities in its foreign policy toolbox. Achieving that optimal balance does *not* dictate that the country be a great or even middle power.[84] What it mandates is only that Nigeria punches within its capability weight in international human rights duties, rather than below, as is the case now. As non-big states like Costa Rica and even South Africa demonstrate, pursuit of a principled foreign policy is not predicated on the luxury of size, wealth, or power, or the intersection of these attributes.[85]

Take Costa Rica as example. At the UN alone, the country "has played a part in virtually every major human rights initiative and institution—vastly disproportionate to its size, wealth, and power."[86] Major highlights of its commitments to international human rights include its instrumental role leading to the establishment in 1993 of the Office of the UN High Commissioner for Human Rights,[87] its campaign for the Optional Protocol to the Convention against Torture, adopted by the UN in December of 2002,[88] and its sponsorship of the First World Conference on Human Rights in 1982.[89] Next to South Africa, in the period since its achievement of majority rule in 1994, the country has "hosted

[83] Alison Brysk, *Global Good Samaritans: Human Rights as Foreign Policy* (New York: Oxford University Press, 1998), *passim* (case study of six states and a coalition of six groups, some of them states).

[84] For one position on the small, middle, and great-power doctrine in international relations, see Gareth Evans, "Middle Power Diplomacy," lecture delivered in Santiago, Chile (June 29, 2011), http://www.gevans.org/speeches/speech441.html (positing that, while *middle power diplomacy* is a useful concept in international relations, identifying the countries which form these *middle powers* with any precision "is an exercise fraught with peril").

[85] Brysk, note 83, p. 118.

[86] Ibid., p. 96.

[87] Ibid., p. 97.

[88] Ibid., p. 98.

[89] Ibid., p.106.

an unprecedented series of global and regional conferences."[90] Major highlights of its contributions to the international human rights regime include the hosting of the UN Conference on Racism in 2001.[91] Moving forward, the country has displayed a willingness to endure reprisals for its principled promotion of international law. For example, in 2003, Pretoria chose a reduction in US aid rather than sign an impunity agreement with the US concerning the International Criminal Court.[92]

In contrast, dating back to its independence, including under the Fourth Republic since 1999, Nigeria has punched below its weight in its contribution to international human rights. Activities weighted excessively in multilateralism, at the expense of bilateral tools, betray a lack of readiness for principled foreign policy. Belief in the usefulness of the United Nations as an instrument for safeguarding the independence of small states ranked among the objectives of Nigerian foreign policy during the early years of Nigeria's independence.[93] The thinking is testimony to a foreign policy hued toward multilateralism that should no longer dictate policy sixty-three odd years as of this book after the country's independence within which period petroleum products have replaced agricultural exports as mainstay of Nigeria's economy.

To consolidate its fledgling democracy and contribute its due quota to the international human regimes, to the benefit of democracy and human rights in its homeland, Nigeria needs more bilateral activities in its foreign policy toolbox. To achieve the status of principled foreign policy state, Nigeria must accumulate more bilateral activities. A dependent, insufficiently-funded, volunteer program, riddled with administrative issues, including the late or non-payment of allowances,[94] does not do that. The inadequate funding of the MFA to which the TAC is inseparably tied, takes away from its ability and effectiveness as a bilateral tool in the conduct of Nigeria's foreign policy. In its 37 years of operation as

[90] Brysk, note 83, p. 173.

[91] Ibid., p. 173.

[92] Ibid.

[93] See Ibrahim A. Gambari, *Party Politics and Foreign Policy: Nigeria Under the First Republic* (Zaria, Nigeria: Ahmadu Bello University Press, 1980), 55–56.

[94] Samuel Akpan, "Nigerian TAC Volunteers Protest Non-Payment of Allowances in Gambia," *Cable* (Lagos) (May 19, 2023), https://www.thecable.ng/nigerian-tac-volunteers-protest-non-payment-of-allowances-in-gambia.

of this book, the performance of the TAC has not worked to change the quintessentially multilateral character of Nigerian foreign policy.

There is no suggestion that Nigeria gives up the multilateral instruments—peacekeeping tied mostly to ECOWAS—that it now depends upon largely to implement its foreign relations. To the contrary, it should streamline those tools along the lines of international human-right standard laid out in Chapter 4 on reconstructing national interest in readiness for human-right duties, while increasing the bilateral contents of its overall relations with other countries. Multilateral policies are important in a globalized world where sometimes states need to stick together to effectively tackle human-right challenges. At the same time, Nigerian external relations are overly hued in the multilateral angle, inconsistent with the requirements of a human-right policy in the manner that policy is defined in this book.

Compared to peacekeeping missions, tied to ECOWAS, explored in the previous chapter, the TAC is inherently bilateral. However, the program is still fledgling and lacking in robustness. Information on the program is sketchy, a sketchiness that arguably speaks to small achievements as a bilateral instrument. For one thing, there is little evidence that the scheme is properly funded. The UN recommends a minimum target of 0.7% of a sponsoring country's gross domestic product (GDP) as allocation to foreign aid[95] that, given the falling prices of oil, the mainstay of Nigeria's economy, it is doubtful that the program meets, especially in the light of the domestic needs of the country.

There are paradoxes related to the Nigerian state generally that magnifies the proposition of insufficient bilateralism laid against the TAC. Volunteers of the program display qualities of citizenship, signified by "concern for others," matched against findings that suggest that "Nigerians are not active citizens in their own country."[96] They appear to establish a global form of citizenship, not restricted by national boundaries,[97] even though, to begin with, Nigerians lack the concept of a common citizenship.[98]

[95] See Millennium Project, "What Is the 0.7% Target? 2002–2006," http://www.unmillenniumproject.org/press/07.htm.

[96] Adebanwi, Adebanwi, "International Service and Civic Nationalism in Nigeria and The Gambia," note 13, pp. 63–72 (abstract).

[97] Ibid.

[98] Ibid., pp. 67–68.

In the light of these composite problems, in actuality, the TAC amounted to little more than "a complement to [its] traditional diplomacy."[99] It is a diplomacy which "identified the use of Nigeria's abundant pool of well-trained human resources as a foreign policy instrument and recognized its enormous potential in enhancing cooperation" with ACP countries.[100] The modest, if not pedestrian, goal at its inception was "to establish a reliable and measurable" tool of assistance,[101] in a bid to burnish Nigeria's image much tarnished by extended military rule. One quarter of a century under the Fourth Republic, including the famished years under General Buhari, Nigeria has not moved far beyond this pedestrian destination.

Conclusion

Drawing importantly on the law creating the program, this chapter lays out the nuts and bolts of the TAC, including its location as an agency under the Ministry of Foreign Affairs; volunteers under the scheme juxtaposed with the responsibilities of beneficiary countries; and funding of the program, given the importance of money in the effective administration of any worthwhile project. On the history and evolution of the TAC as a tool of Nigeria's foreign policy, the program reached a high point in September 2014 when beneficiary countries expanded to include Brazil, Venezuela, and Vietnam, three countries outside the ACP fold. Its lowest point came with the contradictions under the Buhari years until 2023. With respect to its possibilities and limits as a human-right tool, two interrelated problems identified and discussed at some length, were insufficient funding, which it shared with the Ministry of Finance as parent agency, and insufficient bilateralism. Regarding the first without at all minimizing the second, portraiture of the TAC as a signature tool for realization of Nigeria's foreign policy, talk less of its human-right content, rings hollow if the scheme is not backed by adequate funding.

To improve its funding situation while building some of the bilateralism Nigeria needs on the road to a human-right policy, the TAC must

[99] Adebanwi, Adebanwi, "International Service and Civic Nationalism in Nigeria and The Gambia," note 13.

[100] Ibid.

[101] See ibid.

transit into an independent agency free from the tentacles of the Ministry of Foreign Affairs, just like the US national government did in 1981 by disentangling the US Peace Corps from the US State Department and making it an independent federal agency.[102] The agency comprises of a head office based in Washington, DC, nine area offices, and overseas operations in 76 countries, utilizing nearly 8,000 volunteers.[103] As of 2023, "more than 210,000 Americans hav[e] served as [US Peace Corps] volunteers."[104]

[102] See "Peace Corps," *Federal Register*, https://www.federalregister.gov/agencies/peace-corps#:~:text=The%20Peace%20Corps%20was%20established,2501%2D1.

[103] Ibid. The history of the agency dates back to November 2, 1960, when, during a speech in San Francisco, President John J. Kennedy proposed "a peace corps of talented men and women" who would dedicate themselves to the progress and peace of developing countries. "Peace Corps," John F. Kennedy Presidential Library and Museum (Boston, MA), http://www.jfklibrary.org/JFK/JFK-in-History/Peace-Corps.aspx. The proposal became a reality when on March 1, 1961, Kennedy signed an executive order creating the organization. The ideological rivalry between the US and the Soviet Union, embedded in the Cold War, had a hand in the creation of the Peace Corps. Kennedy observed that the Soviet Union "had hundreds of men and women, scientists, physicists, teachers, engineers, doctors, and nurses [...] prepared to spend their lives abroad in the service of world communism," whereas the United States had none. Ibid. Therefore, through the Peace Corps, he would involve Americans more actively in the cause of democracy, peace, development, and freedom. Tanganyika (merged into Tanzania in 1964) and Ghana were the first countries to participate in the program. Ibid. On September 22, 1961, Kennedy signed into law a bill passed by Congress that made the Peace Corps a permanent federal agency within the State Department. It remained part of the State Department until 1981 when it became an independent agency. Ibid.

[104] Christopher Hedrick, "The New Peace Corps," Op-Ed, *Yale Journal of International Affairs* (February 26, 2013), https://www.yalejournal.org/publications/the-new-peace-corps.

CHAPTER 8

The Community Court of Justice

Introduction

This chapter integrates the perspective of the ECOWAS Community Court of Justice, referred to abbreviatedly in this book as the Community Court of Justice (CCJ), to the proposal for a human-right policy for Nigeria post-Buhari, taking advantage of the inestimable opportunity afforded by a fortuitous conjunction and intersection of earth-shaking events. These occurrences are symptomized in Nigeria by the reduced influence of the military in the country's body politic, evidenced by General Buhari's departure after two anemic terms in office as President, and abroad by the coronation of a new monarch in the UK. The UK is the creator of modern-day Nigeria and, post-independence, maintains influence and interests in the country, for good or bad, that stretch up to the present day.[1] This chapter is the last of five sample methods—after reconstructing the national interest to improve Nigeria's readiness for human-right duties (Chapter 4), increased respect for human rights

[1] See, for example, UK Government, "UK-Nigeria Development Partnership Summary, July 2023" (Policy Paper) (July 17, 2023), https://www.gov.uk/government/publications/uk-nigeria-development-partnership-summary/uk-nigeria-development-partnership-summary-july-2023#why-and-how-the-uks-development-offer-with-nigeria.

P. C. Aka, *Human Rights in Nigeria's External Relations in the Age of General Muhammadu Buhari and His Successors*,
https://doi.org/10.1007/978-3-031-63231-0_8

in the country (Chapter 5), peacekeeping (Chapter 6), and the TAC (Chapter 7).

A reckonable distinction exists between the CCJ and peacekeeping, two chapters before, as co-methods. Since the creation of ECOWAS in 1975, Nigerian peacekeeping has been conducted via the instrumentality of the economic union, specifically ECOMOG, its military unit. In contrast, the CCJ is an acknowledged organ—or offshoot—of ECOWAS, toe-to-toe like the other key institutions of the organization, such as the AHSG, the CM, the Executive Commission (formerly Secretariat), and the Community Parliament, enumerated in the material on peacekeeping, yet less dependent on its parent entity (at least conceptually), consistent with the character of judicial tribunals.[2] Testament to this proposition is the provision in the ECOWAS Revised Treaty of 1993 mandating the Court to "carry out the functions assigned to it independently of the Member States and the institutions of the Community."[3]

[2] See Office of the UN Commissioner for Human Rights, "Basic Principles on the Independence of the Judiciary," Seventh United Nations Congress on the Prevention of Crime and the Treatment of Offenders held at Milan from 26 August to 6 September 1985 (September 6, 1985), https://www.ohchr.org/en/instruments-mechanisms/instruments/basic-principles-independence-judiciary. In addition to the topic of independence of the judiciary, the principles include freedom of expression and association for judges; their qualifications, selection, and training; conditions of service and tenure; professional secrecy and immunity related to their deliberations and to confidential information acquired in the course of their duties in non-public proceedings; and discipline, suspension, and removal from office. Ibid. There are twenty of these basic principles altogether, including, but not limited to: guarantee of judicial independence enshrined in the Constitution or law of the country, and respect of that independence by government authorities; ability of judges to decide matters before them impartially, based on the facts and in accordance with the law, free of direct or indirect interference from government authorities; jurisdiction over all issues of a judicial nature and exclusive authority by judges to decide whether issues before them for adjudication is within their competence as defined by the law; absence of any inappropriate or unwarranted interference with the judicial process, including subjection of judicial decisions to revision, inconsistent with the law; requirement that the judiciary ensure that judicial proceedings are conducted fairly, including respect for the rights of the parties; and the duty of UN member-states to provide adequate resources to facilitate performance of judicial functions. Ibid. Adoption of these principles was inspired by the expressed belief that "judges are charged with the ultimate decision over life, freedoms, rights, duties and property of citizens." Ibid., preamble.

[3] Economic Community of West African States (ECOWAS), Revised Treaty of the Economic Community of West African States (ECOWAS) (July 24, 1993) [hereinafter ECOWAS Revised Treaty], art. 15(3), http://www.refworld.org/docid/492182d92.html.

Moving forward, unlike the materials on reconstructing Nigeria's national interest to increase the country's readiness for human-right duties (Chapter 4), and increased respect for human rights in the Nigerian homeland (Chapter 5), the CCJ looks every bit like a method, much in the league of peacekeeping (Chapter 6), and the TAC (Chapter 7). The CCJ's being part of ECOWAS speaks to the crucialness of the customs union as an instrument of Nigeria's foreign policy. Countries with weak legal and judicial systems especially need a human-right court.[4] Therefore, the CCJ's integral-ness with ECOWAS is as well an implicit testament to the willingness of Nigeria and its fellow members in ECOWAS, free of undue sensitivity for sovereignty, to submit their domestic systems to the rule of law, a democratic ideal oftentimes linked to the judiciary.[5]

West Africa is a subregion rife with dependent judiciaries vis-à-vis the executive and legislative co-branches of the government. Courts in the subregion are subject to undue influences, both direct and indirect, which have the overall effect of weakening whatever independence is provided for them in their national constitutions.[6] This dependence accounts for the analogization of judiciaries in the subregion to mere "arm of the executive."[7] Complicating the suboptimal environment is a minimal regard for the rule of law, indicated, for example by a high level of corruption and

[4] See Alter et al., "A New International Human Rights Court for West Africa: The ECOWAS Community Court of Justice," *American Journal of International Law*, 107(4) (October 2013), 737, 752 (examining the transformation of the ECOWAS Community Court of Justice into a new international human rights court for West Africa). Put differently, the article shed light on the "ironic result" of how an international court, established to promote regional economic integration, metamorphosed into a human-right court, specifically "why West African governments, which set up the ECOWAS Court in a way that has allowed persistent flouting of Community economic rules, later delegated to ECOWAS judges remarkably far-reaching human rights jurisdiction." Ibid., pp. 738, 740.

[5] See United States Courts, "Overview—Rule of Law," https://www.uscourts.gov/educational-resources/educational-activities/overview-rule-law#:~:text=Rule%20of%20law%20is%20a,Independently%20adjudicated (defining the rule of law as "a principle under which all persons, institutions, and entities are accountable to laws that are: publicly promulgated, equally enforced, independently adjudicated, [...], consistent with international human rights principles").

[6] Adedamola Adeosun, Measuring the Quality of the International Judiciary: The ECOWAS Community Court of Justice. Ph.D. Dissertation, School of Law (London, UK: Open University, May 2023), 202, https://oro.open.ac.uk/86967/1/Measuring%20the%20Quality%20of%20the%20International%20Judiciary%20PDF.pdf.

[7] Alter et al., note 4, p. 763.

abuse of political powers that cuts across all branches of the government, including the judiciary itself.[8]

The CCJ is one of nine regional courts in the world, and one of several judicial tribunals affiliated to a customs union (see Table 8.1). Although, as we see shortly, its jurisdiction encompasses human rights, the CCJ is not a specialized human-right court in the sense, for example, of the African Court of Human and Peoples' Rights, the European Court of Human Rights, or the Inter-American Court of Human Rights. In addition to this introduction and a conclusion, the ensuing discussion comprises two main sections: the history and evolution of the CCJ, and the degree of its amenability as a tool for the application of human rights in Nigeria's external relations in the age of Buhari and his successors, with a view to improving that amenability. The extendedness of the discussion in this chapter speaks to its importance, matched against the preceding four chapters and co-methods. An appendix on key dates in CCJ history seals the conversation.

History and Evolution of the CCJ

The humanitarian interventions in Liberia and Sierra Leone, beginning in the late 1980s, marked key stages in the history and evolution of ECOWAS with ramifications for the CCJ and its place in a projected human-right policy for Nigeria post-Buhari. The interventions unearthed gaps in the architecture of ECOWAS's legal instruments that left room for broader overhaul of the Community.[9] As well, they marked a departure in the balance between national sovereignty (à la noninterference) and more altruistic goals, one in the direction of altruistic goals that, overtime, morphed into "broader conception of regional conflict prevention," including "constitutional transitions of power, good governance, and human rights."[10]

It was in the light of these revelations that, in 1991, ECOWAS set up a Committee of Eminent Persons to take stock of the progress of the economic union's journey toward economic cooperation and integration in the subregion and make appropriate recommendations for

[8] Adeosun, note 6, pp. 201–202.

[9] Alter et al., note 4, p. 771.

[10] Ibid.

Table 8.1 Juxtaposing the CCJ with co-regional courts in the world

Item No.	*Court name*	*Seat*	*Date established*	*Is it affiliated to a customs union?*	*Special features*
Africa					
1.	African Court of Human and Peoples' Rights	Arusha, Tanzania	2010, but first judges were appointed in 2006	No	Differentiated from the African Commission on Human and Peoples' Rights, a quasi-judicial body[11]
2.	East African Court of Justice	Arusha, Tanzania	2001	Yes	Affiliated to the East African Community[12]
3.	ECOWAS Community Court of Justice	Abuja, Nigeria	2001	Yes	Affiliated to ECOWAS
Asia: None					
Europe					
4.	European Court of Human Rights	Strasbourg, France	1959	Yes	Affiliated to the Council of Europe, and governed by the European Convention on Human Rights. Full-time court since 1981

(continued)

[11] For a statement on the distinction between the two human-right institutions, see note 146 and accompanying text below.

[12] For more on this court, see note 147 and accompanying text below.

Table 8.1 (continued)

Item No.	*Court name*	*Seat*	*Date established*	*Is it affiliated to a customs union?*	*Special features*
5.	Court of Justice of the European Union (CJEU)	Luxembourg City, Luxembourg	1952	No	Comprises two Courts: Court of Justice, and General Court[13]
6.	European Free Trade Agreement Court	Luxembourg City, Luxembourg	1994	Yes	Affiliated to the European Free Trade Association, made up of Iceland, Liechtenstein, Norway, and Switzerland
The Americas (North and South America)					
7.	Caribbean Court of Justice	Port of Spain, Trinidad and Tobago	2001	No	Hybrid tribunal: municipal, and international courts
8.	Central American Court of Justice	Managua, Nicaragua	1991	No	Settles disputes among its four member-states: Guatemala, Honduras, El Salvador, and Nicaragua. Incarnation of the tribunal existed from 1907 to 1918
9.	Inter-American Court of Human Rights	San José, Costa Rica	1979	Yes	Affiliated to the Organization of American States, and governed by the American Convention on Human Rights

[13] As a Court of Justice, the CJEU handles requests for preliminary rulings from national courts, as well as certain actions for annulment and appeals. As a General Court, the CJEU rules on actions for annulment brought by individuals, companies, and, in some cases, EU governments. In practice, this means matters like agriculture, competition law, trade, and trademarks. European Union, "CJEU Court of Justice of the European Union (CJEU)," https://european-union.europa.eu/institutions-law-budget/institutions-and-bodies/search-all-eu-institutions-and-bodies/court-justice-european-union-cjeu_en.

improvement.[14] The committee was chaired by General Yakubu Gowon of Nigeria, Head of State of Nigeria at the time ECOWAS was created in 1975 and one of the prime movers of the economic union.[15] The committee put equal stress on security and economic issues; it defined security broadly to include peace and stability within states in the context of a new wave of democracy across the world, marked by the mainstreaming of human rights in many areas of human endeavor, including economic cooperation and integration.[16] This reassessment and stocktaking coincided with the decision of ECOWAS member-states "to put security issues on a firmer legal footing."[17]

The net result was that vis-à-vis the 1975 treaty, which lacked any human-right language, the 1993 Revised Treaty, published in the wake of the Eminent Persons' Committee review and mirroring its recommendations, incorporated such language in good measure. In addition to "recognition, promotion and protection of human and peoples' rights, in accordance with the provisions of the African Charter on Human and Peoples' Rights,"[18] the revised treaty also included human-right-oriented values like "accountability, economic and social justice and popular participation in development,"[19] as well as promoting and consolidating democracy in each member-state, consistent with the Declaration of Political Principles in July 1991, among the "fundamental principles"

[14] See ibid.

[15] See, for example, "Yakubu Gowon and Ecowas's Restoration," *This Day* (Lagos) (February 28, 2024), https://www.thisdaylive.com/index.php/2024/02/28/yakubu-gowon-and-ecowas-restoration; and Jerry Fisayo-Bambi, "Nigeria's Yakubu Gowon, the Last Living Founding Father of ECOWAS Calls for Its Rescue," *Africa News* (February 22, 2024), https://www.africanews.com/2024/02/22/nigerias-yakubu-gowon-last-living-founding-father-of-ecowas-calls-for-its-rescue/.

[16] Alter et al., note 4, p. 771; and Frans Viljoen, *International Human Rights Law in Africa*, 2nd Ed. (New York and London: Oxford University Press, 2012), 482 (positing that "as the winds of democracy swept authoritarianism and militarism from the continent in a post-Cold War world, [. . .] human rights became mainstreamed into all forms of subregional cooperation"). Following the transmutation of the OAU in 2001 into the African Union, numerous organizations emerged in the region that built their missions on human rights. These include the Pan African Parliament, and the African Peer Review Mechanism of the New Partnership for Africa's Development, among others. Ibid. (abstract).

[17] Alter et al., note 4, p. 771.

[18] ECOWAS Revised Treaty, note 3, art. 4(g).

[19] Ibid., art. 4(h).

ECOWAS member-states sought to achieve in their pursuit of subregional economic cooperation and integration.[20] Individually and collectively, these developments welled up to the CCJ's acquirement of jurisdiction over human rights by 2005.

The CCJ threw its judicial doors open for business on January 30, 2001, when its first seven judges were sworn-in at Bamako, Mali, by Alpha Oumar Konaré,[21] then President of Mali and ECOWAS Chairperson. As of 2020, the CCJ delivered 261 judgments out of a total of 496 cases filed before the Court since 2003.[22] A breakdown of its accomplishments shows that within the seventeen-year period, the Court held 1102 sessions, delivered 261 rulings, issued 32 orders and four advisory opinions, as well as rendered 19 decisions on applications for judgment revision out of the 35 applications on its docket.[23]

Scholars like Karen J. Alter and her colleagues praised the jurisprudence of the CCJ, rich in human rights, as "active and bold."[24] It is an assessment that other followers of ECOWAS events share. These include the organizers of the Global Freedom of Expression competition at Columbia University who, in 2022, awarded the Court the prize of "significant legal ruling" for its decision in *Amnesty International & 7 Others v. The*

[20] Ibid., art. 4(j).

[21] Community Court of Justice, "Membership of the Court," http://www.courtecowas.org/members-of-the-court/. The Court swore-in these judges in Mali, rather than Abuja, because, as of this date, as the story goes, ECOWAS leaders were still consulting regarding location of the seat of the Court. Pan-African News Agency (Dakar), "West Africa: Konare to Swear in ECOWAS Judges" (January 29, 2001), https://allafrica.com/stories/200101290396.html. The Court was initially located in Lagos, but moved to its permanent headquarters in Abuja after Nigeria was designated in 2002 as the host country of the Court. Alter et al., note 4, p. 748, n.69. The seven judges sworn in were: Alfred Anthony Benin (Ghana, Vice President from 2007 to 2009), Awa Nana Daboya (Togo), Hansine N. Donli (Nigeria, President from 2001 to 2007), Amina Mallé Sanogo (Mali, President from 2007 to 2009), Soumana Dirarou Sidibé (Niger, Vice President from 2004 to 2007), El Hadj Mansour Tall (Senegal, Vice President from 2001 to 2004), and Barthelemy Toé (Burkina Faso). Community Court of Justice, "Judges 2001–2009," http://www.courtecowas.org/judges-2001-2009-2/.

[22] See Community Court of Justice, "ECOWAS Court Issues 2020 Judicial Statistics," http://www.courtecowas.org/2021/01/21/ecowas-court-issues-2020-judicial-statistics/.

[23] Ibid.

[24] Alter et al., note 4, p. 737. See also Adeosun, note 6, p. 108 (stating that since its creation, the CCJ "has positioned itself as a dominant catalyst for the development of legal order in the West African [sub]region, especially" in human rights).

Togolese Republic.[25] The decision involved a shutdown of the Internet by the Togolese government during a protest in the country in September 2017.[26] In extending this honor, these competition organizers reasoned that, in the light of the rise of Internet shutdowns by certain governments across the globe, the ruling created a useful binding precedent in West Africa, particularly ECOWAS member-states.[27]

A slate of legal frameworks has been adopted related to the work of the CCJ. One conceivable way, therefore, to approach this discussion on the history and evolution of the CCJ, the one chosen here, is to analyze the provisions of these documents and related materials. In chronological order, these instruments are eight-fold: the treaty of 1975 setting up ECOWAS, the Protocol on the CCJ of 1991, ECOWAS's revised treaty of 1993, First Supplement to the 1991 Protocol adopted in 2005, Second Supplement to the 1991 Protocol adopted in 2006, institutional reforms since 2006, overview of a sample of key CCJ judgments, and a summation statement that recapitulates the kernel of the presentation in this section. We take these legal sources in turn (Table 8.2).

ECOWAS's 1975 Treaty

This treaty laid the foundation stone for the human-right jurisdiction of the CCJ. But this is not a clearcut proposition. Here is why. The treaty created a Tribunal of the Community,[28] mandated to "ensure

[25] Community Court of Justice, *Amnesty International and 7 Others v. the Togolese Republic*, Suit No. ECW/CCJ/APP/61/18, Judgment No. ECW/CCJ/JUD/09/20 (June 25, 2020), https://www.eods.eu/elex/uploads/files/642e998c687ef-JUD-ECW-CCJ-JUD-09-20-Amnesty-Int.-TOGO-7-ORS-vs.-REP.-OF-TOGO-25_06_20-vA.pdf.

[26] Ibid. (in the case, the complainants, Amnesty International and seven other parties, including a journalist-activist and blogger, alleged that, following a protest in the country related to presidential term limits, the Togolese government shut down the Internet, thereby impeding the right to free expression, contrary to the African Charter on Human and Peoples' Rights as well as international human-right instruments like the ICCPR Togo is a state party of); and Columbia University, Global Freedom of Expression, "Global Freedom of Expression Prize Winners 2022: Awards Ceremony," https://globalfreedomofexpression.columbia.edu/prizewinners2022/.

[27] See Global Freedom of Expression Prize Winners 2022, note 26.

[28] Economic Community of West African States (ECOWAS), Treaty of the Economic Community of West African States (ECOWAS) (May 28, 1975) [hereinafter ECOWAS 1975 Treaty], art. 4(d), https://www.refworld.org/legal/constinstr/ecowas/1975/en/63881. See also art. 11(1).

Table 8.2 The CCJ's transition to a human-right court: constituting legal instruments, salient provisions, and related matters

Item No.	*Legal instrument or source*	*Date*	*Salient provisions and related matters on the road to human-right jurisprudence*
1.	ECOWAS Treaty	1975	The Treaty created a Tribunal of the Community, something in the mold of an ad hoc court
2.	Protocol on the Community Court of Justice	1991	The Protocol is integral to the ECOWAS Treaty of 1975. This document made the CCJ a permanent judicial tribunal, and established it as "the principal legal organ of" ECOWAS charged with the responsibility of "ensur[ing] the observance of law and justice in the interpretation and application of the [1975] Treaty"
3.	ECOWAS Revised Treaty	1993	This Treaty reaffirmed the status of the CCJ as a permanent court, as well as created it, among others, as a key institution of ECOWAS. Building on the Protocol of 1991, it also formally established the Court and made its judgment binding on member-states, institutions of the Community, as well as on individuals and corporate bodies. Setting the stage for what would come in 2005, this legal instrument embodied human-right values, dressed up as fundamental principles, that ECOWAS member-states committed themselves to

Item No.	*Legal instrument or source*	*Date*	*Salient provisions and related matters on the road to human-right jurisprudence*
4.	First Supplementary Protocol	2005	First of two amendments to the 1991 Protocol on the CCJ, notable for expanding the mandate of the Court into human rights, specifically its provision that the Court has jurisdiction over "violation[s] of human rights that occur in any Member State" (i.e., individuals and NGOs may bypass national courts and seek remedies directly from the CCJ). The expansion in the Court's jurisdiction came in the wake of *Olajide Afolabi v. Federal Republic of Nigeria* (2004) where the Court pled lack of jurisdiction
5.	Second Supplementary Protocol	2006	Through this instrument, ECOWAS member-states enhanced the supranational character of the customs union by making Community protocols directly applicable in national legal orders without the need for country-to-country ratifications. The document comprised seven paragraphs embodied in three articles. The changes relate to a proposed restructuring of the Court, including justifications contained in the preambles and the precise format of those changes, bearing on composite matters like the makeup of the Court, qualifications for judges, the role of the Judicial Council in the selection of judge, including the composition of the Council, as well as the term of office of judges, and procedure to be followed when a judge resigns. At this point the composition of the Court remained unchanged at seven members
6.	Post-2006 Reforms	Since 2007	Proposals to reduce the size of the Court to five members on efficiency grounds and related matters

the observance of law and justice in the interpretation of the provisions of" the treaty, as well as "the responsibility of settling such disputes as may be referred to it in accordance with Article 56 of" the treaty.[29] Article 56 laid down procedures for settling disputes in ECOWAS.[30] The Treaty specified that "[t]he composition, competence, statutes, and other matters relating to the Tribunal shall be prescribed by the" AHSG of the economic union.[31] The Tribunal created here has the look of an ad hoc court, compared to the permanent tribunal 16 years down the line under the Protocol of the CCJ next below.

Protocol on the Community Court of Justice

Under this legal instrument, the CCJ evolved into a permanent tribunal.[32] It was established as "the principal legal organ of" ECOWAS charged with the responsibility of "ensur[ing] the observance of law and justice in the interpretation and application of the [1975] Treaty."[33] The Protocol was executed by the AHSG in Abuja on July 6, 1991,[34] but did not enter into force until November 1996, by which date the ratification by seven member states needed to bring it into effect took place.[35] The Protocol is annexed to the treaty and is integrated into it.[36] Many of the instrument's provisions track those of the Statute of the International

[29] Ibid., art. 11(1).

[30] Ibid., art. 56 (providing that "[a]ny dispute that may arise among the Member States regarding the interpretation or application of this Treaty shall be amicably settled by direct agreement," failing which "the matter may be referred to the Tribunal of the Community by a party to such disputes and the decision of the Tribunal shall be final").

[31] Ibid., art. 11(2).

[32] See Community Court of Justice—ECOWAS, "About Us," http://www.courtecowas.org/site2012/index.php?option=com_content&view=article&id=2&Itemid=5.

[33] Community Court of Justice, Protocol A/P..l/7/91 on the Community Court of Justice (July 6, 1991), preamble [hereinafter Protocol on the CCJ], http://www.courtecowas.org/wp-content/uploads/2018/11/Protocol_AP1791_ENG.pdf.

[34] See Protocol on the CCJ. The document comprised a set of four preambles and 34 articles dealing with an assortment of subject matters, some of them covered in the following discussion inside the text, from definitions (Chapter 1) to entry into force (Chapter 34). Ibid.

[35] Alter et al., note 4, p. 747.

[36] See Protocol on the CCJ, note 33, art. 34(3) ("The Protocol is annexed to the Treaty and shall form an integral part thereof").

Court of Justice, integral to the UN Charter, and adopted by the global organization in 1945.[37]

First the preambles. Key insights from the material that we consider instructive are references to Article 11 and Article 4(e) of the 1975 Treaty, and a statement regarding "the essential role" of the CCJ. Article 11 of the document refers to the Tribunal of the Community.[38] Article 4(e) of the Treaty is a proverbial "necessary and proper" clause, drawing from the playbook of US constitutionalism, permitting the creation of "such other Commissions or bodies as may be established by the [AHSG] or are established or provided for by this Treaty."[39] Coming to "essential role," the preamble indicated the "aware[ness]" of the AHSG, the contracting parties, to the effect that that role "is to ensure the observance of law and justice in the interpretation and application of the Treaty" and related legal documents, including "responsibility for settling such disputes as may be referred to it in accordance with the provisions of Article 56 of the Treaty and disputes between States and the Institutions of the Community."[40]

Next, the main document. For us, the instrument embodies several instructive provisions. First is the set aside, as indicated before, of the CCJ as "the principal legal organ of the Community."[41] Another relates

[37] See International Court of Justice, Statute of the International Court of Justice (1945), https://www.icj-cij.org/statute. The statute comprises 70 articles, 69 of which are divided into 5 chapters as follows: Chapter I, Organization of the Court (Articles 2–33), Chapter II, Competence of the Court (Articles 34–38), Chapter III, Procedure (Articles 39–64); Chapter IV, Advisory Opinions (Articles 65–68); and Chapter V, Amendment (Articles 69–70). Ibid. One key provision is Article 38(1) which lists four sources that the court may apply to decide a case, namely: treaties, customary international law, general principles of law, and judicial decisions and academic writing as a subsidiary source. See ibid., art. 38(1). These sources are qualified by Article 59 which states that the ICJ's decisions are binding only to the parties in that case, and Art. 38(2) which allows the court to decide a case *ex aequo et bono* [translatable into based on "what is fair and good" or equity], if the parties agree to use this arrangement. For a text of the UN Charter, see Charter of the United Nations, 59 Stat. 1031, T.S. 993, 3 Bevans 1153 (1945), https://www.un.org/en/about-us/un-charter, specifically Chapter XIV, integrating Art. 38.

[38] ECOWAS 1975 Treaty, note 28, art. 11(1).

[39] ECOWAS 1975 Treaty, note 28, art. 4(e). See also ibid., art. 4(2) (specifying that "[t]he institutions of the Community shall perform the functions and act within the limits of the powers conferred upon them by or under this Treaty and by Protocols thereto").

[40] Protocol on the CCJ, note 33, preamble.

[41] Ibid., art. 2.

to composition: The Court "shall be composed of independent judges selected and appointed by the [AHSG] from nationals of the Member States who are persons of high moral character, and possess the qualification required in their respective countries for appointment to the highest judicial officers, or are jurisconsults of recognized competence in international law."[42] It shall comprise seven judges, "no two of whom may be nationals of the same State."[43] It must be headed by a President, assisted by a Vice President, that its judges elect "from among their number who shall serve in that capacity for a term of three years."[44] The judges must be 40–60 years old, and no judge over 65 is eligible for reappointment.[45] The judges serve a five-year term in office and may be eligible for reappointment for just one other five-year term.[46] They may not "exercise any political or administrative function or engage in any other occupation of a professional nature."[47] During their time in office, judges "enjoy privileges and immunities identical to those enjoyed by diplomatic missions and diplomatic agents in the territory of Member States, as well as those normally accorded to international courts and the members of such courts."[48] These include freedom from "prosecution or arrest for acts carried out or statements made in the exercise of their functions."[49]

With respect to jurisdiction, the Court is required to "ensure the observance of law and of the principles of equity in the interpretation and application of the provisions of the" 1975 Treaty,[50] including disputes under Article 56 of the treaty relating to the procedures for settling disputes, brought by member-states or the Authority or other institutions of the Community pertaining to interpretation or application of

[42] Ibid., art. 3(1). A jurisconsult is a master of jurisprudence, especially in the international law related to regional integration. US Legal, "Jurisconsult Law and Legal Definition," https://definitions.uslegal.com/j/jurisconsult/.

[43] Protocol on the CCJ, note 33, art. 3(2).

[44] Ibid., art. 3(2).

[45] Ibid., art. 3(7).

[46] Ibid., art. 4(1).

[47] Ibid., art. 4(11).

[48] Ibid., art. 6(1).

[49] Ibid., art. 6(2).

[50] Protocol on the CCJ, note 33, art. 9(1).

the treaty.[51] To this effect, on behalf of its nationals, a member-state may bring action "against another Member State or Institution of the Community, relating to the interpretation and application of the provisions of the Treaty, after attempts to settle the dispute amicably have failed."[52]

These are powers within the domain of its contentious jurisdiction.[53] In addition, the Court is empowered to issue advisory opinions.[54] An advisory jurisdiction exists when the judicial tribunal involved renders an opinion "at the request of the government or an interested party indicating how the court would rule on a matter should adversary litigation develop."[55] In other words, such an opinion is "an interpretation of the law without binding effect."[56] An advisory jurisdiction supplements and completes a contentious jurisdiction. The Protocol specifies that "[t]he Court may, at the request of the Authority, Council, one or more Member States, or the Executive Secretary, and any other institution of the Community, express, in an advisory capacity, a legal opinion on questions of the Treaty."[57] In addition, the CCJ has arbitral or arbitrational jurisdiction. As we see below in the discussion on the Supplementary Protocol promulgated in 2005, pending the establishment of the Arbitration Tribunal for the Community, the Court is empowered to act as arbitrator.

[51] Ibid., art. 9(2).

[52] Ibid., art. 9(3).

[53] As its name implied, a contentious jurisdiction is the authority of a court to decide a case before it limited to matters in controversy between the parties, as opposed to uncontested matters. "Definitions of Contentious Jurisdiction," *World Law Dictionary*, https://dictionary.translegal.com/en/contentious-jurisdiction/noun. The bulk of the CCJ's work belongs in this category.

[54] See Protocol on the CCJ, note 33, art. 10(1)–(4) ("Advisory Opinion").

[55] "Advisory Opinion," *Black's Law Dictionary*, 6th Ed. (Eagan, MN: West Publishing, 1991), 35.

[56] Ibid.

[57] Protocol on the CCJ, note 33, art. 10(1). Such a capacity is necessary to give the Court a role, in concert with co-institutions in ECOWAS, in nipping disputes and related conflicts in the bud before they occur, thereby facilitating its judicial mandate to interpret provisions of the Treaty. See Community Court of Justice, "Mandate and Jurisdiction," http://www.courtecowas.org/mandate-and-jurisdiction-2/ (referencing art. 10 of the Protocol).

The Protocol also permits the CCJ to write up and apply its own rules of procedure.[58] ECOWAS is mandated to "appoint and provide the Court with the necessary officers and officials to enable it carry out its functions."[59] Under the Protocol, the ASHG determines "the remuneration, allowances and all other benefits of the" CCJ,[60] but operational expenses of the Court are charged to the budget of the Executive Secretariat of the Community,"[61] subsequently renamed Executive Commission.

The AHSG determines the seat of the Court,[62] but "where circumstances or facts of the case so demand, the Court may decide to sit in the territory of another Member State."[63] In adjudicating the cases that come before it, the Court must be guided by the Treaty and its rules of procedure, but it may also apply, where "necessary, the body of laws

[58] Protocol on the CCJ, note 33, art. 32. These are rules of order, regulations of an institution, in this case a court, which the institution in question uses to facilitate the conduct of its business. "Rules of Procedure: Definition and Legal Meaning," *Black's Law Dictionary*, 2nd Ed., https://thelawdictionary.org/rules-of-procedure/. Proceedings before the CCJ can be oral or written. Oral proceedings comprise the hearing of parties, agents, witnesses, experts, advocates, and counsel. Written proceedings comprise materials like applications entered in the Court, notification of the application, defense, reply or counter-statement, rejoinder and related supporting briefs or documents. See Franca Ofor, "Presentation on [the] Community Court of Justice, ECOWAS," Office of the UN High Commissioner for Human Rights, Strasbourg. Until her retirement in October 2020, Ofor was a Principal Legal Research Officer at the CCJ. See Community Court of Justice, "Pioneer Staff of ECOWAS Court Praised for Their Role in Its History and Transformation" (October 26, 2020), http://www.courtecowas.org/2020/10/26/pioneer-staff-of-ecowas-court-praised-for-their-role-in-its-history-and-transformation/. In response to court closure and other businesses induced by the COVID-19 pandemic, in 2020, the CCJ established an electronic case management system, including the introduction of a new electronic case filing platform and the conduct of virtual court sessions. The Court's President, Edward Amoako Asante of Ghana, explained that digitization aligns the Court's case management system with international best practices, enables remote case filing, and reduces the travelling cost for litigants to the seat of the Court. News Agency of Nigeria, "ECOWAS Court Begins Full Digital Operations January 2021," *World Stage* (November 25, 2020), worldstagenews.com. While a notable improvement, in the view of the researcher Adedamola Adeosun, digitizing the Court's management did not remove the challenges of establishing a fully functioning digital library and maintaining a world-class website, which remain suboptimal. Adeosun, note 6, p. 111.

[59] Protocol on the CCJ, note 33, art. 29(3).

[60] Ibid., art. 28.

[61] Ibid., art. 30.

[62] Ibid., art. 26(1).

[63] Ibid., art. 26(2).

as contained in Article 38 of the Statute of the International Court of Justice."[64] It must hear evidence and render its judgment in public but may also "sit in camera at the request of one of the parties or for reasons which only the Court may determine."[65] Decisions of the Court must "be read in open court and shall state the reasons on which they are based."[66]

Subject to certain limitations, including those pertaining to revision of a prior judgment, decisions of the Court are "final and immediately enforceable."[67] Judgments of the Court are subject to revision but only under certain exceptional circumstances.[68] An application for revision "may be made only when it is based upon the discovery of some fact of such a nature as to be a decisive factor, which fact was, when the decision was given, unknown to the Court and also to the party [seeking] revision, provided always that such ignorance was not due to negligence."[69] Even so, "[t]he proceedings for revision shall be opened by a decision of the Court expressly recording the existence of the new fact, recognizing that it has such a character as to lay the case open to revision and declaring the application admissible on this ground[,]"[70] and the Court "may require prior compliance with the terms of the decision before it admits proceedings in revision."[71] At any rate, the decision of the Court is binding only "between the parties and in respect of that particular case,"[72] and no revision application will be entertained by the Court if made "after five years from the date of [that] decision."[73]

Member-states and institutions of the Community are "mandated to take immediately all necessary measures to ensure execution of the"

[64] Ibid., art. 19(1). Regarding Article 38 of the Statute of the International Court of Justice, see note 37.

[65] Protocol on the CCJ, note 33, art. 14(3).

[66] Ibid., art. 19(2).

[67] Protocol on the CCJ, note 33, art. 19(2).

[68] See Protocol on the CCJ, note 33, art. 25(1)–(5).

[69] Ibid., art. 25(1).

[70] Ibid., art. 25(2).

[71] Ibid., art. 25(3).

[72] Ibid., art. 25(5).

[73] Ibid., art. 25(4).

Court's decision.[74] They should also "refrain from any action likely to aggravate or militate against" resolution of an ongoing dispute before the Court.[75] Still on remedies, in cases before it, the Court may, in its discretion and sound judgment, "order any provisional measures or issue any provisional instructions which it may consider necessary or desirable."[76] Also, a member-state which believes that it has an interest "that may be affected by the subject matter of a dispute before the Court, [...]" may make an application for permission to intervene to the Court.[77]

The Revised Treaty of 1993

This treaty reaffirmed the status of the CCJ as a permanent court.[78] Solidifying the permanence, it created the CCJ, among others, as a key institution of ECOWAS.[79] While leaving out its composition and related details as issues for another day to be spelled out in a future protocol,[80] the treaty provided that the Court shall carry out functions assigned to it independently of the member-states and the institutions of the community,[81] and that its judgment shall be binding on member-states and institutions of the Community, as well as on individuals and corporate bodies.[82] Along with the Protocol of 1991, this Treaty gave the Court original and final jurisdiction, in other words, making its judgments not subject to appeal.[83] The treaty also created an Arbitration Tribunal of

[74] Ibid., art. 22(3).

[75] Ibid., art. 22(2).

[76] Protocol on the CCJ, note 33, art. 20.

[77] Ibid., art. 21.

[78] ECOWAS Revised Treaty, note 3, art. 15(1).

[79] Ibid., art. 6(1)(e). See also ibid., art. 6(2) (specifying that these institutions "shall perform their functions and act within the limits of the powers conferred on them by this Treaty and by the Protocols relating thereto").

[80] Ibid., art. 15(2).

[81] Ibid., art. 15(3).

[82] Ibid., art. 15(4).

[83] Ibid., art. 76; and Protocol on the CCJ, note 33, art. 19.

the Community,[84] along with specification to the effect that its status, composition and related matters will be set out in a future protocol.[85]

Other notable provisions of the treaty include the one relating to judicial and legal matters,[86] involving an undertaking by member-states "to co-operate in judicial and legal matters with a view to harmonizing their judicial and legal systems"[87]; and another relating to settlement of disputes. Under this latter, without prejudice to the provisions of the treaty and relevant protocols, "[a]ny dispute regarding the interpretation or the application of the provisions of [the] Treaty shall be amicably settled through direct agreement,"[88] failing which, "either party or any other Member State or the Authority may refer the matter to the [CCJ] whose decision shall be final and shall not be subject to appeal."[89] Consistent with the new wave of democracy across the world throwing its effects of multipartyism and human rights across the world, as indicated earlier in this chapter, this document bore several values centered on human rights that ECOWAS member-states committed themselves to, including recognizing and promoting human and peoples' rights, in accordance with the provisions of the African Charter on Human and Peoples' Rights; integrating the values of accountability, socioeconomic justice, and popular participation into development; as well as promoting and consolidating democracy in each member-state, consistent with the Declaration of Political Principles of 1991.[90]

The Supplementary Protocol of 2005

This legal instrument is notable for expanding the mandate of the Court into human rights, specifically for embedding a provision that the Court has jurisdiction over "violation[s] of human rights that occur in

[84] ECOWAS Revised Treaty, note 3, art. 16(1).

[85] Ibid., art. 16(2).

[86] See ECOWAS Revised Treaty, note 3, art. 7(1)–(2), including art. 7(2), indicating that the modalities for implementation of this provision are to be worked out in a future protocol.

[87] Ibid., art. 7(1).

[88] Ibid., 76(1).

[89] Ibid., 76(2).

[90] See notes 18–20 and accompanying texts.

any Member State,"[91] meaning that individuals and NGOs may bypass national courts and seek remedies directly from the CCJ. The instrument is the first of two sets of amendments to the 1991 Protocol on the CCJ. Adopted at Accra, Ghana, on January 19, 2005, by AHSG, this protocol followed a memorandum by the CCJ to the Council of Ministers (which body advises the AHSG).[92] The instrument amended the preambles and other specified provisions of the English version of the 1991 Protocol.[93] A notable statement from the preambles revolves around a proclaimed desire by the AHSG "to take all necessary measures to ensure smooth operations of the Court and guarantee effective implementation of its decisions."[94]

Next to the main document, we have already referred to the provision of the document to the effect that the CCJ has jurisdiction over "violation[s] of human rights that occur in any Member State,"[95] in practical terms, permitting individuals and NGOs to bypass national courts and seek remedies directly from the CCJ. This amendment broadened the competence of the Court beyond the more limited areas of jurisdiction specified in the 1991 Protocol on the CCJ. From interpreting and applying the ECOWAS treaty, at this point its authority to hear and resolve disputes lengthened to include matters related to the legality of subsidiary legal instruments adopted by ECOWAS, such as regulations, directives, and decisions; failure of member-states to honor their obligations under the Treaty, conventions, protocols, regulations, directives, and decisions of ECOWAS; action for damages against a community institution or official of the community for any action or omission in the exercise

[91] ECOWAS, Supplementary Protocol A/SP.1/01/05, Amending the Preamble and Articles 1,2,9, and 30 of Protocol A/P.1/7/91, Relating to the Community Court of Justice and Article 4, Paragraph 1, of the English Version of the Said Protocol (January 19, 2005), art. 3(4) [hereinafter ECOWAS Supplementary Protocol A/SP.1/01/05], http://www.courtecowas.org/wp-content/uploads/2018/11/Supplementary_Protocol_ASP.10105_ENG.pdf.

[92] The document comprised preambles (of ten items) and 12 articles, all but one uncaptioned. Ibid.

[93] See ibid. (caption of document).

[94] Ibid.

[95] Ibid., note 91.

of official functions; and power to adjudicate allegations of human-right violations that occur in any member-state.[96]

The greenlight for individuals and NGOs to file directly with the Court came in the wake of *Olajide Afolabi v. Nigeria*.[97] There, the Court gave a strict construction of the 1991 Protocol on the CCJ that denied direct access to private litigants.[98] In the case, Olajide Afolabi, a Nigerian trader entered into a contract to purchase goods in Benin, an ECOWAS member-state, but could not consummate the transaction because the Nigeria government unilaterally closed the border between the two countries.[99] Afolabi filed suit with the CCJ, alleging that the border closure violated the right to free movement of persons and goods.[100]

The Court ruled that it lacked the jurisdiction to hear the case,[101] even though it acknowledged that the complaint raised "a serious claim touching on free movement and free movement of goods."[102] It reasoned that ruling otherwise will be predicated on a ECOWAS legal instrument that expressly grant the Court jurisdiction; in other words, only ECOWAS member-states can authorize the Court to review complaints from private entities.[103] Nonetheless, the complainant challenged an issue of "blatant noncompliance with ECOWAS free-movement rules,"[104] and the case paradigmatically illustrated "the serious physical and legal barriers" importers, exporters, and other traders face in West Africa.[105] Little wonder that in its wake, "ECOWAS judges, civil society groups, and ECOWAS officials lobbied [ECOWAS] member states to expand the Court's jurisdiction."[106]

[96] Ibid.

[97] Community Court of Justice, *Olajide Afolabi v. Nigeria*, ECW/CJ/JUD/01/04 (April 27, 2004), *reprinted* in *African Human Rights Case Law Analyzer*, https://caselaw.ihrda.org/en/entity/6dp0llnd6hr82kc18ylbjiqkt9?page=6.

[98] See Alter et al., note 4, p. 749.

[99] *Olajide Afolabi v. Nigeria*, note 97.

[100] Ibid.

[101] Ibid.

[102] Ibid., ¶ 55.

[103] *Olajide Afolabi v. Nigeria*, note 97.

[104] Alter et al., note 4, p. 748.

[105] Ibid., p. 749.

[106] Ibid., p. 748.

Less than nine months after the judgment, ECOWAS adopted this first amendment of the 1991 Protocol on the CCJ. In what seemed like an overrule of *Afolabi*, the amendment permits individuals to directly access the Court with allegations of human-right abuses, provided the application is not anonymous or made while the same matter is pending before another international court.[107] However, parties can institute action even when a suit is pending in a domestic court in the member-state, an occurrence some scholars state may encourage forum shopping by aggrieved parties.[108] This challenge of a border closure imposed by Nigerian authorities was the Court's first case. The Court's dismissing the case catalyzed "a campaign by bar associations, NGOs, Community officials, and ECOWAS judges, which resulted in the 2005 Protocol that gives the Court broad human rights jurisdiction."[109]

Two events leading to the *Afolabi* case, all of which took place in 2001, need to be mentioned here. Individually and collectively, these developments lent human rights advocates "a legal foothold when they later lobbied to give the Court a human rights jurisdiction."[110] The first, referenced before in Chapter 6 on ECOWAS within the context of peace-keeping, was the adoption of the Protocol on Democracy and Good Governance, aimed at deterring military coups and related unconstitutional changes of government.[111] The Protocol "wove multiple references to human rights into the fabric of an ambitious regional effort to promote democracy, accountability, transparency, and the rule of law."[112] With particular reference to the CCJ, it featured a clause which specified that the jurisdiction of the Court "shall be reviewed so as to give the Court the power to hear, *inter alia*, cases relating to violations of human rights, after all attempts to resolve the matter at the national level have failed."[113]

[107] ECOWAS Supplementary Protocol A/SP.1/01/05, note 91, art. 4(d)(i)–(ii).

[108] Adeosun, note 6, p. 94.

[109] Alter et al., note 4, p. 740.

[110] Ibid., p. 745.

[111] Economic Commission of West African States, *Protocol A/SP1/12/01 on Democracy and Good Governance: Supplementary to the Protocol Relating to the Mechanism for Conflict Prevention, Management, Resolution, Peacekeeping and Security* (Dakar, Senegal: ECOWAS, December 2001), https://www.eisa.org/pdf/ecowas2001protocol.pdf. See also Chapter 6, note 118.

[112] Alter et al., note 4, p. 745.

[113] Ibid.

The second event was the formation by NGOs of the West African Human Rights Forum, an umbrella organization that gained accreditation from ECOWAS and attempted to influence Community policymaking. As part of the overhaul emanating from the Revised Treaty of 1993, member-states agreed to broaden public participation in ECOWAS by expanding access for civil society groups. National NGOs were precluded from participating in Community policymaking, but regional civil society groups could be accredited to observe public meetings, make presentations, and circulate documents. These institutional reforms created an incentive for civil society groups to mobilize within ECOWAS and to create regional advocacy bodies. These opportunities for regional mobilization provided an avenue in 2004 for human rights groups to contribute to proposals to expand the Court's jurisdiction. NGO access was also important five years later when the Gambian government, unhappy with Court's rulings against it, proposed curbing its newly-acquired authority to hear human rights cases.[114]

Other notable provisions linked to the Supplementary Protocol of 2005, proverbial icing on the cake to the direct access on allegations of human-right violations for individuals and NGOs, include the specifications that, "[p]ending the establishment of the Arbitration Tribunal provided for under Article 16 of the [1993] Treaty, that the Court shall have the power to act as arbitrator for the purpose of Article 16 of the Treaty,"[115] and that "[a]ny action by or against a Community Institution or any Member of the Community shall be statute barred after three years from the date when the right of action arose."[116] Yet others are that the Court "shall have jurisdiction over any matter provided for in an agreement where the parties provide that the Court shall settle disputes arising from the agreement,"[117] and that the AHSG "shall have the power to grant the Court the power to adjudicate on any specific dispute that it may refer to the Court other than those specified in this Article" [dealing with the CCJ's jurisdiction].[118]

[114] Ibid.

[115] ECOWAS Supplementary Protocol A/SP.1/01/05, note 91, art. 3(5).

[116] Ibid., art. 3(3).

[117] Ibid., art. 3(6).

[118] Ibid., art. 3(8).

Complementing these provisions are two more amendments, one related to implementing judgments of the Court, and the other to the budget. Article 6 of the Supplementary Protocol, embodying a new Article 24, specifies that "[j]udgments of the Court that have financial implications for nationals of Member States or Member States are binding";[119] and that the "execution of [a] decision of the Court shall be in form of a writ of execution" from the Court's Registrar to the member-state involved,[120] subject to enforcement upon verification that the writ is from the Court.[121] To facilitate receipt and processing of execution, every member-state must mark out a competent national authority charged with this task, and notify the Court accordingly.[122] A "writ of execution issued by the Community Court may be suspended only by a decision of the Community Court of Justice."[123]

Next to budgetary matter, Article 8 amended Article 30 of the 1991 Protocol. As changed, the new provision read, somewhat opaquely, that the budget "shall be dealt with in accordance with the relevant provisions of the Revised Treaty."[124] This is in place of the requirement in 1991 that "the operational expenses of the Court [...] be charged to the budget of the Executive Secretariat of the Community." Important, though less momentous than the foregoing, rather than limited to English and French, the official languages of the Court was changed to now include Portuguese.[125]

[119] Ibid., art. 6(1).

[120] ECOWAS Supplementary Protocol A/SP.1/01/05, note 91, art. 6(2).

[121] Ibid., art. 6(3).

[122] Ibid., art. 6(4).

[123] Ibid., art. 6(5).

[124] Ibid., art. 8.

[125] Ibid., art. 9.

The Supplementary Protocol of 2006

Through this instrument, ECOWAS member-states enhanced the supranational character of the customs union by making Community protocols directly applicable in national legal orders without the need for country-to-country ratifications.[126] The instrument is the second of two sets of amendments to the 1991 Protocol on the CCJ. Adopted at Abuja on June 14, 2006, it comprised seven paragraphs embodied in three articles.[127] The changes relate to a proposal for restructuring the Court, including justifications for the restructuring embodied in the preambles as well as the nature of those changes, such as the composition of the Court, qualifications for judges, the role of the Judicial Council in the selection of judge (including the composition of the Council), the term of office of judges, and procedure to be followed when a judge resigns. At this point the size of the Court remained unchanged at seven members.

First the preambles. For us, several statements therein stand out. The first is the reference to directives contained in the final reports of the 53rd and 55th sessions of the Council of Ministers on restructuring the CCJ; the directives provided that the Court "shall be restructured in such a way as to enable the judges devote themselves to their main duties."[128] Another is the statement to the effect that, with the restructuring, "the Court shall be equipped with an organizational chart which will enable it [to] perform its duties optimally, ensure harmonization of tenure with statutory positions in other institutions of the Community and include the position of judge in the general plan for rotating statutory posts among member states."[129]

[126] See Alter et al., note 4, p. 775.

[127] ECOWAS Supplementary Protocol A/SP. 2/06/06, Amending Article 3 Paragraphs 1, 2 and 4, Article 4 Paragraphs 1, 3 and 7 and Article 7 Paragraph 3 of the Protocol on the Community Court of Justice (June 14, 2006) [hereinafter ECOWAS Supplementary Protocol A/SP.2/06/06], https://journal.cfcomlaw.com/wp-content/uploads/2021/10/scan0003.pdf.

[128] Ibid., preamble.

[129] Ibid., preamble.

A third is "[c]onsidering the need to appoint to the CCJ competent judges, who can contribute through the quality of their decisions, to the development of Community Law, capable of consolidating and speeding up the regional integration process."[130] A fourth is "[c]onsidering [...] the need to ensure that the judges of the CCJ are persons of high moral standing upon assumption of duty and to guarantee that this quality is maintained by the judges through their term of office."[131] A fifth relates to "concern[] with providing the [CCJ] with functional organs and suitable human resources."[132] Last but not least is "[d]esirous[ness] of adopting recruitment modalities based on criteria which would allow for selection and appointment of the most suitable persons as judges of the CCJ and to adopt any measure that will enhance the functioning of the court."[133] A trade tying these six-odd preambles is justification of the proposed restructuring of the CCJ. We return to this matter in the next subsection dealing with post-2006 reform measures.

Next to the main text of the document, this discussion focuses on the seven paragraphs (or amendments) embedded in the three articles: paragraphs 1, 2, and 4 of Article 3 of the Protocol (under Art. 2 of the document); paragraphs 1, 3, and 7 of Article 4 of the Protocol (under Art. 3 of the document); and paragraph 3 of Article 7 of the Protocol (under Art. 5 of the document). Article 2 amended Art. 3 of the Protocol of 1991 (dealing with the composition of the Court, qualification for judges, and the role of the Judicial Council related to recruitment of judges) in three pertinent paragraphs.[134] The changes are that: the Court "shall be composed of seven independent judges [...] appointed by the Authority from nations of the states who are persons of high moral character and possess the qualification required in their respective countries for appointment to the highest judicial offices, or are jurisconsults of recognized competence in international law, particularly in areas of Community Law or Regional Integration Law."[135] They must have a total of no less than 20 years of professional experience; members of the Court shall elect a

[130] ECOWAS Supplementary Protocol A/SP.2/06/06, note 127, preamble.

[131] Ibid., preamble.

[132] Ibid., preamble.

[133] Ibid., preamble.

[134] ECOWAS Supplementary Protocol A/SP.2/06/06, note 127, art. 2.

[135] Ibid., art. 2.

President and Vice-President from among their numbers who shall serve in those capacities for renewable terms of two years; and no two members of the Court shall be nationals of the same member-state.[136]

Recruitment relating to the remaining three slots will fall on the Judicial Council of the Community made up of Chief Justices of the Supreme Court of member-states to which posts have not been allocated or the representatives of these Chief Justices.[137] The Council will select the three from member states who do not have judges on the Court, interview those candidates and make recommendations for their appointment to the Authority through the Council of Ministers.[138] More on this Council in the subsection below on the post-2006 reforms of the CCJ.

Article 4 equally amended three paragraphs of Article 4 of the Protocol of 1991 (dealing with terms of office of Court members).[139] The changes are that judges be appointed for a four-year, nonrenewable, term; that a judge whose term expired must remain in office until the appointment and assumption of office of their successor; that the discipline of judges, including questions regarding their inability to perform their duties, whether by reason of physical or mental instability, shall be brought before the Judicial Council of the Community for consideration; and that the composition and modalities for the functioning of the Council in disciplinary matters shall be defined by a decision of the Authority.[140] Article 5 amends paragraph 3 of Article 7 of the 1991 Protocol on the CCJ (dealing with resignation of judges).[141] The changes are to the effect that when a judge resigns from the Court, its President must inform the President of the Executive Commission who then reports to the Chairman of the Judicial Council, who, in turn, recommends a replacement.[142] The new judge serves the unexpired term of his or her predecessor and shall also be a national of the same country.[143]

136 Ibid.

137 Ibid.

138 Ibid.

139 ECOWAS Supplementary Protocol A/SP.2/06/06, note 127, art. 4.

140 Ibid., art. 4.

141 Ibid.

142 Ibid.

143 Ibid.

Post-2006 Reforms

These reforms are little more than glosses on the proposal by the Council of Ministers for restructuring the CCJ laid out in the previous legal source (and subsection), including the justifications for the reforms contained in the preamble of the Supplementary Protocol of 2006 and details of the restructure, such as the composition of the Court, qualifications of its judges, and the recruitment role of the Judicial Council, among others. More specifically, the latest proposal came from the Ad Hoc Ministerial Committee on Institutional Reform whose justification touted a "streamlined and efficient organizational structure[] capable of achieving cost savings whilst improving service delivery,"[144] in other words, efficiency along with effectiveness. The following discussion focuses on the change in the size of the Court from the seven in the last section to five, the judges' term of office, the work of the Judicial Council, and criticisms of the justifications for the restructuring set forth by the Council of Ministers focused on the reduction in the size of the Court and their term of office. To put the matter in greater perspective and present some benchmark for comparison, Table 8.3 summarizes the features of the highest courts in the fifteen member-states of ECOWAS, juxtaposed with those of the African Court of Human Rights, and the East African Court of Justice.

[144] Quoted in Trust Africa Foundation, "Rethinking the Proposed Restructuring of the ECOWAS Community Court of Justice," *Issue Lab* (December 1, 2017) [hereinafter Africa Trust, "Rethinking the Proposed Restructuring of the CCJ"], https://search.issuelab.org/resource/rethinking-the-proposed-restructuring-of-the-ecowas-community-court-of-justice.

Table 8.3 Features of the highest courts in ECOWAS member-states, juxtaposed with those of the African Court of Human and Peoples' Rights, and the East African Court of Justice

Item No.	*Court name*	*Date established*	*Seat*	*No. of judges*	*Term length*	*Special features, if any*
1.	African Court of Human and Peoples' Rights[145]	2004	Arusha, Tanzania	11	Six-year term, renewable one time only	Different from the African *Commission* on Human and Peoples' Rights[146]
2.	East African Court of Justice	1999	Arusha, Tanzania	10	Seven-year non-renewable term	Two judges from each member state[147]
3.	Supreme Court of Benin	1993	Cotonou	No more than 15	Mandatory retirement age of 65	The country also has a Constitutional Court, made up of members who serve a 5-year term, renewable one time only
4.	Supreme Court of Burkina Faso	1960	Ouagadougou	Not indicated	Appointments mostly controlled by the president of the country and judges have no term limit	The country also has a Constitutional Court appointed for a 9-year term, with one-third of its membership renewed every three years
5.	Supreme Court of Cape Verde (Cabo Verde)	1980[148]	Praia	8	Life tenure	The country also has a Constitutional Court
6.	Supreme Court of Côte d'Ivoire	1994	Abidjan	13	Life tenure	The country has a Constitutional Council, comprised of 9 members, plus former Presidents of the country[149]

(continued)

Table 8.3 (continued)

Item No.	*Court name*	*Date established*	*Seat*	*No. of judges*	*Term length*	*Special features, if any*
7.	Supreme Court of The Gambia	1851[150]	Banjul	7	Life tenure, subject to a mandatory retirement age of 75	
8.	Supreme Court of Ghana	1876[151]	Accra	14[152]	Mandatory retirement age of 70, but a judge may also retire at 60	
9.	Supreme Court of Guinea	1990	Conakry	14	Nine-year term until age 65	
10.	Supreme Court of Guinea-Bissau	1974	Bissau	9	Life tenure	
11.	Supreme Court of Liberia	1839	Monrovia	5	Mandatory age of 70	
12.	Supreme Court of Mali	1969	Bamako	19	Five-year term (no indication regarding renewability)	The country also has a Constitutional Court of 9 members who serve for a 7-year term renewable once
13.	Supreme Court of Niger	1999	Niamey	Not indicated	Not indicated	The country also has a 7-member Constitutional Court, whose judges have a six-year, nonrenewable term, with one-third of the membership renewed every 2 years
14.	Supreme Court of Nigeria	1963[153]	Abuja	16	Mandatory retirement at 70	

Item No.	*Court name*	*Date established*	*Seat*	*No. of judges*	*Term length*	*Special features, if any*
15.	Supreme Court of Appeal of Senegal[154]	1960	Dakar	13	Mandatory retirement at 68, but a judge may also leave at 65	The country also has a Constitutional Council of 7 members; judges serve 6-year terms, with renewal of 2 members every 2 years
16.	Supreme Court of Sierra Leone	1960	Freetown	5	Mandatory retirement at 65	
17.	Supreme Court of Togo	1960	Lomé	Not indicated	Not indicated	The country also has a Constitutional Court made up of nine members, appointed for a renewable, seven-year term

[145] As of March 2023, 34 out of 55 African countries, who are member-states of the African Union, are state parties of the 2004 Protocol establishing the Court. See Amnesty International, "Why the African Court Should Matter to You" (June 9, 2023), https://www.amnesty.org/en/latest/campaigns/2023/06/why-the-african-court-should-matter-to-you/#:~:text=ESTABLISHMENT%20OF%20THE%20COURT&text=The%20Protocol%20came%20into%20force,from%20all%20over%20the%20continent.

[146] To minimize confusion, here is the difference between these two complementary institutions. Established by the African Charter on Human and People's Rights (1981), the African Commission on Human and Peoples' Rights was inaugurated on November 2, 1987, in Addis Ababa, Ethiopia, from where it subsequently moved its headquarters to Banjul, The Gambia. Unlike the Court, peopled and filled by judges, the members of the Commission are Commissioners, like the Court incidentally numbering eleven. More elaborately, the African Commission is tasked with promoting and protecting human rights by interpreting the African Charter and considering individual complaints. The Commission hears cases from the 53 member-states of the African Union (all African countries but South Sudan). It reports to the Assembly of Heads of State and Government of the AU. Its eleven Commissioners serve in their personal capacities for six-year terms that may be renewed once. Its jurisdiction spans the rights set out in the African Charter. Its duties include examining national reports on the situation of human rights which each member-state is required to submit to it every other year, adopting resolutions and declarations, country visits, and resolving communications (i.e., complaints) submitted by member-states, as well as by individuals, and NGOs. To facilitate performance of its duties, the Commission has developed a system of "special measures," including Working Groups which monitor and investigate specific questions linked to the its work. Testament to the nature of the relationship between this Court and the Commission, the latter submits cases to the African Court. See Open Society Justice Initiative, "Fact Sheet: African Commission on Human and Peoples' Rights," https://www.justiceinitiative.org/publications/african-commission-human-and-peoples-rights#:~:text=The%20African%20Commission%20is%20tasked,(all%20except%20South%20Sudan.

For its part, the African Court on Human and Peoples' Rights is a judicial body that delivers binding judgments on compliance with the African Charter. It was established by the Protocol to the African Charter on Human and Peoples' Rights, adopted in June 1998, by member-states of the then OAU in Ouagadougou, Burkina Faso. The Protocol entered into force in January 2004, following the required ratification by 12 member-states. The court hears cases from the 26 AU member-states that have ratified the Protocol establishing the Court: Algeria, Burkina Faso, Burundi, Cote d'Ivoire, Comoros, Congo, Gabon, Gambia, Ghana, Kenya, Libya, Lesotho, Mali, Malawi, Mozambique, Mauritania, Mauritius, Nigeria, Niger, Rwanda, South Africa, Senegal, Tanzania, Togo, Tunisia, and Uganda. Article 3 of the Protocol extends the Court's jurisdiction to "all cases and disputes submitted to it concerning the interpretation and application of the Charter," the Protocol and other human-right instruments that states have ratified. In addition, Article 4 gives the Court jurisdiction to issue advisory opinions on "any legal matter relating to the Charter or other relevant human rights instruments." The first eleven judges of the Court were elected and sworn in in 2006. Each judge serves a six-year term and can be re-elected once. All judges, except the President of the Court, serve on a part-time basis. In 2004, out of concern over the proliferation of AU institutions, the AU integrated the Court with the African Court of Justice, creating an African Court of Justice and Human and Peoples' Rights. The expectation is that when it becomes fully operational, the consolidated Court will form the principal judicial organ of the AU. See African Court on Human and Peoples' Rights, "About Us," https://www.african-court.org/wpafc/; and African Court on Human and Peoples' Rights, "Basic Information," https://www.african-court.org/wpafc/basic-information/.

[147] The member-states are Burundi, Kenya, Rwanda, Tanzania, and Uganda. The Court hears cases from these member-states related to violations of the rule of law, one of the fundamental and operational principles set out in the East African Community Treaty, which established the Court. The Court was inaugurated in November 2001 and heard its first case in 2005. It has two chambers and sits in Arusha, Tanzania. The Court has no explicit jurisdiction relating to human rights. However, the fundamental and operational principles of the East African Community, set out in Articles 6–8 of the Treaty, include good governance, signified by "adherence to the principles of democracy, the rule of law, accountability, transparency, social justice, equal opportunities, gender equality, as well as the recognition, promotion and protection of human and peoples' rights in accordance with the provisions of the African Charter on Human and Peoples' Rights." See Open Society Justice Initiative, "Fact Sheet: East African Court of Justice," https://www.justiceinitiative.org/publications/east-african-court-justice; and East African Court of Justice, "About Us," https://www.eacj.org/?page_id=19.

[148] The court originated as the National Council of Justice, established on July 5, 1975, following the country's independence the same day. Supremo Tribunal de Justica, "History of the STJ in Cape Verde," http://www.stj.cv/historia.html [archived].

[149] Until its creation in 1994, the Supreme Court had a Constitutional Chamber which covered the duties of this Council. Washington University Manual of International Legal Citation, "Republic of Côte d'Ivoire (Republicque de Côte d'Ivoire)," https://apps.law.wustl.edu/GSLR/CitationManual/countries/ivorycoast.pdf.

[150] Note that this court became the highest court in The Gambia only in 1997 with the adoption of a new constitution that year. Before then, litigants could appeal decisions of the Supreme Court at the West African Court of Appeal based in Sierra Leone, and from thence to the Judicial Committee of the Privy Council, based in London. Following the country's independence in 1965, this arrangement persisted, but with the West African Court of Appeal replaced by the Court of Appeal of The Gambia. For a history of the Gambian legal system, see Flora Ogbuitepu Ngo-Martins, "Update: Researching Gambian Legal Information," *GlobaLex* (May/June, 2021), https://www.nyulawglobal.org/globalex/Gambia1.html (especially the discussion on "the Judicature").

[151] Until 1960, the Supreme Court was not the highest court in Ghana, given that, like in The Gambia, there was a right of appeal to the Judicial Committee of the Privy Council

By this latest package of reforms, the size of the Court was reduced by two judges to five with their term of office still four-year, non-renewable, tenure from the last period.[155] This is the size as of this book. In its succinct expression, the CCJ "is composed of five independent Judges who are persons of high moral character, appointed by the [AHSG], from nationals of Member States for a four-year non-renewable term upon the recommendation of the Community Judicial Council."[156] Building on changes percolating since the adoption of the Protocol of the CCJ in 1991,[157] neither the judges, nor other members of the Court, may be "regarded as representatives of their Governments or government of any other ECOWAS member state."[158] These judges, who may come from private practice or from the academia, must be armed with "at least twenty years professional experience," who "possess the qualifications for appointment to the Supreme Court or the highest judicial office [in their own countries], or are jurisconsults of recognized competence

in London. See Judicial Service of Ghana, "The Republic of Ghana Judiciary," https://www.judicial.gov.gh/index.php/component/content/article/101-history/235-summary.

[152] The 1992 gave a specification of no less than 10 judges; otherwise, there is no limit on the number of judges appointed to the Supreme Court, even though there have been calls for a cap on the number that, on the other hand, some judges objected to due to the responsibilities spelled out for the court by the 1992 constitution. See Justice Agbenorsi, "Don't Cap Supreme Court Judges—Chief Justice, Spohia Akuffo Proposes," *Graphic Online* (December 8, 2022), https://www.graphic.com.gh/news/general-news/don-t-cap-supreme-court-judges-chief-justice-spohia-akuffo-proposes.html.

[153] This was the date, specifically October 1 of that year, that appeals from the Federal Supreme Court to the Judicial Committee of the Privy Council were abolished, at which point the Supreme Court became the highest court in the country. Learn Nigerian Law, "History of the Nigerian Legal System," https://www.learnnigerianlaw.com/learn/legal-system/history.

[154] In 1992, the Supreme Court was abolished and replaced by four specialized bodies that, in addition to the Supreme Court of Appeal, include the Council of State, the Constitutional Council, and the Accountability Court, similar to the system in France. Abdou Khadre Lo, "The Senegal Case Study," UNAM, https://archivos.juridicas.unam.mx/www/bjv/libros/6/2748/15.pdf.

[155] Community Court of Justice, "Membership of the Court," note 21.

[156] Community Court of Justice, "About Us," http://www.courtecowas.org/about-us-2/#:~:text=The%20Court%20is%20composed%20of,of%20the%20Community%20Judicial%20Council.

[157] See notes 42–47 and accompanying texts.

[158] Community Court of Justice, "Membership of the Court," note 21.

in international law, especially community law or law of regional integration."[159] As of this book, the members of the Court are: Edward Amoako Asante (Ghana, President), Gberi-bè Ouattara (Côte d'Ivoire, Vice President), Dupe Atoki (Nigeria), Keikura Bangura (Sierra Leone), and Januária Tavares Silva Moreira Costa (Cape Verde).[160]

Critics of this cache of latest reforms of the CCJ consider them as lacking in merit and legal basis.[161] These critics include members of the Court itself like current President, Edward Amoako Asante of Ghana. We will look at his insights and next those of Africa Trust Foundation, a nonprofit based in Dakar, Senegal.[162]

Asante called for restoration of the seven-judge Court that existed before the latest reforms,[163] a position shared by Femi Falana, a Nigerian human rights lawyer and frequent CCJ counsel, who shared spotlight with him at the venue where the President made the call; Falana wanted the Court size increased to fifteen judges.[164] Asanta said the reduction to five from seven is "of grave concern" to him and his colleagues because it is "having an adverse effect on the operations of the Court."[165] He

[159] Ibid.

[160] Community Court of Justice, "Current Judges," http://www.courtecowas.org/current-judges-2/.

[161] See, for example, Alliances for Africa, "Strengthening the ECOWAS Court of Justice: Enhancing Access to Justice in the West African Region," https://alliancesforafrica.org/strengthening-the-ecowas-court-of-justice-enhancing-access-to-justice-in-the-west-african-region/#:~:text=It%20was%20a%20unanimously%20agreed,that%20has%20no%20legal%20force; and Africa Trust, "Rethinking the Proposed Restructuring of the CCJ," note 144.

[162] Trust Africa, "Shaping the Future We Want for Africa," https://trustafrica.org/about-us/#:~:text=TrustAfrica%20is%20a%20Pan%20African,the%20continent's%20most%20pressing%20challenges. Trust Africa touts itself as a pan-African organization "founded with a commitment to strengthen African agency in addressing the continent's most pressing challenges[,]" and rooted in a conviction "that Africans must work together to set their own development priorities, informed by the aspirations of African citizens." Ibid. Its program focuses "on strengthening democracy and democratic governance, promoting equitable development, and advancing African philanthropy." Ibid. Akwasi Aidoo is the founding Executive Director of the organization. Ibid.

[163] "ECOWAS Court: President Asante, Falana Call for More Judges," *Vanguard* (Lagos) (November 22, 2021), https://www.vanguardngr.com/2021/11/ecowas-court-president-asante-falana-call-for-more-judges/.

[164] Ibid.

[165] Ibid.

observed that because many of the cases before the Court border on abuses of human rights in ECOWAS member-states, Court members "carry [a] burden of exigency which only five justices cannot meet in record time."[166] He pointed out that with only five justices, simultaneous or multiple court sittings are impossible, given that a minimum of three justices are needed for such sittings.[167] Yet the adjudication business of the Court must proceed apace, no beat missed. Despite the Court's best efforts, "the number of cases pending before the Court continues to grow astronomically."[168] Because of "the increasing caseload of the Court," he said, "a Court composed of only five members cannot cope," adding that since a complete chamber requires a minimum of three judges, "[i]t is also difficult to form more than one chamber in the Court."[169]

Court President Asante's appeal for a return to the status quo ante includes review of the tenure of justices from the new four-year, non-renewable, term to the initial five-year term renewable for another five-year term.[170] He opined that no international court or tribunal maintains such tenure for its judges, and advised ECOWAS not to model the tenure of its judges after that of Commissioners of the specialized technical commissioners who he said are political appointees.[171] "The tenure of judges is four years, before the judge settles it is about six months and six months before he leaves he cannot settle cases, so effectively judges just work for three years. But when the tenure is made seven years just like most of the international and regional courts, you have a very long time to make the jurisprudence of the court solid and stable."[172]

The criticism by Africa Trust Foundation is more robust although, unlike Asante's, focused mainly and exclusively on the proposal to downsize the CCJ to five judges. Its overall assessment revolves around the thrust that the Court has successfully applied its jurisprudence "to

[166] Ibid.

[167] Ibid.

[168] Ibid.

[169] Ibid.

[170] "ECOWAS Court: President Asante, Falana Call for More Judges," note 163.

[171] Ibid.

[172] Quoted in Unini Chioma, "ECOWAS Court Strengthens Reparations, Enforcement," *Nigerian Lawyer* (July 9, 2019), https://thenigerialawyer.com/ecowas-court-strengthens-reparations-enforcement/.

strategically speak to regional situations."[173] Rather than produce efficiency, the change is a "misguided" undertaking that could effectively "dismantle" the CCJ.[174] The change is hard to justify because "a five-member Court can constitute one court session only, and two arbitration sessions concurrently," thereby creating an "unnecessary case backlog" for the Court that will make "constitution of an appellate chamber impossible."[175]

In short, downsizing the CCJ to five judges is inconsistent with the purpose and role of the Court.[176] The rationale for the restructure hinges on facilitating the achievement of the Treaty's objectives relating to increased integration across the subregion.[177] However, this amounts to a narrow scope for the evaluation of the efficiency of the Court as an ECOWAS institution that does not take into consideration its evolution, in its own right, as a Court of Justice, specifically a human-right court, a marked departure from the initial conceptualization as a tribunal designed solely to help build a common market.[178] "[I]f the [...] Court's performance is measured against its original professed role," it maintained, "then [it] will be found lacking, mainly because the initial set[-]up of the [...] Court by [the member-states] allowed for the persistent flouting of community economic rules, which in turn have resulted in the [sub]region making very little progress toward its professed goal of regional economic integration."[179]

Equally, the efficiency measurement "fails to take into consideration the fact that since its establishment ECOWAS member states have yet to challenge barriers to intraregional trade before the [Court]."[180] The Foundation cited the proven track record of the Court as another reason why the downsizing makes little sense.[181] In its current status as a human-right court, the Court affords citizens of West Africa, particularly those

[173] Trust Africa, "Rethinking the Proposed Restructuring of the CCJ," note 144.

[174] Ibid.

[175] Ibid.

[176] Ibid.

[177] Ibid.

[178] Ibid.

[179] Ibid.

[180] Ibid.

[181] See ibid.

of member-states, "an additional independent supra-national mechanism through which they can seek remedy for human rights violations."[182] Since acquiring jurisdiction over human rights complaints in 2005, the Court has issued more than 100 judgments that have condemned human rights violations by member-states, including Nigeria.[183] Add to these achievements the fact that most recently, the Court has transformed itself into a promoter of women rights in Africa.[184] In short, because it has used its jurisprudence "to strategically speak to regional situations," the Court deserves "commendation and further strengthening," not a downsizing that stands to make it inefficient, undermine its effectiveness, and weaken the status it has won for itself as an international court by dint of its hard work.[185] To enhance the efficiency and effectiveness of the Court, ECOWAS leaders should leave the size as it is or increase it.[186] Going further, they should improve their financial support for the Court, enhance their cooperation with it, and work to promote speedier implementation of its judgments.[187]

The only missing element needed to complete this discussion on the post-2006 reforms, to which topic we now turn, is the Judicial Council of the Community, abbreviatedly here called the Judicial Council or the Council. The conversation builds on insights from the previous subsection related to the Council.[188] As indicated therein, the Council comprises Chief Justices from ECOWAS member-states not already represented on the then seven-member Court.[189] The body is charged with responsibility for recruiting and disciplining CCJ judges; in this role, it shortlists and interviews candidates for judges and makes recommendations for appointment to the AHSG.

Proper appreciation of the Judicial Council is predicated on understanding of judges as statutory appointees under the dispensation of

[182] Trust Africa, "Rethinking the Proposed Restructuring of the CCJ," note 144.

[183] Ibid.

[184] Ibid.

[185] Ibid.

[186] Ibid.

[187] Ibid.

[188] See note 137–138 and 140 and accompanying texts.

[189] See note 137 and accompanying text.

the post-2006 reforms. Statutory appointments are high-level positions that rotate among ECOWAS member-states.[190] Governments of these member-states decide which country is next in line for a statutory appointment to the Court.[191] The Legal Affairs Directorate then follows through by advertising for the position and collecting submissions from eligible applicants. Applications which meet specified criteria are forwarded to the Judicial Council, which vets those applications and interviews candidates, following which it then selects three candidates and forwards their names, together with rankings determined based on points, to the AHSG, which makes the actual appointments to the Court.[192] For judges seated already on the Court, the Council is tasked with reviewing complaints alleging judicial bias and other forms of improprieties.[193] This arrangement "provid[es] a layer of political insulation for ECOWAS judges against whom such charges are filed."[194] Specifically, the Judicial Council's participation in judges' recruitment and discipline "increases the influence of national judges in the selection process for the CCJ," and lays down procedures for reviews of misconduct which "insulate judges from attempts by governments to remove them from office."[195]

Contrary to criticism of the changes in the term of office tied to the Judicial Council, ECOWAS officials and stakeholders, including those in the Executive Commission, view this and related reforms like the creation of the Judicial Council as one way to harmonize judicial appointments with other statutory appointments in ECOWAS, while improving the quality of judges who apply to sit on the Court.[196] They equally perceive the reduction in the term of office positively, noting, for example, that shorter, nonrenewable terms, increase the opportunity of all member-states of ECOWAS to appoint judges to the Court.[197] Even the size of a court is not written in stone. Instead, as Table 8.3 on the features of the highest courts in ECOWAS member-states shows, noticeable variations

[190] Alter et al., note 4, p. 760.

[191] Ibid.

[192] Ibid.

[193] See ibid.

[194] Alter et al., note 4, p. 760.

[195] Ibid.

[196] Ibid.

[197] Ibid., pp. 760–761.

exist in the composition of courts. Judicial tribunals outside Africa are no different. The Judiciary Act of 1789, which established the US federal court system created a Supreme Court of six judges,[198] whose number grew, across seasons, over the years to the current nine justices on the Court.

Sample of Historic Decisions by the CCJ

A picture is worth a thousand words. Guided by this adage, a sample of seven cases over a fourteen-year period from 2008 to 2022 across four ECOWAS member-countries—The Gambia, Mali, Niger, and Nigeria—is used to illustrate the decisions that exemplify the CCJ's human-right jurisprudence. The seven cases break down into: one each from The Gambia and Mali, two from Niger, and three from Nigeria. Because the choice of cases is intuitive, rather than scientifically determined or derived, the historic-ness of the sample is more subjective than objective. For example, *Amnesty International & 7 Others v. The Togolese Republic*, for which the CCJ in 2022 won the honor of "significant legal ruling" is not included here,[199] partly because we have before now commented on it. The cases in recentness, from most to least, are: SERAP and 176 Other Concerned *Nigerians v. Nigeria*,[200] (ii) *Fodi Mohamed & Others*

[198] See Legal Information Institute (LII), Cornell Law School, "Judiciary Act of 1789," https://www.law.cornell.edu/wex/judiciary_act_of_1789#:~:text=The%20Judiciary%20Act%20of%201789,Congress%20sees%20fit%20to%20establish.

[199] See notes 25–27 and accompanying texts.

[200] Suit No. ECW/CCJ/APP/23/21 (July 14, 2022) [hereinafter SERAP Twitter Case]. The case consolidated four lawsuits, namely: Suit No. ECW/CCJ/APP/29/21 filed by Mrs Mojirayo Ogunlana-Nkanga on behalf of Media Rights Agenda and four other non-governmental organizations; Suit No. ECW/CCJ/APP/23/21 (filed by Mr. Femi Falana, on behalf of SERAP), a Lagos-based NGO, and 176 Nigerians; Suit No. ECW/CCJ/APP/26/21 filed by Mr. Patrick Elohor, President of One Love Foundation, an NGO; and Suit No. ECW/CCJ/APP/24/21, filed by Chief Malcolm Omirhobo, a Lagos-based human rights lawyer. Center for Journalism Innovation and Development, "MRA Calls on Federal Government to Implement ECOWAS Court Judgment in Twitter Ban Suits," Press Release (July 19, 2022), https://thecjid.org/mra-calls-on-federal-government-to-implement-ecowas-court-judgment-in-twitter-ban-suits/.

v. Niger,[201] (iii) *Kadiaton Siby v. Mali*,[202] (iv) *SERAP v. Nigeria*,[203] (v) *SERAP v. Nigeria and Anor.*,[204] (vi) *Hadijatou Mani Koraou v. Niger*,[205] and (vii) *Manneh v. The Gambia*.[206] In the natural order of things, including variations in complexity, some of the cases draw more discussion than others. The extended commentary should not be read to mean that they are more important than any of the other cases, because all seven cases rank equal in significance.

SERAP and 176 Other Concerned Nigerians v. Nigeria

From June 5, 2021 to January 13, 2022, the Nigeria national government under General Muhammadu Buhari imposed an official ban on Twitter,[207] a social media website based in the US, since July 2023 known as X. The ban effectively blocked access to the platform, a micro-blogging site, for many residents in a country that has a reputation as Africa's tech hub; Nigeria hosts many areas where there are many businesses related

[201] Suit No. ECW/CCJ/APP/27/19, Judgment No. ECW/CCJ/JUD/19/21 (June 24, 2021), https://caselaw.ihrda.org/en/entity/pcaiwdusd5?page=1 (text in French).

[202] Suit No. ECW/CCJ/APP/42/19, Judgment No. ECW/CCJ/JUD/15/21 (June 22, 2021), *reprinted* in African Human Rights Case Law Analyzer, https://caselaw.ihrda.org/en/entity/16tp7b9q7l7h (text in French).

[203] Suit No. ECW/CCJ/APP/08/09, Judgment ECW/CCJ/JUD/18/12 (December 14, 2012), https://caselaw.ihrda.org/en/entity/pftlz3gneo0wxsgq0kdszto6r?page=30 [hereinafter SERAP Environmental Protection Case].

[204] Suit No. ECW/CCJ/APP/12/07, Judgment No. ECW/CCJ/JUD/07/10 (November 30, 2010) https://www.worldcourts.com/ecowasccj/eng/decisions/2010.11.30_SERAP_v_Nigeria.htm [hereinafter SERAP Public Education Case].

[205] Suit No. ECW/CCJ/APP/08/08, Judgment No. ECW/CCJ/JUD/06/08 (October 27, 2008), http://www.courtecowas.org/wp-content/uploads/2023/12/JUD-ECW-CCJ-JUD-06-08-Dame-Hadijatou-Mani-Koraou-c.-La-R%C3%A9p-du-NIGER-27_10_08-vA-1.pdf.

[206] Suit No. ECW/CCJ/APP/04/07, Judgment No. ECW/CCJ/JUD/03/08 (June 5, 2008), https://www.worldcourts.com/ecowasccj/eng/decisions/2008.06.05_Manneh_v_Gambia.htm.

[207] See Ruth Maclean, "Nigeria Bans Twitter After President's Tweet Is Deleted," *New York Times* (June 5, 2021), https://www.nytimes.com/2021/06/05/world/africa/nigeria-twitter-president.html; and Danielle Paquette, "Nigeria Suspends Twitter After the Social Media Platform Freezes President's Account," *Washington Post* (June 4, 2021), https://www.washingtonpost.com/world/2021/06/04/nigeria-suspends-twitter-buhari/.

to technology, with potential for creation of more in the future.[208] The trouble began when, on June 1, 2021, General Buhari, then President of Nigeria, tweeted: "Many of those misbehaving today are too young to be aware of the destruction and loss of lives that occurred during the Nigerian Civil War. Those of us in the fields for 30 months who went through the war, will treat them in the language they understand."[209] He directed his threat to insurgents in Igbo Southeast Nigeria campaigning for a separate state outside Nigeria, resurrecting a similar campaign from 1967 to 1970 that overlapped Nigeria's bloody civil war.[210] The tweet revived memories of the atrocities of the conflict and was interpreted by many persons within the country and beyond as a threat against ethnic Igbo who fought as Biafrans to secede from Nigeria from 1967 to 1970.[211]

Shortly thereafter, Twitter flagged and removed the president's tweets for violating its terms regarding violence.[212] In retaliation, on June 5, 2021, the Nigerian national government "indefinitely suspended" Twitter.[213] The suspension was announced by Lai Mohammed, then Minister of Information and Culture, who indicated that the government

[208] See Statista, "Number of Active Technology Startup Hubs in Africa as of 2019, by Country" (April 28, 2023), https://www.statista.com/statistics/1294785/number-of-active-tech-hubs-in-africa-by-country/#:~:text=As%20of%202019%2C%20more%20than,78%20and%2056%20hubs%2C%20respectively (pointing out that, in 2019, Nigeria had 90 of the estimated 640 hubs in Africa that supported technology-based startups; this was the highest number of active tech hubs, followed by South Africa with 78 and Egypt with 56).

[209] Quoted in Obinna Chukwunenye Nweke, "Hunger as a Weapon of War: Biafra, Social Media and the Politics of Famine Remembrance," *Third World Quarterly*, 45(2) (2024), 314. https://doi.org/10.1080/01436597.2023.2182283.

[210] Nweke, note 209.

[211] Ibid.

[212] Alexis Akwagyiram, "Twitter Removes Nigerian President's 'Abusive' Civil War Post," *Reuters* (June 3, 2021), https://www.reuters.com/world/africa/twitter-removes-nigerian-presidents-abusive-civil-war-post-2021-06-02/; and "Twitter Deletes Nigerian Leader's 'Civil War' Post," *BBC News* (June 2, 2021), https://www.bbc.com/news/world-africa-57336571.

[213] See Nimi Princewill and Stephanie Busari, "Nigeria Bans Twitter After Company Deletes President Buhari's Tweet," *CNN* (Updated June 5, 2021), https://www.cnn.com/2021/06/04/africa/nigeria-suspends-twitter-operations-intl/index.html; Kim Lyons, "Twitter Blocked in Nigeria After Deleting a Tweet by Its President" (Updated June 5, 2021), https://www.theverge.com/2021/6/5/22520166/twitter-suspended-nigeria-delete-tweet-president-violate-rules; and Ruth Olurounbi and William Clowes, "Nigeria Condemns Twitter for Deleting President Buhari's Tweet," *Bloomberg* (Updated

acted out of a concern that "the persistent use of the platform" could "undermin[e] Nigeria's corporate existence."[214] The government also threatened to arrest and prosecute anyone using Twitter in the country to the point that Nigeria's National Broadcasting Commission (NBC), which regulates broadcasting in the country, asked all broadcast stations to suspend the patronage of Twitter.[215]

Many Nigerians, individuals and groups alike, opposed the ban.[216] These critics included the Nigerian Bar Association, whose then President, Olumide Akpata, tweeted on June 4, 2021, that his association "note[s] with great concern the extraordinary decision of the [Nigerian] Federal Government to suspend the operations of @Twitter in Nigeria and, by necessary implication, the right of Nigerians to freely express their constitutionally-guaranteed opinions through that medium."[217] Outside Nigeria, critics included the European Union (EU), Canada, Ireland, the UK, and the US; the five entities issued a joint statement through their diplomatic missions in Nigeria, wherein they expressed disappointment over the Nigerian government's suspension of the social media platform.[218] The diplomatic missions expressed their support for human rights of free expression and access to information, which rights they indicated applied both online and offline.[219] Despite the wellspring of disapproval within and outside Nigeria, it took seven months for

June 2, 2021), https://www.bloomberg.com/news/articles/2021-06-02/nigerian-president-threatens-crackdown-after-spate-of-attacks.

[214] See Alexis Akwagyiram, "Nigeria Says It Suspends Twitter Days After President's Post Removed," *Reuters* (June 5, 2021), https://www.reuters.com/technology/nigeria-indefinitely-suspends-twitter-operations-information-minister-2021-06-04/.

[215] Committee to Protect Journalists (CPJ) (New York), "Nigerian Broadcast Regulator Orders Outlets to Stop Using Twitter Amid Nationwide Block" (June 8, 2021), https://cpj.org/2021/06/nigerian-broadcast-regulator-orders-outlets-to-stop-using-twitter-amid-nationwide-block/.

[216] See "Nigerians on Twitter React to Nigeria's Twitter Suspension," *Alja Zeera* (June 5, 2021), https://www.aljazeera.com/news/2021/6/4/nigerian-twitter-users-blast-govt-ban-of-social-media-giant.

[217] Quoted in Princewill and Busari, note 213.

[218] US Embassy and Consulate in Nigeria, "Joint Statement from the Diplomatic Missions of Canada, The European Union (Delegation to Nigeria), The Republic of Ireland, The United Kingdom, and The United States of America" (June 5, 2021), https://ng.usembassy.gov/partners-joint-statement-re-twitter-suspension/.

[219] Ibid.

the Buhari government to lift the ban.[220] To get around the restrictions and inconveniences created by the ban, many Nigerians creatively accessed Twitter with the aid of a Virtual Private Network (VPN),[221] i.e., create a secure connection between two networks, using an insecure communication medium like a public Internet.

Along with 176 Nigerians who denominate themselves "concerned," the Socio-Economic Rights and Accountability Project (SERAP), a Nigerian NGO and nonprofit, sued the Nigerian government before the CCJ challenging the ban.[222] The plaintiffs alleged that the ban on Twitter violated their various right to freedom of expression and those of many other Nigerians. "The suspension of Twitter is aimed at intimidating and stopping Nigerians from using Twitter and other social media platforms to assess government policies, expose corruption, and criticize acts of official impunity by the agents of the Federal Government."[223] Contending that "the free communication of information and ideas about public and political issues between citizens and elected representatives is essential," they urged the Court to declare the Nigerian government's action

[220] Ruth Maclean, "Nigeria Lifts [Seven]-Month Ban on Twitter," *New York Times* (January 13, 2022), https://www.nytimes.com/2022/01/13/world/africa/nigeria-lifts-twitter-ban.html. Such is the lack of trust between the rulers and the ruled in Nigeria that many citizens attribute a sinister reason for the government's decision to lift the ban, namely, was the upcoming general election in 2023 and the government's intention to use the platform for its campaign. Ameh Ejekwonyilo, "Why ECOWAS Court Declared Twitter Ban by Nigerian Government Illegal," *Premium Times* (Abuja and Lagos) (July 14, 2022), https://www.premiumtimesng.com/news/headlines/542696-why-ecowas-court-declared-twitter-ban-by-nigerian-govt-illegal.html.

[221] Ejekwonyilo, note 220.

[222] SERAP Twitter Case, note 200. The Socio-Economic Rights and Accountability Project (SERAP) is a Nigerian NGO and nonprofit formed in 2004 and based in Lagos. Firm in its conviction regarding the still "unexplored potential of international human rights law for increasing transparency, accountability and protection of economic and social rights in Nigeria," the NGO seeks to use the human-right tool, including anticorruption laws and standards, "to encourage the government and [the Nigerian peoples] to address developmental and human rights challenges such as corruption, poverty, inequality and discrimination." SERAP, "About SERAP," https://serap-nigeria.org/who-we-are/. SERAP offers "free legal advice and services for victims of corruption and economic and social rights," and works to assist these victims to redress abuses of these rights. In pursuit of its mission, the group uses means like advocacy in print and electronic media, litigation, capacity building, and promotion of educational awareness. Ibid.

[223] Ejekwonyilo, note 220.

unlawful.[224] This is not to mention the economic cost, signified by the fact that "[t]he arbitrary action by the Federal Government and its agents [...] negatively impacted millions of Nigerians who carry on their daily businesses and operational activities on Twitter."[225] They said Twitter's suspension was "arbitrary" as "there is no law in Nigeria [...] permitting the prosecution of people simply for peacefully exercising their human rights through Twitter and other social media platforms."[226] For its part, the Nigerian government urged the court to dismiss the suit because, in its view, the CCJ lacked the jurisdiction to hear it.

The Court agreed with the plaintiffs.[227] It ruled that suspending the operation of Twitter "violates the rights of SERAP and 176 concerned Nigerians to the enjoyment of freedom of expression, access to information and the media, as well as the right to fair hearing."[228] It is also inconsistent with the provisions of the ACHPR, and of the ICCPR, both of which instrument Nigeria is a state party to.[229] The Court ordered the Nigerian national government under General Buhari to take necessary steps to align its policies to give effect to the fundamental rights and freedoms of Nigerians by, among other means, ensuring that such a ban does not happen again.[230]

[224] Ibid.

[225] Ibid.

[226] Ibid.

[227] SERAP Twitter Case, note 200.

[228] Ibid.

[229] Ibid. For the ACHPR, the relevant provision is Art. 9, guaranteeing "every individual" the right to receive information, as well as to express and disseminate opinions within the law. Organization of African Unity (OAU), African Charter on Human and Peoples' Rights ("Banjul Charter") (June 27, 1981), CAB/LEG/67/3 rev. 5, 21 I.L.M. 58 (1982), art. 9, https://www.refworld.org/docid/3ae6b3630.html. For the ICCPR, the cited provision is Art. 19, which guarantees "everyone," the right to hold opinions as well as to freedom of expression, including the freedom to seek, receive, and impart information and ideas, orally or in print, without undue restrictions. UN General Assembly, International Covenant on Civil and Political Rights, UNTS, vol. 999 (December 16, 1996), art. 19, https://www.refworld.org/docid/3ae6b3aa0.htm.

[230] SERAP Twitter Case, note 200.

Fodi Mohamed & Others v. Niger

This case involved Fodi Mohammed, a woman enslaved by the Takaboune Idiabaz family from childhood for over thirty years.[231] Zainabu, one of Fodi's daughters, given out as a wedding gift to Idiabaz's granddaughter, filed legal proceedings requesting freedom, but Niger prosecutor minimized the gravity of the offense by treating it as a misdemeanor, with, for example, no restitution considered for the victims.[232] This was despite the fact that Niger has in its statute book, a law passed in 2003 that outlawed slavery.[233] In addition, the country was a state party to the Banjul Charter, the African Charter on the Rights and Welfare of the Child (1990),[234] and the ICCPR, all of which instruments Niger ratified.[235]

The CCJ found Niger to be in violation of the right of Fodi and her children to dignity, and their right to fair trial.[236] It also ruled that Niger failed in its duties to protect the best interest of her six children, all of them minor between four and fifteen years at the time the case was filed in June 2019, along with their right to development, inconsistent with provisions of the above three treaties that Niger ratified.[237] It ordered the Niger government to pay damages and make restitution to the Mohamed family in the sum of 63 million FCFA [Franc of the Financial Community of Africa], about US$114,000.[238] As a step toward implementing the judgment, by October 25, 2021, the Niger government reportedly

[231] Judgment No. ECW/CCJ/JUD/19/21 (June 24, 2021), note 201.

[232] Ibid.

[233] The law in question was Article 270.1-5 of the Nigerien Criminal Code. Legal Information Institute (LII), Cornell Law School, "*Hadijatou Mani Koraou v. Republic of Niger*," https://www.law.cornell.edu/women-and-justice/resource/hadijatou_mani_koraou_v_republic_of_niger [hereinafter Legal Information Institute, The Karaou Case].

[234] African Union, African Charter on the Rights and Welfare of the Child (July 1990), https://au.int/sites/default/files/treaties/36804-treaty-african_charter_on_rights_welfare_of_the_child.pdf.

[235] Niger ratified the African Charter on the Rights and Welfare of the Child in 1999, the African Charter on Human and Peoples' Rights in 1986, and the ICCPR in 1986.

[236] Judgment No. ECW/CCJ/JUD/19/21 (June 24, 2021), note 201.

[237] Ibid.

[238] Ibid.

paid reparation worth about 30 million FCFA (about US$53,000) to the slavery victims, as a step toward implementing the judgment.[239]

Despite this applaudable turn of events from the Niger government, this case strikes a chord of dismay. As of the Mani case of 2008, surveyed below, an estimated 43,000 people lived their lives as slaves,[240] filled with the indignities attached to the status. It speaks to the intractableness of the culture of slavery in Niger where, in this modern age, some persons are still "born to be slaves."[241] A stubborn disease requires a drastic regimen of treatment. This means that, as one BBC Correspondent then posted in Niger, wrote, "[e]nding slavery in Niger would require a social revolution."[242] In her instructive elaboration, given that "[t]he slave owners, and the establishment," cannot be trusted to do the job, "[a]n entire section of the population would have to be taught that they are not intrinsically inferior to others, but that is what they have believed for generations."[243]

Kadiaton Siby v. Mali

This case involved a Malian widow, Kadiaton Siby, who was entitled to inherit her husband's property following his death in 2013. But because she refused to marry Souleymane Siby, her husband's brother, her in-laws beat her up and chased her away from her home. She filed a complaint that the Malian police ignored. Instead, her case languished in Malian

[239] See Julia Sloth-Nielsen, "Remedies for Child Rights Violations in African Human Rights Systems," *De Jure Law Journal* (2023), 625, 643, http://dx.doi.org/10.17159/2225-7160/2023/v56a36.

[240] "Former Niger Slave Launches Legal Case," *Reuters* (April 7, 2008), https://www.reuters.com/article/idUSL07612649/ (citing Anti-Slavery International, a UK-based human-right group founded in 1839). See also Horace S. Adjolohoun, "The ECOWAS Court as a Human Rights Promoter? Assessing Five Years' Impact of the *Koraou* Slavery Judgment," *Netherlands Quarterly of Human Rights*, 31(3) (2013), 342, 351.

[241] Hilary Andersson, "Born to Be a Slave in Niger," *BBC News* (February 11, 2005), http://news.bbc.co.uk/2/hi/programmes/from_our_own_correspondent/4250709.stm (quoting a study that found that "almost 8 [percent] of the population are slaves"). For a background account of slavery in the land, see "Niger Slavery: Background," *Guardian* (London) (October 27, 2008), https://www.theguardian.com/world/2008/oct/27/humanrights1.

[242] Andersson, note 241.

[243] Ibid.

local courts for years until November 2019, when two human-right groups filed a case on her behalf.

The CCJ found that Mali violated Kadiaton's right to dignity and the right for her case to be heard in a reasonable time.[244] It ruled that Mali had failed to protect her and her family as well.[245] The Court ordered Mali to try the case in a reasonable time, to liquidate the estate of Kadiatou's husband, and to pay her damages in the amount of one hundred million FCFA,[246] at the time about US$181,000.

SERAP v. Nigeria (2012)

SERAP filed a case against the Nigerian government and seven oil companies, including the state-owned Nigerian National Petroleum Corporation (NNPC).[247] The suit detailed specific environmental damage caused by oil spills that in certain cases lasted for days and were not properly cleaned up.[248] As a result, the land and water that traditionally supported agriculture and fishing in the communities these spills occurred were polluted, creating health issues for residents that included respiratory problems.[249]

[244] Judgment No. ECW/CCJ/JUD/15/21 (June 22, 2021), note 202.

[245] Ibid.

[246] Ibid.

[247] SERAP Environmental Protection Case, note 203. The remaining six are Shell Petroleum Development Company (SPDC), Elf Petroleum Nigeria Ltd., Agip Nigeria Plc., Chevron Oil Nigeria Plc., Total Nigeria Plc., and Exxon Mobil Corporation. The judgment was delivered by a panel of six judges, comprising Justices Awa Nana Daboya, Benefeito Mosso Ramos, Hansine Donli, Alfred Benin, Clotilde Medegan, and Elian Potey. Amnesty International, "Groundbreaking ECOWAS Court Judgment Orders Government to Punish Oil Companies Over Pollution," Press Release (December 16, 2012), https://www.amnesty.org/en/latest/press-release/2012/12/ground-breaking-ecowas-court-judgment-orders-government-punish-oil-companie/.

[248] SERAP Environmental Protection Case, note 203, ¶¶ 13–18.

[249] Ibid., ¶ 18. This is one of several cases on environmental damage in Nigeria alone that the Court addressed. For others tangentially connected to the right to a satisfactory environment under Article 24 of the Banjul Charter, see Community Court of Justice, *Nosa Ehanire Osaghae & 3 Others (on Behalf of Niger Delta People) v. Nigeria*, Suit No. ECW/CCJ/APP/2015, Judgment No. ECW/CCJ/JUD/03/07 (October 10, 2017), https://caselaw.ihrda.org/en/entity/5rot9qij7oijzfuyfghr1i3sor?page=1 (focused on allegations of corruption and killings by the military); Community Court of Justice, *Rev. Fr. Solomon Mfa & 11 Others v. Nigeria and 5 Others*, Suit No, ECW/CCJ/APP/11/16, Judgment No. ECW/CCJ/JUD/06/19 (February 26, 2019), https://caselaw.ihrda.org/en/entity/y1vuecy8gz; Community Court of Justice, *Raymond Oguche & 4 Others v. Nigeria*, Suit No. ECW/CCJ/APP/11/15, Judgment No. ECW/CCJ/JUD/24/18

The CCJ held that the Nigerian government violated various provisions of the Banjul Charter that it is a state party to by failing to adequately prevent and repair environmental harms from oil spills that devasted the environment in Nigeria's Niger Delta region.[250] These provisions are Article 21 on the right to wealth and natural resources,[251] and Article 24 on the right to a general satisfactory environment.[252] "The quality of life of people is determined by the quality of the environment. But the government has failed in its duty to maintain a general satisfactory environment conducive to the development of the Niger Delta region."[253] These provisions, particularly Art. 24, mandates "every State to take every measure to maintain the quality of the environment [...] such that the state of the environment may satisfy the human beings who live there, and enhance their sustainable development."[254] It reasoned that in addition to enacting laws to regulate the extractive industry,

(July 4, 2018), https://caselaw.ihrda.org/en/entity/v7dx0uzx5h36xsri94ojn61or?page=1; and Community Court of Justice, *Rose M. Ako v. West African Monetary Agency and 4 Others*, Suit No. ECW/CCJ/APP/01/14/SUPP, Judgment No. ECW/CCJ/JUD/2815 (December 2, 2015), https://caselaw.ihrda.org/en/entity/jcp55cz4kcrjbp0nc7bck57b9?page=2.

[250] SERAP Environmental Protection Case, note 203, ¶ 112. The Niger Delta refers to the vast low-lying region through which the waters of the Niger River drain into the Gulf of Guinea. It is Nigeria's largest wetland, and the third largest wetland in the world, with an estimated population in 2006 of over 40 million people, accounting then for more than 23% of the country's total population of over 140 million, one of the highest population densities in the world (265 people per square kilometer). Jean Balouga, "The Niger Delta: Defusing the Time Bomb," *International Association for Energy Economics* (First Quarter 2009), 8, https://citeseerx.ist.psu.edu/document?repid=rep1&type=pdf&doi=b89b353dac321fb7af47dbd06364896f72c5bda3#:~:text=The%20Niger%20Delta%20region%20is,National%20Population%20Commission%2C%202006. Based on information from Nigeria's National Population Commission, the region comprises nine states, made up of all six states in the South-South geopolitical zone plus Abia, Imo, and Ondo states.

[251] African Charter on Human and Peoples' Rights, note 229, art. 21(1) ("All people shall freely dispose of their wealth and natural resources. This right shall be exercised in the exclusive interest of the people. In no case shall a people be deprived of it"). Art. 21(2) next specifies that "[i]n case of spoliation, the dispossessed people shall have the right to the lawful recovery of its property as well as to an adequate compensation." Ibid.

[252] Ibid., art. 24 ("All peoples shall have the right to a general satisfactory environment favorable to their development").

[253] SERAP Environmental Protection Case, note 203, ¶¶ 100, 112.

[254] Ibid., ¶ 101. The CCJ defined environment as "an indivisible whole, comprising the biotic and abiotic natural resources, notably air, water, land, fauna and flora and the interaction between [them]." Ibid., ¶ 100.

creating agencies charged with implementing the laws, and allocating monies for such implementation, states must unveil "concrete measures" designed to prevent environmental damage and to make effective reparations when such damage takes place.[255] The Court further reasoned that, "[d]espite all the laws it has adopted and all the agencies it has created," the Nigerian national government "was not able to point out in its pleadings a single action that has been taken in recent years to seriously and diligently hold accountable any of the perpetrators of the many acts of environmental degradation which occurred in the Niger Delta Region."[256]

The Court dismissed the claims against the companies involved because, in its view, only member-states of ECOWAS and ECOWAS institutions can be sued before the court for human-right violations.[257] However, it denied the Nigerian national government's "attempt to shift the responsibility on[to] the holders of a license of oil exploitation," finding that available evidence showed that "the core of the problem in tackling the environmental degradation in the Region of Niger Delta resides in lack of enforcement of the legislation."[258] It was the lack of enforcement, signified in a failure to act, it ruled, that gave rise to Nigeria's failure to afford the citizens of the Niger Delta the right to a general satisfactory environment laid down in the Banjul Charter.[259]

The Court ordered the defendant to restore the environment of the Niger Delta and prevent further damage to the environment while ensuring that perpetrators of the damage are brought to book.[260] It denied Nigeria's challenge that a three-year statute of limitations had passed since some of the spills had taken place, reasoning that since the effects of the spills were ongoing, given that they had not been effectively cleaned up, the violation was "persistent and continuous" and the suit was not time-barred.[261] Contemplating the nature of compensation to be awarded to a group in situations of a breach of environmental rights,

[255] Ibid., ¶ 105.

[256] Ibid., ¶ 108.

[257] See SERAP Environmental Protection Case, note 203, ¶ 108.

[258] Ibid.

[259] Ibid.

[260] Ibid.

[261] Ibid.

the Court deemed monetary damage inappropriate here and in future cases. Awarding mass damages to the sum of US$1 billion in damages as the applicants demanded would be impractical "in terms of justice, morality, and equity" because the applicants had not identified particular victims entitled to that award.[262] Instead, it found that what is necessary is "a collective benefit adequate to repair, as completely as possible, the collective harm" caused by "a violation of a collective right."[263] The UK-based human-right group, Amnesty International, hailed the judgment as "ground-breaking."[264] With the basic public education case, next below, on socioeconomic human rights, this collective right case ranks among the most progressive decisions from the fountainhead of the CCJ's human-right jurisprudence.

SERAP v. Nigeria (2010)

In this case, SERAP sued the Nigerian national government and the Universal Basic Education Commission over issues related to public basic education in Nigeria.[265] SERAP contended that the destruction of Nigeria's natural resources through large-scale corruption is the sole cause of the problems denying the majority of the citizens access to quality education.[266] The applicant further contended that the "allegations of high-level corruption have contributed to series of serious and massive

[262] Ibid., ¶¶ 113–115.

[263] Ibid.

[264] Amnesty International, "Judgment Orders Government to Punish Oil Companies Over Pollution," note 247.

[265] SERAP Public Education Case, note 204. The judges in this case were Hansine N. Donli, Anthony A. Benin, and Sournana D. Sidibe, with Justice Donli (President 2001–2007) from Nigeria, listed as President in the judgment. As indicated in note 21, Donli was among the seven founding judges of the CCJ.

[266] SERAP Public Education Case, note 204. In making this argument, SERAP pointed to a report by the Independent Corrupt Practices Commission (ICPC), which uncovered corrupt practices in the management of funds allocated for education. The Commission was created in September 2000, at the inception of Nigeria's Fourth Republic, in the perennial attempt to reduce or eliminate corruption in public life in Nigeria. The Commission receives and investigates reports of corruption and, in appropriate cases, prosecute the offenders; examines, reviews, and enforces the correction of corruption-prone systems and procedures of public bodies, with a view to eliminating corruption in public life; educates and enlightens members of the public on and against corruption and related offences with a view to enlisting

violations of the right to education, including lack of access to quality primary education in Nigeria."[267] It alleged that the Nigerian national government "contributed to these problems by failing to seriously address all allegations of corruption at the highest levels of government and the levels of impunity that facilitate corruption in Nigeria."[268] The situation, in turn, had contributed to the denial of the right of the peoples to freely dispose of their wealth and natural resources, to the detriment of socioeconomic rights, including enjoyment of the right to education.[269]

The Court disagreed with the proposition of Nigerian officialdom to the effect that education is "a mere directive policy of the government and not a legal entitlement of the citizens."[270] Instead, it ruled that "every Nigerian child is entitled to free and compulsory basic education."[271] It explained that, although non-justiciable under the Nigerian Constitution, the right to basic education is justiciable under the Banjul Charter.[272] The Court reasoned that embezzlement or theft of part of the funds allocated to the basic education sector will have a negative impact as the shortage of funds will impede performance at the level for which the budget was approved.[273] However, this, by itself, is not determinative. The most that could be said, as a matter of middle ground, is that while steps are being taken to recover the funds or prosecute the suspects who stole, diverted, embezzled, misapplied, or in other respects, mismanaged, the monies appropriated for basic education in the ten states of Nigeria the plaintiffs complained about, the Nigerian national government "should take the necessary steps to provide the money to cover the shortfall to ensure a smooth implementation of the education program, lest a section

and fostering public support for the fight against corruption. See The Corrupt Practices and Other Related Offenses Act 2000, Act No. 5, *Laws of the Federation of Nigeria*, https://web.archive.org/web/20100312232055/http://www.nigeria-law.org/Corrupt%20Practices%20and%20other%20Related%20Offences%20Act%202000.htm ("An Act to prohibit and prescribe punishment for corrupt practices and other related offenses").

267 SERAP Public Education Case, note 204.

268 Ibid.

269 Ibid.

270 Quoted in Sloth-Nielsen, note 239, p. 642.

271 SERAP Public Education Case, note 204, ¶ 26.

272 Ibid.

273 SERAP Public Education Case, note 204.

of the people should be denied a right to education."[274] In their important study on the CCJ, Alter and her coauthors commented on the CCJ's "circumspection with regard to remedies,"[275] specifically their wariness "in interpreting international law and in modulating the remedies that they award to successful applicants."[276] This is one such instance.

Amnesty International praised the decision as "an important restatement of the principles of universality and indivisibility of all human rights established in both the [Banjul Charter] and the [UDHR]," as well as a signification of "an important step forward in the progressive realization of economic, social and cultural rights in Nigeria in particular, and the West Africa sub-region in general."[277] It advised the Nigerian national government to "publicly acknowledge that it is bound by the decision made by the ECOWAS Court and that it will take immediate steps to enforce it," as well as "to address corruption in the education sector in order to ensure the right to education."[278] To promote the effectiveness of the CCJ and with it the growth of human rights in West Africa, it advised, all ECOWAS member-states should use their influence to ensure that the Nigerian government complied with the decision.[279] Additionally, consistent with their international obligations, these countries should also "take steps to ensure that the right to free and compulsory basic education is upheld in their own countries."[280]

[274] Ibid., ¶ 28.

[275] Alter et al., note 4, p. 766.

[276] Ibid., p. 777.

[277] Amnesty International, "Nigeria: ECOWAS Court Affirms Nigeria Accountable for Ensuring the Right to Education," Amnesty International Public Statement (December 6, 2010), https://www.amnesty.org/en/wp-content/uploads/2021/07/afr440322010en.pdf.

[278] Ibid.

[279] Ibid.

[280] Ibid.

Hadijatou Mani Koraou v. Niger

In this case, the Niger government enacted a law, part of its criminal code, that outlawed slavery.[281] The law made slavery a crime punishable by 10–30 years imprisonment and a fine of 1–5 million CFA in Nigerien law.[282] The law made Niger one of few countries in West Africa and beyond to outlaw slavery.[283] However, the Niger government enforced this law laxly.

Thus, when the judicial system failed to convict her "owner" under this law, Mani, then 24 years old, proverbially took the law into her own hand by bring her case before the CCJ for resolution, taking advantage of a provision of the ECOWAS Supplementary Protocol of 2005, which gave individuals and NGOs direct access to the Court to vindicate human-right concerns.[284] Hadijatou was born into an established slave class and like all slaves in Niger, was inherited, sold, and made to work without pay.[285] She was also used as a sexual slave by her master.[286] In 1996, when Hadijatou was about twelve, she was sold to a local tribal chief, El Hadj Souleymane Naroua.[287] The transaction took place in accordance with a customary practice in Niger called "Wahiya," which allows for young girls, generally slaves, to be acquired to work as a servant and as a concubine.[288] A slave bought under these conditions is known as a "Sadaka" and is regarded by her "master" as being available to engage in sexual relations at any time.[289] During the nearly ten years Hadijatou was enslaved by Naroua, she gave birth to four children, all fathered by him, two of which children

[281] See note 233 and accompanying text.

[282] Ibid.

[283] Jeroen Beirnaert, "West-African Court Slavery Judgment," *International Union Rights*, 16(2) (2009), 19, https://www.ilo.org/sites/default/files/wcmsp5/groups/public/@ed_norm/@declaration/documents/publication/wcms_140854.pdf.

[284] See note 96 and accompanying text.

[285] The text of this judgment is available in French, one of three ECOWAS working and official languages; the other two are English and Portuguese. Because this author does not speak French, these comments draw on sources written in English, including the excellent case by Interights, a London-based NGO, now closed. See Interights, "*Hadijatou Mani v Niger*," https://www.interights.org/niger-slavery/index.html.

[286] Interights, "*Hadijatou Mani v. Niger*," note 285.

[287] Ibid.

[288] Ibid.

[289] Ibid.

survived.[290] In August, 2005, Hadijatou was told she was free to leave, but when she tried to do so and married a man of her choice, Naroua had her charged for bigamy for which she spent time two months in jail.[291]

The CCJ ruled that Hadijatou was unquestionably "held in slavery for 9 years, in violation of the prohibition" on slavery in both international and domestic law, including Nigerien domestic law.[292] The judgment reaffirmed the long-established prohibition of slavery in international law, including the *erga omnes* nature of the obligations relating to slavery as being owed to the community of nations as a whole,[293] and its status as a peremptory norm forbidding the creation of any "modern forms of slavery."[294] It ordered the Nigerien government to pay Hadijatou the sum of 10 million CFA, about US$19,000–$20,000, in damages, as reparation and as restitution for the harm she suffered.[295]

It reasoned that, through its government, the Niger state had not lived up to its legal responsibility to protect Hadijatou from slavery under domestic and international laws.[296] Instead, it had passively, but no less destructively, tolerated the practice. The Court stressed the need for the state to take positive measures to protect its citizens from slavery. It put on record the failure of the judiciary in this case to condemn the practice of slavery, when Hadijatou's case came to its attention, a failure to act to protect her that it analogizes to tolerance or acceptance of slavery.[297] Although the CCJ did not specify in detail the nature of the state's positive obligations to prevent slavery, it noted the obligation of the authorities to take adequate measures to contain or eradicate slavery.[298] To the contrary, at several points, the Niger government failed through its judicial and administrative authorities to perform its protective human-right obligations.[299] The Court rejected the argument of Niger's counsel

[290] Ibid.

[291] Ibid.

[292] Interights, "*Hadijatou Mani v. Niger*," note 285 (citing ¶ 80 of the judgment).

[293] Ibid.

[294] Ibid.

[295] Ibid.

[296] Legal Information Institute, The Karaou Case, note 233.

[297] Interights, "*Hadijatou Mani v. Niger*," note 285 (citing ¶ 84 of the judgment).

[298] Ibid.

[299] Ibid. (citing ¶¶ 85–86).

related to the exhaustion of local remedy, making it incumbent upon a judicial tribunal to intervene only where the state in question had failed to protect the right of an aggrieved person.[300]

This case is one of the most celebrated in the wellspring of the CCJ's human-right jurisprudence, and one of the first cases of slavery adjudicated in an international court. The judgment was delivered in Niamey, Niger's capital on October 27, 2008, rather than in Abuja, the headquarters of the CCJ, to dramatize the importance of the case. On practical grounds, deciding the case in Niamey lent critical access to the victim, her witnesses, and civil society to the court proceedings, with ramifications for the debate on slavery in Niger and beyond.[301] Because CCJ judgments are binding on all member-states of ECOWAS, it was expected to have an effect in many other West African states. The occurrence created a moment of international standard embedded in the application of human rights in external affairs for ECOWAS member-states, including Nigeria, focus of this book.

The case gained a high level of publicity, setting the precedent for minority groups, especially women, to fight back against the traditional slavery practices common to Niger as well as other ECOWAS nations.[302] It also bestowed personal honors on Hadijatou for mustering the determination and good sense to bring it. In 2009, she was honored by the US State Department with the "International Woman of Courage" award.[303] Then US Secretary of State Hilary Clinton praised her as "an inspiring person."[304] Similarly, she was named by *Time Magazine* as one of the top 100 most influential people in 2009.[305]

The Niger government acknowledged that the judgment was binding on it and pledged to respect it.[306] Thus, on March 17, 2009, the government fully paid the compensation due to Hadijatou, enabling her to rebuild the fragments of her life marred or impeded by her negative experiences as a slave, and dismissed the pending criminal case of bigamy

300 Ibid.

301 Interights, "*Hadijatou Mani v. Niger*," note 285.

302 Legal Information Institute, The Karaou Case, note 233.

303 Interights, "*Hadijatou Mani v. Niger*," note 285.

304 See ibid.

305 Interights, "*Hadijatou Mani v. Niger*," note 285.

306 Ibid.

against her.[307] Unfortunately, as the French saying goes, the more things change, the more they manage to remain the same. While developments have been made toward holding Hadijatou's former master accountable for her enslavement, for many, progress in this respect has been uneven and suboptimal. While Naroua was found guilty of slavery, the punishment was light, given the gravity of the crime involved.[308] On March 31, 2009, he was sentenced to 12 months in prison, with a fine of 500,000 francs CFA, and 1 million CFA in damages awarded to Hadijatou.[309] At this point, Naroua appealed to the Tribunal Correctionelle of Konni, which, after hearing the case on June 30, 2009, sentenced him to a three-year suspended sentence and reduced the amount he was ordered to pay by half to 500,000 CFA.[310]

Maneh v. The Gambia

In this case, Ebrimah Manneh, a journalist with the *Daily Observer* newspaper based in Banjul, The Gambia, was accosted by two plainclothes officials of the country's National Intelligence Agency at the premises of the newspaper on July 11, 2006.[311] He was arrested without charges and detained indefinitely.[312] Manneh was believed to have disclosed information critical of the government that appeared in a news article. He disappeared until January 2007, when reports emerged that he was being detained at a local police station.[313] Intelligence and police officials denied that he was in their custody.[314]

In May 2007, Media Foundation for West Africa (MFWA) filed a complaint with the ECOWAS Court charging The Gambian government with numerous human-right abuses, with a demand for Manneh's release,

[307] Ibid.

[308] Ibid.

[309] Ibid.

[310] Ibid.

[311] Judgment No. ECW/CCJ/JUD/03/08 (June 5, 2008), note 206, ¶ 5 ("Summary of the Facts").

[312] Ibid.

[313] Ibid., ¶¶ 7–8.

[314] Ibid.

as well as compensation for his injuries.[315] The MFWA is an NGO, based in Accra, Ghana, with a network of national partner organizations in sixteen countries in West Africa, with a branch in The Gambia. Manneh was detained under dehumanizing conditions, including sleeping on a bare floor in overcrowded cells, solitary confinement, and denial of access to medical care.[316] The Gambian government refused to respond to the complaint and ignored multiple requests to appear or file documents, as well as a plea from his counsel on March 16, 2007 for his release.[317]

The Court ruled for Manneh, ordering The Gambian government to release him from "unlawful detention without any further delay," and pay him US$100,000 in damages.[318] It reasoned that the actions of the government violated specific provisions of the Banjul Charter, of which The Gambia is a state party, including the presumption of innocence until proven guilty, the right to defense by counsel of his choice, the right to be tried within a reasonable time by an impartial tribunal, and the right to petition for redress.[319]

The Gambia ignored the judgment, for which it was roundly criticized in the media. The International Press Institute (IPI), criticized the Gambian government's "flagrant disregard" of the ruling.[320] The IPI is a global network of editors, media executives, and leading journalists, who dedicate their energies to the defense of media freedom and support for independent journalism. Equally, the African Commission on Human Rights lent its voice with an appeal for The Gambian government "to immediately and fully comply" with the judgment.[321] In the midst of this fracas, in March 2011, Gambian authorities announced that Manneh had died, but denied any involvement in his death.[322]

The case here is actually two in one; the other proverbially joined to it at the hips, for reasons that become obvious soon, is *Musa Saidykhan*

[315] Ibid., ¶¶ 9, 19.

[316] Ibid.

[317] Ibid.

[318] Ibid., ¶ 44.

[319] Ibid., ¶ 41.

[320] Quoted in Alter et al., note 4, p. 762.

[321] Ibid.

[322] Committee to Protect Journalists, "Chief Ebrima Manneh," https://cpj.org/data/people/chief-ebrima-manneh/.

v. The Gambia in 2010,[323] which involves the detention and torture of Musa Saidykhan.[324] After a coup attempt in 2006, a nongovernment newspaper published the names of individuals that the Gambian National Intelligence Agency had arrested. Shortly thereafter and without a warrant, soldiers and policemen arrested Saidykhan, the newspaper's editor, and took him to a detention center, where he was tortured and held for twenty-two days. Eventually, intelligence officials released Saidykhan, but continued to monitor his movements and threatened his family, ultimately causing Saidykhan and his family to flee the country.

Supported by the MFWA, in 2007, Saidykhan filed a complaint before the CCJ, seeking a declaration that his arrest and detention were illegal and that he had been tortured and denied a fair hearing. This time around, unlike in *Manneh*, the Gambia government responded. This "was harder for the government to ignore, because the plaintiff was alive, exhibited clear evidence of torture, and pursued the case from the safety of another country."[325] It asked the Court to dismiss the suit on the grounds that it lacked jurisdiction over the case, that the Court's intervention was "an affront to [its] sovereignty," and that the suit should be heard by a national court, part of the reason being that the Court's intervention posed "an affront to [The Gambia's] sovereignty."

The CCJ rejected these arguments. This was context for the Gambian government's campaign in 2009 to narrow the human-right jurisdiction of the Court.[326] The attack on the Court occurred while the merits phase of Saidykhan was pending. Gambian officials expressed that they were "aggrieved" by the judgment in the Manneh case and that they had "set the political process in motion to […] get the decision set aside."[327] In September 2009, the Gambia called for a Meeting of Government Experts to revise the 2005 Protocol and restrict the Court's authority.[328] Specifically, Gambia leaders sought to limit the

[323] Suit No. ECW/CCJ/APP/11/07, Judgment No. ECW/CCJ/JUD/08/10 (December 16, 2010), https://caselaw.ihrda.org/en/entity/froafttgl56tn7350qszzd7vi.

[324] Ibid., ¶ 41.

[325] Alter et al., note 4, p. 762.

[326] See ibid., pp. 761–762.

[327] Quoted in ibid., pp. 762–763.

[328] Alter et al., note 4, p. 763.

CCJ's human-right jurisdiction to treaties ratified by the respondent state and to require exhaustion of domestic remedies.[329]

However, the attempt failed. The ECOWAS Committee of Legal Experts recommended against narrowing the Court's human rights jurisdiction.[330] The Council of Justice Ministers endorsed the committee's recommendation, and so too did the Council of Foreign Ministers.[331] In sum, The Gambia's proposals aimed at revisiting the 2005 Protocol with the intent to limiting the CCJ's human-right jurisdiction to treaties ratified by member-states and requiring plaintiffs to exhaust local remedies before approaching the Court failed.

In December 2010, in the aftermath of that unsuccessful attempt to restrict its authority, the CCJ held the Gambian government responsible for the illegal detention and torture of Saidykhan and ordered it to pay him US$200,000 in damages.[332] However, The Gambia refused to comply with either the Saidykhan or the Manneh judgments.[333] Instead, in 2011, in addition to denying responsibility for Manneh's death, it asked the Court to set aside both judgments.[334] Rather than do so, the Court reaffirmed the two judgments and remedial orders.[335] Despite this stout political opposition, proverbially, the worst is over, mostly thanks to the strong support of local and regional NGOs and the sagacity of the Court, including its deft "circumspection with regard to remedies."[336] For, in the keen assessment of Alter and her colleagues, in the period after the Court successfully staved off the attempt from The Gambia to stem its jurisdiction, its authority "rested on a more solid foundation than when" it first got it in 2005.[337]

[329] Ibid.

[330] Ibid., p. 763.

[331] Ibid.

[332] Judgment No. ECW/CCJ/JUD/08/10 (December 16, 2010), note 323, ¶¶ 46–47.

[333] Alter et al., note 4, p. 764.

[334] Ibid.

[335] Ibid.

[336] Alter et al., note 4, p 766.

[337] Ibid., p. 765.

Final Word on Legal Instruments and Related Matters

Recall the transition of the CCJ, recounted above, from adjudicating disputes relating to interpretation and application of Community acts to cases involving violations of human rights that occur in any member-state.[338] Acquiring human-right jurisdiction made the CCJ "one of the most transformed international courts in terms of functions, structure, and processes."[339] It is an occurrence that some commentators, speaking to the reorientation "in a new direction" that the process involved, praise as "redeployment,"[340] yet in other respects veritably gradualist.

> ECOWAS's contested involvement in humanitarian intervention brought human rights concerns into Community politics. Eager to prevent civil wars and violent unrest in the region, ECOWAS assumed a conflict prevention role and then expanded its activities to include promoting constitutional transitions, good governance, and human rights. These developments created a permissive environment for civil society groups and ECOWAS judges to lobby member states to give the Court a human rights jurisdiction, in part by arguing that doing so would also further economic integration.[341]

In short, by implication, the coalition of governmental leaders, Community officials, and NGOs so central to the life and work of the Court made choices that served to "maintain[] the barriers to judicial enforcement of regional economic rules while facilitating a wave of human rights complaints by private litigants[.]"[342] Plainly, taking the gradualist interpretation route, there were more practical factors at play embedded in the reality that individuals must be granted direct access to the Court for it to become fully operational.[343] Before the supplementary protocol

[338] See note 95 and accompanying text; and Community Court of Justice—ECOWAS, "About Us," note 32.

[339] Trust Africa Foundation, "Rethinking the Proposed Restructuring of the ECOWAS Community Court of Justice," note 144.

[340] Alter et al., note 4, p. 772.

[341] Ibid., p. 775.

[342] Ibid.

[343] *Bringing Justice Home: The Road to Final, Appellate and Regional Court Establishments*, ed. Cheryl Thompson-Barrow (London, UK: Commonwealth Secretariat, 2008), 44 (citing Franca Ofor).

of 2005, which amended the Protocol of the Community Court of 1991, few cases wend their way to the Court, and because they came directly from individuals, those cases were struck out for want of jurisdiction.[344] That was how, coupled with the jettison of the mandate to exhaust local remedies through national courts, the 2005 amendments made the CCJ "one of the busiest courts in Africa."[345]

The emergence of the CCJ from an ad hoc tribunal charged with interpreting and applying Community acts to a permanent Court that adjudicates cases involving violation of human rights in every ECOWAS member-state made it what Open Society Foundations, the US-based nonprofit consortium, likened to four-courts-in-one: a human-right court, a court for resolution of inter-state disputes, an administrative court for ECOWAS, and a court of arbitration.[346] What is more, the authority did not come through judicial lawmaking.[347] Instead, the route to that authority involved a coordinated campaign wherein bar associations, NGOs, and ECOWAS officials, joined with CCJ judges, mobilized to secure member-states' consent to the transformation.[348]

No different from their counterparts in other subregional courts in Africa, adjudicating human rights affords the CCJ "an opportunity to expand their dockets, develop legal doctrine, and issue rulings that are relevant to stakeholders. If the courts' decisions also complement or extend the norms of the African Charter, so much the better."[349] And because of this occurrence or in spite of it, vis-à-vis their counterparts in

[344] Ibid.

[345] Adeosun, note 6, pp. 68–69.

[346] Open Society Foundations, "Fact Sheet: ECOWAS Community Court of Justice" (June 2013), https://www.justiceinitiative.org/publications/ecowas-community-court-justice.

[347] Timothy Endicott, "How Judges Make Law," in *The Foundations and Future of Public Law: Essays in Honor of Paul Craig*, eds. Elizabeth Fisher et al., 127–144 (New York: Oxford University Press, 2020) (abstract) (portraying case law as "something that springs from the imagination of the judge"). Judicial lawmaking comes in a range of activities that includes "developing, adapting, modifying, filling gaps, interpreting, or even branching out in a new direction." ICJ Judge Sir Robert Jennings, quoted in Mohamed Shahabuddeen, *Precedent in the World Court* 91 (London, UK: Cambridge University Press, 2007).

[348] Alter et al., note 4, p. 738.

[349] Ibid., p. 778.

other African subregions, the change has been attended by little political backlash from the governments of ECOWAS member-states.[350] For Nigeria, window into the world in this book, this is a quintessential moment in the promotion of international standards to the benefit of application of human rights in external relations.

Although not a human-right court by design, the CCJ belongs on the list of any human-right tribunals.[351] The Court personifies "an international institution created to achieve one objective which evolved to take on very different functions," including a role that "constrains the discretion of" its creators.[352] Not only did ECOWAS member-states give the CCJ a broad human-right jurisdiction, from every indication so far, "they have [also] eschewed opportunities to narrow the Court's authority."[353] Because CCJ judges "address[] many issues that have yet to come before the African Commission or Court," they make "important contributions

[350] See Alter et al. note 4, 750–753 (commenting on "the Coordinated Campaign by Nonstate Actors to Redesign the ECOWAS Court, and the Surprising Absence of Member State Opposition" in the aftermath of the Afolabi case decided April 27, 2004). See also Karen J. Alter et al., "Backlash Against International Courts in West, East, and Southern Africa: Causes and Consequences," in *The Performance of Africa's International Courts: Using Litigation for Political, Legal, and Social Change*, ed. James Thuo Gathii (Oxford University Press, 2020), https://doi.org/10.1093/oso/9780198868477.003.0008 (arguing that variations in the mobilization efforts of community secretariats, civil society groups, and sub-regional parliaments explain why efforts to eliminate the three courts or narrow their jurisdiction were defeated in ECOWAS, scaled back in the EACJ and largely succeeded in the SADC). Alter and her coauthors analyzed attempts by three African governments (The Gambia in West Africa, Kenya in East Africa, and Zimbabwe in Southern Africa) to restrict the jurisdiction of three similarly-situated subregional courts in response to politically controversial rulings. In West Africa, when the Court of the Economic Community of West African States (ECOWAS) upheld allegations of torture by opposition journalists in Gambia, that country's political leaders sought to restrict the Court's power to review human rights complaints. The other Member States ultimately defeated Gambia's proposal. In East Africa, Kenya failed in its efforts to eliminate the East African Court of Justice (EACJ) and to remove some of its judges after a decision challenging an election to a sub-regional legislature. However, the member-states agreed to restructure the EACJ in ways that have significantly affected the Court's subsequent trajectory. In Southern Africa, after the Southern African Development Community (SADC) Tribunal ruled in favor of white farmers in disputes over land seizures, Zimbabwe prevailed upon SADC Member States to suspend the Tribunal and strip its power to review complaints from private litigants.

[351] Alter et al., note 4, p. 775.

[352] Ibid., p. 768.

[353] Ibid., p. 738.

to regional human rights jurisprudence."[354] Overall, vis-à-vis subregional community courts elsewhere in Africa, the CCJ's "status as a human rights court is far more settled [...]."[355] And whether dramatic or gradualist, these changes are more long-lasting than fluky.[356]

This is not to suggest that everything is smooth sailing or pain-free for the Court, because it is not. Rather, no different from other ECOWAS institutions, the CCJ has challenges, some of those unique to it, others difficulties that it shares with likeminded institutions. One shared difficulty is inadequate funding.[357] Like ECOWAS of which it is an organ, the Court is funded through a self-funding mechanism consisting of funds generated through a 0.5% levy placed on goods imported into the subregion that member-states then remit to a specified ECOWAS account to cover the operational costs of the community.[358] For the rest of its budget, ECOWAS and the Court then rely substantially on the payment of levies and voluntary donations from member-states.[359]

For all the financial independence that it embodies,[360] the problem with the levy system is the lack of commitment by member-states to honor their financial obligations to the Community, evident in the accumulation of arrears, detrimental to the growth of the economic union, by these member-states.[361] The arrangement is blamed for the chronic deficit that has befallen the Community dating back to 2000.[362] In 2016, the

354 Ibid., p. 768.

355 Ibid.

356 Reflecting on the depth of the CCJ's commitment to human rights, Alter and her colleagues introspect, based on interviews with government officials, human rights groups, and lawyers, that ECOWAS member-states "will eventually specify which human rights treaties can be adjudicated by the ECOWAS Court, add an exhaustion of domestic remedies requirement, and create an appellate review mechanism." Alter et al., note 4, p. 778. They added instructively that "[t]hese revisions, if they do occur, should not be seen as rebukes of either the Court or its judges[;] [r]ather, such revisions are more likely to reflect a maturing legal system that is evolving in conjunction with fundamental reorientations of ECOWAS objectives." Ibid.

357 See Adeosun, note 6, pp. 113–114.

358 Ibid.

359 Ibid.

360 ECOWAS is reputed as one of the most financially independent organizations in Africa. See Adeosun, note 6, p. 114.

361 Ibid.

362 Ibid.

account of the economic union was in the red; the budgetary deficit coincided with the drastic deterioration of Nigeria's economic fortunes due to a steep fall in the world's oil market.[363] Unfortunately, besides Nigeria, only few countries like Côte d'Ivoire and Ghana provide contributions high enough to keep the economic union financially buoyant.[364]

Next to problems unique to the CCJ as an institution, one that readily comes to mind is noncompliance with its judgments,[365] that even CCJ judges themselves complain about.[366] Unlike tribunals, such as the CJEU, the CCJ lacks reliable mechanisms for enforcing its policies and fostering compliance with its decisions. ECOWAS instruments provide little guidelines on the remedies that the Court can utilize in making whole litigants who approach it for relief.[367] Instead, while the decisions of the Court (like those of the AHSG and the CM) are binding, they have no legal force on member-states who, instead, are merely encouraged, never mandated, to synchronize their laws and policies with the aims of the Community, including facilitating execution of the Court's judgment. Commentators like the researcher Adedamola Adeosun lament that leaving enforcement of the Court's decision to the goodwill and related idiosyncrasies of member-states is a thing of gamble that just doesn't work.[368]

Alter and her colleagues put the matter more nuancedly. While conceding the problem as "formidable,"[369] they also believe that, given the infancy of the CCJ and other subregional judicial tribunals in Africa, vis-à-vis their counterparts in Europe and the Americas (North and South

[363] Ibid.

[364] Ibid.

[365] See ibid., pp. 111–113.

[366] See, for example, "West African Countries Disregard ECOWAS Court Rulings—Judge," *Vanguard* (Lagos) (November 22, 2021), https://www.vanguardngr.com/2021/11/heifer-in-talks-with-diaspora-investors-for-livestock-production (referencing Amoako Asante, President of the Court).

[367] See Tony Anene-Maidoh, "Enforcement of Judgments of the ECOWAS Court of Justice," *National Institute for Legislative and Democratic Studies (NILDS)* (2018), 58, 70, https://ir.nilds.gov.ng/bitstream/handle/123456789/387/ENFORCEMENT%20OF%20JUDGMENTS%20OF%20THE%20ECOWAS%20COURT%20OF%20JUSTICE.pdf?sequence=1&isAllowed=y.

[368] Adeosun, note 6, p. 112.

[369] Alter et al., note 4, p. 777.

America), the difficulty needs to be put in closer perspective.[370] Plus, they point out, CCJ judges have exhibited sagaciousness and political savviness in various ways, bound to make the issue of noncompliance less deeply felt, including narrowly tailoring the remedies they award to successful plaintiffs.[371]

Even with less than full compliance, CCJ judgments have rich political and social values: they are tool of "political mobilization" through which marginalized communities, tapping into international law, "increase[d] their out of court political leverage."[372] The decisions trigger "domestic debates" within member-states.[373] And while these countries may not fully implement the judgments due to constraints like lack of financial or human resources, the Court "enjoys the grudging respect" of member-states, rather than readily dismissed by disagreeable member-states.[374]

Several factors account for why, despite the attempt to curtail its jurisdiction, the CCJ still stands on strong political and legal grounds compared to other judicial tribunals in Africa; how it manages to deliver "legally and politically consequential decisions,"[375] unscathed by the rough and tumble of politics in Africa. First, the Court weathers challenges that come its way by mobilizing supportive constituencies, moderating the remedies it awards to successful litigants, and overall nudging governments publicly, yet gently, to implement its decisions.[376] Second, its jurisprudence embedded in human rights "enjoys the strong support of the ECOWAS Commission," whose officials, well versed in "the political landscape" of the Community, are able to "redirect opposition to the Court in ways that address member states' concerns without compromising the judges' independence."[377] Third, since 2006,

[370] Ibid.

[371] Ibid.

[372] Obiora Chinedu Okafor et al., "On the Modest Impact of West Africa's International Human Rights Court on the Executive Branch of Government in Nigeria," *Harvard Human Rights Journal*, 35 (2022), 170.

[373] Solomon Ebobrah, "The ECOWAS Community Court of Justice: A Dual Mandate with Skewed Authority," in *International Court Authority*, eds. Karen J. Alter et al. (New York: Oxford University Press, 2018), 82, 94.

[374] Okafor, note 372, p. 170.

[375] Alter et al., note 4, p. 765.

[376] Ibid., pp. 738–739, 766.

[377] Ibid., p. 777.

Community protocols apply directly in national legal orders without the need for country-to-country ratification.[378] In their coalescence, these factors speak to the huge asset-hood of the Court in the realization of international standard embedded in the application of human rights in external affairs for Nigeria nay other ECOWAS member-states, dealt with more fully in the next section.

The CCJ and the Application of Human Rights in Nigeria's External Relations: Possibilities and Limits

The key word in this chapter, as set out in the introduction, is the amenability of the CCJ as a tool for the application of human rights in Nigeria's external relations. Vis-à-vis the other two visible co-methods (peacekeeping and the TAC), the CCJ offers itself as the most promising technique for that application. Used in tandem with the other two, it is formidable. This is one instance where potential or apparentness, rather than actual result now, counts for so much.[379] Approaching this conversation from the perspective of a search for the international standards embedded in human rights, the possibilities related to application of human rights in external relations for Nigeria and other ECOWAS member-states are plentiful matched against conceivable limits.

In the wake of the adoption of the treaty in 1993 and supporting protocols, ECOWAS activities are said to have been underlain with concepts of democracy, human rights, and the rule of law.[380] No singular institution of the Community typifies this fortuitous and auspicious development like the CCJ with its human-right jurisprudence. "Although the ECOWAS Court exercises jurisdiction over fewer states, it is [...] at least as active in adjudicating human rights violations as are [the African Commission on Human and Peoples' Rights and the African Court

[378] See note 126 and accompanying text.

[379] An insight that comes to mind here is the thought of King David, the psalmist when he observed from his mind's eyes that "the hills [were] clothed with gladness," with the meadows and valleys "shout[ing] for joy," each, in its singularly distinctive manner, bearing witness to God's creative work. Psalm 65: 12–13, *Holy Bible*, New International Version.

[380] See Table 8.2 , especially the last column titled "salient provisions and related matters on the road to human-right jurisprudence."

on Human and Peoples' Rights]," both continent-wide institutions.[381] By rendering in a timely manner, legally and politically consequential decisions that "provide[] legally binding remedies to victims who have direct access to the Court without exhausting local remedies[,]" and addressing "issues that have yet to come before the" African Commission on Human and Peoples' Rights or the Court, binding on ECOWAS member-states and institutions of the Community, without the need for country-to-country ratifications, the CJJ contributes importantly to subregional human-right jurisprudence.[382]

This is a good instance of application and export of international standards embedded in human rights, not only for Nigeria, but also for other ECOWAS member-states. What is more, the CCJ's human-right jurisprudence "enhances [...] the clarity of international law and raises [...] human rights protections in West Africa."[383]

> For *civil society groups*, the ECOWAS Court and other subregional tribunals offer a way to minimize the obstruction, haggling, [and] delay that many observers associate with the continental human rights system [internal quotes omitted]. For *lawyers*, subregional litigation provides a corrective to the limited avenues of legal recourse available to victims of rights abuses in Africa. [And] *[f]or judges* on subregional courts, the adjudication of human rights provides an opportunity to expand their dockets, develop legal doctrine, and issue rulings that are relevant to stakeholders. If the courts' decisions also complement or extend the norms of the African Charter, so much the better.[384]

In the aftermath of the Supplementary Protocol of 2005, which broadened the jurisdiction of the Court to embrace determination of cases of human-right violations "that occur in any member state," the Court has assumed a level of activity in the adjudication of human rights issues some legal scholars praise as second to none in Africa.[385] It has "become a go-to alternative for litigants who do not have faith in the judiciaries in

[381] Alert et al., note 4, p. 756.

[382] Ibid., p. 775.

[383] Ibid., p. 778.

[384] Ibid. Emphasis added.

[385] Alter et al., note 4, pp. 737–779.

their member states."[386] Given that many member-states of ECOWAS "face the challenge of a lack of functional judicial systems as a result of various social and political instabilities," the CCJ has become the forum of choice for litigants on matters that sound on human rights. Many of these litigants are Nigerians.

What sets this Court apart from other subregional judicial tribunals, such as the East African Court of Justice, the Tribunal of the South African Development Community, and the continent-based African Court of Human and Peoples' Rights, are its three distinctive features, namely: (i) direct access for private parties, including NGOs; (ii) absence of ECOWAS-specific human-right instrument or standards, a phenomenon scholars denominate "indeterminate human rights jurisdiction"; and (iii) absence of any requirement for litigants to first exhaust domestic remedies, such as in national courts, or administrative agencies, before approaching the Court.[387] Each of these concepts bears some elaboration. First, direct access to litigants. Through various means, including rebuffing arguments that human rights are matters essentially within a state's domestic jurisdiction, that ECOWAS legal instruments, such as treaties and protocols, have no domestic effect, and that direct access for NGOs should be denied because litigants have no standing to challenge human-right violations before national courts, the CCJ has successfully rejected attempts by the governments of ECOWAS member-states to circumvent the direct-access provision.[388] But where, with respect to NGOs, the Court appears to draw the line is that "no corporate body can bring a human rights case before this court as a plaintiff as an alleged victim of human rights abuse."[389] As Alter et al. point out, this feature is "unusual [i.e., innovative] for a new human rights [C]ourt."[390]

Next to indeterminate jurisprudence, the CCJ's lack of a designated human-right charter to apply presents both risk and benefit for the

[386] Adeosun, note 6 (abstract).

[387] Alter et al., note 4, pp. 753–756.

[388] Ibid., pp. 753–754.

[389] Community Court of Justice, *Starcrest Investment Ltd. v. President of ECOWAS Commission,* Case No. ECW/CCJ/APP/01/08, ECW/CCJ/JUD/06/11, ¶ 17 (July 8, 2011), https://www.worldcourts.com/ecowasccj/eng/decisions/2011.07.08_Starcrest_Investment_Ltd_v_President_of_ECOWAS_Comm.htm.

[390] Alter et al., note 4, p. 753.

Court.[391] The benefit is that it precludes political controversy over which rights the Court could review.[392] The potential risk from the lack is that application of human rights could be challenged as an overbroad delegation to interpret an ever-evolving area of international law—or, more basically, expose the Court to the accusation that it is applying human-right instruments that are not legally binding.[393] However, CCJ judges view the lack of a designated human-right instrument not as a criticism as such but rather as an "opportunity to define and delimit the scope and legal parameters of [the Court's] human rights mandate in its own image."[394] Even so, the jurisprudence is less indeterminate than it appears on the surface given that, as some have argued, over the course of its work, the CCJ appears to have adopted the African Charter on Human and Peoples' Rights as its human rights bill, pursuant to Art. 4(g) of the 1993 Revised Treaty.[395]

Finally on the lack of a requirement to first exhaust domestic remedies, the absence helps the CCJ. Human-right petition systems, regional and UN, require individuals to first seek relief in domestic venues like national courts or administrative, or, in the alternative, explain that such remedies are futile because they are unavailable, ineffective, or insufficient, failing which the complaint in question stands dismissed.[396] This requirement has several benefits, including that it gives domestic institutions a proverbial first bite of the apple in addressing the complaint in question, reduces forum shopping and precludes needless rivalry between domestic and international courts, reduces the risk of conflicting decisions, and prevents international tribunals from being overburdened by a deluge of human-right cases.[397]

But, like with direct access to private litigants, CCJ judges have firmly rebuffed argument to the contrary, insisting that the non-exhaustion rule

[391] See Alter et al., note 4, pp. 754–755.

[392] Ibid.

[393] Ibid.

[394] Ibid., p. 754, quoting Tony Anene-Maidoh, then Chief Registrar of the Court.

[395] See ECOWAS Revised Treaty, note 3, art. 4(g) (including "recognition, promotion and protection of human and peoples' rights in accordance with the provisions of the African Charter on Human and Peoples' Rights, among the "fundamental principles" of ECOWAS).

[396] Alert et al., note 4, pp. 755–756.

[397] Ibid.

is a deliberately settled upon, rather than an accidental happenstance, in the CCJ's architecture of human-right jurisprudence.[398] For this rule, as for direct access for private litigants and NGOs, CCJ judges would discontinue application of this rule only if ECOWAS adopts an amendment to the 2005 amendments to the 1991 Protocols that take them away, something that ECOWAS has not done yet, rather than through the artfulness of implication or related judicial construction.[399] Yet still on the non-exhaustion rule, the risk of conflict is mitigated by the CCJ's consciousness and alertness, an occurrence that it also asserts repeatedly, that it is not an appellate court and will, therefore, not generally review challenges to national court decisions.[400]

Something else about the CCJ as tool for the application of human rights in Nigeria's external relations: Judgments of the court "enjoy direct enforceability in the municipal sphere" of ECOWAS member-states, an occurrence that, as the Koraou decision relating to modern forms of slavery in Niger is testament, gives them "a fairly acceptable level of compliance,"[401] that minimizes the problem of noncompliance of CCJ decisions. Specifically, "through the binding nature of its judgments on all branches of the defendant state, executive, legislature and judiciary [...] as well as their superiority and precedence over domestic courts' decisions, and their direct enforcement," CCJ judgments "generate influence on [the] domestic systems" of ECOWAS member-countries.[402]

As indicated elsewhere, the activism of the CCJ in human rights since 2005 is a positive story for judicial independence in Nigeria.[403] "A subregional outfit yet located right inside Nigeria, the Community Court of Justice provides an alternative adjudicative point for litigants, especially on human rights issues, while putting pressure on Nigerian domestic courts

[398] Ibid.

[399] See ibid.

[400] Ibid., p. 756, n. 132.

[401] Adjolohoun, note 240, pp. 342–371, 351.

[402] Ibid., p. 351.

[403] See Philip C. Aka, "Judicial Independence Under Nigeria's Fourth Republic: Problems and Prospects," *California Western International Law Journal*, 45 (Fall 2014), 37–45 (commenting on two factors of Nigerian politics with potential implications for judicial independence, "the invigoration of the ECOWAS Community Court of Justice" being the "potentially positive" force).

in a manner that represents a boon to judicial independence."[404] Nigerian Fourth Republic leaders helped to instigate the grant of increased authority for the Court.[405] These leaders probably calculated that it was in the country's national interest to support a permanent court (rather than an ad hoc tribunal) that adjudicates the trade and related disputes of economic integration, while simultaneously dealing with human rights issues within national borders with potential to militate against regional security, if left unaddressed.[406] Whatever the reason, no less than the leaders of fellow member-states, they have shown no indication so far that they disapprove its active human-right jurisprudence.[407]

Through politically and legally consequential decisions like its judgment on basic public education and on the right to a healthy environment, guided by the Banjul Charter, the Court has contributed to the protection and promotion of socioeconomic human rights in Nigeria and by extension other member-states of ECOWAS, to the benefit of the application of human rights in external affairs. All this harks back to what scholars like Solomon T. Ebobrah and Victor Landon characterize as a backup mechanism Africa's international courts, including the CCJ, lend in supporting national courts in the protection of constitutional orders.[408] These courts accomplish the protection through four means: by flagging violations and acting as an early warning system, by expanding the normative and institutional scope of human right protection, by developing norms, and by setting boundaries of acceptable behavior.[409]

[404] Ibid., p. 45.

[405] Alter et al., note 4, p. 747.

[406] Ibid., pp. 772–773.

[407] Ibid., pp. 758–761.

[408] Solomon T. Ebobrah and Victor Landon, "Africa's Sub-Regional Courts as Back-Up Custodians of Constitutional Justice: Beyond the Compliance Question," in *The Performance of Africa's International Courts: Using Litigation for Political, Legal, and Social Change*, ed. James Thuo Gath (New York and London: Oxford University Press, 2020), 178–210.

[409] Ibid., pp. 206–210.

Conclusion

This chapter brings to a close the exploration in Part II of this book dedicated to methods for a human-right policy for Nigeria post-Buhari; the material began with Chapter 4 on reconstructing the country's national security in readiness for human-right work. Of the three obvious methods isolated for examination in this book, the CCJ appears to hold the most potential in the journey for principled foreign policy for Nigeria. Both peacekeeping and the TAC are work in progress. Peacekeeping is ridden with problems related to violations of human rights and humanitarian law that denude the otherwise signature tool of Nigerian foreign policy of critical human-right merits. For its part, the TAC is both inadequately funded (like its principal, the Ministry of Finance) and insufficiently bilateral. In contrast, the CCJ is not infected with any of these disabilities.

In one fell swoop, the founders of ECOWAS did two things bearing on the CCJ with ramifications for international standards embedded in human rights, including the application of human rights in external affairs, that drive this book. They created the CCJ to adjudicate inter-state economic disputes. One such notable trouble with immense bearing on human rights was the "tit for tat" revolved around the expulsion of supposedly illegal aliens from member-states that Nigeria conducted during a period of economic difficulties under its Second Republic from 1979 to 1983, in seeming retaliation of Ghana's own expulsion of Nigerian workers earlier on.[410]

More than the first, the second deed here, emblematized by the humanitarian interventions in Liberia and Sierra Leone from the 1980s to the 1990s, was a sheer act of serendipity. ECOWAS's peacekeeping initiatives, designed to minimize the regional impacts of the crises in Liberia and Sierra Leone in the 1980s and 1990s, led to human-right abuses by peacekeeping forces, including looting, expropriation, theft, and sexual exploitation of women and children.[411] These violations highlighted the

[410] See Jean-Marie Henckaerts, *Mass Expulsion in Modern International Law and Practice* (Leiden, Netherlands: Martinus Nijhoff Publishers, 1995), 66–71 (study of the problems of mass expulsion of aliens, migrant workers, and stateless persons in international law, including several case studies, one of them Nigeria's mass expulsion of migrant workers). Ironically, this was the type of arbitrary expulsion that Art. 27 of ECOWAS's 1975 treaty (providing for elimination of obstacles militating against the free movement of people and goods), was designed to prevent.

[411] Alter et al., note 4, p. 772.

need in the West African subregion for conflict resolution mechanisms, including the necessity for human rights to guarantee regional security.[412] Animated by a concern for human rights in a subregion like West Africa "where the judiciary is an arm of the executive," human-right NGOs were a major factor in the securement of approval in 2005 to broaden the CCJ's jurisdiction to include human rights.[413]

The humanitarian interventions in Liberia and Sierra Leone coincided with increased NGO involvement in regional policymaking, one made possible by the Community's new openness to civil society, which these human-right NGOs tapped into, using an existing institution to promote their objectives.[414] They latched on a provision in the Good Governance Protocol of 2001 that suggested that the Court, at the time not yet operational, might one day hear "cases relating to violations of human rights, after all attempts to resolve the matter at the national level have failed."[415] While at the time "such a possibility seemed remote," by 2005, "vague promise turned into reality."[416] In a word, to the overall and ultimate benefit of human rights, including the generation and application of these values in external relations, the humanitarian interventions in Sierra Leone and Liberia engendered enlightened "conceptions of regional security" that effectively "expanded the [CCJ's] mandate and created concomitantly greater constraints on state sovereignty."[417] In-between the two developments of adjudicating interstate economic disputes, and abuses from Nigerian-led humanitarian interventions necessitating the application of human rights to guarantee regional security, the puzzle, revolved around "how an international tribunal, initially established to help build a common market, [became transmuted into] a human rights court,"[418] was fortuitously (re)solved.

[412] Ibid., pp. 750–753, 772.

[413] Ibid., p. 763.

[414] Alter et al., note 4, p. 748.

[415] Economic Commission of West African States, *Protocol on Democracy and Good Governance*, note 111, art. 39 ("Protocol A/P.1/7/91 adopted in Abuja on 6 July 1991 relating to the Community Court of Justice, shall be reviewed so as to give the Court the power to hear, inter-alia, cases relating to violations of human rights, after all attempts to resolve the matter at the national level have failed").

[416] Alter et al., note 4, p. 748.

[417] Ibid., p. 770.

[418] Alter et al., pp. 738, 769.

Chapters 6 on peacekeeping points up the risk in the pursuit of principled foreign policy when the policy is built excessively on multilateral implements, and insufficiently balanced with bilateralism (vide Chapter 7 on the TAC). The lesson of this chapter is that it all depends: as the chronicle of the human-right jurisprudence of the CJ makes obvious, in a setting where judicial decisions are binding without the need for country-to-country ratifications, a multilateral tool can provide a compass and opportunity for application of human rights in external affairs that goes beyond the applicator. In other words, in and of itself, multilateralism is not automatically a problem, unless we make it so.

With examination of the five methods now complete, the coast is clear for Part III of this book on objections to the argument of this book revolved around the exigency for principled foreign policy for Nigeria in the wake of General Buhari's departure from the Nigerian political scene. The rebuttals of these objections are contained in the next two chapters: 9 on the necessity for thoroughgoing reforms in domestic and foreign policies aimed at relieving or closing the gap between the aspirations of Nigerian citizens and the performance of their leaders, and 10 on achievements of the book with a look into the future related to this topic, including the subtitle of loving the foreigner as oneself key to the thrust of this book. First to Chapter 9 we turn.

Appendix: Key Dates in CCJ History

Date	*Event*
1975	ECOWAS's founding treaty adopted on May 28 of this year by ECOWAS founding fathers incorporates a mandate for a Tribunal Committee to adjudicate disputes arising from the interpretation and operation of the legal instrument
1991	The CCJ is created by a Protocol on July 6 of this year
1993	ECOWAS leaders released a revised treaty which features the CCJ among the key institutions of ECOWAS. A provision of the treaty, art. 16, also creates an Arbitration Tribunal

(continued)

(continued)

Date	Event
2000	In December of this year, ECOWAS member-states appointed the first seven judges for the CCJ. One of them, Hansine Donli, from Nigeria, was elected as President of the Court. Donli was considered "a natural choice to lead the Court" because "[a]s a Nigerian with a network of contacts in the country, it would be easier for her to arrange for the infrastructure and administrative support that the judges required"[419]
2001	On January 31, 2001, the seven judges were sworn in in Bamako, Mali, by the then president of the country, who was at the time Chairperson of ECOWAS
2004	This year on April 27, the Court gave its judgment in *Afolabi v. Nigeria*, its first where it ruled that it lacked jurisdiction. The case challenged border closure by Nigerian authorities and involved a Nigerian trader who had entered into a contract to purchase goods in Benin. Afolabi could not complete the transaction because Nigeria unilaterally closed the border between the two countries. He filed suit with the ECOWAS Court, alleging that the border closure violated the right to free movement of persons and goods. Nigeria challenged the Court's jurisdiction and Afolabi's standing, arguing that the 1991 Protocol did not authorize private parties to litigate before the Court. The CCJ sided with the Nigerian government and dismissed the suit, on the theory that it lacked jurisdiction. The case catalyzed the Court's ultimate transformation into a human-right Court
2005	On January 19 this year, ECOWAS adopts the first of two supplementary protocols amending the 1991 Protocol on the Community Court. The amendments codify the Court's jurisdiction over human-rights cases laid out in the Protocol of 1991. It broadens the jurisdiction of the Court to encompass determination of cases of human-right violations "that occur in any member state"
2006	ECOWAS releases the second amendment to the 1991 Protocol on the Community Court
2008	On October 27 this year, the CCJ released its judgment in *Hadijatou Mani Koroua v. Niger*, dealing with slavery
2008	On June 5 this year, the CCJ released its judgment in *Manneh v. The Gambia*, involving the torture of a journalist. This case preceded Musa Saidykhan v. The Gambia, involving another torture and indefinite detention of a journalist, decided by the Court on December 16, 2010
2009	On October 27 this year, the CCJ released its judgment in *SERAP v. Nigeria*, the basic public education case
2011	On this date too, the CCJ published its first law report. It covered all its decisions for ten years from 2000 until 2010
2012	On December 14 this year, the CCJ released its judgment in *SERAP v. Nigeria*, the SERAP Environmental Case
2018	The Court is reorganized and its judges reduced from seven to five

(continued)

[419] Alter et al., note 4, p. 748.

(continued)

Date	*Event*
2020	The Court established an electronic case management system in response to the physical closure of the Court as a result of the COVID-19 pandemic. This development introduced a new electronic case filing platform and the conduct of virtual court sessions
2021	On June 22 this year, the Court released its judgment in *Kadiatou Siby v. Mali*
2021	On June 28 this year, the CCJ released its judgment in *Fodi Mohammed and Others v. Niger*, like Koroua in 2008 on slavery
2022	On July 14 this year, the CCJ released its judgment in SERAP and 176 Other Concerned Nigerians v. Nigeria, the Twitter Ban case.
2022	Columbia University, via its Global Freedom of Expression, conferred on the CCJ the prize of "significant legal ruling" for its decision in *Amnesty International & 7 Others v. The Togolese Republic* (2020), involving the shutdown of the Internet by the Togolese government during a protest in the country in September 2017

PART III

Rebuttable Objections

CHAPTER 9

Enacting Serious Reforms at Home and Abroad

Introduction

Human rights has an influence in Nigeria's external affairs. But it is an inchoate influence with little force at home to ground and sustain it. Instead, to use peacekeeping, one of the five methods highlighted in this book as means to principled foreign policy, Nigeria keeps peace abroad that it does not have at home. This condition of beautiful abroad but ugly at home creates an unsatisfactory spottiness of "now you see it, now you don't"[1] begging for resolution if the country is to grow human rights at home to the benefit of democracy therein, take its proper role in Africa and the larger world, and generally boost its contribution to international human rights.

This is the first of two chapters devoted to rebuttal of conceivable objections to the argument for Nigeria to build on its journey to principled foreign policy from where it stopped after General Buhari, taking advantage of the inestimable opportunity signified by the declining influence of military rule in Nigeria that Buhari's departure signified, as well as developments abroad, such as the rise of a new monarch to the

[1] Robert Charles Smith, *Racism in the Post-Civil Rights Era: Now You See It, Now You Don't* (New York: SUNY Press, 1995), *passim* (commenting on racism in the US in the post-civil rights era).

P. C. Aka, *Human Rights in Nigeria's External Relations in the Age of General Muhammadu Buhari and His Successors*, https://doi.org/10.1007/978-3-031-63231-0_9

throne in the UK, Nigeria's creator and former colonizer. Two main issues this chapter covers relate to objections built around the "But So What" rejoinder to the argument in this work for a human-right policy for Nigeria in the wake of General Buhari's departure from the Nigerian political scene, and the type of change Nigeria needs for principled foreign policy to the benefit of democratic consolidation within the Nigerian homeland.

But So What: Two Rebuttable Objections to the Argument in This Book

There are two interconnected objections to the argument for increased application of human rights in Nigeria's external affairs made in this study. These objections are that Nigeria needs to meet domestic needs first before it can worry about applying human rights abroad, and that the application of human rights in external affairs is an issue of unclosed gap between words and action infecting domestic and foreign policies that even major states like the United States, at the risk of the charge of hypocrisy, still struggle with. However, as the ensuing discussion elaborates, each of these objections lacks merit and is unavailing. With a twist of counter-intuitiveness, each of these objections assume added keenness in the wake of the completion of General Buhari's eight years in office as President which some analysts posit set Nigeria back decades from a developmental standpoint.[2]

Objection Pointing to Unmet Domestic Needs

The first objection is that it is premature to talk about human rights in foreign affairs for a country where, as of 2022, over 88 million people, numbers large enough to form a large country, lived below poverty

[2] See Chapter 1, note 9, and accompanying text. See also Nathaniel Shaibu, "Buhari Set Nigeria Five Decades Backward—Clark," *Punch* (Lagos) (January 19, 2024), https://punchng.com/buhari-set-nigeria-five-decades-backward-clark/ (quoting the position of Edwin Clark, leader of an Ijaw sociocultural organization to the effect that Buhari's eight years as President was "a period of complete and total retrogression" that set the country "five decades backward").

line.[3] This is a reality that even data that Nigerians themselves generate concede.[4] Put differently, wouldn't the elevated requirements of human rights[5] in foreign affairs amount to an overkill for fledgling legal and political communities like Nigeria, whose hands are already full, struggling to secure these super-rights at the domestic level. This objection tracks the concern in some part of the literature that a certain threshold of development and security necessary for state survival and welfare needs may have to be sufficiently satisfied to permit the pursuit of a human-right policy.[6]

The answer is that Nigeria, a state born in international relations via British colonialism in Africa, has the capability to pull through principled foreign policy, if it reduces wastes and rationalizes its human and material resources better than it does now. Infusing more human rights into Nigeria's foreign affairs will facilitate the work of democracy at

[3] See "Number of People Living in Extreme Poverty in Nigeria from 2016 to 2022, by Gender," *Statista*, https://www.statista.com/statistics/1287827/number-of-people-living-in-extreme-poverty-in-nigeria-by-gender/#:~:text=In%202022%2C%20an%20estimated%20population,at%2043.7%20million%20for%20women. See also Chapter 5, notes 70–71 (commenting on the scarcity of socioeconomic rights in Nigeria under the Fourth Republic since 1999).

[4] See National Bureau of Statistics, "Nigeria Launches Its Most Extensive National Measure of Multidimensional Poverty," Press Release (November 17, 2022), https://nigerianstat.gov.ng/news/78 (showing that 63% of persons living within Nigeria, amounting to 133 million people, are multidimensionally poor).

[5] *Human rights* and other key terms in this study are defined in Chapter 2, the first of two chapters on the exigency for a human-right policy for Nigeria post-Buhari. The elevation part comes in because, as one human rights scholar after another has observed, these rights are super-rights. See, for example, Louis Henkin, "Human Rights: Ideology and Aspiration, Reality and Prospect," in Samantha Power and Graham Allison eds., *Realizing Human Rights: Moving from Inspiration to Impact* (New York: St. Martin's Press, 2000), 5 (praising these rights as "claims as of right," "limitations on democracy" that, although not absolute, can "trump even a public interest duly determined in a democratic society"); Jack Donnelly, *International Human Rights*, 4th Ed. (Boulder, CO: Westview Press, 2013), 20 (contending that "[t]o assert one's human rights is to attempt to change political practices [...] so that it will no longer be necessary to claim those rights as human rights").

[6] Alison Brysk, *Global Good Samaritans: Human Rights as Foreign Policy* (New York: Oxford University Press, 2009), 7.

home—just as it does for countries like Costa Rica[7] and Canada[8]—while enriching, adding color, and providing a higher shooting target for Nigerian leaders and foreign policy officialdom in conducting foreign policy. We live in a world where the Responsibility to Protect (referred to colloquially as "R2P"), has emerged as a norm.[9] Under this shaping rule, "while sovereign states ha[ve] the primary responsibility for protecting human rights in their jurisdictions, if [these] states prove[] unwilling or unable to prevent gross violations, outside parties ha[ve] the responsibility to become involved."[10] Countries which make serious efforts to incorporate human rights into their foreign affairs stand a better chance of shouldering this arguably added burden, compared to states which do not.

As indicated in Chapter 5 on increased respect for human rights in Nigeria as one of various methods to a human-right policy, what the more than two decades of the Fourth Republic has demonstrated is that civilian rule does not automatically result in high-quality governance. Because principled foreign policy is arguably more onerous than one *not* anchored

[7] This is one of the six countries that Professor Brysk profiled in her work. See Brysk, note 6, pp. 95–118, especially pp. 116–117. In a play on or parody of the children story, Thomas the Tank Engine, Brysk called Costa Rica "The Little Country That Could." Ibid., p. 95. Costa Rica is instructive because with a population of only 3 million people (vis-à-vis Nigeria's 135 million denizens as of 2009 when the Brysk study was published), ibid., pp. 8–17, and with an economy based mainly on tourism, agriculture, and export of electronic products, the country lacks the size and resource endowments of Nigeria.

[8] See Andrew Lui, *Why Canada Cares: Human Rights and Foreign Policy in Theory and Practice* (Montreal, Canada: McGill-Queen's University Press, 2012), 173 (disclosing that besides contributing to the international human rights regime, Canada has a "more selfish, inward-looking reasons for [its] international behavior on human rights" embedded to improve its federal system).

[9] See David P. Forsythe, *Human Rights in International Relations*, 3rd Ed. (New York: Cambridge University Press, 2012), 4–5.

[10] Ibid. For a similar view, see Francis M. Deng, "Reconciling Sovereignty with Responsibility: Basis for International Humanitarian Action," in *Africa in World Politics: The African State System in Flux*, 3rd Ed., eds. John W. Harbeson and Donald Rothchild (Boulder, CO: Westview Press, 2000), 353, 357; and Francis M. Deng et al., *Sovereignty as Responsibility: Conflict Management in Africa* (Washington, DC: Brookings Institution Press, 1996), 1–33 (mapping out the "Normative Framework of Sovereignty"). According to Deng, a government should not claim sovereignty, embedded in the doctrines of territorial integrity and non-interference in the internal affairs of the country that it serves, if it is not able to establish legitimacy by meeting minimal standards of good governance and responsibility for the security and general welfare of its citizens.

on those values, application of human rights in external relations adds more quality to governance at home and puts to rest the paradox of "ugly at home and beautiful abroad" that now passes for Nigerian human-right policy. Political communities who visit ill on "strangers" abroad will have no difficulty finding maleficent strangers at home.[11]

Moreover, stipulating universal threshold of development and security to be met before pursuit of a human-right policy may impose preconditions that for some countries should productively be synchronized with the implementation of such policy. Studies on the behaviors of states who consistently apply human rights in their foreign policies have shown that "good citizens are made, not born"[12]; in other words, "although some national values and experiences harmonize readily with human rights, foreign policy projection of those norms must be learned and mobilized."[13] Also, there is no requirement that the mobilization of those norms be perfect,[14] given that every state has its "blind spots and insufficiencies" in human rights.[15] Instead, principled foreign policy states need only to be "good-enough Good Samaritans,"[16] who, for example, "foster bridges between areas of strength and lagging sectors."[17]

There is no requirement that Nigeria punch above its weight in applying human rights in external affairs the way global Good Samaritans like Costa Rica have impressively done. However, given its human and material endowments, Nigeria punches below its weight. At the very least, at this point in its national history, Nigeria should be ranking among the regional "tigers" from the global South that Brysk indicated are aspiring to take their place in the conduct of human-right-based foreign policies.[18] For Nigeria, the requisite national value harmonizing with human

[11] See Mae C. King, *Basic Currents of Nigerian Foreign Policy* (Washington, DC: Howard University Press, 1996), 3–31, 237–241 (commenting on "relations with strangers," externally as well as internally, including that "Nigerian nationalism constantly seeks to reconcile differences that are a source of estrangement among citizens").

[12] Brysk, note 6, p. 221.

[13] Ibid.

[14] Ibid., pp. 221–222 (discussing the lesson of "Good-Enough Good Samaritans").

[15] Ibid., p. 222.

[16] Ibid., pp. 221–222.

[17] Ibid., p. 222.

[18] Brysk, note 6, p. 230. The tigers, four of them altogether, are Argentina, Brazil, Chile, and South Korea. Ibid.

rights that can form the basis for principled foreign policy learning would include its experience in peacekeeping and its habit of eschewing the use of force in disputes with neighbors. It could also include resources anchored on the rule of law, such as "persuasion by ideas, openness to civil society," and "dedicated diplomats," among others.[19]

The aspect of this objection regarding a certain threshold of development and security supposedly necessary to ground a human-right policy brings up a power-status distinction (whether great, middle, or small) that is inapplicable here, even inappropriate, particularly with respect to Nigeria. This is because a country might be a great power and not apply human rights in its external affairs. An example here would be Japan that Brysk included in her case study. Japan applies human rights weakly in its external affairs.[20] And its records caution against the undue expectation that "as countries develop or democratize or Westernize[,] they will automatically reach out to help strangers and build global governance[.]".[21]

In contrast, there are comparatively small powers—of which Costa Rica and South Africa come to mind—which more robustly apply human rights in their external affairs. Costa Rica does not even have an army,[22]

[19] Ibid., p. 118 (commenting on "latent resources" Costa Rica possesses, other countries can adopt, all of which factors "can be assisted externally," and can "help to strengthen democracy at home as well as abroad").

[20] During a special-topics course in political science, International Human Rights Law and Politics, this writer taught at Chicago State University in spring 2014, where the Brysk book featured among the required texts, the class questioned the status of Japan as global Good Samaritan, given several statements on the "limitations of Japan's global citizenship." Grounds for that uncertainty included the very title of the Japan chapter, "Peace without Justice," Brysk, note 6, p. 148; the revelation that "Japan has been a leading aid provider and multilateralist, but a slow and even reluctant human rights advocate[,]" ibid., p. 149; and the finding that "Japan is a consumer rather than a generator of international law, and international law has been imported by civil society groups rather than systematically adopted by government as a constitutive feature of national identity[,]" ibid., p. 162. See also Yozo Yokota and Chiyuki Aoi, "Japan's Foreign Policy Toward Human Rights: Uncertain Changes," in *Human Rights and Comparative Foreign Policy*, ed. David P. Forsythe (New York: United Nations University Press, 2000), 115–145 (characterizing the country's human rights policy as "uncertain").

[21] Brysk, note 6, p. 221.

[22] The country abolished its army in 1948. See Tanisha Ellis Hayles, "Costa Rica—A Country Without an Army and Proud of It," *Jamaica Observer* (Kingston) (March 2, 2014), http://www.jamaicaobserver.com/columns/Costa-Rica---a-country-without-an-army-and-proud-of-it_16147133; David P. Barash, "Costa Rica's Peace Dividend: How Abolishing the Military Paid Off," *Los Angeles Times* (December 15,

the symbol of great-power status for many countries in our still realist-dominated international community.[23] Professor Donnelly delved into this matter in his book on international human rights, commenting on differences in human-right policies.[24] He took issue with the claim by the Norwegian writer and politician, Jan Egeland, to the effect that "small and big nations are differently disposed to undertaking coherent rights-oriented foreign policies."[25] Following thoughtful examination of the matter, Donnelly concluded:

> Differences between the United States and the like-minded countries are largely matters of choice. Norway and the Netherlands place a relatively high value on international human rights not because they are small and weak but because of how their citizens understand themselves, their place in the world, and the obligations associated with their identity.[26]

Similarly, power status has little relevance regarding whether or not Nigeria adopts a human- right-oriented foreign policy. In sum, the proposition regarding a threshold of development and security necessary for the implementation of a human-right policy mistakes capability to apply human rights in external relations with power status—when in actuality some materially poor states like Costa Rica maintain a respectable human rights foreign policy while supposedly rich ones like Japan lack or maintain that policy nominally.

2013), http://articles.latimes.com/2013/dec/15/opinion/la-oe-barash-costa-rica-demilitarization-20131208. The result is that "[t]o this day, Costa Rica has no army, navy or air force, no heavy weapons of any kind. *There are local police forces but no national defense force.*" Ibid. Emphasis added.

[23] See Forsythe, note 9, pp. 317–343 (commenting on "the politics of liberalism in a realist world"). Professor Forsythe posits that "[t]he international law of human rights is based on liberalism, but the practice of human rights all too often reflects a realist world." Ibid., p. 317.

[24] Donnelly, note 5, pp. 130–133.

[25] Quoted in ibid., p. 130. Specifically, Egeland posited that the measured human rights accomplishments of the United State are "because of, rather than in spite, of her superpower status." Donnelly, note 5, p. 130, quoting Jan Egeland, *Impotent Superpower-Potent Small State: Potentialities and Limitations of Human Rights Objectives in the Foreign Policies of the United States and Norway* (Oslo, Norway: Norwegian University Press, 1988), 3, 5.

[26] Donnelly, note 5, p. 133.

Finally, applying human rights in external relations resonates with the indivisibility of these rights, one of the byproducts of the World Conference on Human Rights in Vienna (WCHR) in June of 1993.[27] The declaration and program of action adopted at the end of that conference indicated that "[a]ll human rights are universal, indivisible and interdependent and interrelated."[28] While making room for variations between and within regions, the declaration stated that "it is the duty of States, regardless of their political, economic and cultural systems to promote and protect all human rights and fundamental freedoms."[29]

In the aftermath of the WCHR in 1993, "all states, regardless of national history and mythology" have become "compelled to confront the international law and diplomacy of human rights."[30] These states include the likes of China which in 1993 opposed the concept of universal rights and viewed such rights as intervention into the domestic affairs of other nations.[31] Just as the spread of human rights forbids demarcation between political-civil rights and socioeconomic rights, today countries must infuse their relations with other countries with human rights, rather than limit themselves to enforcement of human rights domestically.

Such extension of human rights into external relations, continuation of domestic policy by other means,[32] rhymes with the injunction of the Vienna declaration for the international community to "treat human

[27] See Office of the UN High Commissioner for Human Rights, "World Conference on Human Rights, 14–25 (June 1993), Vienna, Austria," http://www.ohchr.org/EN/ABOUTUS/Pages/ViennaWC.aspx; and "World Conference and the Vienna Declaration," *BBC World Service*, http://www.bbc.co.uk/worldservice/people/features/ihavearig htto/four_b/treaties_vienna.shtml.

[28] Office of the UN High Commissioner for Human Rights, Vienna Declaration and Program of Action (June 25, 1993), http://www.ohchr.org/EN/ProfessionalInterest/Pages/Vienna.aspx, ¶ 5.

[29] Ibid.

[30] David P. Forsythe, "Introduction," in Forsythe, ed., *Human Rights and Comparative Foreign Policy*, note 20, pp. 3–4.

[31] Ibid. In 1998, China ratified the International Covenant on Economic, Social, and Cultural Rights, the same year it *signed* the International Covenant on Political and Civil Rights, but has yet to ratify. See Human Rights Watch, "China: Ratify Key International Human Rights Treaty" (October 3, 2013), https://www.hrw.org/news/2013/10/08/china-ratify-key-international-human-rights-treaty.

[32] See Peter Calvert, *The Foreign Policy of New States* (New York: St. Martin's Press, 1986), viii (maintaining that foreign policy is "ancillary to domestic policy and serves its needs").

rights globally in a fair and equal manner, on the same footing, and with the same emphasis."[33] It calls to mind the Biblical enjoinment, one theme of this book, about loving the foreigner as ourselves in a complexly interdependent world that counsels against drawing sharp divisions between domestic and foreign policies, given the blurring of the line between the two policies. For a time now the talk has been about how to move from inspiration to impact in realizing human rights.[34] Application of these rights in foreign policy is one practical way to effect that transition.

Objection as to Unclosed Gap

Another conceivable objection to the argument in this book for a human-right policy for Nigeria relates to the complaint about unclosed gap between domestic and foreign policies. The objector will argue that even democratic heavyweights like the US have such gaps. There is some merit to that argument. No one can minimize the setback to international human rights posed by the abdication of US's leadership in the field, before the terrorist attacks of September 11, 2001,[35] that got arguably worse in the aftermath of those attack.[36] The changed tone in US foreign during the presidency of Barack Obama from 2009 until 2017 did little to change the general picture of abdication or inattentiveness.[37] Nor did events under Joseph R. Biden, president since 2021. In a more-broadly-themed speech he gave in Abuja on November 19, 2021, on building a partnership with Africa, Secretary of State Antony J. Blinken stated,

> I know I'm hardly the first American secretary of state to come to Africa and promise different and better engagement. Too many times, [African

[33] "Vienna Declaration and Program of Action," note 28, ¶ 5.

[34] See Power and Allison, eds., *Realizing Human Rights*, note 5, *passim*.

[35] See Henkin, note 5, p. 38, n.61.

[36] Michael Ignatieff, "Is the Human Rights Era Ending?" in *Perspectives on Terrorism: How 9/11 Changed U.S. Politics*, ed. Allan J. Cigler (Boston, MA: Houghton Mifflin Co., 2002), 103–106 (making the pointed observation that, with the war against terror that attended the terrorist attacks against the US in September 2001, "[t]he new element in determining American foreign policy is what assets—bases, intelligence[,] and diplomatic leverage—it can bring to bear against Al Qaeda").

[37] Philip C. Aka, "The *Country Reports on Human Rights Practices* and U.S. Human Rights Policy in a Changing World," *Perspectives on Global Development & Technology*, 14 (2015), 241.

> countries] have been treated as junior partners—or worse—rather than equal ones. Too often, we ask our partners to help uphold and defend an international system that they don't feel fully reflects their needs and aspirations. And we're sensitive to centuries of colonialism, slavery, exploitation that have left painful legacies that endure today.[38]

Conceivably, it is this occurrence that necessitated the scout for "global good Samaritans" to fill some of the gap in the US's leadership of the international human rights movement.[39]

But such comparison of Nigeria to the US can be overstretched. The US is a nation "in search of itself" in an ongoing attempt to realize its founding principles,[40] and a state that played an instrumental role in the evolution of the modern human rights movement,[41] drawing on a natural rights doctrine in its Declaration of Independence that goes back to the

[38] Antony J. Blinken, "The United States and Africa: Building a 21st Century Partnership," US Embassy and Consulate in Nigeria (November 12, 2021), https://ng.usembassy.gov/the-united-states-and-africa-building-a-21st-century-partnership/.

[39] See Brysk, note 6, *passim*.

[40] Theodore H. White, *America in Search of Itself: The Making of the President 1956–1980* (New York: Harper & Row, 1982), *passim*. Then President Barack Obama made this same point in an address at the 66th session of the UN General Assembly on September 14, 2014, in New York, where he advised US enemies not to exploit the troubles in Ferguson, Missouri, to deflect attention from their own human rights abuses. See White House, Office of the Press Secretary, "Remarks by President Obama in Address to the United Nations General Assembly" (September 28, 2014), www.whitehouse.gov/the-press-office/2014/09/24/remarks-president-obama-address-united-nations-general-assembly [hereinafter Obama's UN General Assembly Address]. Ferguson gained notorious international attention when on August 9, 2014, a white police officer shot an unarmed black teenager to death, sparking widespread protests and civil unrest that went on for months. See, for example Dara Lind et al., "An Uneasy Peace in Ferguson," *Vox* (August 21, 2014), www.vox.com/2014/8/11/5988925/mike-brown-killing-shooting-case-ferguson-police-riots-st-louis. Obama conceded with critics that the US occasionally "have failed to live up to [its] ideals," but nevertheless maintained that, unlike many countries in the world, within "the open space of democracy," "America is a country that has steadily worked to address [its] problems, to make [its] union more perfect, [and] to bridge the divides that existed at the founding of this nation." Obama's UN General Assembly Address.

[41] Mary Ann Glendon, *A World Made New: Eleanor Roosevelt and the Universal Declaration of Human Rights* (New York: Random House 2001), *passim*.

British philosopher John Locke.[42] These include the propositions that all humans are created equal and "endowed by their Creator with certain unalienable Rights," including "Life, Liberty and the Pursuit of Happiness" (i.e., property); and that "Governments are instituted among Men" and charged precisely with the obligation to secure, rather than destroy, these rights.[43] In contrast, for all its enormous potentials, Nigeria still has a long way to go in these efforts, a shortfall that necessitates academic and policy-oriented attention of the type this work fosters.

Nigeria perceives itself as "giant of Africa" and potential leader of the Black world. In the words of one foreign minister of the country, there is no black story, "unless it is a Nigerian *success* story."[44] This is a role Nigerian leaders accepted in the first decade of the country's independence before oil displaced agriculture as mainstay of the country's economy. It is also as well a role that these leaders in the Fourth Republic since 1999 have not shown any indication to abandon, not even with unceasing criticisms from the media and enlightened citizens of the country's foreign policy, for too long centered on Africa, as insufficiently driven by national interest.[45] Adopting principled foreign policy will put more meaning into Nigeria's self-image as giant of Africa than it does now. The country boasts norms and experiences harmonizing with human rights that it now needs to mobilize in its external relations.

[42] See Philip C. Aka, Review of Lutz Oette, ed., *Criminal Law Reform and Transitional Justice: Human Rights Perspectives for Sudan* (Burlington, VT: Ashgate Publishing 2011) *Africa Today*, 59 (Summer 2013), 135–136, n.1.

[43] *Declaration of Independence* (July 4, 1776), http://www.archives.gov/exhibits/charters/declaration_transcript.html.

[44] Ojo Maduekwe, foreign minister from 2007 to 2010, cited in Monday Dickson, "Citizen Diplomacy in President Umaru Musa Yar'Adua's Nigeria, 2007–2009: An Assessment," *International Journal of Politics and Good Governance*, 1 (2010), 5, http://onlineresearchjournals.com/ijopagg/art/59.pdf.

[45] See Reuben Abati, "The Gains of Jonathan's Diplomacy," *Premium Times* (Abuja) (September 9, 2012), http://www.premiumtimesng.com/news/99498-the-gains-of-jonathans-diplomacy-by-reuben-abati.html (arguing that "[t]he world had changed a lot since Nigeria distributed its oil wealth to other countries and asked for nothing in return" and that "[t]he new strategy[,]" which he said Goodluck Jonathan, President from 2010 to 2015 favors, "called for partnership, mutual respect, enhanced and innovative diplomacy, and constructive exchange").

Consolidating Democracy at Home by Doing Good Abroad

The rank of global Good Samaritans who apply human rights consistently in their foreign affairs is wide open.[46] These states produce important international human rights goods,[47] including the buildup of "global governance" and "reshap[ing] the meaning of sovereignty" to the benefit of human rights as a norm of legitimacy.[48] Nigeria can join the rank of these global Good Samaritans and contribute to the international human rights regime. But, although important, that is not the main import of this work. Application of human rights in external relations is also valuable because of what it does for Nigeria in its own right at home. This study is an account on human rights in Nigerian foreign policies that necessarily includes a narrative of the domestic forces that drive those foreign policies.

Promoting human rights abroad can bolster Nigeria's democracy at home the same way it has done for Costa Rica and Canada, especially Canada which, like Nigeria, has a federal system of government. In addition to contributing to the international human rights regime, Canada uses application of human rights in external relations in a targeted attempt to cement individual rights as the cornerstone of its federalism as well as to mitigate friction between the country's diverse social groups, including communities in French-speaking Quebec.[49] In contrast, under the Fourth Republic as before it, Nigeria is a state held down by its Lilliputian leaders.[50] The country needs to close the gap between the aspirations

[46] See Brysk, note 6, *passim.*

[47] As Professor Brysk explains, the influence of these states "can be critical for framing and ratifying treaties, creating and staffing multilateral institutions, monitoring and sanctioning offenders, assisting victims, directing resources, implementing peace processes, catalyzing transnational initiatives or emerging issues, and introducing new understandings of rights to the global agenda." Ibid., p. 3.

[48] Ibid., p. 4.

[49] See Andrew Lui, *Why Canada Cares: Human Rights and Foreign Policy in Theory and Practice* (Montreal, Canada: McGill-Queen's University Press, 2012), 7, 32.

[50] See Adekeye Adebajo and Abdul Raufu Mustapha, eds., *Gulliver's Troubles: Nigeria's Foreign Policy After the Cold War* (Scottsville, South Africa: University of KwaZulu-Natal Press, 2008), 2 (lamenting the disconnect between the country's high-minded aspirations for a leadership role abroad juxtaposed with the petty ambitions, kleptomania, and small-mindedness of some Fourth Republic leaders).

of its citizens and the performance of its leaders. It should be a state "worthy of its [peoples'] dreams,"[51] both those in Nigeria and the sizable population in the Diaspora.

Human rights can build Nigeria[52]; embracement of international standards embedded in human rights is the key to attaining that mark. Given its checkered history of instability, including numerous coups, countercoups, and a vicious civil war, Nigeria is a country noted for its dubious mastery of "the art of dancing on the precipice without falling over."[53] But such flirt with disaster is not sustainable. And should Nigeria disintegrate due to unrelieved human rights abuses, successor states to the parent state will still grapple with the same problem of human rights challenges, without the benefit of a large republic that an incoherent Nigeria now affords.[54] Herein lies the significance of this book.[55]

[51] William J. Clinton, "Remarks Following Discussions with President Olusegun Obasanjo of Nigeria and an Exchange with Reporters in Abuja, Nigeria, Aug. 26, 2000," in *Public Papers of the Presidents of the United States: William J. Clinton, 2000–2001* (Washington, DC: Best Books, 2000), 1701. The term "peoples'" is bracketed because Clinton used "people's."

[52] See Fran Quigley, *How Human Rights Can Build Haiti: Activists, Lawyers, and the Grassroots Campaign* (Nashville, TN: Vanderbilt University Press, 2014), *passim* (focusing on Haiti).

[53] John Campbell, *Nigeria: Dancing on the Brink* (Lanham, MD: Rowman & Littlefield Publishers, 2013), xxiv.

[54] For Nigeria, this notion of a "large republic" can be easily overstretched. This is because, as the US Senator Eugene McCarthy (1916–2005) indicated in 1969, urging the intervention of the US government in the Nigerian civil war on the side of breakaway Biafra, Nigeria is populous enough to allow for more than one viable state. See his May 16, 1969 speech, reprinted in A.H.M. Kirk-Greene, *Crisis and Conflict in Nigeria: A Documentary Sourcebook 1966–1969*, Vol. 2 (London: Oxford University Press, 1971), 401–403. McCarthy believed that Nigeria has resource advantages that make it "viable without the eastern region." Ibid., p. 404. For the seceding eastern region, he said, "[e]ven without some minority tribes, Biafra would be a populous country by African standards, larger than three-fourths of the African countries. Only [ten] of some [forty] African countries would be larger." Ibid. Given the large population of each of the three major ethnic groups, numbering into the tens of millions, the statement is no less true today than it was more than 50 years ago.

[55] This point helps explain the proposition for "another independence" for Nigeria, in the form of a "start-over" dissolution, in a bid to fix it. See Uzodinma Iweala, "Nigeria's Second Independence: Why the Giant of Africa Needs to Start Over," *Foreign Affairs* (July/August 2022), https://www.foreignaffairs.com/articles/africa/2022-06-21/nigeria-second-independence. For a newspaper story on this seemingly enigmatic proposition, see Wale Odunsi, "Okonjo-Iweala's Son, Uzodinma

Nigeria needs a human-right policy with more breadth and depth to match its aspirations for a credible leadership role in Africa and the world. Over six decades since its independence in 1960, the tool that mainly drives Nigeria's external relations is an unreformed peacekeeping. This is inadequate for a country rich in human and natural resources that aspires for a leadership role in the West African subregion and beyond. Although principled foreign policy is an integral component of general foreign policy, the application of human rights in external relations is a more demanding target that Nigeria needs to shoot for.

To be sure, applying human rights is not painless. Instead, it could bring discomforts, such as disruption in normal diplomatic relations, limited commercial opportunities, infliction of domestic economic hardship, alliance structures that may be strained, or retaliation by a target state.[56] However, it is the viable way forward for Nigeria. In short, increased application of human rights in Nigeria's foreign relations will: remove the solecism of abuses at home, and a nominal commitment to international law abroad that currently fronts as human-right policy[57]; bring increased harmonization to domestic and foreign policies; and inject

Suggests Nigeria's Dissolution Months to 2023 Elections," *Daily Post* (Lagos), (June 28, 2022), https://dailypost.ng/2022/06/28/okonjo-iwealas-son-uzodinma-suggests-nigerias-dissolution-months-to-2023-elections/. *Foreign Affairs* is a two-monthly magazine published by the Council on Foreign Relations, an American think tank specialized in US foreign policy and international relations, with offices in New York City and Washington, DC. The context for the proposal was the lead up to the 2023 elections. Iweala, son of former Nigerian Finance Minister, Ngozi Okonjo-Iweala, posits that a conceivable solution to the myriad of political troubles Nigeria confronts is its dissolution. He urged the Nigerian people to decide if they want Nigeria, which he called a "patchwork entity," to continue or to fold up. "Nothing should be off-limits for discussion—even the dissolution of the country," he opined. He contended that the question is "reasonable [...], given that the country is the arbitrary product of colonial boundaries." Iweala, "Nigeria's Second Independence."

[56] David Gillies, *Between Principle and Practice: Human Rights in North–South Relations* (Montreal, Canada: McGill-Queen's University Press, 1996), 50.

[57] Philip C. Aka, "Human Rights in Nigeria's External Relations: Exigency, Methods, and Rebuttable Objections," *Buffalo Human Rights Law Review*, 21 (2014–2015), 25; S.O. Akinboye, Beautiful Abroad but Ugly at Home: Issues and Contra[di]ctions in Nigerian Foreign Policy, University of Lagos Inaugural Lecture Series (2013), www.unilag.edu.ng/opendocnew.php? (criticizing Nigeria's tendency to "exhibit acts of benevolence abroad" while spotting a domestic environment "marked by ugliness[,]" including "a sheer lack of direction on how to achieve development"); and Douglas C. Lovelace, Jr., "Foreword," in Clarence J. Bouchat, *The Causes of Instability in Nigeria and Implications for the United States* (Carlisle, PA: Strategic Studies Institute & U.S. Army War

a more credible accent to its foreign policy initiatives and aspirations for a leadership role in Africa and beyond that will turn it into a giant with real, rather than clay or cripped, feet.[58]

When was the last time that a Nigerian leader used the language of human rights in formulating domestic or foreign policy?[59] Nigerian governments at all levels, civil society (non-governmental sector), and the general public must get into the habit of using human rights in their debates on domestic and international issues.[60] Nigeria needs to embrace the type of serious reforms at home and abroad that the assets of international human rights make possible. Nigeria is a microcosm of Africa and mirrors some of the problems the region faces, and "a good place to begin," in search of answers to those difficulties.[61] As a result, unless Nigeria embraces and implements comprehensive reforms that stretch into external relations, talk about any "renaissance" in the continent in this century will remain just talk.[62]

College, August 2013), iii (characterizing Nigeria's portraiture as "international influence and domestic paralysis").

58 See, for example, Eghosa E. Osaghae, *Crippled Giant: Nigeria Since Independence* (Bloomington, IN: Indiana University Press, 1998), *passim* (commenting on structural impediments predating the country's independence that turned it into a "crippled giant").

59 The insight that inspires this question is South Africa where, under Nelson Mandela, an exchange ensued regarding application of human rights in the country's foreign policy. See Tiyanjana Maluwa, "Human Rights and Foreign Policy in Post-Apartheid South Africa," in *Human Rights and Comparative Foreign Policy*, ed. David P. Forsythe (New York: United Nations University Press, 2000), 250–275.

60 Chidi A. Odinkalu, "Why More Africans Don't Use Human Rights Language," *Human Rights Dialog*, 2 (December 1999), www.carnegiecouncil.org/publications/archive/dialogue/2_01/articles/602.html.

61 See Oladimeji Aborisade and Robert J. Mundt, *Politics in Nigeria*, 2nd Ed. (New York: Longman, 2002), xi–xii (stating that "[n]either Nigeria nor any other country can stand for all of Africa, for Africa is marked by great diversity. Still, if to know Nigeria is not necessarily to know Africa, it is a good place to begin, for there will be little that is surprising in politics elsewhere on the continent to one who is well acquainted with the Nigerian experience").

62 The notion of *renaissance* is one anchored in Africa's pan-Africanist past, back to the very beginning of the last century, that some African intellectuals, most prominently Thabo Mbeki, former South African president, have resurrected. In a speech, "I am African," marking this recent movement, that he gave in Cape Town, South Africa, on May 8, 1996, Mbeki stated that to make the twenty-first century the century for Africa the continent must, first, "capture the intellectual space to define its future and therefore the imperative to develop its intellectual capital." Quoted *in* Lazarus Sauti, "Thabo Mbeki's

The foreign affairs analyst Fareed Zakaria took a position several years ago in the debate regarding the seeming decline of United States global power.[63] Zakaria decried the "kind of unreflective ancestor worship" that appears to have taken hold of the American mind.[64] Those who wrote the United States' Constitution, he said, were individuals who "constantly adapt[ed] their views"; they were versed in the favorite American pastime of "contemplating decay" and thinking "a great deal about decline" when things are still going well.[65] In a nutshell, the framers of the US Constitution were individuals who advised "bold, persistent experimentation," always aware that America "was a work in progress, an unfinished enterprise that would constantly be in need of change, adjustment, and repair."[66]

The same advice is enjoined upon Nigeria. To borrow the "urgency of now" analogy of Dr. Martin Luther King Jr., this is no time to inebriate "the tranquilizing drug of gradualism."[67] Instead, to thrive as a state in the twenty-first century, its leaders need to enact reforms in several areas of the country's national life all the way to external relations with the same spirit of bold, and persistent experimentation.

The tale that comes to mind here is that of beautiful restoration analogizable to Kintsugi, the ancient Japanese art form wherein an artist takes broken pottery (usually tea ware) and pieces the shards back together with lacquer, threading gold into the cracks.[68] As the renowned Japanese

Legacy to Africa," *Herald* (Zimbabwe) (September 16, 2013), http://www.herald.co.zw/thabo-mbekis-legacy-to-africa/. Next, it must "rebuild and sustain [its] universities and other centers of learning, attract back to Africa the intelligentsia that has migrated to the developed North, build strong links with the intelligentsia in the African Diaspora and give" these individuals "the time and space they need to help" shape the future of Africa. Ibid.

[63] See Fareed Zakaria, "Are America's Best Days Behind Us?" *Time* (March 3, 2011), http://content.time.com/time/magazine/article/0,9171,2056723,00.html.

[64] Ibid.

[65] Ibid. Zakaria opined that it is this state of mind that stimulated the type of innovative reforms that had kept the US globally competitive. Ibid.

[66] Ibid.

[67] Martin Luther King Jr., "I Have a Dream" (August 28, 1963), *reprinted* in *NPR* (Updated January 16, 2023), https://www.npr.org/2010/01/18/122701268/i-have-a-dream-speech-in-its-entirety.

[68] See Makoto Fujimura, *Art + Faith: A Theology of Making* (New Haven, CT: Yale University Press, 2021).

artist Makoto Fujimura elucidates, Kintsugi "does not just 'fix' or repair a broken vessel; rather, the technique makes the broken pottery even more beautiful than the original."[69] The implementation of Kintsugi dates back centuries ago when a warlord's favorite cup was destroyed and then beautifully restored using this restorative technique.[70] Within the context of Nigeria, this all boils down to the "consistent agenda of reform," shorn of cosmetic or window-dressing changes, Chinua Achebe set forth in his diagnoses over forty years ago on "the trouble with Nigeria."[71]

The alternative to comprehensive reforms that spans all the way to external relations with minimal regard for sharp distinctions between domestic and foreign affairs is dire, reading from the phenomenon of *Japa*, the urgency of departure that, as of this book, grips the cream of Nigerian youth.[72] *Japa* is a Yoruba term for "to run," or "to flee," that has become distinctly synonymous with persons leaving Nigeria; since it seized the popular imagination circa 2020, the term has been analogized to the desperation of middle-class youth, defined as persons 34 years and below, to leave the country.[73] The urge to flee kicks in when, in the words of the historian Toyin Falola, the youth involved feels the sense that "prolonged discomfort cannot be endured any further," the result of a break down in the "balance between patience, endurance, and the desire to succeed" that impels the individual gripped by this emotion to want

[69] Ibid. The imagery this story brings to mind is Phoenix, the imaginary bird which, as the ancient myth goes, burns itself to ashes every five hundred years and is then born again. See Roel B. van den Broek, *The Myth of the Phoenix, According to Classical and Early Christian Traditions*, translation by I. Seeger (Leiden, The Netherlands: E. J. Brill, 1972).

[70] Fujimura, note 68.

[71] Chinua Achebe, *The Trouble with Nigeria* (Enugu: Fourth Dimension Press, 1983), 1. Achebe wrote, "The trouble with Nigeria is simply and squarely a failure of leadership. [...] The Nigerian problem is the unwillingness or inability of its leaders to rise to the responsibility, to the challenge of personal example which are the hallmarks of true leadership." Ibid.

[72] Jing Jing Liu, "*Japa*, or to Flee or to Run: Nigerian Youth and the Urgency of Departure," MoLab Inventory of Mobilities and Socioeconomic Changes, Max Planck Institute for Social Anthropology, Halle/Saale (2023), https://doi.org/10.48509/MoLab.6432.

[73] Ibid.

to flee.[74] Many, particularly many in the youth population who engaged in this practice, also call this tendency "checking out."[75] But whether the youth exodus outside Nigeria is denominated *Japa* or checking out, the effect remains the same.

However, in concert with attentive citizenship, there are just few problems good leadership cannot resolve,[76] which is the main point of this book. "With good leadership and citizenship, the nation and its people can *japa* [as in immunize themselves] from situations that create a desperate craving for *japa*."[77] Starting with good leadership, a political structure, no matter how creatively designed, is as good as the men and women who run it. Leaders are distinguished from mere power holders. Instead, they are office holders capable of producing social change that will satisfy the authentic yearnings of their followers.[78]

Building on these thresholds, the government must work harder to eliminate the push-factors that make individuals want to leave, rather than remain in, Nigeria, including improving the living conditions of citizens; promoting infrastructure and schemes that allow businesses, whether small- or medium-scale, to thrive; and revitalizing the education system by, for example, resolving the issues that drive labor unions to strike repeatedly.[79] Unless these steps are implemented, "Nigerians will continue to *japa* to escape from *sapa* [i.e., being broke and living in poverty and bondage]."[80]

For their part, citizens need to know that not all individuals seized with an urge to leave can do so, given the reality that not all Nigerians can leave.[81] This is where good citizenship kick in—by the masses of the people assuming the responsibility to take on that role: they must kick

[74] Toyin Falola, "*Japa*!" *Premium Times* (Lagos) (September 2, 2022), https://www.premiumtimesng.com/opinion/551986-japa-by-toyin-falola.html.

[75] Adaobi Tricia Nwaubani, "The Nigerians Hoping to Check Out of Their Country," BBC (February 28, 2022), https://www.bbc.com/news/world-africa-60393076.

[76] See the proposition of Chinua Achebe on leadership in note 71.

[77] Falola, note 74.

[78] See James MacGregor Burns, *Leadership* (New York: Harper Torchbooks, 1978), 4–5.

[79] Falola, note 74.

[80] Ibid.

[81] Ibid.

against "bad leadership, *japa* from drugs, *japa* from crime, *japa* from 419 [i.e. pervasive scam artistry], *japa* from political lethargy, and be disposed to entrepreneurship."[82] Good citizenship, driven and corralled by good leadership, was the impetus behind the seven steps to a human-right policy for Nigeria post-Buhari expounded in Chapter 5 on the need for increased human rights within Nigeria. We will return to this trade related to impulse to leave among the youth in Chapter 10 in the reflections on prospects for the future that rounds off this book.

Conclusion

This chapter is the first instalments out of two discussions dedicated to rebuttal of possible objections to the argument in this book revolved around the urgency of a human-right policy for Nigeria in the wake of the end of the Buhari presidency. Two main concerns this chapter addressed relate to the "But So What" rejoinder to the argument in this work, and the type of change Nigeria needs for principled foreign policy. The first dealt with the objection pertaining to unmet domestic needs and unclosed gap in terms of nonalignment between domestic and foreign policies tantamount to hypocrisy. Next to the type of change Nigeria needs, the chapter articulated bold and persistent experiment in several areas of national life all the way to external relations, with small regard for sharp demarcation between domestic and foreign policies in a globalized international system like ours marked by complex interdependence. The alternatives to comprehensive reforms, such as growing migration by the cream of young people, by whatever name, whether *Japa* or checking out, are just too dire to contemplate.

Chapter 1 laid out four research questions that drive this book, namely: factors which make embracement and internalization of international standards in governance, signified by increased application of human rights in external affairs, exigent for the country; quantifiable influence of human rights in Nigeria's external relations (i.e., how far does the country have or need to go to join the hallowed club of "global Good Samaritans" who consistently apply human rights in their external affairs); conceivable methods to facilitate the application of more human rights in Nigeria's

[82] Ibid. On 419, see, for example, Erika Eichelberger, "What I Learned Hanging Out with Nigerian Email Scammers," *Mother Jones* (March 20, 2014), http://www.motherjones.com/politics/2014/03/what-i-learned-from-nigerian-scammers.

external relations; and possible objections to the case for more human rights in Nigeria's external relations and conceivable rebuttals of those objections. This chapter dealt with the last of these research questions, leaving the analytical coast clear for the first three, along with prospective issues, for Chapter 10, which also doubles as the conclusion of this book.

CHAPTER 10

Conclusions and Prospects for the Future

This chapter is one of two materials dedicated to rebutting possible objections to the argument of this book revolved around a human-right policy for Nigeria in the wake of General Buhari's departure from the political scene in the country, an occurrence that for us heralds the decline of praetorianism in Nigerian politics dating back to 1966. The sole purpose of this final chapter, no different from any other finale, à la conclusion, is to recapitulate the achievements of the book with an introspective look into the future. There are three aspects to the discussion: continuation and completion of the conceivable objections and rebuttals to the book focusing on three remaining questions from the research questions that frame this study, restatement of the achievements of the book, and prospects for the future.

Revisiting the Research Questions That Framed This Study

There are four such questions, referencing Chapter 1, which laid out the argument of the book. Chapter 9 dealt with the objections revolved around unmet domestic needs and unclosed gaps between domestic and foreign policies, an occurrence not unique to Nigeria, which objections the chapter also addressed. That leaves us with three remaining questions,

P. C. Aka, *Human Rights in Nigeria's External Relations in the Age of General Muhammadu Buhari and His Successors*,
https://doi.org/10.1007/978-3-031-63231-0_10

namely: the influence of human rights in Nigeria's external relations, the exigency for increased infusion of human rights in Nigeria's external relations, and conceivable methods for facilitating application of human rights in Nigeria's external relations.

Influence of Human Rights in External Relations

Like in anything, as indicated in Chapters 1 and 2, going to the purpose of this book,[1] human rights exerts certain influence in Nigeria's external relations. But it is an effect that, as this whole book shows, is spotty, sporadic, and/or incidental. It is a nominal influence that needs to be systematized to optimize the contribution of the country to the international human rights regime, to the overall benefit of the work of democracy and human rights at home, without which Nigerians at home and in their swelling numbers in the Diaspora,[2] stand little chance of making their country a state worthy of the dreams of its diverse peoples.

More than Part I which sketched the imperativeness of a human-right policy for Nigeria, the gristmill for gauging any influence is Part II on the methods for the realization of that principled foreign policy. We begin with Chapter 4 on reconstructing Nigeria's national interest in readiness for human-right duties. Vis-à-vis the "default" worldview of Political Realism, doctrinal (re)orientation of Nigeria's foreign policy toward Constructivism is less pain-free because of the plasticity of Constructivism embedded in its allowance of human-right values into external affairs, based on its perception of the national interest as what the state

[1] See Chapter 1, notes 64–90 (making the case for a human-right policy for Nigeria) and Chapter 2, notes 76–116 (commenting on rudimentary infrastructure for human-right work).

[2] See, for example, Jing Jing Liu, "Africans in China Are on the Move," *Africa Is a Country* (June 7, 2022), https://africasacountry.com/2022/06/africans-in-china-are-on-the-move (China); Oreva Olakpe, "Nigerian Migrants in China: Changing the Narrative," *Heinrich Böll Stiftung* (Cape Town, South Africa) (October 2018), https://za.boell.org/en/2018/10/09/nigerian-migrants-china-changing-narrative (China); Victoria Ojeme, "Nigerians are One of the Most Populous Immigrant Community Doing Excellency [sic] Well—Japanese Ambassador," *Vanguard* (Lagos) (January 20, 2022), https://www.vanguardngr.com/2022/01/nigerians-are-one-of-the-most-populous-immigrant-community-doing-excellency-well-japanese-ambassador/ (Japan); and Dreux Richard, "The Other Side of Tokyo's Nigerian Community," *Japan Today* (August 2, 2011), https://japantoday.com/category/features/lifestyle/the-other-side-of-tokyos-nigerian-community (Japan).

makes to be. Moreover, to begin with, Nigerian foreign policy mostly still centered on Africa, does not comply strictly with Realist precepts and commandments.

Next to reshaping Nigeria's foreign policy machinery, that is a work in progress below international standards, given the lack of popular input and lack of elite cohesiveness that mark policymaking and implementation in Nigeria. The same failure of international standards embedded in human rights apply to the steps to the haven of increased human rights at home in Chapter 5—maintaining civilian rule; increasing citizen attachment to democracy through extension of socioeconomic rights; taking group rights seriously for a country that is a patchwork of ethnic groups; taking decentralization, à la political restructuring, seriously for a country with numerous ethnic groups where, because three of the largest ethnic groups (the Igbo in the East, the Yoruba in the West, and the Hausa-Fulani in the North) unceasingly "vie with each other for political predominance and economic favor,"[3] federalism was introduced in the country before independence; stemming the influence of religion whose salience coincided with the abandonment of the Settlement of 1960 which strove to keep the country secular; and election of competent governments able and willing to get the job done. In the light of these dysfunction, the auxiliary protection of external assistance is necessary to maintain the suboptimal system.

The same lack of international standards characterized peacekeeping, Chapter 6, whose multilateralism the use of ECOWAS deepened. The TAC, Chapter 7, tempered somewhat by multilateralism, but, as we saw, with the Ministry of Foreign Affairs to which it was inseparably tied, the scheme was insufficiently funded and, partly for this reason, insufficiently bilateral in its operation. This leaves the CCJ, Chapter 8, among these methods as the most promising. However, that is relatively rather than in an absolute sense. The reason is because, although Nigeria and other ECOWAS member states are willing to submit their domestic systems

[3] Robert L. Tignor, *Capitalism and Nationalism at the End of Empire: State and Business in Decolonizing Egypt, Niger, and Kenya, 1945–1963* (Princeton, NJ: Princeton University Press, 1998), 195. Analysts like John Campbell, one time US ambassador to Nigeria, commented on the elite competition that have undermined Nigeria's democratic institutions and alienated vast segments of its impoverished population. John Campbell, *Nigeria: Dancing on the Brink*, Updated Edition (Lanham, MD: Rowman & Littlefield, 2013). That competition mostly takes place within these largest ethnic groups, especially Hausa-Fulani and Yoruba since the civil war more than half a century ago.

to the rule of law, a democratic ideal oftentimes linked to the judiciary, the CCJ's being part of ECOWAS speaks to the key-ness and relative indispensability of the customs union as an instrument of Nigeria's foreign policy.

Exigency for Increased Infusion of Human Rights in Nigeria's External Relations

Although Chapters 1 and 2 laid down justifications for this urgency, with Chapter 2 commenting on incipient infrastructure for a human-right policy, those reasons can bear recapitulation here. For one thing, broadly speaking, Nigeria is a state invented by human rights. To whom much is given, much is expected. Secondly, Nigeria can punch more within its weight, rather than below it, by contributing more through its word and action, especially the latter, to international human rights. Thirdly, for Nigeria, application of human rights in external affairs may be the only practical opportunity to contribute to the international human rights regime. Fourthly, injecting more human rights into Nigeria's external relations could harmonize the country's domestic and foreign policies, to the benefit of democracy at home. Infusing more human rights into Nigeria's foreign relations will help to build a culture of the rule of law necessary to consolidate democracy in the land. For how long can Nigeria stretch its luck, dancing on the precipice without falling over?[4] Plus, Nigeria has the infrastructure to conduct a human-right policy, if it rationalizes its resources well.

Conceivable Methods for Facilitating Application of More Human Rights in Nigeria's External Relations

Part II of this book, comprising Chapters 4–8 identified and exhaustively discussed a sample of five possible methods—reconstructing Nigeria's national interest, guided by the Constructivist worldview, to improve its amenability to human-right work; the charity begins at home of increased human rights within Nigeria; peacekeeping; the TAC; and the CCJ—that Nigeria can use to facilitate application of human rights in its external relations. No minimizing the importance of the other portions, the salience of

[4] Campbell, note 3.

these materials places them at the centerpiece of this book. And although some of the materials, such as Chapter 6 on peacekeeping, Chapter 7 on the TAC, and Chapter 8 on the CCJ, on first appearance seem more method than the others, all of them, regardless of their obviousness to the naked eye, are equally important and part of a seamless whole. In the discussion on increased respect for human rights at home, we stressed the necessity to synchronize, rather than implement the seven measures sequentially. The same advice applies with all five methods.

Achievements of This Book

Simultaneously, this book:

- advances a compelling argument for the adoption of international standards symbolized by the application of human rights in Nigeria's external relations after the famine years of General Buhari under the Fourth Republic, taking advantage of momentous events at home and abroad, among them the reduced influence of the military in Nigeria's body politic that Buhari's departure signified, and the coronation of a new monarch in the UK, given the lingering influence and interests of the UK in Nigeria in the postcolonial period;
- articulates and develops five sample methods for such application, including reconstructing Nigeria's national interest to improve its readiness for human-right duties, increased respect for human rights in the Nigerian homeland, peacekeeping, the Technical Aid Corps (TAC), and the ECOWAS CCJ; and
- responds to conceivable objections against the argument for principled foreign policy in Nigeria post-Buhari, all of them strongly rebutted in the last two chapters of the work, couched in the tone of consolidating democracy at home by doing good abroad, sensitive to the blurring of domestic and foreign policies in a globalized world, marked by complex interdependence.

In shorthand, the book is a proposal for thoroughgoing reforms in all aspects of Nigeria's national life, all the way to external relations, packaged in the less arcane and more accessible constitutional language of international human rights.

Chapter 1 laid down the argument of the book, including the domestic and external events that provide the context for the work. Part I, comprising Chapters 2 and 3, meant to answer the why question in this research, built on that argument. A major takeaway from Chapter 2 is that, despite its known disabilities, nonetheless, Nigeria has the potential infrastructure for the conduct of a human-right policy, if it rationalizes its resources more properly. Chapter 3 unearths five discernible periods in Nigeria's foreign policy since independence with an eye on their human-right contents. To start the story from its proverbial beginning and provide more depth in time duration necessary for thorough understanding, the discussion includes the precolonial and colonial eras.

Part II of the book, made up of Chapters 4–8, and dedicated to answer the how question of this research, set forth five methods that Nigeria can use to pursue principled foreign policy in the age of Buhari and his successors under the Fourth Republic, with each chapter throwing in its perspective on the journey to that destination. Chapter 4 focused on reconstructing Nigeria's national interest to improve its readiness for human-right work. Doctrinally speaking, this spells a choice of Constructivism over Political Realism or Idealism, given its enhanced plasticity indicated by the extent to which, vis-à-vis the two rivals, the theory permits interjection of human rights in external relations. Key takeaways from the chapter include strategies for reconstructing Nigeria's national interest to make it human right-compliant, including reshaping the country's foreign policy machinery.

Chapter 5 contributed increased respect for human rights as its perspective on Nigeria's road to principled foreign policy with a justification that included enumeration of seven steps, ranging from the "default" step of maintaining civilian rule through popular attachment to civil-democratic rule through progress in socioeconomic rights, attention to group rights, power devolution, to minimizing the salience of religion in politics and external support for democracy, designed to facilitate achievement of that target. Key takeaway lessons from this chapter are that charity begins at home (Nigeria cannot seriously export abroad values that it neither produces nor practices at home), and that the Nigerian homeland should be the starting point in the journey toward a human-right policy. The inclusion of this, as a co-method alongside four others, speaks to the need for scholars and diplomats alike to refrain from erecting sharp distinctions between domestic and foreign policies.

Chapter 6 integrated the perspective of peacekeeping as a method in the journey to principled human right for Nigeria. The lesson from this chapter is that for Nigeria peacekeeping is mostly a multilateral instrument conducted through ECOWAS that becomes even more multilateral when achieved through the agency of ECOMOG, its monitoring group, complete with the humanitarian abuses in some locations like Sierra Leone and Liberia where Nigerian troops practiced their peacekeeping wares. As a foreign-policy implementation tool, peacekeeping reached its apogee with Nigeria's interventions in Liberia and Sierra Leone, the first to stop a civil war, and the second to restore an overthrown civilian government. This was the context in which President Bill Clinton, during a highly-publicized state visit to the country in August 2000, at the inception of the Fourth Republic, commended Nigerian leaders for their creativity in "building the record of a moral superpower."

Chapter 7 integrated the perspective of the Technical Aid Corps (TAC), a volunteer program as the fourth of five methods in the proposal for a human-right policy for Nigeria. It is a critical assessment of the possibilities and limits of the program related to the application of human rights in Nigeria's external relations in the age of General Buhari and his successors. To punch within its weight, rather than below it, Nigeria needs a mixture of multilateral and bilateral activities in its human-right foreign policy toolbox fit for a would-be global Good Samaritan which infuses and enriches its external relations with human-right deeds in the sense we use this term in this book. More than for peacekeeping, the question for this tool is whether, in additional to being human-right-compliant, it is also bilateral enough to get the job of international human-right job properly done. The answer was no, given that the scheme, tied inseparably to the Ministry of Foreign Affairs, is both inadequately funded and inadequately bilateral in execution.

Chapter 8 integrated the perspective of the CCJ in the proposal for a human-right policy for Nigeria post-Buhari. The Court is a key institution of ECOWAS, created under a revised treaty of the subregional economic organization adopted in 1993. It hears cases from Nigeria and other member-states and adjudicates human-right violations, either by individuals or corporate bodies, although its jurisdiction on human-right abuses does not extend to complaints pertaining to violations of regional economic rules. And while still a multilateral tool, vis-à-vis its obvious co-methods (i.e., peacekeeping, and the TAC), the CCJ holds tremendous promise with respect to application of human rights in Nigeria's external relations. The chapter is the last of five sample methods—after reconstructing the national interest to improve its readiness for human-right duties, increased human rights in Nigeria, peacekeeping, and the Technical Aid Corps.

Chapters 9–10, grouped under Part III of the book, addressed the so what? question of this book, specifically conceivable objections to the argument of this book and possible rebuttals to those objections. Legitimate objections to this manner of foreign policy for Nigeria revolve around the concern about whether the country possesses the wherewithal for the formulation and implementation of an effective human-right policy, given the many existential problems it faces at home. The answer to these objections, as Chapter 9 fields them, lies in a calibrated yes answer embedded in reforms: serious changes at home and abroad, including increased harmonization of domestic and foreign policies, designed to help the country punch within its weight, rather than below it, and by so doing, enhancing its contribution to international human rights to the dual benefit of its own domestic well-being and in foreign policy related to its known aspirations for a leadership role in Africa and beyond. Therefore, as indicated in Chapter 9, last before this one, Nigerian leaders will need to enact reforms in multiple areas of the country's national life, all the way to external relations in a spirit of bold and persistent experimentation. Along with the masses of the citizenry, they must do so guided by the thrust and analogy of Nigeria as "a work in progress, an unfinished enterprise that would constantly be in need of change, adjustment, and repair."[5]

This chapter, this very material, recapitulates the achievements of the book with an introspective reflection into the future, as indicated in the next section below. In an era of complex interdependence, such as the world finds itself, eight years of ruinous rule can spell existential threats for ordinary citizens, with ramifications for their relations with other countries. In the wake of Buhari's presidency under the Fourth Republic from 2015 until May 2023, the exigency for a human-right policy for the betterment of domestic policy has increased while the means for attaining that policy in several areas, including peacekeeping, have measurably diminished.

[5] Chapter 9, note 66, and accompanying text (referring to the US).

Prospects for the Future

Predicting the future can be a hazardous undertaking given that, as the Jamaican reggae singer and songwriter Bob Marley (1945–1981) warned long ago, only time will tell—even for those whose conditions under the current scheme of things are optimal,[6] much less so for Nigeria as this book shows. Keeping this cautionary well in mind, the discussion here delves into a mix of composite dynamics, signified by the irrelevancy of the state, accelerated by mass exodus out of the country, especially by youth, by whatever name, in a complexly interdependent world, driven by globalization, where some countries are unveiling creative immigration policies, in due testament to the subtitle of this book revolved around loving the foreigner as oneself, and Constructivism, the exploratory-cum-explanatory framework that drives the work. We take these issues in turn, focusing on the irrelevant state, mass exodus, permissive immigration policies, and loving the foreigner as oneself.

Irrelevant State

Even in the best times, many African countries, including Nigeria, lack the capability to accomplish basic tasks associated with statehood, such as providing security protection to citizens and levying and collecting taxes from them. These are countries that decades ago the political scientists Robert H. Jackson and Carl G. Rosberg labelled "juridical states"; these countries derive their sources of legitimacy from doctrines of international law, such as sovereignty, rather than empirical forces embedded in the ability to get the job done governance-wise[7] As this phenomenon deepened over the years, rather than abate, scholars coined new terms to

[6] Bob Marley and The Wailers, "Time Will Tell," *Genius* (1978), https://genius.com/Bob-marley-and-the-wailers-time-will-tell-lyrics ("Time alone, oh, time will tell/Think you are in heaven, but you're living in hell [...]") (chorus).

[7] See Robert H. Jackson and Carl G. Rosberg, "Why African Weak States Persist: The Empirical and the Judicial in Statehood," *World Politics*, 35(1) (October 1982), 1–24; and Robert H. Jackson, *Quasi-States: Sovereignty, International Relations, and the Third World* (Cambridge, UK: Cambridge University Press, 1990). See also Robert H. Jackson and Carl G. Rosberg, *Personal Rule in Black Africa: Prince, Autocrat, Prophet, Tyrant* (Berkeley, CA: University of California Press, 1982).

describe it, such as "crippled giant,"[8] "dancing on the brink" without falling off,[9] and "irrelevant." The last came from the political scientist Julius O. Ihonvbere who observed, in the context of ethnicity and the quest for nation-building in Nigeria and other African countries, that "[t]he limited hegemony of the post-colonial state, its inability to meet the basic needs of the vast majority, and its heavy reliance on violence and coercion to maintain control, make it very 'irrelevant' to the existential conditions of the vast majority."[10]

Mass Exodus Out of Nigeria

While Nigerians or groups within the country such as the Igbo, Yoruba, and Edo, have a history of migration that goes back in time, what is motivating this exodus are "[a] dearth of local prospects, and a desire for individual prosperity," meshed with a "palpable sense of national despair."[11] But the phenomenon "increases inefficiency, causes brain drain, and stalls development."[12] Besides the medical and banking sectors, the brain drain affects almost all sectors of the Nigerian economy, because the persons seeking to leave "are mostly highly skilled individuals with specific talents across different industries."[13] In 2020, youth unemployment (i.e. unemployment among persons 15–34 years old) stood at 35%, with a further 28% of young people in the labor force underemployed (i.e. youth working 20–39 hours a week), and only 37% working full time (40 or more hours per week).[14]

[8] Eghosa E. Osaghae, *The Crippled Giant: Nigeria Since Independence* (Bloomington, IN: Indiana University Press, 1998).

[9] Campbell, note 3 (focusing on US-Nigerian relations).

[10] Julius O. Ihonvbere, "The 'Irrelevant' State, Ethnicity, and the Quest for Nationhood in Africa," *Ethnic and Racial Studies,* 17(1) (1994), 42–60, 10.1080/01419870.1994.9993812.

[11] Jing Jing Liu, "*Japa*, or to Flee or to Run: Nigerian Youth and the Urgency of Departure," MoLab Inventory of Mobilities and Socioeconomic Changes, Max Planck Institute for Social Anthropology, Halle/Saale (2023), https://www.eth.mpg.de/6221762/japa_or_to_flee_or_to_run#:~:text='Japa'%2C%5B1%5D,youth%20to%20leave%20the%20country, 10.48509/MoLab.6432.

[12] Toyin Falola, "*Japa!*," *Premium Times* (Abuja) (September 2, 2022), https://www.premiumtimesng.com/opinion/551986-japa-by-toyin-falola.html.

[13] Ibid.

[14] Quoted in Liu, note 11, footnote 6.

Surveys show that in 2021, about 73% of Nigerians expressed an intention to leave the country.[15] The number dropped a little bit to 69% in a 2022 survey by a polling organization, the Africa Polling Institute, compared to 39% in 2019, who indicated they would relocate out of the country if given the chance.[16] Many who have already emigrated can't imagine moving back.[17]

In addition to workers in the healthcare system, these include thousands of students who chose not to participate in the higher educational system reeling from the effect of inadequate funding and strikes by instructors protesting poor conditions of service, including non-payment of basic salaries.[18] Many fleeing are also leaving because of biting economic hardships, including high unemployment, especially among the youth.[19] The urge to leave "stresses the inability to survive in an environment in which one's own personal efforts are constantly undermined by political and economic effects," a desperation hastened by a massive depreciation of the Naira, the country's national currency.[20] Thus, in the words of the Nigerian lawyer and human-right activist Dele Farotimi, the individuals leaving are "escaping," not migrating in the real sense of the

[15] Falola, note 12.

[16] Larry Madowo et al., "Many Talented Young Nigerians are Leaving: Halting the Exodus Will Be a Task for the Next President," *CNN* (February 24, 2023), https://www.cnn.com/2023/02/24/africa/nigeria-japa-exodus-trend-election-intl-cmd/index.html. Persistent insecurity, a crumbling economy and rampant corruption are the leading issues for the next government, according to a pre-election survey of voters by SBM Intelligence, based in Lagos. Ibid. Coupled with the high cost of living and unemployment, these concerns make the country so unattractive for many citizens who pine to leave. Ibid. See also Ore Ogunbiyi, "A Young Person's Guide to Escaping Nigeria," *Economist* (February 24, 2023), https://www.economist.com/1843/2023/02/24/a-young-persons-guide-to-escaping-nigeria.

[17] Madowo et al., note 16.

[18] Falola, note 12.

[19] See ibid.

[20] Liu, note 11.

term.[21] In his elaboration, at least from the standpoint of material well-being, it is so "functionally insane to remain in Nigeria" that any Nigerian who can afford to live abroad and refuses to go "is a mad" person.[22]

The mass exodus dilemma is a problem universal to all African countries that Nigeria, as a microcosm of the continent, only exemplifies. One analyst likened rising youth unemployment in Africa to a "ticking time bomb."[23] With "[o]ne of three young Africans [being] unemployed," how can African countries create jobs for the young to preclude unrest, in a region where the youth population is projected to double by 2050?[24] Remittances from abroad provide life-saving economic cushions at home for families of migrants, but the phenomenon comes with broader economic repercussions that the band-aid cushions from remittances fail to make up. This is because, due to the brain drain, to turn their countries around, "even good leaders with considerable political skills will have [...] to wait to create entire[ly] new cohorts of trained professionals to tackle problem areas."[25]

Permissive Immigration Policies

On March 26, 2024, German lawmakers enacted a citizenship law, the Act on the Modernization of Citizenship Law, signed into law by President Frank-Walter Steinmeier, Head of State of Germany, that takes

[21] Dele Farotimi, "Anyone Who Can Afford to Live Abroad and Has Refused to Go Is a Mad Man," Teju BabyFace Deep Dive Podcast (March 26, 2024), https://www.youtube.com/watch?v=ITNqS_VnWTE.

[22] Ibid.

[23] Stella Mapenzauswa, "In Africa, Rising Youth Unemployment Is a Ticking Time Bomb," *New Decoder* (August 11, 2022), https://news-decoder.com/in-africa-rising-youth-unemployment-is-a-ticking-time-bomb/.

[24] Ibid. A well-known name among the Igbo is *azi-ki-we*, meaning that the youth are more prone to anger than older persons because of a built-in comparative advantage, indicated by an ability to hold more grudge that can be more toxic for society: they are younger and have more time to draw blood from detractors with their grudge. Instructively, Azikiwe is the last name of Nnamdi Azikiwe, a foremost figure in the decolonization movement in Nigeria and Africa as a whole. Azikiwe was Nigeria's Governor-General (1960–1963) and President (1963–1966).

[25] National Intelligence Council, "Mapping Sub-Sahara Africa's Future," CR 20050-2 (March 2005), 5, http://www.au.af.mil/au/awc/awcgate/nic/africa_future.pdf.

effect on June 26, 2024.[26] The law reduced the minimum period of German residence necessary for naturalization from eight years down to five years, and even three years in exceptional circumstances.[27] The law also permits German citizens to hold multiple citizenship in place of the current situation where dual citizenship is possible only in rare circumstances.[28] The expectation, where our point kicks in, is that this will increase uptake of German citizenship, given that many potential citizenship applicants are citizens of other countries currently barred from naturalizing without giving up their current citizenship.[29] There is also the expectation that this law will facilitate access to German passport, making the country a more attractive labor market for foreign talents.[30] Due to these features of expansiveness, some analysts understandably describe the law as "monumental."[31]

The German law follows on the heel of countries like Canada with comparatively permissive immigration policy that some analysts point to as a model for other countries; foreign-born persons make up close to one-quarter of Canada's population.[32] For the most part, the Canadian public holds favorable views of immigration.[33] As of 2022, Canada admitted new permanent residents under four main categories as follows: 58% of immigrants through economic pathways, 22% through family sponsorship, 17% as refugees and protected persons, and 2% for humanitarian

[26] "Germany's Dual Citizenship Law Goes Into Effect at End of June 2024," *Arnall Golden Gregory* (March 27, 2024), https://www.agg.com/news-insights/publications/update-germanys-dual-citizenship-law-goes-into-effect-at-end-of-june-2024/; Olivia Logan, "Dual Citizenship Law Effective from June After German President Signs Bill," *I Am Expat* (March 27, 2024), https://www.iamexpat.de/expat-info/german-expat-news/dual-citizenship-law-effective-june-after-german-president-signs-bill; and "Germany: New Citizenship Law to Enter into Force in June 2024," *Fragomen* (March 26, 2024), https://www.fragomen.com/insights/germany-new-citizenship-law-to-enter-into-force-in-june-2024.html.

[27] "Germany: New Citizenship Law to Enter into Force in June2024," note 26.

[28] Ibid.

[29] Ibid.

[30] Ibid.

[31] Logan, note 26.

[32] Diana Roy and Amelia Cheatham, "Backgrounder: What Is Canada's Immigration Policy?" Council on Foreign Relations (Last updated March 28, 2024), https://www.cfr.org/backgrounder/what-canadas-immigration-policy.

[33] Ibid.

or other reasons.[34] Canada is also notable for its relative openness to foreigners seeking asylum.[35]

Loving the Foreigner as Yourself

The Scriptures admonishes that "The foreigner residing among you must be treated as your native-born. Love them as yourself, for you were foreigners in Egypt."[36] The statement leading to this enjoinment precludes mistreating the foreigner. "When a foreigner resides among you in your land, do not mistreat them."[37] The enjoinments are on a list of various laws in this book. Leviticus is one of the 66 books of the Bible, third on a list that begins with Genesis in the Old Testament and ends with Revelation in the New Testament.[38] The book of Leviticus is the provenance of the laws and regulations God gave to Israel. As opposed to religious beliefs as such, the commandments in Leviticus emphasize ritual, legal, and moral practices that, nonetheless, embody the worldview of the creation story in the book of Genesis that God wishes to live with humans.

There are two meanings for this book that we take from the love-the-foreigner-as-yourself theme. The first relates to minimizing the gap between domestic and foreign policies to facilitate integration of human rights in external relations in a world like ours marked with complex interdependence that the demarcation between domestic and foreign policies blurs to the point of indistinction. With its theme of thorough-going change ensconced in loving the foreigner, this book bridges the gap between domestic and foreign policies. The second meaning is that human rights can save Nigeria because of the benefits emanating from the international standards embedded in human rights that can enrich and add needed value to democracy at home.

[34] Ibid.

[35] Ibid.

[36] *Holy Bible*, New International Version, Leviticus 19:34.

[37] Ibid., Leviticus 19:33.

[38] Of the Bible's 66 Books, 39 comprise the Old Testament and 27 the New Testament.

Constructivism

This book ties Nigeria, a key state in Africa, brainchild of British colonial experiment, into the literature on human rights in comparative foreign policy.[39] Using Nigeria as window into the world, it contributes to the campaign to treat human rights as genuine national interest, rather than a sporadic appendage to general foreign policy.[40] Compared to the rival theories juxtaposed with it in Chapter 2, Constructivism boasts "a wider remit of how interests are defined,"[41] including allowances that anarchy (the lack of a world government) is what states make of it, foreign policy is what states make of it, and the national interest may be what the state and its citizens are interested in, not always state security.

Because, vis-à-vis its rivals, Constructivism perceives the contexts in which states interact in external relations to range from cooperative to competitive, in a manner that permits them to respond in many different ways, the approach affords the most scope for application of human rights in external relations. The significance of this book lies in the fact that it joins the list of works dealing with the application of human rights in external affairs, some of which also utilized Constructivism as theoretical framework. Given that Nigerian foreign policy since independence for so long centered on Africa does not follow the strict commandment of Political Realism, embracement of Constructivism is relatively painless.

In his work on Canada, among the studies surveyed in Chapter 2, Andrew Lui maintained that "constructivism has difficulty explaining the rhetoric-reality gap in Canadian human rights politics," elaborating that, while the theory "offers a useful explanation of the underlying motivations behind human rights pursuits, it falls short of addressing

[39] See David P. Forsythe, "Introduction," in *Human Rights and Comparative Foreign Policy,* ed. David P. Forsythe (New York: United Nations University Press, 2000), 17 (stating that "[w]ith an unlimited budget and a multi-volume project, we could have added numerous states that merit study: France, Norway, Germany, *Nigeria*, Kenya, Mexico, Brazil, Pakistan, Israel, the Philippines, etc.") (emphasis added).

[40] Jack Donnelly, *International Human Rights*, 4th Ed. (Boulder, CO: Westview Press, 2013), 139–147.

[41] Andrew Lui, *Why Canada Cares: Human Rights and Foreign Policy in Theory and Practice* (Montreal, Canada: McGill-Queen's University Press, 2012), 116.

the inherent trade-offs and competing priorities of statecraft."[42] We are unable to corroborate such finding with respect to Nigeria. For one thing, there is insufficient evidence. Unlike their counterparts in Canada and elsewhere, Nigerian leaders hardly use the language of human rights in their formulation and execution of domestic and foreign policies.

More than Political Realism or Idealism, Nigerian foreign policy behavior faulted by many of its citizens as "doing too much in the African continent without corresponding positive outcome"[43] fits with Constructivism. Still, given the trailblazing character of this work, firm conclusions on the extent to which Constructivism helps us understand Nigeria's foreign policy behaviors are premature at this point and must await future studies. Social science research views the world as it is, but also as it should be in instances when agreed-upon criteria exist among social scientists and legal scholars for the ideals of what should be. This research combines the best of what is and what should be, describing the application of human rights in Nigerian foreign policy the way it is now while prescriptively incorporating suggestions on the way forward.

Final Word

Nigeria's traction in the journey toward a foreign policy imbued with human rights hit a nadir during General Buhari's two terms in office from 2015 until 2023. His presidency is also a negative watershed and marked the end of military influence in Nigerian politics dating back to the first military coup in the country in 1966. Under Buhari, trending into the Tinubu presidency, severe deteriorations have occurred in Nigeria's domestic and external fortunes. The set of circumstances afforded an inestimable opportunity and context for the analysis in this book. Nigeria began the second century of its existence on January 1, 2015. As it steps into this second century of its existence as a country, there is urgent need for its leaders to mend their human-right ways. Nigeria is a country born

[42] Lui, note 41, p. 163. Based on the observation, Lui reached the conclusion that "a conceptual framework that centers on identities and international norms cannot explain those instances in which behavior differs markedly from the underlying narrative." Ibid.

[43] Hadi Y. Al-Hassa, "Evaluating Nigerian Foreign Policy at 50," *Gamji* [no date indicated, but probably published in 2010], http://www.gamji.com/article/9000/news9139.htm.

in foreign affairs, the result of British imperialism, whose claim to existence more than one century after its forced amalgamation still verges on "juridical statehood," more than empirical indicators of performance.[44]

To become a liberal democratic state that respects the human rights of all its citizens, without distinction, based on ethnicity, religion, gender, class, or other grounds, Nigeria cannot afford to stumble through episodes of massive human-right violations in the second century of its existence as it did in the first. The answer is application of human rights in its external affairs to the benefit of what it does at home. All this is consistent with appeals for Nigerian leaders to address domestic challenges that impinge the country's external relations and image, including pursuit of foreign policies that put the masses of the Nigerian peoples at the center of policy formation and implementation.[45]

In the light of current developments, Nigeria is an irrelevant state with every potential to degenerate into a failed state.[46] If its no-good leaders at all levels, national, state, and local, do not act proactively to arrest the weight of dysfunctionality they confront, the country could degenerate into a failed state with effects that could be felt within and beyond the West African subregion. All this will be taking place in an international system where countries like Germany and Canada are crafting immigration policies specifically designed to attract foreign talents, many of them from Nigeria and other portions of the developing world, of a manner arguably consistent with Biblical enjoinment about foreswearing the distinction between natives and foreigners. Complicating nation-building for Nigeria, disaffected groups like the Igbo long excluded

[44] See note 7 and accompanying text.

[45] See Usman A. Tar and Sharkdam Wapmuk, eds., *Nigerian Foreign Policy [Sixty] Years After Independence* (Cham, Switzerland: Palgrave Macmillan, 2023).

[46] A "failed state" is a condition of "state collapse," where the state in question is no longer able to perform its basic security and development functions nor demonstrate effective control over its territory and borders. "Crisis, Fragile, and Failed States Definitions Used by the CSRC," LSE (Crisis States Workshop, London) (March 2006), https://www.lse.ac.uk/international-development/Assets/Documents/PDFs/csrc-background-papers/Definition-of-a-Failed-State.pdf. Such a condition is present when the state is no longer able to "reproduce the conditions for its own existence." Ibid. It does not mean a state that is poorly performing. The flipside of a failed state is an enduring one, although it is difficult to pinpoint the line that divides the two, given that even in a failed state, some elements of the state, such as organizations at the local level might continue to exist. Ibid.

from the mainstream of the country's political and socioeconomic life, today spend more effort in self-determination campaigns designed to exit the country than they do to build it.[47]

To stave off self-imposed irrelevance verging into failed statehood, Nigerian leaders must timely implement changes in domestic policies with ramifications that extend to foreign relations, and changes in foreign relations with positive ramifications for democracy at home. Otherwise, they will lose many of the cream of their citizens who will choose to escape abroad, thereby swelling the already sizable population of Nigerians in the Diaspora that includes faraway countries like China and Japan until recently not destinations of choice and complicating its already-bad brain drain, to the detriment of developmental efforts at home.

This goes too to reducing, if not removal, of the line between domestic and foreign policies that keep blurring. In a globalized world rife with complex interdependence, driven by globalization, Nigerians have every right to go abroad to improve their conditions. But not to leave home to flee away from all types of reparable social injustices, including economic inequalities, a helplessly falling local currency, and a higher education system in the age of Artificial Intelligence, riddled with striking lecturers, and other distortions. Given the element of external assistance or support that we laid out among the steps to increased human rights in Nigeria in Chapter 5, this is an approach that major countries like the US should, from a more altruistic standpoint,[48] support. As the analyst Fareed Zakaria opined, commenting on the phenomenon of illiberal democracies (i.e., nominal democracy shorn of constitutionalism), such support will make *democracy* safe for the world, rather than the world safe for democracy.[49]

[47] Philip C. Aka, *Navigating the Tension Between Sovereignty and Self-Determination in Postcolonial Africa: Blueprints for the Midcentury* (Cham, Switzerland: Palgrave Macmillan), 173–260 ("Sovereignty and Self-Determination in a Non-Constitutionalized Setting: Nigeria in Comparative Perspective").

[48] On the possible role of altruism in International Law and Relations, see Jason Rudall, *Altruism in International Law* (London and New York: Cambridge University Press, 2021).

[49] Fareed Zakaria, "The Rise of Illiberal Democracy," *Foreign Affairs*, 76(6) (November–December 1997), https://doi.org/10.2307/20048274.

References

Aaron, Kiikpoye K. 2023. Buhari's Eight Years of Governance Disaster. *Guardian* (Lagos). May 24. https://guardian.ng/opinion/buharis-eight-years-of-governance-disaster/.

Abati, Reuben. 2024. Cardoso, CBN, and the Nigerian Economy. *Premium Times* (Abuja). February 6. https://www.premiumtimesng.com/opinion/665839-cardoso-cbn-and-the-nigerian-economy-by-reuben-abati.html.

Abati, Reuben. 2016. Why We Need to Restructure Nigeria to Save It. *Info Square* (Online). June 3. http://infosquare.com.ng/why-we-need-to-restructure-nigeria-to-save-it-by-reuben-abati/.

Abati, Reuben. 2016. The President as Chief Diplomat. *YNaija* (Lagos). April 17.

Abati, Reuben. 2012. The Gains of Jonathan's Diplomacy. *Premium Times* (Abuja). September 9. http://www.premiumtimesng.com/news/99498-the-gains-of-jonathans-diplomacy-by-reuben-abati.html.

Abati, Reuben. 1999. What Is Obasanjo's Foreign Policy? *Guardian Online* (Lagos). August 29.

Abegunrin, Olayiwola. 2009. *Africa in Global Politics in the Twenty-First Century: A Pan-African Perspective*. New York: Palgrave Macmillan.

Abegunrin, Olayiwola. 2003. *Nigerian Foreign Policy under Military Rule, 1966–1999*. Westport, CT: Praeger.

Abdulsalam Abubakar. *Online Nigeria*. http://www.onlinenigeria.com/abubakar.asp.

Aborisade, Oladimeji, and Robert J. Mundt. 2002. *Politics in Nigeria*, 2d Ed. New York: Longman.

P. C. Aka, *Human Rights in Nigeria's External Relations in the Age of General Muhammadu Buhari and His Successors*, https://doi.org/10.1007/978-3-031-63231-0

Abubakar, Atiku. 2016. Restructuring Nigeria for Greater National Integration and Democratic Stability. Paper Presented at the Umaru Musa Yar'Adua Memorial Hall, Kaduna. July 30. http://www.elombah.com/index.php/special-reports/9123-how-to-restructure-nigeria-written-by-atiku-abubakar.

Abubakar, Atiku. 2016. Restructuring for Nigeria's National Unity. Remarks During a Book Launching at the Yar'Adua Center, Abuja. May 31. http://opinion.premiumtimesng.com/2016/05/31/173089.

Accept Democracy as Lifestyle, Not Government[al] System, Buhari Urges Nigerians. 2015. *The Will*. June 19. http://thewillnigeria.com/news/accept-democracy-as-lifestyle-not-government-system-buhari-urges-nigerians/.

Achebe, Chinua. 2012. *There Was a Country: A Personal History of Biafra*. New York: Penguin Press.

Achebe, Chinua. 1983. *The Trouble with Nigeria*. Ibadan, Nigeria: Heinemann.

Adebajo, Adekeye. 2013. Sad Deterioration of Nigeria's Foreign Policy. *B[usiness] D[ay] Live* (Johannesburg). May 6. http://za.news.yahoo.com/sad-deterioration-nigeria-foreign-policy-051439591.html.

Adebajo, Adekeye. 2010. Nigeria. In *Providing Peacekeepers: The Politics, Challenges, and Future of United Nations Peacekeeping Contributions*, eds. Alex J. Bellamy and Paul D. Williams, 245–268. New York: Oxford University Press.

Adebajo, Adekeye. 2002. *Liberia's Civil War: Nigeria, ECOMOG, and Regional Security in West Africa*. Boulder, CO: Lynne Rienner Publishers.

Adebajo, Adekeye. 2002. *Building Peace in West Africa: Liberia, Sierra Leone, and Guinea-Bissau*. Boulder, CO: Lynne Rienner Publishers.

Adebajo, Adekeye, and Abdul R. Mustapha, eds. 2008. *Gulliver's Troubles: Nigeria's Foreign Policy after the Cold War*. Scottsville, South Africa: University of KwaZulu Press.

Adebayo, Bukola. 2018. Nigeria Overtakes India in Extreme Poverty Ranking. *CNN*. June 26. https://www.cnn.com/2018/06/26/africa/nigeria-overtakes-india-extreme-poverty-intl/index.html.

Adedeji, Adebayo. 1976. *Report of the Committee on the Review of Nigerian Foreign Policy, Including Economic and Technical Cooperation*. Lagos: Government Printer.

Adedeji, Lanre. 2015. Telecommunications and the Nigerian Economy. *Lawyers Chronicle*. http://thelawyerschronicle.com/telecommunications-and-the-nigerian-economy/. Last visited March 23.

Adeleye, Adisa. 2013. The Old and the New: Which Way Forward? *Vanguard* (Lagos). November 15. http://www.vanguardngr.com/2013/11/old-new-way-forward/.

Ademoyega, Adewale. 1981. *Why We Struck: The Story of the First Nigerian Coup*. Ibadan, Nigeria: Evans Brothers Ltd.

Adeniji, Adesoji. 2015. Peacekeeping Contributor Profile: Nigeria. *Providing for Peacekeeping*. April 24. http://www.providingforpeacekeeping.org/2015/04/24/peacekeeping-contributor-profile-nigeria.

Adeosun, Adedamola. 2023. Measuring the Quality of the International Judiciary: The ECOWAS Community Court of Justice. Ph.D. Dissertation. School of Law. London, UK. Open University. May. https://oro.open.ac.uk/86967/1/Measuring%20the%20Quality%20of%20the%20International%20Judiciary%20PDF.pdf.

Adetayo, Chris. 2023. A Foreign Policy Guide for President Tinubu. *Cable*. June 13. https://www.thecable.ng/a-foreign-policy-guide-for-president-tinubu.

Adetayo, Olalekan. 2015. Nigerians Won't Regret Electing Me, Says Buhari. *Punch* (Lagos). June 4. http://www.punchng.com/news/nigerians-wont-regret-electing-me-says-buhari-2/.

Adetula, Victor A. O. 2010. Between National Security Considerations and Good Neighborliness: Nigeria and the Challenge of Cross-Border Crime in West Africa. In *Governance and Border Security in Africa,* eds. Celestine Oyom Bassey and Oshita D. Oshita, 295–308. Lagos: Malthouse Press.

Adebanwi, Wale. 2011. *Globally-Oriented Citizenship and International Voluntary Service: Interrogating Nigeria's Technical Aid Corps Scheme*. Discussion Paper No. 71. Uppsala, Sweden: Nordiska Afrikaininstitutet.

Adebanwi, Wale. 2009. International Service and Civic Nationalism in Nigeria and The Gambia. In *Youth Service in Comparative Perspective*, ed. Amanda Moore McBride, 65–72. St. Louis, MO: Center for Social Development, Washington University in St. Louis.

Adebanwi, Wale. 2005. Government-Led Service: The Example of the Nigerian Technical Aid Corps. *Voluntary Action: The Journal of the Institute for Volunteering Research*. 7(2). https://www.bl.uk/collection-items/government-led-service.

Adewunmi, James Falode. 2019. The Military and Nation-Building in Nigeria: The General Ibrahim Babangida Regime, 1985–1993. *International Letters of Social and Humanistic Sciences*. 85: 37–48.

Adichie, Chimamanda N. 2006. *Half of a Yellow Sun*. New York: Alfred A. Knopf.

Adjolohoun, Horace S. 2013. The ECOWAS Court as a Human Rights Promoter?: Assessing Five Years' Impact of the Koraou Slavery Judgment. *Netherlands Quarterly of Human Rights*. 31(3) (2013), 342–371.

Adler, Emanuel. 1997. Seizing the Middle Ground: Constructivism in World Politics. *European Journal of International Relations*, 3(3): 319–363.

Adler, Jonathan E., and Catherine Z. Elgin, eds. 2007. *Philosophical Inquiry: Classic and Contemporary Readings*. Indianapolis, IN: Hackett Publishing Co., Inc.

Advisory Opinion. 1991. *Black's Law Dictionary*, 6th Ed. Eagan, MN: West Publishing.

African Court on Human and Peoples' Rights. About Us. https://www.african-court.org/wpafc/.

African Court on Human and Peoples' Rights. Basic Information. https://www.african-court.org/wpafc/basic-information/.

African Economic Community (AEC). *AU Watch News*. https://www.au-watch.org/african-economic-community-aec/#:~:text=The%20commitments%20in%20this%20Plan,Ordinary%20Session%20of%20the%20Assembly.

Agbakwuru, Johnbosco, and Joseph Erunke. 2015. Senate Urges Buhari to Review Nigeria's Foreign Policy. *Vanguard* (Lagos). June 3. https://www.vanguardngr.com/2015/06/senate-urges-buhari-to-review-nigerias-foreign-policy/.

Agbenorsi, Justice. 2022. Don't Cap Supreme Court Judges—Chief Justice, Spohia Akuffo Proposes. *Graphic Online*. December 8. https://www.graphic.com.gh/news/general-news/don-t-cap-supreme-court-judges-chief-justice-spohia-akuffo-proposes.html.

Ahmadu-Suka, Maryam. 2012. Nigeria: 186 Soldiers for Guinea Bissau Peacekeeping Mission. *Daily Trust* (Abuja). November 22. http://allafrica.com/stories/201211220936.html.

Aiyede, Emmanuel Remi. 2021. Nigeria's Electoral System is Still Broken. *Conversation*. May 9. https://theconversation.com/nigerias-electoral-system-is-still-broken-heres-a-list-of-whats-urgent-159693.

Ajaebili, C.N. 2011. The Option of Economic Diplomacy in Nigeria's Foreign Policy. *International Journal of Humanities & Social Science*. 1: 277–280. http://www.ijhssnet.com/journals/Vol_1_No_17_Special_Issue_November_2011/30.pdf.

Ajala, Aderemi Suleiman. 2009. Yoruba Nationalism: Culture, Politics[,] and Violence in South-Western Nigeria (1900–2009), Institut für Ethnologie und Afrikastudien, Johannes Gutenberg-Universität, Mainz, Germany. Working Paper No. 107. http://www.ifeas.uni-mainz.de/Dateien/AP107.pdf.

Ajere, Jonathan. 2012. Regional Voluntarism: The Sustainability of Nigerian Afrocentrism. *E-International Relations*. July 19. http://www.e-ir.info/2012/07/19/regional-voluntarism-the-sustainability-of-nigerian-afrocentrism/.

Aka, Philip C. 2023. *Navigating the Tension Between Sovereignty and Self-Determination in Postcolonial Africa: Blueprints for the Midcentury*. Cham, Switzerland: Palgrave Macmillan.

Aka, Philip C. 2022. *Bosnia as Civic State and Global Citizen: Alternative Futures Outside the EU*. Lanham, Boulder, New York, and London: Rowman & Littlefield.

Aka, Philip C. 2019. Fidel Castro and Socioeconomic Human Rights in Africa: A Multi-Level Analysis. *Fordham International Law Journal.* 43(1): 41–78.

Aka, Philip C. 2018. Why Nigeria Needs Restructuring Now and How It Can Peacefully Do It. *Denver Journal of International Law and Policy.* 46(2): 123–157. Winter.

Aka, Philip C. 2017. *Human Rights in Nigeria's External Relations: Building the Record of a Moral Superpower*. Lanham, Boulder, New York, and London: Lexington Books.

Aka, Philip C. 2016. Bridging the Gap Between Theory and Practice: Seven Practical Steps to Humanitarian Integrity in Nigeria. *CIHA Blog*. February 25. http://www.cihablog.com/bridging-the-gap-between-theory-and-practice-in-humanitarian-action-seven-practical-steps-to-humanitarian-integrity-in-nigeria/.

Aka, Philip C. 2015. The *Country Reports on Human Rights Practices* and U.S. Human Rights Policy in a Changing World. *Perspectives on Global Development & Technology.* 14: 238–260.

Aka, Philip C. 2014–2015. Human Rights in Nigeria's External Relations: Exigency, Methods, and Rebuttable Objections. *Buffalo Human Rights Law Review.* 21: 1–26.

Aka, Philip C. 2014. Judicial Independence under Nigeria's Fourth Republic: Problems and Prospects. *California Western International Law Journal.* 45(1): 1–78.

Aka, Philip C. 2013. Review of Lutz Oette, ed., *Criminal Law Reform and Transitional Justice: Human Rights Perspectives for Sudan* (Burlington, VT: Ashgate, 2011). *Africa Today.* 59(4): 131–137. Summer.

Aka, Philip C. 2009–2010. NEPAD and the Movement for Popular Participation in Development (MPPD) in Africa. *Human Rights & Globalization Law Review.* 3: 79–148.

Aka, Philip C. 2009. Introductory Note to the Human Rights Action Plan for China (2009–2010). *International Legal Material.* 48: 841–845.

Aka, Philip C. 2006. Analyzing U.S. Commitment to Socioeconomic Human Rights. *Akron Law Review.* 39(2): 417–463.

Aka, Philip C. 2004. Prospects for Igbo Human Rights in Nigeria in the New Century. *Howard Law Journal.* 48(1): 165–266. Fall.

Aka, Philip C. 2003. Human Rights as Conflict Resolution in Africa in the New Century. *Tulsa Journal of Comparative & International Law.* 11: 179–209. Fall.

Aka, Philip C. 2003. Nigeria Since May 1999: Understanding the Paradox of Civil Rule and Human Rights Violations under President Olusegun Obasanjo. *San Diego International Law Journal.* 4: 209–276.

Aka, Philip C. 2002. The Military, Globalization, and Human Rights in Africa. *Journal of Human Rights.* 18: 361–438. Summer.

Aka, Philip C. 2002. The "Dividend of Democracy": Analyzing U.S. Support for Nigerian Democratization. *Boston College Third World Law Journal.* 22(2): 225–280. Spring.

Aka, Philip C. 2001. Education, Economic Development, and Return to Democratic Politics in Nigeria. *Journal of Third World Studies.* 18(1): 21–38.

Aka, Philip C. 2000. Nigeria: The Need for an Effective Policy of Ethnic Reconciliation in the New Century. *Temple International & Comparative Law Journal.* 14(2): 327–361.

Aka, Philip C., and Joseph Abiodun Balogun. 2022. *Improving Disability Laws under Nigeria's Fourth Republic: Ten Measured Steps into the Future*. Lanham, Boulder, New York, and London: Lexington Books.

Aka, Philip C, and Joseph Abiodun Balogun. 2022. *Healthcare and Economic Restructuring: Nigeria in Comparative Perspective*. Gateway East, Singapore: Palgrave Macmillan.

Akande, Tunji. 2014. Youth Unemployment in Nigeria: A Situation Analysis. Brookings. September 23. https://www.brookings.edu/articles/youth-unemployment-in-nigeria-a-situation-analysis/.

Ake, Claude. 1996. *Democracy and Development in Africa*. Washington, D.C.: Brookings Institution.

Akinboye, S.O. 2013. Beautiful Abroad but Ugly at Home: Issues and Contra[di]ctions in Nigerian Foreign Policy. University of Lagos Inaugural Lecture Series. www.unilag.edu.ng/opendocnew.php?

Akindele, Richard A., and Bassey Ate, eds. 2000. *Selected Readings on Nigeria's Foreign Policy and International Relations*. Lagos: Nigerian Institute of International Affairs and Vantage Publishers.

Akinrefon, Dapo. 2012. Let's Return to Aburi Accord—Adeniyi. *Vanguard* (Lagos). January 30. http://stephendieseruvwe.com/2012/03/14/lets-return-to-aburi-accord-adeniyi/.

Akinyemi, Akanmi I. 2023. Nigeria's Growing Population Can Be an Advantage, with Better Data and a Policy Focus on Young People. *Conversation*. July 11. https://theconversation.com/nigerias-growing-population-can-be-an-advantage-with-better-data-and-a-policy-focus-on-young-people-209530#:~:text=The%20country%20has%20the%20largest,under%20the%20age%20of%2015.

Akpan, Ani. 2008. Nigeria Hands Over Oil-Rich Bakassi to Cameroon. Reuters. August 14. https://www.reuters.com/article/us-nigeria-cameroon-bakassi/nigeria-hands-over-oil-rich-bakassi-to-cameroon-idUSLE14871520080814.

Akpan, Samuel. 2023. Nigerian TAC Volunteers Protest Non-Payment of Allowances in Gambia. *Cable* (Lagos). May 19. https://www.thecable.ng/nigerian-tac-volunteers-protest-non-payment-of-allowances-in-gambia.

Akwagyiram, Alexis. 2021. Nigeria Says it Suspends Twitter Days after President's Post Removed. *Reuters*. June 5. https://www.reuters.com/technology/nigeria-indefinitely-suspends-twitter-operations-information-minister-2021-06-04/.

Akwagyiram, Alexis. 2021. Twitter Removes Nigerian President's "Abusive" Civil War Post. *Reuters*. June 3. https://www.reuters.com/world/africa/twitter-removes-nigerian-presidents-abusive-civil-war-post-2021-06-02/.

Alabi, Mojeed Olujinmi A. 2006. Law Making in Pre-Colonial Yorubaland. In *The Yoruba in Transition: History, Values, and Modernity*, ed. Toyin Falola and Ann Genova, 112–124. Durham, NC: Carolina Academic Press.

Alfred, Charlotte. 2015. Boko Haram Actually Kills More People in Terror Attacks than ISIS. *Huffington Post*. November 18. http://www.huffingtonpost.com/entry/boko-haram-isis_us_564cd890e4b00b7997f8c15d.

Al-Hassa, Hadi Y. Circa 2010. "Evaluating Nigerian Foreign Policy at 50." *Gamji*. http://www.gamji.com/article9000/news9139.htm.

Alliances for Africa. Strengthening the ECOWAS Court of Justice: Enhancing Access to Justice in the West African Region. https://alliancesforafrica.org/strengthening-the-ecowas-court-of-justice-enhancing-access-to-justice-in-the-west-african-region/#:~:text=It%20was%20a%20unanimously%20agreed,that%20has%20no%20legal%20force.

Allison, Graham. 1971. *Essence of Decision: Explaining the Cuban Missile Crisis*. Boston, MA: Little Brown.

All Progressives Congress. About APC. http://apc.com.ng/index.php/about-apc.

Alter, Karen J., James Thuo Gathii, and Laurence R. Helfer. 2020. Backlash Against International Courts in West, East, and Southern Africa: Causes and Consequences. In *The Performance of Africa's International Courts: Using Litigation for Political, Legal, and Social Change*, ed. James Thuo Gathii. Oxford University Press. https://doi.org/10.1093/oso/9780198868477.003.0008.

Alter, Karen J., Laurence R. Helfer, and Jacqueline R. McAllister. 2013. A New International Human Rights Court for West Africa: The ECOWAS Community Court of Justice. *American Journal of International Law*. October. 107(4): 737–779. https://doi.org/10.5305/amerjintelaw.107.4.0737.

Amnesty International. 2023. Why the African Court Should Matter to You. June 9. https://www.amnesty.org/en/latest/campaigns/2023/06/why-the-african-court-should-matter-to-you/#:~:text=ESTABLISHMENT%20OF%20THE%20COURT&text=The%20Protocol%20came%20into%20force,from%20all%20over%20the%20continent.

Amnesty International. 2015. *Stars on Their Shoulders[,] Blood on their Hands: War Crimes Committed by the Nigerian Military*. June 3. http://www.amnestyusa.org/research/reports/stars-on-their-shoulders-blood-on-their-hands-war-crimes-committed-by-the-nigerian-military.

Amnesty International. 2012. Groundbreaking ECOWAS Court Judgment Orders Government to Punish Oil Companies Over Pollution. Press Release.

December 16. https://www.amnesty.org/en/latest/press-release/2012/12/ground-breaking-ecowas-court-judgment-orders-government-punish-oil-companie/.

Amnesty International. 2010. Nigeria: ECOWAS Court Affirms Nigeria Accountable for Ensuring the Right to Education. Amnesty International Public Statement. December 6. https://www.amnesty.org/en/wp-content/uploads/2021/07/afr440322010en.pdf.

Amuwo, 'Kunle. 2001. Introduction: Transition as Democratic Regression. In *Nigeria during the Abacha Years (1993–1998)*, eds. 'Kunle Amuwo, Daniel C. Bach, and Yann Lebenu, 1–56. Lagos: IFRA-Nigeria.

Amstutz, Mark R. 1999. *International Ethics: Concepts, Theories, and Cases in Global Politics*. Lanham, MD: Rowland & Littlefield Publishers.

Analysis: Nigeria's Sharia Split. 2003. *BBC News*. January 7. news.bbc.co.uk/2/hi/Africa/2632939.stm.

Anderson, Carol. 2003. *Eyes on the Prize: The United Nations and the African American Struggle for Human Rights, 1944–1955*. New York: Cambridge University Press.

Anderson, J.N.D. 1976. *Law Reform in the Muslim World*. London: Athlone Press.

Andersson, Hilary. 2005. Born to Be a Slave in Niger. *BBC News*. February 11. http://news.bbc.co.uk/2/hi/programmes/from_our_own_correspondent/4250709.stm.

Anene-Maidoh, Tony. 2018. Enforcement of Judgments of the ECOWAS Court of Justice. National Institute for Legislative and Democratic Studies (NILDS). https://ir.nilds.gov.ng/bitstream/handle/123456789/387/ENFORCEMENT%20OF%20JUDGMENTS%20OF%20THE%20ECOWAS%20COURT%20OF%20JUSTICE.pdf?sequence=1&isAllowed=y.

An-Naim, Abdullahi. 1993. The National Question, Secession and Constitutionalism: The Mediation of Competing Claims to Self-Determination. In *Constitutionalism and Democracy: Transition in the Contemporary World*, eds. Douglas Greenberg, Stanley N. Katz, Melanie Beth Oliviero, and Steven C. Wheatley, 105–125. New York: Oxford University Press.

Anya, Anya O. 2010. Nigeria: The Human Capital Challenge. *African Journal of Physics*. 3: 5–30. http://sirius-b.ncat.edu.ncat.edu/asn/afps/ajp/ajp-ISOTPAND10/Proc%20ISPD%20book5-30.pdf.

Anyaoku, Emeka. 2013. Nigeria's Current Drift Towards Chaos. *Vanguard* (Lagos). November 12. http://www.vanguardngr.com/2013/11/nigerias-current-drift-towards-chaos-emeka-anyaoku/#sthas.3H7LjLA6.dpuf.

Anyaoku Proposes Reduction of Nigeria's 36 States into 6 Units. 2016. *Sun* (Lagos). February 3. http://sunnewsonline.com/new/anyaoku-proposes-reduction-of-nigerias-36-states-into-6-units/.

Aribisala, Femi. ECOWAS Imperative for Nigeria. 2015. *Nigeria Development and Finance Forum*. Last visited February 28. http://www.nigeriadevelopmentandfinanceforum.org/PolicyDialogue/Dialogue.aspx?Edition=63.

Asadu, Chinedu. 2024. What is ECOWAS and Why Have [Three] Coup-Hit Nations Quit the West Africa Bloc? *Associated Press*. January 29. https://apnews.com/article/mali-burkina-faso-niger-ecowas-africa-d2e8b1e5448d9a7823e6b9d3d8ec774b.

Asadu, Chinedu. 2023. Nigeria's Supreme Court Refuses to Void President's Election and Dismisses Opposition Challenges. *AP News*. October 26. https://apnews.com/article/nigeria-election-supreme-court-abubakar-tinubu-ad610050879e5a0178bcb52934c56054.

Asadu, Chinedu. 2023. Nigeria's President Faces New Challenge to Election Victory as Opposition Claims He Forged Diploma. *AP News*. October 5. https://apnews.com/article/nigeria-tinubu-abubakar-election-challenge-ba0fd3483678b84747bd38aba53d5bf9.

Ashiru, Olugbenga. 2011. Seminar to Review Nigeria's Foreign Policy. July 28. http://www.mfa.gov.ng/news_one.php?article=41.

Associated Press. 1985. Expelled Foreigners Pouring Out of Nigeria. *New York Times*. May 4. http://www.nytimes.com/1985/05/05/world/expelled-foreigners-pouringout-of-nigeriaby-the-associated-press.html?pagewanted=print.

Atlantic Charter. 1941. August 14. http://avalon.law.yale.edu/wwii/atlantic.asp.

Awojide, Dipo. 2023. Solutions to Challenges Plaguing Tertiary Education in Nigeria. *LinkedIn*. November 20. https://www.linkedin.com/pulse/solutions-challenges-plaguing-tertiary-education-nigeria-awojide-r4hfe/.

Ayitogo, Nasir. 2022. Military Influence "Dwindles" in Nigerian Elections. *Premium Times* (Abuja). July 9. https://www.premiumtimesng.com/news/headlines/541716-2023-military-influence-dwindles-in-nigerian-elections.html.

Ayoade, J.A.A. (2010). Nigeria: Positive Pessimism and Negative Optimism: A Valedictory Lecture. *Nigerian Voice*. Vol. 2. September 17. http://www.thenigerianvoice.com/print/34992/1/nigeria-positive-pessimism-and-negative-optimism-a.html.

Ayua, Ignatius Akaayar, and Dakas C.J. Dakas. 2005. Federal Republic of Nigeria. In *Constitutional Origins, Structure, and Change in Federal Countries*, eds. John Kincaid and George Alan Tarr, 239–275. Montreal, Canada: McGill-Queen's University Press.

Azikiwe, Ifeoma. 2013. *Nigeria: Echoes of a Century: 1914–1999,* Vol. 1. Bloomington, IN: AuthorHouse.

Babalola, Samiu. 2011. Nigeria's Technical Aid Corps: Pearl of South-South Cooperation. *Africa Platform for Development Effectiveness*. December 21.

http://www.africa-platform.org/resources/nigerias-technical-aid-corps-pearl-south-south-cooperation.

Babarinde, Olufemi A. 1999. Regionalism and African Foreign Policies. In *African Foreign Policies,* ed. Stephen Wright, 215–236. Boulder, CO: Westview Press.

Babatunde, Aishat, and Yusuf Akinpelu. 2020. Nigeria Underfunding Diplomatic Missions, Weakening Foreign Policy—Experts. *Premium Times* (Abuja). December 11. https://www.premiumtimesng.com/news/headlines/430537-nigeria-underfunding-diplomatic-missions-weakening-foreign-policy-experts.html.

Babatunde, Oyediji O. 2014. Hausa/Fulani Pre-Colonial Political System in Nigeria. *Word Press.* March 30. http://www.profseunoyediji.wordpress.com/2014/03/30/hausafulani-pre-colonial-political-system-in-nigeria.

Baehr, Peter R. 2009. Foreign Policy. In *Encyclopedia of Human Rights.* 5: 237–247. New York: Oxford University Press.

Baehr, Peter R. 2000. Trials and Errors: The Netherlands and Human Rights. In *Human Rights and Comparative Foreign Policy: Foundations of Peace*, ed. David P. Forsythe, 49–86. New York: United Nations University.

Baehr, Peter R. 1998. Mobilization of the Conscience of Mankind: Conditions of Effectiveness of Human Rights NGOs. In *Reflections on International Law from the Low Countries*, ed. Peter R. Baehr, 135–155. Leiden, Netherlands: Brill Publishers.

Baehr, Peter R., and Monique Castermans-Holleman. 2004. *The Role of Human Rights in Foreign Policy,* 3rd Ed. New York: Palgrave Macmillan.

Ball, Terence, Richard Dagger, and Daniel I. O'Neill. 2014. *Political Ideologies and the Democratic Ideal,* 9th Ed. Boston, MA: Pearson.

Balouga, Jean. 2009. The Niger Delta: Defusing the Time Bomb. *International Association for Energy Economics.* First Quarter. 8–11. https://citeseerx.ist.psu.edu/document?repid=rep1&type=pdf&doi=b89b353dac321fb7af47dbd06364896f72c5bda3#:~:text=The%20Niger%20Delta%20region%20is,National%20Population%20Commission%2C%202006.

Bannister, Tom. 2017. Volunteering, A Participatory Approach to South-South Cooperation. *UN Volunteers.* April 11. https://www.unv.org/news/volunteering-participatory-approach-south-south-cooperation.

Barash, David P. 2013. Costa Rica's Peace Dividend: How Abolishing the Military Paid Off. *Los Angeles Times.* December 15. http://articles.latimes.com/2013/dec/15/opinion/la-oe-barash-costa-rica-demilitarization-20131208.

Bassey, Celestine Oyom, and Charles Quarker Dokubo. 2011. *Defense Policy of Nigeria: Capability and Context: A Reader.* Bloomington, IN: AuthorHouse.

Basic Information. ECOWAS. www.ecowas.int/about-ecowas/basic-information/.

Basic Writings of John Stuart Mill: On Liberty, the Subjection of Women, and Unilateralism. 2002. New York: Modern Library.

Beard, Charles A, and G.H.E. Smith. 1934. *The Idea of National Interest: An Analytical Study in American Foreign Policy*. New York: Macmillan

Beaumont, Peter, and Isaac Abrak. 2018. Oil-Rich Nigeria Outstrips India as Country with Most People in Poverty. *Guardian* (London). July 16. https://www.theguardian.com/global-development/2018/jul/16/oil-rich-nigeria-outstrips-india-most-people-in-poverty#:~:text=According%20to%20the%20authors%2C%20energy,with%20India's%2073%20million%20people.

Beehner, Lionel. 2007. "The Coalition of the Willing." Council on Foreign Relations. Updated February 22. http://www.cfr.org/iraq/coalition-willing/p9340.

Beirnaert, Jeroen. 2009. West-African Court Slavery Judgment. *International Union Rights*. 16(2): 18–19. https://www.ilo.org/sites/default/files/wcmsp5/groups/public/@ed_norm/@declaration/documents/publication/wcms_140854.pdf.

Bellamy, Alex J., and Paul D. Williams, eds. 2013. *Providing Peacekeepers: The Politics, Challenges, and Future of United Nations Peacekeeping Contributions*. New York: Oxford University Press.

Bello, Ademola. 2010. Umaru Yar'Adua: A Mediocre Administrator, the Least Prepared Nigerian President Since Shehu Shagari. *Huffington Post*. May 13, Updated May 25, 2011. http://www.huffingtonpost.com/ademola-bellow/umaru-musa-yaradua-a-medi_b_575125.html.

Bennett, John C. 1966. *Foreign Policy in Christian Perspective*. New York: Scribner's 1966.

Berman, Larry, and Bruce Allen Murphy. 2013. *Approaching Democracy*, 8th Ed. New York: Pearson Education, Inc.

Bhattacherjee, Anol. 2012. *Social Science Research: Principles, Methods, and Practices*. Scholar Commons Textbooks Collection.

Biography of Alhaji Shehu Usman Aliyu Shagari. *The Biography*. http://thebiography.us/en/shagari-alhaji-shehu-usman-aliyu.

Black, Eric. 2012. Why the Constitution's Framers Didn't Want Us to Directly Elect the President. *Minn. Post*. October 17. https://www.minnpost.com/eric-black-ink/2012/10/why-constitution-s-framers-didn-t-want-us-directly-elect-president.

Blas, Javier. 2014. Victim of Shale Revolution, Nigeria Stops Exporting Oil to U.S. *Blogger*. October 2. http://blogs.ft.com/beyond-brics/2014/10/02/victim-of-shale-revolution-nigeria-stops-exporting-oil-to-us/.

Blinken, Antony J. 2021. The United States and Africa: Building a 21st Century Partnership. US Embassy and Consulate in Nigeria. November 12. https://ng.usembassy.gov/the-united-states-and-africa-building-a-21st-century-partnership/.

Boko Haram Fast Facts. 2016. *CNN Library*. Updated February 19. http://www.cnn.com/2014/06/09/world/boko-haram-fast-facts/.

Borenstein, Seth. 2023. US Oil Production Hits All-Time High, Conflicting with Efforts to Cut Heat-Trapping Pollution. *AP*. Updated October 20. https://apnews.com/article/oil-fossil-fuels-climate-change-biden-df27160fc81f28d21fbf1fc5575b77bc.

Bova, Russell. 2010. *How the World Works: A Brief Survey of International Relations*. New York: Longman.

Brief Notes on Nigeria. *Online Nigeria*. http://www.onlinenigeria.com/history.asp.

Brooker, Paul. 2009. *Non-Democratic Regimes: Theory, Government, and Politics*, 2d Ed. New York: Palgrave Macmillan.

Brown, Ryan Lenora. 2015. A Top Nigerian Export: Fervent Christianity. *Christian Science Monitor*. September 28. http://news.yahoo.com/top-nigerian-export-fervent-christianity-135101567.html.

Brysk, Alison. 2009. *Global Good Samaritans: Human Rights as Foreign Policy*. New York: Oxford University Press.

Building Security in Southern Africa: An Update on the Evolving Architecture. 1999. Monograph No. 43. Pretoria, South Africa: Institute for Security. November.

Bukola, Akintola. 2007. Nigeria and the World: A Review of Nigeria's Foreign Policy (1960–2007). *Nigerian Army Quarterly Journal*. 3: 438–371. December.

Bump, Micah. 2006. Ghana: Searching for Opportunities at Home and Abroad. *Migration Information Source*. March 1. http://www.migrationpolicy.org/article/ghana-searching-opportunities-home-and-abroad.

Burns, James MacGregor. 1978. *Leadership*. New York: Harper Torchbooks.

Calvert, Peter. 1986. *The Foreign Policy of New States*. New York: St. Martin's Press.

Campbell, Ian. 1994. Nigeria's Failed Transition: The 1993 Presidential Election. *Journal of Contemporary African Studies*. 12(2): 179–199. https://doi.org/10.1080/02589009408729556.

Campbell, John. 2018. Obasanjo's Costly Failed Third-Term Bid. Council on Foreign Relations. September 27. https://www.cfr.org/blog/obasanjos-costly-failed-third-term-bid.

Campbell, John. 2013. *Nigeria: Dancing on the Brink*. Updated Edition. Lanham, MD: Rowman & Littlefield Publishers.

Campbell, Keith. 1978. Nigerian Foreign Policy and the Economic Community of West African States (ECOWAS). Occasional Paper. South African Institute of International Affairs. September.

Cárdenas, Emilio J., and María Fernanda Cañás. 2001. The Limits of Self-Determination. In *The Self-Determination of Peoples: Community, Nation, and*

State in an Interdependent World, ed. Wolfgang Danspeckgruber, 101–118. Boulder, CO: Lynne Rienner.

Carter, Jimmy. 2000. The American Road to a Human Rights Policy. In *Realizing Human Rights: Moving from Inspiration to Impact*, ed. Samantha Power and Graham Alison, 49–61. New York: St. Martin's Press.

Cassel, Douglass. 1998. The Universal Declaration at 50: Changing the World? *Christian Century*. December 23–30. 1249–1251.

Chazan, Naomi, Peter Lewis, Robert A. Mortimer, Donald Rothchild, and Stephen John Stedman. 1999. *Politics and Society in Contemporary Africa,* 3rd Ed. Boulder, CO: Lynne Rienner Publishers.

CEN-SAD Celebrates 13th Anniversary. *Pana Press*. http://www.panapress.com/CEN-SAD-celebrates-13th-anniversary---12-756752-29-lang2-index.html.

Census History. 1993. In *Nigeria: A Country Study,* Helen Chapin Metz. Washington D.C.: GPO for the Library of Congress. https://countrystudies.us/nigeria/30.htm.

The Centenary Project. Colonial Footprints: Lagos, Then and Now. *Google Arts and Culture*. https://artsandculture.google.com/story/colonial-footprints-lagos-then-and-now/LAUBxuvCARsA8A.

Center for Energy Economics. *Gas Monetization in Nigeria*. http://www.beg.utexas.edu/energyecon/new-era/case_studies/Gas_Monetization_in_Nigeria.pdf.

Center for Journalism Innovation and Development. 2022. MRA Calls on Federal Government to Implement ECOWAS Court Judgment in Twitter Ban Suits. Press Release. July 19. https://thecjid.org/mra-calls-on-federal-government-to-implement-ecowas-court-judgment-in-twitter-ban-suits/.

Chigozie, Chilaka Francis, and Odoh Samuel Ituma. 2015. Nigerian Peacekeeping Operations Revisited. *Singaporean Journal of Business Economics & Management Studies*. Vol. 4. www.singaporeanjbem.com/pdfs/SG_vol_4_(2)/1.pdf.

Chima, Obinna. 2014. Nigeria's Unemployment Rate May Rise by 2%. *This Day* (Lagos). January 7. http://www.thisdaylive.com/articles/nigeria-s-unemployment-rate-may-rise-by-2/168227.

China: Ratify Key International Human Rights Treaty. 2013. *Human Rights Watch*. October 3. https://www.hrw.org/news/2013/10/08/china-ratify-key-international-human-rights-treaty.

Chioma, Unini. 2019. ECOWAS Court Strengthens Reparations, Enforcement. *Nigerian Lawyer*. July 9. https://thenigerialawyer.com/ecowas-court-strengthens-reparations-enforcement/.

Chothia, Farouk. 2015. Who are Nigeria's Boko Haram Islamists. *BBC News Africa*. May 4. http://www.bbc.com/news/world-africa-13809501.

Chuku, Gloria. 2013. Olaudah Equiano and the Foundation of Igbo Intellectual Tradition. In *The Igbo Intellectual Tradition: Creative Conflict in African and African Diasporic Thought*, ed. Gloria Chukwu, 33–65. New York: Palgrave Macmillan.

Churchill, Winston. 2008. *Churchill by Himself: The Definitive Collection of Quotations*. Edited by Richard M. Langworth. New York: Public Affairs.

CIA *World Factbook*. Nigeria. 2023. Last updated September 5. https://www.cia.gov/the-world-factbook/countries/nigeria/.

CIA *World Factbook*. Nigeria. 2014. Last updated November 19. https://www.cia.gov/library/publications/the-world-factbook/geos/ni.html.

Clapham, Andrew. 1993. *Human Rights in the Private Sphere*. New York: Oxford University Press.

Clapham, Christopher. 1993. Democratization in Africa: Obstacles and Prospects. *Third World Quarterly*. 14(3): 423–438.

Clark, Andrew. Mali. *Encyclopedia Britannica*. http://www.britannica.com/place/Mali/Government-and-society#ref1180547.

Claude Jr., Inis L. 1965. *The Changing United Nations*. New York: Random House.

Clinton, William J. 2000. Remarks to a Joint Session of the Nigerian National Assembly in Abuja. *American Presidency Project*. August 26. https://www.presidency.ucsb.edu/documents/remarks-joint-session-the-nigerian-national-assembly-abuja.

Clinton, William J. 2000. Remarks Following Discussions with President Olusegun Obasanjo of Nigeria and an Exchange with Reporters in Abuja, Nigeria, August 26, 2000. In *Public Papers of the Presidents of the United States: William J. Clinton, 2000–2001*, 1701–1705. Washington, DC: Best Books.

Clinton, William J. 2000. Remarks to a Joint Session of the Nigerian National Assembly in Abuja, August 26, 2000. In *Public Papers of the Presidents of the United States: William J. Clinton, 2000–2001*, 1705–1710. Washington, DC: Best Books.

Clinton, William J. 2000. Remarks at a State Dinner Hosted by President Olusegun Obasanjo of Nigeria in Abuja, August 26, 2000. In *Public Papers of the Presidents of the United States: William J. Clinton, 2000–2001*, 1711–1712. Washington, DC: Best Books.

Clinton Praises "New Nigeria." 2000. *BBC News*. August 26. http://news.bbc.co.uk/2/hi/africa/897423.stm.

Cohen, Michael. 2024. Why Nigeria Currency Exchange Mess Is So Hard to Fix. *Bloomberg*. January 29, updated January 30. https://www.bloomberg.com/news/articles/2024-01-29/why-nigeria-s-naira-currency-exchange-regime-mess-is-so-hard-to-fix.

Cohen, Ronald, Goran Hyden, and Winston P. Nagan, eds. 1993. *Human Rights and Governance in Africa*. Gainesville, FL: University Press of Florida.

Collective Security. *Encyclopedia Britannica*. http://www.britannica.com/topic/collective-security.

Columbia University. Global Freedom of Expression. 2022. Global Freedom of Expression Prize Winners 2022: Awards Ceremony. https://globalfreedomofexpression.columbia.edu/prizewinners2022/.

Committee to Project Journalists (CPJ). 2021. Nigerian Broadcast Regulator Orders Outlets to Stop Using Twitter Amid Nationwide Block. New York. June 8. https://cpj.org/2021/06/nigerian-broadcast-regulator-orders-outlets-to-stop-using-twitter-amid-nationwide-block/.

Committee to Protect Journalists. Chief Ebrima Manneh. https://cpj.org/data/people/chief-ebrima-manneh/.

Common Market for Eastern and South Africa. http://www.comesa.int/.

Community Court of Justice. 2020. Pioneer Staff of ECOWAS Court Praised for Their Role in Its History and Transformation. October 26. http://www.courtecowas.org/2020/10/26/pioneer-staff-of-ecowas-court-praised-for-their-role-in-its-history-and-transformation/.

Community Court of Justice. 2020. *Amnesty International and 7 Others v. the Togolese Republic*. Suit No. ECW/CCJ/APP/61/18. June 25. https://www.eods.eu/elex/uploads/files/642e998c687ef-JUD-ECW-CCJ-JUD-09-20-Amnesty-Int.-TOGO-7-ORS-vs.-REP.-OF-TOGO-25_06_20-vA.pdf.

Community Court of Justice. Current Judges. http://www.courtecowas.org/current-judges-2/.

Community Court of Justice—ECOWAS. About Us. http://www.courtecowas.org/site2012/index.php?option=com_content&view=article&id=2&Itemid=5.

Community Court of Justice. ECOWAS Court Issues 2020 Judicial Statistics. http://www.courtecowas.org/2021/01/21/ecowas-court-issues-2020-judicial-statistics/.

Community Court of Justice. Judges 2001–2009. http://www.courtecowas.org/judges-2001-2009-2/.

Community Court of Justice. 2022. *SERAP and 176 Other Concerned Nigerians v. Nigeria*. Suit No. ECW/CCJ/APP/23/21. Judgment No. ECW/CCJ/JUD/40/22. July 14.

Community Court of Justice. 2021. *Fodi Mohamed & Others v. Niger.* Suit No. ECW/CCJ/APP/27/19. Judgment No. ECW/CCJ/JUD/19/21. June 24. https://caselaw.ihrda.org/en/entity/pcaiwdusd5?page=1 (text in French).

Community Court of Justice. 2021. *Kadiaton Siby v. Mali*. Suit No. ECW/CCJ/APP/42/19. Judgment No. ECW/CCJ/JUD/15/21. June 22. *Reprinted* in African Human Rights Case Law Analyzer. https://caselaw.ihrda.org/en/entity/16tp7b9q7l7h (text in French).

Community Court of Justice. 2020. *Amnesty International and 7 Others v. the Togolese Republic*. Suit No. ECW/CCJ/APP/61/18. Judgment No. ECW/CCJ/JUD/09/20. June 25. https://www.eods.eu/elex/uploads/files/642e998c687ef-JUD-ECW-CCJ-JUD-09-20-Amnesty-Int.-TOGO-7-ORS-vs.-REP.-OF-TOGO-25_06_20-vA.pdf.

Community Court of Justice. 2019. *Rev. Fr. Solomon Mfa & 11 Others v. Nigeria and 5 Others*. Suit No. ECW/CCJ/APP/11/16. Judgment No. ECW/CCJ/JUD/06/19. February 26. https://caselaw.ihrda.org/en/entity/y1vuecy8gz.

Community Court of Justice. 2018. *Raymond Oguche & 4 Others v. Nigeria*. Suit No. ECW/CCJ/APP/11/15. Judgment No. ECW/CCJ/JUD/24/18. July 4. https://caselaw.ihrda.org/en/entity/v7dx0uzx5h36xsri94ojn61or?page=1.

Community Court of Justice. 2017. *Nosa Ehanire Osaghae & 3 Others (on Behalf of Niger Delta People) v. Nigeria*. Suit No. ECW/CCJ/APP/2015. Judgment No. ECW/CCJ/JUD/03/07. October 10. https://caselaw.ihrda.org/en/entity/5rot9qij7oijzfuyfghr1i3sor?page=1.

Community Court of Justice. 2015. *Rose M. Ako v. West African Monetary Agency and 4 Others*. Suit No. ECW/CCJ/APP/01/14/SUPP. Judgment No. ECW/CCJ/JUD/2815. December 2. https://caselaw.ihrda.org/en/entity/jcp55cz4kcrjbp0nc7bck57b9?page=2.

Community Court of Justice. 2012. *SERAP v. Nigeria*. Suit No. ECW/CCJ/APP/08/09. Judgment ECW/CCJ/JUD/18/12. December 14. https://caselaw.ihrda.org/en/entity/pftlz3gneo0wxsgq0kdszto6r?page=30.

Community Court of Justice. 2011. *Starcrest Investment Ltd. v. President of ECOWAS Commission*. Suit No. ECW/CCJ/APP/01/08. Judgment No. ECW/CCJ/JUD/06/11. July 8. https://www.worldcourts.com/ecowasccj/eng/decisions/2011.07.08_Starcrest_Investment_Ltd_v_President_of_ECOWAS_Comm.htm.

Community Court of Justice. 2010. *Musa Saidykhan v. The Gambia*. Suit No. ECW/CCJ/APP/11/07. Judgment No. ECW/CCJ/JUD/08/10. December 16. https://caselaw.ihrda.org/en/entity/froafttgl56tn7350qszzd7vi.

Community Court of Justice. 2010. *SERAP v. Nigeria and Anor*. Suit No. ECW/CCJ/APP/12/07. Judgment No. ECW/CCJ/JUD/07/10. November 30. https://www.worldcourts.com/ecowasccj/eng/decisions/2010.11.30_SERAP_v_Nigeria.htm.

Community Court of Justice. 2008. *Hadijatou Mani Koraou v. Niger*. Suit No. ECW/CCJ/APP/08/08. Judgment No. ECW/CCJ/JUD/06/08. October 27. http://www.courtecowas.org/wp-content/uploads/2023/12/JUD-ECW-CCJ-JUD-06-08-Dame-Hadijatou-Mani-Koraou-c.-La-R%C3%A9p-du-NIGER-27_10_08-vA-1.pdf.

Community Court of Justice. 2008. *Manneh v. The Gambia*. Suit No. ECW/CCJ/APP/04/07. Judgment No. ECW/CCJ/JUD/03/08. June 5. https://www.worldcourts.com/ecowasccj/eng/decisions/2008.06.05_Manneh_v_Gambia.htm.

Community Court of Justice. 2004. *Olajide Afolabi v. Nigeria*. Judgment No. ECW/CJ/JUD/01/04. April 27. *Reprinted* in African Human Rights Case Law Analyzer. https://caselaw.ihrda.org/en/entity/6dp0llnd6hr82kc18ylbjiqkt9?page=6.

Community Court of Justice. 1991. Protocol A/P.l/7/91 on the Community Court of Justice. July. 6. http://www.courtecowas.org/wp-content/uploads/2018/11/Protocol_AP1791_ENG.pdf.

Community Court of Justice. Mandate and Jurisdiction. http://www.courtecowas.org/mandate-and-jurisdiction-2/.

Community Court of Justice. Membership of the Court. http://www.courtecowas.org/members-of-the-court/.

Constitution of the Federal Republic of Ethiopia, 1995. *Reprinted* in *Ref World*. August 21. http://www.refworld.org/docid/3ae6b5a84.html.

Constitution of the Federal Republic of Nigeria, 1999. *Constitute Project*. https://www.constituteproject.org/constitution/Nigeria_1999.

Constitution of the Federal Republic of Nigeria (Promulgation) Decree No. 24. 1999. May 5.

Constitution of the Federal Republic of Nigeria. 1979. *Constitution Net*. www.constitutionnet.org/files/nig_const_79.pdf.

Constitution of the Federation of Nigeria, 1960. *Law Nigeria*. https://constitution.lawnigeria.com/2018/03/26/1960-constitution-of-nigeria-the-nigerian-constitution-hub/.

Constitution of the Federal Republic of Nigeria. 1963. *Law Nigeria*. https://constitution.lawnigeria.com/2018/03/26/1963-constitution-of-nigeria-the-nigerian-constitution-hub/.

Constitution of the United States of America. 1789. https://www.usconstitution.net/const.html.

Council on Foreign Relations. 2008. Fact Sheet on Africa Contingency Operations Training and Assistance (ACOTA). June 15. http://www.cfr.org/africa-sub-saharan/fact-sheet-africa-contingency-operations-training-assistance-acota/p22318.

Countries in the World by Population (2023). *Worldometer*. https://www.worldometers.info/world-population/population-by-country/.

Crabb Jr., Cecil V. 1972. *American Foreign Policy in the Nuclear Age*, 3rd Ed. New York: Harper & Row.

Craven, Matthew. 2015. Between Law and History: The Berlin Conference of 1884–1885 and the Logic of Free Trade. *London Review of International Law*. 3: 31–59.

Crawford, Emily, and Alison Pert. 2015. *International Humanitarian Law*. New York: Cambridge University Press.

Crawford, Neta C. 2002. *Argument and Change in World Politics: Ethics, Decolonization, and Humanitarian Intervention*. New York: Cambridge University Press.

Crisis, Fragile, and Failed States Definitions used by the CSRC. 2006. LSE. Crisis States Workshop, London. March. https://www.lse.ac.uk/international-development/Assets/Documents/PDFs/csrc-background-papers/Definition-of-a-Failed-State.pdf.

Cross, Ben. Performance Legitimacy for Realists. 2022. *Philosophy East and West*. Project MUSE. https://doi.org/https://doi.org/10.1353/pew.0.0241.

Crude Tactics. 2016. *Economist* (London). January 30. http://www.economist.com/news/middle-east-and-africa/21689584-cheap-oil-causing-currency-crisis-nigeria-banning-imports-no.

Curtis, Mark. 2004. *Unpeople: Britain's Secret Human Rights Abuses*. New York: Vintage Books.

Customs Union. *Britannica Money*. https://www.britannica.com/money/customs-union.

Dada, Jacob Abiodun. 2012. Impediments to Human Rights Protection in Nigeria. *Annual Survey of International & Comparative Law*. 18: 67–92.

Daldorph, Brenda. 2015. Muhammadu Buhari: "The Converted Democrat?" *France 24*. Latest update April 13. http://www.france24.com/en/20150401-nigeria-buhari-president-elections-coup-africa.

Danfulani, John. 2014. The End of Apartheid: A Redefinition of Nigerian Foreign Policy. *IQSRJ Journal of Humanities & Social Science*. 19: 53–57. http://iosrjournals.org/iosr-jhss/papers/Vol19-issue11/Version-3/I0191135357.pdf.

Danziger, James N. 2013. *Understanding the Political World: A Comparative Introduction to Political Science*, 11th Ed. New York: Pearson.

Davidson, Basil. 1994. *Modern Africa: A Social and Political History*, 3rd Ed. New York: Longman.

Declaration of Independence. 1776. July 4. http://www.archives.gov/exhibits/charters/declaration_transcript.html.

Definitions of Contentious Jurisdiction. *World Law Dictionary*. https://dictionary.translegal.com/en/contentious-jurisdiction/noun.

Deng, Francis M. 2000. Reconciling Sovereignty with Responsibility: Basis for International Humanitarian Action. In *Africa in World Politics: The African State System in Flux*, 3rd Ed., eds. John W. Harbeson and Donald Rothchild. Chapter 14. Boulder, CO: Westview Press.

Deng, Francis M., Sadikiel Kimaro, Terrence Lyons, Rothchild Donald, and I. William Zartman. 1996. *Sovereignty as Responsibility: Conflict Management in Africa* Washington, DC: Brookings Institution Press.

DeYoung, Karen. 2010. Obama Redefines National Security Strategy, Looks Beyond Military Might. *Washington Post.* May 27. http://www.washingtonpost.com/wp-dyn/content/article/2010/05/27/AR2010052701044.html.

Diamond, Larry. 2001. Foreword. In Rotimi T. Suberu, *Federalism and Ethnic Conflict in Nigeria*, x–xv. Washington, DC: United States Institute of Peace.

Diamond, Larry, Anthony Kirk-Greene, and Oyeleye Oyediran, eds. 1997. *Transition Without End: Nigerian Politics and Civil Society under Babangida.* Boulder, CO: Lynne Rienner.

Diamond, Larry. 1995. Nigeria: The Uncivic Society and the Descent into Praetorianism. In *Politics in Developing Countries: Comparing Experiences with Democracy,* 2d Ed., eds. Larry Diamond, Juan Linz, and Seymour Martin Lipset, 417–491. Boulder, CO: Lynne Rienner.

Diamond, Larry. 1988. Nigeria: Pluralism, Statism, and the Struggle for Democracy. In *Democracy in Developing Countries: Africa*, Vol. 2, eds. Larry Diamond, Juan Linz, and Seymour Martin Lipset, 33–91. Boulder, CO: Lynne Rienner.

Dickovick, J. Tyler, and Jonathan Eastwood. 2013. *Comparative Politics: Integrating Theories, Methods, and Cases.* New York: Oxford University Press.

Dickson, Monday. 2010. Citizen Diplomacy in President Umaru Musa Yar'Adua's Nigeria, 2007–2009: An Assessment. *International Journal of Politics & Good Governance*, Vol. 1, http://onlineresearchjournals.com/ijopagg/art/59.pdf.

Directorate of Technical Aid Corps. About DTAC. https://www.dtac.gov.ng/DTAC/dtac/aboutDTAC#first.

Directorate of Technical Aid Corps. Welcome to the Directorate of Technical Aid Corps. http://www.dtac.gov.ng/DTAC/dtac/aboutDTAC.

Dixon, Robyn. 2010. Umaru Yar'Adua Dies at 58; Nigerian President. *L. A. Times.* May 7. http://articles.latimes.com/2010/may/07/local/la-me-umaru-yaradua-20100507/

Donnelly, Jack. 2013. *International Human Rights,* 4th Ed. Boulder, CO: Westview Press.

Donnelly, Jack, and Debra Liang-Fenton. 2004. Introduction. In *Implementing U.S. Human Rights Policy*, ed. Debra Liang-Fenton, 3–25. Washington, DC: United States Institute of Peace Press.

Donnelly, Jack. 2000. An Overview. In *Human Rights and Comparative Foreign Policy,* ed. David P. Forsythe, 310–334. New York: United Nations University Press.

Donnelly, Jack. 1998. *International Human Rights,* 2d Ed. Boulder, CO: Westview Press.

Dougherty, James E., and Robert L. Pfaltzgraff. 1990. *Contending Theories of International Relations: A Comprehensive Survey,* 3rd Ed. New York: Harper & Row.

Dowd, Caitriona, and Clionadh Raleigh. Mapping Conflict across Liberia and Sierra Leone. *Accord*. 23:13–18. https://rc-services-assets.s3.eu-west-1.amazonaws.com/s3fs-public/CON1222_Accord_23_2.pdf.

Dreams of Our Founding Fathers. Independence Day Speech by Tafawa Balewa. https://www.facebook.com/notes/fela-durotoye/dreams-of-our-founding-fathers-independence-day-speech-by-tafawa-balewa-october-/10150259870812185/

Dzirutwe, Macdonald. 2022. Tinubu Says It is His Turn to Rule Nigeria in Election Appeal to Buhari. *Reuters*. June 3. https://www.reuters.com/world/africa/tinubu-says-it-is-his-turn-rule-nigeria-election-appeal-buhari-2022-06-03/#:~:text=%22It%20is%20my%20time%2C%20I,t%20have%20become%20the%20president.%22.

East African Community: One People, One Destiny. http://www.eac.int/.

East African Court of Justice. About Us. https://www.eacj.org/?page_id=19.

Eboh, Camillus. 2023. Nigerian Supreme Court Affirms President Tinubu's Election Win. *Reuters*. October 26. https://www.reuters.com/world/africa/nigerian-supreme-court-upholds-president-tinubus-election-win-2023-10-26/#:~:text=ABUJA%2C%20Oct%2026%20(Reuters),victory%20was%20marred%20by%20irregularities.

Ebobrah, Solomon T., and Victor Landon. 2020. Africa's Sub-Regional Courts as Back-Up Custodians of Constitutional Justice: Beyond the Compliance Question. In *The Performance of Africa's International Courts: Using Litigation for Political, Legal, and Social Change*, ed. James Thuo Gath, 178–210. New York and London: Oxford University Press.

Ebobrah, Solomon. 2018. The ECOWAS Community Court of Justice: A Dual Mandate with Skewed Authority. In *International Court Authority,* eds. Karen J. Alter, Laurence R. Helfer, and Mikael Rask Madsen. New York: Oxford University Press, 2018. Chap. 4.

Echono, Adoba. 2023. Nigeria's Foreign Policy Giant Strides under President Buhari Administration. *Voice of Nigeria*. Last updated May 23. https://von.gov.ng/nigerias-foreign-policy-giant-strides-under-president-buhari-administration/.

ECOMOG: Peacekeeping or Participant? 1998. *BBC News*. February 11. news.bbc.co.uk/2/hi/Africa/55719.stm.

Economic Community of Central African States. http://www.ceeac-eccas.org/index.php/fr/.

Economic Community of West African States (ECOWAS). http://www.ecowas.int/.

Economic Community of West African States (ECOWAS). *ECOWAS in Brief*. http://www.comm.ecowas.int/sec/index.php?id=about_a&.

Economic Commission of West African States (ECOWAS). 2022. *ECOWAS Vision 2050: ECOWAS of the Peoples: Peace and Prosperity for All*. Abuja. https://ecowas.int/wp-content/uploads/2022/09/Vision2050_EN_Web.pdf.

Economic Commission of West African States. 2001. *Protocol A/SP1/12/01 on Democracy and Good Governance Supplementary to the Protocol relating to the Mechanism for Conflict Prevention, Management, Resolution, Peacekeeping and Security*. Dakar, Senegal: ECOWAS. December. https://www.eisa.org/pdf/ecowas2001protocol.pdf.

Economic Community of West African States (ECOWAS). 1993. Revised Treaty of the Economic Community of West African States (ECOWAS). July 24. http://www.refworld.org/docid/492182d92.html.

Economic Community of West African States (ECOWAS). 1975. Treaty of the Economic Community of West African States (ECOWAS). May 28. https://www.refworld.org/legal/constinstr/ecowas/1975/en/63881.

ECOWAS at 40: The Driving Philosophy of Multinationalism. 2015. *Guardian* (Lagos). June. http://www.ngrguardiannews.com/2015/06/ecowas-40-the-driving-philosophy-of-multinationalism//

ECOWAS. Basic Information. www.ecowas.int/about-ecowas/basic-information/.

ECOWAS Court: President Asante, Falana Call for More Judges. 2021. *Vanguard* (Lagos). November 22. https://www.vanguardngr.com/2021/11/ecowas-court-president-asante-falana-call-for-more-judges/.

ECOWAS. History. www.ecowas.int/about-ecowas/history/.

ECOWAS. 2006. Supplementary Protocol A/SP.1/06/06 Amending the Revised Treaty. Abuja. June 14. https://journal.cfcomlaw.com/wp-content/uploads/2021/10/scan0004.pdf.

ECOWAS. 2006. Supplementary Protocol A/SP.3/06/06 Amending Protocol AP.2.8/94 Relating to the Community Parliament. June 14. https://journal.cfcomlaw.com/wp-content/uploads/2021/10/scan0005.pdf.

ECOWAS. 2006. Supplementary Protocol A/SP. 2/06/06, Amending Article 3 Paragraphs 1, 2 and 4, Article 4 Paragraphs 1,3 and 7 and Article 7 Paragraph 3 of the Protocol on the Community Court of Justice. June 14. https://journal.cfcomlaw.com/wp-content/uploads/2021/10/scan0003.pdf.

ECOWAS. 2005. Supplementary Protocol A/SP.1/01/05, Amending the Preamble and Articles 1,2,9, and 30 of Protocol A/P.1/7/91, Relating to the Community Court of Justice and Article 4, Paragraph 1, of the English Version of the Said Protocol. January 19. http://www.courtecowas.org/wp-content/uploads/2018/11/Supplementary_Protocol_ASP.10105_ENG.pdf.

ECOWAS. Vision 2020. www.ecowas.int/about_ecowas/vision-2020/.

ECOWAS Vision 2020: Toward a Democratic and Prosperous Community. 2010. June. www.ecowas.int/wp-content/uploads/2015/01/ECOWAS-VISION-2020.

ECOWAS Parliament. Parliament at a Glance. https://www.parl.ecowas.int/ecowas-parliament-at-a-glance/#:~:text=COMPOSITION%20OF%20PARLIAMENT,on%20the%20basis%20of%20population.

Editorial Board, *Guardian*. 2022. The Muslim-Muslim Ticket Challenge. *Guardian* (Lagos). June 17. https://guardian.ng/opinion/the-muslim-muslim-ticket-challenge/.

Edwards, Chris, Christopher Preble, and Tad DeHaven. Department of Defense Timeline. *Downsizing the Federal Government*. https://www.downsizinggovernment.org/defense/timeline#:~:text=1946%3A%20The%20War%20Department%20establishes,Department%20of%20Defense%20in%201949.

Effiong, Joseph. 2012. Reflections on Nigeria's Foreign Policy, *Journal of Social & Psychological Sciences*. Vol. 5. www.questia.com/read/1G1-314443206/reflections-on-nigeria-s-foreign-policy.

Egbejule, Oromo, Ope Adetayo, and Ruth Olurounbi. 2023. "Squandered Goodwill": How Buhari Failed Nigeria a Second Time. *Alja Zeera*. May 29. https://www.aljazeera.com/features/2023/5/29/squandered-goodwill-how-buhari-failed-nigeria-a-second-time.

Egbo, Steve. 2003. *Nigeria and the World: A Treatise on Foreign Policy*. Enugu, Nigeria: John Jacobs Classic Publishers.

Eichelberger, Erika. 2014. What I Learned Hanging Out with Nigerian Email Scammers. *Mother Jones*. March 20. http://www.motherjones.com/politics/2014/03/what-i-learned-from-nigerian-scammers.

Ejekwonyilo, Ameh. 2022. Why ECOWAS Court Declared Twitter Ban by Nigerian Government Illegal. *Premium Times* (Abuja). July 14. https://www.premiumtimesng.com/news/headlines/542696-why-ecowas-court-declared-twitter-ban-by-nigerian-govt-illegal.html.

Ekwe-Ekwe, Herbert. 2022. Africans Had No Business Fighting in Either the 1914–1918 War or the 1939–1945 War. *Journal of Asian and African Studies*. 57(1): 11–28. https://doi.org/10.1177/00219096211054907.

Ekwe-Ekwe, Herbert. 2006. *Biafra Revisited*. Dakar, Senegal: African Renaissance.

Embassy of the Federal Republic of Nigeria, Washington, DC. Nigeria: Past, Present[,] and Future. http://www.nigeriaembassyusa.org/index.php?page=nigeria-past-present-and-future.

Endicott, Timothy. 2020. How Judges Make Law. In *The Foundations and Future of Public Law: Essays in Honor of Paul Craig*, eds. Elizabeth Fisher, Jeff King, and Alison Young, 127–144. New York: Oxford University Press.

Energy Information Administration. 2023. Petroleum and Other Liquids. April 26. https://www.eia.gov/international/content/analysis/countries_long/Nigeria/#:~:text=Nigeria%20held%20an%20estimated%2037.1,at%20the%20beginning%20of%202023.&text=Nigeria%20produces%20mostly%20light%2C%20sweet,global%20markets%20(Table%202.

Eniola, Toluwani. 2014. Nigeria Now 39th Most Corrupt Nation, Says TI. *Punch* (Lagos). December 4. http://www.punchng.com/news/nigeria-now-39th-most-corrupt-nation-says-ti/.

Equiano, Olaudah. 1995 [1789]. *The Interesting Narrative of the Life of Olaudah Equiano: Written by Himself*. Edited with an intro. by Robert J. Allison. New York: Bedford/St. Martin's Press.

Ernest Shonekan, Nigeria's Most Fugacious Leader. *Nairaland Forum*. http://www.nairaland.com/1336063/ernest-shonekan-nigerias-most-fugacious.

Esedebe, P. Olisanwuche. 1994. *Pan-Africanism: The Idea and Movement 1776–1991*, 2d Ed. Washington, DC: Howard University Press.

Ethnicity and Race by Countries. *Infoplease*. http://www.infoplease.com/ipa/A0855617.html.

European Union. CJEU Court of Justice of the European Union (CJEU). https://european-union.europa.eu/institutions-law-budget/institutions-and-bodies/search-all-eu-institutions-and-bodies/court-justice-european-union-cjeu_en.

Evans, Gareth. 2011. Middle Power Diplomacy. Lecture delivered in Santiago, Chile. June 29. http://www.gevans.org/speeches/speech441.html.

Eze, Osita C. 1984. *Human Rights in Africa: Some Selected Problems*. Lagos: Nigerian Institute of International Affairs and Macmillan Nigeria.

Eze, Osita C., and Peter A. Egom, eds. 2009. *Foreign Policy and Nigeria's Economic Development*. Lagos: Nigerian Institute of International Affairs.

Ezeaku, Calista. 2013. Should the Six Geopolitical Zones Become Federating Units in Nigeria? *Tide* (Lagos). February 11. http://www.thetidenewsonline.com/2013/02/11/should-the-six-geopolitical-zones-become-federating-units-in-nigeria/.

Ezirim, Gerald E. 2011. Fifty Years of Nigeria's Foreign Policy: A Critical Review. *Sacha International Academic Journal*. http://www.academia.edu/345652/Fifty_Years_of_Nigeria_s_Foreign_Policy_A_Critical_Review.

Faal, Courtney. Balewa, Sir Abubakar Tafawa (1912–1966). *Black Past*. http://www.blackpast.org/gah/balewa-sir-abubakar-tafawa-1912-1966.

Fafowora, Dapo. 2015. Review of Nigeria's Foreign Policy. *Nation*. June 14. http://thenationonlineng.net/review-of-nigerias-foreign-policy/.

Fafowora, Dapo. 2013. Lord Lugard and the 1914 Amalgamation of Nigeria. *Nation*. February 28. http://thenationonlineng.net/lord-lugard-and-the-1914-amalgamation-of-nigeria-2/.

Fagoyinbo, Joseph Babatunde. 2013. *The Armed Forces: Instrument of Peace, Strength, Development[,] and Prosperity*. Bloomington, IN: AuthorHouse.

Falana, Femi. 2022. Making Chapter II of the Constitutional Justiciable. *This Day* (Lagos). March 2. https://www.thisdaylive.com/index.php/2022/03/02/making-chapter-ii-of-the-constitution-justiciable

Falola, Toyin. *Japa!* 2022. *Premium Times* (Abuja). September 2. https://www.premiumtimesng.com/opinion/551986-japa-by-toyin-falola.html.

Falola, Toyin. 1998. *Violence in Nigeria: The Crisis of Religious Politics and Secular Ideologies*. Rochester, NY: University of Rochester Press.

Falola, Toyin, and Adebayo Oyebade. 2010. *Hot Spot: Sub-Saharan Africa*. Santa Barbara, CA: ABC-CLIO.

Falola, Toyin, and Matthew M. Heaton. 2008. *A History of Nigeria*. New York: Cambridge University Press.

Falola, Toyin, A. Ajayi, A. Alao, and B. Babewale. 1994. *The Military Factor in Nigeria, 1966–1985*. Lewiston, N.Y.: Edwin Mellen

Faraclas, Nick. 2013. *Nigerian Pidgin*. New York: Routledge.

Farotimi, Dele. 2024. Anyone Who Can Afford to Live Abroad and Has Refused to Go is a Mad Man. Teju BabyFace Deep Dive Podcast. March 26. https://www.youtube.com/watch?v=ITNqS_VnWTE.

Fasan, Olu. 2022. Buhari Wants Tinubu as Next President; He's Nigeria's Worst Enemy. *Business Day* (Lagos). November 28. https://businessday.ng/columnist/article/buhari-wants-tinubu-as-next-president-hes-nigerias-worst-enemy/.

Fatton, Jr., Robert. 1990. Liberal Democracy in Africa. *Political Science Quarterly*. 105(3): 455–473. Autumn.

Faul, Michell. 2014. Nigeria: Economy $510B, Biggest in Africa. *USA Today*. April 6. http://www.usatoday.com/story/money/business/2014/04/06/nigeria-economy-510-billion-biggest-in-africa/7389395/.

Fawole, Alade W. 2003. *Nigeria's External Relations and Foreign Policy under Military Rule, 1966–1999*. Ile-Ife, Nigeria: Obafemi Awolowo University Press.

Fearson, James D. 2003. Ethnic and Cultural Diversity by Country. *Journal of Economic Growth*. 8:195–212. June. https://web.stanford.edu/group/fearon-research/cgi-bin/wordpress/wp-content/uploads/2013/10/Ethnic-and-Cultural-Diversity-by-Country.pdf.

Federal Capital Abuja. 2003. *Online Nigeria*. December 2. http://www.onlinenigeria.com/links/abujaadv.asp?blurb=387.

Federal Republic of Nigeria. 1977. *Report of the Constitution Drafting Committee Containing the Draft Constitution*, Vol. 1. Enugu, Nigeria: Ministry of Education & Information, Printing Division.

Ferree, William J. 1997 [1948]. *Introduction to Social Justice*. Arlington, VA: Center for Economic and Social Justice. https://www.cesj.org/wp-content/uploads/2012/08/introtosocialjustice.pdf.

Field, Martha A. 1992. The Differing Federalisms of Canada and the United States. *Law & Contemporary Problems.* 55: 107–120.

Fisayo-Bambi, Jerry. 2024. Nigeria's Yakubu Gowon, the Last Living Founding Father of ECOWAS Calls for its Rescue. *Africa News.* February 22. https://www.africanews.com/2024/02/22/nigerias-yakubu-gowon-last-living-founding-father-of-ecowas-calls-for-its-rescue//.

Fisher, Max. 2013. A Revealing Map of the World's Most and Least Ethnically Diverse Countries. *Washington Post.* May 16. https://www.washingtonpost.com/news/worldviews/wp/2013/05/16/a-revealing-map-of-the-worlds-most-and-least-ethnically-diverse-countries/.

Fleischman, Janet (Human Rights Watch). 2003. ECOWAS: Troops to Liberia Must Respect Human Rights. Letter to President John Kufuor, then Chairman of ECOWAS. July 18. https://www.hrw.org/news/2003/07/18/ecowas-troops-liberia-must-respect-human-rights.

Fombad, Charles Manga. 2008. Transitional Justice in Africa: The Experience with Truth Commissions. Hauser Global Law School Program. May/June. http://www.nyulawglobal.org/globalex/Africa_Truth_Commissions.html.

Ford, John. 2014. The Origins of Boko Haram. *National Interest.* June 6. http://nationalinterest.org/print/feature/the-origins-boko-haram-10609.

Foreign Policy Association. How U.S. Foreign Policy is Made. http://www.fpa.org/features/index.cfm?act=feature&announcement_id=45&show_sidebar=0.

Foreign Relations. 1991. In *Nigeria: A Country Study*, ed. Helen Chapin Metz. Washington DC: GPO for the Library of Congress. https://countrystudies.us/nigeria/80.htm.

Foreign Relations. 1992. In *Nigeria: A Country Study,* 5th Ed. Helen Chapin Metz, ed. Washington, DC: Library of Congress. https://www.marines.mil/Portals/1/Publications/Nigeria%20Study_1.pdf.

Forsythe, David P. 2012. *Human Rights in International Relations,* 3rd Ed. New York: Cambridge University Press.

Forsythe, David P., ed. 2000. *Human Rights and Comparative Foreign Policy.* New York: United Nations University Press.

Forsythe, David P. 2000. Introduction. In *Human Rights and Comparative Foreign Policy,* ed. David P. Forsythe, 1–18. New York: United Nations University Press.

Forsythe, David P. 1998. Human Rights Fifty Years after the Universal Declaration. *PS: Political Science & Politics.* 31: 507–511. September.

French, Howard W. 1995. Nigeria Executes Critic of Regime; Nations Protest. *New York Times.* November 11. http://www.nytimes.com/1995/11/11/world/nigeria-executes-critic-of-regime-nations-protest.html?pagewanted=all.

Frynas, Jedrzej G. 2000. *Oil in Nigeria: Conflict and Litigation Between Oil Companies and Village Communities.* Hamburg & London: Lit Verlag.

Fujimura, Makoto. 2021. *Art + Faith: A Theology of Making*. New Haven, CT: Yale University Press.

Gaadi, Donald Terfa. 2013. Ethnic Groups and Geo-Political Regions in Nigeria. *Eagle Reporters* (Abuja). December 28. http://eaglereporters.com/2013/12/28/ethnic-group-and-geo-political-region-in-nigeria-by-donald-terfa/.

Gaffey, Conor. 2016. Biafra Protests Prompt Separation Anxiety in Nigeria. *Newsweek*. March. http://www.newsweek.com/2016/03/11/nigeria-biafra-nnamdi-kanu-protests-432002.html.

Gambari, Ibrahim. 2008. From Balewa to Obasanjo: The Theory and Practice of Nigeria's Foreign Policy. In *Gulliver's Troubles: Nigeria's Foreign Policy after the Cold War*, eds. Adekeye Adebajo and Abdul Raufu Mustapha, 58–80. Scottsville, South Africa: University of Kwazulu-Natal Press.

Gambari, Ibrahim A. 1991. *Political and Comparative Dimensions of Regional Integration: The Case of ECOWAS*. Atlantic Highlands, NJ: Humanities Press.

Gambari, Ibrahim A. 1989. *Theory and Reality in Foreign Policy Making: Nigeria after the Second Republic*. Atlantic Highlands, NJ: Humanities Press, Inc.

Gambari, Ibrahim A. 1980. *Party Politics and Foreign Policy: Nigeria under the First Republic*. Zaria, Nigeria: Ahmadu Bello University Press.

Ganiyu, Adam. 2023. Ministry of Foreign Affairs Job Recruitment (2024–2026)—105 Positions. *Intel Region*. December 29. https://www.intelregion.com/jobs/ministry-of-foreign-affairs-job-recruitment/.

Garba, Joe. 1991. *Diplomatic Soldiering: The Conduct of Nigerian Foreign Policy, 1975–1979*. Ibadan: Spectrum Books.

Gauchet, Marcel. 1997. Right and Left. In *Realms of Memory: Conflicts and Divisions*, eds. Pierre Nora and Lawrence D. Kritzman, 242–245. New York: Columbia University.

Gavin, Michelle. 2023. Nigeria Security Tracker. Council on Foreign Relations. Last updated July 1. https://www.cfr.org/nigeria/nigeria-security-tracker/p29483.

Gbulie, Ben. 1981. *Nigeria's Five Majors: Coup d'état of 15th January 1966, First Inside Account*. Lagos: Africana Educational Publishers.

Geertz, Clifford, ed. 1963. *Old Societies and New States: The Quest for Modernity in Asia and Africa*. New York: Free Press of Glencoe.

George, Alexander L., and Andrew Bennett. 2005. *Case Studies and Theory Development in the Social Sciences*. Cambridge, MA: MIT Press.

Germany's Dual Citizenship Law Goes into Effect at End of June 2024. 2024. *Arnall Golden Gregory*. March 27. https://www.agg.com/news-insights/publications/update-germanys-dual-citizenship-law-goes-into-effect-at-end-of-june-2024/.

Germany: New Citizenship Law to Enter into Force in June 2024. 2024. *Fragomen*. March 26. https://www.fragomen.com/insights/germany-new-citizenship-law-to-enter-into-force-in-june-2024.html.

Gesinde, Seyi. 2015. Nigeria's Foreign Policy in the Eye of Global Challenge. *Tribune Online* (Lagos). May 28. http://tribuneonlineng.com/content/nigeria%E2%80%99s-foreign-policy-eye-global-challenge.

Gettleman, Jeffrey. 2011. After Years of Struggle, South Sudan Becomes a New Nation. *New York Times*. July 9. www.nytimes.com/2011/07/10/world/africa/10sudan.html?pagewanted=1&r=2&hp&adxnnlx=1310234502-5nvX4GUBg0fK28Wp4F.

Gilles, David. 1996. *Between Principles and Practice: Human Rights in North-South Relations*. Montreal, Canada: McGill-Queen's University Press.

Glahn, Gerhard von, and James Larry Taulbee. 2012. *Law among Nations: An Introduction to Public International Law*, 10th Ed. New York: Routledge.

Glendon, Mary Ann. 2001. *A World Made New: Eleanor Roosevelt and the Universal Declaration of Human Rights*. New York: Random House.

Gordon, April A. 2003. *Nigeria's Diverse Peoples: A Reference Sourcebook*. Santa Barbara, CA: ABC-CLIO.

Greer, Scott. 1969. *The Logic of Social Inquiry*. Chicago: Aldine Publishing Company.

Grigsby, Ellen. 2012. *Analyzing Politics: An Introduction to Political Science*, 5th Ed. Belmont, CA: Wadsworth Cengage Learning.

Gutmann, Amy. 2001. Introduction. In *Human Rights as Politics and Idolatry*, ed. Michael Ignatieff, vii–xxviii. Princeton, NJ: Princeton University Press.

Gutting, Gary. 2012. How Reliable Are the Social Sciences? *New York Times*. May 17. https://archive.nytimes.com/opinionator.blogs.nytimes.com/2012/05/17/how-reliable-are-the-social-sciences/.

Haass, Richard. 2023. The World's Stake in American Democracy. *Project Syndicate*. January 24. https://www.project-syndicate.org/commentary/world-still-depends-on-us-leadership-by-richard-haass-2023-01.

Haass, Richard. 2014. *Foreign Policy Begins at Home: The Case for Putting America's House in Order*. New York: Basic Books.

Haile Selassie 1892–1975, Former Ethiopian Emperor. *Encyclopedia*. http://www.encyclopedia.com/topic/Haile_Selassie.aspx.

Halper, Evans, and Toluse Olurunnipa. 2023. U.S. Oil Production Hit[s] a Record under Biden: He Seldom Mentions It. *Washington Post*. December 31. https://www.washingtonpost.com/politics/2023/12/31/us-oil-production-has-hit-record-under-biden-he-hardly-mentions-it/.

Hamilton, Alexander. 1788. Federalist No. 70. Bill of Rights Institute. https://billofrightsinstitute.org/primary-sources/federalist-no-70.

Hamilton, Alexander. 1788. Federalist No. 78. National Constitution Center. https://constitutioncenter.org/the-constitution/historic-document-library/detail/alexander-hamilton-federalist-no-78-1788.

Hamilton, Lee H. 1998. Defining National Interest. *Christian Science Monitor.* March 30. http://www.csmonitor.com/1998/0330/033098.opin.opin.2.html.

Hamman, Suleiman, Ibrahim Khalid Mustafa, and Kayode Omojuwa, 2014. The Role of Nigeria in Peacekeeping Operations from 1960 to 2013. *International Affairs & Global Strategy.* 21: 42–45.

Hanhimäki, Jussi, and Odd Arne Westad, eds. 2004. *The Cold War: A History in Documents and Eyewitness Accounts*. New York: Oxford University Press.

Hannum, Hurst, S. James Anaya, and Dinah L. Shelton. 2011. *International Human Rights: Problems of Law, Policy, and Practice,* 5th Ed. Alphen aan den Rijn, Netherlands: Wolters Kluwer.

Harbeson, John W., and Donald Rothchild. 2000. The African State and State System in Flux. In *Africa in World Politics: The African State System in Flux,* 3rd Ed., eds. John W. Harbeson and Donald Rothchild, 3–21. Boulder, CO: Westview Press.

Hastedt, Glenn P. 2006. *American Foreign Policy: Past, Present, Future,* 6th Ed. Upper Saddle River, NJ: Pearson Prentice Hall.

Hatto, Ronald. 2013. From Peacekeeping to Peacebuilding: The Evolution of the Role of the United Nations in Peace Operations. *International Review of the Red Cross.* 95: 495–515.

Hayles, Tanisha Ellis. 2014. Costa Rica—A Country without an Army and Proud of It. *Jamaica Observer* (Kingston). March 2. http://www.jamaicaobserver.com/columns/Costa-Rica---a-country-without-an-army-and-proud-of-it_16147133.

Haynes, Jeff. 2014. Religion. In *Politics in the Developing World,* 4th Ed., eds. Peter Burnell, Vicky Randall, and Lise Rakner, 119–131. New York: Oxford University Press.

Healey, Joseph G. African Proverb of the Month November 2001. *Afriprov.* http://www.afriprov.org/african-proverb-of-the-month/27-2001proverbs/172-nov2001.html.

Heath, Elizabeth. Berlin Conference of 1884–1885. 2010. In *Encyclopedia of Africa*, eds. Henry Louis Gates, Jr., and Kwame Anthony Appiah. New York: Oxford University Press. https://www.oxfordreference.com/display/10.1093/acref/9780195337709.001.0001/acref-9780195337709-e-0467.

Hedrick, Christopher. 2013. The New Peace Corps. Op-Ed. *Yale Journal of International Affairs*. February 26. https://www.yalejournal.org/publications/the-new-peace-corps.

Henckaerts, Jean-Marie. 1995. *Mass Expulsion in Modern International Law and Practice*. Leiden, Netherland: Martinus Nijhoff Publishers.

Henkin, Louis. 2000. Human Rights: Ideology and Aspiration, Reality and Prospect. In *Realizing Human Rights: Moving from Inspiration to Impact*, eds. Samantha Power and Graham Alison, 3–38. New York: St. Martin's Press.

Henkin, Louis. 1998. The Universal Declaration and the U.S. Constitution. *PS: Political Science & Politics.* 31(3): 512–515. September.

Holy Bible. New International Version.

Holy Bible. English Standard Version.

How Nigeria Won Its First Democratic Power Transfer. 2015. *Economist* (London). April 6. http://www.economist.com/blogs/economist-explains/2015/04/economist-explains-2.

Howard, Rhoda E. 1986. *Human Rights in Commonwealth Africa.* Lanham, MD: Rowman & Littlefield.

Human Rights Watch. 1993. *Waging War to Keep the Peace: The ECOMOG Intervention and Human Rights.* June. https://www.hrw.org/legacy/reports/1993/liberia/.

Human Rights Watch. 2003. Bilateral Immunity Agreements. June 25. http://www.hrw.org/legacy/campaigns/icc/docs/bilateralagreements.pdf.

Human Rights Watch. 2005. *"Rest in Pieces": Police Torture and Deaths in Custody in Nigeria.* July. https://www.hrw.org/reports/2005/nigeria0705/.

Human Rights Watch. 2013. China: Ratify Key International Human Rights Treaty. October 3. https://www.hrw.org/news/2013/10/08/china-ratify-key-international-human-rights-treaty.

Hurst, Ryan. Congo Civil War (1960–1964). *Black Past.* http://www.blackpast.org/gah/congo-civil-war-1960-1964.

Icelandic Human Rights Center. The Role of Non-State Entities. http://www.humanrights.is/en/human-rights-education-project/human-rights-concepts-ideas-and-fora/human-rights-actors/the-role-of-non-state-entities.

IGAD. http://www.igad.org/.

Igboin, Benson Ohihon. 2014. "The President of Nigeria Has No Final Say": Sharia Law Controversies and Implications for Nigeria. *Central & East European Online Library.* 265–290. http://www.ceeol.com/search/article-detail?id=180187.

Ignatieff, Michael. 2002. Is the Human Rights Era Ending? In *Perspectives on Terrorism: How 9/11 Changed U.S. Politics,* ed. Allan J. Cigler, 103–106. Boston, MA: Houghton Mifflin Co.

Ihonvbere, Julius O. 1994. The "Irrelevant" State, Ethnicity, and the Quest for Nationhood in Africa. *Ethnic and Racial Studies.* 17(1): 42–60. https://doi.org/10.1080/01419870.1994.9993812.

Ikeke, Nkem. 2016. [Seventeen] Hilarious Nigerian Pidgin Proverbs and Their Meanings. *Legit.* September 29. https://www.legit.ng/987866-17-nigerian-pidgin-proverbs-will-leave-rolling-floor-laughter-photos.html.

Imhonopi, David, and Moses Urim Ugochukwu. 2013. Leadership Crisis and Corruption in the Nigerian Public Sector: An Albatross of National Development. *African Symposium: An Online Journal of the African Education*

Research Network. 13(1): 78–87. June. http://www.ncsu.edu/aern/TAS13.1/TAS13.1_Imhonopi.pdf.

Immigration and Refuge Board of Canada. 1994. Nigeria: Information on the Civil Liberty Organization (CLO), Its Leadership, Its Activities, the Arrest of Its Members and Its Involvement in Demonstrations that Followed the Annulment of the 12 June 1993 Elections. March 1. http://www.refworld.org/docid/3ae6ab3a24.html.

Inamete, Ufot Bassey. 2001. *Foreign Policy Decision-Making in Nigeria*. Selinsgrove, PA: Susquehanna University Press.

Institute for Security Studies. Profile: Economic Community of West African States (ECOWAS). https://www.issafrica.org/AF/RegOrg/unity_to_union/ecowasprof.htm.

Intelligence Reform and Terrorism Prevention Act, Pub. L. 108–458, 118 Stat. 3638. December 17, 2004.

International Committee of the Red Cross. What is the Difference between Humanitarian Law and Human Rights Law? https://www.icrc.org/eng/resources/documents/misc/5kzmuy.htm.

International Court of Justice. 2002. Land and Maritime Boundary between Cameroon and Nigeria (Cameroon v. Nigeria: Equatorial Guinea Intervening). October 10. http://www.icj-cij.org/docket/index.php?p1=3&p2=3&k=74&case=94&code=cn&p3=4.

International Court of Justice. 1945. Statute of the International Court of Justice. https://www.icj-cij.org/statute.

International Crisis Group. 2006. *Nigeria: Want in the Midst of Plenty*. Africa Report No. 113. July 19. http://www.crisisgroup.org/~/media/Files/africa/west-africa/nigeria/Nigeria%20Want%20in%20the%20Midst%20of%20Plenty.

Isichei, Elizabeth. 1995. *A History of Christianity in Africa: From Antiquity to the Present*. Grand Rapids, MI: Wm. B. Eerdmans Publishing, 1995.

Isichei, Elizabeth. 1976. *A History of the Igbo People*. New York: Palgrave Macmillan.

Isichei, Elizabeth. 1973. *The Ibo People and the Europeans: The Genesis of a Relationship—To 1906*. New York: St. Martin's Press.

Isiugo-Abanihe, Uche Charlies. 2020. Why Nigeria Can't Fix Its Development Agenda: And Where the Solutions Lie. *Conversation*. October 25. https://theconversation.com/why-nigeria-cant-fix-its-development-agenda-and-where-the-solutions-lie-123638.

Iweala, Uzodinma. 2022. Nigeria's Second Independence: Why the Giant of Africa Needs to Start Over. *Foreign Affairs*. July/August. https://www.foreignaffairs.com/articles/africa/2022-06-21/nigeria-second-independence.

Jackson, Robert H. 1990. *Quasi-States: Sovereignty, International Relations, and the Third World*. Cambridge, UK: Cambridge University Press.

Jackson, Robert H., and Carl G. Rosberg. 1982. *Personal Rule in Black Africa: Prince, Autocrat, Prophet, Tyrant*. Berkeley, CA: University of California Press.

Jackson, Robert, and Carl Rosberg. 1982. Why Africa's Weak States Persist: The Empirical and the Juridical in Statehood. *World Politics.* 35: 1–24.

Jang, Se Young. 2012. The Causes of the Sierra Leone Civil War. *E-International Relations Students.* October 25. http://www.e-ir.info/2012/10/25/the-causes-of-the-sierra-leone-civil-war-underlying-grievances-and-the-role-of-the-revolutionary-united-front.

Jebuni, Charles D., Olawale Ogunkola, and Charles C. Soludo. 1999. A Case-Study of the Economic Community of West African States (ECOWAS). In *Regional Integration and Trade Liberalization in Sub-Saharan Africa: Regional Case Studies,* Vol. 3, eds. Ademola Oyejide, Ibrahim Elbadawi, and Stephen Yeo, 24–65. London: Macmillan.

Jervis, Robert. 1999. Realism in the Study of World Politics. In *Explorations and Contestation in the Study of World Politics*, eds. Peter J. Katzenstein, Robert O. Keohane, and Stephen D. Krasner, 331–352. Cambridge, MA: MIT Press, 1999.

Jonathan, Goodluck. 2011. Address at the Retreat on the Review of Nigeria's Foreign Policy. August 1. http://www.nigeriavillagesquare.com/index.php?option=com_content&allposts=1&catid=590&id=19313&view=article&Itemid=1719.

Joseph, Richard. 1999. Nigeria and the Challenge of Leadership. *Tell* (Lagos). July 5.

Joseph, Richard A. 1987. *Democracy and Prebendal Politics in Nigeria: The Rise and Fall of the Second Republic.* New York. Cambridge University Press.

Judge, Edward H., and John W. Langdon. 2010. *The Cold War: A Global History with Documents,* 2d Ed. Upper Saddle River, NJ: Prentice Hall.

Judicial Service of Ghana. The Republic of Ghana Judiciary. https://www.judicial.gov.gh/index.php/component/content/article/101-history/235-summary.

Kalu, Uduma. 2013. Nigeria is 33rd Most Corrupt Country—Transparency International. *Vanguard* (Lagos). December 4. http://www.vanguardngr.com/2013/12/nigeria-33rd-corrupt-country-transparency-intl/.

Kaduna, Nigeria. *Encyclopedia Britannica.* 2023. December 10. https://www.britannica.com/place/Kaduna-Nigeria.

Karl, Terry Lynn. 1997. *The Paradox of Plenty: Oil Books and Petro-States.* Berkeley, CA: University of California Press.

Kazah-Toure, Toure. 2007. Nigeria: Challenge to the State and Ways of Breaking through the Quagmire. In *Beyond State Failure and Collapse: Making the State Relevant in Africa,* ed. George Klay Kieh Jr., 170–194. Lanham, MD: Lexington Books.

Kennedy, Anthony. 2006. Justice Kennedy Address. CSPAN. August 5. Keynote Address by Justice Anthony M. Kennedy at the Meeting of the American Bar Association, Honolulu, HI. www.c-span.org/video/?193757-1/justice-kennedy-address.

Kennedy, John F. 1961. Inaugural Address of President John F. Kennedy. John F. Kennedy Presidential Library and Museum. January 20. http://www.jfklibrary.org/Research/Research-Aids/Ready-Reference/JFK-Quotations/Inaugural-Address.aspx.

Keohane, Joseph S., and Robert O. Nye. 1977. *Power and Interdependence: World Politics in Transition*. Boston, MA: Little, Brown, and Company.

Kerstein, Mark. 2011. The U.S. and the ICC: Towards a Closer Relationship? *Justice in Conflict*. April 10. http://justiceinconflict.org/2011/04/10/the-us-and-the-icc-towards-a-closer-relationship/.

Kevin-Alerechi, Elfredah. 2021. Nigerians Experiencing Worst Security Crisis since Civil War: Buhari. *People's Gazette* (Abuja). October 1. https://gazettengr.com/nigerians-experiencing-worst-security-crisis-since-civil-war-buhari/.

Kew, Darren, and Peter Lewis. 2013. Nigeria. In *Introduction to Politics of the Developing World,* 6th Ed., ed. Mark Kesselman, 188–241. Boston, MA: Cengage Learning.

King, Mae C. 1996. *Basic Currents of Nigerian Foreign Policy*. Washington, DC: Howard University Press.

King Jr., Martin Luther. 1963. I Have a Dream. August 28. *Reprinted* in *NPR*. Updated January 16, 2023. https://www.npr.org/2010/01/18/122701268/i-have-a-dream-speech-in-its-entirety.

Kirk-Greene, A.H.M. 1971. *Crisis and Conflict in Nigeria: A Documentary Sourcebook,* Vol. 1. London: Oxford University Press.

Kirk-Greene, A.H.M. 1971. *Crisis and Conflict in Nigeria: A Documentary Sourcebook 1966–1969,* Vol. 2. London: Oxford University Press.

Kirk-Greene, Anthony. 1997. The Remedial Imperatives of the Nigerian Constitution, 1922–1992. In *Transition Without End: Nigerian Politics and Civil Society under Babangida*, Larry Diamond, Anthony Kirk-Greene, and Oyeleye Oyediran, 31–53. Boulder, CO: Lynne Rienner Publishers.

Klobucista Claire, and Mariel Ferragamo. 2023. Backgrounder: The Role of Peacekeeping in Africa. Council on Foreign Relations. Last updated December 12. https://www.cfr.org/backgrounder/role-peacekeeping-africa.

Kumolu, Charles. 2013. Constitution[al] Amendment: National Assembly Moves to Restructure Nigeria. *Vanguard* (Lagos). January 13. http://www.vanguardngr.com/2013/01/constitution-amendment-nassembly-moves-to-restructure-nigeria/.

Krasner, Stephen D. 1982. Structural Causes and Regime Consequences: Regimes as Intervening Variable. *International Organization*. 36: 185–205. Spring.

Kuhn, Thomas. 1996. *The Structure of Scientific Revolutions,* 3rd Ed. Chicago: University of Chicago.

Kühne, Winrich. 2010. The Role of Elections in Emerging Democracies and Post-Conflict Countries. *Friedrich Ebert Stiftung*. August. https://library.fes.de/pdf-files/iez/07416.pdf.

Kuranga, David Oladipupo. 2012. *The Power of Interdependence: Lessons from Africa*. New York: Palgrave Macmillan.

Kwame Nkrumah's Vision. 2000. *BBC World Service*. September 14. www.bbc.co.uk/worldservice/people/highlights/000914_nkrumah.shtml.

Kwarteng, Kwasi. 2012. Nigeria's Current Troubles and Its British Colonial Roots. *Globalist.* March 9. http://www.theglobalist.com/nigerias-current-troubles-and-its-british-colonial-roots/.

Lacey, Marc. 2000. Clinton in Nigeria to Show Support for Civilian Rule. *New York Times*. August 27.

Lauren, Paul Gordon. 2011. *The Evolution of International Human Rights: Visions Seen*. Philadelphia, PA: University of Pennsylvania Press.

Law, Robin. 1991. *The Slave Coast of West Africa 1550–1750: The Impact of the Atlantic Slave Trade on an African Society*. Oxford, UK: Clarendon Press.

Lawal, Salahu Mohammed. 2015. An Appraisal of Corruption in the Nigerian Electoral System. *European Scientific Journal*. 11: 256–273.

Learn Nigerian Law. History of the Nigerian Legal System. https://www.learnnigerianlaw.com/learn/legal-system/history.

Leaving No One Behind: A Social Protection. 2016. New York: UN Development Program. October 6.

Legal Information Institute (LII). Cornell University. Color of Law. https://www.law.cornell.edu/wex/color_of_law.

Legal Information Institute (LII). Cornell Law School. *Hadijatou Mani Koraou v. Republic of Niger*. https://www.law.cornell.edu/women-and-justice/resource/hadijatou_mani_koraou_v_republic_of_niger.

Legal Information Institute (LII). Cornell Law School. Judiciary Act of 1789. https://www.law.cornell.edu/wex/judiciary_act_of_1789#:~:text=The%20Judiciary%20Act%20of%201789,Congress%20sees%20fit%20to%20establish.

Legge, James. 1971. *Confucian Analects, the Great Learning, and the Doctrine of the Mean*. Mineola, NY: Dover Publications.

Leonhardt, David. 2023. *Ours Was the Shining Future: The Story of the American Dream*. New York: Random House.

Le Pere, Garth. 2008. Review of *Gulliver's Troubles: Nigeria's Foreign Policy after the Cold War*, eds. Adekeye Adebajo and Abdul Raufu Mustapha (Scottsville, South Africa: University of KwaZulu-Natal Press, 2008), *African Journal of Conflict Resolution*, 8 (2008). http://www.accord.org.za/publications/book-reviews/638-gullivers-troubles-nigerias-foreign-policy-after-the-cold-war.

LeVan, A. Carl, and Oladimeji Aborisade. 2014. Politics in Nigeria. In *Comparative Politics Today: A World View*, 11th Ed., eds. G. Bingham Powell, Jr., Russell J. Dalton, and Kaare Strom, 631–674. New York: Pearson.

Liang-Fenton, Debra. 2004. Conclusion: What Works? In *Implementing U.S. Human Rights Policy*, ed. Debra Liang-Fenton, 435–461. Washington, DC: United States Institute of Peace Press.

Liberia: Conflict. *Peace Direct*. http://www.insightonconflict.org/conflicts/liberia/conflict-profile/.

Lillich, Richard B., James Anaya, and Dinah L. Shelton. 2006. *International Human Rights: Problems of Law, Policy, and Practice*, 4th Ed. New York: Aspen Publishers.

Lind, Dara, German Lopez, Lauren Williams, and Amanda Taub. 2014. An Uneasy Peace in Ferguson. *Vox*. August 21. www.vox.com/2014/8/11/5988925/mike-brown-killing-shooting-case-ferguson-police-riots-st-louis.

Linz, Juan J., and Alfred Stepan. 1997. Toward Consolidated Democracies. In *Consolidating the Third Wave Democracies: Themes and Perspectives*, eds. Larry Diamond, Marc F. Plattner, Yun-han Chu, and Hung-mao Tien, 14–33. Baltimore, MD: Johns Hopkins University Press.

Linz, Juan J., and Alfred Stepan. 1996. *Problems of Democratic Transition and Consolidation: Southern Europe, South America, and Post-Communist Europe*. Baltimore, MD: Johns Hopkins University Press.

Lippman, Walter. 1943. *U.S. Foreign Policy: Shield of the Republic*. Boston, MA: Little Brown.

Literacy Rate by Country (2023). *Wisevoter*. https://wisevoter.com/country-rankings/literacy-rate-by-country/.

Liu, Jing Jing. 2023. *Japa*, or to Flee or to Run: Nigerian Youth and the Urgency of Departure. MoLab Inventory of Mobilities and Socioeconomic Changes. Max Planck Institute for Social Anthropology, Halle/Saale. https://doi.org/10.48509/MoLab.6432.

Liu, Jing Jing. 2022. Africans in China Are on the Move. *Africa Is a Country*. June 7. https://africasacountry.com/2022/06/africans-in-china-are-on-the-move.

Lo, Abdou Khadre. The Senegal Case Study. UNAM. https://archivos.juridicas.unam.mx/www/bjv/libros/6/2748/15.pdf.

Logan, Olivia. 2024. Dual Citizenship Law Effective from June after German President Signs Bill. *I Am Expat*. March 27. https://www.iamexpat.de/expat-info/german-expat-news/dual-citizenship-law-effective-june-after-german-president-signs-bill.

Lovelace Jr., Douglas C. 2013. Foreword. In Clarence J. Bouchat, *The Causes of Instability in Nigeria and Implications for the United States*, iii–iv. Carlisle, PA: Strategic Studies Institute & U.S. Army War College Press. August.

Lovejoy, Paul E. 1992. Historical Setting. In *Nigeria: A Country Study,* 5th Ed., ed. Helen Chapin Metz, 1–84. Washington, DC: Library of Congress. https://www.marines.mil/Portals/1/Publications/Nigeria%20Study_1.pdf.

Luckham, Robin. 1971. *The Nigerian Military: A Sociological Analysis of Authority and Revolt, 1960–1967*. New York: Cambridge University Press.

Lugard, Frederick J.D. 1922. *The Dual Mandate in British Tropical Africa.* London: Frank Cass & Co.

Lugard, F.D., and A.H.M. Kirk-Greene. 1968. *Lugard and the Amalgamation of Nigeria: A Documentary Record*. London: Cass.

Lui, Andrew. 2012. *Why Canada Cares: Human Rights and Foreign Policy in Theory and Practice*. Montreal, Canada: McGill-Queen's University Press.

Lund, Susan, and Arend van Wamelen. 2015. Lions on the Move: 10 Things You Don't Know about Africa's Booming Economy. In *Current Debates in Comparative Politics,* eds. J. Tyler Dickovick and Jonathan Eastwood, 42–45. New York: Oxford University Press.

Lyakurwa, William, Andrew McKay, and Nehemiah Ng'eno. 1997. Regional Integration in Sub-Saharan Africa: A Review of Experiences and Issues. In *Regional Integration and Trade Liberalization in Sub-Saharan Africa: Framework, Issues, and Methodological Perspectives, Vol. 1*, eds. Ademola Oyejide, Paul Collier, and Ibrahim Elbadawi, 159–209. London: Macmillan Press Ltd.

Lyons, Kim. 2021. Twitter Blocked in Nigeria after Deleting a Tweet by its President. Updated June 5. https://www.theverge.com/2021/6/5/22520166/twitter-suspended-nigeria-delete-tweet-president-violate-rules.

Maclean, Ruth. 2022. Nigeria Lifts [Seven]-Month Ban on Twitter. *New York Times*. January 13. https://www.nytimes.com/2022/01/13/world/africa/nigeria-lifts-twitter-ban.html.

Maclean, Ruth. 2021. Nigeria Bans Twitter After President's Tweet Is Deleted. *New York Times*. June 5. https://www.nytimes.com/2021/06/05/world/africa/nigeria-twitter-president.html.

Macmillan, Harold. 1960. Speech at the South African Parliament, Cape Town. http://www.bbc.co.uk/archive/apartheid/7203.shtml (video).

MacMillan, Margaret. 2003. *Paris 1919: Six Months that Changed the World*. New York: Random House.

McMahon, Robert. 2003. *The Cold War: A Very Short Introduction*. New York: Oxford University Press.

Madeleine Albright Extended Interview. 2006. *PBS*. May 19. http://www.pbs.org/wnet/religionandethics/2006/05/19/may-19-2006-madeleine-albright-extended-intreview/2838/.

Madison, James. 1787. The Federalist No. 10. Bill of Rights Institute. November 22. https://billofrightsinstitute.org/primary-sources/federalist-no-10.

Madowo, Larry, Bethlehem Feleke, and Fridah Okutoyi. 2023. Many Talented Young Nigerians are Leaving: Halting the Exodus Will Be a Task for the Next

President. *CNN*. February 24. https://www.cnn.com/2023/02/24/africa/nigeria-japa-exodus-trend-election-intl-cmd/index.html.

Mahmood, Abba. 2013. Nigeria's Africa Policy in Perspective. *Leadership*. December 26. leadership.ng/columns/Thursday-column/343/nigerias-africa-policy-in-perspective.

Maja-Pearce, Adewale. 2014. Nigeria Does Generate More Electricity Now than It Did 15 Years Ago. *Africa Check*. November. https://africacheck.org/reports/nigeria-does-generate-more-electricity-now-than-it-did-15-years-ago/.

Maja-Pearce, Adewale. 2014. Changing Nigeria's Cruel Police Culture. *New York Times*. October 7. http://www.nytimes.com/2014/10/08/opinion/adewale-maja-pearce-changing-nigerias-cruel-police-culture.html.

Maluwa, Tiyanjana. 2000. Human Rights and Foreign Policy in Post-Apartheid South Africa. In *Human Rights and Comparative Foreign Policy*, ed. David P. Forsythe, 250–275. New York: United Nations University Press.

Mandara, Mairo. 2012. Family Planning in Nigeria and Prospects for the Future. *International Journal of Gynecology & Obstetrics*, 117: 1–4. February 20.

Manor River Union. About Us. http://manoriverunion.int/About_Us.html.

Mantey, Comfort Assa. 2013. Ensuring Free Border Movements in ECOWAS Integration: Challenges to National Security, M.A. Thesis, University of Ghana. July.

Mapenzauswa, Stella. 2022. In Africa, Rising Youth Unemployment is a Ticking Time Bomb. *New Decoder*. August 11. https://news-decoder.com/in-africa-rising-youth-unemployment-is-a-ticking-time-bomb/.

Marley, Bob, and The Wailers. 1978. Time Will Tell. *Genius*. https://genius.com/Bob-marley-and-the-wailers-time-will-tell-lyrics.

Martinez, Michael. 2013. Kerry: Nigeria Acknowledged Human Rights Abuses in Terror Fight. *CNN*. May 25. www.cnn/com/2013/05/25/world/africa/nigeria-kerry-human-rights.

Martinez, Jenny S. 2011. *The Slave Trade and the Origins of International Human Rights Law*. New York: Oxford University Press.

Maxfield, Michael G., and Earl R. Babbie. 2015. *Research Methods for Criminal Justice and Criminology*, 7th Ed. Stamford, CT: Cengage Learning.

May, Clifford D. 1984. Military Rule is Contagious in Africa. *New York Times*. May 6. Section 4, p. 4.

Mays, Terry M. 2015. *Historical Dictionary of International Organizations in Africa and the Middle East*. Lanham, MD: Rowman & Littlefield.

Mays, Terry M., and Mark W. Delancey. 2002. *Historical Dictionary of International Organizations in Sub-Saharan Africa*. Lanham, MD: Scarecrow Press.

M'Bet, Allechi. 1999. The CEAO and UEMOA within ECOWAS: The Road Ahead Toward West African Economic Integration. In *Regional Integration and Trade Liberalization in Sub-Saharan Africa: Regional Case Studies*, Vol.

3, eds. Ademola Oyejide, and Stephen Yeo, 66–85. London: Macmillan Press Ltd.

McCarthy, Colin. 1999. Regional Integration in Sub-Saharan Africa: Past, Present and Future. In *Regional Integration and Trade Liberalization in Sub-Saharan Africa: Synthesis and Review,* Vol. 4, eds. Ademola Oyejide, Benno Ndulu, and David Greenway, 12–44. London: Macmillan Press Ltd.

McElroy, Robert W. 1992. *Morality and American Foreign Policy.* Princeton, NJ: Princeton University Press.

McFadden, Robert D. 2011. Odumegwu Ojukwu, Breakaway Biafra Leader, Dies at 78. *New York Times.* November 26. http://www.nytimes.com/2011/11/27/world/africa/odumegwu-ojukwu-leader-of-breakaway-republic-of-biafra-dies-at-78.html?_r=0.

McKenna, Amy. Goodluck Jonathan, President of Nigeria. *Encyclopedia Britannica.* http://www.britannica.com/biography/Goodluck-Jonathan.

McLoughlin, Gerald, and Clarence J. Bouchat. 2013. *Nigerian Unity: In the Balance.* Carlisle, PA: Strategic Studies Institute & U.S. Army War College Press. June. http://www.strategicstudiesinstitute.army.mil/pdffiles/PUB1159.pdf.

Melly, Paul. 2023. Niger Coup Underlines Challenge to Democracy across West Africa. Chatham House. August 18. https://www.chathamhouse.org/2023/08/niger-coup-underlines-challenge-democracy-across-west-africa.

Members of the IC. Office of the Director of National Intelligence. http://www.dni.gov/index.php/intelligence-community/members-of-the-ic.

Meredith, Martin. 2011. *The Fate of Africa: A History of the Continent Since Independence.* Revised and updated edition. New York: Public Affairs.

Michnik, Adam. 1993. After the Revolution. *New Republic.* April 17. https://newrepublic.com/article/89495/revolution-poland-communism-christianity.

Milakovich, Michael E., and George J. Gordon. 2013. *Public Administration in America,* 11th Ed. Boston, MA: Wadsworth Cengage Learning.

Millennium Project. What is the 0.7% Target? 2002–2006. http://www.unmillenniumproject.org/press/07.htm.

Miners, Norman J. 1971. *The Nigerian Army, 1956–1966.* London: Methuen.

Mingst, Karen A., and Margaret P. Karns. 2012. *The United Nations in the 21st Century,* 4th Ed. Boulder, CO: Westview Press.

Ministry of Foreign Affairs. *Connect Nigeria.* www.connectnigeria.com/businesses/ministry-of-foreign-affairs-14273.html.

Ministry of Foreign Affairs, Headquarters Abuja. Our History. https://foreignaffairs.gov.ng/about-us/our-history/#:~:text=On%20attainment%20of%20a%20Republican,the%20Ministry%20of%20Foreign%20Affairs.

Mitter, Siddhartha. 2016. To Find Progress in Nigeria, Think Local. *Foreign Policy.* May 26. http://foreignpolicy.com/2016/05/26/to-find-progress-in-nigeria-thinklocal/.

Mollenkamp, Daniel Thomas. 2022. Social Justice Meaning and Main Principles Explained. *Investopedia*. Updated July 8. https://www.investopedia.com/terms/s/social-justice.asp.

Morgenthau, Hans J. 1978 [1948]. *Politics Among Nations: The Struggle for Power and Peace*, Revised 5th Ed. New York: Alfred A. Knopf.

Morgenthau, Hans J. 1977. The Pathology of American Power. *International Security* 1: 3–20. Winter.

Morse, Edward L. 2014. Welcome to the Revolution. *Foreign Affairs*. May/June. https://www.foreignaffairs.com/articles/2014-04-17/welcome-revolution.

Muhammed, Murtala. 2013. Africa Has Come of Age. Speech to the OAU Extraordinary Summit Conference, Addis Ababa. January 11. *Africa Youth Union*. December 3. https://www.facebook.com/Africanyouthunion/posts/726490580710778.

Mundt, Robert J., and Oladimeji Aborisade. 2000. Politics in Nigeria. In *Comparative Politics Today: A World View*, eds. Gabriel A. Almond, G. Bingham Powell, Jr., Kaare Strom, and Russell J. Dalton, 680–728. New York: Longman.

Mustapha, Abdul Raufu. 2001. Civil Rights and Pro-Democracy Groups in and Outside Nigeria. In Nigeria During the Abacha Years (1993–1998), eds. 'Kunle Amuwo, Daniel C. Bach, and Yann Lebenu, 143–183. Lagos: IFRA-Nigeria.

Nabakwe, Ruth. 2002. France Continues Peacekeeping Initiatives for Africa. Pan African News Agency. January 23. https://www.globalpolicy.org/component/content/article/199/41018.html.

Nathaniel, Soonest. 2023. Increasing Coups in West Africa: Falana Explores Key Issues Ahead of ECOWAS Summit. *Channels TV* (Lagos). Updated August 10. https://www.channelstv.com/2023/08/10/increasing-coups-in-west-africa-falana-explores-key-issues-ahead-ecowas-summit/.

National Bureau of Statistics. 2022. Nigeria Launches its Most Extensive National Measure of Multidimensional Poverty. Press Release. November 17. https://nigerianstat.gov.ng/news/78.

National Counterterrorism Center. 2022. Boko Haram. October. https://www.dni.gov/nctc/ftos/boko_haram_fto.html#:~:text=OVERVIEW&text=Boko%20Haram%2C%20which%20aims%20to,it%20was%20established%20in%202002.

National Human Rights Commission. 2022. Ojukwu Urges Lawmakers to Make Socio-Economic Rights Justiciable. March 28. https://www.nigeriarights.gov.ng/nhrc-media/news-and-events/320-ojukwu-urges-lawmakers-to-make-socio-economic-rights-justiciable.html.

National Institute for Policy and Strategic Studies. Objectives. http://nipsskuru.gov.ng/index.php/similar-tags.html.

National Intelligence Council. 2005. Mapping Sub-Sahara Africa's Future. CR 20050-2. March. http://www.au.af.mil/au/awc/awcgate/nic/africa_future.pdf.

National Interest: Meaning, Components[,] and Methods. *Your Article Library*. http://www.yourarticlelibrary.com/international-politics/national-interest-meaning-components-and-methods/48487/.

National Security Strategy, United States. 2004. *Encyclopedia of Espionage, Intelligence & Security*. http://www.encyclopedia.com/doc/1G2-3403300516.html.

Nda-Isaiah, Sam. 2014. Is Nigeria a Poor Country of Rich Men or a Rich Country of Poor Men? *Leadership* (Abuja). April 7. http://leadership.ng/columns/363727/nigeria-poor-country-rich-men-rich-country-poor-men.

Ndujihe, Clifford, Henry Umoru, and Joseph Erunke. 2015. Power Sector: Senate Probes OBJ, Yar'Adua, Jonathan. *Vanguard* (Lagos). August 14. http://www.vanguardngr.com/2015/08/power-sector-senate-probes-obj-yaradua-jonathan/.

News Agency of Nigeria. 2020. ECOWAS Court Begins Full Digital Operations January 2021. *World Stage*. November 25. worldstagenews.com.

Ngo-Martins, Flora Ogbuitepu. 2021. Update: Researching Gambian Legal Information. *GlobaLex*. May/June. https://www.nyulawglobal.org/globalex/Gambia1.html.

Niger. *One World Nations Online*. http://www.nationsonline.org/oneworld/niger.htm.

Niger Slavery: Background. 2008. *Guardian* (London). October 27. https://www.theguardian.com/world/2008/oct/27/humanrights1.

Nigeria. 2010. *Ethnologue: Languages of the World*, 17th Ed., ed. M. Paul Lewis. Dallas, TX: SIL International. http://www.ethnologue.com/country/NG.

Nigeria. 2006. In *World Police Encyclopedia,* Vol. 2, eds. Dilip K. Das and Michael Palmiotto, 619–625. New York: Routledge.

Nigeria: Africa's New Number One. 2014. *Economist*. April 12. http://www.economist.com/news/leaders/21600685-nigerias-suddenly-supersied-economy-indeed-wonder-s-are-its-still-huge.

Nigeria Angry at Being Rated Second Most Corrupt. 2003. *IRIN*. October 9. http://www.irinnews.org/report/46630/nigeria-nigeria-angry-at-being-rated-second-most-corrupt.

Nigeria Becomes Africa's Largest Economy. 2014. *Al Jazeera*. April 6. http://www.aljazeera.com/news/africa/2014/04/nigeria-becomes-africa-largest-economy-20144618190520102.html.

Nigeria Becomes Africa's Biggest Economy. 2014. *BBC News*. April 6. http://www.bbc.com/news/business-26913497.

Nigeria Cedes Bakassi to Cameroon. 2008. *BBC News*. August 14. http://news.bbc.co.uk/2/hi/africa/7559895.stm.

Nigeria: Fears Over Population Growth as World Hits [Eight] Billion. 2022. *Africa News*. Last updated November 15. billionhttps://www.africanews.com/2022/11/15/nigeria-fears-over-population-growth-as-world-hits-8-billion//.

Nigeria Independence Act, 1960. 1960. 8 & 9 Eliz., 2 Ch. 55. July 29. www.legislation.gov.uk/ukpga/1960/55/pdfs/ukpga_19600055_en.pdf.

Nigeria—Ministry of Defense. *Global Security*. http://www.globalsecurity.org/military/world/nigeria/mod.htm.

Nigeria Oil. *Worldometer*. https://www.worldometers.info/oil/nigeria-oil/.

Nigeria Population (Live). *Worldometer*. https://www.worldometers.info/world-population/nigeria-population/.

Nigeria Republican Act 1963. 1963. 1963 Ch. 57. December 18. http://www.legislation.gov.uk/ukpga/1963/57.

Nigeria (Republic) Bill. 1963. H.L., Deb. Vol. 254 cc208–14 *Hansard*. December 17. hansard.millbanksystems.com/lords/1963/dec/17/Nigeria-republic-bill.

Nigeria (Republic) Bill, H.L. Deb. 1963. Hansard, Vol. 245, cc208–14. December 17. hansard.millbanksystems.com/lords/1963/dec/17/Nigeria-republic-bill.

Nigeria. *World Atlas*. http://www.worldatlas.com/webimage/countrys/africa/ng.htm.

Nigeria's Muhammadu Buhari in Profile. 2015. *BBC News*. March 31. http://www.bbc.com/news/world-africa-12890807.

Nigeria's Technical Aid Corps for ACP Countries to Expand to Brazil, Venezuela, Vietnam. 2014. *ACP*. September 10. http://www.acp.int/content/news-nigerias-technical-aid-corps-acp-countries-expand-brazil-venezuela-vietnam.

Nigeria's 2023 Election Eroded Voters' Trust: EU Observers. 2023. *Alja Zeera*. June 29. https://www.aljazeera.com/news/2023/6/29/nigerias-2023-election-eroded-voters-trust-eu-observers.

Nigerian Army Education Corps and School. 1992. *History of the Nigerian Army 1863–1992*. Abuja: Nigerian Army Headquarters.

Nigerian Army Peacekeeping Center. About Us. http://www.napkc.org/training.php.

Nigerian Army Peacekeeping Center. Highlight. http://www.napkc.org/training.php.

Nigerian Embassies and Consulates. *Embassies*. https://embassies.net/nigeria-embassy#:~:text=Nigeria%20currently%20maintains%20about%20102%20diplomatic%20representations%20worldwide.

Nigerian Institute of International Affairs. About Us. http://niianet.org/aboutus.htm.

Nigerian Institute of International Affairs. Director-General's Message. http://niianet.org/dgmessage.htm.

Nigerian Military Leader Ousts Interim President. 1993. *New York Times.* November 18. http://www.nytimes.com/1993/11/18/world/nigeria-military-leader-ousts-interim-president.html.

Nigerian Technical Aid Corps Act. 1987. *Laws of Nigeria.* October 1. https://lawsofnigeria.placng.org/laws/N135.pdf.

Nigerians Abroad: Secret Weapon. 2015. *Economist* (London). June 20. http://www.economist.com/news/special-report/21654360-nigerias-diaspora-source-money-markets-skills-and-ideas-secret-weapon.

Nigerians on Twitter React to Nigeria's Twitter Suspension. 2021. *Alja Zeera.* June 5. https://www.aljazeera.com/news/2021/6/4/nigerian-twitter-users-blast-govt-ban-of-social-media-giant.

Noble, Kenneth. 1993. Nigerian Military Rulers Annul Election. *New York Times.* June 24. http://www.nytimes.com/1993/06/24/world/nigerian-military-rulers-annul-election.html.

Nohlen, Dieter, Michael Krennerich, and Bernhard Thibaut, eds. 1999. *Elections in Africa: A Data Handbook.* London: Oxford University Press.

Northedge, F.S. 1969. The Nature of Foreign Policy. In *The Foreign Policies of the Powers,* ed. F.S. Northedge, 9–39. Westport, CT: Praeger.

Nossiter, Adam. 2015. In Town of Missing Girls, Sorrow, but Little Progress. *New York Times.* May 12. http://www.nytimes.com/2014/05/12/world/africa/in-town-of-missing-girls-sorrow-but-little-progress.html.

Number of People Living in Extreme Poverty in Nigeria from 2016 to 2022, by Gender. *Statista* https://www.statista.com/statistics/1287827/number-of-people-living-in-extreme-poverty-in-nigeria-by-gender/#:~:text=In%202022%2C%20an%20estimated%20population,at%2043.7%20million%20for%20women.

Nwabueze, Ben. 2015. Corrupt Practices: Igbo Leaders' Position on Probe of Past Governments. *Vanguard.* August 13. http://www.vanguardngr.com/2015/08/corrupt-practices-igbo-leaders-position-on-probe-of-past-govts/.

Nwanolue, Bonn O., and Victor C. Iwuoha. 2012. A Reflection on Nigeria's Past: Africa as the Centerpiece of Nigeria's Foreign Policy Revisited. *Developing Country Studies.* (2): 78–79. http://www.iiste.org/Journals/index.php/DCS/article/view/1756/1709.

Nwanze, Cheta. A Short History of the Nigerian Police Force. *Trent Online.* http://www.thetrentonline.com/cheta-nwanze-short-history-nigeria-police-force/.

Nwaubani, Adaobi Tricia. 2022. The Nigerians Hoping to Check Out of Their Country. BBC. February 28. https://www.bbc.com/news/world-africa-60393076.

Nweke, Obinna Chukwunenye. 2024. Hunger as a Weapon of War: Biafra, Social Media and the Politics of Famine Remembrance. *Third World Quarterly.* 45(2): 314–331. https://doi.org/10.1080/01436597.2023.2182283.

Nwogu, Nneoma. 2007. Regional Integration as an Instrument of Human Rights: Reconceptualizing ECOWAS. *Journal of Human Rights*. 6(3): 345–360. https://doi.org/10.1080/14754830701531112.

Nwogugu, E. I. 2014. *Family Law in Nigeria*. Ibadan, Nigeria: HEBN Publishers.

Nwokedi, Emeka. 1994. Nigeria's Democratic Transition: Explaining the Annulled 1993 Presidential Election. *The Round Table*. 83(330): 189–204. April. https://doi.org/10.1080/00358539408454202.

Nwokoro, Silver. 2022. Falana, Others Call for Enforcement of Socio-Economic Rights of Nigerians. *Guardian* (Lagos). March 8. https://guardian.ng/features/falana-others-call-for-enforcement-of-socio-economic-rights-of-nigerians/.

Nye, Jr., Joseph S. 2008. *Understanding International Conflicts: An Introduction to Theory and History*, 7th Ed. New York: Longman.

Obadare, Ebenezer. 2023. Paper Truths and Counterfeit Lives. Council on Foreign Relations. October 10. https://www.cfr.org/blog/paper-truths-and-counterfeit-lives.

Obadare, Ebenezer. 2023. Why Buhari Failed. Council on Foreign Relations. May 22. https://www.cfr.org/blog/why-buhari-failed.

Obaje, Nuhu George. 2009. *Geology and Mineral Resources of Nigeria*. Berlin, Germany: Springer-Verlag.

Obama, Barack. 2009. Speech in Ghana on African Development 3. July 12. http://www.voanews.com/wm/live/special-events/english-obama-ghana-event/vb.asx.

Obasanjo, Olusegun. 1987. *Nzeogwu: An Intimate Portrait of Major Chukwuma Kaduna Nzeogwu*. Ibadan: Spectrum Books.

Obi, Emeka A. 2006. *Fundamentals of Nigerian Foreign Policy: A Study on the Role of National Interest in Foreign Policy Making*. Abingdon, U.K.: Bookpoint Ltd.

Obiagwu, Chinonye, and Chidi Anselm Odinkalu. 2003. Nigeria: Combating Legacies of Colonialism and Militarism. In *Human Rights under African Constitutions: Realizing the Promise for Ourselves*, ed. Abdullahi Ahmed An-Na'im, 211–250. Philadelphia, PA: University of Pennsylvania Press.

Obiezu, Timothy. 2023. Opposition Parties Reject Nigeria's Presidential Election Court Verdict. *VOA News*. September 7. https://www.voanews.com/a/opposition-parties-reject-nigeria-s-presidential-election-court-verdict-/7258597.html.

Obituary: President Yar'Adua. 2010. *BBC News*. May 6. http://news.bbc.co.uk/2/hi/africa/6187249.stm.

O'Cléireacáin, Séamus. 1999. Sub-Saharan Africa's Trade Liberalization Experience. In *Regional Integration and Trade Liberalization in Sub-Saharan*

Africa: Synthesis and Review, Vol. 4, eds. Ademola Oyejide, Benno Ndulu, and David Greenway, 50–73. London: Macmillan Press Ltd.

Odeh, Godwin Onuh. 2021. Nigeria's Technical Aid Corps Engagement in The Gambia, 1987–2012: A Neglected Aspect of Nigerian Foreign Relations. In *Culture and Nigeria's Foreign Relations in a Globalizing World*. Abuja: National Institute for Cultural Orientation Agency (NICO). Chap. 14. https://www.researchgate.net/publication/353946774_Nigeria's_Technical_Aid_Corps_Engagement_in_The_Gambia_1987-2012_A_Neglected_Aspect_of_Nigerian_Foreign_Relations.

Odeh, Lemuel Ekedegwa. 2010. A Comparative Analysis of Global North and Global South Economies. *Journal of Sustainable Development in Africa*. 12(3): 338–348.

Odinkalu, Chidi A. 2001. The Management of Transition to Civil Rule by the Military in Nigeria (1966–1999). In *Nigeria During the Abacha Years (1993–1998)*, eds. 'Kunle Amuwo, Daniel C. Bach, and Yann Lebenu, 57–99. Lagos: IFRA-Nigeria.

Odinkalu, Chidi A. 1999. Why More Africans Don't Use Human Rights Language. *Human Rights Dialog*, Vol. 2. December. www.carnegiecouncil.org/publications/archive/dialogue/2_01/articles/602.html.

Odiogor. Hugo, and Abiodun Alade. 2015. "I Cannot Rest When the World Is Being Terrorized—Prof. Ibrahim Gambari." *Vanguard* (Lagos). June 21. http://www.vanguardngr.com/2015/06/i-cannot-rest-when-the-world-is-being-terrorised-prof-ibrahim-gambari/.

Odunsi, Wale. 2023. Nigeria Deploys 2,500 Technical Aid Volunteers to ACP Countries. *Daily Post* (Lagos). February 2. https://dailypost.ng/2023/02/02/nigeria-deploys-2500-technical-aid-volunteers-to-acp-countries/.

Odunsi, Wale. 2022. Okonjo-Iweala's Son, Uzodinma Suggests Nigeria's Dissolution Months to 2023 Elections. *Daily Post* (Lagos). June 28. 2022. https://dailypost.ng/2022/06/28/okonjo-iwealas-son-uzodinma-suggests-nigerias-dissolution-months-to-2023-elections.

Office of the UN High Commissioner for Human Rights. 1998. Declaration on the Right and Responsibility of Individuals, Groups[,] and Organs of Society to Promote and Protect Universally Recognized Human Rights and Fundamental Freedoms. Res. 53/144 adopted by the UN General Assembly on December 9. http://www.ohchr.org/EN/ProfessionalInterest/Pages/RightAndResponsibility.aspx.

Office of the UN High Commissioner for Human Rights. 1993. Vienna Declaration and Program of Action. June 25. http://www.ohchr.org/EN/ProfessionalInterest/Pages/Vienna.aspx.

Office of the UN High Commissioner for Human Rights. World Conference on Human Rights, 14–25. June 1993. Vienna, Austria. http://www.ohchr.org/EN/ABOUTUS/Pages/ViennaWC.aspx.

Office of the UN Commissioner for Human Rights. 1985. Basic Principles on the Independence of the Judiciary. Seventh United Nations Congress on the Prevention of Crime and the Treatment of Offenders held at Milan from 26 August to 6 September 1985. September 6. https://www.ohchr.org/en/instruments-mechanisms/instruments/basic-principles-independence-judiciary.

Office of the UN High Commissioner for Human Rights. What We Do. http://www.ohchr.org/EN/AboutUs/Pages/WhatWeDo.aspx.

Office of the UN High Commissioner for Human Rights. Good Governance and Human Rights. http://www.ohchr.org/EN/Issues/Development/GoodGovernance/Pages/GoodGovernanceIndex.aspx.

Ofor, Franca. Presentation on [the] Community Court of Justice, ECOWAS. Office of the UN High Commissioner for Human Rights, Strasbourg.

Ogbeidi, Michael M. 2010. A Culture of Failed Elections: Revisiting Democratic Elections in Nigeria, 1959–2003. *Historia Actual Online*. 21: 43–56.

Ogunbiyi, Ore. 2023. A Young Person's Guide to Escaping Nigeria. *Economist*. February 24. https://www.economist.com/1843/2023/02/24/a-young-persons-guide-to-escaping-nigeria.

Ogunlesi, Tolu. 2014. Abuja, Nigeria's Capital City, Grows and Flourishes. *Financial Times* (London). May 4. http://www.ft.com/intl/cms/s/0/68c28016-bb16-11e3-948c-00144feabdc0.html#axzz3n50kTd6W.

Ohaegbulam, Festus Ugboaja. 1982. *Nigeria and the United Nations' Mission to the Democratic Republic of the Congo: A Case Study of the Formative Stages of Nigeria's Foreign Policy*. Gainesville, FL: University Press of Florida.

Ohuocha, Chijioke. 2023. Explainer: What is Pushing the Nigerian Naira to Record Lows? *Reuter*. October 27. https://www.reuters.com/markets/currencies/what-is-pushing-nigerian-naira-record-lows-2023-10-27/.

Ojameruaye, Emmanuel. A Tentative Analytical Evaluation of President Obasanjo's Performance (May 1999–May 2007). *Gamji*. http://www.gamji.com/article6000/NEWS7024.htm.

Ojeme, Victoria. 2022. Nigerians are One of the Most Populous Immigrant Community Doing Excellency [sic] Well—Japanese Ambassador. *Vanguard* (Lagos). January 20. https://www.vanguardngr.com/2022/01/nigerians-are-one-of-the-most-populous-immigrant-community-ng-excellency-well-japanese-ambassador.

Ojukwu, Emeka Odumegwu. 1994. Nigeria: The Truths Which Are Self-Evident. *Sunday Magazine* (Lagos). March 6. 15–23. https://nigeriaworld.com/feature/speech/ojukwu_archives.html.

Ojukwu, Emmanuel C., and Chuka Enuka. 2020. Nigeria and African Development Agenda: The Technical Aid Corps (TAC) Initiative. *Journal of African Studies and Sustainable Development*. 3(6), 107–119. https://doi.org/10.13140/RG.2.2.29758.72006.

Okafor, Chiamaka. 2024. Naira Depreciation Ridicules Increased Budgetary Allocation for Nigeria's Foreign Missions. *Premium Times* (Abuja). January 11. https://www.premiumtimesng.com/news/657697-naira-depreciation-ridicules-increased-budgetary-allocation-for-nigerias-foreign-missions.html.

Okafor, Chiamaka. 2022. Gambari Explains Buhari's Foreign Policy Mindset. *Premium Times* (Abuja). August 15. https://www.premiumtimesng.com/news/headlines/548864-gambari-explains-buharis-foreign-policy-mindset.html#:~:text=According%20to%20Mr%20Gambari%2C%20Mr,the%20rest%20of%20the%20world.

Okafor, Obiora Chinedu, Udoka Owie, Okechukwu Effoduh, and Rahina Zarma. 2022. On the Modest Impact of West Africa's International Human Rights Court on the Executive Branch of Government in Nigeria. *Harvard Human Rights Journal*. 35 (2022): 170–232.

Okafor, Victor Oguejiofor, ed. 2008. *Nigeria's Stumbling Democracy and Its Implications for Africa's Democratic Movement*. Westport, CT: Praeger.

Okogwu, L.E., and A. Akpuru-Aja. 2004. *Nigerian Diplomacy and the Conflict of Laws: An Insight into the Practice of Nigeria's Foreign Policy*. Abakaliki, Nigeria: WillyRose & Appleseed Publishing Co.

Okonkwo, Rudolf Ogoo. 2012. Achebe Administers a Sacrament for Biafra. *Nairaland Forum*. October 9. https://www.nairaland.com/1069497/rudolph-okonkwo-reviews-chinua-achebes.

Okoro, Stevens. 2012. Nigeria and the Concept of National Interest. *Daily Independent* (Lagos). July. http://dailyindependentnig.com/2012/07/nigeria-and-concept-of-national-interest/.

Olakpe, Oreva. 2018. Nigerian Migrants in China: Changing the Narrative. *Heinrich Böll Stiftung* (Cape Town, South Africa). October. https://za.boell.org/en/2018/10/09/nigerian-migrants-china-changing-narrative.

Olawale, Salami B. 2014. The Preclude to Babangida Regime's Foreign Policy Initiatives. *Mediterranean Journal of Social Sciences*. 5(3): 81–85. http://www.mcser.org/journal/index.php/mjss/article/view/2120.

Oloka-Onyango, J. 2015. *Battling Over Human Rights: Twenty Essays on Law, Politics and Governance*. Bamenda, Cameroon: Langaa Research & Publishing.

Olonisakin, 'Funmi. 2000. *Reinventing Peacekeeping in Africa: Conceptual and Legal Issues in ECOMOG Operations*. London: Kluwer Law International.

Olujobi, Bethel. 2024. Nigeria Opens Door for Medical, Other Volunteer Missions Abroad. *Business Day*. January 3. https://businessday.ng/news/article/nigeria-opens-door-for-medical-other-volunteer-missions-abroad/#:~:text=The%20Federal%20Government%20of%20Nigeria,TAC)%20recruitment%20exercise%20for%202024.

Olukoya, Sam. 2001. Nigeria's Trigger-Happy Police. *BBC News*. May 11. http://news.bbc.co.uk/2/hi/africa/1322017.stm.

Olurounbi, Ruth, and William Clowes. 2021. Nigeria Condemns Twitter for Deleting President Buhari's Tweet. *Bloomberg*. Updated June 2. https://www.bloomberg.com/news/articles/2021-06-02/nigerian-president-threatens-crackdown-after-spate-of-attacks.

Olusanya, G.O., and R. A. Akindele, eds. 1990. *The Structure and Processes of Foreign Policy Making and Implementation in Nigeria, 1960–1990.* Lagos: Nigerian Institute of International Affairs.

Olusanya, G.O., and R.A. Akindele. 1986. *Nigeria's External Relations: The First Twenty-Five Years.* Ibadan: Ibadan University Press.

Olutoyin, Babatunde Isaac. 2004. Treaty Making and Its Application under Nigerian Law: The Journey So Far. *International Journal of Business & Management Invention.* 3(7). http://www.ijbmi.org/papers/Vol%283%293/Version-3/B033307018.pdf.

Oluwasanjo, Ahmed. 2024. Naira Falls to ₦1,600 Per $1 as Tinubu's Economic Collapse Continues. *Peoples Gazette* (Abuja). February 15. https://gazettengr.com/just-in-naira-falls-to-n1600-per-1-as-tinubus-economic-collapse-continues/.

Omotola, J. Oshola. 2010. Elections and Democratic Transition in Nigeria under the Fourth Republic. *African Affairs.* 109: 535–553.

O'Neil, Patrick H., Karl J. Fields, and Don Share. 2012. *Cases in Comparative Politics,* 4th Ed. New York: W. W. Norton & Co.

Onishi, Norimitsu. 1999. What War Has Wrought: Sierra Leone's Sad State. *New York Times.* January 31. http://www.nytimes.com/1999/01/31/world/what-war-has-wrought-sierra-leone-s-sad-state.html?pagewanted=all.

Open Society Foundations. 2013. Fact Sheet: ECOWAS Community Court of Justice. June. https://www.justiceinitiative.org/publications/ecowas-community-court-justice.

Open Society Justice Initiative. Fact Sheet: African Commission on Human and Peoples' Rights. https://www.justiceinitiative.org/publications/african-commission-human-and-peoples-rights#:~:text=The%20African%20Commission%20is%20tasked,(all%20except%20South%20Sudan.

Open Society Justice Initiative. Fact Sheet: East African Court of Justice. https://www.justiceinitiative.org/publications/east-african-court-justice.

Operation Iraqi Freedom. 2003. *White House.* March 27. http://georgewbush-whitehouse.archives.gov/news/releases/2003/03/20030327-10.html.

Organization of African Unity (OAU). 2000. Constitutive Act of the African Union. OAU Doc. CAB/LEG/23.15. July 11. http://www.africa-union.org.

Organization of African Unity (OAU). 1981. African Charter on Human and Peoples' Rights ("Banjul Charter"). June 27. CAB/LEG/67/3 rev. 5, 21 I.L.M. 58 (1982). https://www.refworld.org/docid/3ae6b3630.html.

Organization of African Unity (OAU). 1963. Charter of the Organization of African Unity. 479 U.N.T.S. 39. Entered into force September 13. http://www1.umn.edu/humanrts/africa/OAU_Charter_1993.html.

Osaghae, Eghosa E. 1998. *The Crippled Giant: Nigeria Since Independence*. Bloomington, IN: Indiana University Press.

Ostien, Philip, and Albert Dekker. 2010. Sharia and National Law in Nigeria. In *Sharia Incorporated: A Comparative Overview of the Legal Systems of Twelve Muslim Countries in Past and Present*, ed. Jan Michiel Otto, 555–612. Leiden, Netherlands: Leiden University Press.

Ottaway, David B. 1978. Carter Arrives in Nigeria on State Visit. *Washington Post*. April 1. https://www.washingtonpost.com/archive/politics/1978/04/01/carter-arrives-in-nigeria-on-state-visit/bd7821e0-271a-49c6-b16d-0252f1efeb74/.

Owete, Festus. 2014. Between Jonathan's National Conference and Obasanjo's National Political Reform Conference: What You Need to Know. *Premium Times* (Abuja). February 16. http://www.premiumtimesng.com/news/155237-between-jonathans-national-conference-and-obasanjos-national-political-reform-conference.html.

Oyekanmi, Babatunde. 2015. 2015 General Elections and the Role of INEC. Paper Presented at a Conference in July. http://www.inecnigeria.org/wp-content/uploads/2015/07/Conference-Paper-by-Tunde-Oyekanmi.pdf.

Ozekhome, Mike A. A. 2014. The Nigerian Judiciary—15 Years of Democracy. *Point Blank News*. Last visited November 24. http://pointblanknews.com/pbn/articles-opinions/the-nigerian-judiciary-15-years-of-democracy/.

Ozoigbo, Bonaventure I. 2008. Federal Balancing in Nigeria: A Paradigm for Democracy. *African Journals Online*. 66–84.

Pan-African News Agency (Dakar). 2001. West Africa: Konare to Swear in ECOWAS Judges. January 29. https://allafrica.com/stories/200101290396.html.

Papp, Daniel S. 2001. *Contemporary International Relations: Frameworks for Understanding*, 6th Ed. Upper Saddle River, NJ: Pearson.

Paquette, Danielle. 2021. Nigeria Suspends Twitter after the Social Media Platform Freezes President's Account. *Washington Post*. June 4. https://www.washingtonpost.com/world/2021/06/04/nigeria-suspends-twitter-buhari/.

Patterson, Thomas E. 2013. *The American Democracy*, 11th Ed. New York: McGraw-Hill.

Patterson, Thomas E. 2008. *The American Democracy*, 8th Ed. New York: McGraw-Hill.

Peace Corps. *Federal Register*. https://www.federalregister.gov/agencies/peace-corps#:~:text=The%20Peace%20Corps%20was%20established,2501%2D1.

Peace Corps. Boston, MA: John F. Kennedy Presidential Library & Museum. http://www.jfklibrary.org/JFK/JFK-in-History/Peace-Corps.aspx.

People's Democratic Party (PDP). *Encyclopedia Britannica.* http://www.britannica.com/topic/Peoples-Democratic-Party-political-party-Nigeria.

Pham, J. Peter. 2007. Nigeria's Foreign Policy: An Inquiry into Sources and Prospects. Paper Prepared for Presentation at an International Conference in Lisbon, Portugal. November 8–9. www.ipri.pt/eventos/pdf/JPeterPham_paper.pdf.

Pine, Atah. 2011. Nigerian Foreign Policy, 1960–2011: Fifty Years of Conceptual Confusion. *Modern Ghana.* October 4. http://www.modernghana.com/print/354264/1/nigeria-foreign-policy-1960-2011-fifty-one-years-o.html.

Pine, Atah. 2009. Parliamentary Diplomacy and Foreign Policy in Nigeria's Fourth Republic. *Blogger.* July 1. http://atahpine.blogspot.com/2009/07/parliamentary-diplomacy-and-foreign.html.

Pitts, Chip. 2005. "Mobilizing Shame" Can Bring Abuses Up Short. *Topeka Capital-Journal.* March 11. http://cjonline.com/stories/031105/opi_pitts.shtml.

Plato. 2007. The Myth of the Cave. In *Philosophical Inquiry: Classic and Contemporary Readings,* eds. Jonathan E. Adler and Catherine Z. Elgin, 23–26. Indianapolis, IN: Hackett Publishing Co., Inc.

Podesta, James. 1994. Haile Selassie 1892–1975. *Contemporary Black Biography.* http://www.encyclopedia.com/topic/Haile_Selassie.aspx.

Pogoson, A.I. Leadership Roles and Foreign Policy: A Study of President Shehu Shagari's Foreign Policy Posture. *Africa Bib.* http://www.africabib.org/rec.php?RID=170748693.

Politics in the Crisis Years. In *Nigeria: A Country Study,* ed. Helen Chapin Metz. Washington, DC: GPO for the Library of Congress. http://countrystudies.us/nigeria/74.htm.

Political Map of Nigeria. *Nations Online.* https://www.nationsonline.org/oneworld/map/nigeria-political-map.htm.

Political Realism in International Relations. 2010. *Stanford Encyclopedia of Philosophy.* July 26, revised April 2, 2013. http://plato.stanford.edu/entries/realism-intl-relations/.

Political Transition. In *Nigeria: A Country Study*, ed. Helen Chapin Metz. Washington, DC: GPO for the Library of Congress. http://countrystudies.us/nigeria/74.htm.

Pope Francis. 2015. Text of Address to a Joint Session of the US Congress. September 24. http://www.politico.com/story/2015/09/pope-francis-speech-to-congress-transcript-text-video-214016.

Poverty in Nigeria: Rich Country, Poor People. 2012. *Poverties.* March, Updated April 2013. http://www.poverties.org/poverty-in-nigeria.html.

Power, Samantha, and Graham Allison. 2000. Introduction. In *Realizing Human Rights: Moving from Inspiration to Impact,* eds. Samantha Power and Graham Allison, xiii–xxvii. New York: St. Martin's Press.

Princewill Nimi, and Stephanie Busari. 2021. Nigeria Bans Twitter after Company Deletes President Buhari's Tweet. *CNN*. Updated June 5. https://www.cnn.com/2021/06/04/africa/nigeria-suspends-twitter-operations-intl/index.html.

Profile: African Union. 2012. *BBC News*. February 1. http://news.bbc.co.uk/2/hi/africa/country_profiles/3870303.stm.

Profile: ECOMOG. 2004. *BBC News*. June 17. http://news.bbc.co.uk/2/hi/africa/country_profiles/2364029.stm.

Protests in Biafra: Go Your Own Way. 2015. *Economist* (London). November 28. http://www.economist.com/news/middle-east-and-africa/21679210-half-century-after-war-angry-biafrans-are-agitating-again-go-your-own-way.

Przeworski, Adam. 1991. *Democracy and the Market*. New York: Cambridge University Press.

Purefoy, Christine. 2011. Goodluck Jonathan: By Name and Nature? *CNN*. April 17. http://www.cnn.com/2010/WORLD/africa/05/06/nigeria.jonathan/.

Queen Elizabeth II Has Died. 2022. BBC. September 8. https://www.bbc.com/news/uk-61585886.

Quigley, Fran. 2014. *How Human Rights Can Build Haiti: Activists, Lawyers, and the Grassroots Campaign*. Nashville, TN: Vanderbilt University Press.

Quist-Arcton, Ofeibea. 2006. Nigeria Rejects Term-Limit Change in Constitutions. *NPR*. May 17. http://www.npr.org/templates/story/story.php?storyID=5410583.

Ramcharan, B.G. 2002. *The United Nations High Commissioner for Human Rights: The Challenges of International Protection*. Leiden, Netherlands: Martinus Nijhoff.

Rasiulis, Andrew P. 2001. The Military Training Assistance Program (MTAP): An Instrument of Diplomacy. *Canadian Military Journal*. 63–64. Autumn. http://www.journal.forces.gc.ca/vo2/no3/doc/63-64-eng.pdf

Rectification of Names. *Cultural China*. http://www.cultural-china.com/chinaWH/History/en/165History878.html.

Redmond, Paul. 2003. Transnational Enterprise and Human Rights: Options for Standard Setting and Compliance. *International Law*. 37: 69–101.

Reforming Nigeria: A Conversation with Ngozi Okonjo-Iweala. 2014. *Foreign Affairs*. March/April. http://www.foreignaffairs.com/discussions/interviews/-nigeria.

Report of the Commission Appointed to Inquire into the Fears of Minorities and the Means of Allaying Them. 1958. London: Her Majesty's Stationery Office.

Return to Military Rule. 1991. In *Nigeria: A Country Study*, ed. Helen Chapin Metz. Washington, DC: GPO for the Library of Congress. https://countrystudies.us/nigeria/30.htm.

Reuters. 2016. A Year on From Nigerian Election Victory Buhari's Reforms Founder. *New York Times*. February 25. http://www.nytimes.com/reuters/2016/02/25/world/africa/25reuters-nigeria-politics.html?_r=0.

Reuters. 1945. Lord Lugard, 87, African Pioneer; Former Governor General of Nigeria Dies—Occupied Uganda, Fought Slavers. *New York Times*. April 12. https://www.nytimes.com/1945/04/12/archives/lord-lugard-87-african-pioneer-former-governor-general-of-nigeria.html.

Rich, David. 2024. With ECOWAS Exit, Mali, Burkina Faso, and Niger Leave Democratic Transition in Limbo. *France 24*. February 2. https://www.france24.com/en/africa/20240202-with-ecowas-exit-mali-burkina-faso-and-niger-leave-democratic-transition-in-limbo.

Richard, Dreux. 2011. The Other Side of Tokyo's Nigerian Community. *Japan Today*. August 2. https://japantoday.com/category/features/lifestyle/the-other-side-of-tokyos-nigerian-community.

Rioting in Nigeria Kills at Least 11. 1993. *New York Times*. July 7. http://www.nytimes.com/1993/07/07/world/rioting-in-nigeria-kills-at-least-11.html.

Robinson, Mary. The Business Case for Human Rights. http://www.unhchr.ch/hurricane/huricane.nsf/0/e47d352dedc39697802566de0043b28e?OpenDocument.

Rocha, José Luís. 2010. Cape Verde and ECOWAS: The Challenge of Regional Integration. *Portuguese Journal of International Affairs*. 3–7. Autumn/Winter.

Rosenau, James N. 1968. National Interest. *International Encyclopedia of the Social Sciences*. http://www.encyclopedia.com/doc/1G2-3045000855.html.

Rosenberg, Matt. Non-Members of the United Nations. *About*. http://geography.about.com/od/politicalgeography/a/nun.htm.

Rosenthal, Elisabeth. 2012. Nigeria Tested by Rapid Rise in Population. *New York Times*. April 14. https://www.nytimes.com/2012/04/15/world/africa/in-nigeria-a-preview-of-an-overcrowded-planet.html.

Ross, Will. 2015. Nigeria Elections: Buhari Scores Historic Win. *BBC News*. April 1. http://www.bbc.com/news/world-africa-32141703.

Roth, Kenneth. 2000. Human Rights Organizations: A New Force for Social Change. In *Realizing Human Rights: Moving from Inspiration to Impact*, eds. Samantha Power and Graham Alison, 225–248. New York: St. Martin's Press.

Rotimi-John, Alade. 2015. The Nigerian Question and Its Resolution. *Guardian* (Lagos). November 18. http://www.ngrguardiannews.com/2015/11/the-nigerian-question-and-its-resolution/.

Roy, Diana, and Amelia Cheatham. 2024. Backgrounder: What Is Canada's Immigration Policy? Council on Foreign Relations. Last updated March 28. https://www.cfr.org/backgrounder/what-canadas-immigration-policy.

Rudall, Jason. 2021. *Altruism in International Law.* London and New York: Cambridge University Press.

Rules of Procedure: Definition and Legal Meaning. *Black's Law Dictionary*, 2d. Edition. https://thelawdictionary.org/rules-of-procedure/.

Rupert, James. 1998. Corruption Flourished in Abacha's Regime. *Washington Post.* June 9. A1. http://www.washingtonpost.com/wp-srv/inatl/longterm/nigeria/stories/corrupt060998.htm.

Saha, Tushar Kanti. 2010. *Textbook on Legal Methods, Legal Systems and Research.* New Delhi: Universal Law Publishing.

Salami, B. O. 2012. Evaluating the Nigerian Technical Aids Corp Scheme, 1987–1993. *Journal of History and Diplomatic Studies.* 9(2012). https://www.ajol.info/index.php/jhds/article/view/96974.

San Diego Foundation. 2022. What Is Social Justice? September 24. https://www.sdfoundation.org/news-events/sdf-news/what-is-social-justice/.

Sanusi, Sanusi Lamido. 2022. Buharism: Economic Theory and Political Economy. *Gamji.* July 22. http://www.gamji.com/sanusi/sanusi26.htm.

Saro-Wiwa, Ken. 1996. *A Month and a Day: A Detention Diary.* London: Penguin Books.

Saunders, Paul J. 2016. The Five Most Abuses Foreign-Policy Cliches. *National Interest.* January 20. http://nationalinterest.org/commentary/the-five-most-abused-foreign-policy-cliches-9978.

Sauti, Lazarus. 2013. Thabo Mbeki's Legacy to Africa. *Herald* (Zimbabwe). September 16. http://www.herald.co.zw/thabo-mbekis-legacy-to-africa/.

Schell, Jonathan. 2003. *The Unconquerable World: Power, Nonviolence, and the Will of the People.* New York: Henry Holt & Co.

Schifferes, Steve. 2003. U.S. Names "Coalition of the Willing." *BBC News.* March 18. http://news.bbc.co.uk/2/hi/americas/2862343.stm.

Schmidt, Brian C. 1998. *The Political Discourse of Anarchy: A Disciplinary History of International Relations.* Albany, NY: State University of New York Press.

Schmidt, Steffen W., Mack C. Shelley, and Barbara A. Bardes. 2005. *American Government and Politics Today 2005–2006 Edition.* Belmont, CA: Thomson Wadsworth.

Scientific Research in Education. 2002. Washington, DC: National Academies Press.

Segun, Joshua, Dominic Azuh, and Faith Olanrewaju. 2015. University-Industry Collaboration: A Panacea to Graduate Unemployment in Nigeria. BVIMSR's *Journal of Management Review.* 7(1), 17–25.

Sen, Amartya. 2006. Democracy as a Universal Value. In *Readings in Comparative Politics: Political Challenges and Changing Agendas*, eds. Mark Kesselman and Joel Drieger, 171–181. Boston, MA: Cengage Learning.

Senate Asks Buhari to Review Nigeria's Foreign Policy. 2015. *Premium Times* (Abuja). December 8. http://www.premiumtimesng.com/news/top-news/194812-%E2%80%8Bs%E2%80%8Benate-asks-buhari-to-review-nigerias-foreign-policy.html.

SERAP. About SERAP. https://serap-nigeria.org/who-we-are/.

[Seventy-Nine] Countries. 2019. *Business ACP*. December. https://businessacp.com/wp-content/uploads/2019/12/79-countries-OACPS.pdf.

Shagaya, John N. 2003. *Governance in Nigeria: The IBB Era: An Insider's View*. Lagos: Viewpoint Communications Ltd.

Shahabuddeen, Mohamed. 2007. *Precedent in the World Court*. London, UK: Cambridge University Press.

Shaibu, Nathaniel. 2024. Buhari Set Nigeria Five Decades Backward—Clark. *Punch* (Lagos). January 19. https://punchng.com/buhari-set-nigeria-five-decades-backward-clark/.

Sharp, Paul. 2009. *Diplomatic Theory of International Relations*. New York. Cambridge University Press.

Sheehan, Michael. 1996. *Balance of Power: History and Theory*. New York: Routledge.

Shikyil, Sylvester S. 2000. Human Rights in Foreign Policy: Nigeria's Experience since 1979. Doctoral dissertation, Department of Law, University of Jos. http://datad.aau.org/handle/123456789/42302?show=full.

Shinn, David H. Reversing the Brain Drain in Ethiopia. 2002. Address to the Ethiopian North American Health Professionals Association. November 23. http://chora.virtualave.net/brain-drain8.htm.

A Short Definition of Democracy. *Democracy Building*. http://www.democracy-building.info/definition-democracy.html.

Sierra Leone. *Global Security*. http://www.globalsecurity.org/military/world/war/sierra_leone.htm.

Sikkink, Kathryn. 1993. The Power of Principled Ideas: Human Rights Policies in the United States and Western Europe. In *Ideas and Foreign Policy: Beliefs, Institutions, and Political Change*, eds. Judith Goldstein and Robert O. Keohane, 139–172. Ithaca, NY: Cornell University Press.

Simpkins, John. 2004. The Role of Constitution-Building Processes in Democratization: Case Study Nigeria. Sweden: Institute for Democracy & Electoral Assistance.

Siollun, Max. 2021. Nigeria's Military Is Part of the Problem[;] It's Also the Solution. *Foreign Policy*. June 7. https://foreignpolicy.com/2021/06/07/nigerias-military-is-part-of-the-problem-its-also-the-solution/.

Siollun, Max. 2016. Nigeria is Coming Apart at the Seams. *Foreign Policy*. February 8. https://foreignpolicy.com/2016/02/08/nigeria-is-coming-apart-at-the-seamsbiafra/.

Siollun, Max. 2009. *Oil, Politics, and Violence: Nigeria's Military Coup Culture (1966–1976)*. New York: Algora Publishing.

Sklar, Richard L. 1963. *Nigerian Political Parties: Power in an Emergent African Nation*. Princeton, NJ: Princeton University Press.

Slave Coast. *Encyclopedia Britannica*. http://www.britannica.com/EBchecked/topic/548212/Slave-Coast.

Slavery Fact Sheets. *Digital History*. www.digitalhistory.uh.edu/disp_textbook.cfm?smtID=11&psid=3807.

Sloth-Nielsen, Julia. 2023. Remedies for Child Rights Violations in African Human Rights Systems. *De Jure Law Journal*. 625–645. https://doi.org/10.17159/2225-7160/2023/v56a36.

Smith, Daniel Jordan. 2008. *A Culture of Corruption: Everyday Deception and Popular Discontent in Nigeria*. Princeton, NJ: Princeton University Press.

Smith, David. 2015. Muhammadu Buhari: Reformed Dictator Returns to Power in Democratic Nigeria. *Guardian* (London). March 31. https://www.theguardian.com/world/2015/mar/31/muhammadu-buhari-military-dictator-nigeria-new-democratic-president.

Smith, Robert Charles. 1995. *Racism in the Post-Civil Rights Era: Now You See It, Now You Don't*. New York: SUNY Press.

Smith, Steve. 2001. Foreign Policy Is What States Make of It: Social Construction and International Relations Theory. *In Foreign Policy in a Constructed World*, ed. Vendulka Kubálková, 38–55. Armonk, NY: M.E. Sharpe.

Social Protection. UNICEF. https://www.unicef.org/social-policy/social-protection.

Sodaro, Michael J. 2008. *Comparative Politics: A Global Introduction*, 3rd Ed. Boston, MA: McGraw-Hill.

South-South Galaxy. African, Caribbean and Pacific Group of States (ACP). https://my.southsouth-galaxy.org/en/data/african-caribbean-and-pacific-group-of-states-acp.

Southern African Development Community: Toward a Common Future. http://www.sadc.int/.

Soyombo, Fiyaso. 2015. How Will Nigeria Fare under Buhari? *Al Jazeera*. June 9. http://www.aljazeera.com/indepth/opinion/2015/06/nigeria-fare-buhari-150607105418906.html.

Soyombo, Fisayo. 2014. Why is Nigeria's Jonathan Worried? *Al Jazeera*. November 27. http://www.aljazeera.com/indepth/opinion/2014/11/why-nigeria-jonathan-worried-2014112310431381 8965.html.

Speech of Sir Abubakar Tafawa Balewa. October 1, 1960. *Reprinted* in *Black Past*, August 20, 2009. https://www.blackpast.org/global-african-history/1960-sir-abubakar-tawafa-balewa-independence-day/.

Statehood Dates. *50States*. http://www.50states.com/statehood.htm#.VoL53xUrKls.

State and Local Governments. *American Government.* http://www.ushistory.org/gov/12.asp.

States of the United States. *Statoids.* http://statoids.com/uus.html.

Statista. 2023. Number of Active Technology Startup Hubs in Africa as of 2019, by Country. April 28. https://www.statista.com/statistics/1294785/number-of-active-tech-hubs-in-africa-by-country/#:~:text=As%20of%202019%2C%20more%20than,78%20and%2056%20hubs%2C%20respectively.

Sterling-Foster, Jennifer, ed. 2013. *Making Sense of International Relations Theory*, 2d Ed. Boulder, CO: Lynne Rienner.

Strayer, Joseph R. 2005. *On the Medieval Origins of the Modern State.* Princeton, NJ: Princeton University Press.

Stremlau, John J. 2015. *The International Politics of the Nigerian Civil War, 1967–1970.* Princeton, NJ: Princeton University Press.

Stromberg, Roland N. Collective Security. *Encyclopedia of the New American Nation.* http://www.americanforeignrelations.com/A-D/Collective-Security.html.

Suberu, Rotimi T. 1999. *Public Policies and National Unity in Nigeria.* Ibadan, Nigeria: Development Policy Center.

Supremo Tribunal de Justica. History of the STJ in Cape Verde. http://www.stj.cv/historia.html. Archived.

Sussman, Alison. 1993. Babangida, Ibrahim 1941–. *Contemporary Black Biography.* http://www.encyclopedia.com/doc/1G2-2870600010.html.

Swarns, Rachael L. 2002. African Leaders Drop Old Group for One that Has Power. *New York Times.* July 9. http://www.nytimes.com/2002/07/09/international/africa/09AFRI.html.

Switzerland's Political System and Government. *All About Switzerland.* http://swiss-government-politics.all-about-switzerland.info/.

Tamuno, Tekena N. 2003. The Nigeria Police Force and Public Security and Safety: Major Challenges and Opportunities since 1930. In *Security, Crime, and Segregation in West African Cities Since the 19th Century,* eds. Laurent Fourchard and Isaac Olawale Albert, 119–140. Paris, France: Karthala Editions.

Tanzania (1961–Present). University of Central Arkansas. http://uca.edu/politicalscience/dadm-project/sub-saharan-africa-region/tanzania-1961-present/.

Tar, Usman A., and Sharkdam Wapmuk, eds. 2023. *Nigerian Foreign Policy [Sixty] Years After Independence.* Cham, Switzerland: Palgrave Macmillan.

Thomas, Daniel C. 2001. *The Helsinki Effect: International Norms, Human Rights, and the Demise of Communism.* Princeton, NJ: Princeton University Press.

Thompson-Barrow, Cheryl, ed. 2008. *Bringing Justice Home: The Road to Final, Appellate and Regional Court Establishments.* London, UK: Commonwealth Secretariat.

Tignor, Robert L. 1998. *Capitalism and Nationalism at the End of Empire: State and Business in Decolonizing Egypt, Niger, and Kenya, 1945–1963*. Princeton, NJ: Princeton University Press.

Timberg, Craig. 2006. Bid to Allow Nigerian a Third Term Hits Snag. *Washington Post*. May 13. http://www.washingtonpost.com/wp-dyn/content/article/2006/05/12/AR2006051200518.html.

The Corrupt Practices and Other Related Offences Act 2000. Act No. 5. *Laws of the Federation of Nigeria*. https://web.archive.org/web/20100312232055/http://www.nigeria-law.org/Corrupt%20Practices%20and%20other%20Related%20Offences%20Act%202000.htm.

The First Republic. 1991. In *Nigeria: A Country Study*, ed. Helen Chapin Metz. Washington, DC: GPO for the Library of Congress. https://countrystudies.us/nigeria/68.htm.

The Gowon Regime. In *Nigeria: A Country Study*, ed. Helen Chapin Metz. Washington, D.C: GPO for the Library of Congress. https://countrystudies.us/nigeria/25.htm.

The Legacy of the Frontline States, Building Security in Southern Africa, Monograph No. 43 (November 1999). https://www.issafrica.org/pubs/Monographs/No43/TheLegacy.html.

The Nigerian Diaspora. *Nigerian Diaspora*. http://www.nigeriandiaspora.com/nigerian-diaspora.php.

The Obasanjo Years: His Legacy. *Lawyers Chronicle*. http://thelawyerschronicle.com/the-obasanjo-years-his-legacy/.

The Organization of African, Caribbean, and Pacific States. Homepage. https://www.oacps.org/.

The Perils of Liberian Peacekeeping. 2003. *BBC News*. August 4. http://news.bbc.co.uk/2/hi/africa/3113009.stm.

The Transformation of Technical Aid Corps Scheme. 2014. Sun (Lagos). August 20. http://sunnewsonline.com/new/the-transformation-of-technical-aid-corps-scheme/.

Treaty of the Economic Community of West African States (ECOWAS). 1975. May 28. http://www.internationaldemocracywatch.org/attachments/351_ecowas%20treaty%20of%201975.pdf.

Truman Signs the National Security Act. 1947. *This Day in History*. July 26. http://www.history.com/this-day-in-history/truman-signs-the-national-security-act.

Trust Africa. Shaping the Future We Want for Africa. https://trustafrica.org/about-us/#:~:text=TrustAfrica%20is%20a%20Pan%20African,the%20continent's%20most%20pressing%20challenges.

Trust Africa Foundation. 2017. Rethinking the Proposed Restructuring of the ECOWAS Community Court of Justice. *Issue Lab*. December 1. https://search.issuelab.org/resource/rethinking-the-proposed-restructuring-of-the-ecowas-community-court-of-justice.

Túb`ọsún, K´ọlá. 2023. Nigeria's Last General Departs the Political Stage. *Foreign Policy*. May 30. https://foreignpolicy.com/2023/05/30/nigeria-democracy-elections-tinubu-bulhari/.

Twitter Deletes Nigerian Leader's "Civil War" Post. 2021. *BBC News*. June 2. https://www.bbc.com/news/world-africa-57336571.

Uchenna, Tony. 2010. Osu Caste in Igboland. *Vanguard* (Lagos). October. http://www.vanguardngr.com/2010/10/osu-caste-in-igboland/.

Ukaigwe, Jerry. 2016. *ECOWAS Law*. New York: Springer.

UK Government. 2023. UK-Nigeria Development Partnership Summary. Policy Paper. July 17. https://www.gov.uk/government/publications/uk-nigeria-development-partnership-summary/uk-nigeria-development-partnership-summary-july-2023#why-and-how-the-uks-development-offer-with-nigeria.

UMA. http://www.maghrebarabe.org/en/.

Umoru, Henry. 2010. Nigeria Lost 2,000 Soldiers, $10 [Billion] in Peace-keeping Operations. *Vanguard* (Lagos). October 25. http://www.vanguardngr.com/2010/10/%E2%80%98nigeria-lost-2000-soldiers-10-bn-in-peace-keeping-operations/.

Umozurike, U. Oji. 1997. *The African Charter on Human and Peoples' Rights*. Leiden, Netherlands & Boston, MA: Brill Publishers.

UN Economic Commission for Africa. African Union (AU) and Regional Economic Communities (RECs) in Africa. http://www.uneca.org/oria/pages/african-union-au-regional-economic-communities-recs-africa.

UN General Assembly. 1966. International Covenant on Civil and Political Rights. UNTS, vol. 999. December 16. https://www.refworld.org/docid/3ae6b3aa0.htm.

UN General Assembly. 1966. International Covenant on Economic, Social and Cultural Rights. UNTS, vol. 993. December 16. https://www.refworld.org/docid/3ae6b36c0.html.

UN General Assembly. 1948. Universal Declaration of Human Rights. G.A. Res.217 A (III). U.N. GAOR, 3d Sess., U.N. Doc. A/810. December 10.

UNITAR. About Us: The Institute. http://www.unitar.org/the-institute.

UNMIL Background. United Nations. http://www.un.org/en/peacekeeping/missions/unmil/background.shtml.

United Nations. Charter of the United Nations. 1945. 59 Stat. 1031, T.S. 993, 3 Bevans 1153. https://www.un.org/en/about-us/un-charter.

United Nations. Department of Peacekeeping Operations. 2008. *United Nations Peacekeeping Operations: Principles and Guidelines*.

United Nations Economic Commission for Africa. African Union (AU) and Regional Economic Communities (RECs) in Africa. http://www.uneca.org/oria/pages/african-union-au-regional-economic-communities-recs-africa.

United Nations. Member States. http://www.un.org/depts/dhl/unms/cms.shtml.

United Nations. Peace and Security. http://www.un.org/en/peacekeeping/.

United Nations. Republic of the Congo: United Nations Operation in the Congo. (ONUC). July 1960–June 1964. http://www.un.org/en/peacekeeping/missions/past/onuc.htm.

United Nations. What is Peacekeeping? http://www.un.org/en/peacekeeping/operations/peacekeeping.shtml.

United Nations Peacekeeping. Principles of Peacekeeping. https://peacekeeping.un.org/en/principles-of-peacekeeping.

University of Minnesota. Human Rights Library. 2015. Ratification of International Human Rights Treaties—Nigeria. http://www1.umn.edu/humanrts/research/ratification-nigeria.html. Last visited February 26.

United States Courts. Overview—Rule of Law. https://www.uscourts.gov/educational-resources/educational-activities/overview-rule-law#:~:text=Rule%20of%20law%20is%20a,Independently%20adjudicated.

US Embassy and Consulate in Nigeria. 2021. Joint Statement from the Diplomatic Missions of Canada, The European Union (Delegation to Nigeria), The Republic of Ireland, The United Kingdom, and The United States of America. June 5. https://ng.usembassy.gov/partners-joint-statement-re-twitter-suspension/.

U.S. Energy Information Admin. 2013. *Nigeria*. December 30. www.eia.gov/contries/and/analysisbriefs/Nigeria/nigeria.pdf.

U.S. Freezes $458 [M][illion] Stolen by Sani Abacha. 2014. *Vanguard* (Lagos). March 6. http://www.vanguardngr.com/2014/03/us-freezes-458-mn-stolen-nigeria-dictator-abacha.

US Legal. Jurisconsult Law and Legal Definition. https://definitions.uslegal.com/j/jurisconsult/.

van den Broek, Roel B. 1972. *The Myth of the Phoenix, According to Classical and Early Christian Traditions.* Translation by I. Seeger. Leiden, The Netherlands: E. J. Brill. Vasquez, John A., and Colin Elman, eds., 2005. *Realism and the Balance of Power: A New Debate*. Upper Saddle River, NJ: Prentice Hall.

Viljoen, Frans. 2012. *International Human Rights Law in Africa*, 2d. Edition. New York and London: Oxford University Press.

Vincent, R.J. 1986. *Human Rights and International Relations*. New York: Cambridge University Press.

Volle, Adam. 2023. Allied Powers. *Encyclopedia Britannica*. May 17. https://www.britannica.com/topic/Allied-powers-World-War-II.

Wachuku, Jaja Anucha. *S9.Com Biographical Dictionary.* http://www.s9.com/Biography/Wachuku-Jaja-Anucha.

Wallace, Paul, and Michael Cohen. 2015. Buhari Bounce Becomes Bust as Nigeria Policies Irk Investors. *Bloomberg*. November 26, updated November 27. https://www.bloomberg.com/news/articles/2015-11-26/buhari-bounce-becomes-bust-as-nigeria-policies-annoy-investors#xj4y7vzkg.

Walker, Andrew. 2009. The Story of Nigeria's "Untouchables." *BBC News*. April. http://news.bbc.co.uk/2/hi/africa/7977734.stm.

Walton Jr., Hanes, and Robert C. Smith. 2010. *American Politics and the African American Quest for Universal Freedom*, 5th Ed. New York: Longman.

Wando, William M. 2012. Challenges, Benefits, and Recommendations for Continued Nigerian Peacekeeping, Paper for the Naval War College, Newport, R.I. November 2. http://www.dtic.mil/dtic/tr/fulltext/u2/a569419.pdf.

Washington University Manual of International Legal Citation. Republic of Côte d'Ivoire (Republicque de Côte d'Ivoire). https://apps.law.wustl.edu/GSLR/CitationManual/countries/ivorycoast.pdf.

What is a "State." *Global Policy Forum*. https://www.globalpolicy.org/nations-a-states/what-is-a-state.html.

What is the 0.7% Target? 2002–2006. Millennium Project. http://www.unmillenniumproject.org/press/07.htm.

Weber, Max. 1968. *Economy and Society: An Outline of Interpretive Sociology*. New York: Bedminster Press.

Weissbrodt, David, Fionnuala Ni Aolain, Joan Fitzpatrick, and Frank Newman. 2009. *International Human Rights: Law, Policy, and Process*, 4th Ed. San Francisco, CA: LexisNexis.

Wendt, Alexander. 1999. *Social Theory of International Politics*. New York: Cambridge University Press, 1999.

Wendt, Alexander. 1992. Anarchy Is What States Make of It: The Social Construction of Power Politics. *International Organization*. 46: 391–425.

West African Countries Disregard ECOWAS Court Rulings—Judge. 2021. *Vanguard* (Lagos). November 22. https://www.vanguardngr.com/2021/11/heifer-in-talks-with-diaspora-investors-for-livestock-production.

When Rape Becomes Genocide. 1998. *New York Times*. September 5. http://www.nytimes.com/1998/09/05/opinion/when-rape-becomes-genocide.html.

Whisky, Ayakeme. 2014. The South-South Position: A Stitch in Time Saves Nine.
Vanguard (Lagos). June 5. http://www.vanguardngr.com/2014/06/south-south-position-stitch-time-saves-nine/.

White, Theodore H. 1982. *America in Search of Itself: The Making of the President 1956–1980*. New York: Harper & Row.

The White House. Advancing American Energy. https://www.whitehouse.gov/energy/securing-american-energy.

The White House, Office of the Press Secretary. 2014. Remarks by President Obama in Address to the UN General Assembly. September 28. www.whitehouse.gov/the-press-office/2014/09/24/remarks-president-obama-address-united-nations-general-assembly.

Why Did the Americans Choose the British System of Government for the Japanese, Instead of the American System? *Reddit*. https://www.reddit.com/r/AskHistorians/comments/1b6gys/why_did_the_americans_choose_the_british_system/?rdt=61002.

Williams, Alabi. 2016. It's Time to Review Nigeria. *Guardian* (Lagos). June 12. http://guardian.ng/opinion/its-time-to-review-nigeria/.

Wilson-Keenan, Jo Anne. 2015. *From Small Places: Toward the Realization of Literacy as a Human Right*. Rotterdam, Zuid-Holland, The Netherlands: Sense Publishers.

Wilson, Frank L. 1996. *Concepts and Issues in Comparative Politics: An Introduction to Comparative Analysis*. Upper Saddle River, NJ: Prentice Hall.

Wind of Change Speech. *About*. http://africanhistory.about.com/od/eraindependence/a/wind_of_change1.htm.

Winston Churchill, Churchill by Himself: The Definitive Collection of Quotations, ed. Richard M. Langworth. New York: Public Affairs, 2008.

Wiseman, John A. 1990. *Democracy in Black Africa: Survival and Revival*. Salt Lake City, UT: Paragon.

Wittkopf, Eugene R., Christopher M. Jones, and Charles W. Kegley. 2008. *American Foreign Policy: Pattern and Process*, 7th Ed. Belmont, CA: Thomson Wadsworth.

World Bank. 1996. *Nigeria—Poverty in the Midst of Plenty: The Challenge of Growth with Inclusion: A World Bank Poverty Assessment*. Washington, DC: World Bank Group. http://documents.worldbank.org/curated/en/582991468759320261/Nigeria-Poverty-in-the-midst-of-plenty-the-challenge-of-growth-with-inclusion-a-World-Bank-poverty-assessment.

World Conference and the Vienna Declaration. *BBC World Service*. http://www.bbc.co.uk/worldservice/people/features/ihavearightto/four_b/treaties_vienna.shtml.

Yakubu Gowon and Ecowas's Restoration. *This Day* (Lagos) (February 28, 2024). https://www.thisdaylive.com/index.php/2024/02/28/yakubu-gowon-and-ecowas-restoration.

Yokota, Yozo, and Chiyuki Aoi. 2000. Japan's Foreign Policy Toward Human Rights: Uncertain Changes. In *Human Rights and Comparative Foreign Policy*, ed. David P. Forsythe, 115–145. New York: United Nations University Press.

Your Article Library. National Interest: Meaning, Components[,] and Methods. http://www.yourarticlelibrary.com/international-politics/national-interest-meaning-components-and-methods/48487/.

Yusuf, Hakeem O. 2013. Human Rights Violations Investigations Commission, the Oputa Panel (Nigeria). In *Encyclopedia of Transitional Justice*, eds. Lavinia Stan, and Nadia Nedelsky, 161–165. New York: Cambridge University Press.

Yusuf, Kabir. 2023. Scorecard: Key Metrics Show Buhari Failed as Nigeria's President. *Premium Times* (Abuja). May 28. https://www.premiumtimesng.com/features-and-interviews/600912-scorecard-key-metrics-show-buhari-failed-as-nigerias-president.html.

Yusuf, Kabir. 2023. Analysis: Trend of Low Voter Turnout Continues in Nigerian Elections. *Premium Times* (Abuja). March 5. https://www.premiumtimesng.com/news/top-news/586193-analysis-trend-of-low-voter-turnout-continues-in-nigerian-elections.html.

Yusuf, Kabir. 2022. Fact-Check: How True is Buhari's Claim that Nigeria is Better off Today Than in 2015? *Premium Times* (Abuja). July 4. https://www.premiumtimesng.com/news/headlines/540682-fact-check-how-true-is-buharis-claim-that-nigeria-is-better-off-today-than-in-2015.html

Yusuf, Mohammed. 2023. ECOWAS Unity Put to Test as West African Coup Crisis Deepens. *VOA News*. September 11. https://www.voanews.com/a/ecowas-unity-put-to-test-as-west-african-coup-crisis-deepens-/7263280.html.

Yusuf, Mohammed. 2022. Africans Say Goodbye to Queen Who Led Britain into Post-Colonial Era. *Voice of America*. September 9. https://www.voanews.com/a/africans-say-goodbye-to-queen-who-led-britain-into-post-colonial-era/6738394.html.

Zakaria, Fareed. 2011. Are America's Best Days Behind Us? *Time*. March 3. http://content.time.com/time/magazine/article/0,9171,2056723,00.html.

Zakaria, Fareed. 1997. The Rise of Illiberal Democracy. *Foreign Affairs*. 76(6): 22–43. November/December. https://doi.org/10.2307/20048274.

Zane, Damian. 2015. Nigeria's Goodluck Jonathan: Five Reasons Why He Lost. *BBC News*. March 31. http://www.bbc.com/news/world-africa-32136295.

Index

P. C. Aka, *Human Rights in Nigeria's External Relations in the Age of General Muhammadu Buhari and His Successors*, https://doi.org/10.1007/978-3-031-63231-0